SWIFT INJUSTICE

The
CRAIG
TITUS
Story

TRACY MITCHELL-MILAM

TMM PUBLISHING

The opinions expressed in this manuscript are solely the opinions of the author and do not represent the opinions or thoughts of the publisher. The author has represented and warranted full ownership and/or legal right to publish all the materials in this book.

Swift Injustice
The Craig Titus Story
All Rights Reserved.
Copyright © 2015 Tracy Mitchell-Milam
v2.0

Cover Photo © 2015 Jason Mathas. All rights reserved - used with permission.

This book may not be reproduced, transmitted, or stored in whole or in part by any means, including graphic, electronic, or mechanical without the express written consent of the publisher except in the case of brief quotations embodied in critical articles and reviews.

TMM Publishing

ISBN: 978-0-578-16457-1

PRINTED IN THE UNITED STATES OF AMERICA

Contents

Introduction 1

Section One:
The Making of the Bad Boy of Bodybuilding

Chapter 1: Titus Family Meeting 71
Chapter 2: Growing up Titus 79
Chapter 3: Chasing his Dream 97
Chapter 4: The Catch 22- Steroids and Bodybuilding 104
Chapter 5: The Return of Craig Titus 110
Chapter 6: Craig and Kelly- The Making of a Power Couple 122
Chapter 7: The Empire that Titus Built- Emperor Enterprises 127
Chapter 8: Commotion behind the Scenes 134
Chapter 9: Losing a Grip on Reality 140
Chapter 10: Free Fall 150
Chapter 11: Ostracized 159

Section Two:
December 2005- 44,640 Minutes of Devastation

Chapter 1: Beginning of the End 169
Chapter 2: Room #232 176
Chapter 3: Dib & Dab with the Devil 188
Chapter 4: Home Alone: Kelly and Melissa 194
Chapter 5: Detonation 200
Chapter 6: Grave Decisions 207

Chapter 7: With Friends Like These 218
Chapter 8: From Dusk 'til Dawn 240
Chapter 9: Identifying Melissa 251
Chapter 10: Arrogance Does Not Make a Person a Murderer 253
Chapter 11: Cop Killers Investigating a "Murder" 268
Chapter 12: Crashing with Schwimmer for the Week 270
Chapter 13: Blindsided by the Autopsy Report 274
Chapter 14: Mandy Polk: A Believable Witness 282
Chapter 15: Spinning Their Wheels 289
Chapter 16: Running From Their Problems 306

Section Three:
Just say that Craig did this thing- if you want to walk!

Chapter 1: The Interrogation 337
Chapter 2: Ron Avidan interviews Matt Cline 363
Chapter 3: Due Process? 369
Chapter 4: The Binion Connection 376
Chapter 5: Checkmate 393
Chapter 6: The Arraignment & Bail Hearings 408
Chapter 7: The Grand Jury Testimony 419
Chapter 8: Spackling the Holes in the Prosecution's case 441
Chapter 9: Entrapment & Solicitation for Murder 457
Chapter 10: Who wants to be a Celebrity Judge? 469
Chapter 11: Book Deal or Murder Plot? 476

Section Four:
Corruption in the System

Chapter 1: Prosecutorial and Judicial Misconduct 493
Chapter 2: Out with the old, and in with the De-new 517
Chapter 3: The Dynamic Defense Duo 522
Chapter 4: Cruel and Unusual Punishment 532

Chapter 5: Making Sense out of Nonsense- The Case Against
 Ron Brady Jr. 544
Chapter 6: Exposing the Unbelievable Truth 549
Chapter 7: Judge Jackie Glass refuses to step down 560
Chapter 8: That would be a Conflict of Interest! 567
Chapter 9: Daskas, Brady, Titus: Lives intertwined 574
Chapter 10: The Plea Deal & Sentencing 598
Chapter 11: After the Verdict 612

Introduction

Do you want to change lives? Become a school teacher; or so I was told twenty years ago when deciding on a major in college. I am not sure how many lives have been changed due to me teaching high school English, but I would like to think that I have rid the world of one less run-on sentence. One thing all teachers have in common, myself included, is the countdown to summer. Every school year seems to drag from month to month, but when summer finally arrives, the wait proves to be worthwhile! Exhausting as the last day of school may be, with kids running wild, checking-in text books, and taking everything down off of the walls; there is a definite rush from all of the excitement!

Two and a half years ago, that last day of school seemed to be no different from all of the years before. At the end of the day, with boxes of miscellaneous objects in my arms, I made my way out the front door, and into the faculty parking lot. I was exhausted, yet revitalized, with the knowledge that school was out for the summer and in a matter of minutes there would be an alcoholic beverage in my hand. Daydreaming about a whole lot of nothing, I got in my car, turned up my CD player and sang along with Pink Floyd, "We don't need no education," at the top of my lungs. Flooring the gas, my wheels screeched out of the parking lot, as I raced to my house.

I had been divorced for over two years, and my son had graduated from High School the year before. Some people fear the empty nest; I had a countdown going since he was in the seventh grade. Summer was here, and I had absolutely nothing to do: no trips to take, no dinners to cook, and no ball games to watch, halleluiah! Summer break was going to be all about me, and my three-month vacation in the back yard lying out by the pool and drinking margaritas. Because it was getting dark outside, the pool unfortunately would have to wait until the next day; I had a date with a box of left-over pizza, can of Dr. Pepper, and my television.

The second I walked through the front door, my bra and shoes were discarded, and the television was turned on. Immediately multi-tasking, with one hand in the refrigerator and the other on the Television remote control, I scrolled through the ID (Investigation Discovery) Channel's Friday night line-up, and was disappointed to find that I had already watched every one of the shows. Thank God for TiVo; I had set the DVR to record every murder mystery that week. After raiding the refrigerator, I made my way down the hall to my bedroom with enough food to hibernate for the summer. With food and beverage in hand, I shut the bedroom door with my foot, grabbed the remote control with my mouth, and plopped myself down on the bed. "What to watch, what to watch?" Browsing through all of the recordings, this proved to be a difficult question; I felt like a kid in a candy store sifting through all of the options trying to find the perfect show.

I read the program details for *Dateline, 20/20, Snapped, On the Case with Paula Zahn,* and *Wicked Attraction*; but nothing caught my eye, until I got to a *48 Hours Murder Mystery* called "Vegas Heat". The description read: "Two Vegas hard bodies, hard partying ways end in an unthinkable murder and the downfall of a fitness powerhouse." A "who-done-it" murder mystery with hot bodybuilders, rock stars, drugs and sexual escapades; this show had my name written all over it!

For years, true crime television shows had provided a little excitement to my less than exciting life. Being a school teacher from Nowhere, Texas, with the same mundane routine day after day, the only scandal that ever came my way was on the television screen; and by damn it, I was going to make the most out of it! This was not just my guilty pleasure; it was my retreat from the real world. While watching these shows, I would become a detective, lawyer, and judge all rolled into one for a short period of time (an hour with commercials and 47 minutes without). From the cops apprehending the "perp" (for ID

INTRODUCTION

virgins- perpetrator) to the prosecutors presenting the case in court, justice was served by the "moral authority" after the judge slammed the gavel, and put the criminal behind bars.

In the end, tears would pour down my face, as if I was actually a family member; and then with the click of the remote control, it was onto the next show. At no time did it ever cross my mind that these were real people, with real emotions, and real lives. As shallow as it may sound, they were simply my entertainment for the evening, nothing more, nothing less; but on that particular evening, that was all about to change.

Lying on my bed, I hit play on the remote control and watched the drama unfold. It was the all too familiar tale of a celebrity making it big, becoming famous and then spiraling out of control on drugs. In this case, it featured the celebrity bodybuilding couple, Craig Titus and Kelly Ryan, the tragic death of their friend Melissa James and their drug-fueled frenzy to cover up her death. All three were abusing drugs. Melissa had several arrests in Florida and Nevada, and her addiction seemed more advanced because she was no longer able to hold a job, and had become financially dependent on Craig Titus and Kelly Ryan. Craig and Kelly appeared to be "functioning" addicts that were able to maintain their jobs and appearances, but were only steps away from disaster.

On December 13, 2005 disaster struck. With the three drug addicts living together under one roof, tempers flared, and a physical altercation broke out between the two women, Melissa James and Kelly Ryan. Ryan's husband, Craig Titus, stepped in and broke the fight up. Melissa then went to her bedroom to pack her things and take a nap. Later that afternoon, Craig Titus and Kelly Ryan found Melissa James dead in her bedroom from what appeared to be a drug overdose. Out of their minds on drugs, the couple tried to cover up the overdose by putting Melissa's body in the trunk of their Jaguar, and torching the vehicle in the desert.

The prosecution testified that Melissa James did not die from an accidental overdose; rather, she was the victim of a love triangle gone wrong. A pre-meditated murder, planned out by Craig and Kelly, ending with Melissa in a trunk, set a-flame in the desert. And so the Murder Mystery began: Did she really overdose on drugs? Or was Melissa James murdered by Craig Titus and Kelly Ryan?

The Autopsy Report said the cause of death was "Undetermined, with the Significant Contributing Factor being Opiate Intoxication." Melissa James had a lethal combination of alcohol and drugs in her system when she died, and it was confirmed that she had been abusing methamphetamines for a number of years. Without the cause of death being ruled a homicide, the prosecution would need a substantial amount of physical evidence to prove that a murder had actually taken place.

There was an ample amount of physical evidence; however, unfortunately for the State, this evidence only proved there was a cover-up, not a murder. The prosecution did not have any physical evidence linking Craig Titus and Kelly Ryan to the murder of Melissa James. When the lead prosecutor, Robert Daskas, was questioned about this on *48 Hours*, he said that it was hard to determine the actual cause of death because the victim had been "tasered, beaten, choked, injected with drugs, and then set on fire."

After hearing this, I thought to myself, "This can't be right, there should have been some physical evidence left behind, especially if all of the acts of violence described above actually took place." Understandably, some of the evidence went up in flames, but the prosecution still should have found some physical evidence to link Craig Titus and Kelly Ryan to this alleged murder. How do you have a murder, a first-degree murder nonetheless, and not have one piece of physical evidence to prove "beyond a reasonable doubt" a murder really took place?

If the victim was shot with a taser, there surely would have been fingerprints on the gun, substantiating that Craig or Kelly pulled the trigger. If she had been beaten or body-slammed, an x-ray would have confirmed it because there would have been some broken bones or a fractured skull. And what about the physical evidence on the murder suspects' bodies?

INTRODUCTION

If Craig Titus and Kelly Ryan did in fact beat this girl to death, they should have had cuts or bruises on their hands, right? Because of the fire, there would understandably not be any visible ligature marks around the decedent's neck; however, her hyoid bone would have been compressed, distorted, or broken if she had been strangled or choked to death. Finally, there was mention of hypodermic needles scattered throughout the house; if Craig and Kelly injected Melissa James with drugs, there should have been some DNA evidence on the hypodermic needles found in Melissa's room, with Craig's DNA on one end and Melissa's on the other.

The prosecution did not have any physical evidence to prove a murder had taken place, but they did have one trick up their sleeve, a confession! Well, sort of. They did not have a direct confession from Craig Titus or Kelly Ryan; rather, an in-direct admission presented to the grand jury by the State's "number one" witness, Megan Pierson Foley. According to Megan Pierson Foley, she was not in the house when Melissa overdosed, but she testified before a grand jury that Kelly had confessed to killing Melissa James in a conversation between the two women.

Soon after that, Megan's testimony was printed in the newspaper. Strangely, even with Megan's words taken out of context and exaggerated in print, the statements quoted in that article still became the facts of the case. Even *48 Hours'* entire premise revolved around Megan Pierson Foley's "hear-say" recollection of the events; even though her testimony had never been challenged in an adversarial system with both the prosecution and defense presenting their case before an impartial jury.

According to Megan Foley's interview on *48 Hours*, she had gone to Craig and Kelly's house seven hours after Melissa James had already passed away. Megan said the couple confessed to murdering Melissa James after a physical altercation erupted between the two women over jealousy and money. Kelly Ryan attacked Melissa with a taser gun, and Craig Titus body-slammed her into the ground; soon after, Craig strangled Melissa and Kelly punched her in the face.

In the end, according to Megan, the couple actually murdered Melissa by holding her down and injecting her with drugs. After hearing Craig and Kelly confess to the murder, Megan said she was scared out of her mind, and started to run out the front door. Before Megan had a chance to escape, Craig handed her a black gym bag, and instructed her to take it home. Megan asked him what was in the bag, and Craig told her it contained the taser gun used on Melissa James. Megan said she took the bag directly to her lawyer, who in turn handed it over to the police.

While watching all of this unfold on the television, I was thinking to myself, "Every word that comes out of this woman's mouth is absurd, and the entire story does not make any sense; without any physical evidence to prove the couple murdered Melissa, the end result seems obvious."

Predicting an acquittal, I continued to watch the last ten minutes of the show, but what happened next completely caught me off guard; Craig Titus and Kelly Ryan took a plea deal. Why would they do that? If they had gone to trial, a jury would have found them "Not Guilty" because there was not enough evidence to convict them of first degree murder and kidnapping; nonetheless, Craig Titus and Kelly Ryan shocked the world and pleaded guilty to a lesser charge of second degree murder, kidnapping, and arson.

When it came time for the judge to sentence the couple, the camera zoomed in on Judge Jackie Glass. I had to hit "pause" on the remote control; this judge looked so familiar, where had I seen her before? I typed the judge's name into my cell phone and discovered she had been a celebrity court television judge on *Swift Justice with Jackie Glass*. According to the introduction of the show, she was "the same judge that put O.J. Simpson behind bars for 33 years." I made a mental note of this interesting tidbit, and continued watching the sentencing phase of the trial.

The words that came out of Judge Jackie Glass' mouth were startling. I have never heard a judge talk to a defendant that way before. The judge was like a bully on the playground when she addressed Craig Titus in the courtroom and said, "Mr. Titus came into court a big man,

INTRODUCTION

with lots of muscles, and money, and now look at him- he is nothing." In addition to her cruel words, the entire time Judge Jackie Glass was belittling Craig Titus, her gestures and expressions were over-the-top; she was so theatrical, it seemed as if she was auditioning for a part in a Broadway production. Then I realized, that's exactly what she was doing. And sure enough, this would be her audition tape for *Swift Justice*, and I will be damned if she did not get the job!

The sentence Judge Jackie Glass handed down was neither "swift" nor "just". The punishment did not match the crime, and Craig Titus was facing the possibility of spending the rest of his life behind bars. At the end of *48 Hours*, the camera scanned the courtroom, and paused for a moment on Maura James, the mother of Melissa James. She sat stoic, staring straight ahead. She appeared apathetic when the defendants were sentenced. The void in her heart from the loss of her daughter could not be filled by excessively punishing Craig Titus with a crime that he did not commit. This mother's heart was undoubtedly broken, and my heart went out to her. As a mother however, I would want justice in the form of the truth, not vengeance in the form of a lie.

Just a couple of seats over, and one row up in the courtroom, there was a woman that was noticeably distraught as tears poured down her face. Shaking her head in disbelief, this attractive, middle-aged woman appeared inconsolable after Craig Titus was sentenced. Looking at her downward turned, almond shape eyes, it was clear that this was Craig Titus' mother. Craig had his mother's eyes, and her eyes told a story of anguish; despair over losing her first born son. Watching this mother grieve, I had to disagree with the Judge's malicious rant; Craig Titus is somebody; he is somebody's son.

There were so many holes in this story, I was left with an empty resolve in the end; something needed to be done, but I didn't know what. Possible solutions ran through my head. I thought to myself that maybe I could research the case and then later write a blog, an article, or perhaps even a book about the injustice that seemingly took place in that courtroom.

I went to the internet, and tried to make sense of the case. When I typed in Craig Titus' name on the computer, I was immediately bombarded by thousands of articles with twists and turns that had never even been addressed on *48 Hours*. Where in the hell would I start? Feeling overwhelmed by the enormity of it all, I began to question myself and what I was doing. Seriously, if this guy did this horrible thing, he should be in jail, right? For the cover-up yes, but for kidnapping and murder, I just did not think so.

If the State's lead witness lied about what happened to Melissa James, and the prosecution wrongfully convicted Craig Titus of murder, then somebody needed to take a closer look at this case- somebody other than me.

Who am I to investigate and expose prosecutorial misconduct in the Nevada Judicial System? I am a teacher, not a journalist; hell, I don't even read the local newspaper! My heart was telling me to look into this, but my head was telling me that it was a waste of time. I would spend my entire summer researching the case, and then what? Write a book? Yeah right, who would read a book written by me?

I thought about that "voice of reasoning" in the back of my head and the handicap it had been to me my entire life. Any time my heart asked, "What if?" My head would counter back with "Why try?" For as long as I can remember, I have never wanted to upset anyone, or ruffle feathers; I have always been a rule-following, people-pleaser who held my tongue, even if I had a different opinion. This voice of reason has held me back for so long; but this time, I was going to follow my heart!

To begin I needed to take a closer look at the television program again, and ask myself, "What was it that bothered me the most about this story?" The obvious answer: "The prosecution's key witness was not telling the truth." Other things did not add up, and I had my reservations about how truthful other people were being as well; but the prosecution's entire case was based on Megan Foley's testimony. Megan Foley's hearsay confession became the facts of the case and the only evidence the prosecution had to convict Craig Titus of murder. In the end, this witness alone, Megan Foley, was the only thing standing between Craig Titus and freedom.

INTRODUCTION

The first time I watched Megan being interviewed on 48 Hours, all of her statements appeared to contradict each other, and it seemed as if she was not being truthful. I wondered if perhaps she was just not real bright; or maybe she was confused, and was not able to clearly articulate her thoughts on camera. However the more I watched, it became evident that she was not freezing on camera; on the contrary, it was apparent that Megan Foley loved the media attention! She posed three different times, engaged in various activities with revealing outfits. She was obviously a confident woman; yet no matter how hard she tried, Ms. Foley did not appear to be an honest woman.

I have always considered myself an expert on lying because I taught school for nearly twenty years. Students lied to me on a daily basis, and I could always read right through them with a 3-step "lie detector" test. First step: "If it doesn't make sense, it's probably not the truth;" and when a person's story didn't add up, an alarm would go off in my head. Second, I would become as observant as possible, paying close attention to that person's words and actions by watching their face and listening for cues in their speech. If that person hesitated, seemed nervous, avoided eye contact, changed the subject, or excessively used the words, "like" and "uhm;" more likely than not, that person was not telling the truth. Finally, I would have the person repeat back the story they just said, word for word. If the story was different, more likely than not, I would conclude that they were lying.

This has been my fool-proof "lie detector" test in both the classroom and in life; and I was about to test it out on Megan Foley's statements on *48 Hours*. But how was I going to compare her words in this story to her words in another story? Simple! I would compare what she said on *48 Hours* to her Grand Jury testimony. That would be the ultimate fool-proof test because one of us would definitely end up looking like a fool. If the stories did not match up, then she would look like a fool because she either lied on national television or under oath in front of a grand jury. However, if they did match up, then she was telling the truth, and I would look like a fool.

On my end, being a fool would actually be advantageous because I could drop this whole thing with a clear conscience, and get back to my plan of enjoying the summer sipping margaritas by the pool. For

Megan Pierson Foley however, if she lied and a man was sitting in prison for the rest of his life because of that lie, I would do whatever needed to be done to turn this story upside down, and expose the truth! While watching 48 hours, I would analyze all of the problems, and document every detail about the case. The focal point would be on Megan Foley's interview; I would scrutinize her words and body language, taking special note of when her actions did not match her words.

Summary & Observations: *48 Hours Murder Mystery:* "Vegas Heat"

The scene opens with a fireman driving his vehicle down a dirt road. The fireman explains that on December 14th 2005, around 4 am, he was dispatched to put out a brush fire about fifteen miles outside of Las Vegas in the Desert. Once there, he recognized it was not a brush fire, but a burning car. After he extinguished the fire, he discovered a dead body in the back of the car.

The camera zooms in on a burned out Jaguar, and two detectives begin discussing what could have happened. One detective states that the license plate and registration connected back to a Kelly Ryan. *48 Hours* shows pictures of Kelly Ryan in Fitness Competitions, and the narrator says, "Kelly Ryan was one of the best Fitness athletes in the world." The camera then cuts back to the other detective saying that he assumed it was Kelly Ryan in the back of the car. The opening credits appear, the picture fades out and the narrator says, "And the mystery continues in 90 seconds."

After the commercial break, Clark County Coroner Mike Murphy is introduced in the receiving area of the Clark County Coroner's Office. The video footage shows a body bag being unzipped while the Coroner explains that the charred remains of the body were placed on this gurney (points to a gurney) and was taken into the very room we stand in.

CBS Correspondent Peter Van Sant asks the Clark County Coroner, "Was there a recognizable face on this body?" And Mike Murphy replies, "Unfortunately there was not." The scene fades out to a dirt road, and Van Sant narrates, "Clark County Coroner Mike Murphy had

INTRODUCTION

a mystery on his hands. A charred corpse discovered on Sandy Valley Road. And it would take weeks to make a positive identification."

The video returns to the Detectives at the burned out Jaguar, and Van Sant narrates, "It was dawn on December 14th 2005 when Las Vegas Homicide detectives Robert Wilson and Dean O'Kelley came upon the smoldering car." Detective Wilson states, "In our investigations, the sooner you can identify the victim, the sooner you can identify the suspects." With his hand on the burned out Jaguar, Wilson shook his head, looked over at Detective O'Kelley and said, "There was a lot of damage done to this car because of the fire. I sure am glad she was dead before the fire happened; that would be a terrible way to go." (Remember this quote when Craig Titus is convicted of murder by the judge. During the trial, Robert Daskas told the judge that the investigators never could determine if Melissa James was dead before they burned her body in the trunk of the car.)

In the next scene, the video shows a car driving down a street pulling up in front of Craig and Kelly's house. Detective Wilson is reenacting what he did when he got out of the car, and knocked on Craig & Kelly's front door on Adobe Arch Court. Wilson said, "A female opened the door, and said that she was Kelly Ryan."

The camera cuts away to a woman in black with bleached blonde hair, wearing a thick coat of make-up with heavily penciled in eyebrows. Sitting for an interview with Van Sant, the woman says that she (Kelly Ryan) was an amazing athlete. With video footage of Kelly Ryan performing a past Fitness routine, Van Sant introduces the woman being interviewed as Megan Foley (She is Megan Foley here; however, she went by Megan Pierson in December of 2005, and Megan Pierson-Foley during her grand jury testimony. She is now divorced from Jeremy Foley and goes by the name Megan Michelle Pierson). Van Sant says that Megan Foley trained with Kelly Ryan, and was her best friend.

The camera returns to the view of Craig and Kelly's house, and Detective Wilson is reenacting his initial contact with Kelly Ryan. Wilson said that Kelly invited the detectives into her home. Once they were inside, the detectives started asking her questions and then Craig Titus walked down the stairs.

SWIFT INJUSTICE

Bodybuilding clips are shown of Craig Titus while Van Sant describes him as being, "The Bad Boy of Body Building." Van Sant states, "Craig Titus was such a star in fact, he was even hired by Vince Neil to help train him for a special that was aired on VH-1." Vince Neil then talks about Craig Titus and says that Titus shot him up with steroids to get fit for the show. Neil indicated that Craig was, "The Rock Star of Bodybuilding."

The video goes back to Detective Wilson continuing his conversation with Kelly Ryan. Wilson states that he asked Kelly if she knew where her car was, and Kelly told him that she didn't know, but thought maybe her assistant took it. Wilson states, "That was the first time that we heard about someone named Melissa James." *48 Hours* shows a picture of Melissa, and Van Sant narrates, "Melissa James was Craig and Kelly's 28 year old live-in assistant, and Kelly told the detectives that Melissa had left Las Vegas the day before to spend Christmas with her mother in New Jersey."

The camera is now on Melissa's Mother, Maura James, in New Jersey. With an airplane flying overhead, Van Sant narrates, "Maura James had gone to Newark Airport to pick Melissa up. She was a little late and did not see her daughter anywhere. The airport stated that Melissa had never gotten on the plane. Maura tried to call Melissa, but she was not answering her phone. Later in the afternoon, Maura James got a call from the morgue regarding an "unidentified body that was found in the trunk of Craig and Kelly's Jaguar outside of Las Vegas."

The footage returns to the detectives at Craig and Kelly's house discussing what happened next. Detective Wilson states, "At this time we knew that Craig and Kelly were probably involved in this so we began to question them separately." *48 Hours* shows a video of Melissa James dancing while Van Sant narrates, "Melissa loved to dance, especially ballet; and at just 19 years old, Melissa opened a dance studio in her home town of Panama City, Florida. Melissa was in her mid-twenties when she first met Craig Titus at a bodybuilding competition in Panama City, Florida in 2001." With a video of Craig prepping to go on stage, Van Sant explains, "Melissa was fascinated by the bodybuilding world. In 2005 Melissa fell on hard times and

INTRODUCTION

lost her dance studio, and was broke. With nowhere to turn, Craig invited Melissa to Las Vegas to help them launch a new clothing store."

The camera focuses back on Megan Foley, and this time she is walking her large dogs at a park, wearing a tight and revealing white tank top. The tank top is short, and her shorts hung low, exposing both her cleavage and midriff. Ms. Foley briskly walks her dogs with a disheveled bounce against the wind; her hair is blowing everywhere and her leashed dogs are pulling her in two different directions. The camera stays on Foley for 5-10 seconds then Van Sant narrates, "Tensions between Kelly Ryan and Melissa James began to rise." The scene switches; it is still Megan Foley, but she is back in the original interview, wearing all black with Peter Van Sant. Foley states, "Kelly did not like Melissa at all! Craig and Kelly's marriage was most definitely on the rocks. They were like having issues left and right, and a lot of that comes down to the fact that Melissa had moved in to their house."

The camera zooms in on Craig and Kelly's house and a picture of Melissa James, and Van Sant narrates, "Including, bringing Melissa, a beautiful, younger woman into their house. There were whispers of an affair between Craig and Melissa." The camera then focuses on Craig and Kelly's master bedroom, and Van Sant says, "Kelly was at her breaking point."

Van Sant interviews Mandy Polk next; he narrates, "Mandy Polk was a fitness athlete that was training with Kelly Ryan, and renting a home from Craig Titus." (With an all-American, girl next door appearance, Mandy has blonde hair, blue eyes and a bubbly personality.) Mandy Polk explains that the day after Melissa's death, Kelly came over to her house, wrapped her arms around her and started crying. Mandy says that Kelly told her, "Homicide was at our house this morning; they found our car burned in the desert." The camera shows a picture of the burned out Jaguar, and Polk, with a confused laugh says, "I was trying to put the two together. What does homicide have to do with your car? How did it get there? Why are you crying?" Never breaking eye contact with Van Sant, Mandy exclaims, "It was very strange!"

Two days after detectives found the burning Jaguar, Van Sant says that the detectives found surveillance video tapes from Wal-Mart, with

SWIFT INJUSTICE

Kelly Ryan buying lighter fluid. The surveillance also showed Craig Titus helping load the purchase into the Jaguar, hours before the car was discovered in the desert. With the picture of a truck driving down a dirt road, Van Sant narrates, "With Craig and Kelly on the run, the detectives began to build a murder case against the couple. The DNA tests were still out, but police believed the body in that car had to be Melissa James."

The camera returns to Megan Foley, in the white tank top, walking her dogs, and Van Sant narrates, "The most startling piece of evidence came from Megan Foley, Kelly's pal, who went to the police with an astonishing story." The camera is once again on Craig and Kelly's house in the dark, with ominous music in the background. Van Sant narrates, "Megan told police that she was invited to the Titus house the night that Melissa James went missing." Megan then begins to explain her encounter at the house that night. Looking off to the left, with an unsure look in her eyes, Megan Foley begins the story with a high pitch voice, "Craig answered the door. And I was like, where's Kelly? And he, uhm motioned, she was upstairs in her bathroom."

(The inflection in her voice, at the end of every sentence makes it sound like she was asking a question. While she was talking, I was thinking 1980's Valley Girl, or American Pie, "This one time at band camp.")

For a few seconds Megan makes eye contact with Van Sant, and said, "Kelly was drying her hair, like acting, like totally normal, and, uhm, putting on make-up." (Megan's voice starts off deep then progressively gets higher and faster; she sounds unsure about what she was saying, even with basic details.) The video shows Melissa's picture, and Van Sant narrates Megan's words, "Megan said the couple began to talk about their problems with Melissa, accusing Melissa of stealing from them. But Craig then said the problem had been solved!" (The camera goes back to Megan, and I had to hit pause and take a break. I was wishing that Van Sant would just narrate Megan's words the entire time; the bad grammar, and all of the "uhms" and "likes" were about to send me over the edge! But then it occurred to me, if Megan Foley had not been on this show, and I had not heard her tell this story; I might not have thought twice about this trial.)

INTRODUCTION

Megan Foley picks up where Van Sant left off about Craig Titus. Foley looks to the left, then the right, and her eyes get wide as she said, "Craig started joking around saying that she (Melissa) is not going to bother us anymore; you know, she is not going to hurt us anymore. And I was like, whaa, like what do you mean?" After a nervous pause, she mumbled in a low voice, "Oh, she's just not. She's gone. We shipped her back to Florida." The picture then shows a blurry vision moving forward, as if someone is walking through a house, and Van Sant narrates, "But minutes later, Megan said Kelly pulled her into a bedroom closet, out of Craig's ear shot. Kelly then whispered that an argument with Melissa had spiraled out of control. Kelly said that she reached for a taser gun they kept in the house." (Cue taser gun on the screen.)

The camera returns to Megan; her eyes are shifting and nose is twitching, and with her "Valley Girl" inflection said, "Kelly was standing right there, you know, and she, uhm, pulled, like out this taser, and uhm, tried to use it on Melissa." Megan stutters through the next statement, "And I mean, she told me that, and she honestly said, that I did not have it turned up high enough, you know, because she honestly said it didn't do anything. So then she like, turned up the volume on the thing, and uhm, she shot it again; and that is the tru-, uhm, that is honestly what she said!"

(I made numerous observations when Megan Foley made this statement. For one, there is not a "low" or "high" button on a taser gun; that does not make sense. Also, Megan had to inject the phrase, "she honestly told me" into her statement; this is a phrase that a person typically uses right before they tell a lie. Most noteworthy however, was Megan's inability to articulate her words and finish a complete thought or sentence while peppering every sentence with "like" and "uhm.")

Van Sant must have picked up on this as well, because for the first time, he stops Megan, and repeats back what she just said, and asks her about the taser gun. As Megan is shaking her head "yes", Van Sant asks Megan, "So what happens then?" Megan's lower jaw is now moving back and forth, so they don't keep the camera on her long. The camera turns back to Van Sant, but the viewers can still hear her

◄ SWIFT INJUSTICE

talk. Megan states, "That was when Melissa took the taser from Kelly, and that's when Craig grabbed Melissa, and body slammed her." The camera goes back to the blurry image of the front of Craig and Kelly's house in the dark while creepy music plays in the background. Van Sant narrates more of Megan's story, "Then Megan says that Craig pinned Melissa down, while Kelly injected her with narcotics." The cameras are back on Megan; she looks Van Sant in the eyes then looks away, and says with a matter of fact, monotone voice, "Yep, Kelly took a needle, and shot a needle full of morphine in her (Melissa's) leg."

(By this point, I could barely stomach listening to this woman. She just told America about her friends torturing this girl, as if she was talking to a girlfriend on the phone about something that didn't really matter, and shrugging her shoulders like, "Oh well?" What kind of person would go over to a friend's house, listen to this story, and not run as fast as they could straight to the police? Something was not right about this woman and this story. I knew I had to concentrate, and listen closer, because it was clear to me that the only evidence the prosecution had, were the words that came out of this woman's mouth. And I needed to document everything this woman said, so that I could later compare it to her grand jury testimony.)

The producers must have felt my pain because they muffled Foley's voice out, like a Peanuts cartoon, when the teacher is talking, and all you hear is "wha-wha-wha-wha-wha." They also slowly blurred her face out as Van Sant began to narrate, "Megan went on to tell police that Craig busted into the closet with a disturbing tale of his own." The video returns to Megan; she looks rigid and uncomfortable. Megan stammers over her words, but eventually states, "Craig said, that yeah, uhm, it's you know, it's like really funny, it uhm, if you ever want to know how you can kill someone by choking them, I can show you." (Megan does not look at Van Sant one time when she tells him this story, and barely glances at him to see his reaction. Megan rubs her hand over her mouth and then licks her lips with her tongue; she looks like she is about to vomit.)

Then with an extra high pitched voice, Megan blurts out, "And I was like what do you mean? You can show, I mean, uhm, you can kill somebody by choking them?" Megan makes a motion like she is choking someone and mumbles extremely fast, "And he came behind me, like this, and you know, he uhm, like put my head in there, and he went like this, and he squeezed his bicep on me." Megan does not look up at Van Sant this time, until he questions her statement. With a look of confusion, Van Sant strokes his chin, looks at his notes, and slowly asks, "So he is saying, that Melissa is gone, and right after that, he is saying I will show you how you can kill somebody with a choke hold?" Megan incessantly blinks her eyes and affirmatively nods her head; with a creepy smirk she mumbles, "Uh-huh." Van Sant seems to be at a loss for words, and then he asks Megan, "What are you thinking to yourself when he is using a choke hold on you, and saying this is how it is done?" Megan responds, "I thought he was crazy."

After this, the scene is set with the camera moving forward erratically through the house to the front door, giving the viewers the image of a person frantically running out of the house. Then Van Sant narrates Megan's words, "All Megan wanted to do was get out of that house. As she was leaving, Craig pushed a black gym bag into her hands." The camera cuts back to the interview between Van Sant and Pierson. Van Sant states, "So at this point, Craig hands you a bag." Megan, looking off, nods her head "yes." Incessantly blinking her eyes, she replies, "Uh-huh, and at this point I am not asking questions." Van Sant asks Megan, "You didn't ask what was in the bag before you took it home?" Megan stumbles with a reply, and lets it slip that there was someone else with her, "I believe that we did, I mean, I think I did." Staring off in the air, Megan says Craig Titus told her, "It was some work-out equipment, work-out bands, and a taser gun." Picking up where they left off, Van Sant once again narrates Megan's words, "Frightened, Megan took the bag with the taser home. Megan then had her attorney call the police, who went back to Craig and Kelly's house with a search warrant."

(Details are left out that are crucial to the case and the credibility of Megan Foley; more questions needed to be asked! Going through my mind are essential questions such as: How long was Megan Foley at Craig and Kelly's house? Did Megan know that Melissa was dead in the house? Did Megan Foley leave right after Craig and Kelly said they killed Melissa? How long did Megan hold onto the bag before she turned it over to the police? And, why did Megan take the bag to a lawyer who then turned it over to the police? These unasked and unanswered questions would make anyone think Megan Foley is hiding something or is involved in some way.)

As the show resumes, the camera zooms in on the front of Craig and Kelly's house, and the homicide detectives working the case tell what they found with the search warrant. Lead Homicide Detective Dean O'Kelley states, "There were taser dots with serial numbers scattered throughout the house, and the serial numbers on those dots matched the gun Craig Titus gave Megan Foley in the black gym bag." The video shows images of the Las Vegas strip, and Van Sant narrates, "With all of that evidence, the police put out a warrant for Craig Titus and Kelly Ryan; but first they had to find them."

48 Hours shows video footage of the FBI raiding a nail spa where Kelly Ryan was getting a manicure. Van Sant narrates, "Nine days after Melissa's disappearance, the FBI tracked the couple to Boston. Kelly Ryan was arrested in a beauty shop." The camera shows Craig in the back of a police car, and Van Sant says, "Craig Titus was waiting in the truck outside." The camera shows a picture of Kelly Ryan handcuffed, and Van Sant states, "They were charged with Murder, Kidnapping and Arson. And 21 days after the body was found, it was officially identified as Melissa James. But getting justice for Melissa may be difficult. Prosecutors could have a hard time proving their case because the coroner could not say for sure how she died. He could not even say if it was murder."

48 Hours then turns to Craig Titus' attorney, Marc Saggese. The video shows Saggese boxing in a ring while Van Sant narrates, "Craig is fighting back, hiring a heavy hitter to defend him." Marc Saggese dramatically explains and demonstrates how he defends his clients in the courtroom while boxing in the ring. All geared up, Saggese comes out swinging his gloves hard at his sparring partner. After he punches the guy with a few jabs and a left hook, "Sly" Saggese says, "It's you, and it's the other guy. If he is better than you, he kicks your ass, and if you are better than him, you kick his ass."

INTRODUCTION

(This leaves me asking, "What the hell dude?" I was worried at this point; it looked like Judge Jackie Glass was not the only one mailing out audition tapes! I stopped and googled Marc Saggese to see if he was for real. To my surprise, just around this time, when Craig Titus and Kelly Ryan were in the fight of their lives, Marc Saggese and Michael Cristalli (Kelly's attorney) were shooting scenes for a reality show. A reality show based on Saggese and Cristalli's lives as criminal defense lawyers, defending high-profile cases. This reality show was later turned into a CBS Drama series called *The Defenders*.)

The story continues, and the video shows a truck driving down a dirt road, and Van Sant narrates; "Now it was time to hear from Craig Titus to hear what he has to say." A picture of Melissa James is shown, and Van Sant says, "More than two and a half years after Melissa's body was found in a burned out car, Craig Titus tells his story for the first time." (This interview with Craig was before the trial date, and Craig was limited on what he could and could not say to Van Sant with his lawyer by his side.)

Now the interview turned to Craig Titus. With a shaved head, eye glasses, and a blue button up dress shirt, Craig looks like he is still lifting weights and working out. After the attorneys walk in, and everyone shakes hands, Van Sant narrates, "Craig insists it was not murder. He said it all began when he walked into his house and saw a shocking sight." The video shows an image of Craig and Kelly's house, and Craig tells Van Sant his version of what happened that night. Titus states, "My wife is on the ground with taser darts in her leg. There is blood on Kelly's face and her shirt. Melissa is standing over Kelly with a taser gun in her hand. I pushed her to the floor, and I went to help my wife, but Melissa is still coming after us."

The picture breaks away to party pictures of Craig, Kelly, and Melissa, as Van Sant narrates, "Craig said the fight started when Kelly accused Melissa of stealing, and Melissa became enraged." Craig, looking Van Sant in the eyes the entire time, repeats that Melissa was out of her minds on drugs, "and had already shot Kelly multiple times with the Taser gun. When I entered the room, Melissa was physically attacking Kelly."

Craig states that he did everything he could to restrain Melissa, and he was yelling, "Melissa, stop, calm down, shut the fuck up!" Once Melissa stopped attacking Kelly, Craig yelled, "Get the Fuck out of my house Melissa! Pack up all your shit right now! Then that was the end of it."

Zooming in on a blurry version of Melissa's room, Van Sant narrates, "According to Craig, Melissa then ran into her bedroom and slammed the door. He then went upstairs with Kelly, and about 40 minutes passed." The camera returns to Craig, and he says, "It quieted down, we went downstairs, and Melissa was dead." With anguish on his face, and tears in his eyes, Craig says that he tried to revive Melissa, "but I couldn't."

Pictures of Craig and Kelly partying are shown, while Van Sant narrates, "Craig claims that he, Melissa and Kelly had been getting high on cocaine, painkillers, and crystal meth for days leading up to the fight, and Melissa took things too far." The video returns to the interview with Craig Titus. Van Sant questions Craig, "You are telling me that Melissa James over dosed?" Still maintaining eye-contact, and without hesitating, Craig nods his head, and answers, "She O.D.'d; Melissa had been shooting those drugs for months."

The camera turns from Craig to the video of a gurney in the Medical Examiner's Office. Van Sant narrates, "In fact, the autopsy revealed that there were enough drugs in her system to kill her, including, a fatal level of morphine. But how did it get there? Well there's Craig's story that she O.D.'d, and there was what Megan told the police." Next, *48 Hours* returns to Megan Foley, being interviewed by Van Sant. When questioned about that night, Megan Foley says, "Craig held her (Melissa) down, and Kelly put a needle full of morphine in her leg."

The camera goes back to Craig Titus being interviewed, and Van Sant narrates, "Craig insists that everything that happened to Melissa, transpired after they found her dead; they covered up the overdose after the fact because they were scared." Van Sant asks Craig, "Were you panicked?" Craig responds, "Oh my God, we were terrified!" *48 Hours* shows pictures of Craig working out while Van Sant narrates,

INTRODUCTION

"Yet, Craig and Kelly had enough sense to plant the debit card, buy the lighter fluid, burn the Jaguar, and falsely accuse Melissa of stealing money from them." Van Sant then looks at Craig and states, "That does not sound like two people that are panicked, it sounds like you are meticulously thinking this through."

(Now, I don't know about you, but from my perspective, this is an extremely biased remark from a neutral journalist, before a trial ever took place. I completely disagreed with Van Sant's comment. It sounded to me like they were panicked, and not thinking straight due to the effects of the drugs. If they were rationally thinking everything out, Craig and Kelly would not have left the debit card lying around that they just used to purchase lighter fluid, they would have destroyed it. If they were planning it out, perhaps they would have used cash at a small "mom and pop" store to purchase lighter fluid earlier in the day. They would not have frantically run to Wal-Mart, with surveillance cameras everywhere, at 3:30 a.m., 30 minutes before they burned the car. This story screams- drug induced, panicked cover-up.)

Craig Titus explains to Van Sant, "Well now we are terrified, and still doing drugs; and it was all bad!" Van Sant replies, "You have lied to cops, you have lied to Melissa's mother, why should I not believe that you are lying to me right now Craig?" Craig looks him square in the eyes, straightens his glasses and states, "I don't know why you should think I am not lying right now, all I can do is tell you that this is what happened."

The interview turns to the prosecutors, Josh Tomscheck and Robert Daskas. They tell Van Sant that there was duct tape all around Melissa's face and body. Van Sant asks, "Who duct tapes a dead body?" Tomscheck replies, "A murderer." Van Sant asks Tomscheck and Daskas if it hurt the prosecution's chance of winning because the Coroner's Report said that Melissa's death was "Undetermined", and could not be labeled a homicide. With a smug look on his face, Robert Daskas says, "I don't think it hurt our chances. When you have a victim that's been beat, tasered, injected, choked, duct taped, then burned in the back of a car, it is tougher for a pathologist to say this is exactly what happened."

SWIFT INJUSTICE

(Remember- Melissa was dead before the car was set on fire, so duct tape and fire were not contributing factors of her death. There is no physical evidence to prove the other allegations, only hear-say evidence from Megan Pierson Foley.)

Craig's attorney, Marc Saggese, seems overly confident when he states, "If you look at the medical evidence in this case, and you separate it from the events that occurred after she died, the State will not be able to prove their case beyond a reasonable doubt: that a murder occurred!" Van Sant narrates, "Their attorneys say that Craig and Kelly are guilty of a panicked cover-up, but not murder! High on drugs, they tried to dispose of Melissa's body, any way they could."

The video cuts back to Craig and Kelly's house as Van Sant narrates, "The prosecutors think that Craig and Kelly's cover-up story is nonsense. They said Craig Titus and Kelly Ryan cleaned up the crime scene, and even tried to get rid of all those taser dots with a vacuum cleaner." (There were still taser dots throughout the house; couldn't this simply mean that Craig and Kelly kept their house tidy? The taser dots are large and bright enough; if they wanted to find every last taser dot, it would not be that difficult.)

In the house, the interview turns to the detectives and the gym bag. Lead Homicide Detective Dean O'Kelley reports that not only was a taser gun found, but another weapon was found, a leather sap. Van Sant picks the leather sap up and reports, "Wow this is really heavy at the end of it; I could do some serious damage with this." The detective replies, "Absolutely!" Van Sant asks Detective Dean O'Kelley, "And what did you find on this leather sap that was significant?" The lead homicide detective, Dean O'Kelley, while looking down at the sap the entire time states, "We had the sap tested for DNA. And on the handle end of the sap was Craig Titus' DNA, and on the striking end of the sap, we found Melissa James' DNA." Van Sant asks the detective, "What does that tell you?" The Detective states, "that means that Craig Titus hit Melissa James over the head with this sap."

(What? This piece of evidence would prove, beyond a reasonable doubt, that Craig Titus beat Melissa to death! So why is it being revealed in a quick blurb at the end of this show? This was never

INTRODUCTION

mentioned by Robert Daskas or Megan Foley. Everything else was just hear-say from Megan Foley; but this would actually be forensic proof that a murder took place. Call me cynical, but this seems sketchy, and I just did not buy it. Certainly a detective wouldn't make something like that up on national television just to make the case against Craig Titus seem more damning than it actually was right before his trial. Right?)

Video clips of Craig and Kelly are shown while Van Sant narrates, "So what is the motive for all of this?" Prosecutors believe it is the oldest one in the book- sex and jealousy." Lead Prosecutor, Robert Daskas states, "That was a recipe for disaster. You've got three people involved with drug abuse. You have the potential of Kelly believing that Craig was in a relationship with Melissa. So in all likelihood, there was a confrontation between Kelly and Melissa. That is probably what started the whole thing." With slow music playing, video footage of Melissa is shown. Van Sant narrates, "Prosecutors want the jury to remember that even though Melissa was not perfect, she did not deserve to die the way she did."

48 Hours shifts gears completely, and shows a video of Craig Titus in the Clark County Detention Center, being pulled out of his cell, strapped to a chair, and blindfolded. Van Sant reports, "This story takes a strange turn when a tactical team hauls Craig Titus out of his room because of a jailhouse rumor of an escape plan." There is a break for a commercial, and *48 Hours* returns showing pictures of Craig Titus as a body builder, then of him naked, strapped down, blindfolded, & restrained in a wheel chair. Van Sant states, "This one time King of Bodybuilding, sat strapped and humbled in his new jail house throne." (From where I sat, this was a degrading comment that said a lot about this journalist, and this entire documentary about the case.)

48 Hours shows pictures of Melissa James as Van Sant narrates, "Two and a half years have passed since Melissa's death, and as the trial is about to begin, everything suddenly changes. Craig Titus and Kelly Ryan end their claims of innocence, and accept a plea deal. Craig pleads guilty to Second Degree Murder, First Degree Kidnapping, and Third Degree Arson; while Kelly gets off easy, pleading guilty to Battery and Arson."

But before he is sentenced, Craig tries to recant his plea in an interview with a local television station. Three days after taking a plea deal in this high-profile murder case, former body builder Craig Titus said that he did not commit the crime." Video footage of Craig being interviewed by a reporter from a phone at Clark County Detention Center shows Craig saying, "I took the plea bargain and admitted something that did not happen so that my wife can go home." The reporter asks, "So you took a plea deal to a crime that you did not commit?" And Craig emphatically replies, "Yes, absolutely!"

48 Hours displays video footage of the court room. Van Sant narrates, "In court, a furious Judge Jackie Glass demands to know if there is a deal or not." The Judge states, "The moment I saw that on the news, I had concerns of whether your plea was really free and voluntarily given. So I am here to find out, before we go through with this, is this what you plead guilty to? Is this what you did?" The camera turns to Craig, he hesitates, and shakes his head "no", then looks over at his lawyer, and lets out a sigh. Then, shrugging his shoulders in defeat, Craig looks down, and in a soft voice, reluctantly says, "Yes ma'am."

(Craig looked at his lawyer, his body language said that he did not want to do this, and his lawyer was shaking his head "yes". At the last minute, it looked like Craig wanted to back out, and his lawyer talked him back into it. It seemed as if Craig did not have a choice, this was the only option, and there was no turning back; but why? There was no physical evidence of murder, just hearsay accusations. Nothing could have been proven beyond a reasonable doubt. This was an easy win for the defense! So why urge Craig Titus to take this plea deal? My head was spinning as I watched this take place.)

With the camera scanning the room, the judge tells everyone to have a seat. As Robert Daskas speaks, he turns around to the packed court room and with a raised voice shouts, "The only thing worse than losing your child, is losing your child in this manner. If your dog, or pet, or goldfish died, you would not give it a burial like this. What they

INTRODUCTION

did was unspeakable!" At this point, Daskas turns back around, looks at the Judge, pauses, and then sits down.

Kelly Ryan and Craig Titus address the court, and the loved ones of the victim speak. After everyone has a chance to speak, it is Judge Jackie Glass' turn to address Craig Titus. Judge Jackie Glass said, "Mr. Titus came into this process as the big man, all kinds of muscles, and famous, and you look at him now, and you see what he has become; he is nothing, nothing but a murderer." (I am sure right when Judge Jackie Glass left the court room after admonishing Craig Titus, she mailed her audition tape straight to Los Angeles.)

Van Sant reports that Craig Titus received the maximum sentence of 21-55 years while Kelly Ryan was given 6-17 years. The video fades to black, and words scroll across the screen: "Craig Titus asked the court to reduce his sentence or let him stand trial. That request was denied. Kelly Ryan divorced Craig Titus later that year."

Reading over the Grand Jury Transcripts

Not only did I read Megan Pierson Foley's testimony that she gave to the grand jury in March of 2005, I also read the entire transcript of the grand jury hearings, at which time I discovered my suspicions were true. The first thing that caught my attention was the leather sap was in fact tested, and according to the Las Vegas Metropolitan Police Department Crime Scene Analysts, there was no DNA evidence found on either end of the sap. The test results read "Inconclusive".

The Lead Homicide Detective, Dean O'Kelley, in the *48 Hours* interview said that the sap was tested, and Craig's DNA was found on one end of the weapon and Melissa James' DNA on the other. This led me to question this investigation all together! What else would this homicide detective mislead the public about in relation to the Craig Titus' case? With this question in the back of my mind, I turned to the key witness, Megan Pierson Foley's statements on National Television and under oath to the grand jury in March of 2005.

After reading Megan Pierson Foley's grand jury testimony, my suspicions were confirmed. Megan either lied on national television or in her grand jury testimony; or she lied in both the interview and testimony. Megan Pierson Foley's statements were riddled with contradictions throughout her entire grand jury testimony; she would say one thing and then three statements later, she would completely contradict herself under oath. Megan Pierson Foley testified under oath that she in fact knew that Melissa James was dead and in the trunk of the car *before* she left that house.

According to her own testimony, Megan knew every detail prior to the cover-up, before it ever happened. She knew the times that everything occurred, the places they went, and the names of everyone involved. Moreover, with that knowledge, Megan Pierson Foley walked out of Craig Titus and Kelly Ryan's house with a bag of evidence, and she did nothing about it.

Megan Pierson Foley's Grand Jury Testimony

(The 6th Amendment's Confrontation Clause- the 6th Amendment to the U.S. Constitution sets out many rights for defendants during a criminal prosecution, including the right of the accused to confront their accusers. The relevant text of the 6th Amendment reads as follows: *In all criminal prosecutions, the accused shall enjoy the right to be confronted with the witnesses against him*. The Confrontation Clause guarantees criminal defendants the opportunity to face the prosecution's witnesses in the case against them and dispute the witnesses' testimony. This unfortunately never happened in this case, and neither Craig Titus nor the Defense was provided the chance to challenge Megan Pierson Foley's grand jury testimony. Listed below in bold print, with Megan Pierson Foley's grand jury testimony, are Craig Titus' comments to Ms. Foley's allegations.)

Having been first duly sworn by the Foreperson of the Grand Jury to tell the truth, the whole truth, & nothing but the truth, Megan Pierson Foley testified as follows:

Q: Megan, how old are you?
A: *I am 25.*

Q: And I actually called you Megan Foley. Is it Megan Pierson?
A: *Yeah, I haven't changed my name after I got married.*

INTRODUCTION

Q: I understand you recently got married, what is your husband's name?
A: *Jeremy Foley*
Titus Answer: Jeremy divorced her the next year for lying under oath.

Q: Do you know someone by the name Kelly Ryan?
A: *Yes, I do.*

Q: How do you know Kelly?
A: *I met her at Baja Fresh in September 2004. She was my best friend.*
Titus Answer: She was her client. Calling Kelly her best friend is ridiculous! Kelly trained her for less than a year. Megan was a totally obsessed fan!

Q: What were the circumstances of how you met Kelly?
A: *I work across the street, walked in there, and saw her standing there. I idolized her for quite a few years, so when I saw her, I struck up a conversation.*

Q: You say you idolized her, Can you explain that?
A: *I do figure competitions and she is a fitness competitor.*

Q: Okay. You had followed her career for a number of years.
A: *Correct, for over six years.*
Titus Answer: Megan was a psycho fan for more than six years. She was obsessed with Kelly, and she turned into a stalker. Megan was never Kelly's best friend- what a joke!

Q: Explain how your relationship progressed from that day.
A: *Previously, I had broken my back, and that day she told me ways to heal, and said she would start training me when I was back on my feet.*

Q: Did you in fact start training under Kelly Ryan at her house?
A: *Yes, I did.*

Q: And about when did you start doing that?
A: *It was sometime in January 2005.*
(To be clear: According to Megan's own testimony, Ms. Foley had been a fan of Kelly Ryan for six years. At the time, Kelly was making

SWIFT INJUSTICE

an appearance at Baja Fresh, across the street from where Megan worked. While Kelly was signing autographs for her fans, Megan just happened to run into her idol, and struck up a conversation with her. Kelly was cordial to her, like she was with all of her fans. Being a trainer, Kelly gave Megan her card, and told Megan to call her when she was able to start working out again. Megan called her four to five months later and then she started training under Kelly Ryan.)

Titus Answer: Megan's already lying; she did not start working out until after Arnold. Kelly didn't train any clients before Arnold because she was focused on training herself. So it was in the middle of March 2005.

(This means that Megan only knew Kelly for 8-9 months before Melissa died.)

Q: Did there come a time when you spoke to Kelly Ryan on a daily basis?
A: *Yes, about a month after I started training with her.*

Q: And by December of 2005, how good of friends were you?
A: *We were best friends; she was supposed to be my maid of honor in my wedding.*

Titus Answer: Kelly thought she was nuts for asking her!
(I tried to make sense of this, but had a hard time wrapping my mind around it. Megan barely knew Kelly Ryan, and asked Kelly to be in her wedding. Most people have life-long friends and family members in their wedding, not someone they have only known for a few months. This says something about Megan, and her lack of friends and real relationships.)

Q: When were you married?
A: *February 12, 2006*

Q: How do you feel about being here today?
A: *Very upset. It's very depressing. Just not, I didn't think (pause) I thought I knew her better than this.*
(After seven months?)

Q: Okay. And when all of this that we are talking about came down, did you give some statements to the police?

INTRODUCTION

A: *Yes I did.*

Q: When was the first time, approximately, when you gave a statement to the police about the events that occurred on December 13th and 14th?
A: *I believe it was a week later, maybe even two.*
(In the *48 Hours* interview, Megan said that after Craig handed her the black gym bag, she ran out the front door and immediately turned it over to the authorities. "A week or two later" is a life time in a police investigation.)

Q: How many statements did you give?
A: *I've given two.*
(In her first statement, sometime between Dec.21st and Dec.28th, Megan told police that she did not believe that Craig or Kelly killed Melissa James because Melissa James died of a drug overdose. So from Megan's first to second story, she did an about-face, and went from stating that Melissa died from an accidental drug overdose to telling the police that Craig and Kelly killed her. This appears to be a huge coincidence because at that time, the prosecution had no evidence to prove that Melissa was killed; instead, the toxicology report supported a drug overdose. The autopsy report stated that Melissa James' manner of death was inconclusive, but a contributing factor in her death was opiate intoxication; in a second autopsy report, it was revealed that Melissa James had toxic levels of both morphine and heroin in her system. If Melissa died of a drug overdose, it would be the end of the road for this murder case; unless the prosecution could turn the overdose around and pin it on the defendants. In Megan's second statement, she said Kelly told her they injected Melissa James' with morphine. The revelation of heroin in Melissa's system came out much later, well after Megan made this second statement. The autopsy report also showed that Melissa was a chronic user of many different narcotics, primarily methamphetamines; and police records indicated that Melissa James had numerous drug arrests in Las Vegas and in Florida. If Melissa James habitually abused drugs, and had already been injecting drugs into her system all day, why would Craig and Kelly hold her down and inject more morphine in Melissa to kill her? This is not like a nurse giving a person a shot of antibiotics in the

ass, these drugs have to go directly into the vein; and after years of being an intravenous drug abuser, finding a healthy vein on Melissa James would have been a difficult task. According to Craig Titus, all three women, Melissa James, Megan Pierson, and Kelly Ryan, injected each other, every day with various drugs. If Kelly Ryan injected Melissa James with drugs the day of her death, this would not have been out of the ordinary- they did this to each other all of the time!)

Q: And is it fair to say that there are some things that you said in your second statement or that you remember today that were not included in the first statement that you gave the police?
A: *Yes, because I was protecting Kelly.*
Titus Answer: Up to this point, I changed my story twice, and Robert Daskas said that I could not be believed because I repeatedly changed my story. Megan changes her story over and over, and she becomes the prosecution's number one witness. Why does Robert Daskas (the prosecutor) not mention that Megan changed her story when he goes on *48 hours*? Because he forced Megan to tell this story; Megan could either say what the prosecution told her to say, or go to jail, period!

Q: Why was that?
A: *Uhm, I believed that the things that I was told about Melissa were true, and with the light of things, I found they're not. So I was just being naïve and tried to protect her in a way that....I didn't think that what I was holding back mattered.*
(Holding back that Craig Titus & Kelly Ryan tasered, body-slammed, beat up, choked, and injected Melissa James with morphine and heroin would probably matter!)
Titus Answer: Because Megan knew there was no murder!!!

Q: Okay, on Monday, December 12th did you speak to Kelly?
A: *Yes I did when I went over to her house to train at 5:00 p.m.*

Q: Did Kelly say anything to you at that time about Melissa and some sort of identity theft or theft?
A: *Not at that time, no.*

INTRODUCTION

(When asked this same question again by a juror at the end of her testimony, Megan said that Kelly told her about Melissa stealing her credit cards on Monday night.)
Titus Answer: Megan is saying exactly what the prosecutor told her to say, and he wants her to say this because he needed to establish a motive.

Q: Did you see Melissa at that time?
A: *Uh- huh, when I was training, yes.*

Q: And prior to December 12th, how many times had you seen Melissa?
A: *Uhm, I probably saw Melissa a total of ten times while I was working out at Kelly's house; and a couple of times outside of there, but that was about it.*
(Megan will contradict herself later in this testimony. Megan goes into detail about private conversations she had with Melissa James. Intimate exchanges between the two women that would have never taken place unless they had a relationship.)

Q: Prior to Tuesday, December 13th, had Kelly ever said anything to you about having any potential problems with Melissa stealing from her?
A: *No*
(This is the second time Robert Daskas asks Megan this question, because she is mixing up "their" story. Megan will change this story a few questions down.)

Q: Did you have any contact with Craig or Kelly on Tues., Dec. 13th?
A: *I don't believe so, no; I tried contacting her but I couldn't reach her; No I take that back, yes I did.*
(Seriously..."No I didn't see Craig or Kelly the day Melissa overdosed!" Oh wait, unless you count those six hours that we watched movies, snorted lines, looked at a dead body in the trunk of the car, and discussed how to cover everything up; in that case, yes I saw them.)

Q: When was the first time you had contact with Craig and Kelly that day?

A: Around I want to say ten o'clock in the morning -ish, somewhere around there.
(-ish?)

Q: What was the nature of that contact?
A: Craig had contacted me earlier than that and was just going into further detail about what they had found in Melissa's room.
(Everyone knew that Craig did not like Megan. Craig never talked to Megan about anything, so why would he call her on the phone to gossip about Melissa? When Kelly and Melissa started fighting that week, Craig did everything in his power to diffuse the situation. He paid for Melissa to stay in a hotel room and bought her a plane ticket home. Craig did not want any added drama to take place before Melissa left to move back with her mother in New Jersey.)
Titus Answer: This conversation did not take place that morning; it took place that evening after MJ (Melissa James) had already overdosed.

Q: What time did Craig call you on Dec.13th?
A: Around 9 a.m.
Titus Answer: I never called Megan in my life; she's a liar!

Q: Was that unusual to you?
A: Absolutely
Titus Answer: Hell yes that's unusual! That makes me furious; the prosecution had her make that up! Check the phone records; they have the phone records for everything else. I never called Megan, period!

Q: How much contact did you have with Craig Titus?
A: Contact at the house when we were in person, but via phone or something like that, not very often at all, once a month if that.

Q: Did you find it unusual that Craig called your cell phone directly?
A: Yes

Q: And what did Craig tell you at that time?
A: That he had gone into Melissa's room and found a lock box that had credit cards, copies of credit cards, a HELOC statement- Home Equity Line of Credit, and copies of IDs.

INTRODUCTION

(A HELOC statement, hmmm- and what does Megan do for a living?)
Titus Answer: Once again, this is a conversation we had that night, after Melissa overdosed. When Megan saw that HELOC statement, she shit her pants because she had embezzled money on our home loan, and was afraid that the police would figure it out!

Q: What was his demeanor like when he was telling you this?
A: *Very pissed, very angry; he said that there are three things you don't mess with: friends, family, and his money.*
(This was something Craig said all the time; this quote was even on his web site.)
Titus Answer: I never called Megan and said that!

Q: Was this a message he left or did you have a conversation with him?
A: *I believe that was the time that he did leave me a message and later on in the morning that was the conversation he and I had.*

Q: So at 9:00 a.m., he leaves you a message?
A: *Uh-huh*
Titus Answer: Oh my God! The Prosecution is attempting to form a time line where I called going into detail about what I found in Melissa's room...then got angry on the day she died... motive to kill on Dec.14th!

Q: Did you call him back?
A: *Uh-huh, around eleven-ish, I believe.*

Q: And that is when you have this conversation?
A: *Uh-huh*
Prosecution: "You need to say "yes" for her (the reporter) because she is taking everything down and she can't get "uh-huh's" and "huh-uh's."

Q: And what time did you have a conversation with Kelly?
A: *Around ten-ish.*

Q: Was this the first time you heard from her about potential problems with Melissa?
A: *Yes*

Titus Answer: Another outright lie, Megan already said that Kelly was complaining about Melissa days earlier.

Q: After you have this conversation with Craig and Kelly, when is the next time you attempt to contact Kelly?
A: After I had my final at U.N.L.V, which I want to say was around two o'clock.
Titus Answer: Is it not convenient for the prosecution that it was 2 o'clock, the same time the taser was being fired? More prosecution coaching!

Q: Why were you calling her?
A: I wanted to see if they wanted to get together for dinner to celebrate me graduating from school.

Q: Did you plan on working out with Kelly that day?
A: Yes, that also was a reason I was calling.
(The day in question is a Tuesday, and Megan said herself that she only worked out on Monday, Wednesday, and Friday. Also, Megan had never called Kelly before when she worked out on those days; she would just show up. Why does she have to call before she comes over now?)

Q: Was it sort of your intention that you were going to work out that day?
A: Yes

Q: Did you get any response back from Kelly prior to 5:00 p.m.?
A: No

Q: Was that unusual?
A: Yes

Q: Did you assume then that you weren't going to work out that day?
A: Yes
(According to both Kelly Ryan and Craig Titus, Megan appears to be someone that pushes herself on Kelly, wanting Kelly desperately to be her best friend. It is hard to imagine that Megan would not go over to Kelly's house after she was finished with school to insist on Kelly

INTRODUCTION

going to her graduation party. Kelly appears to be her only friend after all.)

Q: What did you do instead?
A: *I made dinner reservations at Green Valley Ranch.*

Q: When was the next time you heard from Craig or Kelly?
A: *While we were at dinner, so 6:30 or seven.*
Titus Answer: They never went to the country club to have dinner. Megan went to Tony's house to hang out with his girlfriend, and then she stopped by Greg Ruiz's house to pick up cocaine. Then she came over to our house uninvited with two 8-Balls of Cocaine!

Q: Which one called you?
A: *Craig, from their home phone.*

Q: What was the nature of the conversation?
A: *He was just discussing more stuff about Melissa. Saying that he had bought her a plane ticket, and was sending her to Florida, but then would contradict and say he dropped her at the corner store, that he didn't feel sorry for her and they were kicking her out for stealing their stuff.*

Q: Were there conversations about whether you and Jeremy would go over to their house and get together that night?
A: *Yes, I got about three calls while we were at dinner.*

Q: Who called you next, and what was the nature of the call?
A: *Kelly called because she was pissed off. So we started to compare stories of what Melissa had told me and what, just regarding that I better find a replacement for my maid of honor because Kelly would not be around, and Kelly interpreting that to mean she was going to be dead versus it was regarding, I think her intentions were elsewhere.* (Let me try to interpret what I think Megan is trying to say: "Melissa told both Megan and Kelly something in private. They are now comparing what Melissa said to both of them. Melissa told Megan that she better find someone to replace Kelly as her maid of honor because Kelly wouldn't be around much longer." Even translated this does not make sense. I am not sure if Megan just botched a story that the prosecution made up for her, or if this conversation actually took place.

Remember, Megan said she had only seen Melissa a handful of times in passing, and had never really talked to her. But apparently, in passing, Melissa told Megan that Kelly was going to die before Megan's wedding, and Megan would need to replace her. If this is true, it sounds like a threat from Melissa, so it seems unlikely that Megan would not tell Kelly this before then.)

Q: You don't think that is what Melissa meant?
A: No
(I wish I could have been a fly on the wall when Megan flubbed her lines and said this; I bet the prosecutor's face was priceless!)

Q: Did you and Kelly have a discussion about what Melissa meant by that?
(In a Preliminary Hearing, the Defense would have torn her apart, but this is the prosecution's witness, so she can explain with a one word answer.)
A: Yes

Q: And did Kelly indicate that they were threatened in any other way by Melissa?
A: No

Q: During that conversation, did you discuss going over to Craig & Kelly's house?
A: Yes, I believe that Kelly handed the phone over to Craig and he talked more about Melissa, and he, I could hear him speak to her (Kelly), you know, is it okay if Megan and Jeremy come over? And he came back and was like Kelly is not feeling well, how about you guys come over tomorrow, and then we hung up.

Titus Answer: Megan was the one that called us all day and all night because she wanted to know every detail about what was happening! The phone records will show that; we didn't call her, and I sure as fuck didn't call. Tony had filled her in on some stuff, and Kelly told her a little. I wanted Kelly to shut up about it. I didn't want Megan to know anything because she was a loud mouth! I sure as hell didn't want them to come over to the house. The story is backwards, Megan asked Kelly if they could come over, and Kelly asked me. I said absolutely not, and Megan kept insisting so Kelly told her

INTRODUCTION

she wasn't feeling well, we would get together another time. Megan bothers the fuck out of me, and I was already on edge; I am not exaggerating when I say MEGAN WAS THE LAST PERSON I WANTED TO SEE THAT NIGHT!

Q: Did you get another phone call from them while you were at dinner?
A: *Yes from Kelly.*
(Is this phone call #6 or #7 from Craig and Kelly to Megan?)

Q: What was the nature of that conversation?
A: *More stuff, just reminiscing about stuff that Melissa had said in the past, that if Craig doesn't kill you- you're better off dead anyway type stuff that she was worried about, and so we decided at that point, she's like come over after you guys get done with dinner.* (Let's break this down- the nature of the conversation between Kelly and Megan was "just reminiscing about stuff that Melissa had said in the past"- When Megan was first asked if Kelly had mentioned Melissa stealing from her prior to Tuesday, December 13th, Megan replied "no". Then when asked about her relationship with Melissa, she said she saw her about ten times, but didn't really talk to her. But earlier in the testimony, Megan said Melissa told her that Kelly would be dead before Megan's wedding. So either Megan was lying before, or she is lying now, but either way she is lying. Megan is stirring the pot, and getting Kelly even more worked up and upset with Melissa James. After Megan and Kelly are done "just reminiscing" about Melissa, Kelly tells Megan, "If Craig does not kill you, you are better off dead, type stuff." Most people reminisce about pleasant things, and they don't have conversations about "killing someone type stuff!" Megan had never mentioned the word "kill", and then casually throws this in at the end of the statement where it does not make sense.)

Q: Did you and Jeremy then go over after dinner?
A: *Yes we did. We went over around 10:30-11:00 p.m.*
Titus Answer: It was two hours before that.

Q: Did you stop anywhere between Green Valley Ranch and their house?

A: We went home and changed clothes, got my puppy then went over there.

(Megan and Jeremy's dinner reservations were at 6:30 p.m.; so they were most likely finished around 8:00 to 8:30 p.m. According to Megan's testimony, she and Jeremy arrived at Craig and Kelly's house around 10:30-11:00 p.m. If they actually went to dinner, changed clothes, then went straight over to Craig and Kelly's house, there are at least two hours not accounted for.)

Titus Answer: They didn't go to the country club to eat; before Megan came over, she picked up some weed from Tony and coke from Ruiz.

Q: And what was your impression of why you were going over there?
A: To celebrate graduation, and just to sit there and figure out what had gone on between, you know, compare stories.

(So according to Megan, Craig told her they got rid of Melissa, and Kelly told her that if Craig does not kill you, you are better off dead, and Megan wants to come celebrate her graduation at their house. Megan repeatedly uses the phrase; "We were going to compare stories," yet Megan insists that she had no knowledge of anything prior to arriving at Craig and Kelly's house.)

Titus Answer: Megan brought a bag of weed and two 8-balls of cocaine over to the house. The second she walked in the door, she wanted to snort coke with Kelly and gossip; that's all Megan ever wanted to do!

Q: Now at this particular time when you go over there, are you under the influence of any sort of drugs or alcohol?
A: No drugs. Jeremy and I had shared a bottle of wine at dinner but I wouldn't, we were not driving, uhm, so not, I mean, not drunk or anything like that, no way.

(I tried to read this with a straight face, when she is answering a question about drinking or doing drugs, and Megan slurs her words in the transcript- classic! This was where Craig and the defense knew they had Megan. It was no wonder she was stumbling over her words, because there were many witnesses for the defense that had seen both Megan and Jeremy doing drugs. They were in Craig and Kelly's close circle of friends, all of whom did an excessive amount of drugs together. Craig said that Megan and Kelly would snort and inject each other with cocaine on a daily basis. Megan did not have an ounce of credibility. She would have ended up being the defense's star witness because during cross-examination at the trial, Megan's story, and lies, particularly about her drug abuse, would have been exposed. All that the defense would have needed to do would be a hair follicle test, and Megan would have been out because she lied under oath! I interviewed numerous people myself that confirmed Megan was out of control on drugs; this wasn't a big secret.)

Q: What did you find when you got over to their house?
A: *Craig, you can tell, was a little disturbed. And Craig showed us, you know, this bag with crystal meth, and some bloody needles, and...*
(On *48 Hours*, Melissa did not start her story off with looking at Crystal Meth and needles, she just ran up to Kelly's bathroom to chit-chat while Kelly got ready).
Titus Answer: This happened after Megan, Jeremy, and Kelly all went into the garage and looked at Melissa's body in the trunk of the car later in the evening, not when they first walked in the door. If anything, Megan was showing all of us all the drugs she bought before she came over.

Q: So as you get there, Craig is still talking about what Melissa did or didn't do?
A: *Uh-huh*
(Craig, Craig, Craig- Daskas has a boner for Craig.)
Titus Answer: Not true, they go in the closet to talk. I don't say a word! I was pissed the fuck off that she showed up after I told her not to, and she knew it!

Q: Is that a yes?
A: *Yes. Sorry.*
Titus Answer: Notice how many times Daskas says my name- he is gunning for me and me alone!

Q: Where did you go when you first got to the house?
A: We went upstairs, into the office first which in their house is right next to the master bedroom and then I walked around to the master bedroom.

Q: Where did Jeremy go?
A: He stayed in the office with Craig.

Q: What is Kelly doing in the bathroom?
A: Drying her hair, putting on lotion and make-up; she just got out of the shower.

Q: What happens next?
A: We talk a little bit here and there about class, working out, Kelly mentions a few things about Melissa and what she has done, and I walked back and forth between the office and the bathroom a couple of times. (After you have been talking about a murder all day, would you casually talk about classes at school and working out?)

Q: Does there come a time that Kelly starts to talk to you about what happened potentially to Melissa?
A: Yes

Q: What's Kelly's demeanor like when she tells you this?
A: She keeps her voice very quiet, obviously didn't want Craig to hear anything that she was saying because every time he walked in, she would stop talking.
Titus Answer: I did not want Kelly telling her anything- this is true! I wanted to keep everyone out of it, especially Megan. Kelly was the one that ran her mouth!

Q: So what does she tell you in a hushed voice about Melissa?
A: Kelly said that they had gotten Melissa a hotel room the night before so Craig went over to the hotel to confront Melissa about what he had found. It ended up getting back over to the house. Kelly was sitting upstairs and Melissa and Craig came in, and Melissa supposedly had a taser gun. At some point the taser gun got into Kelly's hands and she turned around and tried to use it on Melissa.
(That story makes absolutely no sense, and does not match her previous stories. Here Megan is saying Melissa had the taser in her hands, and it somehow got into Kelly's hands. Megan is either lying on television or under oath.)
Titus Answer: I did not get MJ a hotel room so that I could confront her about anything, that's a total lie! I got MJ a hotel room the night

before because she and Kelly would not stop fighting. I purchased MJ a plane ticket to New Jersey because I cared about her, but could not have her around anymore; she was toxic. I went back to the hotel the next morning to pick MJ up so she could come home and pack for her flight. I dropped her off and left; phone records and surveillance cameras show that I was still at the hotel room at the time of Melissa's death.

Q: And you said you're not sure which one had the taser?
A: *Melissa had it at first and then Kelly took it from her.*
(I have a big problem with this! The way this was worded in the Las Vegas Review Journal and in his book, *Fire in the Desert- The True Story of the Craig Titus-Kelly Ryan Murder Mystery*, Glenn Puit made it sound as if Kelly Ryan had the taser gun all along, and was brutalizing Melissa James with it. On all of the television shows about the case, Lead Homicide Detective Dean O'Kelley and Lead Clark County Prosecutor Robert Daskas go into great detail about the taser dots found in the house, and how they told the time of death. Every time Robert Daskas was interviewed in the newspaper and national television, he said that Kelly Ryan tasered Melissa James, and that is one big lie! According to the prosecution's witness, Melissa James had the taser and Melissa shot Kelly Ryan with the gun! How could the taser gun be a deadly weapon if Melissa used it on Kelly?)

Q: Okay, What else did Kelly tell you?
A: *She turned on the taser to use it and that it I guess stunned her in the back of the neck, but she didn't have it up high enough, so she yelled for Craig and he came upstairs, picked Melissa up, brought her downstairs into the living room, body slammed her and started beating her up.*
Titus Answer: I walked in and saw Kelly lying on the ground jerking and flopping around. Melissa was tasing Kelly in the leg. A taser gun shoots darts connected to wires, you cannot press it to the neck to shoot it; and there are no settings to increase the voltage to a higher shock!
(When asked if the investigators took fingerprints of the taser gun in the Grand Jury Testimony, of course the answer was "no." So either they seriously compromised the investigation, and did not finger print

a "murder weapon," or they did finger print it, and withheld the information from the defense.)

Q: Now is Kelly able to tell this all to you in one big statement or is it interrupted?
A: Interrupted. Every time Craig came in the room, she stopped talking about it.

Q: What would Kelly start to talk about once Craig entered?
A: What Craig did to Melissa?
(Daskas must be kicking himself for having this woman be their star witness!)

Q: When Craig left the room would she start talking about what happened to Melissa?
A: Immediately.

Q: Did Kelly move you anywhere in the room at one point?
A: When Craig and Jeremy were in the room, we walked into the closet. We walked in there and shut the doors and kept whispering.
Titus Answer: They were in the closet, snorting and shooting the drugs that Megan brought over to the house that night. This was not unusual; Megan and Kelly did this all the time. This is where they always went when I was at home and Megan brought cocaine over. They sat in the closet and gossiped while they did drugs. It pissed me off because I felt like they were doing this behind my back.

Q: Are you asking her any questions at this point?
A: A little bit here and there, but it was just when Craig would walk in that she would stop talking about it, and I was like what, what, what happened now, or how did it happen?

Q: Did Kelly indicate to you why she tasered Melissa in the first place?
A: No
(So for no apparent reason, Melissa pulled out a taser gun from her ass, and just walked in and tasered Kelly for no apparent reason. Then it switched hands and Kelly tasered Melissa in the neck, but it was not turned up high enough so it did not do anything- which, according to the prosecution's experts is not possible.)
Titus answered: I was a guilty man after this lie hit the newspapers.

Q: So at this point Kelly's told you that she called Craig upstairs, Craig took Melissa downstairs and body slammed her in the living room?
A: Correct

(According to Kelly Ryan, Melissa was yelling that she was going to kill her, and Kelly was simply trying to defend herself. Ryan said that Melissa was the aggressor, and she did what she had to do to survive. It was fight or flight, and Kelly Ryan chose to fight!)

Titus answered: I was nowhere around while these two went at it! I was back at the hotel having sex with one of my side girls. I came in after the fact- this body slamming shit never happened! The prosecutor told Megan to say that to save her own ass; and she did! Think about it- I am a professional bodybuilder, if I body slammed Melissa, I would have broken her in half. This would have shown up on the x-rays. She would have had broken ribs or a concussion, but she had nothing, so this is a gross exaggeration in Megan's testimony. Or should I say in Robert Daskas' testimony?

Q: And you said Craig started to beat her up?
A: Uh-huh

Titus answered: Lie, lie, lie! If I beat her up, bones would be broken, and this would be in the autopsy report. I have never hit a woman in my life!

Q: Are those the words that Kelly used?
A: Uh-huh.

Q: Did she tell you anything else that happened to Melissa?
A: *She said that Melissa at some point had taken a Xanax to go to sleep, and while she was sleeping, Kelly went into her room, and punched her in the face.*

Titus Answer: Of all the lies that Megan told, this one was the most outrageous. If Megan was going to make up a lie about Kelly, at least make it believable. Kelly and Melissa did fight and argue non-stop for a week, but it was over Melissa taking her car and being gone for days, and over Melissa being a pig around the house, and expecting Kelly to do everything for her. They did yell at each other, but it never got physical until the end between the two girls. Kelly would not go in and just maliciously hit someone while they were asleep. Kelly was defending herself against Melissa, period!

Q: Melissa took Xanax and went to bed?
A: Yes

Titus Answer: Holy shit! Right there Megan is saying that Melissa took a Xanax and went to bed, and she was very much alive. That tells you- she does not know shit!

Q: Did this make sense to you at the time?
A: No
(Nothing Megan has said up to this point has made any sense; and when something does not make sense, it is usually a lie!)

Q: Did you ask any follow-up questions about that?
A: *Not really, because it started to seem very fishy to me.*
(If in fact Kelly had just told Megan that she tasered Melissa, Craig body slammed her then beat her up, then Kelly beat her up while she was sleeping, who in their right mind would not go check on the girl, or leave the house immediately and call the police? Maybe someone that has something to hide.)

Q: And Kelly tells you she walks into where Melissa is sleeping and hits her?
A: *Uh-huh.*

Q: Is that a yes?
A: *Yes.*

Q: What else does Kelly tell you about what happened to Melissa?
A: *She said that she punched Melissa a couple of times; she showed me marks on her knuckles from it. Then she said that Craig was holding Melissa down and told Kelly to go get the morphine, and Kelly shot a needle of morphine into Melissa's leg. She said that Melissa was very resilient because it did not do anything to her.* (Isn't it interesting that Megan throws in this story about Craig and Kelly injecting Melissa with morphine after the toxicology report listed morphine as a contributing factor in Melissa's death? Megan had never mentioned this before the grand jury hearing, not even in her second statement to the police weeks after the incident. In the second autopsy report, heroin and morphine were both listed as contributing factors in Melissa's death. So what about the heroin Daskas? Did Craig and Kelly inject

Melissa with heroin as well? If so, why does Megan not mention heroin in her grand jury testimony?)
Titus Answer: Kelly and Melissa shot each other up all the time, but so did Megan and Kelly. It is hard to find a vein on yourself, and easier to administer the shot to another person, so those three did this to each other all the time. However, heroin was in Melissa's system, and I know for a fact that none of us have ever touched heroin.

Q: At any time during this evening does Craig indicate to you anything about a physical fight with Melissa?
A: He also said that he beat her up. (We are leaving out a big step-up to now Kelly and Megan were hiding in the closet, and Kelly was whispering this information so Craig could not hear her telling Megan. When do they leave the closet, and why does Craig join in the conversation? Also, Megan starts the sentence with, "he also said," so what did he say before that?)
Titus Answer: After all the questioning about the fight, it just now comes out that I personally said this? And it is only after the prosecution asks if "Craig indicated to you that he was in a physical fight with Melissa?" Robert Daskas keeps leading the witness, and turning everything on me. Megan never said a word about me beating Melissa up until the prosecutor leads her with this question. If I beat her up, why doesn't Megan elaborate on that, and provide details about that beating? Because I didn't beat her up, and Megan knows she can't explain how I beat her up because it's all a lie.

Q: When did this happen?
A. When I was walking back and forth between the master bedroom and the office, I could tell that Craig was informing Jeremy of what had gone on, and Craig told us that, I mean me that, you know, he had beat her up downstairs.
(It is so interesting to me that on the *48 Hours* interview, Megan never mentions Jeremy being there at the house. When she does say "we" she changes it back to "me". Then here she said, "Craig told us, I mean me." Why does she do this?)

Q: And so the whole time that you and Kelly are in the master bedroom, Craig is walking back and forth, where is Jeremy?
A: In the office.

Q: At some point do you ask Kelly where Melissa was at?
A: Yes. She said that she is downstairs, and she whispers it.

Q: And let the record reflect that you are pointing down with your finger.
A: Pointing down because we were right above the garage.
(This is crucial because Megan just acknowledged that she knew Melissa was in the garage. She will try to correct what she said later.)

Q: Is that the motion that Kelly did?
A: Yes

Q: And what was your thought at this point as to where Melissa was?
A: I thought that she was downstairs sleeping in her room.
(Megan just said she was pointing down because they were right above the garage.)

Q: Eventually do you and Kelly leave the master bedroom area?
A: Yes, we then walk downstairs into the kitchen because she wanted to show me her kitchen glasses that she believed Melissa had put morphine in.
Titus Answer: This never happened. I am assuming Megan says this to explain what they were doing in the garage.

Q: What did you do as a result of the fact Kelly was thinking there was something in her glasses?
A: Jeremy and I went out to the garage to look at the water softener.
(Megan just testified that Kelly told her they just tasered, body-slammed, beat up, and drugged Melissa, and put her body in the garage; and now they are all going into the garage to check on the water softener?)
Titus Answer: That's idiotic! Megan, Jeremy, and Kelly went into the garage to look at the dead body in the trunk of the car. Think about it; why did they go into the garage twice? What is so interesting in the garage that keeps them going back? Answer- Melissa's overdosed body in the trunk of the car.

Q: What did Jeremy do?
A: He took the lid off and set it on top of the Jaguar.

Q: Did all four of you go out into the garage?
A: *No, just Jeremy, me, and Kelly.*

Q: What was Kelly's demeanor like when she was in the garage at that time?
A: *Freaked out, like very uneasy. When Jeremy sat the lid down on her car, she about jumped out of her skin, and that again was another hint, where like he and I uhm, you know, started to put things together that something was not right.*
(Grammar disclaimer- It's astounding that "him and I" started to put things together over this, and not everything else mentioned before!)

Q: Did you see anybody in the car?
A: No.
Titus Answer: The Point is… If Megan and Jeremy would have admitted to looking at the body in the trunk of the car, then the prosecution would have to ask, "Why didn't you immediately leave their home? The answer would be… Kelly told us what happened and we could clearly see it was not a murder so we conspired to hide the entire ordeal so their careers would not be ruined!

Q: Do you go then back in the house after the garage?
A: *Yes.*
(When they walked down the stairs, and were right by the front door, that would have been the perfect chance for them to sneak out and go to the police. A normal person would have been scared out of their mind, but they all go into the garage where the dead body is located!)

Q: What do you guys do next?
A: Just keep talking, just small talk to be honest, nothing really. We were going to go upstairs to watch a movie.
(Call me crazy, but this does not seem to be a very good time to, you know, uhm, like, go upstairs for small talk and a watch a movie-ish!)

Q: How do you feel about staying in their house at this point?
A: *I was very freaked out. I was very scared. You could tell by the energy that something was not right, that something had gone on in there.*

(So Megan is so scared and freaked out that she decides to stay a couple more hours, engage in small talk, and watch a movie? If I were Megan, I would just admit that I was on drugs, because only a person on drugs would stay in that house!)

Titus Answer: Not True… Everyone kept doing cocaine… they girls had the TV on while they were talking, and we had music on downstairs. And at one point, when everyone was upstairs, and I was in the kitchen, Megan cornered me and grabbed my dick and told me she was horny. I blew her off, and told her she was disgusting for trying that shit with Melissa overdosed in the car, and it really pissed Megan off. She acted bitchy and pissed off the rest of the night, and I could not wait for her to get the fuck out of my house! As a matter of fact, Kelly told me the next day, Megan even hit on her, and played it off as a joke! Kelly and I discussed on numerous occasions how obsessed Megan was with her. When Megan was sober, she would make passes at Kelly and when she was high she made passes at me.

Q: Are there any more conversations about Melissa?
A: Yes. Later on in the Master Bedroom, Craig showed on Kelly how you can strangle somebody, and I kind of played dumb to see what he was talking about, and I was like what are you talking about, let me see, and he did it on me, and you instantly stop breathing. It scared me, the way he showed it on me.

(Megan said Craig did not want Kelly and Megan to talk about what happened. Then Craig blurted out that he beat Melissa up, and casually mentioned he killed her too. Everyone but Craig then go into the garage, where Melissa's body is located. After that Megan puts it all together, and was so scared that she decided to go back upstairs to watch a movie. But before they do, Craig is showing everyone how he choked Melissa with a demonstration on Kelly. It looked like so much fun, Megan asked Craig to do it on her!)

Titus Answer: Why would I show Kelly how I choked Melissa when she was there, and why would Megan say, "Show Me" if she thought I just killed somebody with a chokehold. Look- you can talk to anyone in Las Vegas and they will tell you that Megan is a compulsive liar. Jeremy even talked to me about it on numerous occasions. This was a prosecutor's wet dream to have a compulsive liar take the stand to testify against me. The problem is, she's stupid, and can't

INTRODUCTION

keep up with what she says from statement to statement; and that would backfire later!

Q: You said later that he did this?
A: *Uh-huh.*

Q: Is that a yes?
A: *yes*

Q: This is after you were in the garage looking at the water softener?
A: *Uh-huh.*

Titus Answer: The Dead Body!

Q: Is that a yes?
A: *Yes.*
(Pay close attention to Megan's statements after she says "uh-huh," this is when she typically tells a lie.)

Q: You said you were going to watch a movie. How do you get back upstairs?
A: *I think we just walked up there.*
(Are you sure a magic carpet didn't take you upstairs? This is the prosecution's key witness!")

Q: What starts the conversation about choking someone?
A: *Craig just walked in and started talking about it, and that's how he started talking more about how he said he killed Melissa.*
(Craig never mentioned choking Melissa before so why would he start "talking more" about choking Melissa. This is the first time Megan says Craig "killed Melissa," and again she talks as if they had already had a conversation about this.)

Q: Did Craig talk about choking Melissa?
A: *Yes.*
(Not according to what Megan just testified. She said that Craig showed Kelly how to choke somebody, and then Megan had Craig show her. Melissa's name was never mentioned.)

Q: And then you also said that he killed Melissa?
A: *Yes.*

SWIFT INJUSTICE

(No, this is the quote: "That's how Craig just walked in and started talking about it, and that's how he started talking more about how he said he killed Melissa." I am trying very hard to follow what this woman is saying, but she does not make any sense!)

Titus Answer: Read her first statements- I NEVER SAID THIS!

Q: What did he say specifically?
(This is your big moment Megan, wow the jurors!)
A: *He said that, uhm, well he said that...pause... like he was joking around, but that is how he, you know, how he killed Melissa, by strangling her.*
(And I typed word for word from the transcript! I don't know what moment is more priceless, when she explains that she did not drink or do drugs that night, or here, when she tells about Craig's big confession!)

Q: You said he demonstrated a chokehold on you. What did he do exactly?
A: *He came behind me, put his arm like this, and squeezed his bicep.*

Q: Is Craig also into fitness competitions?
A: *Yes, he's a bodybuilder. He's huge.*

Q: Did he make any other comments that made you change you impression, that maybe he did kill Melissa?
A: *Yes. Later on he said that we are really going to miss her. I wish that it didn't have to go down like this. Just comments that lead you to believe that when he's saying we're going to miss her, that she is no longer here, not that she was shipped away on a weekend to go to Florida.*

Titus Answer: Oh my God, she is such a FUCKING LIAR. They stayed in our home for 6-7 hours and partied the entire time. They knew that Melissa and Kelly got into a huge fight, and soon after Melissa overdosed. They both knew that I was not there when Kelly and MJ were fighting, and I showed up after she overdosed. They knew it was not a murder; and if Kelly did accidentally kill her in self-defense, I was not there when it happened! Megan knew all of this, hours before she and Jeremy barged in through the front door. Kelly simply confirmed what they already knew! The second Megan came in our house, she was asking to see the body! Megan and Jeremy tried to

INTRODUCTION

act all concerned, and "do what best friends do," to help us cover it up so we would not get in trouble, but really, they just wanted to be in on the know, and have a place to party. **They were shitty friends, and Megan is a shitty human being!**

(After reading Craig's comment, a question popped up in my head. How different would the outcome have been if someone showed up at Craig and Kelly's house other than Megan and Jeremy? What if a real friend walked in that night, someone that truly cared about Craig and Kelly, not a poser abusing drugs? A real friend would have never brought more drugs into the house, and conspire to help them cover up the overdose, or walk out the door with the evidence. A real friend would have called 911. Careers might have been ruined, but Craig wouldn't be facing a life behind bars, and Melissa's family would have been able to bury their daughter with dignity.)

Q: Was there any discussion with you about what they were going to do with Melissa's body?
A: *Yes, Craig said something about it before we left at 2:30.*
Titus Answer: Wait a minute… first Megan said she thought MJ was asleep in the room, now we are discussing what to do with the body. YES BECAUSE MEGAN SAW THE BODY!!!!!

Q: Where were you when he talked about what he was planning for Melissa? (Megan left this part out on National Television!)
A: *In the upstairs office.*

Q: What did he say his plans were for Melissa?
A: *That he was going to drive the Jaguar up to Red Rock, scatter clothes around the car, and set it on fire, to make it look like a rape.*
Titus Answer: This was one of dozens of plans we (Tony, Megan, Jeremy, Kelly, and myself) came up with over the evening to cover up the over dose. Now you can see that there were never any plans to burn the body, only the car! When Tony got out, we were so high, not thinking, he lit it too soon, and Melissa was not supposed to be in there!

Q: Did he discuss what time this was going to happen?
A: *Four o'clock*

(Megan could have prevented the arson if she went straight to the police with this information after she left the house.)

Q: Did he say anything about other times that something was going to happen?
A: *He stated that at five o'clock, eleven p.m. and four a.m.*
(With her own testimony, Megan is an accessory to this crime)

Q: Did he mention Tony Gross' name?
A: *He said that he lent him a thousand dollars and he was going to have Tony dispose of the car.*
Titus Answer: Dispose of the car not a body. In the police reports, they have Tony's phone records because he just set his own car on fire and collected insurance fraud money a week before this happened. He knew right where to go, and how to do it. He was supposed to drop her body off in front of a hospital earlier in the day, but kept calling and chickening out because there were surveillance cameras up everywhere.

Q: Do you know Tony Gross?
A: *Yes I do, through Craig and Kelly.*

Q: Between the times that Craig is demonstrating the choke hold and the time that you leave the house, did you ever go back into the garage?
A: *I believe so, yes.*
(Megan said that Craig and Kelly killed Melissa. Megan knew the body was in the trunk, and said Craig told her that they were going to dispose of her body and burn the car. And now she is saying that they are going back into the garage?)

Q: What was the purpose of going back into the garage?
A: *Kelly said that the posing lights were on, and she did not know why, so she was going out there to turn them off.*

Q: When you went out to the garage, were the posing lights on?
A: *Yes.*

Q: Did you go out to the garage with her to look at the posing lights?
A: *Yes, I did.*

Q: Did Craig and Jeremy go out to the garage?
A: *No, they stayed in the Living Room.*
(If Megan truly believed that Craig and Kelly murdered Melissa, why would Megan leave her fiancé in the living room with one of the "murderers", and follow the other "murderer" out to the garage? Anyone in their right mind would think that Kelly was luring them into the garage to kill them because they knew too much information about the death of Melissa James. Someone in their right mind would not leave their only source of protection, their fiancé, in a room, 25 feet away, with a man that had just "beat, body slammed, injected, and strangled" a female a few hours earlier. If Craig and Kelly had in fact killed Melissa, and Jeremy and Megan stumbled upon Melissa's body, it would make sense that Craig and Kelly would kill them next and get rid of the witnesses. But this never happens! No, someone in their right mind would have bolted out the front door the second they put two and two together, to save their own lives!)

Q: Did you think it was unusual that the lights were still on?
A: *Yes.*

Q: Why is that?
A: *They are never on. They are only on if you are posing.*
(According to her testimony, the first time that Megan and Kelly went into the garage, she knew that something had more than likely happened to Melissa James. The reason to go into the garage the first time is peculiar, yet plausible. The second time, Megan knew for a fact that Melissa was dead in the car. So why in the hell would she go back into the garage to turn the lights off?)

Q: Did you shut the lights off in the garage?
A: *No.*

Q: Did Kelly shut the lights off in the garage?
A: *No.*
(So after all that, they did not even turn off the posing lights in the garage?)

Q: Did Craig go out to the garage?
A: *No*

Q: Do you eventually go back in the house?
A: Yes.
(According to Megan's testimony, Craig and Kelly were sadistic murderers that had tortured and killed Melissa James just hours before Megan and Jeremy arrived at their house to watch movies. And before Megan and Jeremy leave, Megan said that Craig and Kelly were going to burn their jaguar with Melissa in the trunk, spread her clothes out around the scene, and make it look like a rape. This cover up had not even taken place yet, and Megan knew the exact time and location of the arson, and yet she does nothing- and that is okay?)

Q: At some point before you leave, does Craig ask you to take something home?
A: *He had not asked me at the time, no. He had asked Jeremy.*
Titus Answer: Jeremy and Megan both offered to put the taser gun and the sap in the bag with the other items because I was a felon, and I am not allowed to have weapons in my home. They said they would throw them away. Megan took all of the HELOC papers out with that bag, so she could shred them when she got home. We left Melissa's drugs in her room so the police could see that she was a drug addict, but Megan took a lot of the drugs we had around the house in that bag as well.

Q: Okay, when did you come to learn that Craig wanted you or Jeremy to take something from the house?
A: *As we were literally walking out the door.*
(Megan lied about the black gym bag on national television. According to Megan's interview on *48 Hours*, she said that as she was running out the front door (supposedly by herself) when Craig handed her the gym bag. At this time, Megan asked Craig what was in the gym bag, and he replied, "The taser gun." *48 Hours* said the case broke wide open because she immediately took the bag to her lawyer, who turned it over to the police. But according to Megan's grand jury testimony, she and Jeremy (who along with Tony Gross are never mentioned on *48 Hours*) took the gym bag to their lawyer a week or two later. In fact, Megan said that she didn't know what was in the bag, didn't look in the bag until the next day, and after the police repeatedly tried to contact her, she finally turned the bag over to them.)

INTRODUCTION

Q: What happened?
A: *We said our goodbyes, and there was a gym bag right next to my purse. I grabbed my purse, walked out and Craig said, "Hey wait, you forgot this," and I said, "What's this" Craig said, "Oh don't worry about it, Jeremy knows about it."*
Titus Answer: Not true- we talked all night about them taking the bag.

Q: Did you know what was in the gym bag?
A: *No.*
Titus Answer: YES!!!

Q: Did you take the bag home in fact?
A: *Yes.*

Q: Did Craig say why he wanted you to take the bag home?
A: *He said that he knew the police were going to be coming to his house the next day and he said that he did not want whatever was in the bag in the house when the police came.*
(How is this not an accessory to a crime or conspiracy? Tony Gross said that he did not do anything but follow Craig to the desert and give them a ride home (which would be a lie also). Megan knew the details, discussed the soon to be arson, then walked out the door with evidence to hide from the police.)

Q: By the time you leave the house do you know where Melissa is?
A: *Yes*

Q: And how did you come upon that knowledge?
A: *I believe it was Craig that said that she was in the trunk of the car.*
(In the above answer, the prosecutor asked Megan where she thought Melissa was at, and Megan said that she thought Melissa was downstairs sleeping in her room.)
Titus Answer: No, I walked into the garage and caught them looking at the body in the trunk.

Q: When and where does he make that statement?
A: *It was downstairs, maybe an hour before we left.*

(They went into the garage right before Megan and Jeremy left; Megan knew that Melissa was in the trunk of the car when she went out there!)

Q: And what do you guys do at that point?
A: I can't remember exactly, just more talking about it. I think he was saying how he was going to get rid of the body. Before that he said she was in the trunk.

Q: So you leave at this point and you feel like something is wrong?
A: Uh-huh.

Q: Do you call the police?
A: No, because I felt threatened by Craig Titus.
(So threatened that you sat around in the living room for an hour talking about "it", watched a few movies, fished out the HELOC papers, and walked into the garage to look at the body one last time before you went home. The real threat came from the investigation over potentially exposing mortgage fraud; and being charged with conspiracy for participating in the cover-up.)

Titus Answer: The first thing out of their mouth was that you can't call the police because Megan and Jeremy feared that they would get in trouble if the police were called. They knew it was not a murder, and said they wanted to cover it up so that nobody got in trouble. Megan never felt threatened by me; she wanted to have sex with me! What the fuck?

Q: Do you know exactly what went on at this point?
A: From A to Z, no.
(From A to Z, no, but B-Y, yes- she was not there when Melissa overdosed, but she knew about it within an hour of her death Megan did not physically burn the vehicle, but she knew exactly where they were going, what time it was to take place, and specifics on how they were to carry this out.)

Q: Did some of it make sense to you?
A: Absolutely.

Q: Did you ever look in the Nike bag that Craig gave you to take home?

A: *I did the following day so actually it would have been Tuesday afternoon. Or would that have been Wednesday?*

(In Megan Pierson's words, Craig and Kelly "killed" Melissa then placed her body in the trunk of the car; and the car was going to be burned in 2-3 hours. Was Megan not the slightest bit curious about what was in the bag? Even I, a boring by-the-book school teacher, would have unzipped that bag the second I got in the car to drive home. It is obvious from the repeated phone calls with Craig and Kelly, that Megan is a nosey person, and has to know exactly what is going on at all times. Megan called Kelly to "compare" stories that Melissa had confided in the two of them. When Megan was in the closet, she said that she pulled information from Kelly, and was agitated when Craig interrupted the story. Would this same meddlesome woman, on a fifteen minute drive home, sit and hold a bag with evidence from the crime, and never once open it up to see what was inside?)

Q: What was in the Nike bag?
A: *A taser gun, a gym rope, and something else for one of the Taser guns or stun guns. I'm not sure what it was.*
(What about the sap with the DNA of Craig on one end and Melissa on the other?)

Q: Do you eventually hand that Taser gun and the contents of the gym bag over to the police?
A: *Absolutely!*
(Absolutely-ish, uh-huh, two weeks later-ish, after they tried to contact me a dozen times; my lawyer absolutely handed the bag over to the police immediately-ish!)

Q: Do you recall what day it was that you did that?
A: *No. It was the first time I gave a statement.*

Q: After you leave that morning (Wed. Dec. 14th), when is the next time that you have a conversation with Craig or Kelly?
A: *I don't think I spoke to Kelly or Craig. Craig had contacted me from a, he went and bought a pay-as- you- go phone, I didn't answer it because I did not know the phone number, and so it had been at least two to three days.*

Titus Answer: Not True. We did not have prepaid phones until the day we left town.

Q: When was the next time you talked to Craig and Kelly?
A: *Friday at Greg and Diana's house.*

Q: Did you know Greg and Diana?
A: *Yes, through Craig and Kelly. They're business partners.*
Titus Answer: Greg was their drug dealer.

Q: Who all was there?
A: *Pat Franks, Greg & Diana Ruiz, myself, Jeremy, and obviously Craig and Kelly…uhm, Tony Gross with his girlfriend. Oh yeah, and Jeff Schwimmer.*
(With all of these potential witnesses, it is interesting that the prosecution does not call any of them to testify for the grand jury except Megan Pierson Foley.)
Titus Answer: Tony brought the weed and Greg supplied the cocaine and OxyContins. We were all there trying to sort out our problems- everyone was paranoid about how this would affect them. Tony was scared because he sold Melissa the morphine from his dying Grandfather. He was also worried because his finger prints were all over the duct tape. This was probably why he was so adamant about burning Melissa with the car. Tony picked the place to burn the car, close to where he burned his own car for insurance money. Greg was scared because he had sold cocaine to Melissa. Megan was scared because she thought the mortgage company would find out about the fraudulent loan. Jeremy and Megan were both worried about aiding and abetting for taking off with the possible murder weapons. If the investigators tested the bag, it would test positive for all sorts of drugs. Everyone acted like they cared about us and wanted to help us out, but all they cared about was themselves; it was self- preservation. Schwimmer seemed to be the only real friend, and he let us stay with him the entire time. He bought us the pre-paid phones, and hooked us up with lawyers. Schwimmer just gave me the creeps though because he was addicted to crack, and made sexual advances on me when he was high.

INTRODUCTION ➤

Q: Now you're concerned about what has gone down with Craig and Kelly, and you agree to meet them. Why?
A: *I was going to say goodbye to Kelly.*

Q: Where did you think she was going?
A: *To Greece*

Q: How long did you stay at Greg and Diana Ruiz's house?
A: *I would say an hour at the most.*
Titus Answer: Come on Megan- it was all night long- everyone stayed up all night doing cocaine almost until the sun came up the next morning.

Q: Was there any discussion by Craig and Greg Ruiz about selling his house?
A: *He was trying to sell his houses, yes. He asked me if I could get appraisals on his properties quickly that weekend.*

Q: What do you do for a living?
A: *I am a mortgage broker.*

Q: Did you discuss getting quick appraisals?
A: *I said I could try; that is all I said.*
Titus Answer: Megan was coming up with all kinds of schemes and plans in case we needed thousands of dollars in a hurry up front for attorney's fees.

Q: Did you hear Craig ask anyone to buy his house?
A: *Yes, I heard him ask Jeff.*
(Why isn't Jeff Schwimmer a witness?)
Titus Answer: Schwimmer offered to buy all three houses before we left.

Q: During the time that you were at this gathering, did you have any alcohol to drink?
A: *No.*
Titus Answer: Yes, lots of red wine.

Q: Did you or Jeremy take any drugs or anything at that time?
A: *No.*

Titus Answer: Yes- they smoked a lot of weed and snorted a ton of coke. (Perhaps this is why they kept the other participants at the party off of the witness stand, because they would have testified to the contrary- that everyone in that house was doing drugs that evening.)

Q: And just to clarify, when you first went to Kelly and Craig's house after going to Green Valley Ranch, did you do any drugs at their house?
A: No.
Titus Answer: They didn't go to the Green Valley Ranch Country Club; Megan went over to Tony's house to buy weed and Greg's house for coke.

Robert Daskas: "I have no further questions for this witness. Does anyone else have any questions?" A juror asks a question:

Juror Q: You testified that defendant Ryan said that she injected morphine into Melissa James. Was that the first time you had ever heard of them having the drug at their house, or had you seen that drug there before?
A: Craig actually purchased it the day Melissa moved in.
Titus Answer: Tony either sold it to Melissa or gave it to her. I know that he stole it from his dying grandfather on hospice. I never purchased or used morphine! Megan knew for a fact that this morphine came from Tony Gross, she was pissed off that he sold it to Melissa so cheap (or gave it to her) and did not give it to Megan because she wanted it for herself. And she thought that she had a closer relationship with Tony than Melissa. Megan was very jealous of Melissa, and did not like for any of us to show any special favoritism towards her. Megan was a very egocentric human being. What bothered me was that Tony was a people pleaser, so he wanted people to like him, but how you could steal from your own grandfather, something that is making him comfortable in his last days, how you could live with yourself?

Juror Q: To your knowledge did Titus or Ryan take any type of steroid or drug on regular basis?
Prosecutor: I am going to ask you not to answer that- irrelevant.

INTRODUCTION

Titus Answer: Megan was using growth hormones and primobolan depot which I injected in her twice a week while she was training with Kelly.

Juror Q: You stated that your workouts were usually scheduled at five p.m. Was that Monday, Wednesday, Friday or Tuesday, Thursday, Saturday?
(Looks like the Juror just figured out the discrepancy in the workout schedule.)
A: *Monday, Wednesday, Friday.*

Juror Q: You testified that when you arrived at the house, the defendant showed you crystal methamphetamine and some bloody needles?
A: *Uh-huh.*

Juror Q: Did he also show you any of the credit cards or that HELOC statement you said that he talked about on the phone?
A: *Yes he did.*
(Would Craig bring out bloody needles, crystal meth, and credit card / HELOC statements into the living room to show Megan and Jeremy, or would it not make more sense that he took them into Melissa's room to show them all of these things after the overdose?)
Titus Answer: I found the crystal meth, bloody needles, credit cards, and HELOC statements after she over dosed; I never talked about it on the phone.

Juror Q: While you were having dinner and you got these phone calls from either Mr. Titus or Ms. Ryan, did they say how much money either one of them thought had been taken from them?
A: *They said that there was a wire for twenty-three thousand. Craig could not account for that and he called Green Point, who is the owner of the loan, and they said that they did not know where the wire was going. And I know that that's, as a loan officer that that's incorrect.*

Juror Q: So that's the only dollar figure that was mentioned?
A: *Uh-huh, $23,000.*

Juror Q: Okay. At those early telephone conversations, did you ever tell him that he ought to call the police and report these thefts and the identity thefts and the credit card action?
A: *Yes. Because he told me before that she had a warrant out for her arrest out of Florida for identity theft.*
(This woman would have ended up being the prosecutions down fall. If you question her long enough, the "truth-ish" will eventually come out. Now just imagine if this went to trial!)

Juror Q: About what time did you go into the garage the second time?
A: *I would probably say around maybe one-ish.*
Titus Answer: 11:30 p.m.

Juror Q: So between One and Two a.m.?
A: *Yeah, One and Two.*
Titus Answer: The DA wants to establish that they left soon after they were in the garage just in case it comes out that they saw the body.

Juror Q: Did you ever go into Melissa's room?
A: *No, I did not.*
Titus Answer: Bullshit!!!

Juror Q: Do you know where her room is located?
A: *Right next to the garage.*

Juror Q: Do you walk past Melissa's room when you go to the garage?
A: *Uh-huh.*

Juror Q: Was the door to Melissa's room open or closed?
A: *It was shut.*
Titus Answer: It was wide open because we were discussing how MJ destroyed her room after finding out she was not going to be allowed back in our home after Christmas. Megan personally made the comment about how ungrateful she was to tear up everything that did not belong to her like she was a teenager. Then Megan said that she never could stand her.

Juror Q: And you had initially been told by Kelly that's where Melissa James was, in the room?
A: *Yes, that is what I assumed when she said downstairs, yes.*

INTRODUCTION

(No, in your testimony, you said that you assumed she was in the garage. The prosecutor asked you directly, and Megan said, "Pointing down because we were right above the garage." All of these contradictions in one testimony is nuts!)

Juror Q: Prior to December 13th, did you have an occasion to observe the relationship between Craig and Melissa?
A: Uhm, they were friends. Melissa was actually annoyed with Craig because he would demand a lot of her. He would ask her to do one thing and five minutes later ask her to do another thing, and she would get very upset with him.
Titus Answer: How does Megan know this? Megan already stated she barely knew MJ and never spoke with her.

Juror Q: Was Melissa an employee of the couple; was she paid by them?
A: She was not paid like a salary or anything like that. She got to stay at their house free, and ate their food and she was given money. But she was brought in to help them with Women's Physique International, which was a federation they were opening, and Ice Gear Clothing that they were opening with Greg and Diana Ruiz.

Juror Q: Would it be correct to say that when you were at Craig and Kelly's house, you spent most of the evening discussing what they had done to Melissa James?
A: Not the whole time, no we talked about lots of things. They were talking about the federation- one of our close friends was supposed to invest in it. We talked about me graduating and getting married.

Juror Q: But there did come a time when you knew that what they were telling you might have happened?
A: Yes and then we got out of there as quickly as we could.

Juror Q: So they (Melissa, Craig, and Kelly) had been friends for a while?
A: Yes. I believe that she actually lived with them other times but they stopped talking for a couple of years and then she came back into their lives because her boyfriend and she were having problems, and she had been arrested, and was homeless or something like that.

Juror Q: That evening when you were at their house, after you had dinner at Green Valley Ranch, was the first you had heard anything about Melissa stealing?

A: The first time I heard it was actually Monday when I worked out with Kelly. She stated that she noticed some of her credit cards had been used and were missing.

(This contradicts her answers given at the beginning of her grand jury testimony when she was asked this question by the prosecution. I believe she was lying in the beginning, and telling the truth here.)

Juror Q: Just to clarify that, I thought I had asked you that question so I want to make sure we're on the same page. Monday the 12th when you worked out, there was some discussion about Melissa using their credit card or what have you?

A: Yes.

(The Juror called her out for conflicting statements).

Questions need to be answered!

Think about this: at the beginning of the Grand Jury hearing, Robert Daskas gave instructions and definitions to the jurors explaining how to decide if a person was guilty or innocent of a specific offense. After listening to Megan Pierson's own testimony, why was she not charged with the above mentioned crimes?

Aids or Abets- Every person concerned in the commission of a felony, whether he or she directly commits the act constituting the offense, or aids or abets in its commission, every person present who directly or indirectly counsels encourages, hires, commands, induces, or otherwise procures another to commit a crime be accomplished is a principal, and shall be proceeded against and punished against as such.

Conspiracy is an agreement or mutual understanding between two or more persons to commit a crime. To be guilty of conspiracy, a defendant must intend to commit, or to aid in the commission of, the specific crime agreed to. The crime is the agreement to do something unlawful; it does not matter whether it was successful or not. Each member of a criminal conspiracy is liable for each act and bound by

INTRODUCTION

each declaration of every other member of the conspiracy if the act or the declaration is in furtherance of the object of conspiracy.

Why was Megan not charged with a crime? The only plausible explanation would be that she was forced to testify and say exactly what the homicide detectives & prosecution instructed her to say in front of the Grand Jury. Megan Foley was Robert Daskas' puppet, and he thought the rest of the world would be stupid enough to buy her story without reading the details in the case. Unfortunately for her, the story did not make sense and she implicated herself in the crime. The investigators and prosecution seemed to think they could just throw the newspaper a few stories about sex tapes, wife swapping, and backward kissing cousins because it would sell off the racks and keep everyone happy. This would keep the Jerry Springer Simpletons chanting, "Titus is a Murderer;" distracting the public from the truth!

Two sides to every story

With the lines blurred between legitimate news outlets and tabloid journalism, everyone from *Geraldo Rivera* to *Greta Van Susteren* had cameras outside of the courtroom trying to turn this high profile case into a buck. There was no time to double check the facts or sources; being the first to report the information, true or false, made the most money. Glenn Puit, a crime reporter for the Las Vegas Review Journal, became the investigator's own personal hose; leaking the prosecution's version of the truth, straight to the headlines in the newspaper. Puit was always the first to report any scandalous piece of information about the case; but was he reporting the truth, or just the prosecution's version of the truth?

Without any physical evidence, the lead prosecutor rolled the dice, and played the case out in the media. By the time Craig Titus and his defense team had a chance to come up with a strategy, every outrageous story, leaked by the prosecution, had already snowballed out of control. In the eyes of the public, Craig Titus was a guilty man trying to prove he was innocent.

The original defense team's strategy was to keep quiet and to not comment in the press. This would have probably been a smart strategy with most defense cases, but in this case it backfired. Thanks to the prosecution, the media, and the bodybuilding community, lurid details started to spill out from every direction. Craig's "so-called" friends in the bodybuilding community bashed him on message boards, and sold information about him to news magazines.

Feeling as if the national media was trying to take over their turf, local reporters tried to get a leg up by printing anything the police leaked to them about the investigation. Nothing was out of bounds, and the truth was never a concern; the more salacious the gossip, the more likely it was to be printed because smut sells.

Craig Titus made a name for himself in bodybuilding by being the "bad boy with a big mouth" who spoke his mind; otherwise he would have never been successful in that industry. An industry with testosterone, egos, and message boards; where most people seem to get some kind of rush out of putting other people down.

Craig Titus built a reputation on arrogance, and for that reason alone, many people disliked him. The first time the detectives met Craig Titus, they didn't like him either. From day one, they thought he was an overconfident asshole; and unfortunately, because of this, the detectives believed Craig Titus was a murderer as well. However in America, no matter how arrogant or how big of an asshole the guy might be, the detectives and prosecutors do not have the right to charge somebody with "make believe" crimes.

Why did Robert Daskas continue to go after Craig Titus, even after the evidence did not add up? Could he not back up and say, "We screwed up, our bad," and drop the charges? No, in fact, Robert Daskas did the opposite, and instead of throwing out the charges, or charging Craig Titus and Kelly Ryan with a lesser crime, he amended the charges! This "crime of passion" turned into First Degree Murder with Kidnapping tacked on to make it a capital offense. Robert Daskas and the District Attorney would do everything but back up and admit they were wrong because they saw Craig Titus as a stepping stone on their way up the political ladder. While Robert Daskas prepared to run for Congress, Craig Titus' head would make a beautiful trophy over his mantle. The higher the profile case, the bigger the win would

INTRODUCTION

be! With power comes arrogance, and with arrogance comes ego, and it appeared to be ego-vs.-ego.

For the first time in Craig's life, he may have been outmatched. Titus literally had to fight with both hands cuffed behind his back; and he picked a fight with possibly the most powerful man in the Clark County courtroom, only behind the district attorney himself. As a prosecutor in the District Attorney's office, Daskas had a tremendous amount of authority, as prosecutors are arguably the most powerful figures in the criminal justice system. Not only are prosecutors heavily involved in the investigation of crimes, but they are solely responsible for what charges, plea bargains, and sentences a criminal defendant will face. With that much power, prosecutors like Robert Daskas need to be watched closely and scrutinized for every mistake; and if the results have to be rigged to ensure a conviction, something needs to be done.

Books were written that support the prosecution's case even before Craig Titus and Kelly Ryan ever had their day in court. Craig was singled out as a murderer from the minute the homicide detectives walked through his front door; even though the autopsy report indicated that a murder never took place. Instead of a murder, there was an overdose, and this would not draw in the publicity needed to propel the prosecution's careers to the next level. On National television, Robert Daskas said, "All we know is there was an altercation, and Melissa James died as a result. The only people that know the truth are Craig and Kelly; and without a trial, we will probably never know exactly what happened." Regrettably for Mr. Daskas, I am afraid he is wrong. Craig was never given a chance to have a fair trial, and was manipulated into accepting a plea deal (A fact that is sworn by Titus' lawyer, Marc Saggese, in an affidavit.) Without a doubt, the investigators, prosecutors, and the judges do not want the world to know the truth; but today the truth comes out.

Craig Titus: "You can lock me behind bars, and deny my freedom, but you can't keep me from telling the truth; and I am telling the whole fucking story, period!"

Section One:
The Making of the
Bad Boy of Bodybuilding

CHAPTER 1

Titus Family Meeting

After talking to Craig on the phone, he genuinely believed it was important for me to drive to Houston and meet with his mother and sister. They could give me all of his legal work, and provide more intimate details about Craig and his case. Craig said it had been a while since they had sat down with anyone that believed their side of the story, and it would really lift their spirits to visit with me. Craig also shared that his mom is the best cook in the world, and if he could not enjoy one of her home cooked meals, he wanted me to enjoy one for him.

So my girlfriend and I drove ten hours to Houston to meet Craig's mother and sister, Sandi & Nicole. When we first pulled up, they greeted us at the car with warm embraces, and welcomed us into his mother's beautiful home. With a slight Yankee accent, and a hysterically smart-ass sense of humor, Craig's mom quickly had my attention, and we immediately bonded. Both Craig's mother and sister were beautiful; it was hard to tell if they were mother and daughter or sisters.

Speaking over each other, and finishing one another's sentences, it was obvious to me that Sandi and Nicole were close. Their bond with each other, and their love for Craig was clearly stronger than ever. Candidly getting their point across, it was apparent the apple did not fall far from the tree. Sandi calls it like she sees it, and tells everyone exactly what she thinks, without holding anything back.

After a number of laughs, Sandi's eyes filled with tears when she talked about all of the friends and family members that have turned their backs on them because of this whole ordeal. "They either didn't know what to say or wouldn't say anything at all. It's been heartbreaking because after this happened, most of them had absolutely nothing to do with us at all. We felt very alone, and still struggle with the hurt from judgment, even today." Nicole grabbed her mom's hand and said, "We got each other, right? And here are two people that believe us, and are listening, and want to help." Sandi nodded her head, but explained that it has been challenging because there have been people come and go out of their lives, and it had become hard to know who they could trust. "They will promise to write a book, or help Craig out, and for whatever reason they just disappear."

Nicole said, "Well it is usually because they are too scared to write anything, because the deeper you get into it, the scarier it gets." Sandi said that she wanted me to be careful; "Craig mentioned that you were talking about possibly going to Las Vegas to interview people, and just so you know honey, that's a really bad idea. It's not safe, and I don't trust anyone there." I laughed and told them, "You do realize, I am a school teacher; I'm not real important." Sandi said, "Oh honey, you're an angel sent from God, and Craig really believes in you!" I told Nicole and Sandi, "It's obvious that what happened to Craig was wrong, and I will do my best to get to the bottom of it; fingers crossed, I won't get whacked in the process!"

Pulling out a tape recorder, I asked Craig's mother and sister to share with me anything they would like mentioned in the book. The following are their thoughts and statements about Craig and his conviction:

Sandi (Craig's mom): "You know he's my first born, so that makes him a little, extra special. Craig Michael Titus was born to be somebody, and I'm not just saying that because I am his mother either! I mean someone special; a man that is kind-hearted, confident, and ambitious. He was brought up to have values and taught that nothing in life comes easy. He always wore his heart on his sleeve, and he was passionate about everything that he did. Craig wasn't just given his fame and fortune from bodybuilding; he was a hard worker and made his dream of becoming a professional athlete come true. Craig

TITUS FAMILY MEETING

was successful at everything he put his mind to; it was incredible watching his work ethic from a very young age. He would take notes, observe, and map out every detail of his life. Once he reached his goal, he would set another one; he was constantly striving for more- wanting to be the best!"

Sandi paused for a moment then continued, "Everyone sees him and thinks they know him, because they watched him on the stage or in magazines as a bodybuilder. I held him in my arms as a baby. I know my son. They know the superficial; I know his soul and his compassionate heart. His eyes would melt my heart, and he would never leave the house without a hug and a kiss. He watched out for his little brother at school, and would stand up for him when he was picked on or bullied. Craig adored his baby sister Nicole, and with the age difference when they were young, he acted like her father in scaring off her boyfriends, and caring and guiding her through her teenage years. Nicole adored her big brother, and he would do anything for her." Nicole interjected, "And I adored him, I still adore him!"

Sandi: "Craig would never want the bodybuilding world to know this, but he was a 'Mama's boy.' We have always had a special relationship, and I start to cry when I even talk about it today. He was the little boy that would sit in my lap and stroke my hair. When he would see me cry, he would wipe the tears from my eyes, and tears would roll down his eyes. He would bring me flowers, since he was young, and kiss me on the cheek, and tell me, 'This is for being such a great mom!' If Craig saw anyone that was hurting, he would stop and talk to them, touch them, usually cry with them, and most important talk to them. He was so empathetic, and could instinctively feel the pain of others around him, and do everything in his power to help that person. On road trips it would take us at least two extra hours to make our destination, because he would never leave a car stranded on the side of the road, he always helped them get their car started, or gave that person a lift to a mechanic or called a tow truck."

Sandi chuckled, as she said, "Just the other day I got a phone call from one of Craig's friends and he was telling me a story about Craig, and how they nearly got in a wreck and stopped traffic because Craig made him stop his car in the middle of the road. He said that Craig ran over to the side walk and emptied his wallet to this homeless vet without legs in a wheel chair. Gave him a pat on the back, and told him that he hopes that this helps him out. The two guys were going on a trip, and Craig just emptied his wallet, but that was Craig! I just tear up every time I think about him, because Craig is such a softy, and I miss him so much! I don't understand how someone can just make up a charge, without any evidence, and keep my baby from me, that is my baby, will you please help me." (Can I Stop for a minute?)

Nicole (Craig's sister): "Mom has had such a hard time. She just battled breast cancer, and her big fear is not seeing Craig before he gets out. My heart aches for her, but what can we do? I hate it, because I have these beautiful kids, and I know Craig would be such a great uncle, and he is not here. (Nicole showed me a picture of one of her boys). This one here reminds me of Craig so much! I just want him to be a part of their lives; we are all missing out on so much, and for what? It's such bullshit!"

Sandi: "What I want everyone to understand is that I have had the pleasure of being the mother to this beautiful boy from day one, and my love for him has never changed. I have loved him just the same as when he hit a homerun in little league baseball, handed me flowers, and told me I was the best mom ever, when he won the state title in wrestling, when he became a professional body builder, when he was on the cover of over 100 magazines, when he owned his own company. And my love for Craig has not changed when he lost everything and sits behind bars thousands of miles away from my home. If anything, my love is stronger, and I love him today more than I ever have; he is with me every second of every minute over every hour of the day, in my broken heart! Craig's biggest triumphs and ultimate failures came from one thing, his career in bodybuilding. It was a blessing and a curse at the same time." (Long pause)

Sandi continued, "I know who Craig Michael Titus really is, but the only image that everyone sees is that damn 'Bad boy' bodybuilding image. This guy that goes around talking smack and acting tough! Don't get me wrong, Craig is like his mother, and he doesn't take crap from nobody! And that is a good thing, right? Stand up for yourself, believe in yourself! It just became so ridiculous on those bodybuilding blogs, these things these men would say behind a message board, and Craig would confront them face-to-face, like a real man. He was arrogant, but it came with the territory, it was a part of bodybuilding. Add in jealousy, because there's no question that Craig was the best looking in the bunch; so they would lose the girl, and be pissed at Craig. He can't help it if he is better looking than all of them, right? Craig has always been nice looking, and has had multiple girlfriends since kindergarten, a new one every day or two. So they paint him in the media as being a womanizer- the women love him, what's he going to do? These guys that were jealous said things behind Craig's back, and Craig's not that way; he's brutally honest- 'say it to my face, not to my back!' Some of that was Craig being a man, but some of that was a show. Craig sold his image of the 'bad boy of bodybuilding,' and made millions; then the media took it, and portrayed him as a monster to sell their magazines."

Sandi said, "As a Mother it really hurt me to see how the media feeds off all of this, and turns my son into something that he is not; I felt helpless because there wasn't a goddamn thing I could do about it! Now, I am not making excuses, or making light of what happened; but this is the truth, and I have to be blunt and just say it. Craig wanted to be a professional bodybuilder more than anything else in the world, and that cost him his freedom the first time around- when he was using steroids. He became a professional bodybuilder, but had to go to prison, I don't know if it was worth it, because that charge haunted him every day after he got out of prison. I will say this, my son made some bad decisions, but I know for a fact-my son is not a murderer! He is not capable of killing anyone! He has never laid his hand on a woman in his life, and actually took a plea to cover for his own wife, so that she would not have to spend a day in jail."

(Sandi said, "I need a break, just give me a minute honey." Sandi begins to cry, and Craig's sister said she had some things to add).

Nicole: "Craig was the most amazing big brother; I looked up to him in every way, and loved spending time with him in Las Vegas. There were a lot of things my brother tried to shelter me from, and didn't want me to see. Craig was very protective of me; well I say of me, Craig was just protective of his family period. There were some things going on that I did see however, take Melissa James for example. Craig never wanted me to meet her; I think primarily because of her meth addiction, and my age- he just didn't want me to get tangled up in that world. I do know that she would stay with them a lot, both in California and Nevada, sometimes for a couple of weeks and other times for several months. At one time she had her act together, and owned her own dance studio, but Craig said she lost the studio and everything else because of her meth addiction. Craig always felt bad for her, and had a hard time turning her away; he was that way with his friends and family- loyal to a fault, ya know. In any case, I remember this one time I was visiting my brother and we were at his house, I think it was either in 2002 or 2003; and Melissa called Craig, begging him to let her come stay with them again. Everything was fine before Melissa called; we're having fun hanging out, watching movies, and when she called, Kelly flipped her shit, and just started ranting about Melissa."

Nicole said, "Kelly told me that Melissa would call them up every couple of months with an embellished or completely fabricated story, needing money or a place to stay. Melissa would either have some huge, prospective opportunity; whether it be: modeling, dancing, or college. Or she would have some life changing disaster: she went bankrupt, got arrested, was in a coma, or got kicked out of her parents' house. Kelly said there was always some bull shit story behind every single one of Melissa's phone calls. I experienced that first hand when she promised to get me a modeling job with Hawaiian Tropic; and of course, it never happened! At any rate, Kelly was done with Melissa's lies and she couldn't stand her. Kelly didn't care if Melissa was homeless, she did not want her to step foot back in their home. When Craig got off the phone with Melissa, Kelly let him have it. I felt so bad for him!"

In a matter of fact tone, Nicole said, "To tell you the truth, I really don't know how Craig put up with either one of those women. Kelly was so controlling and she would blow up over the tinniest things. In the media, Kelly has been portrayed as this "sweet, girl next door," and I never understood that. It's such a load of crap to hear people say that after Kelly hooked up with Craig she changed. Did any of those people really know Kelly? She was using drugs long before she ever met my brother, and continued to use them throughout their marriage. Kelly Ryan's behavior was erratic, and escalated because of her drug use. My brother has been blamed for everything that Kelly ever did wrong in her life, and there were some things he did not have any control over- like this plastic surgery thing. Craig was so upset when he heard that people were accusing him of forcing Kelly to have plastic surgery; Craig never wanted her to do that, and she did it behind his back. Kelly Ryan was a strong, independent woman that was driven to succeed. She did whatever she needed to do to win, and this included countless procedures under the knife to perfect any imperfections Kelly believed she had. If there was someone controlling that relationship, it was not Craig; it was Kelly Ryan."

Sandi: "Yeah, if there was a controlling one in that house, it wasn't Craig, that's for sure! What's crazy is Craig was just trying to help this girl Melissa out; he was in an impossible situation in between these two women. I don't think Craig realized how bad off this girl was. Let me tell you, I saw the condition of the guest room where she was staying, and I have never seen anything like that! After the investigators were done with the house, we had to get it ready to put on the market to pay for the attorneys; and I bet I found a hundred used needles in that room, and she had only been there for two months. There was filth, like a squatter- a drug home. The entire house is pristine, but this room- it was nasty! I scrubbed that room from top to bottom, and as I was scrubbing, something kept coming to me. If Craig was going to premeditate to kill this girl, why would he buy her a hotel room, and a plane ticket home? The prosecution and media ask, "Why would you not call the police when she was stealing from you?" I say that you don't know his heart. He wanted to help her. She was already in trouble with the law, and he knew what that was like. He did not want Melissa arrested. He tried to help Melissa, but he couldn't, so he bought her a plane ticket home. Kelly told Craig that Melissa James had to go, and my brother bought Melissa a plane ticket that day. I know for a fact that Craig called Melissa's mom and said that Melissa needs help, and you have to promise me you will get her help. Craig told her that Melissa had been stealing from them, but that was okay, he just needs to get her far away, and wanted her mom to promise to put her in a rehab. Craig had already been talking to me about taking time off so that he and Kelly could go to separate rehab facilities before they started this new federation thing they were doing."

Nicole: "I talked to him on the phone about that. Craig told me that he planned on sending Melissa to New Jersey on Tuesday, and then he was going to check both Kelly and himself into rehab. He needed some help pushing back the start of some of his projects. I said when you come back from a rehab, you cannot hang out with those same friends, and I told him they are poison. It was hard though because one of his friends invested in the clothing wear, and the other invested in the gym- it was just all around him. Then we talked about Kelly, and oh my god, getting Megan out of the picture. She had done some fraud/scam thing because she did their mortgage, she came over every day pushing drugs in Kelly's face, and she recently got Kelly a job where she worked. She was a cock roach that I had no idea how to squish really. But you know what, he had a plan!"

CHAPTER 2

Growing up Titus

Craig Michael Titus grew up in Riverview, Michigan, a suburb in the Metro Detroit area, located along the shore of the Detroit River. It was a predominately white, blue-collar community of 10,000 people; where a boy was expected to grow up to be a man, and a man was expected to kick some ass. Craig watched his father and grandfather provide for their families, instilling a strong work ethic in him and his siblings at a young age. Getting their hands dirty, and putting in extra hours was not just expected, it was demanded. This applied to chores at home, school work in the classroom, hobbies on the side, and sports on the field; Craig was demanded to give 100%, with absolutely no excuses. Craig's father ruled the house with an iron fist. His demands of Craig in particular were so, some would say, "over the top" that it made it impossible for Craig to ever please his father, or measure up to his expectations. It did however implant in Craig a desire to dig his feet in, constantly keep his legs moving, pushing forward with all of his strength, knowing he would eventually reach his goal.

At times this made for a difficult home life for Craig. He had his dad berating him to succeed in one ear, and his mother encouraging him to do his best in the other ear. According to one of Craig's friends, "When Craig was a kid, he was the happy-go-lucky class clown. Everybody wanted to hang out with him. But ever since he was little, he was an asshole to play sports with, because he was so fucking intense! And if we didn't win, you don't wanna know!"

From an early age, Craig always out performed everyone around him, and demanded that everyone rise to his level. He was a tough kid, full of energy, tackling every sport that came his way. Strong and agile, Craig was always the best one on the field; with lightning speed, he would zip past his opponents before the whistle was even blown.

Hating to lose, if he couldn't be the best, to hell with it, and on to the next venture; a sport where one athlete depended on others for success, was not for him. Very few people had the "Craig Titus" determination and drive, and he couldn't relate to those who fell short of his expectations. If he passed the ball to someone, that person sure as hell better catch the ball and score. Any drops or fumbles from his teammates were unacceptable and would be followed by an in-your-face, expletive tongue-lashing from Craig.

Titus made no apologies for having a hot temper, and would be the first to admit that he had a "win at all cost" state of mind. Any weakness from his teammates, especially laziness, was unacceptable. While running the mile, he would look on with disgust at any "fat ass" that was out of breath and would start to walk when the coach wasn't looking. Craig was doing his damnedest to run that mile in under five minutes, and he did not understand how someone could be so lazy; they could not just keep their legs moving until they crossed the finish line. It was a mindset that Craig Titus assumed everyone had, but eventually realized that no one was willing to put in the effort that he was willing to put in to ensure success.

Although Craig excelled as the point guard on the basketball court and running back on his Jr. High School football team, Craig had to find a sport where no one held him back. He knew the only person he could count on at the end of the day, was himself. Craig had to find an individual sport where there is an "I" in win and a "me" in team, and he found that sport in Wrestling. Wrestling was actually the perfect fit for Craig, being smaller in size than the other kids; it leveled the playing field.

Wrestling's a combat sport, combining strength and flexibility. Wrestlers must incorporate weight lifting into their training in order to acquire upper and lower body strength to gain the dominant position against an opponent. Also, diet and intense cardio exercise is vitally important in order to sustain the attacks of the competition. Craig's hard work paid off, and in the end, he won a state title in wrestling. Wrestling was important, because it spilled over, and inspired him as he ventured into bodybuilding. In fact, Craig was able to integrate everything he learned from wrestling, and apply it to bodybuilding. After his last season of wrestling in high school, Craig started focusing on bodybuilding, and grew a couple more inches; he had his sights set on one day becoming a professional bodybuilder.

As is usually the case, aspirations and dreams change after high school, and this happened with Craig when he graduated in 1984 and moved from Michigan to Tacoma, Washington. Craig soon became side tracked and fell in love with an older woman named Soosie. For Craig, he was too young, and it happened too fast, but they were "in love" and when he was offered an amazing job opportunity working with his family in Houston, the two love birds headed south. They spent every waking moment with each other, and he poured all of his soul into this new relationship. Craig worked in underground excavation, and made great money at a very young age. It all seemed perfect; Craig worked alongside his Dad every day, and lived closer to his mom and sister, all of whom had moved to Houston earlier in the year. Craig was a family man, and he dreamed about developing a relationship with his father that he never had as a child.

This real life "Urban Cowboy" got hitched, "Bud & Sissy" style. They even took it one step further, and sealed the deal with a baby. Within weeks of the marriage his wife was pregnant; and within months of graduation, Craig's entire life changed. His new life was filled with added pressures, priorities, and responsibilities. His dreams of being a bodybuilder seemed like just that, a dream. Craig was now a full time worker, husband, and soon to be father. Craig's dad was tough to work with, and demanded a lot from his son. Underground excavations were back breaking work, and after the long hours on the job, when he got home, he was exhausted.

Because Craig & Soosie got married so fast, they really didn't know each other when they set up house. Coupled with the immaturity that comes along with being so young, the love affair turned sour fast. The only thing they shared in common was a hot temper, and the two constantly fought about everything. To Craig it seemed like nothing he did was good enough, and every time he walked through the door, he felt like he had done something wrong.

Whether it was dirty clothes on the floor, or boots tracking in mud on the carpet, she busted his balls about everything. She never seemed happy about anything, and depressed about everything. There was just enough air in the room, and she managed to suck all of the life out of it! The honeymoon was over the day they both said, "I do," and he felt trapped in a loveless marriage with a baby on the way.

As his image in the mirror began to fade, and disdain for his wife began to grow, Craig found tranquility, if just for a few hours a day, when he escaped away to his sanctuary, his gym- Bally's President & First Lady in Houston, TX. Craig had everything in common with all of the guys at the gym. They even had their own language, speaking in bodybuilding jargon, that only they understood. Talking shit to each other while doing drop sets, discussing which bodybuilder won the last Olympia and Arnold.

The outside world didn't get it, but every die-hard gym rat understood the other, and their desire to become as fucking ripped as possible! They all talked about moving to Venice Beach one day, lifting weights all day and getting laid. They all dreamed of becoming professional bodybuilders, and being handed the Professional Bodybuilding Card for the IFBB- International Federation of Bodybuilding. As Craig worked out with the guys, he listened to tips and advice from those who have actually competed in bodybuilding events. He would stare at the flyers posted about upcoming competitions all over the gym. He grew to desperately want to take bodybuilding to the next level and enter a competition. Looking around at the posters of all of his bodybuilding idols, Craig hit it hard, and started lifting weights. He stared at his reflection in the mirror, and began to daydream about walking across that stage of Gods and Champions at the next 1988 Olympia. He would shock the bodybuilding world as he broke the four time winning streak of Lee Haney. In his mind he could hear the crowd chanting his name, "Titus, Titus, Titus."

Craig eventually snapped out of it, realizing his name was actually being called over a loud speaker, not at Olympia, but at the gym where he was working out. Craig walked to the front, and the cute receptionist he had been flirting with earlier in the day, said, "It's your wife on line one." He smiled and winked at the cute girl, took a deep breath, rolled his eyes, and said, "Yeah, what?" Soosie told him to come home because he had been "playing" at the gym long enough. She continued, "And pick up some KFC with extra mashed potatoes and dark gravy." Craig had just been asked by the guys to go have a beer after they were through working out, but he knew this was out of the question, so he replied, "Give me thirty", as he kicked the vending machine. Luckily a Dr. Pepper came out, so he wouldn't have to buy her whiny ass a drink to go with her extra mashed potatoes.

As Craig was walking out of the gym, he picked up a brochure with an application for the 1988 Houston Bodybuilding Competition. Craig jumped in his truck, and headed South on I 45. There must have been an accident or some type of late night construction because the cars were at a standstill. His mind veered off, thinking about all the guys at the gym and how goddamned lucky they were. Craig knew none of them had pregnant wives at home, and they could do whatever they wanted whenever they wanted. Most of them had jobs at the gym, a few girlfriends on the side, and their lives revolved around bodybuilding. The more Craig thought about it, the more pissed he got, especially with all of the "ball and chain" jokes. What pissed him off the most was that he knew his wife did have him chained by the balls, and he resented the hell out of her for that!

Craig could not get the upcoming Houston Bodybuilding Championships out of his head. All of his buddies at the gym had already signed up, and were training to compete in it. Even more frustrating, he thought to himself, he knew if he entered the competition, he could beat all of their asses, hands down! Craig looked a million times better than every single person working out at that gym; shit, he could see that by just looking in the mirror. Every one of those guys had been stacking gear for years, adhering to a strict diet of protein and supplements and practicing every pose required to perform and win a competition.

SWIFT INJUSTICE

Just with genetics alone, Craig was already bulked up and had a natural "V" shape. Just imagine if he put a little money into it, without a doubt; done deal, he would get his pro card in no time, and be on stage, kicking everybody's ass! All Craig could think about was, "What if"? The question played out in his mind like a scratched record: "What if ..., What if..., What if..." Fuck the, "what if's", he finally thought. He knew he could not live his life wondering "what if" anymore. He would never win the lottery if he didn't buy a ticket, and he was buying that fucking ticket! As he sat in the 8:00 p.m. North Highway traffic, Craig decided that he was ready to get this bodybuilding plan rock and rolling! He was going to compete in the Houston Bodybuilding Competition, period. Craig began putting his plan into place, that day, while sitting in traffic. He needed to start purchasing the steroids yesterday, and injecting them today, if he had a shot at placing in the competition.

He was starting his diet immediately! He read everything he could get his hands on, to learn what and when he should eat every day, leading up to the next competition. Most important, he needed to spend all of his extra time at the gym. As soon as he could, Craig would quit his job, and get a job at the gym. This would mean a huge pay cut, so he would need to write out a budget, and only buy the necessities. Everything was falling into place in his mind, he just needed to put it to paper, and make it happen! And one other thing, "Billy Bad Ass" would have to break the news to his little lady at home.

After Craig picked up some Kentucky Fried Chicken, he pulled up in the driveway, killed the engine, and walked to the front door. He had made up his mind that he was not going to *ask* his wife if he could do the competition; he was going to tell her. He knew somewhere in the Bible it talks about the woman being submissive to the man, and that was the way it was going to be, period! With a bucket of chicken in one hand, and the application in the other, he opened the front door, walked in and set them both down on the kitchen counter top. Soosie got up off the couch, they exchanged their usual monosyllable, bullshit small talk, and then it happened, her eyes fixed on the piece of paper: the application for the bodybuilding competition. The arsenal in his mind was loaded and ready to fire, as he knew his wife would shoot down everything Craig had to say. She could see in his eyes that something was up. He stared a hole through her with a stoic glare of determination, ready to pounce, the minute she opened her negative ass mouth. Craig was about to stand his ground, and he would be damned if he was going to let her stand in the way of this dream.

Craig walked over to the refrigerator, and just as he turned his back, Soosie, with a sarcastic tone and a laugh of disdain spouted out, "What's this?" Craig thought to himself, "Here we go." He shut the refrigerator door, poured a glass of milk, and asked, "Can't you read? It's an application for the Houston Bodybuilding Competition." Soosie shot back, "Why is it taking up space on my kitchen countertop?" Craig said, "Well Genius, once I eat dinner, I am going to fill it out and pop it in the mail." There was a brief silence, and with a raised voice his wife cynically asked, "Are you fucking kidding me? Tell me this is a joke, because it is pretty fucking funny!" She picked up the application, and started to laugh, and asked again, "This is a joke right?" Craig's face and neck were beginning to blotch bright red as his blood pressure went through the roof.

If there was one thing Craig could not stand, it was to be laughed at, especially over something he has been dreaming about for years. Craig said, "No I am not fucking kidding, and you are the only one that thinks it's funny. Every single person at the gym thinks I have a chance to win." His wife tried to contain her laughter when she asked, "Is it like one of those baby pageants where everyone pays the entry fee, and they all walk away with a piece of shit plastic trophy? If you want a trophy, come home straight from work, without going to the gym or stopping at a bar, and give me a little attention. I will get you a plastic trophy and tape whatever bullshit you want to hear on it to boost your ego." Soosie took the bag of chicken and chunked it in the trash, and yelled, "Goddamn it Craig, you have a fucking baby on the way and you barely make enough money to pay the rent. You are home for a few hours to sleep, and then you are out the door again. Now you want to throw money away, prancing around a stage, just to have a bunch of assholes boost your fucking ego, telling you how great you look."

SWIFT INJUSTICE

With a look of disgust on her face, Soosie yelled, "Grow the fuck up Craig!" She slapped the glass of milk out of Craig's hands, crumpled up the brochure, tossed it in the trash, and yelled, "If you can't be a real man, I will go find me one." Craig shot back, "Good luck finding a dumb ass, willing to fall for your crazy bipolar ass. If you want to get me a trophy, get me one for putting up with you!" Craig dug the brochure out of the trash, went to the desk and pulled out his checkbook.

Craig filled out the application, and the check, licked the envelope, and opened the drawer to find a stamp. While he was digging through the paper clips and coupons to find a stamp, Soosie walked back in the room. She always took great pleasure in tearing Craig down, and by the look on her face, it was obvious she was going to throw one last jab. "Hey, while you are at it, why don't you go take some singing lessons, maybe you can become a rock star. Or better yet, here is a book, why don't you read it, and win the Pulitzer Prize. You do know how to read?" Craig looked her square in the eyes, then looked down, licked the stamp, placed it on the letter, and walked out the door.

Over the next couple of months, Craig spent almost no time at home. His new home was at Bally's working out. If he was not at the gym, he was at his job, making as much side money as he could to provide for his family and hopefully purchase steroids to bulk up for the upcoming bodybuilding competition. Craig dedicated his mind and body to the art of bodybuilding. He listened and watched the veterans of the gym, and did his best to mimic their training and dieting routines. Calling 900 Bodybuilding tip lines, shuffling through all of the magazines, Craig crammed like a college student before a midterm exam.

He was looking leaner from his small portioned, high protein meals, and intense cardio workouts. He bought every popular supplement endorsed by all of the professionals, emptying his pockets, trying to help him gain any type of edge over his competition. The fear of the unknown and the excitement of living out his dream on stage was an adrenaline rush. Craig found himself spending all of his time with the guys at the gym, having them push him to the limit in his cardio and weight training, while critiquing and breaking down each mandatory pose. Outsiders looking in had no idea what all went into "posing" for the judges. It is not just a bunch of guys in speedos flexing their muscles for five seconds with a grimace on their face.

The bodybuilding veterans at the gym who had competed said posing was the most difficult part of the competition; and it can either make or break an athlete. They have to be mentally and physically prepared to know all of the poses the judges are looking for, standing flexed for over ten minutes, heart rates going up, sweat pouring, with muscles cramping. Only the guys that walked the walk and talked the talk could possibly understand, and he found himself inadvertently isolating himself from everyone that was not associated with the gym.

Twelve weeks out from his first competition, Craig was dieting and training like he was taught and trained, and purchased Androl 50 (Androgenic Steroid Oxymetholone) from a buddy, and saw the physical effects immediately. From what he had read, and had been told, Winstrol (Anabolic Androgenic Steroid Stanozolol) was the best AAS used by professionals for contest preparation primarily for its ability to promote muscle growth while speeding up the reduction of fat without water retention. Winstrol was the steroid that would guarantee him the results he wanted, and as luck would have it, 8 weeks out, a novice bodybuilder approached Craig and offered him some Winstrol V for a good price.

Craig jumped on it, and immediately began utilizing one injectable 50 mg a week. The first noticeable enhancement was that his skin dramatically thinned, and took on a dry grainy appearance. His strength and appetite however increased, and he continued to use a high protein low carb diet. There were drastic changes in his physique- he became significantly leaner without losing strength. Over all, Craig's muscle mass stayed the same while his separation and condition drastically changed for the better at a startling rate. (Throughout his competitions in his career, Craig always used both oral and injectable Winstrol, saying it was an essential anabolic steroid that he used every time for contest preparation.)

Craig's wife thought this "bodybuilding stuff" was a phase that he needed to get out of his system. She hoped that after this competition was over he would shake out of it, and focus on things that were more important to her. She could not have been more wrong, this was the most important thing in his life. Craig was on a one-way street, heading in a totally different direction from his wife; his passion was with bodybuilding, leaving little room for anything else. They could feel the weight of this competition on their marriage, splintering their nonexistent bond as each day passed. Craig could not have negative energy in his life at that moment; he had to block her and everything else out of his mind, and focus 100 percent of his energy on bodybuilding. Very soon, they would both be able to tell if this was just a phase in Craig's life, as the competition was then just a day away.

The countdown had begun, and in less than twelve hours, Craig would be up on that stage at the 1988 Houston Bodybuilding Competition. He could hardly sleep; his mind raced in a million different directions. He tossed and turned, rehearsing each pose in his mind while he watched the clock slowly tick away, minute by minute; the anticipation was agonizing! A few hours before the sun came up, Craig jumped out of bed and began to methodically lay out each item he would need before he headed out the door. Everything from hair product to directions to the venue was spread out and placed neatly in a gym bag. After taking inventory, and setting his bag by the front door, he headed to the kitchen to make breakfast. Just the day before he had clipped out a recipe for a protein shake from a muscle magazine, bought all of the ingredients, and had them ready to mix together the next morning. He added each ingredient in a blender: 1 cup of milk, ½ cup of water, ½ cup of plain yogurt, 2 scoops of whey protein powder, three tablespoons of peanut butter, 1 tablespoon of honey, and half a banana.

In the months prior to this big day, Craig had gotten into the routine of following every last detail of instruction verbatim, either from magazines, 900 phone lines, or suggestions given to him by other bodybuilders. Titus also followed a new routine, which he adhered to strictly. He ran 2 ½ miles before work, went to the gym after work, lifted and worked a different muscle group for a couple of hours, then finished with some sort of cardio before he left the gym. With the exception of his job, and everyday life getting in the way, Craig devoted every minute he had to this competition. He kept a journal, and like a mom marking the wall to show how many inches her son had grown in the past month, Craig marked down every last detail of his progress. He had prepared himself, obsessively, for his first competition. He placed his journal in his gym bag, headed to the door, jumped in the truck, and was off to the show.

1988 Houston Bodybuilding Competition

On the day of his first competition, Craig arrived an hour early to the stadium. This gave him a little extra time to mentally prepare, and get the feel for his surroundings. This competition was huge, and it was broken down in weight divisions: Bantamweight: up to 142 lbs., Lightweight: 143-156 lbs., Middleweight: 157-176 lbs., Light Heavyweight: 177-198 lbs., and Heavyweight: over 198 lbs. Most competitors try to compete at the top of their weight class. Craig was told that it is better to compete as a "ripped" Middleweight than a "smooth" Lightweight. Craig knew he would have a much greater impact on the judges by competing ripped and in top shape, than appearing smooth and bulked up, so he competed as a Middleweight, weighing in at 185 pounds.

When Titus first arrived, he went to the mandatory prejudging meeting, where all of the rules and guidelines are discussed, and questions are answered before they hit the stage. He was weighed in, given a number and an official line-up. After that he was off to do some last minute preparations before he hit the stage to make his muscle definition look more defined and distinct. The panel of judges was seated, and the morning portion of the competition was ready to begin.

Bodybuilding contests are divided into two events, the prejudging and the evening show. Prejudging is like a rehearsal for the evening show. The panel of judges was ready to rank all of the competitors on criteria such as symmetry, muscularity, and conditioning... The first round is the symmetry round, and he knew this was extremely important because it was in this round that he would make his first impressions on the judges. Although muscle size is taken into account during the symmetry round, the judges are primarily looking at symmetry, proportion, and definition of the athlete.

Next was the compulsory round, and this was where Craig was able to really show the judges his development. This round consists of seven compulsory poses, each designed to show the judges different aspects of the bodybuilder's physique. Craig had those seven poses down pat before he ever stepped on stage. When his name and number were called, with two other guys, he was first asked to stand with his hands by his side. Even though he was asked to "stand relaxed," he knew there was no relaxing about it. He had to keep his muscles tensed and under control at all times.

With his body flexed the entire time, he was judged from the front, showing off his front double biceps. Here he used the abdominal crunch method by flexing and crunching his abs to show off his ripped midsection. He held his arms in such a fashion as to give each arm an equally balanced look, holding his forearms at almost right angles with his elbows, while twisting his wrists to bring out the peak in his biceps. With his upper arms slightly above parallel with the floor, he bent his knees and tensed his legs to show off every single muscle. He was asked to "quarter turn to the right". Turning ninety degrees to the right, the judges then critiqued the backside of his physique. He made sure his back and legs were as tense as possible. At this time, they asked him again to "quarter turn to the right," where he turned another ninety degrees so the judges could view him from the side. Here the judges focused on his front lat spread, side chest, side triceps, and back double biceps from the other side. Craig made sure to keep every muscle tensed and his abs tight at all times; feeling cramps all over his body, he thought he was going to pass out when asked once again to "quarter turn to the right." Craig was now facing the judges again, and they had one last look at his overall physique. The nine judges ranked each competitor from first to last, and at the end, the competitor with the lowest score, was ranked highest going into the evening show.

After the Preliminaries, Craig waited around for the results to be posted. He felt good about the Preliminaries, but was shocked to see that he was in first place going into the finals. There was little time to revel in the excitement of first place, as he had just a short while to catch his breath, and then start preparing for the evening show, set to begin at 7:00 p.m. Even though it would be the same song and dance as the morning show, he would need to calm down and mentally prepare himself to do it all over again. The adrenaline rush from being in first place squelched his appetite, but he had to eat something before he went back on stage. He knew not to eat too many carbs, or drink too much liquid because it would cause him to swell, and loose that perfect physique that had him in the leader's position. After a quick bite to eat, the music was cranking back up as the auditorium filled with people.

Craig went back on stage, and performed the same routines, but this time he approached his routines with more passion and personality. He had this win in the bag, and he knew it. Craig was already a confident man before he had stepped on that stage, but his confidence was through the rough and bounced off the walls as everybody felt his energy in the audience. After his awe-inspiring performance, five guys, including Craig, were called back on stage for a pose down. The crowd went wild, and Craig felt like a rock star; he flaunted his stuff and posed with a swaggered perfection.

At the end, the emcee called the contestants back on the stage, and Craig's name was announced as the "Overall Champion." From that moment on, the bodybuilding world would never be the same as the blonde haired, blue eyed, massive hunk entered the lives of bodybuilding fans. There was no turning back; not only was Craig hooked, but fans were hooked on him as well. That moment seemed surreal, an out-of- body experience that left him with a craving for more! He would get more, and the world would get more of Craig, but as he headed back to his house, trophy in hand, he knew that he needed to devote some of his energy to his family. He had a baby on the way, and with this contest behind him, he needed to prepare to become a Dad and be more of a husband to his wife.

By the time Craig pulled up to the house, Soosie was already asleep; he knew it would be a short night because they had an early morning appointment in downtown Houston at the Obstetrician's office to check on the baby. The young couple arrived for their appointment a little early. After Soosie was weighed, the nurse took her and Craig back to a cold room with an ultrasound machine. While she was scolding Soosie about not putting on enough weight, the nurse measured around her abdomen, then took her vitals, and left the room for a few minutes. Craig tried to lighten the mood with some of his corny jokes; fortunately for Soosie, the nurse promptly returned to listen to the baby's heartbeat. The nurse sat in the chair next to Soosie, lifted her shirt, and gently placed the stethoscope on her stomach. No matter how hard their feelings were towards each other, the excitement of hearing the baby's heartbeat brought back a little of the love between the two. They held each other's hands, and waited eagerly to hear the nurse's response. The nurse did not say a word. Her eyebrows were furrowed, and the grimace on her face told them that she was concerned. The young couples own hearts stopped as they waited in silence to hear the results of their unborn child's heartbeat. The nurse forced a smile on her face, touched Soosie's arm, and said, "I will be right back with the doctor."

Being a man of extremes, Craig's mind began to jump to conclusions, and all he could do was pace the floor. He was preparing himself for the worst just as the doctor walked in the door. Craig blurted out, "Is anything wrong sir?" The doctor said, "I don't know, let's take a look," and smoothed some blue gel on Soosie's stomach. The doctor placed a wand like instrument called a transducer on his wife's stomach, and began to explain, in great detail, how an ultrasound works. He said, "The ultra sound produces sound waves. They are so high that you can't hear them. They bounce off the baby in order to see shadows and you will be able to see a picture of your baby." As the doctor went on, Craig wished the guy would shut the fuck up already, and tell him if his baby is okay. He really didn't give a shit how the ultrasound worked, only if his baby was healthy and had a heartbeat.

The doctor moved the transducer around her stomach, and said, "Well hmmm." By this time Craig was beside himself in fear, shifting from leg to leg, and amped up on pure emotion. Craig glanced over at the monitor, but it looked like a blob of black and white dots; he had no idea how to read the damn thing! The doctor began to smile, and the nurse giggled with excitement, as the doctor exclaimed, "That's what I thought; you are having twins!" Craig and Soosie burst out with excitement when the doctor interrupted, "Not only that, it looks like you have a football player and a ballerina."

With tears in his eyes, Craig asked, "You mean a boy and a girl?" The doctor said, "That's right Daddy." Even though Craig could only see a blob on the ultrasound, and a bump on his wife's belly; for the first time in Craig's life, he felt love, a love like no other. It was an unconditional love that made his heart race, stomach flutter, and knees buckle. The surreal feeling of pride and humility, and a new found respect for the mother of his children was almost more than he could handle. With affection in his eyes, and adoration in his heart, Craig told his wife, "I love you so much." Perhaps these little lives would bring this couple back together, even closer than before.

After a few months, everyday life kicked back in, and the arguments started back up. It was the same fight over and over again: "We don't have enough money & you spend too much time at the gym...blah...blah...blah." Craig tried to compromise, and worked more, helped out around the house, and spent very little time at the gym. He felt conflicted because he was brought up to be responsible; "man up" and provide for his family, but it seemed like nothing was ever enough.

The gym was like oxygen to Craig; he needed it to keep his blood pumping and to feel alive! Every day he was away from the gym, he felt like he was going crazy. Craig needed that escape; without it, he began to feel depressed and lethargic, lacking the energy needed to work extra to provide for the needs of his family. Craig knew someday he could make a good living in bodybuilding, but for the moment he had to put his dreams of becoming a professional bodybuilder on the backburner. His dream of becoming a daddy to a little princess that would sit in his lap, and a son he could throw the baseball with in the back yard would be his primary focus.

Arrival of the Twins

The weeks before his wife was to deliver, Craig could hardly sleep at night. He knew his life was about to do be turned inside out, and his world would completely change once the twins entered the world. It was a rollercoaster ride of emotions, from excitement to fear, as he thought about bringing children into this world. Every time the

Houston evening news came on, it always began with a murder or some grisly crime; all he could think about was keeping those two safe from harm.

The anticipation was too much, but fortunately for Craig, his wife went into labor and the twins made their grand entrance into the world on July 11, 1988. Craig was the proud daddy of beautiful twins- a boy, Aaron Colby & a girl, Ashley Marie Titus. The best day of his life was when he held those two little beings in his arms. He wore his emotions on his sleeve as he looked in their eyes with amazement. They had perfect little hands, perfect little feet, and perfect little lips; perfect everything!

As with most twins, Aaron & Ashley were premature, dividing the average eight pounds between the two tiny bodies. Aaron was slightly smaller than Ashley, and his heartbeat was irregular, so he was placed on a heart monitor when the babies went home. Premature babies tend to sleep less, and have a hard time nursing in the beginning, and this was true with both Aaron and Ashley. Life at the Titus house was very stressful when the twins came home. Craig worked back-to-back shifts to pay the bills, while Soosie stayed home trying to nurse the twins. Having a newborn is nerve-wracking; double that with twins, and everything is magnified. The fear of being a new parent, coupled with the lack of sleep and postpartum depression, it all took a toll on the young marriage.

Both Craig and his wife felt utterly overwhelmed with exhaustion. Craig's mother and sister were over at their house, helping them as much as possible, but when babies are that small, there are never enough arms to help. Every time one baby would go to sleep, the other would cry, or the heart monitor would go off. To keep his sanity, if he ever had a break, Craig would slip away to the gym. This unfortunately only caused more arguments between the couple.

As the months went by, and the twins slept two to three hours at a time, the environment became more peaceful. Before they knew it, the twins were six months old, eating solid food, and almost sleeping through the night. At their six-month pediatric well check, both the twins were given their shots. They had gained two pounds each since their last visit, and were right on target for where they needed to be-compared to other babies their age. Most exciting, Aaron's heartbeat was no longer irregular, and the doctor decided that he was strong enough to take him off of his heart monitor.

This was a huge relief, as both Craig & Soosie were constantly on edge because the monitor would give off a false alarm two or three times a day making them even more sleep deprived than they already were given the circumstances. Living in constant fear, every time the monitor went off was overwhelming; but it seemed as if they finally made it! That six-month mark and Aaron's heart appearing fine; it seemed that all of those sleepless nights paid off. Maybe then, with a little sleep, they could enjoy parenthood a little more. Life would be less tense, and they could start to have some fun with their new family.

On one particular day, a day that seemed like every other day, Craig came home from a long day's work, and Soosie had cooked them dinner. They ate, played, and gave the twins a bath, and then laid them down to go to sleep for the night. Craig turned on some soft music, and he kissed each baby goodnight. He placed his huge hand on Aaron's head, and caressed his son's soft head and face as he watched him fall asleep. With his other hand, he ran his finger over the top of Aaron's hand. Craig's heart began to melt when those little fingers wrapped around his giant finger, as if to tell his Daddy that he loved him. He stood over him, envisioning all of the fun the two of them were going to have in the years to come. A tear dropped from Craig's eye and landed on his son's forehead while he said a prayer of protection for his baby boy. He whispered, "Daddy loves you", and went to bed feeling so humbled and thankful that this little guy was going to be a part of his life forever.

Craig and Soosie were both exhausted, and they were ecstatic about the possibility of getting a half of night's sleep without a monitor going off. Their bed was so comfortable with cold sheets; they rubbed their toes together and looked forward to a great night sleep. With the spinning sound from the box fan humming in the background, and the comfortable sense of security lying heavy on their eyes, Craig and Soosie quickly fell asleep. The evening turned to early morning in the blink of an eye, and Craig had to rush off to his job. The twins had slept through the night, and Craig tried to be as quiet as possible, as to not wake them.

The next morning, Soosie, being awakened by the sunlight peeking in through the blinds, laid in bed for a few minutes until she heard the cry of one of his babies in the background. It would not be long, and one baby would wake the other, so Soosie rushed into the room and swooped up the baby girl to feed her. Soosie thought to herself maybe Aaron was able to sleep longer since he was taken off the heart monitor. She peaked in the room to check, and she sensed that something was wrong. As she walked over, she realized Aaron's lifeless body was blue, and he was not breathing.

On the morning of January 3, 1989, Craig's son, Aaron Colby, the day after being taken off his home cardiorespiratory monitor, died of SIDS (Sudden Infant Death Syndrome). The loss of his son, who Craig lovingly nicknamed his "boo-boo bear" broke his heart, and was almost unbearable. He felt dead inside, with all of his hopes, dreams, and plans for the future turned upside down. Dazed and numb, he didn't know how to grieve, or how to console those that were grieving around him.

The funeral seemed like an out of body experience, and he doesn't have many recollections about that day. The only thing he can really remember was his dad hugging him and giving him a gold necklace with the Egyptian God of Power emblem. Craig put this around his neck, and it somehow awakened the inner man in his heart. No matter how much it hurt, he had to keep going. He knew that life was too short to live it doing things that don't matter. He wanted to make his mark on this world, drawing inspiration from his son who did not ever have chance to realize his dreams. Like Samson in the bible, Craig grew his hair out, and drew strength from his son's reflection he saw every time he looked in the mirror. The next week Craig started training again, only now he had even more determination than before-this time he was doing it for his baby boy!

CHAPTER 3

Chasing his Dream

Craig entered the Houston Bodybuilding Competition for the second year in a row in 1989. This time he entered as a heavy weight- twenty pounds of muscle heavier, where he not only won the Heavy Weight Division, but swept the Overall title as well. As Craig drove home after his victory, he stopped at a convenience store and purchased every bodybuilding magazine that he could find. Craig pulled into his driveway and walked into his house with his trophy under one arm, and his magazines under the other. He tuned his wife out as she began to nag, and he walked into the bedroom and locked the door.

Craig sat the trophy and magazines on the dresser, and he took off his shirt. Flexing in the mirror, Craig would flip the pages of the magazines, and compare himself to the guys in the magazines. With a confident smirk on his face, Craig knew that he could stand next to these guys and compete, and maybe even win. He had only "half assed" everything so far, and had kicked everybody's ass in Houston- just imagine if he dedicated everything he had to bodybuilding!

Over the next year, Craig poured everything he had into the sport. Staying focused on the prize, Craig worked over time at the job site and at the gym. His entire world revolved around stacking gear, dieting, and training, posing, and saving every dime he had to get the fuck out of Texas! A lot of things are sacrificed when a person dedicates their life to becoming a professional athlete; and in this case it was Craig's marriage to Soosie. On July 31, 1989, Craig and Soosie divorced.

Craig changed gyms, and began to train at World's Gym in Houston. It was at this gym that Craig would meet Lee Haney, and his life would be forever transformed. While training Evander Holyfield, Lee Haney noticed Craig working out. Craig's idol and eight-time Mr. Olympia champion took the time to give Craig some pointers, and told him that he had great potential to make it as a professional bodybuilder. Haney suggested that Craig have gynecomastia surgery. He explained how this would contour the entire pectoral muscle region in his chest. When building muscles for competition, the gland mass becomes more obvious, and it becomes worse with use of anabolic steroids. Lee Haney told Craig that with the surgery, and a move out to California, he was certain Craig would be a successful professional bodybuilder in no time. Craig said, "That was the very moment I chose to pursue and dedicate all my time, and my entire life to bodybuilding."

Venice Beach

After Craig had the surgery, he headed to the West Coast to pursue his dream in Venice Beach, California. Also known as "Muscle Beach" on the South side of the Santa Monica Pier, Craig felt inspired the moment he arrived at the mecca of bodybuilding. Craig was getting to work out alongside his idols at Gold's gym; a huge iron building, three blocks from Venice Beach, with AC/DC blaring in the background. All of the bodybuilders from the muscle magazines were training in this building for competitions that Craig had always dreamed about competing in one day. The backdrop, primarily the atmosphere in Gold's Gym, was the original inspiration for Craig as he burst onto the bodybuilding scene in the 90's. Craig hired a dietician and trainer, and learned from the best on how to make the most out of his gear and workouts.

Although it was an electric atmosphere, it was a cutthroat environment. This was because all of these guys were training next to each other, then competing against each other for a relatively small prize. Finding a loyal friend at Gold's gym or in bodybuilding in general was rare. There was a cloud of cynicism and paranoia hovering over the bodybuilding community, making it impossible to trust others. This was because every professional bodybuilder and a large number of amateur bodybuilders were engaged in the illegal activity of steroid use. AAS is a schedule three drug and a C- III is stamped on each and every steroid made in the USA; and in order to walk on the stage of Olympia, these athletes have to break the law. According to Craig, "It sucks, and I don't think it is right, but that will never change!"

Inevitably, it was every man for himself, and Craig had to watch his own back when he tried to put together a formula for the perfect combination of steroids, HGH, and insulin. Craig said, "Looking back, I cannot remember one time openly discussing any contest prep AAS cycles with other bodybuilders. All of us training together; nobody ever wanted to divulge the chemical warfare that would provide us with the winning edge to achieve championship status." All on his own, Craig obviously knew what he was doing because he came out of nowhere, and immediately made his mark in the competitions along the West Coast. Craig Titus' big break came in 1990 where he was set to compete on a more glamorous stage in front of the cameras at ESPN's Tournament of Champions in Fontana, California. He came to play with the big boys, and entered as a heavyweight. He knew he could win hands down as a middleweight, but he had to step up his game to make it in the "Industry."

Craig Titus not only turned heads, and lured fans in with his stellar poses, but he held everyone captive with his jaw-dropping good looks. It was impossible for anyone to take their eyes off of Craig; men and women alike were infatuated with this beautiful stud of a man. Craig stood out from the others and broke away from the pack with this look. His rugged good looks, combined with his near perfect physique had everyone out of their seats. Craig surprised himself, and everyone around him placing 3rd Overall in the 1990 competition. After the competition, Craig appeared humble, as the cameras caught him in action. He graciously thanked the judges for their hard work. He shook hands and congratulated the winners and other contestants in the competition. He then waited around for hours to make sure he signed every autograph from the fans that supported him. With his deep, gravel voice, Craig managed to charm his way into America's heart after his performance that night on ESPN.

Exploding onto the bodybuilding scene, Craig's life changed overnight, in 1991, when he competed in the Los Angeles' Ironman competition, tipping the scales at just over 200 pounds. When he flashed his soon to be signature "Adonis" pose, everyone in the audience began yelling his name. The best word to describe Craig Titus in this particular competition was "confident!" Confidence is possibly the sexiest trait a man can have, and Craig came out of the womb confident. As he made eye contact with the judges, those blue eyes beamed right through them, and he knew he had every one wrapped around his finger. When Craig looked into the crowd, everyone became a Titus fan as he performed one perfect pose after another. Some of the biggest names in bodybuilding were in the audience, from writers to promoters; everyone was there to witness this kid come out of nowhere and take the Overall title; Craig Titus was the next generation of body building.

The 1991 win in the Ironman competition catapulted Craig into the pseudo-celebrity world in the body building community. Back at Venice Beach the next day, Craig worked out at Gold's gym, and ESPN representatives arrived to interview him. They asked Craig questions and took pictures and videoed him while he worked out. What shocked the representatives that were interviewing Craig was that in addition to his muscles and good looks, Craig was intelligent and articulate. He was a man that knew what he was talking about, and he knew where he wanted to go in life.

This new kid had the bodybuilding world right in front of him, all he had to do was reach out and grab it. In 1993, Craig took his first stab at the IFBB pro card in 1993, when he entered the USA Championships in Santa Monica, California and placed fourth, behind legends: Chris Cormier, Paul DeMayo, Mike Francois, Ken Castagnoli & Dennis Newman. Craig said that after this show, he was swarmed by photographers wanting to shoot him for their publications. Craig said, "I realized that the exposure itself could launch me into a great career in bodybuilding." And he was so right; later he would tell reporters that he would rather be "Mr. Magazine" than "Mr. Olympia" because he

CHASING HIS DREAM

would make a lot more money being "Mr. Magazine." And Craig's first Magazine cover was featured on *Musclemag International* (Nov.93), issue #137.

The next year, in 1994, Craig went back to the USA's and came in second behind Dennis Newman. Craig went on that year to the Nationals, and came in second behind Paul DeMayo. From that point on, Craig was hailed as the number one heavy weight contender for amateur titles. He was appearing on magazine covers all over the world. His only hurdle was that point or two that stood in the way of him, as he attempted to step over from Amateur to Professional. Winning on the Amateur level, as impressive as it may be, would not get a bodybuilder in the club.

In the nineties, to get the pro card, an athlete had to finish first overall in an NPC (National Physique Committee) sanctioned national competition. The NPC is the largest amateur body building organization in the United States. In order to become a professional body builder in the United States, a class must first be won at the NPC Nationals Championships or be the overall winner at the NPC USA Championships. The IFBB stands for the International Federation of Body building and Fitness. It is a competitive bodybuilding, fitness, and figure competition organization that is currently the highest level for competitive bodybuilding in the world. (Today becoming a professional is not as difficult because they take the top 2 or 3 from each weight class.)

1995 Denver NPC Competition

Craig Titus walked onto the 1995 Denver NPC stage predicted to win. He placed second in back-to-back competitions prior to Denver, and intended on walking away the third time with a victory. Craig was competing against Phil Hernon, and he had beaten him every time they had competed in the past.

The only thing standing in Craig's way were the nine judges seated across the stage, and a big secret he chose not to disclose to anybody going into the competition. The problem with secrets, in the backstabbing world of body building, is that if a secret is leaked, there is no chance of winning the overall title; and unfortunately for Craig,

◄ SWIFT INJUSTICE

the Emcee of the event, Lonnie Teper had already blabbed to the judges about what he had heard from an "inside" source in Houston.

The secret, a drug conspiracy charge Craig faced in Louisiana, spread like wild fire. Craig had been going back and forth from Los Angeles to Louisiana battling the charge. Craig did not want his personal battle at the moment to affect his placing in that show or his career in general. Not revealing his drug arrest backfired, and like the game of "telephone", Teper's hearsay version of the incident was blathered across the judge's panel and audience before Craig ever stepped on stage. Craig could hear the muttering, and he knew the source of the exaggerated account; but there was nothing he could do at that point. He wanted to go smack Teper in the face, but he also wanted to win, so that was out of the question.

Craig's only competition was obviously inferior, and so Craig had to trust in the judge's to be fair and make the right decision. The judges were looking for symmetry, muscularity, aesthetics, and proportion with points gained for superiority in each category. And at this particular competition, Craig Titus had all of these things; however, because judging is subjective, anything could happen. One negative comment in the back of a judge's head could determine how he or she votes, which could have held him back from becoming a professional.

Despite being predicted to win this competition after the prior five months in muscle magazines, any sort of gossip that made its way back to the judges could have caused them to vote for someone other than Craig Titus. Titus was not in control of his own destiny at that point; with the gossip circulating, but Craig still thought there was no way he could lose the competition. He dominated the stage with his stellar poses; no one touched Craig Titus. Craig knew it, the crowd knew it, and even Phil Hernon, the only man that came close to Craig in the competition, knew it. The question was, "Would the judges score it?"

Craig believed they would, after all, they were there to decide who had the best physique, not who had been in trouble with the law. And, when it was all said and done, the judges would have to justify their scores. Before the announcement of the winner, Craig believed that this was his moment, and he was certain he would walk away as the overall champion. There was no way the judges could declare him anything but the winner, but the judges had the final word.

And the emcee announced, "With one point separating first and second, your second place winner is..," as the crowd mouthed the name Phil Hernon, the emcee, announced, "Craig Titus." For a second there was a hushed silence, then came an outbreak of "Expletives and Boos" from the crowd. Everyone was shocked, and many were outraged, but none as shocked and outraged as Craig Titus himself. Craig said, "And to pour salt on this open wound, the pussy that spread all the rumors, Lonnie Teper, was the one that announced the results. All I could do was glare at that high school bitch, but I wanted to knock his teeth down his throat!" By losing the heavyweight division to Hernon, Craig Titus had no shot at the overall title. Craig ripped his competition number off, crumpled it up, and tossed it on the ground and then stormed off the stage. Slapping the curtains out of his way, Craig threw the "piece of shit 2nd Place" trophy in the trashcan. He grabbed all of his belongings and walked out of the building as fast as he could, washing his hands of the farce of a competition before he said or did something that he would later regret.

Deshay Ebert, an IFBB/NPC promoter, and judge for over 15 years, reaffirmed what Craig already knew, "because of the drug charges and gossip swirling around the hotel in Denver, the pro card was given to Phil; regardless of the fact that the score cards showed that you beat him." It was bullshit, and everyone knew it; however, one positive thing that resulted from the Denver competition is that from that day on Craig Titus was known as the "Bad Boy of Bodybuilding." A title that helped Craig reinvent himself later in his career, and made him stand out from every other bodybuilder in the IFBB.

CHAPTER 4

The Catch 22- Steroids and Bodybuilding

After a short recess, the judge announced that she was prepared to sentence Craig, "Based on Mr. Titus' testimony, I have decided to reduce his part in the transaction as a 'minor role'. It's the court's intention that you will not spend that time in prison." Instead of prison time, Craig was sentenced to eight months in a halfway house and eight months to home confinement, along with three years of supervised release. Far worse, Craig was forbidden to possess any illegal controlled substance and had to report in for regular testing to ensure his body was free of drugs, including steroids. The judge concluded with a warning to Craig, "I am giving you an opportunity to make a life for yourself, but don't misunderstand; if I'm betting wrong on you, and you test dirty, I'm putting you back in jail! Do you understand that?" Craig replied, "Yes, ma'am." She concluded, "Mr. Titus, I've given you the benefit of the doubt. I will not do that again!" The judge stood up, looked Craig square in the eyes and said, "Steroids in all likelihood will kill you!"

The Halfway House

Craig began serving his 16-month sentence on November 1, 1995, in a half-way house in a suburb of Los Angeles, California. He would be randomly drug tested, and in order to stay out of prison, he had to remain steroid free. But anyone that knew Craig knew that the he was not going to let anything stand in between him and becoming a professional bodybuilder. And everyone that plays the game knows that the only way to get that card is to take a shit load of steroids; so Craig weighed the consequences, and said "fuck it" and juiced up.

The halfway house actually worked in Craig's favor. He was able to concentrate on his body, working out at any time of any day. Additionally, he was still able to compete, with the government flipping the bill for his room and board. Putting 1995 behind him, Craig was ready and willing to do whatever it took to break through to the other side while serving out the rest of his time for the conspiracy charge. Not only did Craig spend his time on weights, cardio and diet, but most important, and often overlooked in the bodybuilding community, he mastered his poses. Craig knew that a great physique was irrelevant if he could not display it properly. Craig bulked up to 300 pounds, adding seventy pounds of pure muscle

Getting his IFBB Pro Card

On June 28th in 1996 at the Terrace Theater in Long Beach, California for the NPC USA Men's Bodybuilding Championships, when Craig Titus walked on the stage, everyone was shocked. His fans were surprised to see him competing because they knew that he had recently been arrested. The assholes writing the articles in the muscle magazines and on the bodybuilding websites declaring that Craig Titus' career was over after Denver, were stunned to see Craig in the best shape of his life. Nobody expected what they were about to see; Craig came to win, and was about to put on the performance of his life.

Craig had worked ten times harder and looked ten times better than he did in the 1995 bodybuilding competition. In fact, Titus had never looked that way before; everything about his physique was perfect from head to toe. Everybody could say what they wanted, the fact of the matter was that Craig Titus was there, and he was ready to compete; it was redemption night for the "Bad Boy of Body Building."

After the fiasco in Denver, and with all of the gossip that had floated around about Craig and his conviction, most men would have been hesitant about returning to the stage, but not Craig. If anything, it pushed him even harder! That is what made Craig even more "bad ass" than everyone else. He did not care what others thought about him; Titus had a score to settle. He didn't give a shit if people loved or hated him; he was there for one thing only, the IFBB pro card, and he was not going home without it in his hand. This was his stage, his moment, and if people did not like it, "they could go fuck themselves."

The moment played out like a WWF moment, as the "Bad Boy" entered the stage, and the Craig Titus show began. Craig took the stage more determined, and massive than ever. It was obvious to the thousands in the crowd that the "bad boy" had reemerged as the "comeback kid", and he came to win. It was a twisted Cinderella Story: boy had everything, boy lost everything, boy was back, and boy kicked everyone's ass! Just the sight of Craig Titus taking the stage made the crowd jump to their feet; there was not a person in the audience that didn't want Craig Titus to take the whole thing home. Seriously, he had been in a halfway house these past few months prior preparing for the show- and look what this guy was doing- it was amazing! There was not a person in the bodybuilding world that could have predicted what was about to happen on that stage!

Motivated by all of the critics and haters, Craig jumped on stage and flaunted every muscle that he had, electrifying the crowd; Craig's body did all of the talking for him on that stage. If he was one point away in Denver, this new body was about to burst through and break records, guaranteeing Craig the win. At the end of the night, Craig heard the words he had been waiting to hear for nearly ten years, "And the Overall Champion is, Craig Titus." This was a moment that Craig would never forget, one of the proudest moments of his life. Every emotion was pumping through him, from elation to gratitude; with sheer heart and determination, Craig achieved his goal, and earned the IFBB Pro Card! In the sea of photographers, reporters, and women swarming Craig, he took the time to address and acknowledge each person that had supported him.

Amidst the whirlwind of excitement, the most touching moment of the night came when Craig told a reporter that he dedicated this victory to his son Aaron, who passed away in 1989. With the IFBB pro card came a photo shoot at Venice Beach's Gold's Gym, a contract with Met-RX, and all of the other amenities that are rewarded to those who have broken through from amateur to professional bodybuilder. Unfortunately this victory would be short-lived, because Craig made

THE CATCH 22- STEROIDS AND BODYBUILDING

a deal with the devil, and the devil was ready to collect. Just like everybody else that became a professional bodybuilder, there was a price to pay: it took hard work, determination, and a shitload of steroids to get to that level.

It was a "Catch-22" for Craig: take steroids and earn the pro card, or don't take steroids and stay an amateur bodybuilder. This was his profession, and he had already invested half of his adult life into it; Craig gambled, and in the end he won and he lost. Regrettably for Craig, taking steroids meant that he had violated the terms of his probation, and was facing the reality of going to prison. Craig knew if he tested positive for steroids, prison was a strong possibility. He weighed the consequences, and becoming a professional bodybuilder was more important to him than losing a year or two of his life to a federal prison.

Dirty Steroid Test- Off to Prison

It was no surprise to Craig, when after failing a steroid test, he found himself once again facing the judge that had sentenced him to probation back in Louisiana. The last time Craig saw this judge, she told him if he had a dirty drug test, she would throw his ass in jail for an extended amount time. Nevertheless, the harshness of the sentence the judge handed down still astonished everyone in the courtroom, including Craig himself. The Judge said, "The court has proved with a preponderance of evidence that Mr. Titus engaged in taking steroids during the time when he was on supervised release. For that reason, Mr. Titus, your supervised release is revoked, and you are sentenced to two years in Federal Prison." Craig looked up in despair, wondering if he made the right decision; certain that everything he had worked so hard for was about to go down the toilet.

Those baby blue eyes of confidence now turned to defeat as he looked up at the judge when she said, "You are remanded to the custody of the United States Marshal to begin service, Mr. Titus." Craig looked back at this Mother, who had been in the stands cheering for him his entire life, as she watched Craig being led off in handcuffs to be incarcerated at a federal penitentiary in California. Craig was off to the Federal Correctional Institution in Lompoc, California, 175 miles northwest of Los Angeles. The average offender at this penitentiary is serving time for a federal drug charge or a non-violent offense. Craig had already made up his mind to do his time as fast possible and then return to bodybuilding soon after.

Craig decided to serve his entire sentence out in prison rather than live on the outside and face the restrictions of drug testing. To do this, Craig would have to endure twenty-one months in the minimum security federal prison. He would, however, be able to pick his life back up when his sentence was completed, without worrying if the government was looking over his shoulder. There would be no way he could pick his career back up and gain some kind of momentum with any type of drug/steroid restrictions placed upon him.

Craig was actually the first professional bodybuilder to serve time in prison. He had already resolved in his mind that he was going to stay focused, and have a positive outlook while he was incarcerated. Sure it was "bullshit" that he got caught doing something almost everybody else in bodybuilding does, but he knew that if he dwelled on the negative, he would get nowhere in life. Instead, Craig knuckled down, and kept himself centered by being positive and looking forward rather than back.

According to Craig, "Prison had a funny way of showing me things that I would never have noticed or appreciated in the free world." Craig learned to appreciate the things in life that he took for granted before, "like walking on the beach or holding hands with the girl you love, or being on stage and performing before a crowd of body building fans. When I am released, I will be a much better father, man and professional body builder, I can guarantee that!" Craig said, " I am using this time in jail to make himself a better man. I'm making this a positive experience- expanding my mind by reading books and learning Spanish." Craig would read every night after he finished his work at the prison.

Craig's prison job was working on an outside construction site from 7 a.m. until 3 p.m., Monday thru Friday. Craig did everything from repairing fences to office work as a clerk. To help pass the time, and keep the fan interest up, he would spend about two hours a day on

THE CATCH 22- STEROIDS AND BODYBUILDING

fan mail. He said, "It is a great feeling to know that so many people stand behind you and can't wait to see you on stage again." Craig answered every letter, which was not an easy task, because he got over 200 letters a day. Craig also trained from 90 minutes to two hours a day; some of the most intense workouts of his life. "Motivation comes easy thinking about my pro debut on the IFBB stage when I walk out of the prison doors."

Craig did everything right: he did what he was told, adhered to a strict diet, and kept in top physical shape. He used every opportunity he had to naturally bulk up either in the gym or by doing physical labor. He had a buddy on the inside that worked out with him, and helped him get through the harsh world of prison. It was not ideal, but having a friend by his side made it bearable. They made jokes, encouraged each other, and made the best of a bad situation. Before Craig knew it, his time in prison was up. Released in February of 1999, Craig was more than ready to pick back up where he had left off, but was the world of bodybuilding ready for him? Would Craig Titus give them a choice?

CHAPTER 5

The Return of Craig Titus

With the biggest obstacle behind him, the road in the IFBB would be tough; Craig was now on the stage with the big boys! Before 1982 most of the bodybuilders were less than 200 lbs.; aesthetics and balance won the prize. The world of bodybuilding changed forever when Lee Haney, Craig's inspiration for becoming a professional, and his monster build emerged on the Olympia Stage. With the combination of steroids, nutrition, and conditioning, Lee Haney compiled eight consecutive Olympia wins from 1984- 1991. At 245 pounds, Haney was the total bodybuilding package: symmetry, size, and proportion.

In 1992 Lee Haney's dominance came to an end, and Dorian Yates became the man of Olympia weighing in at 268 lbs., and winning the Olympia from 1992 until 1997. After Haney and Yates, nobody thought that the world of professional bodybuilding could get any larger. Then the biggest, and according to Craig, "the best ever," took the stage, Ronnie Coleman. Coleman reached a competition weight of 297 pounds and became the joint record holder for Mr. Olympia, winning eight in a row from 1998-2005. Ronnie Coleman also holds the record for the most wins as an IFBB professional with 26 wins.

And it was on this stage with Dorian Yates and Ronnie Coleman that Craig Titus would try to rebuild his career and make a living in "The Industry." Craig understood how difficult it would be returning to the stage, and with these enormous men, the odds were stacked against him. He was significantly smaller than the other pros, and had a huge handicap being labeled a "felon." Craig would have to stand toe-to-toe with the biggest names that had ever walked the stage, and to be able to accomplish that, it would take an extraordinary focus and work ethic.

Meeting Kelly Ryan

Shortly after his release, Craig's friend Lorri surprised him with a birthday/welcome home party. She had Craig and a few other friends picked up in a limousine; included in the limo was an up-and-coming fitness star, Kelly Ryan. Craig first saw her on stage in 1995 at the Fitness America Pageant, and along with the rest of the world, he immediately fell in love with her. Craig said, "I was absolutely mesmerized watching Kelly perform her Popeye the Sailorman routine on stage. She was a star being born that day, flying through the air, doing one armed pushups."

Since then, Kelly had risen up the celebrity ladder in the fitness world, and had gained her IFBB pro card in August of 1999. Craig said that from the moment he laid eyes on Kelly in that limo, he was absolutely smitten with her; and he mercilessly flirted with her over the next few months every time he saw her out and about. Kelly would playfully turn away his advances, and Craig knew it was for the best.

At that point in his life, he did not have time for a relationship. And, after dating numerous girls in the fitness industry over the years, women like Monica Brandt, Debbie Halo, April Moore, Theresa Hessler, and Themis Cliderous, to name a few, Craig had made a promise to himself that he would not get involved with another fitness athlete or model again. To be clear, according to Craig, "A one night stand was not out of the question;" but to get serious with a woman in the fitness industry was something Craig wanted to avoid all together. So Craig flirted on the side with Kelly Ryan, but his attention was on his career. Falling in love was not on the agenda, and falling in love with another fitness competitor was out of the question! Anyone in the fitness industry knows that preparing for shows with a girlfriend is hard enough, but preparing for the same shows, never works. Craig just kept trying to tell himself that; the problem was, a person cannot help who they fall in love with, even the biggest and baddest of them all, Craig Titus.

Craig had to strategically plan his entrance back into the world of body building. Out of federal prison, Craig was still an IFBB pro, but many people were less than enthusiastic about his return. Craig lost his Met-Rx contract, and he lost a lot of the fan support from the community, that had once embraced him, because of his incarceration. In fact, Craig felt like he was being shunned from the industry all together saying, "I was black balled from the community, like a poor boy from the wrong side of the tracks trying to enter a college fraternity." Craig needed to come up with a strategic game plan to win back the sponsors and the fans; but before he did that, he needed to build his body back up to be able to stand on the same stage as the other professionals.

Stacking the Steroids

In pursuit of winning back what he once had, Craig devised a system called "blood volume" training where the emphasis was placed on the intensity during workout sessions using medium weights and hard cardio two times a day on some days, and the other days he lifted heavy weights with low reps. While training, he focused on nutrition- eating large amounts of protein to build muscles, and simple carbs for recovery and energy for work-outs. He also supplemented his meals with whey protein, creatine, and glutamine. Craig began stacking, and injecting Anabolic Steroids Stanozol, Human Growth Hormones and Anti-Estrogen Drugs like Clomid, and Diuretics trying to get his body in top physical competition shape.

Titus knew how the game was played; and though no one person in the IFBB would admit it, and state the obvious truth, Titus was always upfront about the fact that without steroids and other performance enhancing drugs, there would be no IFBB or NPC period! Sure you can be a bodybuilder without AAS but you will not turn pro, and you'll never make a living at it! Titus always believed that he was an athlete with sub-par genetics who achieved his status as a professional bodybuilder because of his ability to stack the right products.

Over the years Craig has had countless discussions with bodybuilding champions in regards to steroids. They would compare their cycles, the timing of using insulin in relation to their work outs, and which diuretics were most effective for pulling water. They discussed what drugs to use to alleviate pain due to sore injection sites. Titus has talked about experimenting with different dosages of HGH and whether to inject the growth hormone prior to bed or first thing in the morning prior to a competition.

The point being, the discussions he has had with other professional body builders have never included practices in diet or training or how much sleep they're getting. Their conversations almost always were engrossed in the topic of performance enhancing drugs. Why? Well, that's really quite simple; every professional bodybuilder worked hard in the gym and typically worked out using the same training methods and philosophies. Professional bodybuilders trained twice a day; utilized nutrition principles that were established long ago, never missed a meal, and pushed themselves far beyond the limits in the gym, enduring as much pain as humanly possible on every set. It would be in fact unfair to say the success of top bodybuilders is only a result of using AAS, but if all champion bodybuilders are acutely the same with their training and diet methods, it is fair to say the chemicals make a huge difference if not THE difference.

Stacking cycles sixteen weeks before a competition for Craig Titus was the following:

Contest Prep for 16 weeks:

4 Weeks-

Sustanon 250 mg x 3= 750 mg weekly

Dianabol 5 mg tabs= 10 tabs daily

Equipoise 50 mg x 6= 600 mg weekly

Winstrol tabs x 10 tabs daily

4 Weeks-

Test Cypionate 200 mg x 3- 600 mg weekly

Primobol depot. 100 mg x 4= 400 mg weekly

Dianabol tabs 5 mg x 10 tabs daily= 450 mg weekly

Winstrol tabs 5 mg x 10 tabs daily= 450 mg weekly

4 Weeks-

Propionate test 100 mg x 4 = 400 mg weekly

Haloteston tabs 10 mg x 4 tabs daily- 280 mg weekly

Winstrol V Injection = 300 mg weekly

Deca Durbolin 100 mg x 6 = 600 weekly

Cytodrene 250 mg tab- Last two weeks of the show

Nolvadex tabs- taken the entire cycle duration

This was the system that worked for Craig, and he considered himself an expert in the field of anabolic steroids because he used almost every steroid made in hundreds of combinations.

Predicting Titus to fail

Everyone watched with great anticipation because no bodybuilder had ever been sentenced to prison for a steroid charge, much less, returned to the stage after a stint in prison. There were a few people cheering for him, but for the most part in the beginning, almost everyone predicted that he would crash, burn, and fail miserably. Bodybuilding, at that time, was a very cut throat business; everyone was stepping on the next guy to advance their own careers. The IFBB pros were not hanging out and training with each other, they were bitching, backstabbing, and throwing each other under the bus to further their own careers. It was a negative environment and a tough profession to stage any kind of comeback, but Craig would find a way to do it one step at a time.

Melissa James

Getting his feet wet again, Craig began guest posing, and one of his first gigs was at a NPC local show in Panama City, Florida in 1999. It was at this show that Craig first met Melissa James, a local bodybuilding enthusiast that volunteered to pick Craig up from the airport and assist Craig during the competition.

Melissa drove Craig around Panama City, introducing him to the town and the locals, and helped him out when he needed anything for his show. Craig and Melissa had an instant connection and became fast friends. When he first met Melissa, Craig and Kelly were not yet "serious", but they had just started to date. Craig was physically attracted to Melissa, but felt more of an emotional connection and bond with James as a person in the beginning.

Craig said, "M.J. was using drugs, but not abusing drugs. She was so easy to talk to, and I found myself drawn to who she was on the inside. Melissa was so positive, talking about her dreams of the future, and working with kids- teaching them to dance. Her enthusiasm and love for others touched me, and had I not been interested in Kelly, I probably would have asked M.J. out. But, I was glad I didn't, because she was a great friend to me. Just a cool person with great advice, and had we been in a relationship, that friendship probably would not have grown. Before drugs destroyed her, M.J. was the most amazing woman." Craig and Melissa stayed in touch, and when Craig returned to Los Angeles, he told Kelly about her, and how he could not wait for the two women to meet and become friends.

At this time, Craig and Kelly were not dating, but were very close friends. Their relationship was not platonic; they were not a couple, but were definitely "friends with benefits". Craig knew he needed to focus solely on his career. He did not want to date anyone in the "industry;" so he was fine with their arrangement. While Kelly had her guard up, and she was hesitant to step into another relationship because she had just been jilted by her long-time boyfriend weeks before she met Craig Titus. This boyfriend cheated on Kelly Ryan with multiple women, and they were both verbally and physically abusive towards each other.

Almost every relationship Kelly Ryan had with the opposite sex was toxic because she was constantly looking for external affirmation. She needed to be validated by men through her sexuality, and if she could not control them, there was no point in keeping them around. Kelly Ryan, in fact, had numerous relationships with men, and they always had an ugly and explosive ending.

According to Kelly Ryan's family and friends, Kelly's unhealthy outlook on relationships can be traced back to her childhood, and the example her parents set in their household. Her father Tom Ryan, and mother Niki, did not have a healthy, normal relationship. A family member described Tom Ryan as, "a manipulator; a superficial man that only cared about the appearance of his family."

At home, Kelly's father was abusive behind closed doors with her mother. Tom berated Niki Ryan every chance he got; he even called her "fat" in front of family and friends. Ironically, Niki was gorgeous from head to toe, and she did not have an ounce of fat on her body. She was a beautiful, petite woman with blonde hair and blue eyes. As the wife of an executive, Tom Ryan demanded Niki to act and look a certain way. In his own words, his wife was to "dress and look like the wife of an executive if he was going to escort her around town." To look the part, Tom Ryan required his wife to work out for several hours a day. She also had to watch what she ate. She was to take in no more than 1500 calories per day, and Tom Ryan counted every calorie Kelly's mother put in her mouth.

As for his children, Tom Ryan swept everything under the rug, or "fixed" any problems they had growing up. This was not done to help them; rather, Kelly's father did this to keep up the appearance of having the "perfect" family. For example, when Kelly was a cheerleader, she missed a number of work-outs and practices. She was already on probation for having an "attitude problem." When Kelly was confronted by the cheerleading coach, and told she was going to be kicked-off the squad, Kelly told the coach a lie. She said that her grandmother had just passed away; when in fact, her grandmother was alive and well.

Kelly was known to lie and manipulate her way out of trouble, so the coach did not believe her. The coach told Kelly to bring some sort of proof about her Grandmother's passing, like an obituary, or death notice. Kelly then told her father what had happened, and he "fixed" the problem for his daughter. Tom Ryan called the cheerleading coach, and said his mother had indeed passed away, and then presented a fake death certificate in order to keep Kelly on the team.

At some point, Tom Ryan's obsession shifted away from his wife Niki, and spilled over onto Kelly. According to Kelly's family, when Kelly Ryan started high school, her freshman year, Tom Ryan bribed his daughter to maintain the same weight all four years of high school. Kelly of course complied, and did everything in her power to stay under the one hundred pound mark set by her father. Every year, Tom Ryan paid Kelly a "bonus" of one-thousand dollars for achieving "her" goal of maintaining her weight. By her sophomore year in high school, Kelly began binging and purging to maintain this unhealthy weight, just to please her father.

Once it came to Tom Ryan's attention that his daughter had Bulimia, he refused to talk about it, and declined to seek professional help for Kelly. The Ryan family did not "talk" about their problems, and they surely did not draw attention to any type of psychological disorder. What would people think about him? Certainly it would have been a reflection on his parenting and their home environment (and it was); so he hid Kelly's sickness so nobody would ever find out. Sadly, Kelly Ryan's parents never picked-up on the fact that this was a cry for help. Eating disorders come from a deep-rooted need to have some semblance of control in an otherwise chaotic and abusive environment. Bulimia, and the desire to look perfect, eventually became a part of Kelly Ryan's downfall at the end of her fitness career.

Instead of direction and tough love, Tom Ryan spoiled Kelly rotten. Her father bought alcohol for Kelly and all of her friends, and allowed her to have parties in their home. In Kelly's ninth grade year book, almost every comment was about her: having sex, being a bitch, and loving the parties she had at her house. They went on to comment about how cool Kelly's parents were because they purchased alcohol, and got drunk with all of them.

Tom Ryan did not care who Kelly dated in high school or college; but when it was time to settle down, Kelly's father was overtly vocal about the man she was going to date and eventually marry. When Kelly was in her late-twenties, and Tom heard that his daughter had been dating Craig Titus, Kelly's dad put his foot down, and tried to once again bribe her into breaking the relationship off. According to close family members, Tom Ryan had an opinion formed about Craig Titus well before he ever met him. His dislike for Craig had nothing to do with Craig being the "Bad boy of Bodybuilding." It was because Craig Titus was a bodybuilder, and Tom Ryan knew how much money a typical "bodybuilder" made in the industry- not much. Tom would have preferred Kelly marry a doctor or a man with a trust fund at the very least. If Craig simply had a career on the "approved list", he would have been welcomed with open arms into the Ryan family.

Tom Ryan was an Executive at Ford Motor Company, and he later worked for Michelin in Greenville, North Carolina. In the late eighties, Tom announced the family was moving back to Michigan. It was later revealed that his long-time mistress, and current wife, Sharon, had just recently divorced her husband. Tom Ryan moved the family back to Michigan to be close to this woman who also worked for Ford Motor Company. Back in Michigan, he was not able to get his position back with Ford, and he bounced around from job to job. According to Kelly's family, the only reason Tom stayed with Kelly's mother, and did not divorce her for Sharon, was because Niki's family was worth millions.

In Tom's narcissistic world, every man cheated; he could not have cared less that Craig Titus had a reputation for being a "womanizer". Tom wanted Kelly to marry into money, and he forbade Kelly from dating Craig Titus. Kelly, however, ignored her father's wishes, and in the summer of 1999 when Tom Ryan finally met Craig Titus, he was furious that Kelly had defied his wishes. For the first time in her life, Kelly rebelled against her father. Craig Titus charmed Kelly Ryan into his life. They were a couple, and there was not a damn thing Tom Ryan could do about it.

Bodybuilding world reacts to Craig and Kelly dating

On June 26, 1999, Craig Titus showed up to the World Pro Fitness Classic in Detroit Michigan, not to participate, but to watch "his girlfriend," Kelly Ryan, compete; and the buzz about the couple spread like wildfire! Gossip hit the message boards and internet websites within days. Lonnie "speak before you think" Teper spoke about the couple on a website saying, "Everyone kind of went, Whoa- wait a minute! Kind, quiet, respectful Kelly is dating Craig, the convicted felon?"

Ron Harris, who Craig had a run-in with over gossiping on the 1-900-Bodybuilding phone lines, before his Denver competition, had some

THE RETURN OF CRAIG TITUS

harsh words about the new couple. Harris said, "Everyone was stunned to see Craig and Kelly together. Craig had a reputation as a womanizer with a bad temper, and Kelly was a soft-spoken, polite southern belle." Harris went on to say, "Everyone was talking & freaking out about why they got together, and hoping it would not last for Kelly's sake."

Kelly was not a "southern-belle;" she had established a "hard-core party" reputation in the bodybuilding community long before she and Craig Titus ever hooked up. Kelly ran with the fast crowd in the "industry;" however, unlike Craig, she kept her personal life private. Titus had also pissed almost everybody off in the "tight-knit" community, including Teper and Harris. Craig Titus was a threat to those around him, and with the Kelly stepping into his world, he became a double threat.

With his beautiful girlfriend on his arm, Craig was ready to pump up his image and jump start his career in the IFBB. To do this, Craig needed to come up with a strategy to make him stand out above the rest. Craig was already the "Bad Boy of Bodybuilding" and he intended on taking full advantage of this title, but he needed to lure the audience back in by ruffling some feathers. Craig would have to use his quick wit, and he would have to be even louder and opinionated than ever. Taunting opponents with below the belt remarks, Craig felt he needed to stir-up controversy every chance he got. It would not make a difference if his fans, or anyone else for that matter, loved or hated him. As long as the industry was talking about him, Craig knew that he was back on the right track.

Even Jerry Springer would tell you that his show became most successful, and beat out Oprah Winfrey in the ratings, when they stirred up controversy; the more "low brow" his show became, the higher he soared in the ratings. Controversial confrontations meant dollar signs to Craig Titus, and this would be his meal ticket. Fuck body building etiquette- Craig was about to take over the bodybuilding world Jerry Springer style.

And it worked. Craig became known as an outlandish shit talker that always spoke his mind. He kept the fickle crowds captivated by his bleached blonde good looks and in your face comments. In an interview, Craig said, "You know all these guys, they talk a big game, they talk a lot of shit. But I don't see any of them ever being an old school guy, and smacking somebody in the face that disrespects them! I think I am the only one who's ever done it. I guess until someone else does it, I will hold that title alone."

Craig realized early on that he did not need to be Mr. Olympia to be the wealthiest man in bodybuilding; he needed to be Mr. Self-Promotion. Still, to be able to promote oneself, placing somewhere close to the top 5 was important. With all of the great bodybuilders of this era all on one stage, that was not an easy job. There was no room for error when it came to steroid cycles, that could mean the difference between 5th & 20th place, and it would be impossible to promote 20th place. Craig had to be smarter than the rest; and he knew the reason why most bodybuilders were not successful with steroid cycles was because they were being duped by dealers.

According to Craig, "The problem with most bodybuilder cycles isn't what they are using or in what dosages. It's that most of the steroids being used on the streets are fake; and nothing more than vegetable oil or a testosterone labeled as Deca or Primobolan." Craig said that these steroid dealers purchase powders from china and manufacture their own private label steroids. These are not real steroids- they are buying a 100 cc bottle of Equipoise from Mexico, then taking that EQ and filling 10-10cc Mill-used vials labeling them as testosterone or Deca or Primobolan and selling them for $150.00 a bottle.

Making it even more confusing, there are a lot of big name bodybuilders selling 100 % fake growth horomone steroids; these are guys that Craig and many others would assume that they could trust. So on top of training, dieting, and picking the right public relations strategy, Craig had to be street smart; he had to stay in the mix, place on stage, and promote himself.

First IFBB competition since released from prison

Craig broke the ice, and reentered the world of bodybuilding in his first IFBB competition since being released from prison on February 19, 2000 at the Ironman/Maiden Pro Invitational in Redondo Beach

California. In this competition, he had developed a perfectly structured mass of a body, with the "V shape" from his shoulders to his toes. Craig had a well-crafted posing routine that stood out above the rest. When he posed, he projected his body as a living, breathing work of art. He would tense every muscle in his body while maintaining a high degree of fluidity between poses, before hitting his perfect, signature Adonis shot. Craig had to walk the walk, and talk the talk. He walked like Adonis, posed like Adonis, and had a cocky attitude like Adonis. Craig's brash attitude, with his lip puckered up on one side, and eye browed, looking down at everyone else beneath him, gave him a look like no other athlete. Everyone loved and hated him, all for the same reason, they wanted to be him. But there was only one Craig Titus, so everyone would just have to sit back and take notes on the new poster boy of bodybuilding. Craig finished solid in the Top 8, and in his next competition in Toronto, only a few months later, he won the Overall title.

CHAPTER 6

Craig and Kelly- The Making of a Power Couple

Craig and Kelly moved in with each other in Venice Beach, and before long, the negative comments waned, and they became the "perfect power couple" of bodybuilding. Kelly seemed to become more popular and marketable after Craig and Kelly started dating. Behind the scenes, Craig was a force in Kelly's career, advising her on everything from business deals to costume choices. With Craig by her side, Kelly's popularity soared, and she became the "it" girl of the fitness world. After her win in Roanoke Virginia, at the Jan Tana Pro Fitness Class, she became unstoppable, collecting win after win.

Rumors about their sex life and drug abuse began to circulate, but everyone was crazy in Venice Beach, so they did not stand out too much in the circus. During this time in her life, the "Venice Beach" days, Kelly's friends described her as " The life of the party- a cyclone onstage and off!" According to Craig, "Recreational drugs seemed like harmless fun," but the endless parties and constant backstabbing got old fast. Every bodybuilder was trying to get one over on another- cranking out reps, battling out poses in the mirror, and slandering the other on the message boards. The trash talk soon turned into physical altercations, and Craig & Kelly were ready to get the hell out of Venice Beach!

CRAIG AND KELLY- THE MAKING OF A POWER COUPLE

Before they moved, Melissa James came to visit, and met Kelly for the first time. Melissa had some auditions for some music videos in Los Angeles. Craig said that the three of them instantly became tight. "Kelly and M.J. acted like they knew each other for years! We had such a great time, until I noticed towards the end of her stay that she was using meth, and this was a huge turn off for me. When she offered us some, I immediately took offense, and said something. I hurt her feelings, but wanted her to know how much I hated meth! It was such a bad deal. Not to say that the drugs I have used in the past are not bad, but meth sucks people in like a poison, and destroys lives. After that visit, it seemed like everything fell apart for M.J., and I blame it all on meth! She lost her teaching job, she was arrested, and everything went to shit for her after that!"

Craig was sure he had dodged a bullet with Melissa, and was more certain than ever, Kelly was the woman he wanted to spend the rest of his life with. And on June 6, 2000, Craig and Kelly were married at the Little White Chapel in Las Vegas, Nevada. Craig and Kelly were truly in love, and complimented each other in every possible way. "Craig was Kelly's biggest fan and Kelly was Craig's biggest fan," recalls Dan Solomon, a former manager turned Internet radio host, who with his wife, frequently socialized with Craig and Kelly. Solomon said, "They supported each other. I would say it was one of the more endearing parts of their relationship. You would sit in a room with the two of them, and it was obvious that they supported each other in a way that was, you know, it was nice to see. And the more time you spent with them together, the more it became obvious why they were married, because they cared deeply about each other."

In an interview with Ron Avidan, Craig said, "Kelly is my best friend. She's the best thing that ever happened to me." Their ying and yang approach to life and their marriage gave them balance and a platform for both of their careers to soar. Craig knew that he could only be as successful as his other half. In the marriage and on the stage, Craig and Kelly were a team. And Craig instinctively knew when to step away from the spotlight, and let Kelly's career shine. Kelly in return, supported Craig one hundred percent; they were each other's biggest fans, and deeply cared about the success of each other's careers.

During this time, Craig Titus and Shawn Ray were good friends. Shawn was with Craig when he saw Kelly Ryan compete for the first time, and he talked him into moving to Vegas after he showed Craig around all of the neighborhoods. Shawn Ray owned a second home in Las Vegas, and not far from him, there were brand new houses being built; Ray called the realtor, and after she showed Craig the floor plan on a house being built at 9539 Adobe Court, Craig was sold.

In 2001, Shawn Ray had also invited Craig to take part in his "muscle camp;" a camp where serious bodybuilders got the chance to work out with the biggest names in the industry. Ray said, "I felt Craig's excitement. Here was this guy, nose wide open and all fired up. The next day we did my muscle camp, and Craig couldn't have been the more consummate professional. He was at home, he was working with the guys, he was very friendly, and even though he didn't do well at the show, he seemed to have a grasp of why he didn't do well and was able to roll with it."

The move to Las Vegas

On February 6, 2002, Craig and Kelly purchased the house on Adobe Arch Court. Needing a change of scenery, Craig believed the move would allow them to surround themselves with positive energy, being able to train and build their careers with the best bodybuilders in the industry. Craig told Ron Avidan of Getbig.com, "The cost of living is low, the house is beautiful, and there are not too many pro bodybuilders living out here. We just wanted to get out of the scene, out of the public eye, and out of the scrutiny of the backstabbing two-faced idiots that live in Venice. Venice is not a good place to live. It is full of jealousy and envy and people who would love to see you fail."

When the house was completed, this gorgeous white stucco home was: "more than 3,000 square feet, two stories, five bedrooms, three bathrooms, fireplace, pool, Jacuzzi, and a three car garage." The centerpiece of their home, custom made for an IFBB professional bodybuilder and his fitness champion wife, was a "400 square foot personal gym outfitted with black-framed equipment with red upholstery. Craig Titus and Kelly Ryan had the latest in body-sculpting gear and state of the art work out equipment customized specifically for Craig and Kelly. This included brand new cutting edge work out equipment including machines by Apex, Powertec, Ivanko, and Troy, from a shoulder press and lat pull-down, to professional quality dumbbells weighing from 5 to 200 pounds."

Once in Las Vegas, the dynamics for Craig's reputation seemed to take a positive spin. After the 2002 Olympics, Craig seemed more modest and focused when he told Flex magazine, "I basically looked like crap, and I consider twelfth place a major gift now that I have taken a gander at the photos;" but he vowed to work his ass off to rebuild his career in his new home town of Las Vegas. Craig's fans loved to hate him, and his outrageous antics made him a super star in bodybuilding. Craig was content with placing in the middle, because his ability to self-promote himself made him one of the wealthiest men in the business. By 2002 Craig had only won one major competition, yet his name was one of the biggest names in bodybuilding, appearing on magazine covers and videos, and scoring countless sponsorships.

The biggest boost for the "Bad Boy's" career happened at the 2001 Ironman when a war of words between King Kamali and Craig Titus stirred up some controversy. According to Craig, Kamali mouthed off, "The West Coast Body builder's egos are bigger than their synthol (site enhancement oil that consists of 85% oil, 7.5% lidocaine, & 7.5% alcohol- injected in muscle to enhance the appearance of muscles) filled arms." Craig Titus and King Kamali would throw jabs back and forth on the internet, and in magazines, and the fans loved it! Everyone took sides and had opinions about the rivalry between the two bodybuilders, and professional bodybuilding as a whole became more popular than ever as a result.

As a couple, Craig Titus and Kelly Ryan became the most commanding and marketable couple in professional bodybuilding. "Their marriage soon evolved into the collaboration of two super hero stars; the names Titus and Ryan merged to become one of the most lucrative businesses in the world of bodybuilding- Emperor Enterprises. The power couple pulled in money from personal training, promotions, endorsement of body building products and supplements, magazine covers, articles and guest performances and posing events all over the world. Not to mention prize money from body building contests.

Kelly got a major endorsement deal with biochem supplement; they said she had a reputation for being a "family oriented type of girl." Craig joined Melvin Anthony as the spokesman for Pinnacle nutrition products. However, the big money came from all of the after- party promotions put on by both Craig and Kelly.

Shortly after relocating from Venice Beach CA to Las Vegas, NV, Craig was asked to be a celebrity host for the 2001 USA Championships after party at "Polo Towers", just off the Vegas Strip. Kelly and Craig both accepted the offer to have their images used on all the after party promotional material as well as host the actual party and participate in the festivities. Craig said that he was being paid, very well, to attend a function that they would have otherwise attended. "I have never been one to turn down a good party, and getting paid for it was clearly a bonus."

The party invitation read: "Midnight Entertainment, Skin After Dark presents: THE ULTIMATE U.S.A. CHAMPIONSHIPS After-Party hosted by Craig Titus & Kelly Ryan...where Fitness meets Fantasy... 10 PM Saturday, July 27th ... Come party with the BIG GUNS AND HOT BUNS of Bodybuilding's Elite at HUSH on top of the Polo Towers. Dance all night under the stars with SKIN AFTER DARK GIRLS and watch yourself and others party as we broadcast this party on a 40 ft. big screen! Featuring: DJ Adam Webb... Ladies, Come as Sexy as you can be, and as Naughty as you dare to be!" The after party turned out to be a huge success with over 1,500 people from the bodybuilding and fitness industry attending. At that time, Craig realized that the after-party production could be extremely lucrative; and he was right, they just got bigger and better, and Craig made a bundle off of the after-parties.

CHAPTER 7

The Empire that Titus Built- Emperor Enterprises

At the next Mr. Olympia after party at the "House of Blues," Craig became more than a host; he was factored into a percentage of the net income. From that point on, Craig produced the entire official after-parties for the NPC and IFBB from the East to the West Coast. From there, Craig started his own business, Emperor Enterprises. Craig was the CEO- no partners, and he controlled every aspect of the company. Craig wanted to build an empire that not only included after-parties, but anything and everything he could lasso in and take over that involved the world of fitness and bodybuilding. He used his street smarts and business sense to build Emperor Entertainment into one of the most profitable and diverse companies in bodybuilding.

Craig had an edge in the form of attitude and charisma that separated him from everybody else. The Bad Boy of Bodybuilding did not just sit back and expect contracts to come to him: Craig Titus busted his ass, marketed himself, and grabbed every contract that crossed his path. To be successful on and off the stage, Craig had to be self-confident and aggressive in the negotiations; making no assumptions, just presumptions of victory. "You can't settle for anything less than you think you are worth. I don't sign a contract for a year, it has to be a multi-year contract- this ensures security."

Craig and Kelly's contracts for sponsorships and endorsements were all diversified; they included: Homebodies Home Gym (all-exclusive, customized gym equipment), Xenadrine (energy and weight-loss products), Cytodone Technologies, Pinnacle (supplements), Pure Form- (Kelly Ryan's own product line of supplements), Apex Fitness (Fitness machines), APT Pro wrist straps (personalized wrist straps for lifting weights), Olympic Competition Tanning Products (tanning beds), Vegas Body & Tan (Salon and Fitness Consultations), Las Vegas Athletic Club (Training and Endorsements), plus ads for Addition 2 Chiropractic.

Craig and Kelly both became featured writers for a monthly column with major bodybuilding websites. Kelly had, "Kelly Ryan's Corner" on Bodybuilding.com. Her first entry was on March 1, 2002, and her last was on December 12, 2005. Kelly answered five questions every month about fitness and training, and gave advice and pointers from her experience as a fitness athlete. Craig began writing a column for Muscular Development called "Titus Talks" where he also answered questions, and gave advice and tips on bodybuilding.

When Titus picked up a new promotional contract with Pinnacle for nutrition supplements, he joined Melvin Anthony as a spokesman. The two men had a falling out when word got back to Anthony a year prior that Craig was making sexual advances towards his wife. After the two men talked, they agreed to drop the whole thing. Craig flirted with everybody; he was known for putting the moves on any beautiful woman that crossed his path. If the woman was not interested, or he stepped on someone's toes, Craig would turn it around as a joke; but if the beautiful woman was into it then Craig would inevitably sleep with her. Craig and Melvin moved past that incident, and actually enjoyed hanging out together, promoting Pinnacle in a small promotional booth at body building events.

The IFBB Pro Undercover

One of the best kept secrets in professional bodybuilding, something that has never been revealed until today: Who was the IFBB Pro Undercover? It was none other than Craig Titus himself! Since June 1, 2003 Craig answered questions on bodybuilding.com as the author:

THE EMPIRE THAT TITUS BUILT- EMPEROR ENTERPRISES

IFBB Undercover. Craig remained anonymous, and no topic was out of bounds; he spoke the truth about everything in bodybuilding.

It was a balancing act however, because Craig Titus had a certain style of writing and speaking, "period". He hated certain people (John Romano, Shawn Ray, and Bob Chick) and thought Ronnie Coleman was the best bodybuilder ever, but could not give up who he was by his personal style of writing and personal preferences. He had to remain anonymous, so if he started to bash Ray too much, and people started to question if the IFBB pro was Titus, he would bash himself as well to throw everyone off.

In the first column, the IFBB Pro Undercover wrote for bodybuilding.com:

"This is the first column I am writing for Bodybuilding.com and I hope it is followed by many more. Being an IFBB pro for many years now, I will be as honest as I possibly can. I will answer any questions you may have about the sport in general, any of its athletes, nutrition, supplementation, verify any gossip that's buzzing around and be straight up about any sport enhancing drug questions. Be assured, I will be very accurate, and 100 percent honest in the contents of this column. If I do not know something, I will not answer the question. Why am I remaining undercover? That is very simple. I do not wish for people to know who I am because the honesty of this column could affect my livelihood." So with that let's get started, and for two years, Craig, or the IFBB Undercover Pro kept the bodybuilding community informed and entertained every month."

Craig continues to write columns to this day from prison for Ironmanmagazine.com. Since 2012, Craig spills everything on *Titus Talks* from his wild sex life to his cycles for steroids- nothing is off limits because he has absolutely nothing to lose! A bullshit prison sentence can't even shut Craig Titus up. After appearing in over one hundred bodybuilding magazine covers, and being featured in thousands of articles, Craig seemed to attain his dream of becoming Mr. Magazine in the IFBB.

Greatest Rivalry in bodybuilding history: King Kamali vs. Craig Titus

The biggest hype of his career was promised and delivered at the May 2003 Night of Champions in New York City. Both Titus and Kamali were taking verbal jabs at each other leading up to the competition. Craig said, "I am going to have Kamali beat down before we even walks on the stage. I will have him so upset backstage verbally that he will need to get a box of tissues before he even walks on stage." Then after the show, "We are going to talk. We are going to go man-to-man, face-to-face. I am putting an end to all of this bullshit! The guy is a big-mouth, piece of crap, and that's it. I have had enough." King Kamali responded to Craig's comments by saying, "I am so tired of hearing about that guy. I hear by Knight Craig Titus, Sir Jackass-a-Lot." With the stage now set, the Night of the Champions, lived up to the hype, and was one of the most exciting bodybuilding competitions of that year.

Craig finished strong, and held up his end of the bargain, when he placed third overall, in front of Kamali who placed fourth. The story brought new life to the Titus-Kamali feud, and was once again the headline story in the body building community. Shawn Ray sang the praises of his "friend" Craig Titus. In a column written for bodybuilding.com, Ray said, "Bad Boy Craig Titus showed up to do battle with EVERYBODY! Craig wanted to serve notice he was not one to be pissed on whether on the internet or by magazines!"

Although the body building competitions were real, Craig would later admit that the words hurled back and forth before and after the competitions were all done for publicity. Craig said, "My battles on stage with King Kamali were legendary, demanding the attention from bodybuilding fans despite the fact we were never considered for the over-all title. Our rivalry was irresistible to the fans, writers, photographers, and all those involved in the bodybuilding world. It often became the main attraction of every competition." Craig said, "When King Kamali first came on the scene, I really disliked him. King had never competed against anyone and then he was popping off about how he was going to win the entire competition. Then his comment about the West Coast body builder's arms being all synthol infuriated me. I truly could not stand this guy at first."

Craig explained that the beef in the beginning was real, but in fact, it only lasted a few weeks. "Truth be told, I had an immense amount of respect for King Kamali as a bodybuilder and a family man. We weren't friends, but we weren't enemies either." When Titus and Kamali saw how their feud took off with bodybuilding fans, they decided to keep it going, even if it was just a façade. Craig said, "King and I had a mutual understanding and were keenly aware that this rivalry provided us both with more opportunities. We understood that our dislike for each other generated drama and that drama created controversy and interest which resulted in financial compensation."

Craig said, "Kelly and I actually sat down for dinner one night in 2004 with Kamali and his wife." They talked about the popularity of their rivalry, and how they were the two most popular bodybuilders because of that rivalry. At every competition, even though they were never called out as "number one and two," when they were called out somewhere in the middle, the crowd went crazy. The duo would actually get more of a reaction from the crowd than the person that won the show. There are still articles written to this day, calling their rivalry one of the greatest of all times in bodybuilding. Craig said, "I respected Kamali because of his work ethic, for his devotion to our craft, for his ability to speak his mind, and most of all for his quest to demolish me on stage."

Craig Titus becoming a VH-1 Reality TV Star
By 2004-2005 Craig had built an empire, becoming a household name, and putting bodybuilding back on the map. So it was not long before Hollywood came knocking on the door, propositioning him with an offer to appear on a Vh-1 reality television show as a personal trainer to a washed up rock star. Craig took them up on the offer, with the caveat that Kelly was provided with a cameo appearance on the show.

In the summer of 2004, Craig began filming the Vh-1 Reality TV Show, *Remaking Vince Neil*. The show began with an introduction, showing the band Motley Crue in action. With the vintage footage rolling, the introduction began: "Back in the 80's, Motley Crue was the biggest, baddest, most extreme rock band in the world. In their prime they sold over 40 million records and played in front of sold out stadiums. No band looked hotter or partied harder, and front man Vince Neil led the charge. But that was 20 years and 40 pounds ago..."

The reality show began with Neil walking into a club/strip mall in Minnesota. Vince was performing solo to a small and aging audience in the middle of the afternoon. The narrator explains how the former front man for Motley Crue had become significantly overweight, had maintained an escalating drinking habit, and was struggling to come up with new music to keep his sound current.

Vince Neil was presented with the opportunity to remake himself on national television, with the goal of playing a grand finale concert that could possibly re-launch his career. VH-1 hired experts from Beverly Hills to Las Vegas and over the next few months Neil had plastic surgery, worked with a world renowned personal trainer and nutritionist to help him shed the pounds and pack on the muscle, received a hair and wardrobe makeover from red carpet stylists, and recorded a brand new song with a legendary music producer. When Vh-1 approached Craig and signed the contracts, they knew it was impossible to make Neil into a rock hard, body builder in 6 weeks, so they all signed a contract agreeing that Craig would train Neil, and he would inject Neil with steroids and human growth hormones. The cameras shot Craig going into Neil's kitchen at his house and chunking all of his junk food then replacing his pantry with healthier foods.

After that, the cameras followed the men as they pumped iron together in Craig and Kelly's home gym. Throughout the program, "Before and After" shots were continuously shown on the screen; as Vince Neil's worn out, forty-three year old body, morphed into a "Rock 'n Roll" hard body in a very short amount of time. While the men worked out, Kelly and Joey, her dog, emerged to give Vince Neil some fitness advice and words of encouragement. Vince Neil made it to his goal, and performed poolside at the Palms in Las Vegas. He came out in black leather pants and a black tank top, and everyone that helped him reach his goals were at the concert to cheer him on, including Craig and Kelly. It was a Hollywood reality show, so there was a lot of tears and bull shit, but Craig had a blast training his rock and roll idol.

THE EMPIRE THAT TITUS BUILT- EMPEROR ENTERPRISES

After the filming wrapped, Craig and Vince remained great friends, and the two guys even started to hang out and party together in Las Vegas. Vince Neil said that when they walked in the door of any bar or club, Craig Titus was the "rock star." The reality show was released on Dec. 31, 2004, temporarily boosting the popularity of Vince Neil, and the pursuit of his solo career. (Vince Neil never went on a solo tour and his career unfortunately went nowhere after the show).

Neil would make several brief appearances on miscellaneous television shows, and one show in particular shocked Craig Titus. Neil went on the *48 Hours* murder mystery and talked about the reality show, and how Craig injected the rock star with steroids and HGH without anybody having any real knowledge about what Craig was doing. Craig responded, "That was bullshit; every single person, including Neil and the producers, knew what was going on, and everyone agreed to it. Everyone wanted a hit reality show, but turning this soft guy who never worked out and ate junk food into what they wanted would take more than will power and hitting the gym a few times a week. Every single person knew, and that is such bullshit for him to act surprised. That would be like Vince Neil saying he was going to the plastic surgeon for a little Botox, and he came out of surgery with a brand new fucking nose. He knew!"

CHAPTER 8

Commotion behind the Scenes

As Craig and Kelly's popularity soared with the fans, the power couple began to have problems behind the scenes, on and off the stage. On March 5-7 2004 at the Arnold Classic, according to the cyber world, both Craig and Kelly were off their game with Craig coming in 6th and Kelly coming in 2nd place. But according to Craig, the problem was not in how they placed at the competition, the problem was with the government breathing down their necks; "they were on a fucking witch hunt to bring down the evil athletes using steroids." Craig had more on the line than everybody else because he already had a prior drug arrest. If he were arrested for using steroids, he could be locked up for a long time.

It also began to play with Kelly's mind, because both she and her husband were using steroids and HGH, and rumors were swirling around the bodybuilding community, about "who was ratting on whom to further their career." Craig and Kelly were scared shitless that law enforcement and the government were coming after the IFBB, and the sacrificial lamb was going to be Craig Titus, knocking out Kelly Ryan by default. Steroid scandals were happening all over the United States, and Craig and Kelly's suspicions became a reality when the DEA began handing out subpoenas at the Arnold.

This hit a little too close to home for Craig, especially with all of the enemies he had accumulated in the bodybuilding world. Craig made money off of his arrogant mouth and his derogatory comments about others bodybuilders, but he legitimately pissed off some "important" people in the IFBB. This would be an easy way to shut the "Bad Boy of Bodybuilding" up for good; or to cut Craig's career short, freeing up more money in bodybuilding for everybody else. Bodybuilders did not make very much money, and everyone wanted a piece of the pie. There were a lot of people that hated Craig's lifestyle, and wanted his endorsements, sponsorships, and after-party revenue for themselves. Throwing Craig to the wolves would knock him out of the game, and allow countless others to step into his shoes.

The DEA goes after bodybuilding

This was not fake drama brought on by Titus for media attention, this was real life drama played out behind the scenes of the Arnold. Federal Agents subpoenaed 20 bodybuilders, including Craig Titus, to testify before a grand jury in Des Moines, Iowa, looking into illegal steroid trafficking in the body building industry. The central figure in the BALCO case, Victor Conte, was at the Arnold Classic, plugging his ZMA mineral supplement. Word leaked out that the DEA visited with Shawn Ray at his house for hours, and soon after their "visit", all of the subpoenas were issued right before the competition. This not only pissed Craig off, but pissed everyone off in the bodybuilding community.

The Grand Jury sessions occurred in secret two weeks later in Iowa, and nothing came out of it, because at the time, their primary target was baseball. This was not to say that the government would not come back around and take out bodybuilding once they were done with baseball; more than likely they would. And the government targeted a few high profile people like Barry Bonds to go after and bury. Craig was officially "on the law enforcement" radar, and he had a bad feeling that those in power would eventually come after him because once "you are red flagged for steroids- everyone with a badge wants the brownie points for being the guy that took the famous athlete down!" Craig could never prove that Ray was responsible for the subpoenas, "but it was extremely convenient how everyone that got a subpoena had been on Shawn Ray's shit list for a while."

◄ SWIFT INJUSTICE

Calling Shawn Ray out

Craig felt like he had the perfect opportunity to call this guy out in front of all the bodybuilders at the Orlando Pro Show in Florida on April 30- May 1, 2004, where Shawn Ray was the Master of Ceremonies. When Craig got to Orlando, he became even more pissed because owners of the popular bodybuilding websites were coming up to him and saying that Ray was signing up anonymously under different pen names, spreading venom about Craig.

Craig said, "Shawn Ray was always the biggest fucking pussy. If he was not coming after me, he was always tearing someone else down! There were so many people that hated that guy, and from what I hear, he is still crying, whining and tattling on everybody else to this day!" The shit hit the fan in Orlando when Craig learned that Ray went up to Wayne De Milia and told him that Craig was posting derogatory remarks about Ray on the internet. "What is this guy, a 10 year old girl, oh my God?" By the time the athlete's meeting was called to order by Shawn Ray, Craig was "ready to call that bitch out!"

With everybody sitting around, the meeting was called to order, and Craig let everyone know that Shawn Ray was a "slimy piece of shit!" Craig said that he was the guy going online running other people down for using fake screen names, but all of the screen names went back to Shawn Ray's IP address. And Craig was just getting started, "Are you kidding me, that is what you do bitch. The truth of the matter is that Shawn is a snitch!" Craig then pressed Ray on what he told the federal agents at his house for hours. Ray responded, "We talked about the convict in this room, like anybody cares." Craig shot back, "This convict is about to break your fucking jaw!"

The "like-hate" relationship between Craig Titus and Shawn Ray came to a head when Ray was attempting to become the first ever, "Official Athlete's Representative for the IFBB". Ray said that he would be serving the interests of bodybuilders who did not get all the spoils of the sport, but Craig called "bullshit on that!" Craig asked, "How could Shawn Ray be trusted to represent all of the bodybuilders, when all he ever had was his best interests at heart?"

In the fall of 2004, shortly before the Olympia, Shawn Ray rented a P.F. Chang's restaurant in Las Vegas and assembled all of the pro bodybuilders willing to approve Ray as their representative. Shawn needed ninety-eight signatures to be able to become the representative. Shawn Ray said that everyone signed the petition, including Craig Titus, but Craig denied ever signing any document to endorse Shawn Ray for anything! Craig said that he not only did not sign it, but someone must have illegally forged his name on the document. The problem was none of the signatures had a name printed below it; so there was no way to verify if Craig Titus did or did not ever sign his name. Then the question changed from "Did you sign it?" to "Will you sign it?" And Craig's answer to this was simple, "Nope!"

Without Craig's signature, Shawn Ray would not be able to become the Athletes Representative. When interviewed by Ron Avidan at Getbig.com, Craig said, "Because of my personality, and the way I am in this sport, and the way I manage mine and Kelly's careers, I don't need a rep. And for somebody to say they are going to represent the athletes was a little bizarre for me to swallow. Who does this guy think he is saying he is going to represent me when I have been doing it myself for a long time?"

Craig was actually on to something, and worried about one man, unchecked, having that much power over all of the athletes. Craig said that he would agree to sign the paper if Ray agreed to bring on a pane of athletes to keep the representative in check. Craig said, "Who could more efficiently represent the bodybuilders, to prevent abuse and allow for better decision-making, than a group of athletes working together, rather than just one individual." The dispute played out over bodybuilding message boards on the internet. At the athlete's meeting before the Olympia, Craig finally agreed to sign the petition after Ray agreed to implement a panel for checks and balances. Ironically on January 2nd, 2005, Shawn Ray resigned as the "Athletes Representative in the IFBB" and posted the following letter on a message board:

SWIFT INJUSTICE

"Dear IFBB Pro Men,

As you all know, I received the majority vote to become the Athletes Representative from 2004-2006. There were 3 official meetings where issues, concerns, problems, and changes could be dealt with. I have personally spoken with those of you who had serious problems and concerns in the matters of: Prize money, Judges, Pay per View, Promoter Failure to Pay, Score Sheets, among other things that needed to be addressed by the federation. This year most of you were expecting a response from me following the Mr. Olympia regarding the "Issues and Concerns" that were placed before the other Officials and the Federation Vice President. I forwarded the detailed items to Jim Manion, the IFBB Vice President eight weeks prior to the contest with other Representatives and Officials. I received an email from an IFBB Official Representative that had the "Formal Representative Meeting" starting at 9 pm Wed. after the athlete's meeting. However, when I showed up for the Men's Meeting starting at 7:30 pm, I was told the Official & Representatives Meeting began at 4:30 pm and was over. I was also told that I should have received an e-mail stating the "Change of Time" on my computer. Sadly, I never did receive an email or a phone call stating the change? I was told I would receive the "Minutes" regarding the meeting; however I have yet to hear or see anything. It is for this reason, I feel the position of "Athlete Representative" for me does not carry equal balance for you the athletes in regard to the federation and promoters. Therefore I am removing myself from the position. I do not feel that I will be able to effectively meet the issues and needs to better assist you in your professional careers!"

Shawn Ray

Ron Avidan interviewed Shawn Ray a couple of months later for getbig.com. Avidan said that Shawn Ray was controversial, arrogant, and outspoken. Avidan stated, "Shawn's views differ greatly from many, including myself, and have amazed and irritated many with his stand at various places- press conferences, bulletin boards, magazines and seminars." In the interview Ron Avidan addressed the topic of Shawn Ray representing the bodybuilders. He asked Ray why he quit the Athlete's Rep position in the IFBB after he had already made the commitment.

Shawn Ray: "Wayne DeMilia had me jump through hoops to get the majority vote. Once I was the rep. I sat in on a couple of meetings until the Olympia came around which is the biggest meeting because it influenced exactly what was going to happen in 2005. I spent five months gathering eight bullet points that were the most important on the athlete's agenda. I wrote a letter to the IFBB Vice President, Jim Manion, and we were to go over the bullet points at the Mr. Olympia meeting. They changed the time of the meeting without calling me or emailing me. This led me to believe that they did not want to address the issues that the athletes were concerned about. I think it was a snow job, and I have too many things that I can do instead of running around chasing my tail"

Ron Avidan: "But why quit?"

Shawn Ray: "There was absolutely nothing that was going to get resolved. This meeting was supposed to resolve the issues for 2005. I never got a phone call from October through January from Jim Manion, and if they truly wanted to work with the athletes, they knew I was willing, ready and prepared."

CHAPTER 9

Losing a Grip on Reality

Kelly was a woman that had been driven to be perfect her entire life. In the fitness world, she strived to be flawless in appearance and routine, many times being too critical of herself. Quite often, being a perfectionist could be beneficial; she was after all one of the most successful fitness competitors of all time. Being able to train, diet, lift, pose, and practice routines day in and day out takes a person with a "perfectionist" mind-set. As a "fitness pro", superiority is the ultimate goal: to look and move a certain way. To be at the top, Kelly had to train and diet excessively; this was a requirement.

There was always someone younger and more skilled knocking at the door. For this reason, Kelly Ryan had to push herself to maintain both her skills and performance on the stage often pushing her body past the pain to maintain her position at the top. In these contests, Kelly had to present a personality that lured the judges and audiences into falling in love with her every time she was on the stage. To win Olympia, the fitness competitor had to be perfect, and Kelly was extremely hard on herself trying to become that perfect fitness athlete. She was overly critical of her appearance, and wanted more than anything to receive affirmation from Olympia, and the muscle magazines, that she was a beautiful in their eyes.

The real motive behind Kelly Ryan's numerous plastic surgeries
Kelly felt discouraged by the major muscle magazines because they all seemed to feature swimsuit models over the actual IFBB pros. (The

IFBB would have an answer for that complaint by creating a category for the bikini models in 2010). Kelly was rarely featured in magazines, and she began to make changes in her appearance to make herself more desirable and sexier, hoping to get more covers, and build her own self-esteem.

Over the years, Kelly began to change her appearance, dying her hair blond from brunette at different points to get magazine exposure. Then, observers in the sport said that she went crazy with plastic surgery, trying to make herself appear sexier; many said it actually backfired because it made her features look comical and exaggerated. It became a hot topic on bodybuilding boards and radio shows.

A popular bodybuilding personality went on air saying that Kelly's low self-image, and subsequent plastic surgeries were Craig Titus' fault. He said, "Craig wanted to change Kelly's appearance from the first day they got together. Craig wanted a fitness athlete that he could mold; a star that was on the rise, and he found that in Kelly."

In response to that comment, Craig said, "When I met Kelly, I saw someone that was beautiful on the inside and out. To me, she was perfection, and I adored everything about her! In Kelly, I found someone I could be a friend to, someone I could protect. I was in love with Kelly, just the way she was in love with me. To me she was perfect, and I never thought about molding her, or changing her; that is fucking ridiculous! Craig said, "Any changes Kelly made to her appearance were her decisions, not mine. She felt that she needed to fit this mold for the IFBB Fitness Judges. I was absolutely against anything Kelly did to change or alter her appearance in any way, period. I loved her just the way she was; God broke the mold when He made Kelly Ryan."

Craig explained that Kelly's obsession with plastic surgery started off simple enough, with cosmetic surgery on her eyelid to repair an infection that had nerve damage. Craig said, "When she had the herpes simplex virus on her eyelid, she needed to have plastic surgery to correct the damaged muscles surrounding the eye. Immediately after she had her stitches removed from the eyelid, she had her lips done without telling me. Kelly fell back into a pattern of obsession over her looks. This was a battle she has had since she was a teenager. When she was 13 years old she had bulimia, and felt like she was overweight. When she confided this in me, I watched her close, to make sure she ate small meals every three hours to give her energy.

Kelly was self-destructive when it came to her looks, and I did everything I could to build her up and let her know that she was the sexiest woman ever!" The person she saw in the mirror and the beautiful woman everyone else saw when they looked at Kelly Ryan were never in sync. Kelly became obsessed with every part of her body, and if she could not fix something herself, she would go under the knife, and have a plastic surgeon fix it for her. Kelly Ryan became addicted to chasing the dream of having an air brushed image and being flawless in the eyes of other people through an endless cycle of plastic surgeries.

Craig said, "The plastic surgeries, and the bills from these surgeries were out of control, and I could not get her to stop!" Yet somehow in the media, including the 48 Hours Murder Mystery, it was turned around on Craig, and he was somehow forcing Kelly to have plastic surgery. Nothing pissed Craig off more than being accused of forcing Kelly to have plastic surgery because it was "an outright lie!"

Craig said, "I absolutely adored my Kelly; in my eyes she could do no wrong! Simply put… she was beautiful, and it broke my heart to see her always trying to change something about herself. The only procedure that I encouraged, after she already had her mind made up to do it, was her breast implants. When I met Kelly she already had Breast implants under the chest muscles. These types of implants restricted Kelly's ability to train, and caused her a great deal of pain. As a result, we decided to have her breast implants placed under her skin, over the muscle; and besides her eyelid surgery, that was the only procedure that I ever agreed to, period! A surgery that was necessary for her career, not to make her sexier, but to help her move better because the breast implants over the muscle allowed her to train and perform at 100 % with absolutely no restrictions."

With tears in his eyes, and conviction in his heart, Craig said in a phone interview,

"I will say it one more time, but after that I am not saying it again, I don't give a fuck who believes it, KELLY RYAN WAS BEAUTIFUL; I ADORED EVERYTHING ABOUT HER, AND WOULD NOT CHANGE ONE FUCKING THING ABOUT HER!"

(After reading Craig's letters and listening to his explanations on the phone, this was a topic he was extremely passionate about. Craig seemed deeply wounded by anyone that accused him of trying to alter Kelly's appearance or wanting to change her in anyway. Craig just wanted to help Kelly to attain her dreams. When Kelly's heart was broken, his heart broke more; and Craig fell on the sword over and over again because of his love for Kelly Ryan.)

In the eyes of her husband, and the eyes of the world, Kelly Ryan was flawless: she was both the name and face of Fitness America. Kelly placed first in almost every competition she participated in; but in the eyes of the perfectionist, those wins meant nothing, if she could not win at Olympia. Year after year Kelly would place second, and walk away discouraged, yet determined to take the judges notes and build the image they wanted to see- whatever it would take to come in first place. The problem with trying to build the perfect body image to suit a panel of judges is that these judges are human and subjective, and women's fitness judging was extremely erratic. There were never consistent guidelines for what they actually wanted from the fitness athletes, and their preferences seem to change from contest to contest.

Craig was faced with a no-win situation, but was going to do whatever it took to give Kelly what she had earned (in his mind) over three times over: the title of Fitness Olympia. Trying to decide how to train Kelly was difficult because Women's Fitness never could come to a consensus on what its competitors should look like. For some, the muscular women were objects of beauty; for others, they were mannish ghouls. Others favored the softer, sexier looks- hard bodied chicks in bikinis. Kelly's second-place finishes at the Olympia suggested that muscular was still a premium, and continued to compete with the dancer's body.

◄ SWIFT INJUSTICE

Setting his career aside to focus on Kelly Ryan

By the end of the summer of 2004, Craig put his bodybuilding career on hold, and decided to pour all of his energy into Kelly, and focus on preparing her for the Olympia 2004. Craig said, "I always put Kelly's career first, and it broke my fucking heart that year after year, they robbed her of the Fitness Olympia title. In 2004 the judges informed us the fitness athletes were becoming far too muscular, and they were going to be penalized if they had too much muscle." Craig worked with Chad Nichols on changing Kelly's weight training routine to decrease muscularity and put together a more feminine physique. Calories were significantly lowered as were the amount of weights Kelly worked out with. Nichols and Titus basically shrank down Kelly's existing muscle.

Craig and Kelly were not going to take any chances this time; Kelly trained day and night in her home gym the entire Summer and Fall leading up to Olympia. Adhering to a strict no-fat, high-protein diet; she attacked her physique with a new intensity. Kelly focused on what many critics saw as her weakness, her upper back and shoulders, creating, according to Kelly, "curves she never had before." Kelly Ryan added curves to her glutes, thus reducing the size of her buttocks, making her waist appear smaller. With this she was able to attain the symmetry and taper that was perhaps the only thing that stood in her way of walking away with the title in the past, and was to guarantee her a win in 2004.

The fitness and bodybuilding community watched with great interest as part of the build-up to the Olympia. Dan Solomon, writing for Bodybuilding.com, visited Craig and Kelly in Las Vegas, Nevada in August of 2004. In the article, he painted a portrait of a couple at the peak of their lives, enjoying a "marriage of strength" that had propelled them to the highest levels of the sport, with all the spoils. Solomon wrote:

When the cherry-red Jaguar pulled up in front of my Las Vegas hotel, the gathering of on-lookers could not help but glance over. This car was hot! As I approached, the driver inside rolled down her window to offer a ride.

LOSING A GRIP ON REALITY

The body behind the steering wheel was nearly as hard as the car's polished steel frame. The Jaguar, built on an assembly line by a team of automotive engineers, paled in comparison to its driver, who was built from a lifetime of sweat and passion. In the case of the driver, her brief stop at my hotel was just a quick detour on her journey toward becoming the best professional fitness athlete her sport has ever seen...

Just like the Jag, Kelly Ryan is driven. As we pulled away, I was introduced to her little dog, a Brussels-Griffon named Joey, who routinely rides shotgun as the fitness diva cruises sin-city. We headed off to the suburbs just past the strip, to an obscure neighborhood that has become home to Kelly and her outspoken husband Craig Titus.

Once we pulled into the garage, Kelly directed me upstairs to a room filled with wall-to-wall cardio equipment, equipped with a large screen television mounted to the wall. Seated just a few feet away from the TV was a sculpted, 260 lb. Craig Titus, going through his daily cardio ritual. Craig was riding the stationary bike while admiring the posing routines and classic physiques of several of his rivals on the 2000 Mr. Olympia video.

The consummate student of body building, Craig studied every move with an obvious attention to detail...Craig is regarded as one of the top 15 professional body builders in the world, but amazingly his accomplishments shy in comparison to those of his illustrious wife of four years.

Kelly Ryan has won nearly everything there is to win within the world of professional fitness. Her stage presence is unmatched and her athleticism and strength are a genetic miracle. Despite popular opinion, Craig does not mind being second best in his own house.

The relationship has transcended far beyond a conventional marriage. These two athletes are business partners, training partners, and best friends who also happen to share a bed.

The couple credits each other for their success. Kelly said, 'Craig's work ethic and tenacity make me want to be the best person and athlete I can be...' Kelly is the cover model on the recently published

Ironman Magazine swimsuit issue, an obvious sign that her career is heading in the right direction.

Craig has recently finalized new endorsements deals for him and his wife with a line of exercise equipment and a major supplement company. The two have also gotten into the party promotion business by forming strategic alliances with contest promoters.

This marriage might be best described as the quintessential mutual admiration society. They are each other's biggest fan. Soon the conversation turned towards Kelly…considered a favorite to claim the upcoming Ms. Fitness Olympia crown. Kelly has dazzled audiences throughout the world with an astounding display of showmanship and athleticism. Her background as an elite level gymnast has forced her competitors to embrace a style that was once unheard of within professional fitness. Her high-kicking, tumbling activity has made Kelly a crowd favorite.

Craig is his wife's biggest supporter saying, 'Kelly has worked harder than you could possibly imagine. I truly believe that she will go down in the history of professional fitness as one of the greatest athletes to ever hit the stage.' In conclusion, the lifestyle of a professional athlete is comprised of sacrifices that few outsiders could possibly fathom. This might explain why this relationship is truly a match made in fitness heaven.

Olympia 2004

After all of the hard work, The Olympia weekend finally arrived, October 29, 2004 in Las Vegas, Nevada at Mandalay Bay; this was the only major fitness competition that Kelly Ryan had never won. It was supposed to be Kelly Ryan's Night. With her biggest rival Susie Curry retired, Kelly had her best shot at victory since she first competed in 1999 on the Olympic stage.

Kelly had always been confident in her routine, and she now had the V-shape body of perfection to match that stellar "Flyin' Ryan Routine." Everyone, including Craig and Kelly, expected nothing less than the ultimate prize, and the bodybuilding world anxiously awaited the performance that was to be Kelly's "performance of her life." Kelly's acrobatic performance routine scored the highest for the night; sporting a fedora, pink and black plaid tights, and a half shirt to show off her ripped abs, the crowd went wild when "Flyin' Ryan" walked on the stage. She wowed the judges and the audience when she flipped high in the air then landed into position to perform her signature one-arm pushups to the beat of Janet Jackson in the background.

Ryan ran away with the highest scores in that round, but according to the judge's score cards, two other girls scored higher in the physique rounds. The other girls did appear more muscular than Kelly, but going in, the judges said that was not what they were looking for; they actually discouraged it in fact. It didn't matter however, victory seemed assured when the competition rounds were over, and everyone knew that Kelly Ryan was the winner.

The time had finally come, and the women all lined up for Lonnie Teper to announce the winner. Teper went down the list starting with the fifth place winner, and next the fourth place; then he announced, "And in third place, Kelly Ryan." There was silence for a minute while Kelly stood there in disbelief in her sparkly, one-piece bathing suit and Lucite high heels. Kelly stood there emotionless, glaring down at the judges. She scraped her fingers across her teeth, then rubbed her hands together and placed them on her hips.

When they handed Kelly the $8,000 check and the third place medal, she had a look of "You have got to be fucking kidding me" on her face. She grabbed the medal, held it down by her side, and looked forward with a scowl on her face. When the crowd erupted in boos, it took the announcer a few minutes to get everyone under control. Everyone in that auditorium was shocked, including the women who placed ahead of Kelly. Teper said, "All I do is read the names, please settle down and let's continue."

All Kelly wanted to do was get the hell off that stage. She posed for the group picture, but didn't place the medal around her neck. Without congratulating or talking to anyone, she simply walked off the stage. According to everyone that witnessed her performance onstage, everything about Kelly that night was perfect; there wasn't a thing she could have done different to change the results.

In an interview with Muscle Mayhem, Kelly aired her frustration, "I am not complaining about the results; I would just like to be able to understand it. People in the industry are brutally honest when it comes to comments about my body. But I would say that over the last couple of years, people have consistently been coming up with very positive comments about the changes I made, and I try to use the trend in comments to guide my progress. I feel that as a whole, people in the industry, such as high-level trainers, diet gurus, and former competitors, feel that I have improved dramatically, but are not sure why I am placing so low."

Ron Avidan agreed, "I would watch a show, and I had Kelly in first place, and then she would come in second. I would wonder if the judges saw the same contest that I just watched. But I'm not the judge. I don't know." Predictably, Craig was outraged. Craig wrote in his January 2004 column of Titus talks, "I realize I am married to Kelly Ryan and my opinion on her may be biased because of that fact. But keep in mind there are individuals who believe Kelly Ryan has won the Olympia several times but will never say it to stay politically correct."

According to Craig after that Olympia, Kelly was never the same again. All he wanted to do was fix the injustice, and make everything okay, but he couldn't! After that experience, both Craig and Kelly lost their desire to have any part of the IFBB. Kelly was bewildered, and disillusioned with the entire bodybuilding world. She literally did everything physically possible to correct any minor flaw with her body, and had the perfect image going into the competition. Kelly took constructive criticism to heart, and fine-tuned every last detail with a positive attitude.

Kelly felt utterly defeated, having poured her whole life into this one competition, only to fall short with no explanation why. Craig tried to build her spirit back up by promising her that together they would build a new women's federation, and take down the I.F.B.B. Craig said that he would support her in whatever she decided to do, "I just wanted her to know that she could still win the Olympia title someday. This one title did not define her stellar career!" The time would come for Craig to challenge those in power; but at that time, they were just going to continue to honor their contracts, compete, and finish the season in the IFBB without burning any bridges.

Kelly addressed critics on her blog when she stated: "It really hurts when a writer destroys all the hard work you put into something with a quick flick of a pen. I spoke to the writer and after I broke down each element, he said, 'Oh, well I guess it was more difficult and impressive than I thought.'

The article has already been printed the way he wrote it, and it was all negative. "As far as him writing that no one was in shape, we get marked down for coming in too muscular or shredded. I had more people say it was the best I had ever looked on stage than I ever had in my whole career, including the other competitors. In any professional sport, you have to develop a thick skin, in order to handle such negativity. I take it all in and re-group, but it definitely hurts!"

Everything about Kelly that night was perfect; there wasn't a thing she could have done different to change the results, but that made it all the more difficult to absorb. It was out of her control, and her whole life, she had been in control. To block out the pain, Kelly slowly distanced herself from her close friends, and the body building community. She surrounded herself with shallow minded drug addicts that would tell her what she wanted to hear. These new friends were about ten years younger than Kelly, and wanted to party all of the time- day and night. Kelly was training for one last competition, but her heart was not into it- she partied harder than ever, and trained a little on the side.

CHAPTER **10**

Free Fall

Losing interest after Olympia

Craig continued to participate in the bodybuilding shows he had already committed to, but his heart was no longer dedicated or even interested in the IFBB. The bullshit battle was getting old. Craig had always spoken the truth, but the more involved he got with the IFBB, the more asses he had to kiss; ass kissing may have worked for Shawn Ray, but it did not work for Craig Titus. Craig was tired of the games; he was not bending over anymore. Titus said, "Anyone that is politically correct is a fucking liar!" Craig was tired of tip-toeing around and being politically correct, and he was ready to phase himself out of the IFBB. With this growing disdain for the IFBB, Craig entered the 2005 Ironman Pro Invitational, not knowing this would be his last competition, and the place where his career and life would take a dramatic turn.

The Ironman Pro Invitational took place on February 19th, 2005 in rainy Pasadena, California. All of the competitors participated in a weigh-in on Friday night at the Fit expo. The bodyweights were announced to the crowds: with Craig's weight at 238 pounds. Craig placed Sixth overall, just behind his rival King Kamali. Shortly after the event, at the 2nd Annual Fix Expo Photo-shoot with Alex Ardenti and Robert Reff, Craig injured his calf, and had to return to Las Vegas immediately.

Once Craig arrived in Vegas, his calf swelled up and turned red; it was so painful to the touch that he could not walk. He immediately knew that he was suffering from an abscess deep within the muscle.

Now, over the years, he had experienced painful injection sites, but never to the extent of this particular shot of steroids. He was not completely sure which specific anabolic caused the abscess, but he was positive that one of the drugs he injected in his calf was contaminated with bacteria and was not sterile.

Addiction to pain medication

The following Monday after competing Saturday night, Craig was bed ridden in the hospital, hooked up to IV bags containing antibiotics. For pain, Craig was given 40mg of OxyContin every four hours around the clock. He left the hospital on crutches totally unaware that he was well on his way to being addicted to OxyContin. After a couple of weeks, Craig was taking double the prescription. Craig said, "My life, the life I worked so hard for, and my career in professional bodybuilding, was unknowingly destroyed forever. You see, nothing good comes from narcotics, nothing. All that I loved, family, friends, and my career now became second to the OxyContin."

Craig then explained, "I found myself canceling appearances, canceling guest-posing gigs, and losing the desire to train altogether. Contrary to what everyone who claimed to know me said, my drug problem came in the form of 80 mg OxyContin; but that's what people do, they run their mouths with total disregard for the truth. These people are the first to judge, and throw rocks out of glass houses… especially people in the bodybuilding community." When Craig realized that he had an intense desire to use more of the drug, and became fixated on where he would be able to get the pills after the prescription ran out, he knew that there was a problem. With the support of his family, Craig secretly checked himself into a rehab to detox himself off of OxyContin. After enduring a month of hell, Craig returned home clean and sober; he felt as if he had regained his life, but it was unfortunately only temporary. When Craig came home, he also came back to the same people that enabled him to do drugs in the first place, along with some additional "friends" that Kelly had picked up along the way.

Back from rehab- home to Megan Pierson Foley

Craig recalled coming back from rehab, and "This random chick, I called her Megan the 'Star Stalker' would never leave the house. I asked Kelly who in the hell is that weirdo, and why won't she leave? Kelly said, 'She's just a client. I think she doesn't have any other friends. I don't know how to make her leave; and I can't be mean, but she creeps me out too!'" Craig said, "Star stalker was like a foot fungus. I could not get rid of that shit, and she was irritating the hell out of me! For God's sake, we tried to give her clues; but she was too stupid to take a hint, and get the fuck out of our lives!"

At first Kelly was flattered. Craig said, "I think she began to grow on Kelly; but towards the end, Kelly could not stand her either! Megan would lure Kelly in by telling her how great she was, and buying her all sorts of gifts. Megan would bring a shit load of drugs over every time she came to the house, and they developed an abnormal friendship (if you could even call it a friendship). The whole fucking Megan thing was so destructive ! I wish to God Megan had never come into our lives. I knew from the minute I met her, she would be a horrible influence on Kelly. I told Kelly time and again that she did not need to be hanging out with 'Star Stalker'; she was bad news!"

Young, dumb, and wanting to party all the time, Megan Pierson Foley was the last thing both Craig and Kelly needed when he returned from rehab. They needed to be around mature friends that would keep them grounded and focused. Kelly's ego was so fragile from the Olympia, she was seeking acceptance from the unacceptable. Megan helped fill a temporary void for Kelly, but Megan was so obsessed with Kelly Ryan the superstar, she told Kelly everything she wanted to hear, when what Kelly really needed was someone telling her what she needed to hear.

Craig said, "The reason I remember when Megan interjected herself into our lives so vividly, or became Kelly's 'best friend' according to her Grand Jury Testimony, is because it was at the worst possible time to have this woman hanging around our house. The last thing we needed was for this woman, who so desperately wanted to be friends with Kelly, showing up with cocaine in her hand every time she walked through the door."

Megan was the "single, white female", and copied everything Kelly did. Craig said, "She called and texted her every minute of the day.

If she did not know where Kelly was, she would stalk her down and find her; she was obsessed with my wife! When I was sober, it was scary, but the more I tried to open Kelly's eyes, the more she wanted to party with Megan. Kelly and I partied before Megan, don't get me wrong, but not every frickin' day! That all changed when Megan came around! The second Megan walked through our doors, everything spun out of control!"

Detaching themselves from bodybuilding

As Megan worked her way into Kelly's inner circle, it was not a total surprise. Kelly had already slowly distanced herself from the bodybuilding community along with her close friends and family. Craig said, "Her new friends were about ten years younger than Kelly, and wanted to party all of the time, day and night. There was no escape from it; instead of fighting, I joined in with my wife and her friends." Craig fell back in with his old crowd as well. Finding other ways to kill the pain, Craig began to party hard with recreational drugs. Craig's best friend Matt Cline openly admitted that he sold drugs, and introduced Craig to Greg, Tony, & Schwimmer before he got sober.

Matt eventually checked himself into a rehab and moved back to Boston; he knew if he got mixed up with these guys, he would get back into his old ways. Matt said that he and Craig had not talked for a couple of months, but had reconnected when Craig was trying to get him involved in the WPI. According to Matt, Greg sold cocaine, and Tony was a low-level hood, committing arson for insurance and selling weed on the side. Jeff Schwimmer was just a crack addict that hung around because he had a crush on Craig, and would throw money around to fit in with the crowd. Old drug friends mixed with new drug friends was a bad combination.

Life at the Titus house turned into one big out-of-control party. With all of the "friends" hanging out, Megan and Jeremy became "couple friends" with Craig and Kelly. They were using cocaine to get high and marijuana to come down. When they all started taking ecstasy, the sexual lines were crossed at times, usually at a night club setting, and typically with Megan coming onto Craig and Kelly together.

◄ SWIFT INJUSTICE

Melissa James moves back in with Craig & Kelly

It was in that toxic environment that Melissa James called Craig and Kelly asking them if she could move back into their house in October of 2005. This was not the first time she had asked to live with Craig and Kelly; as established previously, Melissa lived with Craig and Kelly off and on from 2001-2005. In fact, she first moved in with them when she lost her dance studio in 2001.

Before everything crashed around her, Melissa was a dancer, and she opened a dance studio with a partner when she was 19 years old. It was around this time that Melissa began to do some very odd things, routinely missed practices, and appeared to be on drugs when she was interacting with the children. Soon after some of the parents began to notice Melissa's strange behavior, she was arrested on a drug charge in her hometown of Panama City, Florida. The parents of the children found out about Melissa's drug use and arrests, and pulled their kids out of the studio.

The studio subsequently shut down a few months later. Melissa ended up going bankrupt, and moved in with Craig and Kelly off and on during this time. Melissa moved back to Florida, and she lived with her boyfriend for close to a year. This was when Melissa's bad luck seemed to intensify. After a fight with her boyfriend, he kicked her out of their home, and according to Melissa, her family would not allow her to stay with them because she had a string of arrests for possession of drugs, check fraud & credit card abuse.

After this, Melissa called Craig and Kelly and begged them to help her. She claimed that she had nowhere else to turn; her dad would not let her move in with him in Florida, and her mom would not allow her to stay with her in New Jersey, all rightfully so because Melissa had a severe drug problem. When Kelly asked Melissa about her best friend and party buddy from Panama City, Melissa said that they were in a fight because her friend turned her into the authorities after Melissa "borrowed" her driver's license.

Melissa had arrest warrants out, and she did not want to get arrested. Melissa was a wreck; neither Craig nor Kelly wanted her to come live with them, but where else would she turn? Craig promised Kelly that it would only be a month maybe two, but he did not want Melissa to end up homeless on the streets, which looked like that was her only other option at the time. After Kelly reluctantly agreed, Craig paid for Melissa to fly to Las Vegas from Florida in mid-October, 2005.

Everybody was on edge before Melissa arrived in town, so when she showed up at the house tweaked out of her mind, Craig knew he had made a bad decision. With Craig and Kelly's friends hanging out over at their house, Melissa walked around telling bizarre stories. She chattered incessantly, and appeared as if she had no control over her mouth and body movements. After Melissa had been in town for a couple of hours, she asked if she could borrow a car to go to the strip and play the slot machines. Craig and Kelly wanted her to come down off the meth she had taken; her crazy ass stories were freaking all of their friends out, so they allowed Melissa to take the Jaguar out for a little while. Before Melissa left, she asked Craig for some cash because she did not have any money. This was where it all began; two hours into her stay, demanding money and disappearing for days in Kelly's car.

Regardless of what people have been told, Melissa was not there to manage the opening of their new store; nor was Melissa ever an "assistant", The only thing she assisted Craig and Kelly in doing was spending their money, eating their food, trashing their house, and taking Kelly's car for days. If the media wants to call that being an assistant, then okay; but in all reality she was just a freeloader! At any rate, Melissa told her mom that she was working, and planning on going to college; but certainly her mother had dealt with her daughter enough to know that almost everything that came out of her mouth was not true. This is not a slam on the victim; it is a realistic response about meth addiction supported by statements from eye-witnesses of her behaviors.

In an interview with Ron Avidan from Getbig.com, Matt was asked if he knew Melissa James. Matt said, "I knew Melissa very well. I have known her for years because she had been a friend of Craig's for a very long time. For the last two months, Melissa was staying at Craig and Kelly's house." Matt was concerned about her living there because she had been arrested for identity theft in Las Vegas. "She used identity theft to rent apartments, to turn on cell phones. She worked at a cell phone store one time and stole the identities from all the people there."

Craig told Matt that he might put her to work at the stores he was opening and Matt told him it was a bad idea- just because of her past. Matt said that she could never hold a job anyway because of the crystal meth. She just ran in crazy circles and never got anything done. Matt said that she was a nice girl, but addicted to crystal meth. He said that both he and Craig tried for years to get her help, but "she didn't want the help."

Craig and Melissa had always been close friends, so he was initially happy to see her when she arrived in Las Vegas. At one time, all three of them were very close friends. Craig and Melissa, however, always had a special relationship. Because of the obvious connection between Craig and Melissa, Kelly was overtly hesitant and guarded when Melissa arrived that last time in Las Vegas. And with Megan hanging around, it created an even stranger than usual dynamic.

In the past Melissa, Craig and Kelly were "party buddies", and had "threesomes" on several occasions, but Craig and Kelly had decided that was not going to happen this time around. With everyone doing drugs, there was a heightened sense of paranoia; and the air in the room was always tense. After Kelly told Megan about their threesomes with Melissa in the past, Megan became extremely possessive of both Craig and Kelly. Megan was delusional in thinking that she and Kelly were best friends; and when Melissa walked in the doors, Megan made it a competition.

Megan had both a mental and sexual fixation on Kelly Ryan. She did not want Craig and Kelly to have sex with Melissa, so Megan would do everything in her power to tear Melissa down. Megan would play mind games; and both Megan and Kelly would make fun of Melissa behind her back and to her face. If there were going to be threesomes with Craig and Kelly, Megan wanted to be the third party. Megan pressured both Craig and Kelly into having a sexual encounter with her, but neither person was interested in Megan in that way. This made Megan hate Melissa even more. Her obsession with Kelly spilled over on Craig; to the point of approaching him sexually without her "best friend" Kelly Ryan being present.

With "threesomes" and marriage, there was an unspoken rule that everyone had to be present; no two people could go off and be together or form a relationship. And for the most part, Craig, Kelly, and Melissa always stuck to that over the previous five years. However, when Melissa arrived this last time, Craig put his foot down, and said that there would be no sexual contact between the three. Thinking that Craig was excluding her, and only wanted to have sex with Melissa, Kelly became both suspicious and unnecessarily jealous. After Melissa arrived, and Megan heard about the threesomes from Kelly, Megan upped her game and sexually pursued both Craig and Kelly. After a few nights of hard core partying with ecstasy and cocaine, the three went back to Craig and Kelly's house and had sex together.

As for Melissa and Kelly's friendship, it appeared to bounce back and forth. They did not seem to bond until Melissa introduced Kelly to Meth sometime at the beginning of November 2005. They both tried to keep it a secret from Craig because he absolutely hated Crystal Meth; he knew that it was flat out poison (literally, some of the ingredients are battery acid, drain cleaner, lantern fuel, and anti- freeze).

Even though Craig would never touch the shit, he turned a blind eye because of all the crazy things going on in his life at the time. Craig was trying to put together this new federation, and could not do it if they were fighting, so he pretty much ignored the two of them using meth behind his back. They seemed to be best friends when they were shooting each other up with meth. Craig was not crazy about the dealer, Melissa's supposed boyfriend; he seemed shady, but Craig did not step up and ask questions like he should have; he just let things slide.

Problems began to arise when Kelly began partying with Melissa, and Megan felt left out because Kelly was her "best friend". Megan would try to start shit between the two girls by confiding in one, then going and telling the other what she said; this made both Kelly and Melissa increasingly paranoid about the other. Kelly would split her time snorting/injecting cocaine with Megan and injecting Meth with Melissa, and before long it was a crazy house.

Everyone was strung out on drugs, and they were all talking shit about each other and none of their stories made sense. Kelly became paranoid; she thought that people were trying to poison her, and she constantly looked out the window because she thought that people were watching her. Melissa on the other hand, insisted that she had bugs crawling out of her skin, and picked all of the sores on her body. There was constant movement; and the two women were either up or down, but nowhere in the middle. They would love each other one minute, then an unreasonable distrust would creep in, and they would resent and loathe each other the next minute.

When Craig and Kelly were trying to get everything ready for their grand opening, and were overwhelmed by Melissa coming to stay with them, Melissa assured them that she would not be in the way, and only wanted to help out. Melissa told Craig and Kelly she would stock their inventory and organize all of the products before the Grand Opening, but in the end, she did absolutely nothing to help.

Instead Melissa made messes around the house, left trash and food out, and seemed inconvenienced when asked to pick up after herself. The couple noticed that checks were bouncing, and credit cards were being declined, and Melissa would become defensive, denying any accusations that she was stealing from them. The girls began to argue constantly, and Craig would just leave the house because he hated the bickering between the two women, which had only escalated with all of the drug use.

The real tragedy was the toll that Crystal Meth had taken on Melissa James' life as everyone looked away. According to friends that were with Melissa the last couple of weeks in December, this once beautiful girl with smooth glowing skin, had meth sores and acne all over her face and body. She began to grind her teeth and jaw, which resulted in her back teeth falling out. Melissa became thinner and unhealthier. Staying up for days without sleeping, her moods were back and forth. At times she was happy and would talk nonstop, at other times she was lethargic, and just stared out the window. She had frequent violent outbursts caused by psychosis, which was induced by her drug addiction. If you have ever seen someone become addicted to crystal meth, you will fully understand how it can take someone's life over, and fast.

CHAPTER **11**

Ostracized

Women's Physique International
Craig Titus: "I started a new federation called Physiques International and had my sights set on taking over the bodybuilding and fitness industry. My goal was to basically shut down the IFBB and NPC because they were taking over every facet of bodybuilding, but narcotics destroyed that dream as well!"

On Sept. 21, 2005, Bodybuilding.com Press Release: For all Amateur and Professional Fitness & Figure Competitors, and Female Bodybuilders, a New Organization Has Been Formed! By: Craig Titus & Kelly Ryan

Press Release for "Women's Physique International": Attention! This press release goes out to all Amateur/Professional Fitness/Figure Competitors: "Attention! This press release goes out to all Amateur and Professional Fitness Competitors, Figure Competitors, and Female Bodybuilders. Emperor Enterprises, Inc. has put together the re-creation of Women's Physique Competitions, consisting of Fitness, Figure and Women's Bodybuilding.

Who is this for? *The new generation of women's physique competitions is here! Make sure you e-mail your inquiries right away for any type of state chairman position, show promoter, and/or sponsors that you would like to become a part of. There is an explosion of interest in this new organization.*

Who is joining? The time is now and several internationally known companies and publications have already jumped on board and will be publicly announced very soon. What sets us apart from any current organization is that Athlete Management Firms and Sponsor Representatives will be strictly "PROHIBITED" from judging any female competitors where any association exists resulting in any type of questionable outcome of any show. This organization is the best opportunity for the female competitors to shine in their individual categories, resulting in their much deserved placing, exposure and recognition for their years of dedication to the sport.

Craig Titus and Kelly Ryan, of WPI welcome all those ready for new and positive changes aimed towards benefiting the athletes first and foremost!

What is WPI? WPI was created with the idea and hopes for the athletes both retired and currently competing, bodybuilding, fitness, figure, male or female to become chairman, or promoters in their own state. This is the perfect opportunity for all of you to experience the business side of bodybuilding and fitness and establish financial stability for yourself. WPI was designed by competitive athletes, for you the athletes! The totally hot, urban and official clothing line of Women's Physique International will be Ice Gear. Each member/competitor will receive Ice Gear Clothing and use Ice Gear suits in the physique rounds so the athletes are judged on the physiques and not the suit they are wearing. WPI competitions will launch January '06 2006.

Reasons for starting the WPI

The timing for this new federation may have been off, but the motive behind Craig Titus standing up to the NPC/IFBB was pure. Craig firmly believed that when someone worked as hard as Kelly Ryan did to win the Fitness Olympia, and was denied the title year after year because she was not signed with the right management company; that it was wrong and it needed to change! Even with all of the chaos surrounding Craig and Kelly in the winter of 2005, Craig did everything physically possible to change the makeup of the judging and competitions in fitness and bodybuilding on the professional level.

All They Wanted was a Level Playing Field

"Fair play" is a game changer for most people, and when a person feels that something is unjust, they are more likely to support efforts to change the things around them. People are often willing to do things that go against their own personal interests when they think it is necessary for justice, and that's exactly why Craig took this stand to the very end. Starting this federation was a death sentence for his own career, but the scales of justice were a joke, and Craig was willing to throw everything away to even the scales out.

It was even more important when Craig and Kelly competed because it was so hard to get the pro card; anything less than first place was considered a loss. Craig literally went to prison the first time trying to come in first place to become a professional bodybuilder. Today athletes can come in 2nd, 3rd, and sometimes 4th, and still get their pro card, but when Craig competed, First Place was a big fucking deal! Craig knew this, and it pissed him off that there was an unequal playing field because of the judges. Something needed to be done about it, and nobody else wanted to risk their livelihood to speak out against it, so Craig Titus stepped up to the plate.

According to Craig, "The biggest problem with the judges is that in the sport of bodybuilding & fitness, to this very day, people are allowed to judge who have a vested interest with athletes who are on stage competing. Judges who own supplement companies, or clothing companies, or publishing companies should not be able to judge shows where their endorsed athletes are competing on stage. The biggest conflict of interest was with the JM Management- and how his female fitness athletes are always rewarded with a win or higher placing due to the fact that they are signed with their company, deserving or not. Because Kelly Ryan was not signed with this management company where family members are the head of judging at the Olympia, more than likely, no matter how hard she ever worked, Kelly could not win Olympia."

This battle is still being fought today. Articles have been written and legal actions taken, and the only thing that seems to happen is- those in power destroy the careers of those whom speak out against them. In an article written for Muscleandbrawn.com, Anthony Roberts reported on the corruption: **The Fix is in: Manion and Manion Corruption? By Anthony Roberts**

The fix is in on the story of father Jim Manion and son J.M. Manion, and their curious relationship with the sport of bodybuilding. Father Jim Manion is an IFBB and NPC chairperson and head judge. Bottom line: he oversees who wins, and how athletes are placed in competitions. Son J.M. Manion runs JM Management- a fitness and figure group that assists female competitors, and manages their careers. So let's do the Math... A female pays son J.M. Manion to "manage" her career. Female athletes enter contests, and are judged by father Jim Manion. Son J.M. Manion takes a cut from the female athlete's winnings. Do you see any incentive here for Daddy to help son?

It is here that the story becomes curious Roberts reports, 'One girl who signed with J.M. Manion, Kristen Nunn, went from just earning her pro card in the NPC to placing in the top 5 in her very first pro show (in the much harder IFBB). Another athlete who signed with him immediately went from 7th in the Fitness International to placing in the Top 5 for the remainder of the 2004 year- including the Fitness Olympia. Pretty amazing that someone who could not crack the top 5 at all would sign with the son of the IFBB head judge, and then finish in the top 5 for the remainder of the year.

But of course the most glaring example of J.M.'s stellar ability to 'manage' female athletes (when his father directly decides whether or not they win contests) has been in the Fitness Olympia. Susie Curry (JM Management athlete) held the first place title for four years while Kelly Ryan was in second place for three of those years. Then when Susie retired, Adela Freidmansky (another JM Management athlete) took first (inexplicably bypassing Ryan), and Jenny Hendershott placed in 2nd (JM Management athlete), while Kim Klein (who just signed with JM) moved up into 4th place, from 11th the previous year.

Of course all of this happened immediately after JM signed them, and always in contests his father had influence over, or directly controlled the outcome. This same year, arguably the best figure competitor ever to step on stage, Monica Brant, took second in the figure Olympia... to yes, you guessed it, a JM signed athlete, Davana Medina.

Roberts also noted that the "top 5" placing's in the 2008 Figure Olympia were managed by J.M. Manion. *"It's time for the Manion's to address the issue. This is a conflict of interest for a son to make money off contests that his father judges. Bodybuilding can't be taken seriously when this sort of family involvement is allowed to go on."*

2007 Figure Olympia-
1. Jenny Lynn- Managed by Fitness Management Group & J.M. Manion
2. Gina Aliotti- Managed by Fitness Management Group & J.M. Manion
3. Sonia Gonzales- Managed by Fitness Management Group & J.M. Manion
4. Jennifer Gates- Managed by Fitness Management Group & J.M. Manion

2007 Fitness Olympia-
1. Adela Freidmansky- Managed by Fitness Management Group & J.M. Manion
2. Kimberly Klein- Managed by Fitness Management Group & J.M. Manion
3. Jenn Hendershott- Managed by Fitness Management Group & J.M. Manion

2008 Figure Olympia-
1. Jennifer Gates- Managed by Fitness Management Group & J.M. Manion
2. Gina Aliotti- Managed by Fitness Management Group & J.M. Manion
3. Ziville Raudoniene- Managed by Fitness Management Group & J.M. Manion
4. Jenny Lynn- Managed by Fitness Management Group & J.M. Manion
5. Mary Elizabeth Lado- Managed by Fitness Management Group & J.M. Manion

2008 Fitness Olympia-
1. Jenn Hendershott- Managed by Fitness Management Group & J.M. Manion
2. Adela Freidmansky- Managed by Fitness Management Group & J.M. Manion

◄ SWIFT INJUSTICE

John Romano discusses the hot topic

As much as Craig despises John Romano, on his VPX Sports blog in 2011, Romano had a great point on the topic:

> It is interesting considering how the IFBB was started that they would have such a problem with a rival federation or athletes banding together to civilly force change. I guess in their narrow minds, this can only happen once?
>
> We all know that Joe Weider is the father of bodybuilding. He is the guy who first brought bodybuilding to the world through his publishing efforts under a sheet in his mother's dining room table in the middle of the night on a rented typewriter. While Joe toiled away creating our world, it was his younger brother Ben who created the venerable federation where we would compete, single-handedly creating the IFBB.
>
> In 1946 Joe and Ben were going to put on their first bodybuilding show called the Mr. Montreal. At that time there was no bodybuilding federation to sanction a bodybuilding show. The only organized sanctioning body at the time was the Amateur Athletic Union (AAU) which had bodybuilding fall under the auspice of the weight lifting federation, headed then by Bob Hoffman in the US. Prior to the show, Ben had secured permission from Hoffman to stage the Mr. Montreal bodybuilding contest.
>
> The evening of the show, two of Hoffman's men delivered a notice to the head of the AAU Weight Lifting Committee to the athletes telling them that the show was not sanctioned by the AAU and in order to preserve their amateur status, they needed to leave the theater immediately. Ben had no idea why the AAU would do that, but it was at that moment, in a hail storm of fury, that Joe and Ben created the IFBB. They told the bodybuilders not to leave, that now they have their own governing body and that they were going to make bodybuilding bigger and better than ever, and Ben and Joe were able to convince all the competitors to go with them and defect from the AAU.
>
> So why can't this happen today? What the industry needs now is fair competition, and for the athletes to have a voice and competent

representation without a conflict of interest. The corruption has gotten so bad that the athletes don't give a fuck anymore. Why diet your ass off and go the extra mile when you know you have already won? Or on the other hand, why go the extra mile when you know you will never win because the show is rigged?

Snubbed by the IFBB

On October 26th 2005 at the Olympia in Las Vegas for the first time in five years Kelly was not an Olympian participant; she was not even a spectator in the crowd. Craig and Kelly were blackballed from all IFBB events because they started Women's Physique International. Craig was not even approved to go to the expo to hand out flyers in promotion of the W.P.I.; he handed a few flyers to friends, but they were not allowed to hand them out either. Craig realized that his career was over in the IFBB.

Two nights later, Craig and Kelly hosted the Last Emperor Entertainment after Party at Seven, an upscale nightclub on the Las Vegas Strip. Craig and Kelly were famous for their lavish official IFBB after-parties they put on with Craig's best friend and fellow bodybuilder Matt Cline. This year had a different feel than parties they had hosted in the past because they were no longer able to promote the official IFBB after-parties.

Matt moved back home to Massachusetts, and Craig and Kelly were no longer competing on stage. Craig said that there was nowhere near the attendance of the past after parties, but those who came were their real friends who truly supported them. Everyone was expressing their joy in the fact that Craig and Kelly were starting the W.P.I. Craig said, "It was a bitter-sweet exit from the IFBB, but I am pumped about the new beginning!"

Craig Titus: "Kelly and Melissa got into a physical fight, and Kelly called me to come home. I was not there when the girls were fighting, and the cell phone records prove that. I walked in after Melissa overdosed. We were all high, out of our minds on drugs, and after Megan and Jeremy came over, they brought more cocaine, so we got even higher. Nobody was rational, and everyone was selfish and wanted to protect their own ass, so we covered the whole fucking thing up. It was senseless and heartless, and I own that- it is too bad others can't own their end of the cover-up!"

Section Two:
December 2005-
44,640 Minutes of Devastation

CHAPTER 1

Beginning of the End

Dec. 2005- Thousands of words have been written, but nothing can be erased!
Leading up to that tragic day on December 13, 2005, Craig Titus and Kelly Ryan had the blue prints for fame and fortune in the palm of their hands. The bodybuilding duo was on the cusp of greatness with unimaginable wealth when they began to launch their new federation, Women's Physique International, by going head to head with the Manion Dynasty and the NPC/IFBB. In addition to the federation, they were launching their own clothing line and work out gear, aimed for the bodybuilding community, called "Ice Gear." From the outside looking in, Emperor Enterprises, and the household names of Craig Titus and Kelly Ryan, were the new generation of bodybuilding, and they appeared to be unstoppable, until the week of December 12th when everything seemed to completely unravel.

Ironically the week of December 10th thru 14th, Craig and Kelly were actually scheduled to work at a Bodybuilding Training Camp in Dubai. Fellow bodybuilder Shawn Ray had invited Craig and Kelly to take part in a muscle camp in Dubai organized by Ray. Ray had already lined up several bodybuilder pros and was getting ready to print posters and advertise when he axed the project in early December. Both Craig and Kelly had signed on to participate, but like most of Shawn Ray's business endeavors, the camp was unexpectedly canceled with an excuse to follow.

Monday Morning, December 12th 2005

After marking the "Dubai training camp" out of their plans, it was back to the usual grind for Craig and Kelly on Monday morning, December 12th, 2005. The week was off to a normal start, and it was business as usual when Kelly went in the office & typed up her monthly column, *Kelly Ryan's Corner* for bodybuilding.com. Usually Kelly's monthly column was set up for her to answer five questions about fitness and bodybuilding in detail; her last article however was a self-promo shout-out: "My last announcement before the new year: Craig and I are opening up our first ever clothing store to launch our new clothing line called Ice Gear! We recently signed the lease papers and the store location is in the Village Square Shopping Center at the top of West Sahara Blvd. and Fort Apache. With our Urban Styled workout wear, training gear and sweat suits in the hottest fashions and colors, come check us out, opening December 2005!" Unfortunately this, among other business ventures, would never take off the ground because of unforeseen tragic circumstances lurking around the corner.

While Craig worked on his articles for the *Under Cover Pro* and *Titus Talks*, he was putting together some finishing touches on his new federation, Women's Physique International. Craig started the morning off by making some phone calls to promote and discuss the new federation as he attempted to continue to get the word out and create a "buzz" among those in the bodybuilding community. The first person that Craig called was Ron Avidan, the owner of Getbig.com. If there was one guy that Craig could trust, it was Avidan; a man that Craig believed had integrity, and was the most objective and fair writer in bodybuilding.

Ron's website was the place to go for everything on bodybuilding: News, Contest Schedules and Results, Boards/Forums, Pictures, Rankings; as Craig put it, "You name it and this guy had it! Everybody who was anybody followed Getbig.com!" When Craig called Ron that morning to catch up, and talk to him about the launch of his new fitness organization, Ron was unfortunately away from his desk. Ron was eager to hear about the federation from the always outspoken bodybuilder, and he asked Craig to call him back later in the afternoon to discuss the details.

Craig agreed and then started working on the first contest of the New Year for the WPI. Craig wanted to make sure he knew every rule and regulation like the back of his hand. He had reference books and manuals scattered all over his desk and began to research every detail he could find about judging fitness competitions. He got pumped up just thinking about it! Craig wished Kelly was around to ping a few ideas off of; he loved collaborating and discussing every detail about the federation with his wife. He knew that Kelly needed a break however, so he reluctantly worked through the details by himself. After Kelly had finished her work, she decided to spend the day buying last minute Christmas gifts and then relaxing with a massage at the spa.

The Debit Card

When Kelly first started her car, she noticed the gas gauge was on "Empty". She had filled the Jaguar all the way up to "Full" a couple of days before. Evidently Melissa had been driving the Jaguar around town all night without her permission, and did not bother to fill the car back up with gas. Kelly was not going to let this ruin her day however, and she decided to go fill her car back up with gas without saying a word to anyone. The gas station was around the corner from their house, and it would not take more than five minutes to put some gas in the car; so, as Craig stated, "fuck it, she was giving Melissa a pass!"

Kelly pulled the Jaguar up to the pump and got out of her car with her Wells Fargo Debit card in her hand and unscrewed the gas cap. She swiped her card to pay for the gas at the pump, and to her surprise, the word "DECLINED" scrolled across the screen. She thought there must be some mistake, and she swiped it again; but there was no mistake, the credit card was declined.

Completely pissed off, Kelly now had to go inside the convenience store to pay cash for the gas. Kelly had gotten into the habit of carrying very little cash in her purse because she was afraid Melissa would steal it. Kelly held her breath when she checked her wallet; luckily she had a twenty dollar bill, and she was able to put a little gas in the car. Kelly was irritated the car was out of gas, but livid because her card was declined, and she raced home to confront the problem. The tires on the Jaguar skidded to a stop as Kelly slammed on the brakes when she pulled into the driveway of her house. Kelly went straight upstairs to Craig's office and began to lay into him about what happened with her card, accusing Melissa of being the cause for her card being rejected.

Craig had always been "the fixer," but had grown tired of it all, and just wanted peace in his house. Kelly always wanted to confront Melissa when she "fucked them over", but Craig wanted to know all of the facts before he said anything to her. It would be one thing if this had been a stranger off the street that had supposedly stolen Kelly's debit card, but this was Melissa, their friend; and Craig did not want to accuse their friend of something unless he was absolutely certain she actually did it! Kelly did not care about being fair; in her mind, she had been more than fair, and she was convinced that Melissa was taking advantage of their kindness. Kelly knew Melissa stole the card, and she was fed up with all of Melissa's "bullshit" shenanigans. Kelly was ready to play hard ball; she had been fucked over one too many times; she was ready to fuck over Melissa this time.

Kelly believed the only way Melissa would ever learn a lesson, and stop stealing their fucking stuff, would be if they finally filed a police report. She believed they enabled Melissa, and Melissa just kept "shitting all over them!" Craig on the other hand felt conflicted about Melissa because she was already down on her luck; he did not want to kick his friend while she was down.

Craig knew that it was a problem, and he had already made up his mind, even before this happened, to send Melissa off to an intense six-month drug rehabilitation facility. He had not worked out any details yet, but he was aware of the fact that if he did not check her in somewhere soon, Melissa would eventually overdose. Craig both recognized and acknowledged that he enabled Melissa, and allowed her to continue abusing drugs in his home. It was a double-edged sword, and he had to ignore her behavior if he wanted to get anywhere with the new federation that was starting in a month.

Prior to the incident with Kelly's card, Melissa had been constantly asking for money, and Kelly had become defensive about giving her money after Melissa began taking advantage of them. Craig was giving Melissa more money than Kelly was even aware of, and it had become a delicate situation. Over the few months prior, when Craig would let Melissa use a card, it was always his company card, so Kelly would not see it. This kept both women happy and quiet. The less the other knew, the better off everyone would be in the end. It was now much more complicated because the card in Kelly's hand was not Craig's company card, and he had not given that card to Melissa. He was hoping and praying that it was just a mistake, and it had nothing to do with Melissa; but if Melissa was doing it, he knew she would have to move out of their house immediately.

Craig told Kelly to have a seat and calm down; he would get on the Wells Fargo website to see if extra money had been taken out, or if there were any unauthorized transactions. Kelly could not calm down, much less sit down; she was far too wired. She and Melissa had injected each other with meth before she left to go Christmas shopping. Kelly was edgy and anxious, demanding to know answers immediately.

Craig went to the website listed on Kelly's debit/credit card, and he entered all of her password information, and he was denied access to the account information. Thinking, "Oh shit," Craig called the 800 number, and the representative said that the account recently had security information changed. When Craig inquired about this information, the rep. said that he needed to speak to the owner of the account, and Craig thought, "Oh fuck," as he reluctantly handed the phone over to Kelly. Craig could tell that it was not good just by watching Kelly's face. Kelly verified all of her information, and she was in fact overdrawn.

While Kelly was still on the phone, Craig moved money over from his account to her account, hoping to appease her while he tried to handle the huge mess. After Kelly hung up the phone, Craig said that he wanted to look through all of their financial records before they accused Melissa of anything; and before Craig could finish his sentence, Kelly walked out of the office and down the stairs into Melissa's room. Kelly had the Wells Fargo card in her hand when she barged into Melissa's room and said, "I have never had a card declined in my entire life; but today, this card was declined when I was trying to put fucking gas in my car because it was on empty, again!" Kelly waited for Melissa to respond, but the response only pissed Kelly off more when Melissa said, "And?"

Kelly lost it, and started screaming, "And... you have been arrested for forging checks, stealing credit cards, identity theft, among a list of other things, and today my credit card was declined, and my account is overdrawn." Melissa yelled back that she did not "fucking take her card, or touch her precious money," then Craig ran down the stairs to break up the argument. There was not a physical altercation, but when Craig walked in the room, he could see Melissa's face. He knew that both women were tweaked out of their mind, and had not slept in days. Seeing the look in Melissa's eyes, he knew that it was important to get her out of the house as soon as possible. Craig got in between the two women, and wrapped his arms around Kelly to calm her down.

Craig had Kelly follow him up to their bedroom where he shut the door, and sat down on the bed with her. Kelly, thinking that Craig was going to make excuses for Melissa, and explain away her stealing like he usually did, told Craig, "I am done, either she is gone or I am gone, you decide!" Craig tried to comfort Kelly, hugging her as he whispered, "I know, I get it, listen, you are right; Melissa is out of control." Craig explained, "Let's get her a plane ticket; send her to New Jersey for Christmas. Make her think it is just for Christmas, and once she is there we will tell her that she cannot come back." Kelly couldn't believe it, she had wanted Melissa out of their house for so long, and Craig never would turn her away because he felt sorry for her.

"That's all I want for Christmas is for Melissa to move the fuck out of my house!" Craig said, "Okay, okay, but listen, we can't say a word to her about not being able to come back! There is no way we will get her on a plane if she thinks for a minute that we are not going to let her come back; so you gotta fuckin' swear to me that you won't say a word!" Kelly said, "I swear to God, whatever it takes." Craig said, "I am serious, I saw the look in her eyes. If she has any idea that we are sending her to live with her mother, and we are cutting her out of our life forever, she will do something! She will never leave!"

Kelly nodded like she got it, but Craig knew that if she spilled the beans to anyone, it would not work. Craig said, "And, not a word to Megan, she will try to stir up shit; just hang in there for 24 hours. I will get Melissa a hotel room tonight, and throw her ass on a plane tomorrow! But you gotta be cool, no arguments, promise me that?" Kelly agreed, and Craig walked downstairs to talk to Melissa.

CHAPTER **2**

Room #232

Monday Afternoon, December 12th
Walking in Melissa's bedroom, Craig stepped on piles of trash and clothes; he moved some of the junk off her bed and had Melissa come sit by him. Craig said, "Come sit down sweetheart, and listen. We can't go on like this; we all need a little break." Melissa looked up at him as if nothing had ever happened and asked, "What do you mean?" Craig explained, "This is crazy, and it's not healthy, and I think we all need a little time apart. So how about if I get you a plane ticket to New Jersey?" Melissa started to interject, and Craig said, "Wait, just here me out. Just a break, a little breather; you can spend time with your family for Christmas. I am sure they are missing you, and it would be good for you to get away for a while. I will call your mom, and take care of everything. Once everything has settled down you can come back in a few days, or whatever."

Melissa said that she didn't have any money, and Craig told her that he would take care of everything. Melissa had a blank expression on her face, so he knew he would have to do a little more talking to make her bite, but then to his surprise Melissa blurted out, "Yeah okay, I'll go!" Craig was relieved, and gave her a hug, then said, "Okay, good, I will take care of it and make a few phone calls! But for now, so I can finish this work shit, and have a little peace around the house, I am going to get you a hotel room for tonight." Usually when Melissa was told what she was going to do, she objected, but to Craig's surprise, she agreed. He told her to pack an overnight bag, with just a few things. He told her that he would take her to the hotel after he made reservations online.

Craig left Kelly's room, and walked into the kitchen to get on his laptop computer. He pulled out his credit card and booked Melissa a room at the La Quinta on West Sahara; about five miles away from their house, then booked her one-way ticket to New Jersey that was leaving the next day, December 13, 2005 at 10:00 p.m. on Delta Airlines. He went upstairs and told Kelly the news. Kelly was obviously relieved, and asked when she was leaving to go stay in the hotel. Craig said as soon as she packs her overnight bag, "I will drop her off, check her in, and come right back." Craig kissed Kelly on the head and said that he would be back in a few minutes. Craig then headed back downstairs to take Melissa to the hotel.

(Question for Lead Prosecutor Robert Daskas- Why would Craig pay over a thousand dollars to rent Melissa James a hotel room and buy her a plane ticket across country for the holidays if he planned on murdering her the next day?)

When Craig walked into Melissa's room she seemed confused and irritated as she struggled to find her things to pack for the trip. Craig started to become impatient as he watched her shuffle things around, not making any progress in performing the simple task of packing an overnight bag. Trying not to let on that he was aggravated, Craig told Melissa that she didn't need to pack all of her luggage, "This is overnight, not weeks- just grab a few things!" Melissa replied, "But I don't want to forget anything,"

Craig gently explained, "I will pick you up in the morning around nine, and you will have all afternoon and most of the evening to pack. Just throw a few things in a bag, and let's go," Craig said. When Craig walked over to help her, she told him that she had it, "I will meet you in the truck" Melissa said. She obviously did not want him going through any of her things, which appeared to only be piles of trash; Craig just thought, "What the fuck ever," as he walked out to his truck.

By that point, Craig did not care what the hell she had stolen, nor did he care "what the fuck was in her room." Melissa grabbed a plaid hooded long sleeve shirt and her blue jeans then walked out to Craig's truck. Craig asked if she needed anything else, and she said that she didn't if she would be back the next morning. Craig sighed and said, "Okay," then started to drive Melissa to the hotel. Craig pointed out every shopping center on the way because he wanted Melissa to stay occupied with doing something so she did not wander back to the house, which was only a half a mile away.

Craig suggested that Melissa buy her family some Christmas gifts, and he gave her a wad of cash as they pulled up at the hotel. Craig went to the front desk and got the hotel key for room #232, and paid for two nights with his business credit card. He knew that she was leaving the next morning, but after all of the hell these two women put him through, Craig planned on using the extra night with one of the women he saw on the side. Craig walked Melissa to her room, helped unlock the door, told her to call him if she needed anything, and he would be by later to check on her.

Craig dropped Melissa at the hotel & called radio station to talk about WPI

While everything around Craig was spinning out of control, Craig tried to put on a façade that he had everything under control. Once back at the house, he attempted to dig his way through the mounds of untouched shit that had piled up on his desk over the last few months. Everything was overwhelming, but he could not show any signs of weakness or all that they had worked so hard to build would go up in smoke.

Earlier that day, Craig had told his buddy Dan that he would call his radio show to discuss everything he had going on, but wished he had never made that commitment. He was not prepared to talk to a live national audience about the WPI, and he could not stand Dan's co-host, but he had already made the commitment, so he called into the show on Monday evening anyway.

ROOM #232

When Craig called, the producers put him on hold as Dan Solomon introduced the show: "A big welcome to our worldwide listening audience, from Venice Beach to Las Vegas to New York City and London. Body building fans throughout the world; we promise you another terrific show. I'm your host, Dan Solomon. We are broadcasting live. Talk radio for bodybuilding fans is off and running. Back with us for our twelfth episode, we have the incomparable and wildly entertaining, my co-host, Bob Cicherillo." Craig could not believe he was doing this; he was not prepared at all to discuss his new bodybuilding federation- Women's Physique International, and he hated Bob Cicherillo with a passion.

When they introduced Craig, Dan said, "Bob, you know what the question is: is this show ready, and is our audience ready, for Craig Titus?" Bob said, "Well I don't know if anybody is ever ready for Craig. As everybody knows, Craig is always controversial, very outspoken, and certainly not afraid to speak what's on his mind. The rumor mill is buzzing once again around Craig Titus, and Craig has been uncharacteristically quiet. Nothing on the internet message boards, no appearances, what is going on? I ran into Craig not too long at the USA, and thought he was noticeably down in size coming off that last injury." Dan said, "Well you can call it the calm before the storm, and tonight might be the storm because we have Craig Titus here to tell it like it is. This man always speaks the truth."

After Dan rattled off Craig's professional accomplishments, he welcomed Craig to the show, and Craig said, "what's going on guys?' Dan discussed Craig's success and asked him why he loved bodybuilding. Craig said, "You know, you get hooked. It's either a hundred percent or nothing at all. You're in or you're out, and I just happen to be all in 100 percent." Then Chick, being the asshole he was (according to Craig Titus), pressed Craig on his age, and Craig responded, "You can't say your real age in this sport. If anybody should know that, it should be you Chic! When you turn forty, some of the companies think you are too old; you know and I know that."

When Bob Cicherillo turned the conversation toward Craig's absence on the bodybuilding scene, Craig told him about his calf infection. "Fact is, they wanted to amputate my calf; they wanted to cut my leg off from the knee down. That's what the doctor told me, and I said you have got to be out of your mind, you might as well shoot me in the head." Craig explained how he recovered in a hospital, and at home for the past three months, but he was feeling much better now.

For more than an hour, the three would go back and forth; Dan would build him up, and Bob would tear him down as they discussed Craig's career, legal problems, injuries, and Craig's future venture with the WPI. Craig told the guys, "I don't want to complain about the industry, but do something about it, and that is why I am proud to introduce everyone to World Physique International." Craig said, on air, that he was so angry after the results of the 2004 Olympia when Kelly placed third that he decided to take on the NPC/IFBB as a rival organization.

Megan comes over during the interview

As he was finishing up his interview, Craig could hear Megan's "fucking annoying loud voice" echo off of all the walls in the house as she walked through the front door. It was Monday, and Megan came over to workout with Kelly, but she always arrived early, and stayed late, and they gossiped more than they actually worked out. This time she had arrived late, so it was guaranteed that she would stay late, and Craig did not have time for her bullshit.

Craig always did his best to avoid Megan Pierson. She was scheduled to workout at their house every Monday, Wednesday, and Friday at 5:00 in the evening, so Craig would make a point to be busy or gone on those days. However, avoiding Megan was not always easy. Megan usually popped in whenever she wanted, but as far as Craig was concerned, she was never wanted and could rarely be avoided. When Kelly was around, Megan would just walk into the house and never go home.

The most awkward times however were when Megan would show up for Craig to give her an injection of Human Growth Hormone and Steroids when she was preparing for figure competitions. She always seemed to stop by when Craig's truck was out front, and Kelly's Jaguar was gone, dropping her pants, and grinding up on Craig when he gave her an injection. Sober or drugged, Craig found her so repulsive that he always turned away her advances. After he told Megan not to come over unless Kelly was home, she turned on Craig, and seemed hell bent on breaking them up or getting revenge on Craig in some other way.

After Titus got off the phone with the radio station, Craig sat in the upstairs office, being as quiet as possible, eavesdropping on Megan and Kelly's conversation. The two girls were down stairs and Craig wanted to make sure Kelly did not say anything about M.J. to Megan. He knew Megan would fuck everything up, and stir some kind of shit up before they put M.J. on the plane. Craig did not know how long he could sit quiet and listen though; Megan talked for thirty minutes straight about herself, and it was making him sick!

Craig knew, however, if he sat there long enough, Megan would eventually turn the conversation around, and would start talking about Melissa. Then he heard Megan ask Kelly, "So where is Melissa?" And Kelly responded, "Craig got her a hotel room." Craig instantly yelled out Kelly's name, and she sprinted up the stairs! Craig said, "Don't tell that fucking big mouth anything. Megan is crazy; don't tell her a fucking thing!" Kelly said that she wouldn't, and the girls went back to the gym to do a semi- workout. That was Craig's cue to sneak off!

With Craig gone, Megan knew how to get Kelly to talk, and she pulled out some blow for them to share, and a bottle of wine for Megan to drink. Craig and Kelly did not drink alcohol because they were concerned about the effects of damaging their organs while they were taking steroids and human growth hormones. It became a habit after a while, and neither one of them were ever heavy drinkers. But it was fun to listen to other people share stories after they had a few drinks! The topic of gossip between the two women for the last few weeks had been about Melissa James, but Megan could not get a word out of Kelly all night long after Craig yelled out her name. After a few glasses of wine, Megan told Kelly she thought that Melissa was trying to come in between their friendship. She said Melissa did not want Kelly to be her matron of honor in her wedding. Kelly nodded, and thought, "What the hell?", but didn't say a word.

Megan told Kelly that she has been her idol for six years, and this was a dream come true to have Kelly Ryan be her maid of honor!

Through tears she told Kelly how much she loved her, and said she was worried that Megan was going to come in between them. Kelly once again thought, "What the hell?" and nodded. Megan said that she knew that Melissa was jealous of their friendship; she wanted to break them up. Kelly did not know what to say, but knew she had to say something to make this creepy conversation end, so she patted Megan on the hand and said, "Well that will never happen sweetie."

In Megan's mind, Melissa was a threat the moment she moved in with Craig and Kelly. To make sure Kelly and Melissa were never close; Megan constantly circulated gossip, or made things up to hurt Melissa. Megan told Kelly that she needed to confront Melissa before she left for Christmas, but Kelly said that Craig didn't want her to approach Melissa about anything else. "Craig just wants to get her on the plane, and he doesn't want any more confrontations," Kelly said. "Confrontation is face to face; so let's write Melissa a letter. You can put it in her suit case, and Melissa can read it when her ass is out of Nevada," Megan said. Kelly thought this was a great idea because it would allow her to get everything off her chest. What she didn't realize was that Megan just wanted to know the details about the problems between Kelly and Melissa, and that was Megan's manipulative way to get the scoop out of Kelly.

In the letter, Kelly wrote about Melissa stealing from her, and how disrespectful it was after they had taken her into their home. She talked about Melissa taking advantage of their kindness, and taking them for granted by expecting them to pay for everything, while she did nothing in return. Kelly expressed her disgust over Melissa purposefully pitting her and Craig against each other. In all capital letters, Kelly concluded the letter with, "YOU WILL NEVER BE WELCOME BACK IN OUR HOME OR LIVES EVER AGAIN."

Megan had wished the language was harsher, but she could not write the letter for Kelly, and Kelly had ignored all of her suggestions. Megan was ready to go home. She had one more final to take the next day at UNLV; so she told Kelly to call her sometime tomorrow. Megan wanted to get together for drinks after her last final exam. Kelly gave Megan a hug, and walked her to the front door. After Megan left, Kelly messaged Craig, took a hot bath, and got into her bed to watch television. She was relaxed for the first time in a long while with Melissa away from the house.

Around midnight, Craig went home and saw Megan's car still out front. Craig told Kelly to text him when Megan was gone, and he would come back later. Craig went to the La Quinta to check on Melissa. At the hotel room, Craig gave Melissa her boarding pass and ticket information, and went over every last detail, making sure that she understood all of the times. He told Melissa to put the ticket in her purse because he was afraid that she would disappear to the casinos, and miss her flight. Melissa did not want Craig to touch her purse, and it was obvious that she was "chemically off" and was much more mellow than usual.

Knowing that this would be one of the last times he would hang out with his friend, Craig engaged Melissa in a conversation. He asked about Melissa's mom, and wanted to know if she was excited about her coming home for the holidays. Melissa said that her mom was surprised, but that her mother could tell she was a little upset. Melissa said that her mother asked her if anything was the matter. So she told her mother that she and Kelly were not getting along and Craig bought her a hotel room and a plane ticket. When her mom asked why she and Kelly weren't getting along, Melissa told her that Kelly was flipping out and acting crazy over everything.

Craig explained to Melissa that it was just a very stressful time for everybody. "We are being shunned from the IFBB, and that is all we have ever known. That has been my bread and butter, so it is real scary. Something has to be done, and nobody has the balls but me to step up and get it done, but it is still fucking scary. These are people you do not want to turn on; they can destroy your life just for thinking about messing with their profits! There is a lot of crazy bullshit going on right now; We're headed in a direction where we could become ground breakers in fitness, but one small fuck-up and it's all gone."

Craig could tell that she was not listening to him, so he changed the subject, and brought up something that was really bothering him- Melissa's excessive Crystal Meth habit. He thought if maybe she thought they were all struggling with the same thing, and he mentioned going to rehab himself, she would open up and want help as well. Craig told Melissa, "I am thinking about doing a detox for a week, and then hitting the WPI hard. I just can't think straight on all of this pain killer shit, and lead this company in the direction it needs to go. I want Kelly in a more advanced rehab for 30-60 days, and if you decide that you want it, I will pay for you to go to rehab as well."

Melissa was still spaced out, so Craig had to be clearer, "The point is, we have to clean house, and when we set back up, there can be no drugs in this house ever again, period. We have to all start over clean." Melissa seemed receptive, but he was not sure, she was so fucked up on something, it was hard to tell what did and did not process in her mind. Melissa appeared super calm, with glassy eyes, and, when Craig talked; his words went right through her. Craig grabbed her hands, and noticed an unusual sore on her arm, one that looked different from the rest. In the back of his mind he wondered if she had maybe shot up heroin, but he decided he couldn't worry about it. Melissa was too far gone. He just needed to help her on the plane, and then he had to change his phone number.

After Kelly's bath, she settled in her bed and watched television for a while, when she suddenly realized that she was supposed to text Craig when Megan was gone. Sometime between 2:00- 2:30 p.m., Kelly texted Craig that she was gone and then fell right back to sleep. Craig told Melissa, "I need to go home and get some sleep; I will pick you up tomorrow morning around nine." Melissa was still wired, and pleaded with Craig not to leave, but he was exhausted and turned her away. He gave her a hug and a kiss on the forehead; as he did this, he could smell the odor of meth on her body. As Craig walked away, he thought to himself how sad it was that meth had robbed Melissa of her personality, beauty, and future.

Craig returned home, and went upstairs to take a shower and go to bed. The television was still on, so Craig closed his eyes until he fell asleep. When his phone started to ring at 3:33 a.m., Craig jumped up, grabbed the phone and ran out of the room so it did not wake Kelly. He could see that it was Melissa on the caller ID, and he really did not want to talk to her, but he was afraid that it might be an emergency.

Craig answered the phone in a hushed voice as he walked down the stairs, and Melissa begged him to return to the hotel. She was having second thoughts about flying to New Jersey, and was feeling paranoid about the flight, and being alone without Craig's support. He assured her that everything would be fine tomorrow after everyone got a good night's sleep. Craig said that they could talk about it some more when he picked her up at nine; but he was tired, and she needed to get some sleep as well. Just as he started to walk back up the stairs, Melissa called him back again, still pleading with him to come stay the night with her in the hotel room. Craig told her with a harsher tone not to call back again. He said, "That ain't ever gonna happen; you understand, I can't do that anymore. Now go to sleep and I will see you in a little while." Craig then turned off his phone as he walked back upstairs and went to bed.

Tuesday morning, December 13th

Craig awoke at 8:30 a.m. when his alarm went off. It felt as though he had just gone to sleep. He was exhausted, but so relieved that Melissa would be flying to New Jersey later that evening. Craig put some clothes on, ate a little breakfast, and headed out the door to pick Melissa up from the hotel. As Craig walked out the door, he told Kelly he was going to pick up Melissa. He reminded Kelly, "Look at me, I fucking mean it, not a fucking word! No fighting, be nice, help her pack, but do not say a fucking thing about her not coming back to Las Vegas after Christmas."

Kelly rolled her eyes, and Craig said, "If you blow this, we won't be able to get her on the plane, and she will be living here for the rest of her meth-filled life- so don't fuck it up! Act like you are BFF's and you cannot wait to see her in a few days, okay?" Kelly nodded in agreement, but knew it was going to be the performance of her life, because she had grown to hate Melissa James.

Melissa had never gone to sleep, and had shot up her last hit of meth earlier that morning. It was not enough to make a difference, but enough to help get her out of the bed and over to the house to pack her things. Melissa called Eddie right after she took a hit to make sure he did not forget to pick her up later to get her more shit. During the conversation, they talked about the heroin he had given her the night before, and he asked if she liked it. She said it did not help her go to sleep, and Eddie explained that he had just given her a taste. He said she could "dib and dab with it, until it feels right," but most important, it would help her get through the plane ride to Jersey. He said if she liked it they could buy some more this afternoon when he got her more meth.

In the middle of their discussion, Craig started to call Melissa. It was already nine am; she let Eddie go, and told him to pick her up in a couple of hours then clicked over to talk to Craig. Craig told Melissa that he was on his way. Melissa threw on her long sleeve, plaid shirt with a hoodie and blue jeans. Melissa wanted to make sure her arms and legs were completely covered because Craig hated meth and hated heroin even more, and she didn't want to hear his shit that morning. Melissa grabbed her purse, walked down the stairs, and sat outside by the entry way, lit a cigarette and waited for Craig to arrive.

Craig picks Melissa up from the hotel

When Craig arrived, Melissa was looking at her watch, seemingly on edge to get back, probably because she had some meth in her room, and needed a fix before she started the day. When she got in the truck, Craig began to pull out, and Melissa said, "Shit, I forgot all of my stuff!" Craig said, "Remember, you didn't bring anything, just that shirt and jeans, and you have your clothes from yesterday in that bag." Melissa said that she bought some Christmas presents and left them in the room. She did not appear to have enough energy to open the car door, much less walk back to the hotel room, so Craig offered to run back up there.

When Craig got into the room, he noticed some needles wrapped in a bag, and a drug he had never seen before, that had been melted down, so he assumed it must have been heroin. This was crossing a dangerous line for Melissa, but Craig just wanted her on a plane and gone, and her Mother could deal with it, so he chose not to say a word about it. He grabbed the bags of gifts, and on a notepad next to the gifts, there was an address with prices written to the side and the time 1:00-1:30 p.m. scribbled at the bottom.

Craig grabbed the note to hand to Melissa; this would let her know that Craig knows something is going on. When he got in the truck, he handed her the bags, and handed her the note, and said, "You left this." Melissa obviously did not want Craig to know about that note, so she changed the subject fast, and asked him if he had already checked out of the hotel. Craig told her he would do that later, but in reality, he had the hotel booked for an extra night, and was hooking up with a chick around one that afternoon. Craig was anxious to get Melissa back to the house, packed up, and set for the plane so he could meet up with his lady friend in a few hours.

Craig wanted to put what he and Kelly were about to do to Melissa completely out of his mind. Tricking Melissa into thinking the New Jersey visit would be temporary seemed cruel. Melissa was his friend, and he didn't want her to feel unloved; he in fact did love her with all of his heart, and nothing she could do would ever change that. Out of love, he felt like they had to do this, because at some point, somebody would overdose.

As a drug addict himself, Craig knew that Melissa had to be panicked, wondering where she would get her next fix; she didn't have any friends or connections in New Jersey, and she had to be scared out of her mind. Craig felt conflicted and hated to kick Melissa out of the only real home she ever had; Craig told Melissa he would always be there for, and now he was going back on his word. Melissa was building a life in Las Vegas, and that life was being ripped out from underneath her. When Craig and Melissa talked in the past, she confided in him that she felt abandoned by everyone except him. Craig was overcome with grief because he knew Melissa believed he was abandoning her too, just like everybody else.

CHAPTER 3

Dib & Dab with the Devil

On the ride to the house, Craig told Melissa that he was going to drop her off because he had errands to run all morning, but Melissa begged him to come inside because she didn't feel comfortable with Kelly. The tension was thick, and it was obvious that neither woman wanted to be around the other; so Craig agreed to go in and help break the ice, or if nothing else, keep them separated.

When they pulled up in front of the house, Craig made sure that Melissa still had her ticket/boarding pass he had purchased the night before. Craig told Melissa to send her mom a text now so she didn't forget later. He said, "Tell your Mom that you are on Delta airlines, and your flight will arrive around 8:45 a.m. tomorrow morning. Tell her she should leave her house around 8:00 a.m. to pick you up."

Melissa just stared at Craig with a look of confusion; he asked her where the boarding pass with the flight information was, and Melissa pulled it out of her purse and handed it to Craig. He told Melissa to give him her phone and he would text the flight information to Ms. James. When he flipped the phone open, he saw a text from Eddie that said, "Be there at 11 to pick u up." Craig pretended like he did not see that text, and texted Maura James, "Leave tonight at 10 on Delta. Get to Atlanta at 5:00 a.m. and Newark at 8:42 a.m. tomorrow. Call u later with flight numbers."

Back at the house: Craig, Kelly & Melissa

Craig had a little work he needed to do before he left for the afternoon, so he went into the house ahead of Melissa. He grabbed Kelly's car keys, and told Kelly to keep them put up so Melissa did not take off in the Jaguar. Melissa walked through the garage straight to her room, quivering and physically ill from meth withdrawal. When Melissa became this dope sick, she would typically inject twice the amount, trying to get her body to readjust in half of the time. It was clear to Craig, this was what she had just done because Melissa resurfaced, tweaked out of her mind, about fifteen minutes later with an abundance of wired energy.

Before Melissa emerged from her room, she checked her phone to see if Eddie had texted her yet. When Melissa realized she had been busted by Craig, and that he had read the text from Eddie, she ran upstairs to get a feel for if Craig was pissed about the whole thing. Melissa walked upstairs into the office and asked Craig if he wanted anything to eat; she told him Eddie was about to pick her up to go eat at Kentucky Fried Chicken. Craig said, "Sure that will be great, whatever you are having." She asked Craig if Kelly wanted anything, and Craig said, "I don't know, she is in the shower." Melissa said she would go ask her, and walked into Craig and Kelly's bedroom. Craig didn't have the energy to stop her, and wished he just told her to go ahead and pick Kelly up some food. What would it have hurt, he would have eaten it if Kelly didn't want it. Craig wanted to keep Kelly and Melissa as far apart from each other as possible, and that was not the way to do that.

Melissa spotted Kelly's purse, sitting on a chair to the side of the bed. She opened her wallet, and pulled out Kelly's Wells Fargo Debit Card, and slipped the card into her blue jeans. Melissa knew that she risked being caught; but at the point, she did not care, and blamed Kelly for being kicked out of the house anyway. Kelly forced her hand, and Melissa had no choice but to steal Kelly's debit card. Melissa wanted to make it to New Jersey with enough "medicine" to help her survive the Christmas visit and prevent becoming violently ill from withdrawal. Unfortunately for an addict, no amount is ever enough; life on the hamster wheel, constantly moving and scheming to get more drugs, is just another day in the office. This was what Melissa had to do to survive; and any risk associated with scoring her next week's supply became null and void.

Melissa walked back into the office and asked Craig for some money to buy lunch. He handed her a twenty-dollar bill, but that was not enough. Perturbed, Melissa said, "I need more than this; I have to get shit for the trip, and need money for the week in Jersey. It wasn't like I had a choice about any of this!" From the note and text he read earlier, Craig knew that she was meeting "her boyfriend" to buy drugs; but at this point, he did not care, and handed her the rest of the cash he had in his wallet. She kissed him on the cheek, and went into her bedroom to wait for her ride.

Craig went downstairs to get some clothes out of the dryer, and he overheard Melissa talking to Eddie on the phone about, "scoring 'H' after lunch." Craig knew this meant Melissa was going to purchase heroin, but she abruptly ended the phone call when Eddie pulled into the drive way and honked the horn to pick her up. Melissa saw Craig standing close to the room, and wanted to make sure that he did not think they were going on a drug run, so she told Craig that she would see him in a bit with some food. When Melissa got into the car, she told Eddie to remind her to get an extra plate of food for Craig. They needed to drop the plate back off after they were done because she did not want Craig to become suspicious.

Melissa and Eddie ran around the corner to Kentucky Fried Chicken; Melissa was relieved because it gave them a little time to talk business without Craig breathing down their neck. Once they arrived, Melissa started to place her order when her mother, Maura James, called about her flight. Maura wanted to know more details, but Melissa explained she was at a restaurant, and asked her mom to hang on a minute while she ordered her food. Maura could hear Melissa ask someone if they wanted something to eat, and a man's voice said, "No just a drink." Maura overheard Melissa attempting to place her order, and the staff was apparently bothered because she was trying to talk on the phone and place her order at the same time. Melissa told her Mom that she would call her back when she was done eating, but Melissa never called her mom back.

When they finally sat down, Melissa started eating her plate of food, and Eddie began to talk to her about heroin. He knew that she wanted some morphine, but he did not know where to get his hands on anything but heroin on the street. Melissa listened as Eddie explained how "H" (heroin) would work better for her anyway. It was a fluke that Tony had been able to get her morphine in the past; it just happened that his grandfather was dying and on hospice, and when he passed away, he had a shitload of Morphine- Dialudid, Fentanyl patches, and Infumorph injections 25 mg/ml, and he sold it to Melissa as a bundle package.

At that point, Melissa really didn't care as long as she had something to help take the bitterness out of the crystal methamphetamine sting. Almost every speed junkie needs something to come down from the high; in fact now, after abusing meth for over five years, Melissa's body physically craved something to buffer the edge. With Tony's shit gone, Melissa was in the "panic and seek" mode because her supply had already been depleted. She had been asking Eddie to try and find her some morphine for a while, and he put it off. Now there was no other option, it was heroin or bust.

Even though her body needed something immediately, Melissa was still hesitant about trying heroin. Eddie tried to reassure her by explaining that heroin was one hundred times better than morphine; he personally preferred it over anything else. He said, "H is better than sex; it's like a warm blanket of comfort wrapping itself around you, taking all of your pain away." Also, since Melissa had never used it before, it would not take much to work. Melissa's body had built up a tolerance for morphine, and heroin would give her the balance to smooth out the shakes and jitters from crystal meth.

Eddie had his KFC napkin and pen out to do the math, and he asked Melissa how long she would be in Jersey. She wasn't sure because Craig had not purchased a return ticket. She didn't want to stay more than two or three days, and hoped to fly back before New Year's Eve. Melissa told him to plan for a week, and round up to a month. For Melissa a month supply of drugs was like a week supply for another user. Eddie knew she would need far less heroin to get her by for the week; but Melissa wanted him to get her as much as possible, "just in case!"

By the time Eddie was finished writing everything out on the napkin it was a confusing mathematical mess. Eddie chunked the napkin in the trash, and told Melissa to give him all of her cash, and he would buy everything he could possibly get. But before they made the buy, they needed to drop Craig's food off at the house, a thought that made Eddie sick to his stomach. He was already on Craig's shit list, and did not want to do anything else to further piss off the professional bodybuilder. He told Melissa to just run it in and out without saying a word about where they were going. Eddie did not want to give Craig "240" Titus any reason to start bashing in his face.

Tuesday afternoon, December 13th
Last drug run

It was around noon, and Craig and Kelly's cars were both out front in the driveway. Melissa hurriedly walked through the house, left the food in the kitchen, and then slipped back out the front door. As they were driving off, she sent Craig a text to let him know the food was there, and she would be gone Christmas shopping all afternoon. Craig texted her back, and reminded Melissa to be back at the house to pack for her flight, and she responded with a "K". Assuming that Melissa would be gone all afternoon, Craig saw "sky rockets in sight," and continued to plan his "afternoon delight." The girls would not be home alone together, and he would have time to run to the hotel room, have sex, and come back without anyone noticing.

Once in the car, Melissa told Eddie that she needed to stop by a Wells Fargo ATM machine to get some cash. When they got close to the bank, he asked her to get out of the jeep and walk up so surveillance would not video his jeep. Melissa walked down the block, typed in the pass number, and got out the maximum amount for the day. After she walked back to his jeep, they sat and discussed everything she wanted him to purchase from the supplier, and how much the total would be for all of the drugs. Having no experience with heroin, Melissa was surprised when he said that it would be around a thousand dollars for a week's fix. She asked if that included meth, and

Eddie nodded his head. Melissa gave him everything she had, realizing she would not be able to go Christmas shopping. Oh well, fuck it, she thought, that did not matter; the only priority was having enough "medicine" to be able to function.

They drove across town to a seedy apartment complex to take care of business. Eddie went into an apartment building, and returned with an Easter basket full of an assortment of uppers, downers, and "in-be-tweeners". Eddie jumped back in the jeep, drove out of the neighborhood, and pulled into an outlet mall. As he handed Melissa the dope, Eddie said, "This is a friend of mine, so he gave us a huge fuckin' deal. This is China White H, powder! You don't mix it, just snort it, and when you come back I'll show you how to shoot it. D.D. cut it with quinine, so this mother fuckin' shit is strong. It'll just take a bump, know what I'm sayin'? Mr. Harry ain't the same as Ms. Emma; Harry will stick around longer, feel me?"

Melissa was looking out the window, obviously not listening to a word he was saying. Eddie tapped her on the check, and asked, "You got it?" She nodded and smiled. "This is prime shit, just dib and dab and see how your body feels. When you feel the good sick, stop!" Melissa did not respond, so he raised his voice, asking if she heard him, and she replied with a loud, "Yes!"

As they were driving, Eddie kept repeating the same thing over and over to make sure that she understood. Unfortunately, all that Melissa heard was that it would make her feel better; she had the "super flu" and wanted to get back to the house and treat the symptoms as soon as possible. Eddie gave her some Xanax from his personal stash. He told Melissa to take a bar if she was not in a place where she could use heroin; this would help her get by for a while. Eddie handed Melissa a couple of condoms. He told her to put the "ice" in one condom and the "H" in another, wrap them good in toilet paper and "stick them in like a tampon" right before you leave the house to go to the airport. She rolled her eyes, like she already knew how to do that, but he wanted her to play it safe, and make it to Jersey without getting busted in the airport.

CHAPTER 4

Home Alone: Kelly and Melissa

When Eddie and Melissa pulled up to the house, sometime around 1:30 p.m., Craig's truck was gone, and Melissa was hoping Kelly was not home either. Eddie gave her a hug and said, "See you next week baby; remember what I said about the goods, don't let Mr. Harry smack you flat!" Melissa said, "Yeah, yeah, yeah" nodded her head, and gave him another hug as she wished him a "Merry Christmas." She jumped out of the jeep, and slowly approached the garage.

In a way, Melissa wanted Kelly to be home so that she would not notice Melissa had stolen her debit card. But on the other hand, Melissa was afraid Kelly already knew about the card, and would confront her when she walked through the door. Melissa's hands were shaking with anticipation as she punched in the code on the keypad to the garage. Melissa saw the jaguar in the garage, and thought, "Oh shit, she's here." Oh well, just a few small steps to her room, and Melissa would lock her door to keep that bitch out of her face.

Hoping Kelly did not hear the beeps from the alarm system when she opened the door leading into the house from the garage, Melissa sprinted to her room with her purse and the dope. Once in her room Melissa quietly shut and locked the door behind her. She breathed a sigh of relief, turned around, and noticed a large, empty suitcase on her bed. Melissa walked over to the suitcase; it was not there before she left so Melissa knew it was a hint from Kelly to start packing.

Melissa was not in the room for more than a minute, and Kelly started banging on the bedroom door to let her in. Melissa thought that if she was really quiet, Kelly would go away; but no such luck. Kelly said, "Melissa I can hear you in there, let me in." Melissa did not know if Kelly was going to confront her about the card, or just be a bitch and start a fight. Either way, Melissa did not want to answer the door; she could not stand Kelly Ryan, and Kelly was the last person she wanted to see at that time.

Unfortunately for Melissa, Kelly was not going away, and continued to pound away on the door. Melissa hid her purse and stash in the corner then unlocked and turned the door handle. Kelly forced her way through the door, and told Melissa that she could have the suitcase on the bed for her flight home. Kelly had put her letter in a side pocket and left it unzipped. Kelly wanted to make sure Melissa saw the letter before she got on the plane. Melissa tried to physically shove Kelly back out of her room, but Kelly stiff armed the door, and walked over to the suitcase.

Kelly & Melissa Get into a verbal altercation

Kelly tried to come across as if she wanted to help Melissa "pack her things", but they both knew Kelly was being passive- aggressively condescending, and just wanted her out of the house as soon as possible. Kelly opened the suitcase, then walked over to Melissa's dresser and opened the drawers. Kelly took Melissa's things out of the drawers and then started re-folding Melissa's clothes and placing them in the suitcase. Melissa did not want her help however; she wanted Kelly out of the room, so Melissa just started throwing stuff in the suitcase.

When Melissa would throw something in the suitcase, Kelly would take it back out, fold it neatly, and place it back in the suitcase. Completely disgusted with Kelly, Melissa stopped packing, and crossed her arms as she watched Kelly pack the suitcase. The situation became increasingly hostile as Kelly sarcastically told Melissa that she didn't need to worry about cleaning up the room, and referred to Melissa as an ungrateful teenager. Kelly said, "You treat this place like it's a pig sty, and treat everyone with disrespect. No seriously, don't pick up a fucking thing, I will do it all. God, I'm ready for you to be out of this house and out of our lives!"

As Kelly started to sift through some of the items piled on Melissa's bed, Melissa jerked Kelly's arm away, and told Kelly not to touch her things. Kelly snipped back in a juvenile tone, "This is actually all of my shit, in my house; I can touch them if I want to fucking touch them!" Kelly began to open another drawer, and thought she saw their taser gun, but Melissa slammed the door before Kelly could get a good look at it. They both looked at each other, wondering if the other realized that Melissa had the taser in her drawer. With all of the fights Melissa had been having with Kelly, Melissa kept the taser in her room, in case it ever became physical. Melissa had even practiced shooting the taser gun in her room when Craig and Kelly were gone, and she had the gun ready to fire in case she needed it.

Kelly said, "Fuck it, pack yourself, but I want you out of my house in an hour!" Kelly left Melissa's room to go see if the taser gun was missing from their side table drawer in the master bedroom. Melissa slammed the door behind her, locked the door, and ran over to her stash of drugs, and poured them out all over her bed. Melissa was already wired from the meth, and wanted to take something to calm her down, so she pulled out the powder heroin. Melissa poured some out on her hand and snorted it like cocaine, only without spreading it out and breaking it up into lines or a "bump" like Eddie suggested.

After she snorted the heroin, Melissa sat back on her bed, and waited for the mellow high to ease her pains. She got the drip in the back of her throat, only it was not metallic tasting like coke, it was thicker and heavier, and gave her a strong urge to swallow and wash the drip away with her tongue. Impatient for the immediate high that she would get from a needle, Melissa continued to snort the heroin until she felt her body go numb. Although it had been a few hours since Melissa injected meth into her veins, she had both heroin and meth in her system, which could likely be a death sentence regardless of how much meth she shot into her veins earlier. The heroin alone in Melissa's system could more than likely cause her to overdose. In fact, heroin purchased off the street is about ten times more toxic than morphine administered through intravenous injection.

HOME ALONE: KELLY AND MELISSA

The problem with buying drugs from the streets is that the user has no idea how pure the substance is that they are ingesting. When taking drugs prescribed by a doctor, the patient is aware of how strong the drug is, and has knowledge about what they are putting in their mouth when they take it. The bottle comes with a pamphlet explaining what drugs not to mix, how much to take, and how many hours to wait until another dose is taken again. Instead of a pamphlet, Melissa got verbal instructions from a drug dealer, who got the drugs and instructions from a street middleman, who got the drugs from a street supplier, who cut the drugs with God knows what. Melissa was not too worried about it, she had done a shit load of drugs over the years, and nothing had ever happened before, so why worry about it then?

Melissa sat motionless for a while, just letting it all sink in, when the euphoric sensation turned to panic, and she began to struggle to breathe. She was taking huge gasps of air, but she was not getting any air into her lungs. Melissa's body was fighting the urge to fall asleep when she felt a jolt through her body. Melissa forced her eyes wide open, and jumped out of bed. Still gasping for air, she ran to the bathroom, and flushed water in her face. She was completely unaware that her body was in the process of overdosing. Unlike other drugs, once heroin is in your system, it typically takes a person one to three hours to actually overdose.

After a few minutes, although everything was distorted, Melissa looked through her bags of drugs, and saw Kelly's debit card sitting next to it. Melissa knew she needed to go put Kelly's debit card back before she noticed. Melissa was still tripping, but her heart was not racing anymore. Melissa seemed to have her shit together. Hopefully she had it together enough to go put the card back in Kelly's wallet.

When Kelly left Melissa's room earlier, she stood by Melissa's door and attempted to eavesdrop on her. She could hear baggies shuffling and Melissa snorting something. Kelly wondered what was going on; it was completely silent, and all she could hear was Melissa sniffing. From silence, it would turn to chaos, with things clanking and banging around in her room.

Feeling nervous about the entire situation, Kelly tried to call Craig and tell him what had happened. When she could not reach him on the phone, Kelly called Megan Pierson instead. Megan was always available; and once again Megan pulled through when she answered Kelly's phone call. Kelly sat on the couch, chit-chatting with her "best friend" for about twenty minutes. High on drugs, or lost in the moment, Kelly proceeded to tell Megan everything, even after Craig told Kelly to keep her mouth shut! Megan could not believe it, and the two women gossiped about everything until Melissa rounded the corner of the hall. It was at this time that Kelly quickly changed the subject.

Walking down the hall with Kelly's debit card in her front pocket, Melissa could hear Kelly talking on the phone with someone. She could tell by the tone in Kelly's voice that it was Megan Pierson. When Kelly talked to Megan on the phone, Kelly always sounded hateful and mean-spirited. As Melissa strolled past Kelly, it was obvious they were talking about her, but she just ignored Kelly and kept walking to the staircase. Melissa really didn't care what Megan or Kelly thought about her, and sure as hell did not care that they talked about her.

Megan wanted desperately to be a part of the cool circle in the bodybuilding community, and wanted others to see that Kelly Ryan was her friend. The problem was that Melissa, and everybody else, 25 years and older, did not give a shit! At this point Melissa could not stand either one of them, but she knew that Megan would keep Kelly distracted with her grandiose stories, or "lying gossip" while Melissa put the Wells Fargo debit card back into Kelly's wallet.

While Megan and Kelly continued to talk, Melissa walked up the stairs and went into the master bedroom. Once in the bedroom, Melissa walked over to Kelly's purse and pulled out Kelly's wallet. Megan and Kelly were unfortunately at the end of their conversation, and Kelly whispered to Megan, "Melissa is walking back upstairs; I am going to follow her to see if she puts that taser back in our side table drawer." Kelly quietly jogged up the stairs, walked into her bedroom, and saw Melissa with Kelly's wallet in her hand. Kelly yelled, "What the fuck are you doing?"

Startled, Melissa jerked around and dropped the wallet and the card on the ground. As Kelly went over to pick it up, Melissa had a ready answer, "Craig gave it to me to pick-up lunch from KFC for you guys?" Kelly had her doubts; why would Melissa sneak the card in her wallet if Craig gave it to her? Why would Craig give her Kelly's card, when he has a wallet full of credit cards himself?

Melissa's story was possible but not probable. Craig has been constantly giving Melissa money behind her back, so either way, Kelly was infuriated with both Melissa and Craig. To try and catch Melissa in a lie, Kelly called Craig on her cell phone; but once again, Craig did not pick up his phone. Craig was back at the La Quinta hotel room having sex with a lady he had hooked up with in a bodybuilding chat room. When he heard his cell phone, he ignored it. Feeling rejected from the bodybuilding world, and trying to cope with a broken heart, Craig numbed himself with Cocaine, OxyContin, and sex.

Craig never admitted it to anyone, but he was in love with Melissa before her meth addiction robbed her of her outer and inner beauty. Craig honestly believed if Melissa ever cleaned up her life, and got off meth, they would have been able to build a future together. But Craig's heart was broken; he knew that Melissa was at the point of no return. She was in too deep, so they would more than likely never share a life together. Melissa had even stronger feelings for Craig, and at one point in her life, desperately wanted Craig to leave Kelly so that they could get married. At that time, Craig and Kelly's marriage was also a business, and their two names together meant big money. So Craig and Melissa agreed to step away from each other. After that, everything started turning for the worse because of all of the drugs.

CHAPTER 5

Detonation

The explosive fight between Kelly & Melissa

Kelly called Craig over and over, but he did not answer. With five years of pent up anger built up inside, Kelly waited for her "asshole husband" to pick up the fucking phone so that she could let him have it! Craig never answered, so Kelly began to blast his voicemail with profanity, all the while screaming and slapping at Melissa. Heading towards the stairs, the two women were out of control. They were screaming at the top of their lungs, and physically assaulting each other.

Kelly called Craig again, and the call went straight to voicemail. After the beep, Kelly was hysterical, crying so hard she had a hard time talking. Kelly screamed, "This bitch has stolen my car for the last fucking time!" Over Kelly's voice, Melissa leaned over Kelly into the phone and shouted, "When, when have I ever stolen your fucking car?" Kelly yelled back, "You took it all the time for days, and trashed it. You are a fucking con-artist and thief. There's shit everywhere with tags still on them that you stole from stores." Melissa started screaming at Kelly calling her a "cunt, bitch liar," then Kelly started yelling at Melissa calling her "A fucking prostitute, and a meth whore." Recording the entire message, the voicemail eventually cut off with a long beep, but the two women were still screaming. In a matter of minutes, everything escalated, and Kelly was kicking the shit out of Melissa.

Melissa turned around to run down the stairs. About half way down the stairs, Melissa tripped and fell. Once she hit the bottom of the stairs, she sprinted to her room, and locked the door behind her. Kelly continued to call Craig's work and personal cell phones, and their fight was being recorded on Craig's voicemail. Kelly was not finished with Melissa, and she started banging on the door, telling her to get her ass out here to finish what she started. Melissa screamed back, "Stay the fuck away from me, or I will fucking kill you!" The two women were yelling so loud, the neighbor next door could hear every word they said. Kelly screamed, "I am done with you stealing from me, and lying to my face. I am so fucking tired of paying for your ungrateful ass! I am going to throw all your shit out the front door; you can walk to the fucking airport!"

Just as Melissa was about to open her mouth to respond, Kelly said, "Thank God Craig opened his eyes, and finally bought you a one way ticket home. You can live with your fucking mother the rest of your miserable fucking meth life. Craig didn't want you to know, but I am telling you now; you are getting on the fucking plane, and you will never come back here again!" With those few words, Melissa felt completely betrayed, her vision was fogged by the mirage of drugs flowing through her veins, and Melissa snapped! Kelly was elated, "Melissa finally knew she was about to be out of their lives for good." All Kelly cared about now was Melissa gathering all of her stolen shit, packing it in a suitcase, and when Craig got back, he was going to drop her off at the airport. Kelly chanted, "Bye-Bye" all the way to the living room when Melissa opened her bedroom door and charged at Kelly with the taser gun.

Around 2:15 a.m., before Kelly had a chance to turn around, Melissa shot the taser gun at Kelly, and hit her in the back of the leg. Melissa held on to the trigger as tight as she could, not letting go, sending a continuous shock through Kelly's body for over thirty seconds. Kelly was flopping on the ground, paralyzed by the volts of electricity going through her entire body. After the tasing stopped, Kelly laid dazed on the ground. She was completely drained. Weak and depleted of all her energy, Kelly knew if she came after her, Melissa would probably kill her.

Melissa fell to her knees, and dropped the taser. Her demeanor totally changed. Her eyes were so dilated, they were pitch-black. She looked spaced out, almost as if she was unaware of everything happening around her. In a soft voice, Kelly told Melissa to go in her room and start packing her things, but Melissa stayed put, just staring straight ahead at Kelly. It was as if Melissa could not hear Kelly when she spoke. She put her fingers in her ears, and wiggled them around, as if her ears were ringing.

Kelly tried to talk to Melissa again, and Melissa continued to gaze at her without a reply. Then Melissa muttered, "This house is fucking freezing!" Her teeth were chattering and her lips were blue; she looked cold, with a pale tint to her skin color. Melissa struggled to catch her breath, and made some gurgling noises. Melissa stood up, and walked over to Kelly to help her take the taser hooks out of Kelly's leg, and Kelly told her to get the fuck away! When Melissa's hand touched Kelly's leg, Melissa's hands were burning up. Her pupils were now so small, Kelly could barely see them, and her breathing was labored and shallow. Kelly had seen Melissa fucked up before, but this time was different.

Melissa looked like a zombie as she walked into the kitchen. She fumbled around in the kitchen for a while, and grabbed a bottle of vodka and a clean glass. Melissa told Kelly that she didn't feel good, and was going to rest for a little while. Melissa's ears were ringing, and it was giving her a migraine and making her disoriented as she stumbled from the kitchen to the hallway. Kelly asked Melissa if she was okay, and Melissa screamed, "What the fuck do you care? What the fuck does anybody care?" Once in her room, Melissa kicked the door shut, and screamed, "I wish I were just fucking dead already!" Melissa slammed a couple of vodka shots, and threw the glass as hard as she could against the wall.

Melissa had combined drugs and alcohol in the past with no consequences; this time would be different however, her body was already shutting down, and combining alcohol with the drugs in her system suppressed Melissa's impulse to breathe. Kelly heard the glass shatter when it hit the wall, and could hear Melissa destroying the room, but she did not have the energy to confront her. At this point, Kelly didn't care if Melissa destroyed the entire house, as long as she was on the plane to New Jersey by 10:00 p.m.

After about five minutes, the house got eerily silent, and Kelly became concerned about Melissa's well-being. Kelly was feeling strong enough to stand up, so she walked down the hall to check on Melissa. In the hall, she could hear Melissa's voice. Melissa was talking to someone on her cell phone, and she sounded upset. Kelly could tell it was her drug-dealer boyfriend. Melissa was sobbing, and seemingly begging him to come pick her up. Eddie must have turned her down because Kelly heard Melissa yell, "Fuck you then," as she threw her cell phone up against the wall. Kelly waited a few minutes before she knocked on the door, so Melissa would not think she was listening to her conversation. Kelly stood outside her door, and she could hear Melissa talking to herself and fumbling around through the filth trying to find her drug paraphernalia.

Melissa needed one more hit of meth to help her make it through the day; she found a needle and started to prepare the drugs. Kelly knew Melissa like the back of her hand, and she knew what Melissa was doing. Kelly walked away without talking to her and went back into the living room. Melissa was in her bathroom, trying to shoot meth into a good vein; but her vein collapsed, and it squirted out all over the bathroom sink and mirror. So pissed that she had just wasted a hit, Melissa started to kick and hit the wall as hard as she could with the needle still stuck in her arm. Her mood manically flipped back to anger, and she became physically violent, lashing out at everything around her.

Melissa began slapping everything out of her suitcase onto the ground. She threw the bottle of vodka against the wall, and then looked around, grabbing, ripping, and destroying everything in her path until she had no more energy. She started to struggle to breathe again. Melissa began to projectile vomit the vodka she just drank. Once everything was emptied out of her stomach, she began to dry heave and then aspirate.

In the final minutes of her life, Melissa most likely knew that something was wrong when she was overdosing, but was unable to cry out for help. Her muscles tightened and began to spasm all over her body, and she lost complete control of her bodily functions. The quinine, cut with the heroin, did not dissolve in her system, clogging the blood vessels and triggering Melissa's heart to go from racing to barely pumping. This caused Melissa to stop breathing, and she collapsed forward unconscious, hitting the wall as she fell to the floor. Kelly heard the loud thud, and ran straight to Melissa's room. She tried to open the door, but it was locked. She began to frantically bang on the door, but there was no response.

Sometime around 3:00 p.m. at the hotel, Craig finally looked at his cell phone. Craig saw he had missed a bunch of calls from his wife. Thinking it was just the same old bullshit fighting between Kelly and Melissa, Craig was pissed as he listened to his voicemails. Craig realized this was not the same old bullshit fighting; this was urgent, and he needed to get home as soon as possible.

After Kelly banged on Melissa's door and got no response, she tried to call Craig; Craig was trying to call Kelly at the same time, and neither one could reach the other. Craig sat the phone down, and threw his clothes on; while he was dressing, Kelly called Craig, and he picked the phone up and answered, "What the fuck is going on?"

Desperate and frightened, Kelly told Craig to get home, "I think something has happened to Melissa!" With all of his belongings thrown in a bag, Craig ran down the stairs to the truck, yelling at Kelly on the phone, "What the fuck do you mean something has happened to Melissa? What did you fucking do to her?" Kelly started to become hysterical, and begged Craig to just get home right away.

Craig jumped in the truck, and as he got closer to the house, his heart was racing. When Craig pulled into the driveway, the garage door was shut, so he busted through the front door. Kelly was in the living room, screaming, "She's in her room. I heard a thud, and then it went quiet. The door is locked and I couldn't get in!"

Craig ran to Melissa's room, turned the handle to open the door, but the door was in fact locked. He put his ear up to the door, but he could not hear a thing. Craig knocked on Melissa's door and there was no reply. Craig began to bang on the door, yelling her name, "Melissa, open the fucking door now!" Melissa still did not respond, so he ran into the garage to get a screw driver to unlock the door. Screw driver in hand, Craig walked back in the house, knocked one last time, and then inserted the screw driver in the key hole to Melissa's room. After a few seconds of jiggling, and poking, he heard a pop, and the door was unlocked. Craig turned the handle and tried to push open the door.

As Craig tried to push the door open, he realized something was blocking the entryway; there was a seemingly metallic-like odor in the air, like a combination of vomit, shit, and battery acid, billowing out of her room. Craig pushed the door forward with his fingertips, enough to peek his head through, and he realized it was Melissa's body that was the barrier in the doorway. Craig shouldered his way in the door, lunged forward, flipped Melissa over then crouched down next to his friend. Melissa's eyes were open, so he thought for a split second that maybe she was just injured; but as he tried to talk to her, he realized that her condition was far more serious.

Looking into her eyes, he could see there was nobody there. All of the color appeared to be drained from Melissa's body, and her fingernails and lips were a bluish-grey color. Realizing it must be an overdose, Craig jerked her up at that instant into the sitting position, and slapped her face while he yelled her name, "Melissa, Melissa, Melissa, M.J., M.J., Melissa, oh fuck me, oh my God, Melissa!" Craig pulled Melissa's body close to his to see if she was breathing, but he could not feel her breath. He put his cheek to hers, but again there was nothing. Her skin felt pasty and cold, a stark contrast to her body temperature earlier when she felt like she was burning up.

Craig laid Melissa back on the ground and tried to feel for a heartbeat. His hands were shaking so bad, he had a hard time keeping them steady to feel for a pulse. Craig was so panicked that he thought he felt her pulse, but then soon realized it was actually his own pulse, as his heart felt like it was pounding out of his chest. Sweat and tears poured down his face to her face as he screamed, "What did you do? What did you take? Oh my God, Melissa!" Craig had accidentally left his cell phone in the car; so he yelled at Kelly to find him a phone.

High on drugs, and still in shock, Kelly gazed at Craig and Melissa like a deer in headlights. Kelly wasn't moving, so Craig turned around and screamed, "Go get your phone, my phone, any phone now, right fucking now!"

Craig started CPR on Melissa

Kelly ran back to their room to get their cell phones, and Craig, knowing it was now or never, began CPR on Melissa. Craig tried to remain calm, but was so terrified that his entire body was trembling as he cupped his hand behind her neck and tilted her chin up. He tried to open her mouth to press her tongue down, but her jaw was locked.

Terror turned into panic after Craig tried to pry Melissa's mouth open. Her entire body, including her jaw, made a grotesque squishing noise and then went completely limp. There was vomit clumped in her mouth and throat; Craig turned Melissa on her side and tried to scoop it out with his fingers. As he was doing this, Kelly ran in the room with his phone, and she asked if he wanted her to call 911. Craig had Melissa turned away from the door, and Kelly did not realize how grave the situation was; Craig said, "Don't call 911. Hit contacts, pull up Tony and tell him to come over right now."

CHAPTER 6

Grave Decisions

Craig called Tony Gross to come help him

On Tuesday, December 13th, at 3:28 pm Craig's cell phone called Anthony "Tony" Gross' cell phone, according to the prosecution's evidence presented to the Grand Jury. If anyone knew what to do in this situation, it was Craig's buddy Tony. He always bragged about having a drug in his truck called "Pulp fiction potion;" if someone overdosed he could shoot it in their vein and revive them immediately. When Tony answered the phone, Kelly was too hysterical to talk, so Craig yelled at her to hand him the phone. Craig grabbed the phone and blurted out, "Listen, listen, I need your help, M.J. overdosed; come help me fucking now!"

Tony agreed and said that he was on his way, and Craig told him to hurry! Tony jumped in his truck, but he knew that he was fucked because he always made up stories to impress Titus and the other body builders at the gym. Tony wanted them to think he was a bad-ass drug dealer with family connections to the Chicago/Las Vegas Mafia. There was a little truth behind his stories, but no truth behind having "Pulp Fiction potion" in his truck, and he hoped that Craig was not expecting him to save a person's life.

Craig's gag reflexes were tested when he turned Melissa back over, and she had mucus-like foam coming out of her mouth, and a frothy orange substance coming out of her nose, like blood. He turned her head to the side, attempted to scoop the vomit and foam out of her mouth, then tilted her head back and tried to blow air into her lungs. Not knowing what to do next, his eyes slowly scanned the bedroom, and Craig started a futile attempt at chest compressions. Everything was hazy, with the lines blurred between fiction and reality. Melissa had already gone into cardiac arrest, and with no blood circulating to her brain, she had been clinically dead for over fifteen minutes.

Craig knew she was dead, but he could not stop trying to save her life. He contemplated calling 911, but after looking around, at the clutter and filth in Melissa's room while he performed CPR, it dawned on Craig that he was in deep shit. Every drug imaginable along with used hypodermic needles were strung out across her room; if they called 911 and said "overdose," the police would bust in with the EMT, and they would haul his ass off to jail. He went back and forth in his head, but convinced himself that he was doing the right thing because the paramedics would do the same thing that his friend Tony was about to do, if it were even possible to do anything at all. He knew Tony would be at his house any minute, and there was not enough room for everybody in the bedroom, so Craig decided to move Melissa into the kitchen on the tile floor. As he began to lift her, Kelly walked back in the room. Craig told Kelly, "We gotta move her in the other room, there's too much shit everywhere, and Tony will be here any minute!"

Craig repositioned himself at Melissa's head so that he lifted the heaviest end, but he soon realized that was a bad idea because Melissa looked horrible, and Kelly would be looking right at her face. They squatted down, positioning themselves to lift Melissa up, and Craig said, "On three- one, two, and three." They began to move forward with Melissa's body, and Kelly started gagging like she was about to puke, then she dropped her end when they made it to the hall. Craig wanted to hurry and start administering CPR on her in the kitchen before Tony got there, so he yelled at Kelly to "come on!"

Looking right at Melissa's bloated and discolored face, Kelly became hysterical when she went to lift Melissa for the second time. Craig started to lift Melissa up before Kelly, and when he jerked her up, fluids poured out of her body on Kelly's end, and she started screaming, "I can't do it, let's call 911, please." Craig told Kelly to move, he could get her, and he half carried, half scooted Melissa down the hall as fast as he could because she was leaking shit everywhere. When he made it to the kitchen, he laid Melissa down, and Kelly demanded to know why they didn't just call 911 because they had not done anything wrong! Craig yelled, "Because she is fucking dead, in our fucking house, from fucking drugs!" Kelly was crying so hard, she was hardly able to get out another sentence.

Kelly took a deep breath, with Craig's cell phone in one hand, and her thumb and index finger pressing against her brow, she pleaded with Craig to call the police, "Please, please, we didn't do anything, this isn't our fault!" While he attempted to do CPR, Craig sat upright, slapped his chest, and yelled through uncontrollable tears, "I am a convicted felon. Everything that happens will always be my fault!" Unless a person has been to prison, it is impossible to understand the feeling of living in constant fear for violating parole; especially when something is out of their control, like Melissa's overdose. Fear of going back to prison often times overpowers the voice of reason because that person's mentality instinctively tells them, "fight or flight, but don't fucking call the police!" And that is exactly what happened to Craig Titus.

If Craig Titus had not been convicted of the "conspiracy" drug charge in Louisiana when he gave somebody a phone number in the early nineties, then hell yes he would have called the police when Melissa overdosed. But Craig knew that if the police walked in the door, and there was a dead body, overdosed in a felon's home, they would have automatically searched his house and taken him to jail. Drugs cannot be in their home, no matter who they belong to, and drugs were all over that house. If a convicted felon calls "911" because of an overdose, they are automatically subject to prosecution for "use, possession, or distribution." (According to the National Center for Health Statistics, approximately 38,329 Americans died from a drug overdose in the past year, and only 10-56 percent of people who witnessed an overdose actually called for assistance.) Not calling 911 was a mistake that was not justifiable, but Craig's reasoning behind the choice is however understandable.

Tony Gross arrives at the house

Craig and Kelly heard Tony run in through the front door, and they both breathed a sigh of relief; someone was finally there to help them. When he ran into the kitchen, his reaction to seeing Melissa overdosed on the ground spoke volumes. From where he stood, it was obvious that "there was absolutely nothing that they could to do save her life." Craig was devastated; the totality of it all hit him hard! Melissa's beautiful blue eyes were still open asking Craig why he did not save her. All Craig could do was apologize to Melissa, and express how sorry he was for not being able to save her from herself; there was nothing else that could be done. Craig could not stand having her glare at him any longer, and he had to just get up and walk away. He looked over at Tony and asked, "What now?" Tony, a man that never wanted to let anyone down, especially his buddy Craig, didn't know how to save Melissa, but he did know what to do next, and he was determined to help his buddy, "fix the problem."

How Anthony "Big Tony" Gross was nominated as the voice of reason in this drug induced madness would be anyone's guess. Nonetheless, this 23 year old, barely out of high school, wanna-be gangsta was the man calling the shots, and their fate now rested in his hands. In the past, Tony told exaggerated stories about his life in crime and thug-like behavior, with arson, drug trafficking, and other nefarious activities listed at the top of his resumé. Just a few days before, Tony had talked about his latest racket, taking cars out to the desert and torching them for the insurance money, torching his own vehicle for practice. He torched his own vehicle for practice then filed a police report for a missing car, and collected insurance money.

Tony Gross had big stories about his family's connections to both the Vegas and Chicago outfits, and said that he and all of his friends were untouchable because the D.A. ends up dropping any charges ever brought up against him, his family or friends. Craig never totally believed Tony, and usually thought he was full of shit, but he told each story with such an outpouring of charisma and conviction, Craig figured there had to be some truth in there somewhere. Craig and Kelly were physically and emotionally exhausted, so they all decided to snort a couple of lines before they came up with a plan. When Tony mentioned the smell of the body, Kelly got up immediately to start cleaning. If she kept herself constantly busy, she would not have to think about Melissa's lifeless body inside of her house. Craig looked at Tony, and said, "The fucking smell is horrible, but I don't know what to do!"

Craig and Tony walked over to the body, and just stood there for a few minutes and stared at the ghastly scene on the floor. They decided to take a smoke break outside to think things over. Outside, Tony rambled on about how he would take care of the whole thing, telling Craig not to worry about it, and Craig said, "You keep saying that; talk is shit!" Craig bummed a Marlboro light from him then Tony just picked right back up, and started running his mouth, and Craig tuned him out while he finished his cigarette.

Craig and Tony threw their cigarettes on the ground, and walked back into the house. The pungent odor overpowered the house, and nearly knocked them both over when they stepped in the door. Tony said the smell was getting worse, "we gotta clean this shit up, and get rid of the body!" Tony told Craig that they needed to find some duct tape, rope, and lots of blankets. Kelly rounded the corner, and said she would go find some blankets, and the guys went into the garage to look through Craig's tool box for duct tape and rope. They were not able to find rope, but there was some duct tape, so Tony said that he was going to start, and Craig needed to find something so they could tie up the bundle of blankets, making it easier for Tony to lift the body, and carry it around.

The three were now in a drug-induced frenzy to cover the overdose up. With every step the three took to cover-up the overdose, the deeper a hole they dug for themselves; making it impossible for them to snap out of it, and do the right thing. While Craig was in the garage searching for duct tape, Tony walked over to examine the condition of Melissa's body. Kelly ran the blankets to Tony, and Craig walked back in the house with the duct tape and he tossed it over to Tony. Craig asked Kelly if she knew where some rope was at, and Tony said anything would work so he could tie it together and they could carry her body out.

Kelly went back into a frantic cleaning mode, opening all of the windows and turning on fans trying to air out the house. Craig looked around for something Tony could use, and he found some belts from Kelly and his robes and a telephone cord. Craig ran it down to Tony and saw him putting it around Melissa's head: stunned, Craig asked him, "What the fuck are you doin' brah?" Tony said that her body was going to leak out all over the house, and it would leave D.N.A. behind. "Her puke, piss, shit, that is all D.N.A." Without consulting Craig, and before he had a chance to object, the duct tape was on her face, as Tony continued to shovel both Craig and Kelly even deeper into the hole; one that would ultimately be impossible for Craig to crawl out of. The duct tape would prove to be an insurmountable obstacle for Craig to overcome.

It took the three of them to wrap the blankets around the body. Kelly would have to stop cleaning, and help them, forcing her to face the reality of the situation once again. When they were all three standing around her body, Craig suggested that he and Tony lift her, while Kelly wrapped the body. Moving her was traumatic enough for Kelly, but actually wrapping her up could possibly send her over the edge. Tony thought that was a bad idea, and suggested Kelly just hold Melissa's legs, while he wrapped the body. Kelly, however, started to lose it again, and said she could not do it!

Kelly still wanted to call the police, and made one last plea with the guys, but it fell on deaf ears. Craig said they were all in too deep, "I am a convicted felon with drugs in my house. Tony and Greg have both sold Melissa drugs. You fucking kicked her ass. You, Melissa and Megan have been shooting each other up for the past month! We will all go to prison, and because you injected Melissa with drugs and beat her up, you could go to prison for Manslaughter! Besides that, we did not call 911 after Melissa overdosed; instead we cleaned up the scene, and have her body bound in duct tape! How in the hell do you think that's going to look Kelly? How the fuck would we explain all of this shit hours later? We can't! No fucking way. Period, the end, just shut the fuck up and do what we say!"

Kelly replied, "Melissa was trying to kill me! She has been trying to poison me the past few weeks! She is the one who shot me with the taser; I can show them the taser marks on my leg. I was defending myself! Please, please, please, I cannot do this!" Craig said that he did not want to hear another word; this was what they were doing! Tony agreed with Craig; he was not going to prison for selling drugs to Melissa. Tony said, "Fuck that Kelly! We gotta be smart here. There is no fucking way we can call the police! Besides that, my finger prints are all over the fucking duct tape. Look you gotta trust me; I can make the problems go away, but you gotta trust me." With everyone high on cocaine, there was no voice of reason when they all decided to take part in the cover-up, and everything they did to hide the overdose spun completely out of control.

They spread out two blankets on the ground next to Melissa; Tony put tape over her eyes, and told Kelly not to look up at the body as they lifted her onto the edge of the blankets. Craig and Kelly counted to three, and lifted her off the ground, while Tony wrapped the outer edge of the blankets around her body. Tony used duct tape, and continuously wrapped areas that appeared to be leaking through the blankets. They repeated this process with all of the blankets. Craig then took the cloth belts and wrapped the top and bottom, while Tony took the cord and wrapped it completely around the body, trying to secure it together. This held Melissa's body in the fetal position, so they could place her body in the trunk.

Craig and Tony went back outside to smoke and discuss what to do next, while Kelly went back to "frantic cleaning mode". They sat down; Tony pulled out a cigarette and gave it to Craig, then suggested moving Melissa's body to the back of Kelly's trunk. When it got a little darker, he would go bury the body out in the desert. Craig thought about it for a moment, because that would be the easiest thing to do, and they would never find her body, but shook his head "no", and said that he could not do that to Melissa's mother. Tony tried to convince Craig to reconsider and said, "No body, no crime," but Craig said that was not the problem. "Dumping her body where no one can find her, and have her family looking for her would be fucking cruel!" Tony asked Craig, "Well what then because we gotta get rid of the body." Craig was not sure, but for now they needed to move the body to the trunk, without involving his emotionally fragile wife.

They needed to focus on getting the body out of the house and into the trunk of Kelly's car.

Craig went inside the house and grabbed the keys to Kelly's car. They went in the garage to turn on all of the lights, and to make sure the garage door was still down. In the garage, they realized that the light over Kelly's car was out; Craig slipped over to the side to turn on the big posing light, so they would be able to see better. Craig then popped the trunk, cleared it out, and the guys went back inside to move the body out to the car. The two men positioned themselves on opposite ends to lift Melissa and carry her body to the car. Craig warned Tony about how heavy she was, but Tony obviously was not listening. After a couple of steps, Tony dropped his end; making the excuse that he just lost his grip. Readjusting a little, they gave it another shot and lifted Melissa up while they hustled their way across the house.

Once they were inside the garage, Tony said that he had to set the body down for a minute because he was losing his grip again. Once they caught their breath, the men grabbed the blanket and scooted over to the trunk of the car. They took a deep breath and hoisted the body up into the bed of the trunk. Completely exhausted, Tony said, "That was so fucking heavy," as he walked inside to take a break.

The smell in the house was over taken by bleach, while Kelly meticulously cleaned every square inch of the home. Craig stayed in the garage a few more minutes. Looking at his friend's body with such sorrow, he could not wrap his mind around it all; in the blink of an eye, Melissa's life was stolen from him and the world by something as senseless as drugs. A woman he loved was now gone, and would never come back. Craig shut the trunk of the car thinking this would be the last time he would ever see her again. Craig walked into the house, and tried to push it to the back of his mind so he could take care of the rest and put this horrible accident behind him.

Craig and Tony sat down in the living room to hammer out their next step. Tony mentioned burying her body in the desert one last time, but Craig said, "Absolutely not!" Craig said that he wanted her body to be found, and he did not care if there were consequences involved saying, "I am not going to say it again, and I do not want her to be buried in the middle of nowhere! If you do that, her mom will always wonder if she is dead or alive; I am not doing that!" Tony asked, "What then?" Craig said that he didn't know for sure, but they need to find a place where someone will find her immediately, but cannot be traced back to him. Tony replied, "Fuck, if you want to do that, we should have just called the police to come pick her up!" Craig asked, "What if you dropped her body in front of a morgue or hospital?" Tony asked, "What about that hospital at the end of the street, like in the parking lot or something?" They both agreed that would be a good idea, then Tony said he would go check it out, and come back later in the day to drop her body. Tony said, "Let me go scope out the hospital, and find a safe place to drop her. Then I will go out to the desert and find a good place for us to get rid of the jaguar." Craig thanked Tony, and once again Tony reassured him that he had his back. Craig said, "I know you do brother." Tony told Craig he would call him later to make the final arrangements, and Craig went upstairs to take a shower.

Craig felt better after he had a shower, but he was still anxious about what Tony thought when he drove by the hospital, so he gave him a call. According to the phone records, the second call was placed at 4:39 pm. When Tony answered the phone, Craig asked him what he had found out. Tony said that he had only been gone for twenty minutes, but he drove by the hospital, and he did not think that it would work. Just at that time, Megan Pierson tried to call Craig and her name appeared on his call waiting. She had been trying to call Kelly all afternoon, and had neither spoken to or heard back from her to get the follow-up gossip on Melissa. So a frustrated Megan Pierson then started to call Craig, but he kept hitting "ignore" every time she called.

Having to deal with Megan
Megan was the very last person Craig wanted to talk to right at that moment, and when she realized he was hitting ignore because his phone did not immediately go to voicemail, she called Craig's phone over and over. Tony said that there were surveillance cameras on every pole at the hospital. If he dropped Melissa's body there, he would

most definitely get busted. Tony told Craig to give him some time to drive around; he would come up with an alternative plan, mark the perfect spots, and he would call Craig back in a couple of hours. Craig was disappointed, but went along with Tony and decided not to pester him with anymore phone calls. Craig would have to trust his friend, and wait for him to call him back.

When Megan called again, Craig was completely aggravated, but he clicked over and asked her what she wanted. Megan said she wanted to speak to Kelly; she had been trying to call all afternoon, but her phone was turned off. Craig was never friendly to Megan the few times he was forced to speak with her on the phone; on that day, however, he was especially short with Megan, and Megan could tell that something was wrong. When she asked Craig what was going on, he answered, "Nothing, Kelly will call you back later." Craig told her not to call his phone again, and hung up on Megan as she started to talk, he then went downstairs to check on Kelly. When Craig was no longer answering her phone calls, Megan knew something was wrong, so she called their friends to answer her question.

Megan called Tony's cell phone, and he answered the call; this was a horrible time to get a call from her, but he always answered his phone in case there was an emergency. She asked if he had seen Craig and Kelly today, and he said that he just left their place. Megan was pissed that he had been over to their house, and nobody was answering her phone calls. In Megan's mind, Kelly was her best friend, and she should be the one in the "know", not Tony Gross. Megan knew something was up, and she demanded to know every detail, right that minute. Tony said that it was bad, but he couldn't talk about it right now.

Megan was relentless, and kept pressing him for answers, but he refused to say anything to her. Megan was becoming increasingly frustrated, not because she was worried about Craig and Kelly, but because she always had to know what was going on! Megan decided to take matters into her own hands, and got in her car to drive by Craig and Melissa's house. With the exception of Melissa's room, the house was completely cleaned. Kelly took all of the towels to the laundry room and started washing them. After starting a load of laundry, Kelly saw that the lights were still on in Melissa's room so she instinctively walked over to turn them off. The door was cracked, and when she pushed it open, the stench and view were so overwhelming, she had to briefly turn her head away.

Kelly just stood in front of the bedroom doorway, blown away by the condition of the bedroom. Their guest room looked like the inside of a drug addict's box on skid row. Craig walked up behind her, and told her not to worry about cleaning this room, he would take care of it, but she did not listen to him and started to pick up trash. Craig got some trash bags, handed Kelly a bag, and told her to be careful because there were used hypodermic needles everywhere. With Craig on one side, and Kelly on the other, they circumnavigated the room, swooping up piles of trash and confiscating biohazard materials.

CHAPTER 7

With Friends Like These...

Poking out from underneath Melissa's bed was a huge unlocked, metal lock box. When Craig opened the box, he found a bag of crystalized methamphetamines, dozens of forged checks and credit card applications filled out with Kelly's and her mother Nikki Ryan's personal information including social security and driver's license numbers. There were around twenty-five return-receipts from different stores around Vegas where it appeared as if Melissa had a scam going to steal items then return them for cash. At the very bottom of the lockbox, Craig found several HELOC (Home Equity Line of Credit) statements from Green Point Mortgage. Craig realized that Kelly had taken out a fraudulent loan on the house with the help of her "best friend" Megan Pierson for an extra $100,000. When Craig stood up with the signed documents in his hand, Kelly nearly shit her pants because Craig had no clue the two women had done this.

Megan was a mortgage loan consultant, and according to Kelly, she had fraudulently embezzled $100,000 on their home mortgage ($20,000 of which Megan pocketed for herself). An already paranoid Kelly wondered if Melissa planned on using this information against her, or if she had possibly filed for even more lines of credit with all of the identification information she had stolen from them? Why else would she have copies of this information in her room?

After Kelly made a brief confession to Craig, he shook his head, and said, "We can't worry about that right now!" They both knew there was no time to talk about that right now, but Kelly could not let it go, and she insisted on calling Megan. Craig tried to talk Kelly out of calling her; he did not want Megan to know anything about what was going on. If Megan knew anything, all of Las Vegas would hear about it the next day. Kelly ignored Craig's advice however, and walked into the other room to call Megan about the documents. While Kelly was dialing Megan's number, Craig yelled out, "I don't want that bitch coming over to the house!"

When Megan answered the phone, she immediately asked Kelly what was going on, and Kelly told her about the HELOC papers in Melissa's possessions. Kelly said, "They have our signatures all over them, and the amount we took out. Why would Melissa have that; or what could she have done with that information?" For the first time since Kelly has known her, Megan sat silent, and then she became unnerved; the possibility of being exposed for mortgage fraud sent her over the edge. Megan repeatedly said "Oh fuck." Then she said, "This is so bad Kelly! Somebody's going to find out about what we did now. My career will be fucking ruined, and I just got my degree from UNLV! I have to come over immediately to look at those papers!"

Craig could hear Kelly telling Megan repeatedly not to come over right now. Craig walked into the room, and said in a loud voice, "Bye Megan, talk to you later!" Kelly motioned to Craig that she could not get Megan off the phone, so Craig told Kelly to hand him the phone. When Craig got on the phone, he told Megan, "Everything is alright, but we are busy right now. Kelly will call you tomorrow some time, okay!" Megan started to answer Craig, and for the second time that day, Craig hung up on her. He turned Kelly's phone off, but kept his cell phone on in case Tony tried to call him while they finished cleaning Melissa's room.

Tony scopes everything out

According to the phone records, Tony called Craig at 6:23 p.m. to inform him about everything he had discovered so far. Tony said that there were security cameras everywhere, and he could not find a good place in the city to dump the body without getting caught. Tony suggested that they dump her body at a picnic area ten miles outside of town, then drive five more miles in the desert, just outside of Pahrump, and torch the car. Tony said Craig could follow him out of town sometime between 2:00-5:00 a.m. the next morning and they would get it all done at once.

Craig was fine with the second half of the plan, but Craig wanted Tony to take the jaguar out right now to dump her body. Tony said it would be better to do it all in one drive; Craig disagreed, but didn't have it in himself to argue with anyone right now. Craig told him he was tired; he would call him back in a couple of hours to check back in, and make sure the plans did not change again. Craig hung up the phone with Tony, and as the drugs began to wear off, reality began to creep back into his head.

Craig walked into Melissa's room and sat down on her bed. As upset as he was that Melissa had done all of this to them, he pushed that anger aside, and in her room, with nobody else around, he had a melt down over the loss of his best friend. Nobody knew the connection he had with Melissa, even when she was a full-blown junkie. Craig loved Melissa like nobody he had ever loved before. His heart felt like it had just been ripped out, and he could not bear the thought of never seeing or touching her again. Craig had always dreamed of a future with her, but that was over. It would never happen, they would never be, and at that moment he felt dead inside. Wanting to change the way he felt, he went to find more drugs to snap him out of this reality.

Megan had to find out what was going on, and with Craig and Kelly not talking, she went over to Tony's apartment to find out exactly what happened. Arriving at Tony's apartment on the pretense of purchasing cocaine to take over to Craig and Kelly's house later that evening, she walked in, gave him the cash, and he handed her two eight balls of cocaine. Tony tried to hurry Megan back out of the house before his girlfriend arrived home because he wanted to keep her completely out of it, but Megan was not going anywhere until she got some information from Tony. When she started to question Tony, he gave her as little information as possible, so she just stayed after him until Tony told her something. She misled Tony into believing that she knew more than she actually did by playing her "loyal best friend" card, hoping Tony would confide the rest of the story to her.

Tony told her she could only stay for a little while, subsequently they both walked into his living room to discuss what was going on at Craig and Kelly's house. After they both sat down, Megan told Tony that she could not believe what Melissa did; hoping Tony would bite. Tony told Megan, "We got everything under control; nobody will find out nothin." Not sure exactly what he was talking about, Megan asked, "How's that? What's the plan?" Tony told Megan their plans of dumping the body and catching the car on fire. Megan sat completely dumb founded. In a matter of seconds it went from mortgage fraud to a dead body, and Megan did her best not to act shocked and further engaged Tony in conversation about Melissa. Tony told Megan that they originally wanted to dump the body somewhere public, but he was afraid that they might get caught. He said they had not finalized their plans, but he thought they might drop her body at a rest stop with a picnic area outside of town, and then go catch the car on fire and leave it there.

Megan asked Tony why they had to catch the car on fire, and he told her because Melissa was leaking out all over the place in the trunk. The wheels were spinning, and in her mind, she thought that Melissa must have been murdered by a knife because Craig and Kelly did not own a gun. Unsure about what had happened to Melissa; she began to question Tony when his cell phone rang at 7:46 p.m. Tony turned to Megan and said that it was Craig on the line, don't make any noise. Megan tried to take in as much as she could from the one-sided conversation. When he answered, Craig reminded him that he had agreed not to talk to anyone; Tony said, "Yeah, absolutely," and motioned for Megan to be quiet. Craig was calling to make sure that their plans were still on for early the next morning, and he said, "Yep!"

Tony confirmed their plans by repeating them back to Craig, but said it would have to be as soon as Tony's girlfriend had gone to sleep, so probably sometime closer to 2:00 or 3:00 a.m. Craig said that would work, and that he would call him later to make sure everything was alright. When Tony hung the phone up with Craig, Megan then knew that Craig and Kelly were involved in something bad, but she knew would have to question Kelly later to get all of the details.

When Tony looked up at Megan, she suggested that they make it look like a rape and murder to throw off an investigation in the case. She said, "It could be a carjacking gone wrong, or a murder or suspicious rape. Just take an outfit from her drawer, and throw her clothes around the car. Then catch the car on fire and take off; just make sure you guys wear gloves and don't leave any finger prints." Tony tried to appease Megan, and nodded his head saying he would pass that idea on to Craig. Megan suggested that Tony call Craig right now with her sitting there, just to see his reaction when Tony mentioned it. Tony really didn't want to call Craig, but at 8:02 p.m., and at Megan's insistence, he mustered up some energy and called.

When Craig answered the phone, Tony mentioned the possibility of making it look like a rape, and Craig said, "Absolutely not!" Craig just wanted to keep things as simple as possible, otherwise in all of the confusion, they would fuck up somewhere down the line. Tony agreed and said he would talk to them later. Tony knew that Craig wanted to stick to the plan, but in the back of his mind, he was hoping that when they drove out there, Craig would forget that Melissa was in the trunk. Tony still thought it would be best to just do it all at once, and torch the car with Melissa's body still in the trunk. But for now his only worry was getting Megan out of the house before his girlfriend got home.

Tony escorted Megan to the front door and told her not to forget the cocaine for Craig and Kelly. He said, "They will need a kick to stay up all night to do this." He really only wanted Craig to be high out of his mind and numbed to everything around him by the cocaine. Combined with an adrenaline rush and shear fear, Tony hoped Craig would forget about Melissa's body in the trunk when they drove out to the desert. When Megan said goodbye, she reassured Tony that she had their back, and would take care of Craig and Kelly. As she pulled out, she immediately called Kelly. To her surprise, Kelly picked up the phone, and without delay, Megan told her that she knew about Melissa. When Kelly tried to find out how she heard, Megan asked if she and Jeremy could stop by. Megan had to get to the bottom of this right away, and Jeremy could keep Craig distracted while she talked to Kelly.

Kelly told Megan they could stop by for a little while, but she did not want Megan to say anything, "Just show up; otherwise, Craig will never go for it." Megan agreed and called her husband to see if he was even up to going over to Craig and Kelly's house. Megan got him to agree after she said they were going over there to celebrate her final day of classes at school; Jeremy was a wild man, and he knew a celebration at Craig and Kelly's house meant a party, so he was all in!

Megan Pierson Foley & Jeremy Foley arrive to help Craig & Kelly

Megan went over to pick up Jeremy, and they made their way over to Craig and Kelly's house between 9:15 and 9:30 p.m. to surprise Craig with a visit. After cleaning the house all day, Kelly had just taken a shower and put her clothes on when the doorbell rang. Even though she knew that they would possibly come over, Kelly was so edgy from the combination of paranoia and drugs that her heart dropped when she heard the doorbell.

Craig, not knowing that somebody was coming over, was completely flustered when he moved the blinds to the side and peeked out the window. Besides the police, Megan and her husband were the last people that he wanted to see at his door. Unfortunately for Craig, he couldn't pretend like they were not home because he peeked out the window next to the door.

Megan saw him then waved; Craig opened the door, and let them in the house. He told Megan that Kelly was upstairs in the shower. The three walked up the stairs and into the office, while Megan rounded the corner to go into Craig and Kelly's master bedroom. Craig and Jeremy stayed back in the office to hang out. When Megan walked into the bathroom she showed Kelly the party favors she bought at Tony's house, and lined up some coke on a mirror. After they both snorted a big fat line out of a dollar bill, they wiped the powder off the mirror and rubbed it on their gums. Megan immediately wanted to know where Melissa was at, and Kelly pointed down and mouthed, "In the garage".

Megan said that they wanted to go see the body, and Kelly asked if Jeremy knew about it too; Megan nodded her head "yes". Megan said that she told him a little bit on the drive over, but he didn't believe her so, "Let's go show him that I was fuckin' right!" Kelly shook her head "no", and said that it would piss Craig off, so Megan laughed and said, "Let's go run downstairs and look when he is in the bathroom." Kelly said, "Well give him a line of coke to snort, and he will have to take a shit in the next five minutes."

First trip to the garage
The girls walked into the office, and the guys had already snorted a line. Craig said that he had to go take a shit, and when he walked into the other room, the girls took off down the stairs with Jeremy walking close behind them. Megan was like a kid at the circus, going to see the side show freak, and she appeared giddy with anticipation at sneaking a peak in the trunk of the Jaguar. That is until they opened the door to the garage, and they walked into the smell now encompassing the entire garage. Kelly told her that she did not know the half of it, and Megan asked her what exactly happened. Kelly said that Melissa collapsed and died this afternoon in her room from a drug overdose.

A light bulb went off in Megan's head, and she said, "Ohhhhhh, that makes sense!" The posing lights were still on, and Megan commented on how handy those were because it was so hard to see in that huge garage. Kelly popped the trunk open and the three stood there staring at the body. They could only stand there for a minute because the smell made them all nauseated; the three buried their noses deep in their sleeves as they gawked at the corpse covered in blankets.

They were all in utter disbelief. The smell was even more horrendous because of all the saturated chemicals from the methamphetamines. Just as soon as they had opened the trunk, they slammed it shut just as fast to quickly returned inside the house before Craig discovered them missing. Kelly asked Megan how good the coke was because she could not feel a thing. Megan said that it was the best, she got it from Tony. Kelly replied, "My tolerance is ridiculous. I have to shoot it up to feel anything. Will you help me out?" Megan said she wanted to do that too, and they went into the upstairs closet to shoot up, and talk more about their predicament.

Megan told Kelly to start from where they left off on the phone, and she wanted Kelly to tell her every single detail. Kelly paused for a minute because she had promised Craig she would not talk about it, but rationalized that Megan already knew "the big parts," so what would it hurt to explain everything that happened? Kelly had kept everything bottled up all day long, and she really needed to talk to someone about it all before she exploded. It seemed like Megan truly cared about her, and she wanted to help her get out of their mess. Craig, however, knew that Megan had an ulterior motive, and only cared about covering her own ass! But Kelly needed a friend right then to get everything off of her chest; someone to give her sound advice on how to handle the situation. But, just like Tony, Megan was not going to give her the advice she needed because she would be implicated a long with everyone else.

Kelly and Megan's Discussion behind Closed Doors
With the closet doors shut, Kelly whispered that it was an accidental overdose, and they could not have done anything to save Melissa. "I don't know what all she took; there were drugs and needles all strung out in her room. When we went in there, she was already dead!" Megan told Kelly that it was a good thing they didn't call 911, and Kelly agreed with tears in her eyes, "We would all be in so much trouble, and she was already dead; it would not have done any good." "Oh, don't cry, you guys did the right thing!" Megan made a sad face, and told Kelly that she was her "best friend;" she was there to "help," so she needed every single detail. They could hear Craig talking to Jeremy, and he asked where the girls were. Jeremy said he thought they went off to "shoot more blow".

Craig walked into the master bedroom, but as soon as he saw the closet door closed, Craig turned back around to place a call to Tony. Craig called Tony at 10:34 p.m. Craig asked Tony, "Bro, you're still helping me tonight, right?" Tony said that he was, and asked what time Craig wanted to meet up. Craig said that Jeremy and Megan were at his house, and as soon as they went home, he would give

Tony a call. After Craig was through with the call, he walked back into the bedroom hoping to hear what the girls were talking about.

Kelly stopped talking when Craig entered the room, but once he walked away, she continued whispering the story again to Megan. Kelly explained that she found Melissa putting her debit card in her purse, and that they got into a huge fight that turned physical. "We screamed at each other, and she denied stealing the debit card. I told her that we were sending her fucking ass back to New Jersey, and Craig never wanted her to come back here again."

Kelly said, "I started beating the shit out of Melissa, and her pussy ass ran downstairs to her room. I kept trying to call Craig to get his ass home, and he was not answering." Megan said, "Oh shit, Craig was not there when all of this happened?' Kelly said, "No, I think he was trying to purposefully stay away. He hates when we fight, and Craig knew it would not be pretty when we were packing her ass and shipping her back to Florida, or wherever the fuck she is from." Kelly then explained that Melissa had stolen the taser gun out of their bedroom, and had it hidden in her bedroom. Kelly said, "After I went down stairs, Melissa came out, whacked out of her mind on drugs, and started chasing me with the taser gun!"

Megan said, "You have got to be fucking kidding me! Where you scared out of your fucking mind?" Kelly said, "I knew she wanted to kill me. She had that look in her eyes; so yes, I was shitting my pants! This bitch has been putting some shit in our drinking glasses. She had been trying to kill me for weeks, and after Melissa found out she was never coming back, she wanted me dead!" Megan said, "I believe it; I heard stories- she wanted you out of the picture for fucking sure!" Kelly said, "Hell yeah, Melissa had this whole fucking thing planned out! She wanted me dead, and was running after me with the taser gun." Megan asked, "So what did you do?" Kelly said that she had to stop to turn and run up the stairs, but when she stopped, Melissa shot her in the back of the leg!

Kelly said, "It was so scary; I just flopped on the ground. I had no control over my body. It was so fucking painful- fucking excruciating. I was momentarily paralyzed, and my life was in her hands. After the shot was over, I felt physically drained, and did not have any energy to get up. I thought this is it, Melissa is about to kill me; but instead, she just stared at me. She had a look of confusion on her face; like she did not know what just happened. She was tweaked out of her fucking mind!"

Craig walked by the closet as the two girls were whispering. Once they realized he was standing there, they changed the subject. When Craig walked away, Megan said, "Oh my god, I am dying; what happened next?" Kelly said that Melissa went into the kitchen, got a bottle of alcohol, walked back to her room, and flipped the fuck out. "She was screaming, hitting the walls, and throwing shit everywhere. Then it was quiet for a while, but a few minutes later she would start back up trashing her room," Kelly said. Megan asked, "Was Craig still not home?" Kelly said, "Nope, he didn't come home until after Melissa overdosed. When he finally came home, he tried to do CPR, but she was fucking dead; it was so fucking disgusting."

Megan wanted to know more, but Kelly said that if she described what Melissa looked like, it would traumatize her for life!" Megan said, "No it won't! Please, I want to see what she looks like; I could not see what she looked like with the blankets over her." Kelly shook her head "no," and the girls proceeded to ingest more cocaine before joining the boys in the office.

Craig liked Jeremy a whole hell of a lot more than he ever liked Megan. He always thought Jeremy was a stand-up guy. So when Jeremy asked Craig what he could do to help, Craig was truly touched. He asked Jeremy what he already knew, and Jeremy told him that he knew something happened to Melissa, but he did not know any specifics. Craig told Jeremy, "M.J. & Kelly have been at each other's throats these last few weeks. Melissa was a meth addict, and she was not capable of having a rational conversation. Any time Kelly confronted M.J., it would escalate from yelling and screaming to slapping and hitting; they were both out of fucking control! Melissa was doing meth 24/7, staying awake for days, going to casinos, and looking for her next score. We gave her money any time she asked, but the amount of money she was blowing through was fucking astronomical. We just knew something was up; we didn't know if she was selling drugs or stealing from us, and it turned out, she was probably doing both. She overdosed, and we didn't know what to do because of all the drugs in the house. I would go to prison man."

Jeremy nodded his head in agreement, and Craig said, "The whole thing fucking thing sucks! We were on the cusp of millions of dollars, with all of these businesses, and then I had to deal with the love/hate relationship between Melissa and Kelly. One minute they were shooting each other up, and the next minute they were smacking each other in the face!" Jeremy asked why they shot each other up, and Craig explained, "Their veins, especially Melissa's, were so hard to find because of all the chemicals they had been shooting into each other. It was just easier for them to find each other's veins, and give the injection to the other."

When the two girls entered the office with the guys, Megan immediately inserted herself into the conversation, and began to ramble on without making any sense. From the blips and pieces that Megan said, it was apparent to Craig that Kelly told her everything when they were in the closet shooting up drugs. Kelly knew how to read Craig, and she could tell what was going through his mind. Kelly told Craig that Megan bought some coke from Tony earlier in the day, and Tony told her what happened already. Craig looked at Kelly and asked, "So you filled her in on the rest?" Kelly said, "No, I just filled her in on the missing pieces of the puzzle- to explain what really happened to Melissa."

Craig shows Megan and Jeremy the Meth in Melissa's Room

Craig had already told Jeremy some bits and pieces, so he decided to just let it go. Megan asked Craig what drugs he thought Melissa overdosed on, and he guessed it was either: blow, meth, heroin, or morphine, or all of the above. Megan said she had never seen meth before, and she asked Craig what it looked like. Craig started to describe it, and then he remembered Melissa had some in a zip lock bag in her bedroom. He told them Melissa still had some in her room, and directed them to go downstairs with him, and he would show it to them. They all went into the living room; Jeremy and Kelly sat on the couch, and Megan sat down on the ground. Craig ran into Melissa's bedroom, grabbed the plastic bag, and returned to the living room to show everybody.

When Craig returned to the living room, he showed everyone what meth looked like, and Megan immediately started asking questions about it. She said that it looked like little chunks of dirty crystals, and Craig said that is why they call it "crystal". Megan asked if meth was something new because she had never seen it before; she had only heard about it in the media. Craig said it had been around for a long time, they actually used it in World War II to keep the troops awake. High doses were given to Japanese Kamikaze pilots before their suicide missions. Jeremy opened the bag to take a closer look at it, and he started to heave because of the rancid odor.

They could not believe that it smelled like that; Craig told them it was made from amphetamines, battery acid, rat poison, "so hell yeah it stinks!" Just imagine shooting that shit in your body every day for five years, and then overdosing on it; that smell was the worst smell anyone could ever possibly imagine. Craig said, "Go open the door to the garage if you want to smell something truly nasty; you will really puke then!" When they reacted to Craig's statement, they all acted like they had not already gone out into the garage to look at the body. Megan jumped up and grabbed Kelly to go to the garage, and Jeremy said, "I'm good, you two can go look without me."

2nd Trip to the Garage
The two girls went back out into the garage to look at Melissa's body. When they opened the trunk, the smell was worse than before. Kelly tried to move the blankets back so Megan could get a look at the corpse, but it was tied together with duct tape. Kelly would need scissors to cut the duct tape off, and neither girl could stomach standing in that garage any longer. The girls rushed back to the door, Megan following behind Kelly. Megan asked Kelly if she wanted her to turn off the posing lights, and Kelly said "No, we might need them later."

Walking through the hall, Kelly said, "Craig doesn't know we already looked at the body, so act surprised when we walk back in." Megan agreed, and as they walked to living room, the girls put on a performance, as they discussed the body in the trunk of the car. It was all for naught however, because when they returned to the living room, the guys were not even there. Thinking the girls would be out in the garage for a while, Craig and Jeremy had gone back upstairs to the office to snort some more lines of coke. The girls figured that was where they had gone, so they sat down on the floor and talked some more about Melissa's overdose. When Megan put her hand on the carpet, she noticed some multi-colored dots on her hands, so she asked Kelly what they were. Kelly said that she didn't know for certain, but noticed the dots when she was vacuuming in Melissa's room earlier in the day.

After about five minutes, the guys came back down the stairs, and Kelly asked Craig what the dots were from. He took a close look at the dots in Megan's hand and said they were called taser dots called AFIDS. He said, "When Melissa shot Kelly in the leg, taser dots went out all over the place in the living room- it's like confetti." Kelly asked Craig why the dots were all over Melissa's room. "I noticed them on the carpet in both the living room, and in Melissa's room when I was vacuuming the house," Kelly said. Craig asked Kelly, "Are you sure they looked like this, multi-colored, hole punched circles? Kelly said that they looked exactly like the dots Megan had in her hand. Craig said that Melissa must have been shooting the taser gun in her room. Kelly said, "I knew she had this planned out! She was practicing shooting the taser in her room. Melissa planned on killing me today!" They all nodded their head, and agreed that must have been what happened; Craig and Kelly then followed Megan into Melissa's room to check it out.

Around Midnight- The Cover-Up
When they walked in, Craig said that Melissa had so much trash in her room; it was probably just something that looked like "taser dots". Kelly got down on her knees, and crawled around until she found one; she was determined to prove Craig wrong. She licked her finger, picked the dot up, and showed it to Craig for him to examine; Craig was shocked, Kelly was right! While Megan had Kelly in Melissa's room, she wanted to talk to her about the papers they found in the lock box. Megan was not sure what Craig knew about the loan, so she told Craig to go find Jeremy because she wanted to show him the dots.

Megan knew that it would not take much to follow the paper trail to her, so she had to get to the bottom of it all as soon as possible. She was not about to lose everything she had, much less go to prison over $20,000 sitting in her bank account. When Craig left the room, Megan immediately asked Kelly about the HELOC papers, and Kelly walked over to pull them out. When she handed the papers to Megan, her face turned white, and she said, "Holy shit!" Craig walked back in the room, and saw the documents in Megan's hand, and Kelly told her that Craig already knew about the fraudulent loan. Craig said they needed to figure out what to do next because he was one hundred percent sure that the police would be searching the house the second they found Melissa's body.

Megan suggested that she take the fraudulent mortgage documents with her to shred, and Craig said they needed to decide what else Megan and Jeremy should take out of their house. Craig said, "We will all be in a shit load of trouble if any of this stuff is left behind!" Craig looked Megan square in the eyes, and said, "That includes you! It is in black and white that you took out a loan on our mortgage, and then took out another loan under the table. It won't take a genius to put that together, and they will be knocking down your door too." Kelly said, "Not only that, but Melissa bought a shitload of morphine from Tony, and if that is found in her system, he could be charged with manslaughter. So we all have to be smart, and figure out what to do next!" They all decided to run upstairs, do a couple of lines, and then they would be ready to hammer out the final details.

With the realization that Megan could be facing a little jail time of her own, she suddenly shifted from nosey to desperate; and she was not leaving that house until everyone knew exactly what their role was to be after they dumped Melissa's body. Megan said that if the police started questioning Craig and Kelly, she and Jeremy would tell the police that they also saw Melissa overdose. Craig said not to do that because if they started making stories up, nobody would say the right thing. Craig said, "If, and that is a big if, you are questioned, just say that you don't know anything. We are going to play dumb too; but if the cover is blown, make sure they know that you saw the body after she overdosed. That way we have a witness that it was an overdose."

Both Megan and Jeremy shook their head in agreement, and Craig said, "I will say I walked in while Melissa was tasering Kelly, and threw Melissa off of Kelly. I could see the police turning it around on Kelly, and I don't want that to happen!"

Megan suggested mentioning that Melissa's body was in the front seat of the car, instead of the trunk, and Craig actually thought that was a good idea. However, they would all have to say the same thing, and nobody could change their story. Craig said, "If we don't, we will all be fucked on conspiracy charges, and Kelly could be charged with murder! I feel like this is all my entire fault because Kelly wanted to call the police after M.J. overdosed, and I wouldn't let her do it. I am not going to let my wife take the fall for something she did not do, period!" Megan and Jeremy both agreed. At that point, they just needed to decide what Jeremy and Megan would take out of the house before the police arrived. Craig said that he was not allowed to have drugs or weapons in the house; he said he did not have any weapons, so they needed to go around and find all of the drugs. Megan asked if the stun gun was considered a weapon; Craig assumed that it was, so he ran upstairs to get the "weapon" and grabbed a black Nike bag for them to place everything in.

While he was upstairs, Kelly got a leather sap out of Craig's truck that he had never used, but would still be considered a weapon. Craig came down and told her that was a good idea, and other than the taser and sap, they were fairly certain there were no other "weapons" in their home. They left all of the drugs Melissa had in her room, so when the police came, they could see everything she had used.

The rest of the drugs, all over the house, would be a problem however; so they walked around and picked it all up, and placed it in the black Nike bag. After they had everything together, it was about time for Jeremy and Megan to go home. Craig double checked the bag and noticed the HELOC papers were in there; he was glad that Megan did not forget that; he nearly did. Megan said that she would get rid of "it" first thing in the morning, and Craig and Kelly walked them to the door. For the first time ever, Craig felt like he could actually trust Megan, maybe she was not as selfish as he thought. The guys shook hands and the girls hugged; Craig said they would be in contact in a few days; but they would need to lay low until after the start of an investigation, if there ever was an investigation.

Wednesday early morning, December 14th
Megan and Jeremy leave with gym bag & Craig calls Tony

At 2:31 a.m. Craig called Tony and told him that Megan and Jeremy were gone; and Tony said that he was already driving over to their house. He was about to pull in and buy a beer at Green Point Grocery, and he would be at their house in a few minutes. Craig called him back, and asked if he brought the lighter fluid from his house, and Tony said that he forgot; but he told Craig that he would buy some at the convenience store when he went inside.

When Tony walked into Craig and Kelly's house ten minutes later, he said, "I have good news and bad news, what do you want first? Craig said, "The bad news," and Tony told them that they didn't sell lighter fluid at Green Point. Craig asked, "Okay what's the good news?" Tony showed him the blow in his hand, and they agreed to sit for a minute, snort a few lines, and decide what to do next. Tony took his "Visa Pay-As-You- Go" card out, and chopped it up as fast as possible on their living room table. Tony wanted to get Craig "fucked up on drugs," so he made him a "fat-ass line" of coke that was equivalent to four normal lines. When Craig saw the line, he said, "What the fuck man?" And Tony said, "We are going to need it!" Tony rolled up a dollar bill, and Craig snorted the line after about ten tries. When he cleared his line, he laid his head back, and enjoyed the numbing feeling of the drip, while Tony and Kelly both snorted a line a piece.

After a few minutes, they discussed their plans. Craig suggested that they all go to Wal-Mart, and Kelly could go in and buy the lighter fluid and then they could all take off. Tony told him that he still needed to fill up his gas can; but he could meet them there after he filled up. They agreed that would work best, and decided it was now or never; if they were going to get this thing done before the sun came up, they needed to leave right away.

Craig had one more idea before they left, he said, "We should move Melissa's body to the back of your truck. That would make it easier to get her out in a hurry, and we wouldn't have to stop and open the trunk." Tony didn't think that was a great idea because someone might see her body in the back of his truck. Craig told him that nobody would be able to see her, and it would be easier to dump her at the rest area, without having to lift the trunk. He said, "We would look pretty fucking suspicious, pulling the car over, opening the trunk, and pulling out her heavy body; if somebody saw us, we would be over." Tony reluctantly agreed, and they all walked out to the garage so Tony could pull his truck in; but as soon as they entered the garage, it smelled so bad, they both agreed to just leave her in the trunk.

Wal-Mart

When Craig pulled out, he decided to leave the garage doors open to air the shit-smell out, then he drove on down the road to Wal-Mart. Tony stayed at the house for about five minutes, digging through his truck, trying to find a pack of cigarettes. There was no way he could do this without his cigarettes. He looked everywhere with his flashlight, but he could not find them anywhere. Tony thought, "Fuck it, I will just buy another pack"; but short on funds, he needed to stop at Green Valley Grocery again because they sold the cheapest cigarettes around. Tony drove back to the convenience store and purchased a pack of Marlboro lights.

As he walked back to his truck, he opened the pack to light one up, but he couldn't find his lighter. He grabbed his pants out of habit, but realized he had on pajama bottoms without a pocket. He felt in the pockets of his leather jacket, and found the lighter. After he lit the cigarette, he consciously made an effort to put the lighter right back into his jacket pocket. Tony had never been officially diagnosed with Attention Deficit Disorder, but according to all of his friends, he definitely had it. Because of this "disorder," Tony made a mental note of where he put his lighter, or he would forget and lose it. He thought that would suck to drive all the way out there, and not be able to find the fucking cigarette lighter. Tony started the truck, and drove over to the Shell Gas Station. Once he was there, he had to sit for a few more minutes while he finished his cigarette.

On the drive over to Wal-Mart Craig was trying to calm Kelly down so that she did not rouse anyone's suspicions. When Kelly asked him how many bottles of lighter fluid to purchase, he was not sure because he had never done anything like this before. Craig tried to call Tony to ask him, but he had left his phone in the truck when he went inside the store to buy cigarettes. Not knowing for sure and not wanting to be short, Craig told Kelly to buy as many bottles as they had. Craig told her to buy something to go with it too, so that she did not look suspicious.

After they pulled up, Craig realized he left his wallet back at the house so he asked Kelly if she had any cash in her purse. When she fumbled through to check; she found nothing but the Wells Fargo debit card that Melissa put back in her purse before the altercation. She began to panic, what if Melissa drained this card, and there was no money in her account; she would just hold her breath and keep her fingers crossed. It would have to work because Craig was pulling into the Wal-Mart parking lot by then.

With little to no thought put into what they were doing, Craig dropped Kelly at the entrance, and the security cameras captured Kelly walking in the doors around 3:23 a.m. As she walked down the aisle, "Here Comes Santa Claus" was playing in the background. She followed the signs above her head to the "Lawn & Garden" section located on the east side of Wal-Mart. Being the month of December and Wal-Mart making room for Christmas, there wasn't much to choose from.

Kelly snatched every bottle she could find along with a barbeque tool set as she was instructed, and walked up to the front to check out. According to the sale's receipt, Kelly paid for the items at 3:31 a.m. using her Wells Fargo Visa Debit Credit # xxxx xxxx xxxx 2015 with her name, Kelly A. Ryan on the front of the card.

At 3:35 a.m. surveillance showed Craig pull the jaguar to the front of Wal-Mart; Craig jumped out of the driver's side door, and opened the back door and then loaded the bags that Kelly had just purchased into the car. Craig called Tony as he started to drive around the parking lot to find him, but Tony said that he was still putting gas in the gas can. Craig said, "What the fuck is taking you so long? We will be over there in a second."

At 3:37 a.m. Craig and Kelly pulled out of the Wal-Mart exit, drove down the street, and then pulled into the Shell Gas Station to wait on Tony. At 3:38 am surveillance cameras recorded Tony at the Shell Short Line Express, wearing pajama bottoms and a leather jacket, paying the attendant for his gas.

According to the receipts, Tony put $2.66 in a gas can; Tony put the gas can in the bed of his truck. Then at 3:41 a.m. surveillance cameras showed Tony's truck pull out of the exit, followed by Craig and Kelly's Jaguar. Tony was clearly leading Craig out of the parking lot and to the location in the desert to dispose of the jaguar. (Tony would also deny, and maintain until the end, that he had no idea what they were doing, claiming to just follow along to give his friends a ride.)

Tony filled up a gas can; Craig & Kelly follow Tony Gross out to desert

Nothing made sense anymore, and the situation was so out of control, Craig and Kelly were scared out of their minds; the entire nightmare seemed like a complete mind fuck. Everyone was numb, and the following thirty minutes felt like an out-of-body experience. Craig and Kelly followed Tony out to the desert, and once they were on Blue Diamond Road, at 3:46 a.m., Tony called Craig on his cell phone. Tony hoped that Craig was so wired that he had forgotten that Melissa was in the trunk. He told him the exact location where they were going to catch the car on fire.

Craig was right on Tony's tail because he was unfamiliar with the area, and did not want to lose Tony on the drive out there. Tony told Craig that when they pulled over, he would turn his truck around, and jump out to help him destroy the car. When they hung up, Tony was relieved that Craig never mentioned dropping Melissa's body out first. Tony's plan seemed to work. Craig was so amped up on drugs and scared out of his mind, he completely forgot the body was in the trunk of the car. En route, it appeared that there was not a car in sight, until all of a sudden they found themselves right behind an 18-wheeler that was headed in the same direction. Driving over 100 mph, there was no time to hit the brakes and slow down so the truck and Jaguar blew right past the 18-wheeler. According to the trucker, it appeared as if the vehicles were only inches apart. They were so close together, the trucker thought they were attached to each other with a rope.

At 3:56 a.m. Tony called Craig and told him they were about to pull over on Sandy Valley Road; He said it was at Road Marker 21. Tony started to slow down, put on his blinker, and pulled onto the dirt road. Craig followed close behind, plowing down the dirt road. Craig could not see a fucking thing ahead of him because Tony's truck was kicking up so much dirt in the air; it looked as if there was already a fire in the desert.

After a few minutes, Tony finally slowed down and came to a complete stop and motioned for Craig to stop. Tony made a U-turn in his truck, and stopped parallel with the Jaguar. Kelly jumped out of the car and got over on the passenger side of Tony's truck. Tony then moved the truck up and away from the jaguar, and turned it to face the highway. Craig pulled the car forward about 100 yards, and while he waited on Tony, he opened the bottles of lighter fluid and started pouring them all over the jaguar.

Tony & Craig catch the car on fire

Tony grabbed his flash light from the console, and the gas can from the back of his truck, and sprinted over to help Craig. Tony placed the flashlight on the car's bumper, and then poured out all of the gasoline on the car. Craig was dumping his last bottle out when Tony pulled the lighter out of his coat pocket, and ignited the fire; and in a split second, the car was engulfed in flames. Everything was moving so fast, Craig had forgotten that Melissa's body was in the trunk of the car. As the flames began to devour the car, Craig screamed, "Oh fuck, Melissa!" Craig ran over to the trunk, and tried to pry it open, but it was too hot, and too late! Tony grabbed Craig and pulled him back yelling, "We gotta go! It's going to blow up! Let's go! Let's go! Let's go!" They ran back to the truck, and Craig was still trying to get in the back seat when Tony slammed his foot on the pedal and floored the gas. The tires spun for a few seconds without moving forward, and then it raced forward on the Sandy Valley road, leaving their friend behind in the dust and fire.

SWIFT INJUSTICE

It was difficult to see the highway ahead of them when Tony's truck hit something that felt like pot holes, but it was actually the drop off from the highway. Tony jerked the wheel, and almost flipped the truck over, then hit the gas again when he was back on the road. The eighteen-wheeler that they passed on their way to the desert was now driving past them in the opposite direction. The truck driver just saw huge flames appear out of nowhere, and then he noticed what appeared to be the same truck that passed him earlier, speed by him again, only this time it was driving in the opposite direction. Doing his best to see through the cloud storm of dust, the trucker slowed down and called 911 Emergency and reported a brush fire just outside of the Las Vegas city limits. Dispatch transferred the call to the Mountain Springs Fire Department.

Craig and Kelly watched the glow from the fire over their shoulder as they rode with Tony down the highway. Once it had completely disappeared, they turned back around, and Craig blurted out, "What the fuck man?" He yelled, "M.J. was in the goddamn trunk! Why did you light the car before I pulled her out?" Tony replied, "What's done is done; I fucking forgot- I am sorry brah!" Craig hit the dashboard and yelled, "Fuck! What now?" Tony told him that the plans would not change, but they might need to recalculate a few things. Craig said the important thing was to be consistent, and he and Tony revised the plan on the way back to Vegas.

After Craig calmed himself down and thought for a minute, he said, "Okay, Megan and Jeremy were at our house until 2:30 in the morning, and we thought Melissa was on the plane. We go to bed, and Joey starts barking so Kelly gets up to take her out. When Kelly walks through the garage, she notices that her car is missing. Kelly runs upstairs to tell me the car is gone, and I get out of bed to go look in the garage for myself, and I see that it is missing. We called the cops and," Tony interrupted Craig and said, "No man, don't blow the whistle for no reason. They may never fucking see the car out here; they never found my fucking truck! Just send Melissa a text asking about the car, and show that to the cops if they do find the car." Craig thought this was a great idea, and he sent a text to Melissa's phone at 4:28 a.m. that said, "Where the fuck is my car?" Tony said, "She took your car all the time without permission. Just act surprised, and make them think you were out looking for it."

As Tony pulled into Craig's subdivision, he tried to reassure Craig that it was all better this way. But as they were all coming down from the massive amount of cocaine they had all ingested hours before, they sat in silence; they all knew it wasn't better this way. Tony pulled up to the house, and Craig told Tony that he needed to call Megan and Jeremy. "Tell them what happened, and that we had to change the plans. Make sure they know that we are all saying that we don't know where Melissa went with the car. If that doesn't work, then go to plan B, they saw Melissa overdosed in the car," Craig said.

Tony seemed confused trying to sort all of the new details out, but tried to sound confidant when he said, "Dude, it's all cool, I got your back." He gave Craig a dime bag of cocaine, and said, "Snort this after you get some sleep, you have got to be fucking exhausted! Don't fucking worry about a thing, you got friends behind you." Feeling less than secure about the friends that had his back, Craig nodded, and said, "Thanks, bro." Craig and Kelly got out of the truck, and walked up to the house knowing Melissa was gone, and nothing would ever be the same again.

CHAPTER 8

From Dusk 'til Dawn

The Chaos all around on Wednesday morning, December 14th

The Fire Chief of the Mountain Springs Volunteer Fire Department, Dick Draper, was dispatched around 4:30 in the morning to a reported brush fire at the Mountain Springs Mile Marker 28. Draper immediately responded with his quick attack unit to a fire in the desert just a half a mile south of Sandy Valley, a small town outside of Las Vegas.

When Draper arrived on the scene, it was apparent that it was more than a small brush fire. There was a vehicle engulfed in flames, and Draper ran over to make sure there was nobody inside of the car. When he realized there was no one in the car or around the car, he assumed it was more likely than not arson. This was familiar territory for Draper because he was called out at least ten times a year to put these types of fires out; the owners would typically set the cars on fire to collect the insurance money. With 300 gallons of water and foam, Draper put out the volatile flames that had reached over 1,200 degrees Fahrenheit.

While Draper sprayed the car with one last coat of foam, Melissa James' mother, Maura, arrived at the airport to pick her daughter up at the baggage claim, in New Jersey. Maura had just married, and had only lived in New Jersey for a short time with her new husband. She was still having a hard time finding her way around town on the busy interstates. After driving thirty minutes out of her way, she was relieved to finally see a road sign with an arrow pointing ahead that read "Newark International Airport". Maura pulled into the short-term parking and became flustered driving around for another 15 minutes trying to find a parking space during the holiday season.

After she found a spot, Maura jumped out of her car and hurriedly walked her way towards the baggage claim area where she had arranged the day before to meet Melissa. Once inside, Melissa's mother looked for her daughter, hoping she would not be disappointed that she was nearly an hour late; scanning the baggage claim area, Melissa was nowhere to be found. Maura walked back outside to see if maybe Melissa already had her bags and was smoking a cigarette in front of the airport.

Melissa's mother walked all around the front of the airport, and still could not find Melissa. She sat on a bench and tried to call Melissa's cell phone, but it went straight to voicemail. Thinking that maybe her flight had been delayed or even canceled, Maura walked over to the ticket counter and asked the Delta Representative about her daughter's flight. The representative typed the flight information into the computer, and told Maura that the flight actually arrived early; an hour and a half ago.

Maura James had always been a level headed woman, calm and cool under pressure. When she learned that her flight landed earlier, and Melissa was nowhere to be found, she was certain that Melissa was already in New Jersey, and she just needed to locate her. Her only worry at this point was that Melissa's cell phone was not charged; it was an eight-hour flight after all, and this would make it even more difficult to find her.

The Delta representative typed in Melissa's name in the computer, and told her that Melissa never got on the flight; it was at this point that Melissa's mom started to become apprehensive about the situation, and wondered, "What in the hell is going on?" Maura James asked the man at the counter if he could have Melissa's name announced over the p.a. system, and tell her to come to baggage claim; he was certain that she was not in the airport, but made the announcement because he felt sorry for this mother trying to locate her child. Melissa's name was announced three times over the next fifteen minutes, and while her mother waited to see if she would show up, she repeatedly texted and called Melissa's phone, leaving message after message.

Melissa James' mother wanted to call Craig and Kelly, but did not have their numbers in her phone; she had them written down somewhere back at the office. Contacting them would be her next best bet to get into contact with her daughter, so she decided to drive back to her office and give them a call. Walking back to her car, she tried to convince herself that nothing was wrong; there had to be an explanation for her daughter missing that flight. When she got to the car, she got in and took a deep breath; she decided to double check the flight information that Melissa gave her the day before, hoping maybe she misread a time or date. When she double-checked the information, she realized that there had been no mistake, the flight information was correct.

Meanwhile, back in Vegas, Tony Gross dropped Craig and Kelly off in front of their house on Adobe Arch Court. As they walked inside, they didn't say a word to each other; their silence took on a language of itself. Both Craig and Kelly looked like zombies, dazed with pale skin and black circles under their eyes, walking through the house in slow motion; dehydrated all while craving another dope fix. Seemingly unaware of what was going on around them, they staggered through the motions; but in reality, they felt completely dead inside. Heartbroken because of Melissa's overdose, and horrified by what they had done to cover it up, neither Craig nor Kelly knew what to do next. All they could do was rehearse what they were going to tell the police when they came knocking on Craig and Kelly's front door.

Back in the desert, Dick Draper noticed something strange inside the car. There was a spot in the back seat of the car that continued to burn and billowed black smoke even after he sprayed the area with water and foam. Draper repeatedly sprayed the area, but he could not put it out. Draper went back to the truck, and retrieved a flashlight and a pike pole to stir the ashes and see what was causing this reaction to the water. With a flash light, he saw a suitcase and a barbeque set in the back seat. This seemed odd, because normally when people burn their cars to collect insurance money, they don't leave valuables behind. After he poked around, and looked closer with his flashlight, Draper realized that it was actually the charred remains of a human body. Draper had never seen this before in his forty plus years with the fire department. Startled, he dropped the pole, ran back to his truck, and notified Metro about a possible homicide.

At 5:21 a.m., the Las Vegas Metropolitan Police Department was notified that the Mountain Springs Volunteer Fire Department, under the jurisdiction of the Clark County Fire Department, had responded to a vehicle fire reported on Sandy Valley Road, south of State Route 160. Upon extinguishing the fire, the burned remains of an unidentified person, was discovered in the trunk area of the burned vehicle, a 2003 Jaguar, four-door, X-Type with Nevada License plates 269-PPL.

Driving back to her office in New Jersey, Maura James's "calm, cool and collected" mindset began to shift, and she started to become worried about her daughter's well-being as she was struck with the feeling of helplessness because her daughter was thousands of miles away. After she tried to call Melissa over and over, and her phone went straight to voicemail every time, she debated calling the Las Vegas police department. Maura didn't want to over react, but she didn't want to under-react either. It was a double-edged sword: her daughter had warrants out for her arrest, and calling the police might make Melissa's situation worse; but at the same time, she wanted to make sure that her daughter was safe. If nothing else, they could at least go check on her. Maura pulled up in front of her office; not knowing what to do next, images of her beautiful, brown haired, blue-eyed little girl were flashing in her mind. She hit the steering wheel, and with tears rolled down her face she yelled, "Where are you at Melissa?"

Back at Craig and Kelly's house, Kelly dropped her purse by the front door, and walked upstairs to lie down, while Craig walked around, eyes glazed over, aimlessly picking up the house. He walked into Melissa's room, and moved Melissa's Crystal Meth and some other white shit that belonged to her out in the open. He walked back into the living room and pulled out Kelly's Wells Fargo card that Melissa had been using; hoping that the investigators would investigate and see how much money she had stolen from them. This would end up biting Craig in the ass because he was not remembering that Kelly had used that exact same card at Wal-Mart.

Craig then looked around the room, and thought, "What in the hell am I doing? It doesn't matter, we are so fucked." It had been several hours since Craig had taken any drugs, and he felt like he was having hallucinations of reality; a state of mind where things seemed real yet surreal all at the same time. The reality of everything hit him all at once when he looked over and saw Melissa's stuffed animal that she slept with every night, and Craig began to sob hysterically. Craig wiped his nose with his sleeve, and the smell of the fucking over dose was saturated into his clothes; Craig ran into the bathroom to throw-up.

On Sandy Valley Road, the scene of the crime, first responders began to pour in, starting at 5:30 am. One of the officers present was Metro police officer Jeff Hodgekins. As Officer Hodgekins marked the crime scene off with tape, Mark Passalaqua, a Clark County Fire Investigator, pulled up and started investigating the car. He quickly determined the fire was arson because it was started with an accelerant.

With a body in the trunk, and the fire ruled an arson, the Metro police officer notified Homicide Sergeant Rocky Alby, and briefed him on the findings that they had accumulated to that point. Alby notified the homicide detective on duty, Dean O'Kelley, about the crime. O'Kelley was on rotation to be the lead detective, so he was the first detective to arrive on the scene.

After 7 a.m., the other homicide detectives assigned to the case, Robert Wilson, Cliff Mogg, and Ken Hardy, arrived on the scene and began examining all of the potential evidence. Waiting on the CSI team to arrive so they could open the trunk, Detective O'Kelley turned to his partner and said that whoever had done this, "their objective was not to destroy the vehicle, but to destroy that body in the trunk." From the very beginning, the detectives made up their minds that they were not looking for an arsonist, but a murderer.

Crime scene analysts Jessie Sams and Marnie Carter pulled up behind all of the fire trucks and police cars. One with a note pad, and the other with a camera, they attempted to collect every piece of evidence to help the investigators solve the crime, while making sure that everything was processed and preserved without tainting any evidence.

The first pieces of evidence the crime scene analyst noted was located just outside of the car, a few feet away from the vehicle. A flashlight with initials written with a black sharpie across the side, and an empty beer can were collected, photographed, and dusted for finger prints. (These two items would prove significant later in the investigation because they both belonged to Tony Gross.) Next the CSA team examined the tire marks and footprints around the car. Because the area was soaked by the fire truck prior to the CSA team arriving, they were not able to pull up tire or shoe impressions with a mold. They were however able to determine that there were two different sets of footprints all around the car. In the back seat of the car were the remains of a suitcase along with what appeared to be women's clothing. This led the CSA team to believe that the owner of the bag was a female who was possibly going on some sort of extended trip.

The detectives ran a check on the partial plates they found, and it came back as a match. The Motor Vehicle Department found that the 2003 Jaguar belonged to Las Vegas resident Kelly Ann Ryan. Born on 05/10/1972, Kelly Ryan lived about twenty miles away at the address 9539 Adobe Arch Court. The detectives were anxious to go find out if the owner of the car was the body in the trunk. Before they left to go interview the residents on Adobe Arch Court, the crime scene investigators needed help prying the trunk open. With rubber gloves on their hands, the detectives pried the trunk open with a crow bar, and took a step back as they lifted it up to a horrific scene.

The graphic image of the charred remains sent the hardened veterans to their knees. They all tried to regain their composure without getting physically ill. A few of the workers had to walk away, but the crime scene analysts, with a stoic professionalism, kept their eyes focused, and documented everything that they were witnessing as they processed the scene.

The burned remains appeared to represent the physical size of a small person as indicated by the length of the remaining torso, legs, and small rib cage. Although the head of the victim was covered with what appeared to be a blanket, reddish brown hair was visible on the back side of her head. Pieces of the victim's clothing, a blue hooded sweater, denim jeans, along with items of jewelry, led the analysts to believe it was a young female victim.

Meanwhile, back at the house, Craig Titus ran to the bath room, flipping open the lid to the toilet with such force that it smashed up, down, and back up again, creating a loud boom that echoed throughout the house. Craig became hysterical, as he began sobbing uncontrollably for Melissa; his head was pounding and his face looked as if it was about to explode.

Craig ripped his shirt off in an attempt to distance himself from the stench of death, but it penetrated well beneath the skin. Craig's body tensed up as he began to continuously dry heave; and then all at once, everything came pouring out, as he violently vomited all over the bath room. Craig didn't have the energy to pick up a towel and wipe the mixture of mucous and puke that was all over his face, so he made his way over to the sink to wash it off.

Craig felt like he was about to pass out when he finally made it over to the sink. He grabbed the edge of it with clinched fists, holding on so tight that his arms began to tremble. Paranoia crept in his mind, and he feared that if he let go of the sink he would fall down, and his life would be over. His feet began to go numb, and the sensation of prickling pins shot from his toes up through his legs and torso; his body was paralyzed in fear as he stared in the mirror with a black void in his eyes.

Forcing himself to take his next breath, he no longer had a desire to live, but his body instinctively forced the air down his throat. The air, an odorless, tasteless gas that was necessary for the existence of life, was too much for Craig to swallow. His hands were now completely saturated with sweat, and he began to lose his grip on both the sink and reality. Craig's heart was erratically thumping; his chest sounded like a steel hollow trash can being pounded on with a tire iron. Each thump sent a jolt of ricochets through every nerve of his body, throbbing to the beat of the blaring synthesizers of a hardcore metal band.

Craig's eyes' focused and shifted from his hands to his forearms. The tattoos on his skin seemed to come alive. Each line of ink, in every pore of his skin, was smeared with cruel epithets. From the school yard play ground, being the last one picked because he was too small, to the punk-ass bitches in the prison cell of his mind; every line told a story. He felt every piece of shit parasite that ever pretended to be his friend had sucked the blood out of his entire body, drop by fucking drop! The walls in the bathroom began to close in on Craig, and he realized that once again, he was all alone.

In the confines of the four walls surrounding him, there was nowhere to turn; all he had was the reflection in the mirror. When Craig looked up and saw his image staring him back in the face, he began to realize that he was not in fact alone. Far worse than any nightmare, when he stared into his eyes, he imagined Melissa staring back at him. Her blue eyes tormented him as they screamed at Craig to save her from the self-inflicted prison and death sentence of methamphetamines and heroin. Craig began to sob again and hit the bathroom wall with his fist yelling, "Why, Melissa? Why, Melissa? Why, Melissa?" Craig questioned himself, "How could I have prevented all this? Why didn't I stop her from shooting those drugs into her arms?" There was nothing he could have done. How could Craig stop Melissa from shooting drugs in her arms when he had needles of a different drug sticking out of his own arms? It was so fucked up! Everything was fucked up; Craig was fucked, Kelly was fucked, they were all fucked now!

Sitting in her car, Maura James struggled to gather her composure before she walked inside her office. She wiped the tears from her eyes, and tried to relax by taking long deep breaths; she told herself that there must be a logical explanation for all of this. She traced back the last few interactions with Melissa in her mind hoping to jar something in her memory. Melissa had done things like this before, but this time was different, and her Mother had a bad feeling about it. Two days prior to Maura picking up Melissa at the airport, she remembered that her daughter seemed flat and emotionally removed from their conversation.

In the past, when Melissa talked about Las Vegas and her friendship with Craig and Kelly, she always had a sparkle in her voice. A perhaps unrealistic dream of becoming successful, and finally finding her niche in life, whether it was modeling, dancing, or this last time, prospectively becoming the manager of Craig and Kelly's new product line with Ice Gear.

In her last conversation with Melissa, the spark was gone, and she seemed completely void of emotion. A despondent Melissa told her mother that she didn't think she was coming back to Vegas, and when her mother asked her why, Melissa spaced out, and cut the conversation short. Later that evening when they spoke on the phone again, Maura asked Melissa why she was in a hotel room, and Melissa said that Kelly was flipping out and acting crazy. When her mother tried to talk to Melissa about it, her daughter did not want to go into too much detail. Maura believed that Melissa was excited to be coming home, and was perhaps a little homesick.

Craig Titus walked up the stairs at his house, and took a shower. After he put some clothes on, he laid down with Kelly as she slept. His mind was now somewhat clear of drugs, and he was able to face reality for the first time in 24 hours. Craig put his body next to Kelly's body, and rubbed his fingers through her hair. Staring at the side of her face, Craig knew that everything was over. He began to mentally beat himself up as he thought back over the last twenty-four hours; He asked himself, "Why didn't I just listen to Kelly? It would have been bad, but not this bad." When Melissa overdosed, Kelly wanted to call the police; she begged him in fact, but he didn't listen. He thought, "How could I have been such a fucking idiot?"

Running his fingers through Kelly's hair, tears ran down his face. Craig wished he could go back in time to call 911; nothing would have saved Melissa's life, but had he called, maybe he could have saved Kelly. Craig knew how the law worked, and he knew Kelly would be facing Manslaughter once everything came to light. She had never been in trouble with the law before, and she had no clue what was about to happen next. All Craig could think about was how to save his wife from prison. It never crossed his mind that he would be implicated in anything other than a conspiracy to cover-up an alleged crime.

In Maura James' last conversation with her daughter, Melissa seemed more upbeat, but distracted by the atmosphere. Melissa was at Kentucky Fried Chicken, and she was in line ordering lunch. Maura remembered that Melissa was with someone else because she asked that person if they wanted something to eat. Her mother thought she heard a man's voice answer Melissa at the restaurant; was it Craig Titus' voice, she wondered? "No," she thought, "it couldn't be." Craig has a loud raspy voice, and the man's voice on the other side was not as deep, and may have even had an accent of some kind.

But if not Craig Titus, who was Melissa talking to the restaurant? The last words her mother heard Melissa say was that she had to go because she was ordering food. Melissa said she would call her mom back later; and of course, Melissa never did. This was the last time her mother would ever hear her daughter's voice again.

Craig rolled over from his side to his stomach, put his elbows on the bed, and covered his face with his hands. Kelly opened her eyes, and looked over at Craig, and she asked him if he was okay. Craig said, "Not really! Ya know, our lives as we know it are over; we are in so much fucking trouble. The police are going to be here any minute wanting to know why our car is burning out in the fucking desert with a goddamn body in the trunk! They are going to accuse you of murder, I fucking know it!"

Kelly said, "I did not murder her; when they do a toxicology report they will see that." Craig said, "They will see what they want to see, and conclude what they want to conclude; and I fucking guarantee you, we will go to prison." Kelly said, "But we have a plan! We are going to deny everything." Craig said, "They are not going to believe that Melissa accidentally died in the trunk of our car. That will just buy us time. We need a back- up plan, an air-tight back-up plan." Kelly said, "We came up with a back-up plan with Megan and Jeremy. They are going to say they saw Melissa overdosed in the car." Craig said, "We need more, or I guarantee you, you are looking at a life sentence for Melissa's overdose."

Craig thought for a minute, and said, "Let's make a pact. I am going to say I came home and Melissa was attacking you, and I pulled her off. She then went in her bedroom, and we found her overdosed. We have to say I was there, or you will go to prison for life! If all else fails, we have to stick to that- I was there with you. Got it- I was fucking in the house when all this shit went down!" Kelly said, "Phone records will prove you were not there!" Craig said, "Maybe not! But I want you to know, you have my word. I will not let them take you down, and I will confess to the end that I was in the house with you."

Craig began to cry, he knew where he was when all of this happened. He was riddled with shame; he was fucking a girl in a hotel room when all this happened. He knew the girls had been fighting all week, and chose to stay away. He should have manned up; had he been at the house, none of this would have ever happened. Craig told Kelly, "I feel so fucking guilty; you wanted to call the police, and I would not let you. I am not letting you go to jail for any of this; I will take the fall. But you have to promise me, you will not tell a living soul that I was not in the house when M.J. overdosed."

Kelly nodded her head, and said, "I love you so much!" Craig held his wife, and said, "You have no idea how much I love you. Everything is going to be okay; you just have to trust me. Let's rehearse what we are going to say to the police until they get here." Kelly said, "I just want us to lay here and hold each other for a little while, and then we can do what we need to do to get ready for the police." Craig agreed, and the two lay in bed for what felt like eternity, but was actually a couple of hours.

They got up to rehearse what they would say to the police. Craig told her that after the police came, he would talk to Schwimmer about what they needed to do next. Craig said, "I am going to be honest with him, and tell him everything, with the exception of the little fib about me being at the house. He has lawyers, and he will get us the best!" They were both wiped out, and needed to snort some lines before they finished up around the house. Craig pulled out the blow that Tony gave him, and after a couple of hits, they lay in bed for twenty minutes and rehearsed their lines, then they picked up the house and packed their bags. They were ready to go.

CHAPTER 9

Identifying Melissa

At 10:05 a.m., LVMPD Sergeant Rocky Alba notified the Clark County Coroner's office of a death that had occurred on Sandy Valley Road, 3 miles north of SR160 with an apparent homicide/decedent found in the trunk of a burned up vehicle. The Coroner Investigator, Richard C. Jones' summary of the investigation:

"**Circumstances of Death:** A fire was reported on 12/14/2005 at 0440 hours on Sandy Valley Road near SR 160 in rural Clark County. The Clark County Fire Department responded and extinguished a fire. While searching the vehicle a burned body was found in the trunk of the vehicle. LVMPD Homicide Personnel were contacted and responded at 0630 hours. I pronounced death at 1115 hours. **Body:** I viewed a charred human body lying partially supine in a burned out vehicle trunk. Material was found wrapped around the decedent's head covering the face. The material was soot burned, but did not appear to be burned all the way through. There were remnants of some clothes on the posterior area of the body. The fingers were mostly burned off. A small ring was noted on the left little finger. Two bracelets were noted to the left wrist. There was no rigor mortis perceptible. There were no life signs present, and I pronounced death at 1115 hours. Nevada Funeral Services responded per rotation and the decedent was removed from the vehicle and placed on a new sheet provided by LVMPD and was secured into a body bag using Coroner Seal #550328. The decedent was transported to the Clark

County Coroner's Office at 1130 hours and arrived at the CCCO at 1220 hours."

The Medical Examiner

The body was wrapped in three different blankets. The first blanket appeared to be fleece, the second had tiger print, and the third was a cotton fabric with square patterns. The examiner noticed that the body was folded up in an unusual way. Lying on her side, with her head on the passenger side of the car, her knees were bent, and her feet were on the driver's side. They noticed her left arm was bent underneath her body. There were wires all around the victim, none of which seemed to be ligatures, rather wires that had fallen off the car during the fire. Pictures were taken and notes were written, but they didn't want to disturb the body too much until they had the assistance of the coroner's office.

The Justice of the Peace and the Coroner arrived around 9:30 a.m. to seal the body, and take it back to the Clark County Coroner's office to prepare the body for autopsy. Clark County Coroner Mike Murphy said medical examiners could tell the victim was female, but they had little else to go by when they attempted to identify the body. Murphy said, "Finger prints and facial recognition were not possible because the body had been burned." The medical examiner named the body "Sandy Valley Doe" because of where the body was located; and this would be her name until she could be properly identified.

CHAPTER **10**

Arrogance Does Not Make a Person a Murderer

Homicide Detectives Arrive at Craig & Kelly's House

Unfortunately for the homicide detectives, the condition that the body was in provided few clues as to the identification of the corpse in the trunk of the car. At 10:24 a.m. The homicide detectives arrived at the address that matched the owner of the Jaguar. 9539 Adobe Arch Court Las Vegas, Nevada 89148 was a beautiful, large stucco home in an upscale neighborhood. They got out of their unmarked cars, and walked up to the front door. According to Homicide Detective Robert Wilson, before he even knocked on the door, his mind was made up that it was Kelly Ryan in the trunk of the car; this would be the first of many incorrect assumptions to be made by the detectives.

Detective Wilson knocked on the door, and when Kelly answered the door, he identified himself as Detective Robert Wilson with the Las Vegas Homicide Unit, then introduced his colleagues working with him, and explained that they were looking for a Kelly Ryan. Wilson recalled that the woman at the door said, "Well I'm Kelly Ryan." The detective was stunned, and thought, "If this is Kelly Ryan, then the woman in the trunk of the car must be somebody else." Wilson took a few steps forward into Craig and Kelly's foyer, and the other detectives stood close behind him. The living room was like a studio, and any small noise would echo through the house like an amplifier. When

Craig Titus walked down the stairs and said, "Hey officers what's up," his deep, raspy voice boomed across the entire house.

The detectives were shocked when they looked up and saw this huge hulk of a man walking down the stairs. Trying not to look intimidated, Detective Wilson asked Kelly if she owned a 2003 Jaguar. Kelly responded, "Yes sir." Wilson was intrigued now, and asked, "Okay, well do you know where your car is at?" With that question, the game was on, and Craig held his breath, hoping Kelly would remember everything they had been rehearsing up to this moment. Kelly answered, "No, I don't. I think maybe our friend Melissa took it." This was the first time the detectives had ever heard the name Melissa before. Wilson asked, "Does Melissa have a last name?" Craig spoke over her and said, "Yes sir, James- Melissa James."

Detective Mogg, right behind Detective Wilson asked, "Was the car reported as stolen?" The detective pulled out his notepad to write down every time Craig talked over Kelly. Craig said, "She's our friend and she took the car, so we didn't report it stolen. I mean, she's our friend you know? She was going through a tough time, and we had given her a place to live; so of course we wouldn't call the police! Why, I mean, what's this all about sir?" Detective Wilson explained that Kelly's jaguar was found on fire in the desert early this morning. Craig gasped, put his hands over his face, rubbed his eyes with the palms of his hands, and said, "Holy shit!" Kelly followed with, "Oh my God! Nobody was hurt were they?" Detective Wilson said, "Uhm no, there was a body found in the trunk."

Detective Wilson then suggested they come inside to talk, so Craig and Kelly could sit down and give them a little information. Kelly invited them in, and when the detectives walked into the living room, the first thing they observed was that the house was immaculate; there was not a thing out of place. Everything from the carpet to the appliances looked and smelled brand new; however, it would not have mattered if something had happened at her house or not, Kelly was a neat freak, and she always kept her house in pristine condition.

The detectives all presumed before talking with Craig, given his size, beautiful home, and luxury car that he was a professional athlete of some kind. The moment they walked in the door; they also assumed that Craig probably had something to do with it. One detective could not stand Craig in particular; whether it was his arrogant confidence or his enormous build, Detective Mogg did not like Craig or his attitude. Mogg was chomping at the bit to knock Craig down a few notches when he suggested that Kelly go in the kitchen to visit with Detective Wilson, and he would visit with Craig right there on the couch.

Detective Wilson had been thinking the same thing, because he didn't want Craig to speak over Kelly the entire time they were interviewing them. With that, he followed Kelly into the kitchen, where she offered him a drink, and he declined. Wilson pulled out his pen and paper, as Detective Hardy poked his head in the door. Hardy asked Kelly if she minded if he took a look around the place; he didn't want to ask Craig because he was afraid he would say "no." Kelly replied, "No, I guess that's okay" as she pointed towards Melissa's room and the garage. Kelly said that they wanted to do whatever they could to help the police.

Detective Hardy excused himself and headed down the hall that led to Melissa' room. Craig noticed the detective walk by, and thought, "Where the fuck is that guy going, did Kelly say he could search the house?" When Detective Hardy made his way down the hall, he noticed three closed doors. The first door was to the laundry room, the second was to the garage, and when he opened that door, the security "beep" went off, and this startled Craig. The detective kept walking in and out of the garage, causing the beeping noise to repeatedly go off; this put Craig on edge, but he did not want to appear like he was on edge, so he tried to ignore the noise as he answered Detective Mogg's questions.

Back in Melissa's room, Detective Hardy noticed that the room was in stark contrast with the rest of the house. There was a mattress without any bedding flipped over to the side, drawers opened, food on the ground, and clothes piled up all over the room. When the detective saw that drugs were sitting out in plain sight, Hardy made a call in for a search warrant, and then continued to look through the room. Craig could tell that the detective had moved from the garage to Melissa's room, and to help control his nervous energy, he pulled out a cigarette lighter and flicked it the entire time Detective Mogg asked him questions.

When the detective started off the questioning by asking if Craig was having an affair with the woman that was burned alive in the car, Craig knew he was fucked! He knew that this detective thought he killed Melissa, or had something to do with her death, and Craig became very defensive with his answers from the very beginning. Craig shot back, "Fuck no, she was my friend!" But the asshole would not drop it, and they went back and forth several times until Craig finally stood up and said, "Okay, I'm done and my wife is done! I am not okay with you separating us, and snooping around my fucking house! That cop in there could be planting evidence for all I fucking know, and you are being a fucking dick! We tried to help you guys out, and you fucking blew it dude!"

Detective Mogg knew that without a search warrant, if Craig Titus told them to get the fuck out of his house then they would have to get the fuck out of his house. Mogg originally wanted to show Craig who was in charge and tried to intimidate him with his line of questioning, but Craig wasn't intimidated, he was pissed; so Mogg needed to rethink his strategy before he got all the detectives kicked out of the house.

Detective Mogg told Craig to calm down, and take it easy; he said they just wanted to help find his friend. Mogg asked, "You want us to find Melissa, don't you?" Craig nodded, and sat down, but he knew that was bullshit; Craig was well versed on how the police worked; this was not his first rodeo. Those assholes just wanted to separate Craig and Kelly to see if their stories matched up. Detective Mogg's change of strategy included taking the "I'm your buddy, just looking out for you" approach when he finished questioning Craig. This was the farthest thing from the truth because Mogg could not stand Craig the minute the bodybuilder opened his arrogant mouth, and he was one hundred percent certain that Craig was involved in the death of Melissa James. Mogg thought that even if Craig didn't kill her, he did something to her; and truthfully, he really didn't give a shit if Craig did or didn't kill this girl. In his mind Craig was a piece of shit felon, and there was no doubt, if he broke the law before, he would break the law again. Mogg planned on pussyfooting around Craig's ego, but he fully intended to nail Craig's cocky ass to the wall!

Wednesday afternoon, December 14th
Detective Rob Wilson interviews Kelly Ryan

Meanwhile back in the kitchen, Detective Wilson asked Kelly if she was okay with him recording their conversation. Kelly shook her head "yes", so Detective Wilson pushed the record button and started the interview. Wilson recorded himself, "This is Detective Rob Wilson conducting a witness voluntary statement reference a fire death which occurred on 12-14-05. Person being interviewed is last name Ryan, first name Kelly, middle name Ann. Date of birth is 07-10-1972. This interview is being conducted at the residence of 9539 Adobe Arch Court in the kitchen/dining area. Uhm Kelly, you understand that this interview is being recorded?" Kelly said, "Yes sir."

Detective Wilson asked: "And you live here with your husband?" Kelly nodded her head, "Yes." Detective Wilson then asked, "Okay, and his name is?" Kelly said, "Craig Titus, he does bodybuilding and I do fitness."

Detective Wilson: "And there is a friend of yours that you actually allowed to come and stay in the bedroom downstairs?" Kelly said, "Yes, she is a very close friend, her name is Melissa James."

Detective Wilson: "And how long have you known her?" Kelly said, "Uhm gosh, we lived in Los Angeles, for three years, so I would say seven years."

Detective Wilson: "And how did you meet her originally?" Kelly said, "Uhm, my husband was guest posing or guest appearing at a show in Florida, and she was assigned to help him. There are designated people to help the athletes when they make guest appearances. They drive you around, get your food, stuff like that; she was a real sweetheart."

Detective Wilson: "So you kind of adopted Melissa into your group of friends? How did that work?" Kelly said, "It's more of a situation where right off the bat, we really became good friends. At the time we were living in California, and bodybuilders get real jealous and say things behind your back, so it was a situation where you meet somebody that is real, and not involved in the industry; you cherish that friendship. Melissa is just a really a cool chick! When she owned her own dance studio about five years ago, she really had her shit together."

Detective Wilson: "So how did Melissa end up living in Las Vegas with you?" Kelly said, "She needed to get out of Florida; there are lots of drugs there. She stayed with us several times, whether it was for auditions or work opportunities. Then she actually had a great job and we had her stay with us and pay rent, and she was good about paying rent when things were going good for her. But then things stopped happening for her, and she kept trying to open different businesses. Like one time she tried to open a daycare, and nothing ever happened. So she ended up moving back to Florida, because she couldn't get anything going in Vegas."

Detective Wilson: "So when did she come back out?" Kelly said, "She came back out in the middle of October. She met a guy online named Eddie, a Filipino guy, and she said they dated, but he did crazy shit to her according to Melissa. He was really her drug dealer; I am not sure how that relationship really worked."

Detective Wilson: "So then she fell on hard times?" Kelly said, "Bad, real bad. She said she got Toxic Shock Syndrome and was in a coma for three months, and that was when the crystal meth started back up again. And she changed; the sweet Melissa with the round beautiful face was gone. I said something is not right. Her face was so beautiful a few years ago, she looked like Minnie Driver, with the round, real young face, and shiny hair. But now she has aged, and she looks rough. Life has been tough on her, and it affected her appearance."

Detective Wilson: "When did you notice that she had a drug problem?" Kelly said, "Like we've seen her do it from day one, but we've never really been around tweakers, so we really didn't understand what was going on. But we knew there was a problem when she didn't care who she stole from. Melissa laughed and told us that she stole her best friend's information, and now had her own credit card and driver's license with Samantha's name. If she would do that to her best friend, what would she do to us? And Melissa was not like that before, you know!"

Detective Wilson: So she really didn't hide it or anything? Kelly said, "No, she would go to the bathroom to shoot up and leave blood, and a bloody needle in the sink."

Detective Wilson: "And did she start to steal money from you?" Kelly said, "Oh my God yes, like two weeks ago, things weren't adding up, and the cable was shut off. She had written a check for the cable, but they never got it. She started doing that with a lot of our bills. Our credit cards that we kept in a safe started disappearing. Then there were charges popping up to places that we never go, but Melissa goes all the time like Green Valley Grocery- she would go there every day and play the nickel slots all day long. Then account balances are maxing, hundreds of dollars were gone. I thought we knew her."

Detective Wilson: Are her drugs in the house somewhere right now? Kelly said, "Oh yeah, there is a black pouch like full of blood-filled pins and crystal; lots and lots of crystal. Next to it there is a bundle of hypodermic needles, and there is some white powder she got today when she was with Eddie."

Detective Wilson: "Did Melissa ever drive your car, the 2003 Jaguar?" Kelly said, "Yes all the time because she did not have her own car."

Detective Wilson asked: "Did Melissa know where you kept the car keys?" Kelly said, "Yes, we keep all the keys in the box on the dining room table. That's the rule! She had access to the keys at any time."

And from there, the interview seemed like a casual conversation between friends. With a soft, "friend like" approach, and a sincere smile on his face, Detective Wilson asked Kelly in a gentle voice, "When do you last remember seeing your car?" Kelly thought for a minute and said, "This morning, probably around five when I went out to the garage."

Detective Wilson asked her why she was in the garage at 5 a.m., and Kelly said, "I always wake up early to walk our dog. I remember taking a load of clothes to toss in the laundry, and as I was walking down the hall, I noticed the glow from a light coming through the door. It was real bright! Then I opened the garage door, and turned off the posing lights that I must have left on the night before."

Detective Wilson interrupted, "What are posing lights?" Kelly explained that she and Craig are in the fitness industry. She said, "You could probably tell by looking at him, he is a bodybuilder." The detective affirmed the remark with the nod of his head, and Kelly explained that a big part of bodybuilding was the poses they perform while on stage. She said that in order to practice the poses at home, they shine a light on their body while posing, and they can see the image in the shadow on the wall." Detective Wilson nodded like he understood, even though he had no clue.

Detective Wilson: "You went to the garage," then he motioned his index finger in a circular pattern. Kelly continued, "Well yeah, so then I saw the car was missing, and I knew Craig was upstairs so Melissa must have been the one that took the car." The detective asked what she did next, and she said that she went upstairs and told Craig. She said, "Craig then called his good friend Tony Gross, and they went to look for her and the car." The detective asked if Melissa had taken the car before, and Kelly nodded her head, "Yes."

The detective wanted to be clear, and asked if Melissa lived in this house with both her and Craig at this very moment, and Kelly nodded her head. She then explained that Melissa was living with them because she had nowhere else to go. Kelly said, "She had some legal troubles because of drugs. She had no money, and nobody else would take her in because she would rob them blind to feed her meth habit."

Detective Wilson sat silent as Kelly went into further detail, "She didn't have a place to live, so we let her live with us until she could afford a place to move into. She didn't have a job, so we gave her a job, but she never worked. She didn't have a car, so we would loan her our car. She was family you know, but she took advantage of it. She got to where she expected us to give her things, and she was incredibly ungrateful."

The detective asked if their relationship was strained because of Melissa's behavior. And Kelly said, "Oh yeah! I mean, I don't think she ever intended to move out of our house. She was so bad on meth that she stole from everyone, and traded sex for drugs."

Like most people when they are abusing meth or cocaine, Kelly rambled on without stopping. She did not want there to be any silent pauses, and she feared if she stopped talking, she would appear less confident, and they would start to suspect foul play on her part.

Detective Wilson started to ask Kelly another question, and before he had a chance, Kelly started talking again. She said, "Nothing added up, and Melissa was a compulsive liar, so I couldn't believe a word out of her mouth. Just the other day I tried to use my debit card and it was declined, come to find out Melissa had stolen my card and had been using it. Also new credit cards that I had not applied for started showing up in the mail. We had ATM charges for things we had never purchased. If she stayed much longer, she would have stolen everything we had!"

Detective Wilson smiled compassionately, and said that he was sorry, that must have been difficult. He knew how to work Kelly, and the more endearing he became, the more information Kelly revealed.

Detective Wilson: "So what happened after she confronted Melissa?" Kelly said that Melissa blew up and denied the whole thing. "I even confronted her with bank statements, credit card bills and financial documents she forged, and she looked me in the face and said she didn't know what happened! But in her defense, she was shooting up so many drugs, I don't know if she knew that she was lying. Meth completely changed her personality, it made her violent and unstable; she was out of control."

Detective Wilson: "So what did you do?" Kelly said, "We had to get her out of the house so Craig got her a hotel room on Monday, and booked her a flight on Tuesday," Kelly said. Detective Wilson asked, "Did Craig pay for that?" Kelly said, "Yes, both the hotel room and the airplane ticket. He also gave her a couple of hundred dollars to get by on until she got to her mom's house.

◀ SWIFT INJUSTICE

Detective Wilson asked Kelly how Melissa reacted to being kicked out of the house and Kelly said that Melissa flipped out. Kelly said, "She just lost it, and said that she wouldn't have anywhere to go, her own mother turned her away in the past. But I told her that was not my problem anymore. I mean we helped her out enough, you know?"

Detective Wilson nodded his head and asked, "So when was her flight to go home? Kelly thought for a minute and said, "Her flight was last night around ten I think. You'll have to ask Craig, he bought the ticket, but I think it was around ten. Craig purchased the ticket on his credit card a couple of days ago."

Detective Wilson asked: "What happened before she went to the airport?" Kelly thought for a minute, and then said, "Craig picked her up yesterday from the hotel and brought her back here. I had a list of everything that was missing, and showed it to Melissa. Then I asked her one last time about the money; you know to give her the benefit of the doubt." The detective nodded, and Kelly finished, "I was real nice and said, 'Honey if you took it, and just tell me.' She was real pissed off about it, but I thought she's leaving; I will drop it and help her pack her bags. So I walked into her room and said, 'Hey sweetie I am going to help you pack your bags. You don't want to leave anything behind', and as I folded her clothes nice and neat, she jerked the clothes out of my hand and threw everything in her suitcase." Then Melissa yelled, 'Just take me to the airport now'"

Detective Wilson: "What time did you drive her to the airport?" Kelly said, "Oh no, I drove around the corner, and she wanted me to let her out at Green Valley Grocery; it was around three or four in the afternoon, I can't remember." The Green Valley Grocery is a mix between a 7-11 and a grocery store with slot machines."

The detective looked puzzled and asked, "So you packed her seven hours early, and then dropped her off around the corner?" Kelly said, "She was being real rude, and that's what she wanted, so I wasn't going to fight with her anymore. She probably just needed more drugs to make it on an eight hour plane trip. I think she was meeting her drug dealer there because she couldn't buy them at the airport and risk getting arrested."

ARROGANCE DOES NOT MAKE A PERSON A MURDERER

Detective Wilson asked if it was closer to 3:00 or 4:00 p.m. when she dropped Melissa off at the convenience store. Kelly said, "It was about 3:25 p.m." Detective Wilson repeated back, "3:25 p.m.," to which Kelly nodded her head "yes." He thought that was a strange time to say you dropped somebody off somewhere.

Detective Wilson: "Do you remember what Melissa was wearing when you dropped her off at the grocery store?" Kelly said, "Yes, she was wearing a blue long-sleeved shirt that zipped in the front and had a hood in the back, and blue jeans." Right then the detective knew that it was Melissa in the trunk of the car because that was exactly what the victim was wearing when they found her in the trunk of the car.

Detective Wilson knew that he could possibly be talking with the person that put Melissa in the trunk of that car, so he asked, "Were you and Craig with anyone that could verify your story yesterday?" Kelly said, "Uh-huh, our friends Megan and Jeremy came over last night around ten, and left early this morning, around 2-3. We celebrated her graduating from the University of Las Vegas." The detective asked, "And you were here the entire night with those two people?" Kelly said, "Yeah, they came over and we just hung out and talked until early this morning, then we went to bed."

Kelly asked if he wanted their phone numbers, along with Tony Gross' phone number, and he said, "Yes, please," as he scribbled down the number while she read them off of the contact list on her cell phone. Detective Wilson turned off the tape recorder, put his pen in his pocket, and thanked Kelly for her time and cooperation. Kelly said if there was anything else they could do to let her know because they were worried about Melissa. Kelly was relieved questioning was over, and surprised at how well it went. She had heard Craig and the other detectives in the other room, and hoped it went as well with Craig and his detective as it did with her and Detective Wilson.

Detective Mogg and Craig Titus

It became clear fairly fast that Craig's interview was not going very well. Kelly heard voices being raised, and could tell by the tone of his voice, that Craig sounded both pissed and frustrated. She walked into the living room, and Craig said, "I told you, me and Tony drove around Palace Station to look for her. If you want to find Melissa, find this scum bag first."

Detective Mogg asked Craig if his fiancé was with them when they searched for Melissa, and Craig blew up and said, "For the tenth time, Kelly is my fucking wife, not my fucking fiancée!" Craig wanted to punch this dumbass in the face so bad; but instead, he turned around, took a deep breath, and tried to gather his composure as he walked in the kitchen to find Kelly, and ask all of these assholes to leave. With the veins in his neck bulging, and his face bright red with frustration, Craig looked them all square in the eyes and said, "Look guys that's all we know. We are really tired, so if you don't mind, I have to ask you to leave. We are going to rest, and if there is anything else we can help you with, just give us a call." Craig was saying everything but, "Get the hell out," but the detectives either wouldn't take the hint or just refused to leave.

It was a standoff between Craig and Detective Mogg, and it appeared that even without a search warrant, they were not going to leave. With a look of "I can do whatever the fuck I want because I have a badge," Detective Mogg arrogantly walked around the house with a chip on his shoulder. Mogg knew the other detectives were in the process of getting a search warrant signed by the judge, and he didn't want to leave until they came back. Was this legal? Yes and No; yes in Las Vegas but not anywhere else in America. Craig was outraged, "I invited the detectives into my home, but I did not invite them to look around the house; and when I ask them to leave, I expect them to leave!"

Detective Mogg didn't like Craig the minute he saw him walk down the stairs, and Mogg's actions let Craig know that from the very beginning. The detective made up his mind that Craig had killed Melissa James, and he was going to take him down, no matter what Craig said. After hearing Craig's story about how Melissa was living with them, Detective Mogg jumped to the conclusion that Craig and Melissa were having an affair. He knew if this were true, the detectives would have no problem tying Craig Titus to the murder. A love triangle gone wrong would make a strong motive for murder.

ARROGANCE DOES NOT MAKE A PERSON A MURDERER

Craig never admitted to an affair to Detective Mogg, and no matter how hard the asshole detective tried to get it out of him, the answer was always the same. Craig said, "Look you dumb-fuck, I was not having an affair with Melissa James. What part of that do you not understand?" Throughout the interview, when Craig denied the affair, Detective Mogg would turn off his tape recorder, and penciled it in his notes. The affair that Detective Mogg leaked to the newspaper, and the prosecutor repeated time and again, was never tape-recorded. In fact, Detective Mogg lied about it one time under oath, and then dropped the whole thing after that.

Mogg assumed the two were having an affair, and it would strengthen his case; and like he did time and again with other investigations, he simply wrote down what he wanted the suspect to say, to make himself look like a great detective. Mogg would always get a slap on the back by the Lieutenant for his "clever detective" work, so he figured, "What the hell, just make shit up." he believed Craig Titus was guilty anyway.

Detective Mogg knew that he was pushing Craig's buttons, and he seemed to find some satisfaction in that as he walked around the house. Following Detective Mogg from room to room, Craig grew more irritated as the detectives refused to leave their home. Craig then tried to stop him by saying that he needed to talk to his lawyer, and the detective walked past him, right into Melissa's room, as if he was not even there.

In Melissa's room, Detective Mogg noticed a strong box pried open. Craig explained that they just discovered the box today when they went in to clean her room. Craig began to point out all of the financial papers, PIN numbers, social security numbers; every last detail of their life was in her room on paper. The detective began to dig through things, and Craig told him to be careful, "There are bloody needles all over the place." Craig showed him the empty bottles of drugs and drug paraphernalia, but the detective seemed to discount everything he said. Craig showed the detective Kelly's debit card, and said that she had been stealing money from that account. The detective did seem interested in that detail, but he wrote, "Another motive for murder- when Melissa was at the hotel room on Monday night,

SWIFT INJUSTICE

December 12th, 2005, Craig Titus and Kelly Ryan went through her room and opened the box to see if she was stealing from them. Titus claims she was stealing and using drugs in their house."

Even though it was Detective Mogg, not Detective Wilson that was in the room, Wilson made it sound as if he were there when he was on the *48 Hours* mystery when he said, "He was very intent on me focusing on this card, out of all of the credit cards lying around. So right then I knew that Melissa James was in the trunk of the car, and Craig Titus had something to do with her death." As Detective Wilson confirmed on *48 Hours*, within a couple of hours, the detectives that interviewed Craig Titus that day had already convicted him before an investigation ever really began. No matter how much evidence they would find proving an overdose in the future, they wouldn't care.

The homicide detectives would do whatever they needed to do to make sure that Craig Titus was on his way to prison. Craig knew it, and could see it in the detectives' eyes, so instead of asking the detectives nicely to leave his home, he told them to get the fuck out! However, around 1:30 p.m. just as Craig started to kick them out of his house, the detectives secured a warrant to search the house, and the Crime Scene Investigators started entering his home. Jessie Sams, a Crime Scene Analyst, walked in and started taking pictures of everything the detectives pointed out. Detective Mogg told Craig and Kelly they needed to leave the property while they searched the house. It was obvious that these detectives could do whatever they pleased, so instead of arguing, Craig and Kelly just left.

Craig and Kelly tried to act calm and collected, but they were scared out of their minds when they left their house around two o'clock that Wednesday afternoon. Craig had called Jeff Schwimmer before the police came over, but Schwimmer did not answer his phone. Craig left him a message saying that they were in some trouble and needed to stop by his house later that afternoon. When Jeff got the message, he was extremely concerned, so he tried to call them back right away. Unfortunately, Craig and Kelly were preoccupied, and could not talk on the phone; so Schwimmer called all of their friends to see if they knew what was going on.

ARROGANCE DOES NOT MAKE A PERSON A MURDERER

When Jeff called Tony Gross, he acted very strange, and would not say one way or the other if he knew what was wrong; so he called Greg Ruiz, but he never picked up the phone. The last person he called was Megan Pierson, and she of course blabbed, "Melissa overdosed, and they burned Kelly's car with her body in it because they didn't want to get in trouble for having drugs in the house." Jeff said, "What, are you sure? How do you know Melissa overdosed?" Megan said, "We were over there last night, and I saw her body; she died of an overdose, and Tony was going to meet Craig and Kelly around four this morning to burn the car. The police probably found the car if I was guessing. But hey, don't tell them I said anything, I swore I wouldn't tell anybody." Jeff could not believe it, and decided to wait at his house until Craig called him back. While Megan hopped in the car to circle Craig and Kelly's neighborhood to see if there were police cars out front.

CHAPTER 11

Cop Killers Investigating a "Murder"

Detectives Mogg & Hardy have shot and killed unarmed suspects in the past.
Some of the same homicide detectives in this case have literally gotten away with murder, and have never been held accountable. According to Action 8 News : On May 15, 2006, "A 16- year old suspect got away from homicide detective Ken Hardy, and fled the scene by foot, with his hands handcuffed behind his back. As the teenager was running away, Homicide detectives Ken Hardy and Shane Womack shot and killed Swauve Lopez in the back." Ken Hardy, who's been turned in before for delaying giving Miranda rights during investigations, was identified by witnesses who said that he shot the boy because he could not catch him.

The Las Vegas Journal wrote an article on November 27, 2011, called "To Shoot or Not Shoot is a Quandary for Las Vegas Officers". The Review Journal said, "A review-journal analysis of all 378 officer-involved shootings in Clark County since 1990 showed that about 10 percent of the time a Las Vegas officer fired at an unarmed person." The article mentions Ken Hardy. "Bill Young was the Clark County Sheriff in 2006, when handcuffed, murder suspect Swuave Lopez, 16, escaped from a police car and was shot and killed while running with handcuffs from detectives Shane Womack and Ken hardy. Hardy said they fired because they were physically incapable of catching up to Lopez."

Though the death was ruled "justifiable", (There has never been an outside source that makes these rulings; accordingly, officers are never punished, and not one police officer has ever lost their job over any of these shootings. This "justifiable" attitude is the same attitude the detectives had as they walked through Craig's house after he repeatedly asked for a lawyer and for them to leave.) The sheriff even said that he would not have taken that shot. Ken Hardy was not the only homicide detective in Craig's house investigating the case.

The detective that told Craig, "to go fuck himself," when Craig asked for a lawyer, and told him to get out of the house, Clifford Mogg, was also a part of the "378 officer-involved shootings since 1990."

According to the Las Vegas Review Journal: " Deadly Force When Las Vegas Police Shoot and Kill": "Incident Thursday May 13, 1999 at 2:30 p.m. 6253 S. Dean Martin Drive. Douglas Oswalt, 32, was fatally shot by a Las Vegas police officer hanging onto his car as he attempted to drive off during a marijuana sting investigation. Officer Ziel had his arm in the car, and was refusing to release, and the car began pulling forward. His colleague Clifford Mogg, discharged his weapon two times and killed the suspect."

CHAPTER **12**

Crashing with Schwimmer for the Week

Craig called Schwimmer when he and Kelly were driving away from their house on Adobe Arch Court. Craig asked Schwimmer if they could come over, and he said, "Absolutely, you are always welcome at my home; you don't have to call. Is everything alright, are you guys okay?" Craig said that they were okay, and he would tell him everything when they got there.

Jeff Schwimmer was a friend that always seemed to be there for Craig and Kelly. Craig trained Schwimmer a few years back, and helped him get off hard-core drugs. Jeff always felt indebted to Craig for saving his life. Unfortunately, Jeff had not been off drugs long, when he picked back up where he left off; and he was thrilled when Craig started partying with him again. Schwimmer's admiration became creepy however, when his gratitude turned into attraction. At one point, Schwimmer's advances went too far, and Craig turned him down. Craig began to avoid Schwimmer altogether. Craig was afraid Schwimmer would be pissed at him because Craig did not have anything to do with him over the past few weeks. To his surprise, Schwimmer was compassionate and welcomed both Craig and Kelly to stay at his home.

When Craig, Kelly, and Joey, their dog pulled up to Schwimmer's house in the up-scale, gated community, Jeff had them immediately pull their truck into his garage. Being a drug addict for most of his adult life, Jeff Schwimmer was always overly cautious when it

CRASHING WITH SCHWIMMER FOR THE WEEK

came to law enforcement. Schwimmer's drug of choice was crack, and he was more paranoid and hyped up than both Craig and Kelly combined. No matter how fucked up Schwimmer may have been however, he was a true friend, and allowed both Craig and Kelly to stay at his house the week following the incident. In fact, Schwimmer said that Craig and Kelly could stay with him as long as they needed, and he ordered a couple of pizzas because he knew they were starving. Craig and Kelly sat in his living room, and told him every single thing that happened.

Jeff Schwimmer called his top dollar attorney and told him the situation, and asked for his advice. The attorney told Jeff that it did not look good because of the burned body in the car. Jeff asked his lawyer to give him a worst-case scenario, and the lawyer said, "Worst case scenario, they could be charged with Manslaughter." At the time, Craig and Kelly thought this was the worst possible news they could hear. Little did they know, it was not the worst possible outcome. The worst possible outcome would be first degree murder, kidnapping, and arson.

Craig had tried to call Greg Ruiz earlier to tell him he was running low on blow and tabs. When Craig finally got in touch with him, Greg wanted to know what the hell was going on. Ruiz said that Megan told him about the overdose, and she thought that Tony helped him and Kelly get rid of the body. Greg said, "Dude, Megan is blabbing all over the place, and seems to be enjoying the attention. And then my boy Tony just sleeps and sits around depressed, and he won't talk about it. What the fuck happened?" Craig told Ruiz that he did not want to involve him if he did not have to, but said, "Melissa overdosed on meth, and I think from the morphine Tony sold her. I called Tony to help me. Tony walked in while I was giving Melissa CPR, but she was already dead. We all knew we would be in a shitload of trouble. They are arresting drug dealers when people overdose, and charging them with fucking manslaughter."

Craig explained, "I have a record, so we would have all gone straight to jail if we called the fucking cops after she overdosed. We had done a shitload of your fucking drugs dude, and none of us could think straight. We were dumbasses, and we pulled a bone-head move. Tony knew how to get rid of vehicles, so he helped us get rid of the car, and Melissa was in the back. We are all fucked now! So we have to figure out what to do brah; it's all fucked up mess." Greg was still not completely sure about all of the details, but understood enough to realize that all of his friends were in a lot of trouble. Ruiz had sold drugs to Melissa himself, so he could be in just as much trouble as well.

Craig and Kelly stayed the night at Jeff Schwimmer's house on Wednesday, December 14th, and camped out at his house off and on up until the day they left. Craig saw Jeff in an entirely different light; he was supportive and appeared to be one of the few loyal friends that would be there for Craig all the way. They stayed up late Wednesday night talking, and Jeff came up with some possible solutions to their problems.

Ironically, Jeff and Kelly seemed to become quite close over the next few days. They had never been tight before, so this made Craig feel good. Throughout the week Schwimmer and Kelly would run pick up food together and run errands. Kelly said that she appreciated Jeff so much because he was an ear when she needed to talk; Craig in turn felt blessed to have a friend that truly cared about the both of them.

Without question, when Craig and Kelly were interviewed by the police, they should have been honest from the beginning; however they were not thinking clearly because of being: scared shitless, out of control on drugs, without sleep for an extended amount of time; and now they were all past the point of no return in their minds. They had a false sense of security in believing that the detectives would do the right thing once they got the autopsy report back, and they realized Melissa had actually overdosed.

Regrettably, this could not be farther from the truth! After the autopsy report was concluded, everyone began to spin their wheels as they covered up the facts of the case. With the reality of no physical evidence staring them in the face, the investigators coerced witnesses, unlawfully procured statements, and manipulated the evidence; all in an attempt to pin Craig Titus with a bogus murder. And it all started at that moment, at Craig and Kelly's house, when Craig asked the detectives to leave his home, and they didn't budge. They knew a search warrant was on the way, but when Craig told them to get out of his home, and asked for a lawyer, the detectives violated Craig's Fourth Amendment Constitutional Rights, "The right of the people to be secure in their persons, houses, papers, and effects, against unreasonable searches and seizures, shall not be violated."

These are the fundamentals that everyone in law enforcement learns in basic training. Detective Mogg knew exactly what he was doing when he refused to leave Craig's home, and any statements collected at that time should have been suppressed in a court of law. According to *Mapp v. Ohio*, the Supreme Court held that the states were required to suppress evidence obtained in violation of the Fourth Amendment.

CHAPTER **13**

Blindsided by the Autopsy Report

New Jersey: Maura James' Office
Back in New Jersey, Maura James walked up to her office at the Bristol-Myers Building, sat at her desk, and hunted Craig's phone number down. It did not take long to find, because Craig had called her a few days before to talk to her about sending Melissa to a rehab facility. She jotted the number down, and then looked up the phone numbers of hospitals in Las Vegas. If she had not heard anything from Melissa in the next few hours, she planned on calling all of the hospitals.

Maura called Craig but he did not answer; so she left him a voice message asking Craig to give her a call back. While she did this, her ex-husband, Dennis James (Melissa's father who still lived in Florida), asked her if Melissa was living in Las Vegas. An odd question to ask about your child, it seems like a dad would know where his daughter had been living the past couple of months. Nonetheless, Maura told Dennis that Melissa had been living in Las Vegas, and when she asked him why, he said that someone from the Clark County Coroner's Office had just called him asking him questions about Melissa. Dennis did not ask any questions, he simply told them that he would have Melissa's mother call them back. This was even more bizarre, what parent would not freak out if they received a phone call from a Coroners' office about their child? Most parents would have demanded to know why they were calling, and question the person on the other end about the well-being of their son or daughter.

BLINDSIDED BY THE AUTOPSY REPORT

But for whatever reason, Melissa's dad did not sound worried, and told the Coroner's office that he would contact Melissa's mother and have her return the phone call. Perhaps since both parents were aware of Melissa's drug history, neither would be surprised if she had overdosed. Dennis gave Maura the coroner's number and she called as soon as she hung up the phone with him. She told the Coroner's office who she was, and that she was returning a phone call. A woman on the other line asked Maura, "Is your daughter in Las Vegas?" Maura James affirmed that Melissa had been living there off and on for years, and had recently moved back to Vegas in October. The woman then asked for a description of Melissa. Gathering her composure, Maura took a deep breath, and said, "She is petite with brown hair past her shoulders." Maura paused for a moment to take a deep breath and regain her composure then continued, "She is about 5 foot 3 inches, and she has blue eyes."

The woman on the other line asked if she had any birthmarks or tattoos, and Maura said, "She has a pair of ballet dancers tattooed on her lower back." The woman at the coroner's office said, "Okay, ma'am, just one more question, I know this is difficult, but were your daughter's ears pierced?" Maura closed her eyes, and sighed out the word, "Yes." The coroner's office thanked Maura for her assistance, and told her they would be in touch.

Maura James knew that something had happened to her daughter, so she called Craig again, this time from her company phone. The last time she called it said, "Unknown" on the caller ID. This time, however, when the phone rang, a New Jersey area code was displayed on the caller ID, so Craig hit "ignore," and the call went straight to voicemail. Craig knew it was Melissa's mother on the phone, and he also knew that she must be looking for her daughter, but Craig did not have the courage to talk to her yet.

Craig could not bear the thought of telling Melissa's mother that she had overdosed. Much less explain how they panicked, and tried to cover it up by lighting the car on fire with Melissa still in the trunk. He knew that he had to lie to her, and he was not prepared to do that just yet. Craig's phone made a noise alerting him that there was a voicemail, but he didn't even have the heart to listen to her voice in a recording. Thoughts of losing his own son brought back horrible memories in his mind. He knew what it was like to lose a child, and he would not wish that on his worst enemy, much less the mother of his best friend; yet he did not have the fortitude to answer the phone, and at least console her.

Autopsy of "Sandy Valley Doe"

The next morning at 10:30 a.m., Thursday, December 15th, an autopsy was performed on "Sandy Valley Doe/ Melissa Ann James" at the Clark County Coroner's office by Piotr Kubiczek, M.D., Medical Examiner. The examiner was assisted by Crime Scene Analyst Marnie Carter, Case Number 05-09570. Present at the autopsy were Detective Dean O'Kelley, Detective Robert Wilson, and Sergeant R. Alba. The body was confirmed to be that of an adult female with the same height, weight, and hair color as Melissa James. The victim's clothing and jewelry matched what Kelly Ryan had previously described to police as to what James was wearing the last time she saw her at the house. There was an identification tag around the left ankle with the inscription, "05-9570 Sandy Valley Doe (Melissa Ann James) Date of Death 14 December 2005, time of death 1115 hours, height 62 and weight 107."

The coroner's external examination showed that the deceased was an adult Caucasian woman, and despite the body being 60-70 percent charred, many of her facial features including the length of her nose, and position of her eyes and ears, were still intact. When compared to the physical description provided by Maura James, and the photographs from Melissa James' police records, it seemed highly probable that this was the body of Melissa James. Other examination findings included: "The charred body was wrapped in partially burned fabric material. The fabric around the head was tightly secured by partially burned off-white pieces of fabric. There was a fragment of electrical wire on the right side of the neck. This wire left a patterned impression on the right side of the neck. It was oblique. It ran from the decedent's right to left, downward and measured 5 ¼ inches in length. There was a necklace present on the neck that left a patterned impression around the neck.

The skin of the neck was tan-pink. The face is charred in areas that surround the skin covered with duct tape. This covered area measured

5- ½ x 4 ¼ inches. It extended from just above the eyebrows to just below the lower lip." (According to the autopsy report, the duct tape covered the face, but it did not wrap all the way around her head and neck like the prosecution would lead everyone to believe.) "There were two yellow metal bracelets around the left forearm that left a patterned impression that measured 6 x ¼ inch." The coroner explained that the skin was like plastic, and with the rise of temperature, the cable, most likely a loose wire from the interior of the car, left an impression mark. There was also an impression made from a gold necklace that she was wearing.

According to the coroner, there was no evidence of ligature marks, or an actual ligature. Rather, there was a loose binding (the belt from a robe & telephone cord) that was attached to hold the blanket together. Later in Grand Jury testimony, Marnie Carter, the Crime Scene Analyst assisting the Coroner, told the panel, under oath, that the off-white tube-like cloth with raised square checkered patterns was not a ligature, because the fabric was not directly up against the neck.

The second part of the Autopsy was the Internal Examination. The cardiovascular system was normal; the respiratory system however had some changes to it. The coroner wrote, "Aside from thermal changes, the lungs are 1000 grams, together. The upper and lower have blood-tinged frothy fluid in them." This was common with a heroin overdose. The coroner added, "The mucosal surfaces are smooth, yellow-tan and well developed. There is no soot in the airways. The pleural surfaces are smooth, glistening and well developed." This tells us that she did not die in the fire; she passed away sometime before the car burned. He wrote, "The Digestive/Hepatobiliary System was functioning normal. The esophagus is lined by gray-white smooth mucus. The gastric mucus is arranged in the usual folds, and the lumen contains about 300 milliliters of gray, chunky fluid containing pieces of rice and white meat. The colon contains formed stool."

(Her lunch had already made it to her intestines, and was in the process of digesting when she died. This tells us that she died approximately 3-4 hours after she ate. According to her mother, Melissa called her from KFC before noon, so this would back up Craig and Kelly's claim that she died between three and four in the afternoon.)

The autopsy stated that her Endocrine System was normal. "The pituitary, thyroid, and adrenal glands were well developed." The Genitourinary System was normal as well, and showed that she had not been sexually assaulted. "The renal capsules are smooth, thin, & semitransparent. The calyces, pelves, and ureters are unremarkable. The urinary bladder contains trace amounts of urine. The vagina, uterus, ovaries, and fallopian tubes are unremarkable. The breasts have the usual fibrous and adipose mixture. They are charred 90 percent."

Next, the autopsy looked at the Musculoskeletal System and the Neck. The report said, "Aside from charring described previously, the bony framework, supporting musculature and soft tissues are well developed. Aside from thermal changes, the examination of the soft tissues of the neck, including strap muscles and large vessels, reveals normally developed structures. The hyoid bone and larynx are intact, and there is no soot in the larynx."

(According to the prosecution under oath and on television, Melissa James was strangled; but in the autopsy report, the examiner's findings prove otherwise. After the body was x-rayed, the autopsy said, "Multiple X-Rays of the body showed that no injuries of the bony skeleton can be distinguished." The coroner also found that there was no blunt force trauma to her head or any other part of her body, thus she had not been physically assaulted or beaten.)

The Specimens obtained included: "Heart blood, chest blood, peripheral blood, vitreous fluid, and a blood blot for DNA, upper and lower jaw for identification purposes, hair obtained." The findings from the peripheral blood came back "positive for ethanol, 6-monoacetyl morphine (heroin). And hair was positive for amphetamines." This confirmed that she had an excessive amount of drugs in her system at the time of her death.

The toxicology reports supported a "death by overdose" finding, when it revealed that she had toxic levels of alcohol, heroin, and methamphetamines in her system. The report stated the drugs and amounts: "six monoacetyle morphine, also known as heroin, of which she had 472 nannogram per milliliter. Additionally, there was 13 nannograms per milliliter of morphine, and traces amounts of amphetamines and alcohol. Methamphetamines=1,107 picogram/milligram, and Amphetamine=153 picogram/milligram with 300/300 picogram/milligram Cocaine/Metabolites in her system." Taken separately this amount could potentially be fatal, but taken together; it would undoubtedly be lethal, causing a person to go into cardiac arrest and die within hours. Compounding this, a hair sample would later find the presence of methamphetamines, indicating an ongoing chronic abuse of the drug.

The coroner's findings stated: "Autopsy showed a Caucasian female with charring of the body, which was wrapped in a particularly burned fabric material, with duct tape on her face, and wrapped around her upper neck over a blanket. She was found in the trunk of the burned car in the desert. Her lungs had congestion and edema, common with overdose. Neither blunt force injuries nor natural disease was seen.

Toxicology showed ethanol and a toxic level of opiates in the peripheral blood. In addition, testing of the hair showed the presence of amphetamines indicative of common use. Based on the above-mentioned findings, the Cause of Death is Undetermined, with a significant contributing finding of Opiate Intoxication."

It would have been interesting to be a fly on the wall that day to see the investigators faces when they realized that Melissa James was not murdered after all; she actually died from a drug over dose. This autopsy report has never been made public until now; only select phrases have been printed in the media.

The detectives and prosecutor read this Autopsy Report; yet still prosecuted Craig Titus and Kelly Ryan with murder. Deputy District Attorney, Robert Daskas told the media and the court that Craig Titus choked, beat, body-slammed, and possibly burned Melissa James alive in the trunk of his car. Daskas would repeat this statement, that he knew was not true, time and again. He said it at Craig Titus' arraignment hearing, bail hearing, *and* grand jury hearing. Most alarming though was when Robert Daskas said this statement again, right before the judge was about to sentence Craig Titus for a murder he did not commit.

◄ SWIFT INJUSTICE

Craig and Kelly stay the night at Schwimmer's House

On Thursday morning, December 15th, Craig and Kelly got their first good night of sleep over at Jeff's house. When they got up the next morning, Jeff had breakfast made for them. After a few cups of coffee with some pancakes and bacon in their stomachs, their minds seemed clearer than they had in a while. Kelly commented on her behavior, saying they had been chaotically running around, nonstop for the past 48 hours, and for the past few months Melissa had her so on edge, this was the first time she felt like she could breathe. Kelly said, "I know this is terrible, but I really don't miss Melissa one bit." Craig told her, "It just has not hit you yet, and when it all sinks in..." Kelly then interrupted Craig and said that she didn't think so. Kelly said, "She tried to fucking kill me, Craig! If it wasn't her, it would have been me!"

Craig changed the subject, and told Schwimmer that he was thinking about bouncing for a while. Craig said, "I haven't seen Matt in a while, so it might be fun to go hang out with him for the holidays." Schwimmer said that he heard that Matt had not been much fun for a while, but he thought it would be a good idea for them to get out of town for a while. Craig said, "Nobody's a barrel of laughs when they get out of rehab, but Matt will help me out and maybe liquidate a few things. I want to talk to him about possibly buying me out for the WPI, that's a fucking gold mine, and if I have to be gone for a couple of years, Matt would cut me back in on the profits." Craig pulled out his phone and said he was going to give him a call, but Jeff told him to wait, saying "Let me go run to the store and buy you some pay- as- you- go phones; there is no way to trace that shit."

Jeff Schwimmer ran to Target and bought Craig and Kelly two phones and thousands of minutes for them. After he left, Craig and Kelly talked about staying somewhere else the next couple of nights while they made their final arrangements to leave town. They were comfortable with Jeff, but they were afraid to stay in one place for too long. Craig mentioned going over to Mandy's house. She was Kelly's friend that was currently renting a house from them, but Kelly did not want to get her involved, saying, "She is so genuinely sweet; she doesn't do drugs or cuss- I don't want to drag this world over to her house."

Craig said, "Let me just call and see what she says, and we will tell them we are in trouble but do not want to get them involved." Kelly really did not want Craig to call her, but they were very few options as this point, so he went in the other room and called her on his phone. After he spoke to her, Craig came back in the room and told Kelly that she was totally cool about it. Craig and Kelly were packing a few of their things for an overnight stay, and had their stuff ready to go, sitting in the living room. They heard the garage door, and Jeff walked in and handed them their new phones. They opened the phones up, read the instructions and started charging them. Craig said he was going to make sure they worked, so he called Schwimmer's cell, and it started to ring.

Craig became emotional when he thanked Jeff for everything, and after he and Kelly both gave him a hug, he told him that they were going to split for a couple of days. Jeff seemed disappointed, "Not for good, you will be back won't you?" Craig said, "Yea we will be back off and on, and then stay here the night before we split cross country." Jeff asked when that was going to happen, saying "Everyone will want to see you guys before you leave." Craig said that he thought it would be safe to take off on Sunday, and Jeff agreed. Craig and Kelly gathered all of their stuff, and as they walked into the garage to get in his truck, Jeff yelled, "Keep those phones on you 24-7. I am in constant contact with my lawyer, and I am finding you the best lawyer in Vegas. Even when you are on the road, we have to all be in constant contact, and then you won't get in trouble for fleeing or whatever." Jeff hit the button to raise the garage, and Craig poked his head out and said, "Thank you brother."

CHAPTER **14**

Mandy Polk: A Believable Witness

When Detective Mogg refused to leave Craig's house, even after Craig asked him to leave and stated that he needed his attorney present, Craig knew exactly what was going to happen next. The investigators were not playing by the rules from the second they entered his house and illegally conducted a search without a search warrant.

Craig felt semi- confident that the Coroner would be upstanding, and not taint any of the findings. If that were the case, everyone would see that Melissa had died of an overdose. That was a big "if" however: everyone knew that Metro was connected to the District Attorney's office, and if either side wanted to prove that an innocent man was guilty of murder, they would find a way to manipulate the evidence and the court proceedings to make it happen. Justice was unfortunately not blind in the "Good Ol' Boy" Metro networking town of Las Vegas, and Craig was acutely aware of this, which was why he started to panic.

There was a combination of factors playing out in Craig's mind: there was the legitimate paranoia brought on by the homicide detectives' illegal violations of his rights, and the drug-induced paranoia brought on by abusing stimulants over the past three days. Because the homicide investigators appeared to be focusing on Craig as a murder suspect, he went into "Fight or Flight" mode. This was a common, human instinct, and had Craig not been on drugs, he would have stayed and fought the investigation head on. That was the way Craig

Titus had always operated with any obstacle in the past, he fought and kicked ass, but this time was different.

The combination of excessive drugs plus lack of sleep dulled his perception of reality, and triggered irrational outbursts. Stimulants caused Craig to spin his wheels; the harder he pushed on the gas, the deeper a hole the tires dug, ultimately causing Craig to be stuck. When a person sees trouble ahead, it is human nature to want to avoid it, and that was what Craig did, keeping himself moving to avoid the reality of the situation. In Craig's mind, he could not go home, but he could not stay in one place for an extended amount of time either. So after they stayed Wednesday night and Thursday afternoon with Jeff Schwimmer, they were ready to move somewhere else. Craig had several houses that he rented out to tenants, but unfortunately for Craig they were all occupied at the time. This ticked him off because he owned the houses, so he felt that he should be able to tell those people to get the hell out of his house, but if he did that, it would raise red flags.

So Craig thought about Kelly's friend and client, Amanda "Mandy" Polk who was also Craig's tenant. No doubt, she would let them stay the night; it was Craig's house after all! Around 2:00 p.m. on Thursday afternoon, Craig called Mandy and told her that they were in a "bad situation," and needed to get out of town for a while. Craig said that they would stop by where she was living later to explain the details.

Thursday Evening, December 15th
Craig and Kelly go to Mandy Polk's house

Lauren Amanda "Mandy" Polk from Germantown, Tennessee first started talking to Kelly Ryan in the summer of 2005 on the internet. Polk originally wanted to buy a competition suit from her, but Kelly started giving her advice on an upcoming fitness competition.

According to her Grand Jury Testimony, Mandy "Decided to move to Las Vegas. I placed 5th in my show, and it takes the top two places to turn professional, and Kelly thought that I could turn professional if she worked with me. We agreed that my boyfriend, Ryan Chastain, and I would rent a house from Craig and Kelly, and I would start training with her once I moved to Las Vegas."

Polk said that she and her boyfriend moved to Vegas in mid-October of 2005, and starting the first week that she was there, Mandy trained every day." Mandy Polk said that she considered Kelly a friend, and spoke with her several times a week by phone and a couple of times a week through text messaging.

According to the Grand Jury Transcripts: "On Thursday, December 15th at 2005, Craig called Mandy, and this was unusual because Craig had never called her ever before." Mandy said that Craig had informed her that he and Kelly would be coming over later because they had run into some trouble. It was a long story, difficult to explain, but he was going to have to leave town for a long period of time. Mandy was hesitant because Craig did not ask her if they could come over, he informed her that they would come over. Mandy told him to make sure he called before they came by, and Craig told her they would call around 6:00 p.m.

About three hours later, Craig and Kelly showed up, with their dog Joey, at Mandy and Ryan's house on 9045 Quintessa. It was around 5:30 p.m. Craig rang the doorbell, and Mandy was undoubtedly agitated because Craig did not call before they came over. Mandy was awakened from a nap, so she had to change her clothes before she answered the front door.

When Mandy answered the door, Kelly followed her into the bedroom. Kelly put her arms around Mandy and cried on her shoulder. Mandy asked Kelly what was wrong, and told her she wanted to help. Kelly told Mandy, 'Oh my god, the police found my car burned up with a body in it' and I did not react, because that was not normal. I asked her what happened, but she didn't really answer the question." Kelly told Mandy that her roommate was missing, and they thought it was her roommate who stole the car. Mandy told Kelly, "I didn't even know you had a roommate! Who was it?" Kelly said it was Melissa James, but Mandy still did not know who she was talking about.

When asked by Daskas what Craig was doing and saying, Polk said, "Craig was walking around the house like checking the doors and blinds. If any blinds were open, Craig shut them. Craig was not saying anything at first, but when I asked him what happened, he said, 'the less you know the better, really we don't want to involve you guys. I'll just say that she was a drug addict.' When I turned to Kelly and asked her if Melissa was a drug addict, Kelly said, 'Yeah, she was a meth addict. She was a fucking tweaker.' I had never heard that term before so I didn't know what that meant, but I put two and two together."

According to Mandy, Kelly told her that they had taken Melissa in to try and help her out because she was having a hard time in her life. They let her use their red Jaguar, trying to give Melissa her own space in the house to give her a real sense of freedom to come and go. Mandy said Kelly told her that Melissa was supposed to go back home, but she never did, and they noticed that their car was missing. Soon after, Homicide showed up and told them their car was found on fire in the desert, and Melissa was missing.

Kelly tells Mandy the Truth

Sometime between 7:00- 7:30 p.m., Craig said that he was hungry and wanted some Chinese food, so Kelly jumped in Mandy's car, and the two girls drove to a Chinese restaurant. According to Grand Jury testimony, Mandy said, "Kelly explained how Melissa had been a source of stress in her life, saying that, you know, Melissa was a drug abuser and her behavior was erratic. So I started asking her questions because I was confused, and Kelly said, 'I can't lie to you anymore. We found her dead in her room.' I asked her if she burned her up in a car, and Kelly replied 'yes'. So I asked her why she didn't just call 911 if she found her dead of an overdose. It is obviously not your fault, but now you destroyed evidence of an overdose, and that incriminates you."

Kelly could not answer Mandy; instead Kelly said, 'I'm fucked, I bought seven bottles of lighter fluid with my debit card at Wal-Mart. I thought it was the best idea because of my career; I have already taken so many steps back, you know.' Kelly said that Melissa had been dead for a few hours and couldn't describe what she looked like because it would traumatize me for life. She said that they drove the car 'pretty far out' and took care of it, but didn't specify where they had taken the car, and they got back to the house and were through with everything by 6:00 a.m., and the homicide detectives arrived at 10:00 a.m."

When they got back to the house, the girls took the food upstairs, and then Mandy went back down stairs to get some plates and napkins. Mandy asked her boyfriend if he would help her grab the drinks out of the car, telling Craig and Kelly to stay upstairs and start eating. Once they were outside, Mandy divulged to Ryan everything Kelly had told her in the car; and she asked Ryan, "What do we do?" Chastain said, "I don't know, Craig already asked me if they could stay the night. I told them they could, but they would need to leave first thing in the morning."

Mandy was not okay with them staying the night, but believed she had no other choice. Mandy hesitantly said, "Okay, but you have to help me in the morning; I am not good with this kind of stuff. Craig and Kelly have to be out tomorrow; no exceptions, or we could get in trouble right beside them. First thing in the morning, let's offer to get them a hotel room, start getting all of their stuff together, and load everything in the car." Ryan agreed with Mandy and the young couple went back upstairs to eat their food.

Craig had moved them into the hallway, away from all of the windows, and they all finished their dinner. Craig then started talking about taking some OxyContin that Schwimmer gave him to calm him down. Craig asked Kelly if it was okay for him to take it. Craig explained to everyone that he had been to rehab for pain medication addiction a few months ago. Craig said, "I haven't done it in a long time, but I am freaked out right now." Kelly said, "I guess Craig, that's your thing. I'm pissed at Schwimmer for giving those to you, he knows that you have a problem with pills; but whatever, you don't need my permission to do anything."

Mandy Polk got a glimpse into Craig and Kelly's world, and the people they surrounded themselves with. Mandy thought, "What kind of friend gives a drug addict, fresh out of rehab, more drugs to help calm his nerves?" At no time were these people ever real friends to Craig and Kelly; if the drugs were taken out of the equation, none of these people would have anything in common.

At the end of the night, when Kelly was in the bathroom, she told Mandy that she was really stressed out and scared, "I can't have my name attached to a murder; I did not kill anyone!" Mandy gave Kelly a hug, and told her that everything was going to be okay, and then they decided to go to sleep. Mandy said, "I offered them my bedroom, but they did not want to be alone, so I offered them my bed, but they refused. They preferred to sleep on the floor; they were paranoid."

Friday morning, December 16th
Mandy and her boyfriend help Craig and Kelly rent a hotel room

The next morning, Friday, December 16th when Mandy woke up, Craig was already on the computer and talking to Jeff Schwimmer and his attorney on the phone. When Mandy's boyfriend walked in the room, Craig asked him if he would take them to the La Quinta. Mandy and Ryan both agreed to drive them to a hotel because they wanted Craig and Kelly out of their house.

Mandy started the car and waited for the others while they gathered all of their belongings. She drove them to the La Quinta on West Sahara, and Craig asked Ryan to get out and pay for the room. When Ryan returned, he informed them that they only take credit cards, and Chastain was not going to use his credit card to get them a room. Craig got upset with him, and told him if the tables were turned, Craig would use a credit card for him. Mandy defended her boyfriend, and they had words, then Kelly suggested the Holiday Inn down the street from the La Quinta.

They drove a few blocks up to the Holiday Inn Express. Chastain went inside to pay cash for the room, and while he was inside, Craig went off on him because he was offended that Chastain was reluctant to get involved. Craig turned to Mandy and said, "You know I'm just not like that, I'm not like that with my friends. I will go all-out; it doesn't matter who they are or what has happened." Mandy told Craig that he needed to try and understand his position. She said, "He doesn't even know what he's involved with here, and you're involving him by saying that you need him to get you a room. Of course that puts him in a bad position, especially since he doesn't even really have an understanding of what's going on." Chastain returned to the car, and told them he paid cash for a night; Craig apologized to them, and said they would not be returning home so this would be the last time they would all see each other.

◄ SWIFT INJUSTICE

Mandy calls the police

Later that Friday evening, December 16th, Mandy called Kelly to check on her, but her phone was turned off. Her boyfriend wanted her to leave it alone, and just forget that they ever knew Craig and Kelly. But Mandy could not get it off her mind. After the nine o'clock news, when the story was featured, Mandy picked up the phone and called the Las Vegas Police Department to report a crime. She was transferred to Detective O'Kelly, and he immediately asked her name. She said that her name was Mandy, and that she had information about the body found in the Jaguar, but would like to remain anonymous. After giving him her name, she asked if she could remain anonymous.

Over the phone, Mandy told the detective about Craig and Kelly staying with them, and paying for them to stay in a hotel. She said that Kelly admitted covering up Melissa's overdose by setting their jaguar on fire. The detective told her that if she came forward to be interviewed that she would not be charged with conspiracy, and he recommended that her boyfriend come to the Homicide Office as well. Mandy agreed to come in the next day to speak with detectives.

CHAPTER **15**

Spinning Their Wheels

On Saturday morning, December 17th, the detectives had a lot of ground to make up after the autopsy ruled that Melissa's death was "Undetermined with opiate intoxication as contributing factor." The first thing they did was subpoena Craig and Kelly's cell phone records. (And like the autopsy report, the cell phone records would actually hurt the prosecution, being beneficial to the defense.)

The phone records showed 13 incoming and outgoing calls between Craig and Tony beginning at 3:28 p.m. on 12/13- until 4:28 a.m. on 12/14. The cell records proved that Craig did not just call Tony at 3:00 a.m. in the morning to give him a lift to the desert. Craig called him at 3:28 p.m. right after Melissa had overdosed, which was corroborated by the medical report's time of death of Melissa James.

Around 9:00 a.m., the homicide detectives wanted to hunt down the three people that had allegedly conspired with Craig Titus and Kelly Ryan to dispose of Melissa James' body. They felt that all five could possibly be responsible for Melissa's death; and if they wanted to rebound from the autopsy findings, they needed to talk to: Anthony Gross, Megan Pierson, and Jeremy Foley.

Detective Mogg placed a call to both Megan and Jeremy's home phone number and then their cell phones, but there was no response. He left a voice message stating that he was with Metro homicide and he needed to speak with both Jeremy and Megan about a possible murder. The detectives called Megan five times a day for five days, until they finally decided to go pay the couple a visit at their home. When they arrived at their house, there were cars out front, and movement in the house, but nobody ever came to the door. They called and stopped by for over a week, and the couple would not return their phone calls. The detectives were becoming very suspicious of Megan Pierson and Jeremy Foley.

Detectives call Tony's parents

Around 10:00 a.m., Detective O'Kelley placed a call to Tony Gross; however, he did not pick up either. He also left a message for Tony, then he called his parent's number that was listed on a past incident report. When he called the home of George and Angela Gross at their residence, Mrs. Gross answered the phone.

O'Kelley asked to speak with Anthony Gross. She was the only one that called him Anthony, so she knew that something was wrong. She said, "He's not home right now, this is his mother, can I help you?" Detective O'Kelley said, "Yes ma'am, I am a detective with the Las Vegas Metro's Homicide Department, and I am trying to locate your son." Her heart dropped, and because the officer was from homicide, she thought maybe something had happened to her son, so she asked if Tony was okay, "Has he been hurt?"

O'Kelley said that he just needed to speak with her son, and then asked her if the number he was calling was her son's phone number, and she confirmed that the number was correct. O'Kelley said, "Just to verify, I need to make sure, you are the mother of 23 year old Anthony Remo Gross, correct?" Mrs. Gross said, "Yes, that is correct."

O'Kelley asked his mother what kind of car Tony drove, and she said that his car had recently been stolen so he was currently driving her car until the insurance money came in for him to buy another car. The detective asked if this vehicle was a truck, and if it was registered under her name, and Mrs. Gross confirmed that it was a truck that was registered in her name. He asked her for a description of the truck, and she told Detective O'Kelley, "It's a 2003, charcoal grey, Dodge pick–up truck," then she asked if her son needed an attorney. Detective O'Kelley cut the conversation off, and in a flat tone said,

"Please notify Anthony Remo Gross that Metro Homicide needs to speak with him just as soon as possible."

After they hung up, she tried to call Tony, but his cell phone was turned off. She then tried to call his girlfriend, and his best friend, and neither one of them answered the phone either. His mother decided to go drive over to his girlfriend's house to find Tony, but their cars were not in sight, and nobody answered the door.

Tony's mother was now starting to panic as she drove over to her son's best friend's house. Having a homicide detective call her and question her about Tony was one thing, but he wouldn't answer his phone and she couldn't find him. In a panic with tears streaming from her eyes, she arrived at Greg Ruiz's house, jumped out of her car, and banged on the front door. Startled, Greg jumped up, looked around and made sure he did not have anything illegal lying around, then walked over to the door.

Ruiz had always been a laid back guy, but he was always alert and a little on edge because of his drug business. He would only sell drugs to his friends and acquaintances, so he was not too worried about getting caught, but when someone was pounding as loud as they could on his door, he was nervous in anticipation of who was on the other side. When he looked through the peep hole, he realized that it was Tony's mother. She was crying hysterically, and was visibly upset; but Greg was not too concerned because she had done this before.

Anytime Tony got into an argument with his mom or a fight with his girlfriend, or was in any kind of trouble for that matter, his mom would hunt him down. She would call everyone a million times and then drive all over town until she found Tony's truck. If his truck was outside Greg's house, she would start banging on the door. During the investigation, Greg said, "We all thought it was hysterical! Here is this 23-year old man who lives at home with his parents, and makes shit up all the time about being a wise guy, and his mom is coming over here. It embarrassed the hell out of him, but he was my boy, so I had to say something to him, you know? I would ask him shit like, 'Did you forget to clean your room, change your underwear, or take out the trash?' Just to fuck with him."

So when Greg looked out the window, he thought, "Oh here we go," and didn't think much of Tony's mom at his front door. When he opened the door, he could tell that this time was different. She wasn't mad, she was frantic and obviously scared shitless. She was crying so hard that she had a hard time getting her words out, and Greg put his arm around her and walked her into the house.

Greg was starting to get scared himself when Mrs. Gross said that a homicide detective called her, and she thought that Tony was in some sort of trouble with the law. Ms. Gross said, "He asked me questions like where Tony was at, and what kind of card does he drive. And when I asked him if Tony was in trouble, he would not answer me. He just said he needed to speak to him immediately." She said that something happened with her truck that she had loaned Tony, and Greg knew exactly what she was talking about, but didn't know if he should say anything. He didn't want to get his best friend in trouble. But he was a little put out that Tony was not home, so he would have to talk to his mother. Mrs. Gross asked Ruiz what was going on, and he told her that Craig had told him a girl overdosed at his house, and Tony helped him get rid of the body. Tony's mother broke down, distraught and scared. After she calmed down, she hired an attorney for her son.

Craig trades in his truck

Saturday morning, December 17th, Craig drove to the Integrity Chrysler Jeep Dodge dealership to trade in his recently leased Dodge truck for another vehicle on the lot. Jeff Schwimmer followed him to make sure Craig made it to the dealership without being picked up by the authorities. They arrived around 10:30 am, and met with the same salesman that leased him his truck in April 2005. The salesman, David Levinson, said that he was surprised when Craig told him he wanted to trade in his truck. "Craig had leased a 2005 Dodge SRT-10 quad cab. It's a hot rod truck with a Viper V-10 motor. It had ground effects, a little spoiler in the back of the bed, wide tires. It's a high profile vehicle." Craig told the car dealer he needed a four wheel drive truck with better gas mileage because he was driving up north across country.

The men walked around the dealership to find a replacement vehicle; one that would make it through the rough terrains of Utah and Montana. The salesman showed Craig a 2006 SRT-10 Quad Cab, and Craig said he would take it. After Craig filled out the paper work, and waited for everything to be processed, he put the down payment on his corporate credit card and walked outside to smoke a cigarette with Jeff Schwimmer. Craig told his buddy that they had to take off by the next day. Craig was certain that he was going to get pinned for a make-believe murder. His friend had hooked Craig up with the best attorneys, the same attorney Britney Spears used to get her out of trouble. Schwimmer told Craig that Greg wanted to have a get-together before they left, and that looked like it was going to be tonight. Schwimmer gave Craig a hug, and said he would see him tonight, if not at Greg and Diana's, he would see them when they came over to stay the night later that evening.

Craig calls Maura James

After Schwimmer walked away, Craig mustered up the courage to call Maura James back early that Saturday afternoon. She had tried to call Craig three times, and she sounded frantic in her last message. The DNA evidence was not conclusive at that time; but her mom had already come to the conclusion that it was her daughter in the back of the trunk. Melissa's mother could not disguise the sadness in her voice when she answered the phone.

Craig only wanted to take some of her heartache away when he talked to her. Even though he knew that it was a lie, he told Maura that he was certain it was not Melissa's body in the trunk of his car. Craig said he had a friend who had spoken to Melissa James on the phone, inferring she staged the whole thing so she could gain a new identity. Confused, her mother asked Craig, "Well who is in the trunk of your car then?" Craig didn't have an answer for her, he just wanted to let her know that he loved Melissa, and was sorry about everything, and then he hung up the phone.

Craig went back inside the car dealership; it seemed to take forever, but finally, they gave him the keys to his new truck and Craig ran over to the bank. While he was running his errands, Greg Ruiz called him, and asked if they wanted to meet him for lunch. Craig told him to give him thirty minutes; he had to stop by the bank, and pick up Kelly, and told him they would meet him at Subway around 2:00 p.m.

Craig stopped at the bank, and withdrew $10,000 from his account, then picked Kelly up, and checked out of the hotel. They drove over to meet his buddy, and business partner Greg Ruiz for lunch at Subway. They were running behind, so Greg was inside waiting on Craig and Kelly.

Craig and Kelly meet Greg Ruiz for lunch

At 2:30 p.m., Craig and Kelly sat down with Greg to eat and fill him in on what had happened. Craig felt bad because Greg was his business partner with Ice Gear fitness apparel, and he was feeling that he had let his friend down. Greg told him not to worry about that; "We need to focus on what to do next to help you guys out." Greg asked Craig and Kelly if they wanted to come by tonight; they would invite all of their friends.

Ruiz said, "We can come up with the plans, then get fucking stoned and party before you take off. We all need a fucking laugh, especially Tony; he has not been himself, and he has been real depressed." Craig said, "Tony probably feels bad because he didn't take the body out of the car, so now we are all possibly looking at manslaughter." Greg said, "Yeah, he thinks it is his entire fault, and said he didn't think he could face you again." Craig said, "Tell him that is bull shit; it was a mistake, and we will make it right." Greg said, "That's right brother, I told him the same thing. We all know what happened, and I have your back. When things die down, the truth will come out."

Greg told Craig and Kelly that some homicide detectives called Tony's parents, so he suggested that they all hang low, and not get out anymore unless they had to. Craig and Kelly agreed, and Greg walked them to Craig's new truck and asked, "Where's the Viper?" Craig said that he would tell him about it when they came over later. Greg said that they better not back out, "You mother fuckers better be there!" Craig slapped his hand and said, "Hell yeah, we both need a fucking break; especially Kelly, to lift her spirits. Just don't invite anyone we don't know. You know, only invite our circle of friends that know what's going on." Greg said, "Absolutely!"

As Greg started to walk away, Craig said, "I am low right now, but don't want to call Tony in case they are watching our phones; will you take care of me? Ruiz walked back up and said, "Absolutely! You know I always got you brother. Besides, Tony and I decided that I would sell everything until all of this shit dies down." Craig said that was smart, and asked Ruiz to hook him and Kelly up with some, "O.C., coke, and some bars (OxyContin, cocaine, and Xanax); something easy to take on the road, and keep me going." Greg asked him how long he would be on the road, and Craig said, "I'm not sure, but hook me up with enough shit to last at least a month. And give Schwimmer a call, he needs some shit too." Greg tapped the top of Craig's truck with his hand, and said, "Will do, see you tonight brother."

Mandy Polk and Ryan Chastain give statements to the police

While Craig and Kelly were pulling out of the Subway parking lot, Mandy Polk and Ryan Chastain were walking through the doors of the Metro police department. They told the officer at the desk that they had an appointment with Detectives Dean O'Kelley and Robert Wilson. After a few minutes of waiting, they called Mandy and Ryan back for the interview. Mandy voluntarily gave her statement to detectives at 3:54 pm. They asked her to provide as many details as possible when they asked a question. The following is a paraphrased transcript of the notes from the interview:

Detective O'Kelley: Please state your name and age for the record.
Mandy Polk: "My full name is Lauren Amanda Polk, but my friends call me Mandy; and I am twenty- one years old."

Detective O'Kelley: When did you first meet Kelly Ryan, and tell me about your relationship?
Mandy Polk: "I first started talking to Kelly on the internet this past summer because I wanted to buy one of her competition suits. I am an amateur fitness athlete, and Kelly is a professional fitness athlete. I really, really admired her and looked up to her. She influenced me from the very beginning. She influenced my interest in the sport of fitness competition, and in the way I approached routine training,

by seeing her routines and her willingness and ability to improve every competition. She inspired me to try and do the same. I was in contact with her before my last fitness show, and after the show, we spoke about her helping me prepare for my next competition. And Kelly said that she would absolutely help me. She asked if I wanted to come to Vegas to train for a week, or if I was interested in moving to Las Vegas long-term and renting a house from Craig, and my boyfriend and I decided to just move to Vegas in October. It was a chance of a lifetime because Kelly Ryan is one of the most decorated fitness professionals ever. She's known as the 'routine queen' and she also has the nickname 'Flyin Ryan' because of how she flies through the air when she performs a routine."

Detective O'Kelley: And what do you know about Craig Titus? **Mandy Polk:** "Craig's career in bodybuilding is very impressive. He is probably the most famous body builder in the world right now, in the sense that everyone in the fitness world knows who he is. He is invited to the top shows like Olympia, Arnold, and Ironman, and he is always in the top 5 or around the top 5. He is in all of the magazines and they both have big money endorsements with Pinnacle, Pure Form, and Bio Chem. He is very successful."

Detective O'Kelley: Did Kelly become a close friend after you moved to Vegas?
Mandy Polk: "Actually when we first came to Vegas, we stayed at their house for a week. They were very hospitable and welcoming to us. Kelly and I developed a close bond, we stayed up all night talking, and she was just great!"

Detective O'Kelley: Tell me about the day they came over to stay at your house.
Mandy Polk: "Craig and Kelly came over to the house and talked about their jaguar being stolen, and said that Homicide had found it burned up with a dead body in the trunk on the side of the road. Then they said that their roommate was on drugs, and she was missing. When we started asking questions, Craig said, 'The less we knew, the better.'"

Detective O'Kelley: What did they say about Melissa James?

Mandy Polk: "She told me it was her roommate, and she said that Melissa had been trying to sabotage her relationship with Craig for years. Melissa would tell her something and Craig something else, and she tried to stir shit up so that Craig and Kelly would fight, and then Melissa could swoop in and have Craig. She said that Melissa had been arrested in Vegas and Florida for identity theft, and she was stealing things from them, and selling them to make money for drugs. And that she has a drug dealer, and she trades sex for meth."

Detective O'Kelley: Did she tell you what happened to Melissa James?
Mandy Polk: "Yes, Kelly first told me that Melissa stole her car, and she had overdosed in her house. Then she said that she could not lie to me anymore, and said that Melissa was a drug addict, and she overdosed at their house. Kelly said that she was fucked because they put her overdosed body in the trunk of their car, and bought seven bottles of lighter fluid at Wal-Mart at 3:30 a.m. that morning. They followed a friend out there named Tony, and then drove the car pretty far out, and Craig and his friend Tony took care of it. She said they got back close to 6:00 a.m., and the police were there around 10:00 a.m."

Detective O'Kelley: Did they say anything else?
Mandy Polk: "Kelly said that they were innocent, and she was not going to jail for a murder she did not commit."

Detective O'Kelley: And where did they go that night?
Mandy Polk: "They stayed the night at our house. They slept on the floor in my bedroom; they wanted to be away from the windows. We got them a room the next night, and have not seen them since."

After Mandy was done with the interview, the detectives thanked her and told her they would be in contact with her. Next, they called back her boyfriend, Ryan Chastain. Ryan was interviewed by Detective Robert Wilson, a little after 5:00 p.m.

Detective Wilson: Did Craig or Kelly tell you anything about Melissa James or the death of Melissa James?
Ryan Chastain: "Yeah, Craig told me that someone had stolen their car, and tried to still their stuff, and money. This person had a criminal

record for identity theft and Craig thought she was trying to steal their identities."

Detective Wilson: Where did Craig and Kelly stay that night?
Ryan Chastain: "At our house, but I sent them to a hotel because I wanted them to leave. I paid for their room with cash."

Detective O'Kelley: Did Craig say anything about leaving town?
Ryan Chastain: "Yeah. His best friend lives in Boston, so he was going to trade in his truck and get a car to take them across country. He said that his Viper guzzled too much gas. When we took them to a hotel, they said this would be the last time we would ever see them again. So they were leaving soon, he said not to run away, but to get his finances in order and spend Christmas with his best friend and business partner in Massachusetts."

Anthony Gross hires an attorney

Later that afternoon Tony Gross and his mother met with an attorney to discuss Tony's legal troubles. And according to friends that he confided in later, Tony told the attorney everything. Every detail from finding Craig giving Melissa CPR, to helping him move the body to the trunk of the car, then later burning the car. He said that he felt like he could not say no to Craig, because Craig was his hero. Tony truly wanted to help him. The attorney was honest with Tony, and said that with that story, he was facing possible manslaughter charges.

Gross' attorney said that in this system everything is pleaded out, so the District Attorney's office will stick you with every possible crime, even if they don't apply. He told Tony that he was looking at some prison time, or he could let the police know that Tony was willing to cooperate- tell them something they wanted to hear.

His attorney said, "It's always better to go to the police before they come looking for you. This might mean that you will have to change your story, and turn on your friends. Make it look like they did everything and you had absolutely nothing to do with it!"

Tony was hesitant; he really liked both Craig and Kelly, and didn't want to get them in trouble. When Tony nodded his head "No", his attorney told him to think about it over the weekend, and come back Monday, and they would decide what to do next. The lawyer said that it was important that Tony not talk about this conversation or his involvement with the disposal of the victim's body with anybody. Tony nodded his head and said that he understood.

When Tony left that office, he was more depressed than before. No matter what Tony did, he was fucked! He loved Craig, and looked up to him like a big brother. Tony knew that burning the body was actually his fault, and Craig had not wanted that to happen. Tony did not want to turn into a rat and lie about something he was responsible for. And even worse, a few hours later, he would have to face Craig and Kelly at Greg Ruiz' house. All he knew for certain was that he had to go get high, because he could not face this reality.

Saturday night, December 17th – Sunday early morning, December 18th Party at Greg and Diana's house

Craig and Kelly's "best friends" started trickling in over at Greg and Diane Ruiz' house early, because they wanted to make sure they got their shit before Ruiz ran out. All of Craig and Kelly's drug buddies were pumped to have one last party with them before they took off for Massachusetts the next day.

Craig insisted that Greg only invite people that knew exactly what happened. He did not want to rehash the story one more time, and he said, "The more people that know, the more likely some bullshit story will get out, and they would all get in trouble." Greg honored his request, and only invited their friends that knew about the overdose and cover up. When he talked to the people he invited over, Greg told them that Craig and Kelly were going to take off the next day for Boston. Everyone wanted to come over to say goodbye. Craig trusted Greg, and knew that he had always been cautious by nature because of his line of work, so when they walked up to the door, Craig was not worried about the guest list.

Craig and Kelly were the last to arrive, and were overwhelmed as they walked around the room. Craig was absolutely right; he had nothing to worry about. Everyone there knew exactly what had happened that night, and told Craig and Kelly that they were there to help them out. Craig and Kelly both felt blessed, and for the first time in a while, they were able to relax. These people were their loyal friends, and with them on their side, they believed that everything was going to be alright.

Everyone at the party was doing drugs

There were over a dozen people present, all faces Craig and Kelly longed to see: Greg, Diana, Megan, Jeremy, Tony, Tony's girlfriend, Schwimmer, Pat, and Kessler; together again for one last hurrah! Greg was the man! With a smorgasbord of mind- altering chemicals lined up to choose from: cocaine, ecstasy, tabs, bars and pot. The second a person walked in the door, they purchased some shit from Greg. Nobody bothered to go off to go get high in private, they were all friends, doing the same thing; they snorted, swallowed, injected, and smoked their way through Greg's stash.

These drugs were their bond, and they all wanted to share this experience together one last time. Craig and Kelly realized when they walked around the room that everyone had a huge jump on them, so they decided to shoot up their coke. This would give them an immediate high, and catch them up with all of their friends.

While they were shooting up, they could hear everyone talking and were surprised by what they heard. Everyone seemed to know all of the details about the tragedy, from Melissa's overdose to Tony walking in on Craig giving Melissa CPR. Their information came from second hand text messages that were sent out during the week however, and they were all anxious to hear the facts from Craig and Kelly themselves. In an attempt to confirm the rumors, their friends began to pepper them with questions.

Once their questions were answered, and rumors confirmed, Craig said, "Let's talk about this shit later because I need to fucking party right now, period!" Everyone lifted their glasses and cheered, as they yelled, "Fuck Yeah!" They pumped the music up, and everyone began to party, some a little harder than others. With ecstasy bouncing around, things turned sexual fast for a lot of the guests.

Everyone was laughing, cutting up, and partying like it was their last time to ever party together again. Megan was bouncing off the walls, acting crazy, and throwing herself on Craig in front of both Jeremy and Kelly. She sat him down and gave him a lap dance, and he picked her up and put her on Kelly's lap. After they made out, Megan pulled Kelly over and they both straddled a leg. Craig thought for a minute that this could be hot, but when Megan opened her mouth, he quickly changed his mind.

With her high-pitched voice, she shouted, "Isn't Craig the sexiest man alive?" Then she started to squeeze his biceps, and said, "I'd fuck him!" Humping up on him, she asked Craig if he wanted to fuck her. Craig knew if he was sent to prison for a while, this was not the last face he wanted to see. Craig stood up, and started to walk away, when Megan jumped up and wrapped her arms around Craig, and whispered in a slurred voice, "I love you Craig!" Then Kelly walked over and she grabbed her and said the same thing. They both smiled at her, and she started mumbling to both of them that she loved them, and would do anything for them.

This girl was not right in the head, and Craig was doing his best to get away from her when she started asking Craig, "Why don't you like me?" Craig exaggerated and said that he did like her, and Kelly told her she needed to drink some water. "I am going to get you a water bottle, I will be right back," Kelly said; and Craig thought, "Don't leave me here with this fucking crazy ass bitch alone," and got up and followed Kelly to the kitchen. Craig passed by Greg and asked him, "What the fuck is she on? You need to give her something to calm her ass down; she is annoying as hell!" When Craig and Kelly walked into the kitchen Tony was sitting in a chair talking to his girlfriend. Craig could tell that something was up, so he sat down beside him to check on his friend.

Craig put his hand on Tony's shoulder and asked him if he was okay. Tony knew that he faced an impossible situation in the next few days; either tell the truth and go to jail, or lie and send Craig to jail. It was eating him up, and Craig could see that. Craig told him that everything was going to be okay as long as everyone told the truth. "I got your back and you got my back, and I trust you with my life. I hope you feel the same way about me!" Tony said that he did, he was just having a hard time; "I've been having fucking nightmares since the day it happened. I can't get that fucking image of her out of my head!"

Craig really cared about Tony, and felt like shit for calling him in the first place. Craig told Tony, "I was fucked up out of my mind when Melissa overdosed, and I didn't know what the hell to do, man. It happened so fucking fast; it felt like I was stuck, and couldn't move. I was scared out of my mind, and a fucking coward; I wish I never got you involved man! I am going to do everything I can to make sure you don't get in trouble, period!"

Gross sighed, and took a deep breath; he looked up with tears in his eyes, and said, "I am scared out of my fucking mind! I am so fucked!" Tony looked like a little, terrified kid, and Craig's heart broke for him. Craig put his arm around Tony and said, "No you aren't brother; this is me; I will take the fucking heat, not you. Kelly and I are taking off tomorrow, and if we get arrested, I am not saying your name. I won't say shit! I will take the blame for everything: the duct tape on her face, putting her in the trunk, and burning the car." Tony shook his head and said that he couldn't let Craig do that, "I am responsible for everything, if I had dumped the body like you asked, we wouldn't be facing a fucking murder charge."

Right then, Craig knew that Tony had been talking to a lawyer; why else would Tony say they were facing murder charges? Craig asked him if he had told anyone, and Tony said that he had kept his mouth shut, "But nobody else in the house has, they've all been fuckin' blabbing their mouths, especially fucking big mouth in the other room. Everybody knows that I drove you out there."

Craig said, "Okay, then all I am going to tell the police is that you followed us out there, pulled the car around, and you had no idea what we were doing. You say the same thing, and they can't charge you with shit!" Tony truly trusted Craig, and knew that he would follow through with his word; but he could hardly look him in the face knowing that in the following days he would likely be forced to stab Craig in the back.

SPINNING THEIR WHEELS

As the party slowed down, and the drugs wore off, the mood turned more serious and everyone gathered around to talk about what happened to Melissa. Craig was fairly certain that Tony was lawyered up, and feared he had already talked to the police. He wondered if anyone else had talked to the police also. So he asked the group if the authorities had tried to contact any of them about Melissa's overdose. Megan raised her hand, and said, "Yeah, they've been calling me non-fucking-stop." Craig looked surprised; this was the first he had heard about the authorities trying to call Megan. Craig looked at Kelly, and she said that Megan just told her. Craig asked her what she said when they talked to her, and Megan said, "Oh no, I haven't talked to those assholes, they just keep calling and leaving messages. I didn't want to call you and Kelly to tell you because the mother fuckers probably have our phones wire tapped, or some shit like that."

Megan was still obviously slurring her words, so Craig hoped that she would be lucid when they discussed what to do next. Kelly told her that she was doing everything right, and Craig said, "If they really want to talk to you, they will show up at your house. Don't volunteer anything if you don't have to, you know?" He asked her if she got rid of the bag, and she said, "Absolutely, I fucking chunked that shit a long time ago!"

Tony said that the police had left him messages as well, and Craig's ears perked up as he thought, "I fucking knew it!" Tony said, "They even called my fucking parents, and my mom lost her shit!" Craig knew Tony's mother, and thought, "Now it makes sense; this would explain why Tony would have a lawyer." She was the kind of Mom that never allowed Tony to experience consequences when he messed up, she ran around fixing everything for him. Craig and all the other guys would bust Tony's balls all the time because he was such a pussy, a Mama's boy!

There was no doubt in Craig's mind that if Tony's mother was called, they lawyered up the second she got off the phone. Craig began to wonder if Tony's mafia bullshit wasn't bullshit after all. Craig thought, "My luck would be that fucking bastard was telling the truth, and they have connections with both Metro and the D.A.'s office like he said, and they end up fucking me over so that Tony can walk away a

SWIFT INJUSTICE

free man." Craig said to himself, "Nay, there's no fucking way!" and thought to himself, "I need to get some sleep!"

Craig told everyone about being questioned by the police, and said, "I saw the look in that prick detective's eyes. They want me, nobody else. It's all too heavy right now, we're taking off tomorrow, so those idiots can figure out what the fuck really happened and stop just making shit up. When those assholes would not leave my house, even after I asked for a lawyer, I knew right then and there, these assholes want me to be guilty. They actually want this whole thing to be a murder, and I can't wait to see their faces, when all of the evidence comes out, and I can say, 'I told you so, you morons!' Melissa died from a fucking overdose, period!"

Everyone looked worried, so Jeff spoke up and told everyone that he had been talking to his lawyer here in Vegas about everything, and he had arranged for a lawyer to meet up with Craig in Boston as well, saying "It's all good, everything will be okay!" Craig said that Jeff had been amazing, and Kelly agreed saying, "You see who your real friends are when something like this happens."

Of course Megan had disappeared after everything happened, which was actually for the best. She felt like a jerk, and she wanted Kelly to know that she would always be there for them as well. She was, after all, Kelly's "best friend," or so she wanted everybody to think. So Megan said, "You know I will do anything for you guys. If anyone asks me anything, I'm gonna tell them I saw Melissa overdosed in your car with a needle in her arm. If we say that, it would be completely logical for you guys to go burn the car, I mean it was fucking ruined already, you know." Craig said that would be cool, "But I don't want to have change ups and fuck-ups, because then Kelly and I look like liars." Jeremy said that it's not really a change up or lie, because "technically we saw her overdosed in the car." Everyone agreed to tweak the truth a little to protect their friends; Craig looked at Megan and Jeremy and said, "Okay, so we are all on the same page," and Megan said, "Absolutely."

Jeff was tired and ready to go home. He reminded Craig to park his truck in the garage, and told him he would leave the alarm off until they got to his house. It was already two the next morning, and Craig said, "We should leave too; we need to get a good night's sleep before we hit the road later." Megan started crying, and begged them to stay a little longer, but they told her they really needed to get some sleep. Everyone hugged each other, and swore to be there for each other until the end. Nobody was specific when they said "the end," and for many of them, they were not even loyal until the end of the week.

CHAPTER **16**

Running From Their Problems

Last night in Vegas
Craig and Kelly stayed their last night in Las Vegas at Jeff Schwimmer's house, and on Sunday, December 18th, 2005, Craig and Kelly got packed up and ready to head to Massachusetts. Schwimmer gave them some food and drinks for the road, and told them to take the comforter and pillows from the guest room they slept in to be comfortable on the trip. Schwimmer told Craig to call him every day, "After you call, I will give my lawyer an update. He advised me that if you stay in constant communication with us, you can't be charged with fleeing; especially since there have not been any charges filed against you." Craig agreed that he would, and they gave Schwimmer a hug, and Craig told him, "You are amazing, and I will never forget this."

Headed to Boston
Craig and Kelly got into the truck and pulled out their Google map directions they had printed on Schwimmer's computer. They waved goodbye, and were on their way. On their way to Stoughton, Massachusetts, Craig decided to take the road less traveled, and put the northern route into his GPS. They would take I-15 North, and headed north through Utah, Idaho, and Montana. Once they got to Montana, they would make their way east through North Dakota, Minnesota, Wisconsin, Illinois, Indiana, Michigan, Ohio, and New York to Massachusetts. They would be driving through twelve states, 3,268 miles, in the dead of winter through the ice and snow to get to their destination.

RUNNING FROM THEIR PROBLEMS

On the trip, hardly a word was spoken between the two. They were deep in their own thoughts about everything that had happened, and what would happen next; emotionally exhausted, they just stared straight ahead at the white road in front of them. They took showers at truck stops, and pulled over to watch movies on their DVD's to temporarily take their mind off of everything. All along the way there were people stranded in the snow, and Craig would pull over to help anyone that was stuck. In Montana alone, he pulled out ten cars. They thought they may never get to Boston as that rate, but Craig was not going to leave anyone stranded on the side of the road.

Matt Cline

Craig kept in constant contact with Matt Cline, letting him know that they were on their way; and calling him to have his spirit lifted on the long drive to Massachusetts. After a couple of days, however, the FBI started hounding Matt. Someone in their "close circle of friends" had already sold them out, and told the authorities that they were heading to Boston. Matt called Craig and told him not to call or text anymore because he was afraid that the FBI had his phone tapped. Craig told him when he got to town, he would send him a text message, saying that he was in El Paso, TX, and they agreed to meet up at a shopping center close to Matt's house. Craig knew that it could not be good if someone from the party at Greg's house that night had already turned on him and started talking. He was so relieved that he would soon be with someone that would never rat him out, and would do anything to help him, his best friend, Matt Cline.

According to Craig, "Matt Cline was like my brother. He was the one person I knew that I could count on for anything and trust with my life. He was the kind of friend that would help me, even if it meant himself getting into trouble. Matt and I became best friends back in 1991, and remained best friends right up to the day he passed away. When I tore my pectoral muscle, Matt was there helping me while I went through rehabilitation in Venice Beach. When I did two years at Lompoc Penitentiary, Matt wrote me and talked on the phone with me twice a week the entire time I was in prison. When I got out, he came to California and helped me get back on my feet. When I moved to Vegas, he moved to Vegas, and we joined up to throw the after-parties. We trained together, hung out together, partied our asses off together- I loved him like he was my own brother."

Monday, December 19th
Police get surveillance tapes

On Monday December 19th, Detective Wilson obtained digital surveillance recorded from the Short Line Express Market Shell on the northwest corner of State Route 160 and Rainbow Boulevard. According to the police reports, the video showed Anthony Gross' charcoal pickup followed by Ryan's Jaguar. The truck pulled to the west side of the gas pumps, while the red Jaguar drove to the south side of the store, out of view.

A few hours later, Sergeant Alby obtained a VHS tape and photographs of video surveillance recorded on the morning of December 14th at Wal-Mart Superstore located at Fort Apache Road and Hacienda Ave. He also received a reproduction of a store receipt for a transaction that occurred around 3:31 am wherein six, 64 fluid ounce, bottles of "Kingsford" charcoal lighter fluid and one, 64 fluid ounce bottle of "Premium Quality charcoal lighter fluid was purchased. Also purchased were a barbeque tool set and a bottle of juice.

The purchase was made with a Wells Fargo Visa used by Kelly Ryan. He also obtained a photograph of the barbeque tool set with the same store skew number. The video surveillance photographs show a woman with long, dark hair, wearing a red sweat suit with a white stripe running down the sleeves and down the outside of the pant leg pushing a shopping cart with seven bottles of charcoal lighter fluid.

The video surveillance photographs of the outside of the store following the purchase, show the same woman walking to a red, mid-sized car of similar size to an X-Type Jaguar where she met a male driver after 3:30 a.m. The video surveillance tape shows the male driver wearing a dark shirt with a lighter colored shirt getting out of the car and helping the woman place the purchased items in the back seat of the car. The couple pulled out of the parking lot at 3:36 a.m.

Police interview Greg Ruiz

That same morning, the Investigators called Gregory Ruiz and asked him to meet with them. Greg immediately got in his car and headed to the police station to make a statement. In the interview, the homicide detectives asked Greg Ruiz how he knew Craig Titus. Greg said that he had met him through his brother-in-law, and they became friends and started hanging out together after that.

Greg told them that Craig was real famous in the world of bodybuilding. "We went to a bodybuilding seminar one time, and when it was over, we were walking out with Craig, and swarms of his fans wanted an autograph and pictures with him. I thought, this guy is a big fucking deal. It's pretty cool to be friends with a celebrity you know. He could get you into any nightclub, and I felt like a celebrity because Titus was my friend."

Ruiz said that a few months before, in the summer some time, Craig asked him about going into business with him, selling bodybuilding fitness apparel called Ice Gear. "I was fucking pumped, this guy lives in a mansion, and he wants to partner up with me; hell yeah! It all sounded legit, and we were going to split everything right down the middle, 50/50. People warned me not to go into business with Craig because he was nuts, but by this time; I had already put in thirty grand, so there was no backing out now. I just kept telling myself this is a big fucking star, there is no way this business could fail, and you know what I'm sayin'."

When the homicide detectives asked if he got along with Craig as a business partner, Greg said, "Yeah we were cool, but I was becoming more concerned each day when I noticed that Craig had a drug problem. I mean everyone dabbles in it, you know a little bit; even I splurge on special occasions, but this guy did shit every day, all day long. And I thought to myself, shit, I just went into business with a fucking tweaker!"

The homicide detectives asked Greg about Anthony Gross, and his ties. if any, with Craig Titus. Greg told them that he and Tony were best friends. He said that Tony liked to work out at the gym with Craig; he really admired Craig. Greg laughed saying Tony and Craig liked to get together and smoke pot. He said, "But I started to get worried about Tony. You know, he is young, stupid and impressionable. I see Craig doing this hard core shit, and Tony following his every step, like Craig is his hero, and I started to worry a little about my boy."

The homicide detectives asked Greg if he had any knowledge about Craig and Kelly's "swinger lifestyle?" And Greg said, "Hell yes, everyone knew about that. They were swingers, and would have sex with other women. Kelly liked it too, they both fucked different girls." The police asked if Craig or Kelly had ever had sex with Melissa James, and Ruiz said, "I don't know if they ever had sex with Melissa or not. I know that she was Kelly's long-time, good friend and then all of a sudden they became enemies. Kelly hated this girl; we could not even say her name around Kelly."

Ruiz said that he thought maybe at one time Kelly and Melissa had sex together, but when Megan Pierson came on the scene they stopped. He said that Megan was real possessive of Kelly and Craig for a while, and she would make comments about having sex with both of them, and then she would say terrible things about Melissa. Then Ruiz said, "You know what I have heard Craig talk about a sex tape he made a couple of years back with Kelly and Melissa; and I remember Tony saying that he watched it one time. So yeah, they have had threesomes before, but I don't think anything like that has happened in a while."

The homicide detectives asked Ruiz if he ever saw Melissa James, and Ruiz said, "She (James) came to our house a couple of times, and she would stay outside in the front yard. She would never talk to anybody. Every time I talked to her she wouldn't look me in the face. She was a shady kind of girl. I mean, Melissa was very, very shady, and I know for a fact that she was a big drug user, and she was fucked up on meth all the time. I don't know where she bought that shit because none of us would touch it, you know what I'm sayin'. You have to buy that shit from scumbags, and I know she would take off and be gone for a long time on the streets." Ruiz said that he knew that something was going to happen to that girl because she was a full blown junkie. If it wasn't for Craig and Kelly, she would have been on the streets. He said, "I'll be straight up with you, when I heard that she overdosed, I wasn't surprised."

The police asked Greg if he talked to or saw Craig or Kelly on Tuesday, December 13th. Ruiz said that he had not, but he knew that something was up because Megan called him acting hysterical. Ruiz said. "She called me acting all crazy, asking if I knew anything, and I was like what in the fuck are you talking about. She said that Kelly was not calling her back, and she had been trying to call her all day, and I thought this girl has lost her fucking mind."

She might have been trying to pull information out of Greg, but he had no information to pass on, and that was when she told him that she talked to Tony earlier in the day, and he said Melissa died of an overdose. As if that wasn't bad enough, she said that Tony was helping Craig get rid of the body, so they wouldn't get in any trouble for having drugs in the house. Greg said he thought to himself, "What in the fuck are you talking about? Tony is my boy, you know what I'm sayin', my best friend. I thought that Megan was lying, because she fucking lies all of the time for attention, but she wasn't lying. Tony didn't want to talk about much, but he said she died from an overdose. He even walked in while Craig was giving her CPR with puke and shit going everywhere."

The homicide detectives asked Greg what Tony's demeanor was like, and he said that Tony was extremely depressed. He stated that Tony came over the next day, and he still wouldn't talk about it, and there was something definitely wrong. Greg said, "Tony and I have been best friends for a while, and I have never seen him like that. He was all depressed and shit, and looked sick. He had tears in his eyes, and didn't want to talk to nobody. When I tried to talk to him, Tony would just say, 'Don't worry about it, we took care of it.' He wouldn't say shit, and stayed high all day long; he was like a fucking zombie. My wife even said, 'Tony's not right, something's wrong. Tony is always hyper and crazy, and he seems dead.' He was still in his pajamas, and didn't change them for a few days."

Greg said that Tony's mom came over to his house, and demanded to know what was going on, and why homicide had called her looking for Tony. Greg said that Tony would not say much, and that all he had heard is that a girl overdosed at Titus' house, and Tony helped him get rid of the body. He said, "I felt so fucking bad for her, she went fucking crazy, screaming and crying, and shit."

The homicide detectives asked Greg, "When was the last time you saw Craig Titus and Kelly Ryan?" Greg said, "They met me for lunch that afternoon, and then came over to my house on Saturday night to party with some friends." They asked Greg what they talked about at Subway, and he told them that Craig told him about the accidental overdose, and that he feared that he would get blamed for it. "Craig told me he traded in his truck for another truck; for gas mileage, or some shit like that. Let's see, he talked about putting the truck in Jeff Schwimmer's garage while they stayed at his house, and Jeff got them some high-powered attorney in case the story got twisted, just shit like that. They were scared because they didn't do anything, and were afraid that nobody would believe them, you know."

The homicide detectives asked what they talked about on Saturday night, and Ruiz said, "Some of the same shit. People talked about helping them sell their house if they needed to, and Craig said his best friend would help him do that. He talked about this guy in Boston buying his business, and liquidating their assets."

The detectives asked Greg if Craig ever mentioned fleeing the country, and he said, "Yeah maybe, I think he talked about getting a passport, or some shit like that. Megan, Jeremy, and Schwimmer were having a conversation, and I could hear them talking about selling his rental houses to raise money, and they talked about a passport. Maybe starting his bodybuilding Federation up in Greece because he had family there. They could have been joking, I don't know! You would have to ask Schwimmer about all that." When they asked for Jeff Schwimmer's number, Ruiz wrote it down for them.

Monday afternoon December 19th
Police Interview Schwimmer

The homicide detectives' next phone call was to Jeff Schwimmer, but he would not answer his phone. They decided to stop by and pay him a visit, and Schwimmer opened the door to talk to them. The detectives explained why they were there, and asked him when he last saw Craig and Kelly. Schwimmer did not want them to know that Craig and Kelly had been staying at his house because he could be charged with aiding and abetting, so Jeff said that he last saw them at some friend's house last Saturday night. The detectives asked him the name of the friend's house, and who all were at the house and Schwimmer listed everybody that was there.

They asked him why they all met at Greg and Diana's house, and they also asked if anything was said about the death of Melissa James or Kelly Ryan's car being set on fire. Schwimmer said that everyone knew that Craig and Kelly were leaving for Boston the next morning, so it was a party to say, "Goodbye". Then without an attorney present, and high out of his mind on coke, Schwimmer said, "There were drugs everywhere, every person there was either shooting up or snorting cocaine, taking OxyContins, Ecstasy; there were drugs everywhere. I have never seen so many people shoot up dope in one place before!"

It was unclear why he volunteered all of that information, other than to point a finger at everyone else to take the glare off himself. The entire time he talked, his jaw twitched back and forth, he sounded like he had a cold, and he could not stand still; the detectives knew that they could never use him as a witness, but would take advantage of his running mouth, and write every last thing he said down for future reference. They asked him if Craig or Kelly had any problems with Melissa James, and Schwimmer said that Kelly definitely had a problem with her.

He said, "Kelly was talking about how Melissa was stealing from them, and talked about confronting Melissa about stealing from her and they got into a fist fight. She said that there was a stun gun, and someone was shocked by it. Maybe it was Kelly, and she flopped around then Craig came home and broke them up, or something. Then a little after Melissa collapsed from a drug overdose."

Out of nowhere, Jeff told the police that if they wanted to know the truth, he thought Kelly Ryan was somehow involved in Melissa James' death. He said, "Mark my words, Kelly Ryan was the likely catalyst for the events leading to Melissa James' body being burned in the back of the car. I would bet money that Kelly Ryan killed Melissa James, and she forced Craig into getting rid of her body. Kelly Ryan fucking hated Melissa; I mean hated her! Craig loved Melissa, and I don't know why, but Kelly wanted her dead, and that's my honest belief."

The homicide detectives asked if Schwimmer knew anything about Craig's relationship with Tony Gross. Schwimmer said that they knew each other from the gym, and Tony sold him any drugs he could get his hands on. Schwimmer talked about Tony moving up from selling pharmaceuticals he stole from people's houses, to breaking in the big time, and selling the hardcore shit.

Schwimmer didn't want to mention anything about Greg Ruiz because that was his source. He didn't really give a rat's ass about Tony Gross, and if someone was going to get pinched, Schwimmer wanted it to be Tony Gross. He said, "There was talk of having Tony be the drug mule for some guys in the IFBB, and he would go to Mexico to buy and smuggle in steroids. I tried to warn Tony to stay away from all of that shit, or he would end up behind the eight ball."

The homicide detectives asked if anyone else at the party talked about their involvement with the death of Melissa James, and Schwimmer said that was all everyone talked about all night. He said, "Tony was upset, and didn't say hardly two words. He stayed high the entire time and was completely out of it. He left after a couple of hours, you could tell he was upset, and wanted to go home."

The homicide detectives asked about Megan and Jeremy, and he said that Jeremy was real quiet too and did not say much, but "Megan was a fucking big mouth. She is one of Kelly's crazy, stalker fans; she is not really her friend, but Megan thinks they are best friends, you know. So anywhere Kelly goes, Megan is following right behind her, and she is annoying as hell. Megan hated Melissa because Kelly hated Melissa, so she just talked shit about Melissa all night, and talked about going into the garage, and how disgusting the smell was. That's about it." The detectives asked him how long everyone stayed at the party, and Jeff said that everyone left the next morning between one and two.

RUNNING FROM THEIR PROBLEMS

The homicide detectives asked Jeff if he had talked to Craig or Kelly about the death of Melissa James prior to the party on Saturday night. Schwimmer acknowledged that he had, and told them everything Craig and Kelly told him prior to the party. Schwimmer told the investigators the entire story, "Craig and Kelly showed up at my house scared out of their minds the day the police were searching through their house. They were talking about being blamed for Melissa overdosing on Meth, and being charged with murder when I told them to come in, back up, and tell me what the fuck they were talking about."

So they did, and Craig told me, 'They found Melissa overdosed in her room, and there were drugs and needles everywhere. She had crystal meth spread all over her room, and some powder they had never seen before.' Craig said that Melissa overdosed on all that shit, and he freaked out. So he called Tony to come help him, and they wrapped her up and put her body in the trunk of Kelly's car. Tony left and came back later that night, or earlier that next morning. I am not sure what time, but I know that Megan and Jeremy were over at their house all night long, helping them out." Schwimmer said, "After Megan and Jeremy left, Craig called Tony, and Tony went over to their house. Craig was pissed because Tony was supposed to dump the body earlier but he never did. They left and bought lighter fluid and gas, and then Craig and Kelly followed Tony out to the desert. They met up with Tony to go drop the body and burn the car, but they forgot to take Melissa's body out, and Craig could not get her out of the car."

The detectives asked him what he thought about their revelation, and he said, "I couldn't believe it; I was like, what? That was so incredibly stupid! I told Craig he just fucked up all of the evidence that this girl overdosed. The police are going to think you killed her. Craig got pretty heated and said, 'Melissa was not murdered; she overdosed on drugs!' Craig was so upset; he was beside himself with grief. And the whole time we are talking, Kelly is standing there, with her arms crossed, and a smirk on her face. When I asked her if she was okay, Kelly seemed overjoyed that Melissa was gone. Kelly actually said that she was glad Melissa was dead. When I asked her how she could feel that way, she said, 'Melissa had been trying to kill me; she got hers before she got me.' I couldn't fucking believe what came out of Kelly's mouth! I just shook my head in disgust. How could this woman be so callous about the death of this poor girl. Who cares if she overdosed? Melissa was dead; have a heart! After that I was done with Kelly Ryan. She's a total bitch! If anyone goes down for this, it needs to be her."

Tony Gross would be charged with Murder unless he cooperated

Earlier that morning, Gross' attorney talked to Tony and his parents. He informed them that the district attorney's office would be filing charges in the following twenty-four hours, and Tony would be charged with murder. Nobody in that room could believe it, least of all Tony, who had only helped his friend get rid of an overdosed body; he did not murder anyone. Melissa James was already dead when he arrived at Craig and Kelly's house.

Their attorney asked them if Tony would be willing to cooperate with the prosecution, in exchange for the possibility of having the charges eventually dropped. His parents said that he absolutely would do whatever he needed to do to get off, and Gross nodded his head in agreement. With their confirmation of cooperation, Louis Palazzo spoke with the homicide detectives, and told them that Anthony Gross was ready to make a statement. Palazzo informed the investigators that his client would cooperate, and assist the investigation and prosecution in any way or form that he was needed in order to secure a guilty verdict for Craig Titus.

Palazzo told the detectives they could come to his office and conduct an interview with Mr. Gross, after which time his client would surrender to the authorities. In return for Anthony Gross' cooperation, his attorney requested that the bail be set at the lowest amount possible for a murder charge, which would be $13,000.

Anthony Gross' Interrogation

On Monday, December 19th at 5:00 p.m., homicide Detectives Dean O'Kelley and Robert Wilson arrived at the law office of Louis Palazzo where they met with Tony Gross and his counsel. For nearly an hour, the detectives questioned Tony about his involvement in the death of Melissa James.

RUNNING FROM THEIR PROBLEMS

Detective O'Kelley: "Anthony, do you understand this interview is being recorded?"
Anthony Gross: "Yes sir."

Detective O'Kelley: "Were you contacted by Craig Titus on Dec. 13th?"
Anthony Gross: "Yes."

Detective O'Kelley: "Tell me the circumstances surrounding that contact?"
Anthony Gross: "Yeah, I was at my girlfriend's place, and we had gone to bed. I was sleeping in the bed with my girlfriend, just lying there, cuddling with her. And I keep getting some phone calls around three in the morning, but I wasn't answering my phone. Finally I check my phone. I see that it was Craig. I returned his phone call. He said he needed my help. Come meet me over here. I gotta get some gas. And, uhm, that was it. I basically told him all right, and then went to go meet him at the Blue Diamond and Rainbow gas station. I just had my pajama pants and stuff on. I had pulled in and he was already there waiting for me. I pulled up to the gas pump. I swiped my card, got a little bit of gas. At that time, I believe I got a phone call saying, you know, head out on this road, head out that way on Blue Diamond Road. I pulled out and they kept going down this road for fifteen minutes. And then I got a phone call saying, 'There's a road up here, that's where we're gonna be turning on.' We followed down the road; he stopped. His girlfriend Kelly got out of the car; she come got in my truck and told me to pull around. Craig came to my window, grabbed the gas. Uh, I handed it to him through the window. Kelly told me to pull up, so I pulled up. We were talking and all of a sudden Craig jumps in the car and says, 'Go, go, go.' So that's when I proceeded to go. Then I took them straight to their house and dropped 'em off and nothing was said."

The detectives knew that Tony was lying to them. They had already checked the phone records, and knew that Craig and Tony made over a dozen calls beginning at 3:28 pm on the 13th. When they checked the Green Point Grocery surveillance, they did not ever see Kelly and Melissa, but they did see Tony Gross there two times. And the surveillance at the Shell station clearly showed that Craig and Kelly were not already there waiting on him, he was there getting gas, and then they pulled up. And finally, Tony did not follow Craig and Kelly; Tony clearly pulls out first and Craig and Kelly are following him. And the rest of his story did not make sense; so the detectives figured that he was lying about everything else.

Detective O'Kelley: "Okay, so that was Saturday morning, the 14th. What time did you first talk to Titus on the 13th?
Anthony Gross: "It was about 7:00 or 9:00 p.m."

Detective O'Kelley: "Did he say anything about needing gas at this time?"
Anthony Gross: "Yes."

Detective O'Kelley: "Was he specific about that? Did he say bring that gas can?"
Anthony Gross: "No, he just said that, ah, little can, fill up the little can of gas and meet me at the gas station later."

Detective O'Kelley: "Okay, so what did you do after that?"
Anthony Gross: "So I left my apartment with my pajamas on, and met them at the Shell gas station on Blue Diamond and Rainbow, Craig was already there parked on the side waiting on me."

Detective O'Kelley: "You did not meet up somewhere earlier and follow each other to the gas station?"
Anthony Gross: "Uhm, no." (This was one of the many lies that the detectives would catch him in during their interview- they had Tony Gross on surveillance at Green Valley Grocery, a half a mile from Craig and Kelly's house, between 2:00 a.m.- 3:30 am).

Detective O'Kelley: "Anthony, there is surveillance footage of you pulling into the gas station in your charcoal gray truck in front of the red Jaguar."
Anthony Gross: "Yeah, that's right. It was a coincidence when we pulled in together. So anyway, then I put some gas in the can I bought and put it in the center console."

Detective O'Kelley: "Because Craig asked you to do that?"
Anthony Gross: "Yeah, and then we left. Craig called and said to go right on Blue Diamond. So I did. I didn't get another call from him until just before we got to the road he wanted me to turn on. When he

flashed his lights I pulled over on the right side of the road, and that's when Kelly jumped into the passenger seat of my vehicle. She told me to turn around, which I did, and pull up next to the Jaguar, which I did, and then I passed the gas can out of my window to Craig. Kelly told me to pull forward, so I did."

Detective O'Kelley: "So at this time you have no idea what is going on?"
Anthony Gross: "No, I'm thinking in my head. I'm not, but I wasn't sure. I didn't know what was going on." (Caught in another lie)

Detective O'Kelley: "What were you thinking?"
Anthony Gross: "I'm just wondering what is going on? You know like what did, what did, what did, you know, what is the deal? I don't understand it, you know. I couldn't really put it together. I wasn't thinking, you know, wasn't thinking. I didn't wanna ask. I didn't wanna know. The less you know, the less you know."

Detective O'Kelley: "Were you following Titus, or was he following you?"
Anthony Gross: "I was following Craig; I uhm had no idea what, I mean where we were going. He just told me to turn and keep driving until he called me or something."

Detective O'Kelley: "Why such unquestioning loyalty?"
Anthony Gross: "That's just how it happened, that's all. Anyway, I didn't see what happened from there, because Kelly was talking to me, telling me not to say anything to anyone about what we were doing. Then Craig returned with the gas can in his hand, less than minute after he left, and jumped in the back seat through my door, and yelled, 'Go! Go! Go!'"

Detective O'Kelley: "Where did you go next?"
Anthony Gross: "We drove down the highway, and he flashed his lights and turned. I followed him on a rough, dirt road. Then Craig stopped and told me to turn my truck around the other way. Craig took the gas can, and Kelly got into the truck. Craig ran away with the gas can, and Kelly told me not to turn around. Before she could say anything else, like in less than a minute, Craig came running back,

jumped in the car, and yelled at me to, 'go, go, go.' I don't know what happened, and I never asked."

Detective O'Kelley: We found a kinetic flashlight with your initials on it at the scene. Do you own a kinetic flashlight?
Anthony Gross: "Yes, that's my flashlight; it must have fallen out when Craig jumped in my truck. But anyway, I dropped them off at their house, passed on an invitation to come in, and went back to sleep at my apartment. I was gone for about 45 minutes." (The detectives knew that he was lying because the flashlight was next to the jaguar, by two different sets of footprints. Tony quickly changes the subject, but lies again at the end when he said he was only gone for 45 minutes. It became clear that Tony was more involved than he was letting on, and he helped Craig destroy the car.)

Detective O'Kelley: So you say that neither Craig nor Kelly told you what happened to Melissa or that they were burning the car with her body in it. When did you find out that there was a body in the car?
Anthony Gross: "The next day, or day after that. Craig told my friends Jeff Schwimmer and Greg Ruiz, and they told me about it."

O'Kelley then asked Tony for the phone numbers and addresses of both Jeff Schwimmer and Greg Ruiz, and Tony provided the detective with that information. Detective O'Kelly asked Gross if he would allow Criminalistics personnel and detectives to meet with him to take photographs of his truck. Tony told detectives he had changed the tires on his truck because he had a blowout the day after the incident with Titus and Ryan. This told them that he was trying to cover something up. Other things bothered the detectives about Tony's statements. The detectives found it curious that Gross would agree to meet Titus in the early morning hours, at a time when most people are sleeping, and that he would agree to help him get them a small amount of gas without knowing exactly what it was for.

The homicide detectives also found it hard to believe that Gross would agree to follow Titus and Ryan without knowing what was happening, and that Gross did not ask any questions about Titus catching the Jaguar on fire or ask why he would do such a thing. Detective Dean O'Kelley made this comment to the newspaper after his testimony was leaked, "Sometimes you want to see people hang themselves. I love giving Titus enough rope to hang himself, but not with Anthony, because I had spoken with his parents and they were such good people. Every time Anthony lied I felt terrible for them. I could tell he was scared, but he had a story and he was sticking to it. I am a father of two boys, and I did not want this kid to be charged with murder, especially when I knew that Craig Titus was the murderer." This quote is important because O'Kelley would stand by this statement to the very end. He would make sure that Anthony Gross was not charged with anything, as long as he turned on Craig, and did everything they asked him to do, and what they ask him to do, as you will see, is fucking unbelievable!

Tuesday morning, December 20th
Las Vegas Metropolitan Police Department,
Lt. Tom Monahan
Media Release Tuesday, Dec. 20, 2001 Event # 051214-0619

On December 14, 2005, at approximately 4:40 am, a trucker was traveling on State Route 160 (Blue Diamond Road) from Las Vegas toward Pahrump when he spotted a fire in the desert about a half-mile from the road. When firefighters extinguished the blaze, they observed what appeared to be human remains in the trunk of the car. The remains were confirmed to be that of a human, and under the circumstances, it is being investigated as a homicide.

Media Release Wednesday, Dec. 21, 2001
Event # 051214-0619

Investigation has resulted in arrest warrants being issued for three suspects.

1. Titus, Craig Michael, DOB 01/14/1965, 5 feet 9 inches, 225 lbs. Brown hair, hazel eyes, shaved head.

2. Ryan, Kelly Ann, DOB 07/10/1072, 5 feet 3 inches, 120 lbs. Long brown hair, with green eyes.

Titus has a no-bail arrest warrant charging him with murder and third-degree arson. Ryan has a no-bail arrest warrant charging her with accessory to murder and third-degree arson.

A third suspect has been identified as 23-year old Anthony Remo Gross, who has already been arrested on charges of murder and third degree arson.

Craig Titus and Kelly Ryan are husband and wife and were living in the southwest area of Las Vegas. Both are successful bodybuilders and hold numerous titles in the bodybuilding and fitness industry. At this time it is unclear where the two suspects may have fled.

Tuesday afternoon, December 20th
Schwimmer calls Craig, tells him about warrant

Jeff Schwimmer called Craig immediately to tell him about the warrant, and Craig was completely stunned to hear that he had a warrant out for his arrest for murder. Jeff said that it was all over the national news, and they were talking about "a man hunt for the famous bodybuilding couple that murdered their personal assistant."

Jeff told Craig that the police were harassing him, but he had not said a word. He gave Craig the name of the attorney from Boston, and told him to call the guy right away. Craig pulled over and wrote the information down, and thanked Jeff for being so loyal to him. Whether it was from the guilt of turning on Craig, or the panic of being implicated in a murder, Jeff Schwimmer would never answer another call from Craig Titus again.

Anthony Gross arrested

Later that evening, Anthony Remo Gross was placed under arrest for Accessory to Murder & 3rd Degree Arson, and he was booked into Clark County Detention Center. Gross' lawyer, Louis Palazzo told the media that his client did not run and remained in Las Vegas. "He was honest about his involvement and has completely cooperated with the police." Palazzo and law enforcement knew this was not the case. Every statement he gave to the police was a lie. He tried to act like an unwilling participant, but Palazzo went on to say, "I am not going to let him be a scape goat in connection with this case."

The booking process was excessively slow because there were more crimes and arrests than usual during the holiday season. Being detained in a holding cell with cinderblock walls, one clogged toilet, and metal beds with no mattresses or pillows alongside murderers, rapists, and other violent offenders scared the shit out of Tony Gross.

As the drugs that Gross had used before he turned himself in began to wear off, the more miserable his over 24- hour stay in the holding cell became. These men from different walks of life had one thing in common: they were all "drug sick." When Gross scanned the room, he noticed it was difficult to tell how old most of these men were because years of drug abuse had robbed them of their youth, both physically and mentally. It looked like a mental ward in a third world country, and although Gross wanted to cry, he found the strength to suck it up, and attempted to fall asleep with one eye open.

The smell was unbearable; a concoction of body odor and sewage stink. Tony didn't know how long he would be trapped behind bars, but he had his mind made up that once he got the fuck out of there, he was never coming back! Tony was a mama's boy, and his mama had always fixed everything for Tony in the past.

Tony was told that he would not be able to be bailed out until after Christmas, but he held out hope that his family would pull some strings and get him out early. In order to survive, Tony had to block Christmas out of his mind, and focus on surviving through this stint in the Clark County Detention Center.

One thing that was abundantly clear- Tony Gross would never survive in prison! When his attorney approached him and his parents with a deal to turn on his friend Craig Titus, he told them that he was not going to do it. But after spending less than a day in the county jail holding area, Tony knew that he would do and say anything the detectives and prosecutor instructed him to, just to save his own ass.

Tony shares a cell with Darrin Allen and talks about the cover-up

On Christmas Eve, Tony Gross was finally assigned to and escorted to his new cell. It was apparent that he would not be going home for Christmas, but he was excited to walk out of that stuffed room of crazy people. As he approached his cell, Gross felt anxious and nauseated over the anticipation of seeing who was behind the door. He had seen every episode of *Oz* on HBO, and was scared shitless about having a swastika tattooed on his ass and becoming a white supremacist's bitch.

When the corrections officer unlocked the cell door, and Tony saw a young, scared, middle class 21-year-old white kid sitting on the other bunk, he wanted to give the C.O. a big bear hug and kiss him on the lips! John Darrin Allen extended his hand and introduced himself and then asked Tony, "So whatcha in for?" Tony felt vulnerable and alone being cooped up in the holding cell. There were hundreds of men passing in and out, and he was unable to have a conversation with any of them. So when he was finally able to open up and have a meaningful conversation with someone, he opened up and shared everything with his new friend.

Allen found Gross' honesty to be refreshing. Everyone he had encountered in prison thus far said that they were innocent, when they were clearly guilty. Gross seemed contrite when he talked about his egregious actions that night, and seemed sincere when he vowed to stay away from drugs. He described walking in on his celebrity friend Craig Titus, attempting to give Melissa James CPR, and how traumatized he was after he saw Melissa's body swollen and leaking nasty shit all over the floor. John Allen himself was in jail on a drug charge, and was able to empathize with his cell mate's predicament; but he told Tony that he had never personally witnessed someone die from a drug overdose.

Tony explained how irrational their erratic behavior was as they tried to cover up the overdose rather than report it to law enforcement. He told Allen about Craig attempting to clean up the body with towels, and how shit kept pouring out of her nose and mouth. Allen did not want to seem judgmental, but he could not believe it when Gross described attaching strips of duct tape over her nose and mouth "to make her stop oozing nasty shit everywhere!"

When Allen told Gross, "That's fucked up," Gross agreed and said that he wished he had never answered his phone that afternoon. Gross was straight forward, and told Allen about moving Melissa out to the trunk of the car, and taking the car out to the desert and burning the car. He candidly talked about Kelly Ryan wanting to call the police, and Craig wanting to dump her body in front of a hospital. Tony said he was responsible for Melissa's body being torched in the car. Although Allen was shocked, he told Gross that he admired him for his loyalty, and for "Manning up, and admitting what he did." But Tony did not acknowledge the compliment and changed the subject.

The next day was Christmas, and Tony seemed to be having a really hard time; he was quiet and appeared to be depressed. After visiting hours however, his mood changed, and he seemed to have a more positive outlook on his situation. Tony confided in Allen about his family's connections, and his attorney's deal he had arranged with law enforcement. Gross said that he was hesitant to lie and throw Craig Titus under the bus, but after this stay in jail, he had reconsidered everything.

He tried to rationalize his behavior by saying, "If it weren't for him (Craig Titus) I would never be in this situation. They want his head, not mine; what's the point of everyone going to prison?" For the first time during their stay together, the two men got into a verbal argument after Allen asked Gross, "Do you want to be a pussy ass rat?" Gross told him if it meant saving his own ass from going to prison, then he didn't care, he would rat on anyone.

Allen told him that they were finished, and said, "You and me are nothing alike!" Gross could not stand for someone not to like him, so he tried to retract what he said, and even change the subject, but Allen was done with him. Allen understood right from wrong, and knew that it was wrong for Gross to go along with the police to set Titus and his wife up on false murder charges.

SWIFT INJUSTICE

Megan Pierson and Jeremy Foley retain a lawyer, talk to homicide detectives

On Thursday, December 22nd, 2005, after ignoring repeated phone calls and visits from the Las Vegas Metro homicide detectives, and hearing about the arrest warrants issued for Craig, Kelly, and Anthony, Megan Pierson decided that it was time to talk, not to the police, but to her lawyer. After Megan and Jeremy told their lawyer their version of the truth about what happened at Craig and Kelly's house, their lawyer helped them concoct a story to present to the police.

Once they had their story straight, Megan and Jeremy's lawyer called Metro Homicide and asked the detectives to come to his office to interview his clients. In this meeting, Megan told the detectives that she and Kelly Ryan were best friends, and Kelly was going to be her Matron of Honor at her wedding in February. Megan talked about idolizing Kelly Ryan for years, and in the past few months becoming close with her. She told the detectives that Kelly Ryan and Craig Titus had a darker side to them: They were both struggling with drugs. Pearson said, "They're kinda the cat chasing the tail. He says that she has a problem, and she says that he has a problem. But the difference is, he (Craig) is able to stop, but Kelly is not."

Jeremy Foley said that he invited Craig to his engagement party and, to his shock, Titus was injecting OxyContin intravenously. Megan said that they were both shooting up drugs, but it was mostly Kelly. Pierson said, "I was planning a drug intervention for Kelly. And that was why they went over to Craig and Kelly's house on December 13th, to have an intervention for Kelly." Megan said that even though Melissa James was severely addicted to Crystal Meth, she was always talking to me about Kelly Ryan having an addiction problem.

Megan Pierson said, "Melissa planted in my head about her drug problem that it makes her paranoid. She was just saying that Kelly is becoming severely addicted to cocaine, and Melissa accused me of making the problem worse. Kelly was shooting it every hour, and by the middle of the day, after about 4- 6 injections, Kelly would become paranoid and go crazy."

When asked about Melissa's drug use, Megan said that she was also addicted, but she was addicted to the more hard-core drugs. She said that Melissa was very strange. "At times she was introverted and distant, and other times she tried to cause problems between Kelly and me. Probably because she was jealous that Kelly was my best friend."

When Megan was asked if Kelly talked bad about Melissa, Megan said, "All the time." When asked for an example, Megan said, "Okay well, on the Monday before Melissa overdosed, I was working out with Kelly, and she said that she just got her credit card bill in the mail and it had charges from Ross, Marshalls… places that Melissa constantly shopped at, and that Kelly never shopped at."

The homicide detectives told Megan to tell them about the night of Tuesday, December 13th and their encounter with Craig and Kelly that evening. Megan said, "Jeremy and I were at a restaurant having dinner, celebrating my graduation from UNLV when Craig and Kelly called and invited us over to their house. We went over there, and Melissa was not around. We all went upstairs to the entertainment area, where we watch movies and stuff, and Craig says he found something disturbing in Melissa's room. They show us this bag with tons of bloody needles and Crystal meth."

The detectives asked Megan if she was aware of a fight between Melissa and Craig or Kelly. Megan said, "Not with Kelly, but Craig talked about getting in an argument with her and he picked her up and body-slammed her on the floor in the middle of the living room. They were getting physical, you know, and the rest becomes a blur at some point. Then Melissa supposedly went in her room, took a Xanax, and went to sleep."

The homicide detectives asked if Craig mentioned what he was going to do with the body once the victim was deceased, and Megan said, "Uh-huh." Megan said, "Craig made a reference to James being in the trunk of the car. And, I was like, Well, what are you gonna do with her? And Craig told me they were going to drive her out to the desert, put clothes around her, and make it look like a rape. You know, it was strange. Oh, and Craig kept making the comment, 'There's three things you don't mess with, my family, my friends, and my money.'

And he was very, very, very, very mad at her for taking, I mean stealing. They told me that Melissa forged their names to have money wired to her, and it was pending, but Craig was trying to cancel it. The wire was for Twenty-three thousand dollars, and it was from their Home Equity Line Of Credit."

The homicide detectives asked if Kelly said anything about the victim's death, and she said, "No, she really didn't. She was not commenting on anything Craig said or did. She was just kinda doing her own thing, and staying away from the discussion. I mean she is my best friend, and if she knew anything, she would have told me."

They asked her about Anthony Gross, and she said, "I do know for a fact that Tony helped them dispose of James' body as a repayment for some debt he owed Craig. Supposedly Craig loaned him $1,000, and Craig said that if Tony helped him get rid of the body and the car they could call it even."

When the homicide detectives asked about the black Nike gym bag, Megan Foley said that she never looked in it, and does not know what was inside the bag. She said, "Craig made me take it when we were leaving, and he told me to get rid of it because he can't have that stuff in his house or it violates his probation or parole or something like that, I am not sure."

When they asked her if Craig said anything about using the taser on Melissa James, she said that he never mentioned anything about a taser, and she never looked in the bag, so she did not know there was a taser in the bag. Megan Pierson did make one thing clear to the detectives before she left, she was certain that Melissa died of an overdose, and that Kelly was not involved in any of this. Megan said, "I know in my heart that Kelly Ryan did not do a thing!"

According to the investigators, Megan's statements contained information that solidified the detectives' case against Craig and Kelly. Her statement reiterated the couple's suspicion that Melissa was embezzling from them, and also confirmed that the gym bag contained a taser gun which, the manufacturer would later prove, had been shot six times between 2:10 and 2:12 p.m. on Tuesday, December 13, a time frame during which both Craig and Kelly have said Melissa was in their house.

It was the same taser whose discharge remnants, or AFIDs, would be found by detectives in Melissa's room. (The taser dots found in Melissa's room actually helped the defense because Craig and Kelly were out of town at a convention when the AFIDs date and time were listed. This also supports the defenses' claims that Melissa had stolen the taser from Craig and Kelly's side table drawer in their bedroom, and moved it to her bedroom.)

Kelly had seen the taser gun when she attempted to help Melissa pack her clothes. Melissa had obviously been practicing using the taser, which would lead a person to believe that perhaps Melissa's attack on Kelly was premeditated. If Melissa was trying to kill Kelly, as Kelly suggested to many of her friends, then when Craig came home and pulled Melissa off Kelly, this would have been self-defense; his actions saved his wife's life that night.

Friday, December 23rd
FBI arrive at Matt's house, Craig and Kelly arrive in Massachusetts

Early Friday morning, the FBI arrived at Matt Cline's house and questioned him for over three hours. They told Matt that both Gregory Ruiz and Jeffrey Schwimmer informed them that Craig and Kelly were headed to his house, driving cross-country from Las Vegas, Nevada. They tapped Cline's phones and preceded to in front of Matt's house all day waiting on Craig and Kelly to show up.

Once Craig and Kelly arrived in town, Craig tried to call Matt several times. Matt, however, would not pick up the phone because he knew that his phones were tapped, and the FBI had 24-hour surveillance on him. Craig text messaged Matt and said that they were in El Paso. Matt knew what that meant and hoped that Craig did not show up at his house. He knew Craig and Kelly would try to meet him in the Shaw Shopping Center later in the day, but Matt decided to stay put. That way he would not be followed by the FBI, leading them directly to Craig and Kelly.

SWIFT INJUSTICE

When Craig and Kelly drove over to the parking lot in the Shaw's Plaza Shopping Center in Stoughton, Massachusetts, fifteen miles from Boston, his buddy Matt was nowhere to be found. Craig could feel the presence of the authorities breathing down his neck when he saw unmarked cars driving by and looking at his license plate.

When Craig noticed a black Ford Explorer circling his car, he didn't know if he was just being paranoid or what, but he did not want to take a chance, so Craig pulled out of the parking lot as fast as he could. He drove around for several minutes to make sure that they were not being followed, and then he pulled into an auto repair shop just 400 feet away from the shopping center.

Craig and Kelly went inside, and Craig asked about getting his oil changed. Kelly went into the bathroom to brush her teeth and wash her face while Craig visited with the mechanics. He said that he had just bought the truck, and had driven it across country from Las Vegas all the way to Massachusetts. Since the truck used diesel, they did not have the correct filter in stock for that motor, so they had to turn Craig away without changing the oil.

Craig shook their hands, and they got back into the truck, and had to decide what to do next. Craig and Kelly talked about just taking off and going somewhere else, but Craig said, "We aren't doing a damn thing wrong. We left before the warrant was issued, I have been in contact with a lawyer, and I am here to see my best friend, period." They decided to drive over to the Shaw Plaza one last time to see if Matt was over there, and if he wasn't, they were going to go by their lawyer's office and surrender to the authorities.

As they pulled into the parking lot and drove around, Matt was nowhere in sight. Craig wanted to wait around in the parking lot just in case he showed up. When they stopped, they noticed a nail salon; Craig suggested that Kelly go in and get a pedicure just to pass the time. He said, "After you get a pedicure, if he still is not here, we will take off."

Cramped in a truck for nearly an entire week, Kelly jumped at the chance to have her feet rubbed and toe nails painted; hopefully this would take her mind off of everything if only for a little while. Kelly got out of the truck and walked inside The Touch nail salon, while Craig opened a root beer and took a big swig as his eyes scanned the parking lot.

About thirty seconds after Kelly walked into the nail salon, Craig saw the same Ford Explorer from earlier pull up in front of the building. His first reaction was to get out and run, but right as he opened the door, the FBI surrounded his truck with unmarked cars and a SWAT team van. The federal agents had rifles pointed at his face, the police were pointing their guns, and they were yelling, "Get on the ground, and put your hands in the air!"

The parking lot looked like a light show at a nightclub, and sirens were blaring from both the Canton and Stoughton police department. They quickly hand cuffed Craig and placed him in the back of a Canton police car. When Craig Titus tried to look back to see his wife, there were news cameras running up to the car, recording his image as he was being driven away. The SWAT team also rushed into the nail salon and apprehended Kelly, and she was arrested and taken away to be questioned as well.

Craig and Kelly are arrested and taken into custody for questioning

The Canton police extensively searched the truck after Craig and Kelly were arrested. They confiscated a variety of things including: two pay as you go cell phones, a pack of Marlboro lights and a cigarette lighter, a lap top computer, with the DVD, "The Good, The Bad, and the Ugly" inside it. They also found about twenty CD's and DVD's, plastic bags with clean clothes and dirty clothes, a hair brush, a razor, shaving cream, liquid soap, deodorant, toothbrushes, and tooth paste. Inside a spray can with a false bottom, the police found rolls of cash totaling $8,300.

In the backseat of the truck there were pillows, blankets, and a comforter, along with several books and magazines. All of the items were bagged as evidence and sent off, while Kelly and Craig were being taken to the Norfolk County Correctional Facility in Dedham, Massachusetts at 3:45 p.m. Eastern Time to be booked and charged with the Murder of Melissa James.

Craig Titus: "All Megan, Gross, and Foley had to do was lie and repeat the story the investigators and prosecutor told them to say, and all their charges would be dropped. Those three know the truth; they were just as involved in covering up Melissa's overdose as Kelly and I were- they are just as guilty."

Section Three:
Just say that Craig did this thing- if you want to walk!

CHAPTER 1

The Interrogation

Craig & Kelly were held at the Norfolk County Correctional Facility on a federal charge of unlawful flight to avoid prosecution, due to an arrest warrant issued on December 21st, in Las Vegas, Nevada. The FBI reported that Craig and Kelly were driving to Boston, and planned to liquidate all of their assets with the help of Matt Cline. The FBI claimed they possessed intelligence that Titus and Ryan might have been trying to obtain a passport and fly to Greece where they believed Craig Titus had family members, and where there was not an extradition treaty with the United States.

After the booking process, they were immediately taken into an interrogation room where they were questioned separately by the FBI. Craig immediately asked for a lawyer, and said that his wife wanted a lawyer as well. The FBI does not tape record interviews of suspects, so, they would claim that Craig never asked for a lawyer, and voluntarily gave his statement.

FBI Interrogation
Three FBI agents sat down with Craig in the interrogation room, and informed him that they believed he had given an entirely different account of what happened than when he was first questioned by the Las Vegas detectives on December 14th. According to the FBI, Titus said that he and his wife found Melissa James dead of an overdose in his wife's car on the night of December 13th.

Instead of reporting the death to the police, Titus said that he and Kelly Ryan panicked; because they were worried the news of Melissa James' drug overdose would tarnish their public images and ruin their careers. Titus said that he wrapped the body in blankets and secured the blanket with duct tape and a belt from his robe after Melissa James was already deceased. Then to conceal the drug overdose, Titus and Ryan burned the body in her car in the desert.

After Craig told the FBI agents what happened, he asked them again if he could call an attorney, and they told him he wasn't leaving until he told them the truth. They said that his story was bullshit. Enraged, Craig said that the autopsy report would show that he was telling the truth; "Melissa James died from fucking overdosing on drugs!"

The agents said Craig's reaction, of hiding her body in a car, then burning the car, was not a reaction consistent with finding someone who has overdosed in their house. As the hours ticked by, Craig was starting to experience withdrawals from the pain medication, and was beginning to lose his patience.

On edge, he tried to explain why it would make sense for them to panic and try to get rid of a body that was overdosed in his house. "Look, I fucking panicked! I am a felon, and have already been fucked over by you guys before on bullshit, made-up drug charges! When I found Melissa, I fucking panicked because she had Meth, Coke, needles and shit all over her fucking room! I have a record, and my wife and I are high profile celebrities, if we got arrested our careers would have been over. I could see it in the newspaper now, 'Dead girl, Overdosed in Bodybuilder's house.' We would be fucking ruined, so I panicked, and thought, 'let's put her in the trunk, burn the car, and play stupid.' That's what we did, and I don't give a shit if you believe me, but that is the fucking truth! Period, Finito, End of story!"

Then one of the FBI agents suggested that perhaps Melissa didn't die of an overdose; that perhaps instead she died during rough sex. The agent said, "You admitted to placing duct tape around her face and a ligature around her neck." Craig interrupted him and said, he did not fucking admit to that! "I said that after she overdosed, I wrapped blankets around her and secured it with duct tape. Then I took the

THE INTERROGATION

belt from my robe and tied both ends together so that she would fit in the trunk!"

The FBI agent continued, "Ok there was duct tape, and belts, and you previously admitted to various people that the three of you have had sex together, and you did drugs together. Could this have been a sex act gone wrong? You were having kinky sex. You had her tied up. You were using drugs and maybe she OD'd or maybe you possibly strangled her."

Craig just looked at the guy, and made a smart ass remark, "Yeah, that's it. We were having sex and she OD'd. Let's go with that. That's a good story. Look I am not saying another fucking word unless you get my attorney!" *The most significant, and unjust, thing, out of everything we have shared thus far, occurred immediately following this conversation;* **that FBI agent typed up this "rough sex confession" word-for-word.**

While the rope was being typed around Craig's neck in one room, Kelly Ryan was telling her side of the story in another room; and their stories, in a roundabout way, matched up. They had already decided that if they were arrested, they were going to tell the authorities the truth; Melissa died of an overdose and they panicked- with a few little glitches to keep both Kelly Ryan and Anthony Gross out of trouble.

Since Megan Pierson Foley came up with the story about walking into the garage and seeing Melissa James overdosed in the driver's seat of Kelly's Jaguar; they believed both Megan and Jeremy would stick to that story. Megan and Jeremy were just as involved with the cover-up as everyone else, so it would make no sense for the couple to turn on Craig and Kelly and tell the authorities otherwise. In fact, Melissa's body had already been moved from the house to the trunk of the Jaguar when both Jeremy and Megan saw her body; however, both Craig and Kelly decided to stick with the other story, and lied to the authorities about that fact.

Craig and Kelly also agreed to leave Tony's name out of it altogether because Craig did not want Gross to get in any trouble. They had no idea, however, the homicide detectives and the crime scene analysts already knew about Tony Gross. Phone records showed that Craig called Tony minutes after he arrived home and found Melissa dead. They also had phone records showing Tony and Craig calling each other all day on the day of Melissa's death. The last few phone records showed the men calling each other right before the surveillance cameras captured Tony Gross' image at the Shell Gas Station purchasing the gas that was to be thrown on the Jaguar. In addition, there were finger prints on the adhesive side of the duct tape; along with Tony Gross' finger prints left behind on a few personal items at the crime scene.

Craig also misled the investigators and said he witnessed the physical altercation between Kelly Ryan and Melissa James. When in fact, Craig was at the hotel room with his mistress when the altercation occurred; he walked in on the scene after Melissa James had already expired. He felt so guilty about not calling the police, he wanted to make sure Kelly Ryan was not charged with first degree murder. Craig believed if anything, Kelly would be charged with involuntary manslaughter, and after the toxicology report came out, those charges would be dropped against his wife. Once again, however, Craig miscalculated, and he did not realize the investigators had the phone records to prove he was not in the house after the taser gun was fired and Melissa died of an overdose.

The FBI interrogates Kelly Ryan

In the interrogation room, Kelly explained to the FBI that in the weeks and months before James' death, Kelly suspected that James was stealing from them. "There was activity on the card...large sums of money, and they weren't transactions from my husband or me. Then I got really frustrated because my card didn't work, and I said, you know what, like this is it, the card's not going through; so Melissa got mad at me because she felt like I was treating her like a thief."

In addition to that, Kelly said she believed Melissa James had been trying to poison her over the past few weeks. Kelly stated that Melissa wanted her dead so she could have Craig all to herself. Kelly said, "I found residue on our drinking glasses, and I noticed the water tasted strange. I am not sure what she was trying to poison me with, but I

THE INTERROGATION

have my suspicion; and I know for a fact Melissa was doing something to the drinking water."

Ryan said that on the day she disappeared, Melissa James was staying at a La Quinta hotel that Craig had paid for. Ryan said that the next day Craig brought her back to the house on Adobe Arch to pack for her trip. Kelly said that she caught Melissa with her card, and confronted her about stealing from them, and she and Melissa got into an argument.

When asked why she didn't call the police to report the theft, Kelly said, "She's got a lot of knowledge of how to basically ruin someone's life, and I just didn't wanna leave it… like her angry at us." Ryan continued, "So when I confronted her about stealing, and stuff, she got real mad and started acting crazy. So I told her that she was not welcome to stay at my house anymore, and she just took off and left."

Kelly said that later that night some of their friends came over to party, and they noticed the posing lights were on in the garage. So they all walked out to the garage, and we noticed a smell coming from the car. She said, "Smelled like a dirty diaper; it was just an awful smell. And we walked closer to the car and saw Melissa overdosed in the front seat."

An agent asked Kelly why they didn't call the police when they found her body, and she said that they were afraid to call because her husband was a convicted felon. "I don't know how to explain it, like, uhm, I would say probably we were slightly panicked because… we just, never, ever, ever, had to deal with anything like that before. Then, um, you know, Craig and I started thinking, uh, she's got drugs in the house, uh, he's a felon."

Then Kelly said that, they wrapped her up and put her in the trunk of the car she thought, "Oh my God, what are we gonna do, how are we going to explain this? Like, what, what, you know, what are the cops going to say?" So then we decided we had to just get rid of the car because it smelled so bad, and maybe then the situation would be repairable. Then we all thought, the best way to get rid of the car was to set it on fire, and make it look like she stole the car. So Craig called his friend to follow us, and I went to Wal-Mart and bought the lighter fluid, and he followed us out to the desert. He turned the truck around, and after we set the car on fire, he drove us home.

On the morning of December 23, 2005, Lead Homicide Detective Dean O'Kelley received a message from the FBI special agents in the Boston Massachusetts area that they were closing in on the fugitive couple. Anticipating an arrest within the next few hours, O'Kelley booked a flight from Las Vegas, Nevada to Boston, Massachusetts that would leave that night, and arrive in Boston the next morning on Christmas Eve. Before his lunch hour was even up, he was told: "We've got them." O'Kelley was pumped, thinking all of the evidence up to then had just fallen into his lap. It was clear to him that Craig Titus was his man.

O'Kelley told his colleagues it didn't matter if he missed Christmas, the best Christmas gift for him would be to look Craig Titus in the face and say, "We got you, you mother fuckin' murderer!" Detective Clifford Mogg (who interviewed Craig the first time and refused to leave Craig's home) hated Craig Titus even more than the other detective. Detective Mogg gladly volunteered to accompany Detective O'Kelley to Boston, even on such short notice, "to pay his old friend a visit!" That night the detectives boarded their plane, and were off to Massachusetts. On the plane they read over the FBI's interview with Kelly Ryan and Craig Titus from earlier in the day, and prepared their notes to conduct their own investigation the next morning at the Norfolk Correctional Facility.

Saturday December 24th Homicide Detectives arrive in Boston

The next day, on December 24th, Las Vegas Homicide Detectives Clifford Mogg and Dean O'Kelley arrived in Massachusetts from Las Vegas and drove to the Norfolk County Correctional Facility to interview Craig Titus and Kelly Ryan. It was Detective Dean O'Kelley's first time to see either Craig Titus or Kelly Ryan face to face.

Detective O'Kelley was not present the first time the detectives interviewed Craig and Kelly when they gave their original statements at their house. In his notes, O'Kelley wrote about his first impression of Kelly: "She appears scared, deprived of sleep and suffering from severe drug withdrawal." As for his impression of Craig Titus (a man he accused of murder without ever interviewing him) O'Kelley wrote: "He reeks of arrogance, it oozes out of his every pore; but there is an underlying odor of insecurity, and that's why he is so desperate to always be in control."

According to Lead Detective Dean O'Kelley, the standard procedure for obtaining statements is simple: "We start with a pre-interview, during which time the interviewee freely associates about the concern at hand, and the detective takes some notes; then we pull out a tape recorder and apprise the interviewee that we'll be recording his or her statements; and then we'll all speak on record, confining questions and answers to the essential points."

Yet, Detective O'Kelley said, "There were no pre-interviews with Kelly or Craig in Massachusetts because we were not in our environment, we outside of our setup, so we wanted to get the job done as efficiently as possible." This statement is interesting because over the next three years, it became transparently clear that Detective Dean O'Kelley *does* record interviews *when it suits his purpose*. When it doesn't, he simply takes notes on what the suspect says during the investigation. There are some things he does not want recorded, because then it would be impossible to rewrite the statements to implicate an innocent man.

Homicide Detectives record interviews

One thing was certain however, Detective Dean O'Kelley never advised Craig or Kelly that they would be recorded. The problem was that Massachusetts is governed by a different set of laws for recording statements than Nevada. In the former, a two-party state, an officer is prohibited from recording oral communications without the consent of all parties involved, and in the latter, only one party needs to be aware of the recording, and the one person that is aware of the recording can be the officer himself.

In the transcribed copy of Titus' interview in Massachusetts on December 24, there is no preamble to inform him of the tape recorder, as there is in every other interview that detectives conduct in which they record during their investigation. According to Craig's attorney,

"Not only were Mr. Titus' rights violated when the two detectives recorded a statement from Mr. Titus' jail cell, but the detectives actually *broke the law* when they violated the Massachusetts law, MGL 272, which makes it a felony to tape record a suspect during an interrogation." In addition, Craig Titus *repeatedly* said that he was done talking and wanted his lawyer, yet Detective Mogg continued to violate Titus' rights, taunting him and pressing him for more answers.

Actual excerpts from the illegally taped interview were mysteriously leaked to the media. At the time of the leak, only the investigators and the prosecution had access to the statements, so it doesn't take a rocket scientist to figure out the leaks came from either one or both of those two sources. In fact, this information was leaked well after they were informed by the defense lawyers that it was illegal, a violation of Titus and Ryan's rights, and was to be suppressed.

In an article written by Joshua Lombardy, published on March 23, 2006 for Las Vegas Weekly entitled: "The Deadly Saga of Craig Titus and Kelly Ryan ... Love, Drugs, and Bodybuilding," the author provided the following disclaimer before providing details from the interrogation: "Suppressing statements is a legal matter, for lawyers and judges, and not their opposites, we journalists. And so this is what could've been invoked..."

This attitude, though completely false and naïve, would be the attitude among many journalists in the Las Vegas journalism community in the years leading up to Craig Titus and Kelly Ryan's trial. Beginning in February of 2005, after the prosecution leaked information to Glenn Puit of the Las Vegas Review Journal, the first article was published detailing "inside" information that damaged the defense. There would be articles written weekly with information that should have been privy only to the lawyers handling the case. The articles led to a book published in December of 2006, nearly two years before the case was set to go to trial. Craig Titus was a hot topic, with every cable news show discussing the case and People Magazine publishing a story within a week of their arrests. With no physical evidence to tie Craig Titus to a murder, the prosecution exploited the eager journalists, and had Craig's case tried in the media before he ever had a chance to go to court.

THE INTERROGATION

Puit was assigned to cover the case against Craig Titus in February of 2006 after Frank Curreri left the newspaper. In his article with the headlines: "Kelly Ryan remains loyal to bodybuilding husband after detectives in murder investigation tried to get her to turn on him," Puit wrote about the statements made by Craig Titus and Kelly Ryan during their interrogation by the Las Vegas detectives. So even though the 101-page interrogation was suppressed in court, it became public knowledge through articles written by Puit in February and March of 2006.

Homicide Detectives Dean O'Kelley and Clifford Mogg interview Kelly Ryan

Detective Mogg and Detective O'Kelley sat down to interview Kelly, and tape-recorded the interview without her knowledge. According to the 101- page documented statement, Kelly talked for more than an hour about her and Craig's background, and their relationship with Melissa James.

When Detective Dean O'Kelley started the interview with Kelly, he said, "We've been drawn a fairly clear picture from witness statements and people whom Craig talked to about what happened, and one of the things that's been painted fairly clear to us is your level of involvement here, and we're all of the consensus that, um, there was a point in time where you could have stepped back and said I'm not gonna be a part of this. You know I love you Craig, but I'm not gonna have anything else to do with this. You know?"

Kelly Ryan: "Who have you spoken to?"
Detective O'Kelley: "Quite a few people."
Kelly Ryan: "Like?"
Detective O'Kelley: "Like your friend Mandy, and quite a few others."

Kelly Ryan: "What did they say?"
Detective O'Kelley: "Well, um, we know there's a chance for you to, you know, go on with your career and everything else. So what we'd like for you to do now is explain what happened from your perspective, your story as to what happened."
Kelly Ryan: "Okay."

Detective O'Kelley: "Yeah, let's try to maybe iron some things out before we get your statement. Sometimes we can go forward through a situation, or sometimes even backwards, step by step, and people remember things a little better. And if we talk about that in advance, then, um, then sometimes things are a little clearer in your head before we take the actual statement."

Kelly Ryan: "Okay, do you mind if I use the restroom, I don't feel very good?"

Detective O'Kelley: "Okay, tell me about the afternoon or evening when you and Craig found Melissa James dead?"

Kelly Ryan: "Okay, yes, uhm, we could see the posing lights on in the garage, and when we went out to turn them off, uhm, we saw Melissa's body in the front seat of the car; and she wasn't obviously moving, you know. And you know, when you walk up on someone and obviously they're not moving. It's pretty, pretty scary, and we didn't know what to do because we had never been in that situation before."

Detective O'Kelley: "And when you saw her, what did she look like? I mean how did you know that she had overdosed?"

Kelly Ryan: "Well I mean you can just tell, with her eyes open, and stuff coming out of her nose and mouth. She used the restroom all over herself. And there was a horrible smell from all of that. It was the worst smell I have ever, I mean, it made me physically sick. It wouldn't be anything else, you know."

Detective O'Kelley: "Was her body in the state of Rigor Mortis; was she stiff?"

Kelly Ryan: "Oh no, uhm, no, not at all. When we moved her out of the car, she was still limp, but she was definitely not alive. And, uhm, we moved her body to the living room, and she was so messy and heavy. I mean she was so very, very heavy; and I probably ended up dropping her."

Detective O'Kelley: "And why did you move her body inside the house?"

Kelly Ryan: "Well at first because Craig gave her CPR, but then he had to wrap her up because she was leaking all of this fluid everywhere."

THE INTERROGATION

Detective O'Kelley: "Why didn't you call 911 to get Melissa help?"
Kelly Ryan: "It was too late; there would have been nothing they could have done. We talked about it, but then we were all panicked, and freaking out because she has drugs all in her room, and needles. And Craig could go to jail because she had those drugs in our house and overdosed in our house, you know."

Detective O'Kelley: "So what did you do next?"
Kelly Ryan: "Uhm, the smell was so horrible; we decided to move her out into the garage. Then we thought we might as well put her back in the car because it smelled so bad. But there was no way we could drive that body anywhere if she was inside the car, so we decided to put her in the trunk. Uhm, I remember we wrapped her up and carried her out to the trunk, and uhm she wouldn't fit because my trunk was real small. So we put her in the fetal position with duct tape and something else, then we were able to fit her back there. You know like we had to put her body in a ball because her body was too long, and wouldn't fit."

Detective O'Kelley: "I have several witnesses that say you tried to get Craig to call the police, but he wouldn't let you, and I believe that is true. Was there any point where, after she was in the trunk, you thought, hey let's call the authorities?"
Kelly Ryan: "Well yeah, I thought it the whole time; but with the smell, and her in the trunk, it just got to the point where we felt like it was not repairable."

Detective O'Kelley: "I do understand Kelly. Now, let me just make an observation, and be real truthful, I can see that you are in withdrawal right now, do you use meth as well?"
Kelly Ryan: "Yes."

Detective O'Kelley: "Okay, thank you for your honesty, and while we are on the subject, where did you and Melissa get the methamphetamines from?"
Kelly Ryan: "Uhm, I did not use that stuff very often; my husband hated crystal meth, and it wasn't worth an argument. Plus I hated the way it made me feel. Uhm, but you know, Melissa on the other hand, shot up all of the time.

Detective O'Kelley: "And what led you to believe she shot up all the time?"

Kelly Ryan: "There were needles lying around everywhere. I never bought any, and uhm, Melissa would get it from a guy named Eddie that she said was her boyfriend. They met one night at some casino when she had my car and was tweaked out for several days. We've helped a lot of people in the past that were addicted to drugs; sometimes it works, sometimes it doesn't. But, uhm you know, it's something that Craig and I feel good about. We've been very successful, and it makes us feel good to share that success with others. So basically we came to understand that Melissa had a crystal meth problem and we felt like we could obviously get her off of the drugs. But she kept shootin' up all the time, and that led to her being tweaked out of her mind 24/7."

Detective O'Kelley: "Okay, let's shift gears and talk about that night, after you found Melissa. And I am going to be up front with you, we have already been told what Craig did, and everyone believes that you are covering for him. And let me tell you, I am giving you a chance to tell me what happened. Earlier you said this wasn't salvageable, but I am telling you that it is, but that is only if you allow it to be, and tell me exactly what Craig did?"

Kelly Ryan: "I don't understand what you want me to say."

Detective O'Kelley: "I think that you do. Walk me through the night on December 13th, after Melissa was killed, starting when your friends Megan and Jeremy arrived at your house."

Kelly Ryan: "Okay uhm, Megan and Jeremy came over for a while, and we went upstairs for a couple of hours and talked and stuff, then we went downstairs, and they noticed the smell. We all walked toward the garage and saw the posing lights were on, so we went in the garage, and they saw Melissa's body in the car."

Detective O'Kelley: "I thought you said you already put the body in the trunk?"

Kelly Ryan: "Oh yeah, uhm, I'm sorry, I don't feel good, and I am having a hard time remembering. They saw the body in the trunk, so then we went inside and talked about what we needed to do with the body. They just tried to help us because you know Megan is in fitness,

THE INTERROGATION

and she knows what this would do to my career if there was an overdosed body in the house."

Detective O'Kelley: "Okay, now Megan told us that you and Melissa got into a fight over money, can you elaborate on that a little bit?"
Kelly Ryan: "Yeah, Melissa was stealing our credit cards and debit cards, and she tried to steal our identities. She had done that before with her ex-boyfriend in Florida, and got arrested, you know identity theft. She had stolen her best friend's driver's license and identity, uhm, you can look all that up. But anyway, she has done it before, and she stole my debit card and I caught her putting it back, and we got into a fight, you know, uhm an argument. Then Craig came home, and told her to pack all her things and leave. She wasn't welcome in our house anymore."

Detective O'Kelley: "Did it ever get violent?"
Kelly Ryan: "Not like you are thinking, no; but Melissa was acting crazy, you know, knocking things over, throwing things."

Detective O'Kelley: "Okay, and earlier with Detective Wilson, you said at one time you all were close friends, when did that change?"
Kelly Ryan: "When the meth took over her life, she gradually changed into something else. I mean obviously my husband and I have always trusted her, you know; that's why we welcomed her into our house."

Detective O'Kelley: "Did you pay James to be your personal assistant?"
Kelly Ryan: "No, no, we just took care of her. We made sure that she didn't need for anything, but it got to the point where it was never enough. I mean I know Craig gave her money all the time, and I paid for everything, and she didn't appreciate anything and always wanted more so she started stealing from us."

Detective O'Kelley: "Okay, Let me ask you…" (Kelly interrupts)
Kelly Ryan: "I'm sorry, I just thought about this. There was activity on my Wells Fargo debit card, and my Bank of America credit card. There were large sums of money taken out of my accounts, and they were not transactions that my husband or I did. When we called, they said the pass codes and everything had been changed." Craig didn't think it was a big deal, but I got really frustrated because my cards

didn't work, and I said, 'you know what, this isn't right, now my cards won't even go through.' Then Megan and Jeremy came over and we found a safe thing with all our documents.

Detective O'Kelley: "Okay, and what did you find in the safe?"
Kelly Ryan: Photographs of Craig and my drivers' licenses; and uhm, all of our home equity line of credit, mortgage statements, credit card statements with our numbers on the, copies of our social security cards, and she had our dates of birth." Ryan said that the police should be able to find it in the lock box in Melissa's room."

Detective O'Kelley: "Did you ever report any of the theft to the police?"
Kelly Ryan: "No, she was our friend, and we didn't want her to get in trouble. Craig got her a hotel room and plane ticket, and we were going to send her back to her family, and let them deal with her. We weren't going to let her ever come back to our house again."

Detective O'Kelley: "Did Melissa know that she wouldn't be able to come back?"
Kelly Ryan: "Yeah, after Craig picked her up from the hotel, and brought her back to pack, I basically told her, 'you know what, you are not welcome to stay at my house ever again.'"

Detective O'Kelley: "Okay, now let's talk about after Megan and Jeremy left, and Craig called Anthony Gross to help him get rid of the body and the car? Excuse me wait, let me ask you this first, we can see from the phone records that Craig and Tony had been calling each other all day. During those phone calls, did Craig and Tony plan it all out, I mean, putting the body in the car, and burning it?"
Kelly Ryan: "No, Craig and I planned it out, and he called Tony to help us. If they talked during the day, I mean, I don't know, you would have to ask them."

Detective O'Kelley: "Okay, so after you meet up with Anthony Gross, where did you go, what did you do?"
Kelly Ryan: "Uhm, Craig drove to Wal-Mart, and I went inside and bought seven bottles of lighter fluid and a barbeque set with my debit card."

Detective O'Kelley: "Why'd you get 6 bottles of Kingston and 1 bottle of another brand?"
Kelly Ryan: "That's all they had."

Detective O'Kelley: "Okay, so what happened next?"
Kelly Ryan: "We met up with Tony at a gas station, and then followed him out to a place in the desert, and they burned the car. Then I was like, 'Oh my God, I can't believe what we just did.' Then Tony dropped us off, and we just cried and held each other in bed until you guys showed up."

Detective O'Kelley: "Okay, thank you Kelly, I know this is not easy. I just want you to know that I care about what happens to you. I do not want to see you charged with murder or have to spend the rest of your life behind bars. I have talked to all of your friends, people that love you. I have heard about your amazing career. I know where you have come from, and where you have ended up, and I don't think it is your fault, okay."
Kelly Ryan: "Okay, uhm, thank you."

Detective O'Kelley: "Okay Kelly, look, I am talking to you human being to human being. Okay, I don't want to see you continue to involve yourself in this and go down and have it be the end for you; okay I just don't!"
Kelly Ryan: "Okay."

Detective O'Kelley: "I want you to understand where I am coming from; I'm saying that to you as a human being. And I want you to know that both Detective Mogg and I see your situation as being salvageable; we've already talked about this obviously. Craig made choices. Craig has done this thing, not you, Craig murdered Melissa."
Kelly Ryan: "But he didn't, I swear to God! You can ask anyone, Melissa died of a drug overdose."

Detective O'Kelley: "Now Kelly, listen, we have already talked to witnesses that told us about Craig using the stun gun on Melissa. We know that he choked her, and injected her with drugs. Now we need you to tell us a story that adds up and makes sense. Because what you

have told us contradicts our physical evidence. Because what you've told us goes against what other people have told us they witnessed."
Kelly Ryan: "I don't know what you want me to do, lie and say Craig murdered her? I can't do that. If he did murder her, I would tell you; but I'm not going to make something up, you know. Melissa overdosed, and we panicked; that's it."

Detective O'Kelley: "Okay listen Kelly, we already know that Craig is the guilty one, but we can't help you unless you help yourself. And, uhm ... if you don't take this opportunity, then it's going to be gone; it really will. It will be gone, and you'll sit in a cell and rehearse over and over what you could have said to us. You made a mistake when you tried to cover up what Craig did, but hey here is your chance to own up to the mistake; we all make mistakes, okay. You need to realize that Craig made these choices, not you. Craig has done this."
Kelly Ryan: "I'm not sure where you are going with that."

Detective O'Kelley: "Where I'm going with it is that you can't be held responsible for what another person does unless you choose to. This is your opportunity, a free pass, to back up, as far as you can, and tell us what Craig did and make it right."
Kelly Ryan: "I don't know what I'm supposed to say to that. He didn't do what you're saying."

Detective O'Kelley: "Okay, well we have evidence to prove otherwise, and witnesses lined up to testify against him. Those witnesses are willing to testify that you had very little to do with this. That you were manipulated by Craig, okay, so you would not go to prison, and I don't think you should because Craig is the one who did this."
Kelly Ryan: "Uhm, well..."

Detective O'Kelley: "I am just being brutally honest with you, like I said, human being to human being. I don't want you to regret this someday, years down the line when you are sitting behind bars, and you think, oh this could have all turned out different for me, you know."
Kelly Ryan: "I think I need my lawyer; I don't feel comfortable doing that. Why do you want to pin this on Craig, I don't understand."

Detective Mogg interjected and asked, "So is this something that you and Craig planned in advance, or did it just happen?" (This was obviously a trick question, but it was also a little warning to let Kelly know what was about to happen to her if she didn't cooperate. They were going to pin this on Craig, but they had no problem sticking it to Kelly if she did not tell them what they wanted to hear.)

Kelly Ryan: "I don't want to give a statement without anyone here; I don't want to say anything else without my lawyer present."
Detective O'Kelley: "Okay, you have a small window; let me know if you change your mind. And this concludes our interview with Kelly Ryan."

With the thought of spending the rest of their life in prison or saying what the detectives wanted to hear, it's not hard to see how their friends were coerced into changing their stories. In his notes Detective O'Kelley later added that Kelly Ryan seemed to be in withdrawal, "But still managed to be very slow and tactical with her answers. She has great animosity towards Melissa James. All she wanted to talk about was Melissa James stealing their money or doing drugs. With every question we asked, she found some way to turn it right back to an anecdote about Melissa taking advantage of them."

Interrogating Craig Titus
Las Vegas Detectives Clifford Mogg and Dean O'Kelley interview Craig Titus Soon after the detectives interviewed Kelly Ryan, they interviewed Craig Titus. The following interview took place between the detectives and Craig Titus: **Detective Mogg**: "How you doin'?"
Craig Titus: "I want you guys to explain why you think we murdered somebody!"

Detective Mogg: "Well, you should have told us the truth. Your friends have done a lot of talking; and we know the facts. You should have told us the truth about how everything happened. But we can go over all that now, what happened and why it happened; stuff like that."
Craig Titus: "I have been to prison before. I didn't want to go back. So I was waiting for you guys to look at the toxicology report, and sort all of that shit out."

Dean O'Kelley: "Craig, uhm... I guess the FBI guys talked to you yesterday... and they told us that you gave your story. But one thing... there's some confusion over I guess towards the end of the time you were talking to them, and you said that you need an attorney."
Craig Titus: "Yeah, I said it more than once; I said it over and over again!"

Dean O'Kelley: "Well you know, that is a sticking point with us, as far as whether or not you know, you get the opportunity to talk to us..."
Craig Titus: "Well they told me something that was pretty fuckin' ridiculous."

Dean O'Kelley: "We want to definitely hear your side of the story."
Craig Titus: "This is a fuckin' mess man. Everyone's gettin' it all fuckin' wrong."

Dean O'Kelley: "We just wanna clarify, when you said that you want an attorney, and you were not answering anymore questions..."
Craig Titus: "For those three dicks with the FBI, they were just pulling shit out of their ass and writing whatever the fuck they wanted down. I'll talk to you."

After the detectives read Craig his Miranda rights, they knew that they were walking on thin ice, and they needed to play "good cop, good cop" if they wanted Craig to proceed with the interview.

Detective Mogg: "Uhm, okay, we talked to you at your house, and..."
Craig Titus: "We weren't forthright because we were really scared."

Detective Mogg: "I can understand that."
Craig Titus: "We just started a business called Women's Physique International. It's a federation for women's fitness athletes. My wife is the number one fitness athlete in the world- highly respected. If you think fitness, it's Kelly Ryan, period. So we had this business we were starting, and we poured our life savings into it after we retired from competing. So that was going to be the only income we had, and we walk in our garage and our friend's OD'd in our fucking car. And if that ever got out, we would be ruined man."

THE INTERROGATION

Detective Mogg: "Okay." (After an exaggerated pause, the detectives look at Craig like they don't believe him, and Craig starts to become defensive.)
Craig Titus: "So it's real simple guys. We took her out of the car and put her in the fetal position and put her in the trunk of my car and we burned it. That was it."

Detective Mogg: "First off, this girl, what's her name?"
Craig Titus: "You guys know her name; it's Melissa James."

Detective Mogg: "Okay. Give me a little background on her, like how long did you know her, and where did you meet, stuff like that."
Craig Titus: "I can't remember the actual date, maybe in 2000-2001. I first met her when I guest posed in Florida; she was my driver. And, uhm, she owned a dance studio; she was a really cool girl. She came out to California and stayed in L.A. and hung out with us for like six months after I first met her. Then she lost her dance studio to her partner, so she came back out to California to stay with us. Then she moved in with us a couple of times while we were in Vegas, and this last time she came out to work at Powerhouse Gyms that we were supposed to open up. The gym thing fell through; she got out of control on drugs so we asked her to move out."

Detective Mogg: "What kind of drugs?"
Craig Titus: "Crystal Methamphetamines."

Detective Mogg: "And how long had she been doing that?"
Craig Titus: "She always did it ever since I knew her; but she got real bad on it, and started taking other stuff like cocaine and morphine. And sometime she would steal my Nubain or OxyContin when she ran out of morphine."

Detective Mogg: "The, ah Nubain, what is that?"
Craig Titus: "That one cracks me up, because the police don't even know what it is. It's a non-schedule antagonist narcotic that you can buy right off the internet. It's a pain reliever. It's liquid, injectable. Bodybuilders, pro wrestlers, pro football players, all the fighters, they are all on it. I had a prescription for it and OxyContin because of a surgery that I had on my calf."

Detective Mogg: "Was there some issue, Kelly had brought up to us about Melissa, about using your credit cards and running up some bills?"

Craig Titus: "Yeah, we didn't find that out though until the very end. I would give her cash and let her use my card to buy stuff like Christmas gifts, but Kelly didn't let her use her card. And we found out that she took money out of Kelly's account. And uhm, she charged up some credit cards, and charged up a couple grand, but that wasn't a huge issue. I didn't really sweat it too much."

Detective Mogg: "What was your relationship with Melissa?"
Craig Titus: "Just friends."

Detective Mogg: "Anything more than friends?"
Craig Titus: "Not at the end, nope! Not at the time she was living with us this last time… we were nothing but friends. Now when we first met four or five years ago, that was different. I had sex with her a few times."

(It seems like Mogg has been caught in a lie with that question. He insisted that Craig told him he was having an affair with Melissa when he interviewed Craig at his house. This quote from Mogg was repeated several times, and mentioned in the newspaper. Craig was never recorded saying this; he stated this comment word for word. If Craig was recorded saying that he was sleeping with Melissa before she died, why would Mogg ask him about it now; and when Craig denied they were in a relationship, why didn't Mogg say, 'But you told me that you were having an affair the first time I interviewed you?')

Detective Mogg: "Did you guys ever confront Melissa about using credit cards?"
Craig Titus: "Yep."

Detective Mogg: "And how did that go?"
Craig Titus: "It went fine. Melissa said that she didn't do it; you know, and Kelly said, 'Well, the proof is right here,' and showed her. Melissa just denied it; she was doin' meth, and kept telling us that she wasn't doing meth, but we knew that she was… I showed you guys the bag, remember."

THE INTERROGATION

Detective Mogg: "Was Kelly doing meth?"
Craig Titus: "Fuck no!"

Detective Mogg: "She told us that she was."
Craig Titus: "If you are asking me if she is doing meth, the answer is 'fuck no'; has she tried it with Melissa, a couple of times, 'yes'. But she would never do it in front of me because she knew it disgusted me. That shit ruins more lives than any other drug in the world; you are shooting pure poison in your body with meth!"

Detective Mogg: "So how did you feel about Melissa stealing from you?"
Craig Titus: "Look, it hurt my feelings. I would have given it to her if she just asked; and when I talked to her about it, she would just deny it. I still loved her, but it hurt me; I never got mad or anything about it though. Melissa was a nice girl, just going down the wrong path; I didn't know how to help her. She continually lied about everything. She lied about doing meth, but I knew she was using it. When you're use crystal meth, you isolate yourself and sit in a room all day; and then bust out and be gone for two or three days without telling anyone where you are at. She would stay in that room for days on end, and it stunk like meth and body odor. I begged her to go to rehab, and I told her I would pay for it, but she refused. It's been on my mind, fucking bothering me man. Why would a person do that to themselves? It's so fucked up bro. Anyway, no, it didn't bother me; it just hurt my feelings that she would do that to me because she was my friend. I was closer to her at one time, even more than I was with Kelly, so it hurt."

Detective Mogg: "Okay, so you get her the room at a hotel what happened there?"
Craig Titus: "No sex if that's what you're implying; we just talked and hung out for a couple of hours."

Detective Mogg: "Okay, you checked in on the 12th, when did you check out?"
Craig Titus: "Uhm, I picked her up the next morning and brought her home."

Detective Mogg: "Do you remember what time you brought her home?"

Craig Titus: "I can't remember, some time that morning."

Detective Mogg: "And have you talked to Melissa James' mom recently?"

Craig Titus: "Yeah, she called me a couple of times, so I called her back, sometime before I left town."

Detective Mogg: "Do you recall what day that was?"

Craig Titus: "I don't know it was a couple of days after you guys came to my house, and I could see in your face that you thought I killed Melissa."

Detective Mogg: "Why did you leave town?"

Craig Titus: "Because of you, man! I didn't want this. I knew you guys were gonna bump up charges on me. I knew it the second you came in my house; you had it out for me man. You wanted me to be a murderer, because that makes you look great. You already had your mind made up after talking to me for five minutes, that whoever was in that car, I had something to do with it. And that was bullshit; I'm not going to jail for something I didn't do. So I talked to a lawyer because I wanted to come see my best friend, and he said if there isn't a warrant out for your arrest, you don't have to stay in Las Vegas. I thought, you could sort out the bullshit allegations when you got the autopsy report, and it said that she died of a drug overdose, that's it, nothing else. But I didn't want to sit in jail while you figured all of that out, no fucking way!"

Detective Mogg: "Okay, so what happened to Melissa that afternoon, when you said that Kelly dropped her off at the convenience store the first time?"

Craig Titus: "I don't know man, she just took off. Then our friends came over."

Detective Mogg: "Okay, when we talked the last time, you told me about going through Melissa's room and finding some things."

Craig Titus: "Don't start turning things around. Listen to your tape recorder. I told you we found that shit after Melissa was gone."

THE INTERROGATION

Detective Mogg: "So tell me what happened after your friends came over."
Craig Titus: "We were upstairs in my lounge, partying and shit."

Detective Mogg: "Did you or Kelly tell Megan about money Melissa had stolen?"
Craig Titus: "I didn't, but I think Kelly had talked to her about it several times before. Have you guys talked to Megan and Jeremy?"

Detective Mogg: "Yes."
Craig Titus: "Okay. What did they say?"

Detective Mogg: "Let's not worry about what they said; we are talking to you right now."
Craig Titus: "I can see what's going on; I'm not fuckin' blind! Here we go again, you're fuckin' playin' me!" (Craig slaps his hand on the table and scoots his chair back.)
Detective Mogg: (talks over Craig) and says, "Craig, Craig, wait, hold on, no."

Detective Dean O'Kelley: "Craig, when people come to us concerned for you guys… you know, concerned for Kelly, and concerned for you… they don't expect that when they talk to us that we're gonna then come to you and say, 'Oh, this is exactly what was said.' I want you to trust us, and be honest about everything; it's a whole lot easier that way, wouldn't you agree?"
Craig Titus: "Absolutely, but I wanna know why he (Mogg) has to think I murdered somebody. That is all I want to know, because its bullshit!"

Detective Dean O'Kelley: "Look Craig, our investigation is ongoing. We have not come to any conclusions; we are just trying to collect all the facts."
Detective Mogg: "And when I was trying to collect the facts, look at what happened, okay? When I came out to talk to you the first time…"
Craig Titus: "Yeah and you were playin' all kinds of fuckin' mind games with me and then wouldn't leave my house after I asked you

to leave and said I wanted my fucking lawyer. I could tell what you were doin', I'm not fuckin' stupid."

Detective Mogg: "Well now Craig, you told me something that wasn't entirely true, and I knew that you were lying. So put yourself in my shoes, what would you think? But I am open right now, and you can set the record straight, okay?"

Craig Titus: "Yeah okay, whatever man. So here's what fucking happened. Found her in the fuckin' car dead, stinkin' up the whole garage from the stench. There was piss, shit, all over the place. I panicked, this gets in the newspapers and, we are ruined. 'Dead girl, car, OD'd, Craig Titus, Kelly Ryan'. We're fuckin' ruined, plus the car is fuckin' ruined, not a big deal, but still. So I think, okay, let's put her in the trunk, drop her body somewhere then take the car out somewhere to burn it and then we play stupid. Like I told those guys yesterday and you guys today, that is what fuckin' happened, THE END, PERIOD!"

Detective Mogg: "Was anyone with you when you drove out to the desert?"

Craig Titus: "Yeah, I called my friend Tony Gross, like you know. You have him on film getting gas, and then we followed him on Blue Diamond Road. But Tony didn't have anything else to do with any of this okay. He just drove and showed us where to take the car- so just leave him out of it."

Detective Mogg: "Where else did you go?"
Craig Titus: "You already know that too, we stopped and got lighter fluid at Wal-Mart. Kelly used her debit card, and it is all on surveillance."

Detective Mogg: "So how did you feel after you caught the car on fire?"
Craig Titus: "I was fuckin' beside myself! I forgot to take her out, and I was fuckin' upset. She was my fuckin' friend, man. (Crying) It's so fucked up. Now it's even worse because I panicked. God damn it, she was my fuckin' friend!"

Detective Mogg: "Okay, when you tied Melissa up, was there anything else you used to keep her in that position?"

THE INTERROGATION

Craig Titus: (Craig collects himself) "You know, honestly, this is the God honest truth, when I was tying her up in the cocoon position to get her in the trunk, I used duct tape, and I used the robe ties, you know that wrap around a robe, just a cloth strip. That was to pull her knees to her chest from around her neck. But there was something else I used around her legs that broke, a cord maybe, I can't remember."

Detective Mogg: "And you did this all by yourself…that seems hard to do?"

Craig Titus: "Yeah. Look, I have to say this, if this were really a murder, I would have dug a god-damn hole in the fuckin' desert and dumped her body in the hole, and burned the car by itself. Nobody would have ever found her, and my car would be burned and stolen. You know what I mean? I was scared shitless, and forgot to pull the body out. If I murdered her, I sure as hell wouldn't have burned her body in the fuckin' car. It doesn't take a fuckin' genius to know if you're gonna murder somebody, you don't put the dead body in the car and burn it."

Detective Mogg: "Unless somebody panics."

Craig Titus: "Yeah well unless they're real fuckin' stupid!"

Detective Mogg: "The night that Megan and Jeremy were over at your house, were you horsing around with her at all, wrestling, doing anything like that?"

Craig Titus: "With Megan? (Mogg nods) What the fuck are you talkin' about?"

Detective Mogg: "I'm just curious as to whether or not you were wrestling with her. I don't know, horsing around, putting Megan in any kind of choke hold?"

Craig Titus: "I don't ever go around Megan. She is Kelly's friend; Fuck no, I don't even know what you are talkin' about! Did she say that, or did you just make that shit up? That's stupid as hell! You know what guys, I'm done."

Detective Mogg: "I wanna show you something here."

Craig Titus: "I want an attorney; I'm not saying another word to you until I have my attorney." (This is recorded-Craig asked for an attorney, and they did not stop.)

Detective Mogg: "I got a note for ya Titus."
Craig Titus: "Yeah, yeah, she told you what happened, I want my attorney."

Detective Mogg: "Would it surprise you if it didn't match what you said?
Craig Titus: "Surprise me if Megan lied to you, and said I choked her or something, nope that wouldn't surprise me at all because she is fuckin' nuts! Did she tell you how she kept grabbin' my dick that night too? Well she did. Look I want my fuckin' attorney, and I want to see my wife. We were on the phone with our attorney, and we were going to turn ourselves in when we were arrested."

Detective Mogg: "What is going to happen next is you will have an extradition hearing, and at that time you and Megan decide whether or not you wanna go back to Las Vegas voluntarily."
Craig Titus: "What in the fuck are you talking about, me and Megan? Oh my god, you guys are fuckin' morons."

Detective Mogg: "Did you talk to anyone else, tell anybody else a different story?"
Craig Titus: "I'm all done. How many fuckin' times do I have to ask for my lawyer? You wouldn't leave my house when I asked you to leave, and I asked for a lawyer then, and now you keep asking me questions after I keep saying, 'I want my lawyer.' I don't think you are allowed to do that, and your fuckin' recording yourself doing it. See I'm really perceptive; so perceptive you don't even know. So look, get the fuck outta my face, I'm wasting my time telling you morons anything because you think you already know everything; I'm done, Period!"

Detective Mogg: "Well when you have conflicting stories…"
Craig Titus: "Yep, then I'm a murderer. You are a genius dude! Since I am a murderer, I'm all done talking to you. That's it; fuck it!"
Detective Dean O'Kelley: "And that's going to be the end of the interview."

CHAPTER 2

Ron Avidan interviews Matt Cline

In the world of bodybuilding; the social media of choice was not Facebook, rather, it was bodybuilding website message boards. On these sites, members could sign in and discuss anything and everything going on in the world of bodybuilding.

For the most part, these websites and message boards were helpful and educational; however, all too often, they were used to bash other bodybuilders. Many of these posts were mean spirited and cruel. It would take thick skin to be a part of these message boards because these people, hiding behind keyboards, ripped each other to shreds on a daily basis.

After arrest warrants were issued for Craig Titus and Kelly Ryan, the once beloved power couple were now being vilified on these message boards, and their character was being torn apart. Almost everyone that ever knew Craig and Kelly, from close friends to bitter enemies, threw them under the bus, and cashed in on their fifteen minutes of fame.

However, once Craig and Kelly were arrested in Stoughton, Massachusetts, the guns were being aimed in a different direction, and they were being pointed directly at Craig Titus' best friend, Matt Cline. Ron Avidan, an owner of one of these websites, Getbig.com, wanted to give Cline an opportunity to answer all of the vicious rumors being spread on the message boards, and Cline took him up on that offer on Christmas day, 2005.

So how have you been? I have been better. This whole thing is a fucking nightmare. The FBI basically followed the bread crumbs from Las Vegas to Boston in order to get Craig & Kelly.

I thought you lived in Vegas, when did you move to Boston? I moved to Boston in July 2005 because I had to get away from all of the bullshit - from all of the drugs and all of the drama in the Vegas scene. So I moved to Boston, which is where I was from. After I moved, Craig and I didn't talk for a while. Then a short time ago, we started to talk again because he wanted me to get involved in the WPI with him, and also get involved in this clothing line with distribution and stores, called Ice Gear.

So we know that they caught Craig & Kelly near your house in Boston. What role did you have in that? First of all, let me say that I did not rat out Craig or Kelly? I did not want anything to do with this at all, and in no way was I part of that. Craig has been my friend for over 16 years, and I don't like to hear rumors that I ratted out my friend. It just did not happen.

So what role did you have in this since they were going to meet you? Somehow Craig got the idea that he should drive to Boston, and that I was going to give him some money. He called me after it happened, but didn't tell me what happened. I knew something was wrong, but didn't ask. Craig asked me where I can get some passports for them, and I told them I didn't know. He seemed very flustered. After that, I started getting some weird phone calls. The FBI came to my house for three hours, and I knew they had my phones tapped, and that they were sitting around waiting for him to show up.

It seemed that some people from Las Vegas told the FBI that Craig and Kelly were coming to visit me. I learned that Greg Ruiz, a business partner of ours told the cops, as did other people. The next day, they were in front of my house all day waiting for him, and Craig starts calling me. I am not stupid - I know my phones are tapped, and they have surveillance on me everywhere. They wanted me to talk to Craig, and set up a drop, and I said no way - I am not doing it.

I told them that no way I am going to set up my best friend. You guys are the FBI, you guys do you job, and I am not going to help you on this. I know you are getting every phone call, so do you own work. I started to not answer my phone calls, but then Craig text messaged me. He said he was in El Paso, Texas. In actuality, as I found out later, he was in Revere, Massachusetts. Revere is a town north of Boston.

Friday morning, I started getting phone calls at 8-9 in the morning. I said, "Look don't call me, they have my phones taped, and are sitting outside of my house." He said 'I just talked to my attorney, they don't know anything'. I told him bullshit. Right after this conversation, the feds came over, and they knew he was in the area.

Apparently, he was driving up and down near my house, and he was around a mile away from where I live. He wanted me to meet him at 4:00 p.m., get something to eat with him, but I couldn't do that. They wanted me to do a drop but I said no way. I couldn't meet him because then I would be aiding and abetting. Around 3:30 p.m., as I found out, Kelly went to go get a pedicure. And that is when they got them. I did not help the FBI; I didn't know exactly where they were at any time. I found out later that the feds knew that he traded in his truck for another truck. It was a souped up new truck. There were no plates on the truck, and they got the truck right before they left for Vegas. They actually got them from finding the brand new truck.

And you were not going to help liquidate their assets? No - I heard about that whole 'liquidation of assets'. There was never a liquidation of assets. I was going to go and buy some of his things and perhaps invest in the Ice Gear business because Craig and Kelly were running low on funds. They wanted some startup money to fund the WPI. Originally, Jeff Schwimmer (David Schwimmer of Friend's fame cousin) was going to buy a number of Craig and Kelly's houses before this all came down. I think they own a total of three houses in Vegas. What then happened was that Jeff had to pull out because if that deal went through, then it would look like he was aiding and abetting.

Did you know Melissa James, the victim? I knew Melissa very well. I have known here for years because she had been friends with Craig for a very long time. For the last two months, Melissa was staying at Craig and Kelly's house. Craig told me they caught Melissa stealing from them, and they didn't want her in their house anymore. So Craig got her a hotel room for two nights, and bought her a plane ticket to go back home. Melissa was originally going to be running the new Ice Gear clothing store for them. From what I heard, she called her mom, told her that Kelly went crazy on her, and that she was coming home. Now Melissa is known for stealing, but she is mostly a sweet girl, but she had drug problems.

Stealing? How do you know that Melissa stole from them? Melissa used to do identity theft when she lived in Vegas before at other stores. She has lived in Vegas a few times. She used identity theft to rent apartments, to turn on cell phones. I think she worked at a cell phone store one time and stole some identities from that. I tried to get her off the drugs a number of times, but she kept going back to it. She was addicted. She was doing crystal meth.

Do you think Craig killed Melissa? I honestly do not think Craig did it. I know he didn't do it. Craig used his credit card and purchased two nights at a hotel room, and a plane ticket back home for Melissa to Florida. Now, I don't know what happened after that, I don't know if Melissa went back to their house, but if Craig was going to kill her, he would have done it with his hands, not a noose or duct tape or anything. Craig would have just grabbed her by the neck or chocked her easily. I know how Craig thinks.

I think that Kelly went crazy and lost it and that is what happened. Craig had a soft spot for Melissa. They had an affair about a year back, but they have not been physical for a while. Now, Kelly does know that and she doesn't. Kelly was always really jealous of all the flirting that Craig did, unless she was all fucked up. But when she wasn't fucked up, it hurt her. So she finally probably snapped. Now, no one told me this. Craig never told me exactly what happened. Craig told me that she was not killed, and she was dead from an overdose. Then he hung up the phone, and I didn't hear from him. After a few days, I got a lot of weird calls, and the FBI comes around.

Now Melissa has been in and out of Craig's life for over 6 years. Melissa used to stay in the background, she wasn't one of those people that you would know was around. She was decent looking, but wasn't striking. Kelly probably knew that something was going on, but then Kelly started to get jealous, or they were doing some sort of recreational drugs and Kelly probably snapped.

When I lived in Vegas, Craig tried to keep all of the recreational drugs away from me because I used to freak out on a lot of that stuff, but I'm straight now. So basically, they asked her to move in, she was there about two months, and Kelly just snapped one day. I am not sure if Kelly was on recreational drugs either. I just think that Kelly just lost it pretty bad, and this is what I think happened. I know Craig said to me right after the incident that 'I can't let Kelly sit in jail'. What that meant, I have no idea. I didn't ask any questions, because I knew that I couldn't get involved, so I just shut my mouth and didn't ask. I stopped taking his calls. Now Craig did tell me that they found Melissa overdosed, but I think he was just protecting Kelly.

How did you meet Craig a long time ago? Well, I stayed at Ed Connors house back when I was a teenager, and that's when I met Craig. We had an instant kind of bond and friendship, and we've been best friends ever since, close to 15-16 years. Over the years, I have done a number of business ventures with Craig, including his After Parties. We've had our problems, like others. He tore his pec, I tore my hamstring, he got arrested, I got arrested, and things like that. My ex-girlfriend, she was a witch and she actually said she put a spell on us - three bad things happen to him and to me. It is really weird.

People are accusing you of being a drug user, and a seller of drugs? Are you? Right now I am not and have not for a long time. Have I partied and used drugs? Who in this industry hasn't? But I am clean now and intend to stay that way. I left the Vegas party scene. Some of the people who are accusing me were in the party scene big time also. There is another person who is mad at me for hooking up with his ex-girlfriend after they broke up 10 years ago. So what.

CHAPTER 3

Due Process?

Monday, December 27th
Arraignment Hearing in Stoughton, Massachusetts

On Monday, December 27th 2005 at 12:15 pm Eastern Time, Craig Titus and Kelly Ryan were brought into the Stoughton, Massachusetts Courthouse for their arraignment hearing with their attorneys, Robert George, Steven Boozang, John Gibbons, and Anthony Cardinale by their side.

The hearing was short, and since the State of Nevada did not have enough documents or paperwork to extradite them at the time, they postponed extradition until the Nevada authorities produced the legal papers to have them released into their custody. Craig and Kelly were informed of their constitutional rights, and the charges brought against them in the State of Massachusetts; and they pleaded "Not Guilty" to the charges of unlawful flight to avoid prosecution. These charges would later be dropped because Craig Titus and Kelly Ryan left Las Vegas, Nevada before there was a warrant issued for their arrest.

Craig Titus and Kelly Ryan were denied bail, and continued to be held in the Norfolk Correctional facility in Dedham, Massachusetts. With news crews filming outside of the courtroom, Steven Boozang (Titus' Massachusetts attorney) said, "Craig Titus is looking forward to coming back to Las Vegas and fighting these charges head-on. Craig will not be fighting the extradition hearing, and perhaps, and it might be waived before the court date of January 12th. Everything just happened so fast for Craig; he needed to slow things down, and put together a defense team that he was comfortable with to represent his and Kelly Ryan's best interest. Both Craig and Kelly wish to thank the people that care about them, and are supporting them during this extremely difficult time."

On December 27th Megan was interviewed by the police for the second time

Two weeks after Megan Pierson walked out of Craig and Kelly's house with a black bag full of evidence, Megan Pierson walked into her attorney's office with the bag in her hands and her fiancé by her side. The bag she handed to her attorney, Robert Langford, was much lighter than it was when she left Craig and Kelly's house. It still contained evidence that would get Craig Titus in trouble with the law: the taser gun and leather sap. However, it was now curiously missing items that would implicate Megan in any crimes.

When Megan was interviewed on both December 22nd and December 27th, Detectives O'Kelley and Wilson never used a tape recorder during her statements. Instead, they documented the facts with pen and paper. This was curious, because the detectives seemed to always record the statements that would be beneficial to the prosecution, even if it was against the law, and then "forget" to record important communications that would have been beneficial to the defense.

According to a mutual friend of Kelly and Megan, the detectives started the interview by detailing what they thought happened to Melissa James, then named Greg Ruiz, Jeff Schwimmer, and Tony Gross as providing them with this information much like they did with Kelly when they said Megan had already provided them with her information. It was obvious what they held over Tony's head in order to get him to cooperate. One can assume that drug charges and aiding and abetting charges were held over Greg and Jeff's head.

After law enforcement detailed all of the "facts" of the case, the detective fed Megan the same line he fed Kelly, and said that he knew Craig and Kelly did this, and he was giving her a chance to go back and make this right. Human being to human being, he didn't want to see Megan have to sit behind bars because Craig and Kelly murdered Melissa James.

These detectives did not give a shit about Megan, just like they didn't give a shit about Kelly; when Kelly told the investigators that she would not lie, they hung her out to dry with her husband. If Megan would have told them that she would not lie, her fate would have been the same as Kelly.

So when Megan was officially "interviewed" (or intimidated into making a fabricated statement) and asked if there was anything she wanted to add or take away from her initial interview: Surprise, surprise! She repeated back everything the detectives had just told her. Incongruously enough, according to their written notes, Megan told the investigators a story about Craig putting her in a chokehold, something she left out in her December 22nd interview. Coincidentally, Detective Mogg asked Craig about this on December 24th even though Megan was just now talking about it on December 27th. This would be the third time that Detective Mogg was caught in a lie, and the investigation had just started.

Megan allegedly told the detectives, "Craig came up behind me while he was talking about how he choked her out, and he put his arm around me. When he had me in a choke hold he said, 'Watch how fast, you can't breathe.' I started not to be able to breathe. And I was like, 'Is that what you did to her?' And he walked away and would not answer."

The detectives asked if Craig could have been joking around when he put her in a chokehold, and Megan said, "Possibly, possibly. That's him, he jokes a lot, especially when he is high on drugs, and he was using cocaine all night long."

This accusation of Craig Titus choking Melissa James was not supported by the autopsy report however. Melissa's hyoid bone was still intact, and if Craig had in fact put her in a chokehold with his bicep, this would not have been the case. (Perhaps this was a fantasy that Megan had about Craig; many people had already come forward talking about her sick fascination with Craig.)

Megan explained that she knew more than she originally revealed because she wanted to protect Kelly Ryan. Now Megan completely flipped, and told the detectives that Kelly was directly involved in the death of Melissa James. In the second interview, Megan told detectives that Kelly used the taser gun on Melissa, but did not have it turned up high enough. (This was obviously a lie, because there was not a setting on the taser gun to "turn up.")

Under oath at the grand jury hearing, Megan Pierson Foley made two different statements regarding the taser gun: (1) Melissa used the gun on Kelly, and (2) Kelly took the gun away from Melissa and used it on her. According to the prosecution's amended criminal complaint Craig and Kelly were charged with First Degree Murder, and one of the "deadly weapons" listed was the taser gun. The taser gun was on a long list of the possible methods in which Craig Titus and Kelly Ryan allegedly murdered Melissa James.

Without any physical evidence to prove that Melissa James was murdered, the prosecution relied solely on the testimony from Megan Pierson. And according to the detectives, Megan stated that after someone (either Kelly or Melissa) was shot by the taser gun, Kelly freaked out, and started yelling for Craig. And even though, the phone records, provided by the prosecution for the grand jury, clearly showed that Craig was not in the house (because Kelly called him over a dozen times) Megan said that Craig ran down the stairs, and body-slammed Melissa, and "beat the crap out of her."

Then Megan said Craig commented, "We shipped her back to Florida, and we sure are going to miss her." (Craig clearly would not have made this statement, because he purchased the airline ticket, and knew that Melissa was going to New Jersey to see her mother, not Florida to see her father for Christmas. By chance, Mogg also mentioned this in his initial written report, and said that Craig told him this on December 14th, and Megan made the same error in words when she used this phrase ten days later. Is this yet another coincidence, or would this be another lie that the detective was caught in?)

In this day and age of forensic evidence, it's beyond comprehension how this murder investigation could not turn up any physical evidence to support the murder allegations against Craig Titus. Every person involved in a crime leaves behind some trace evidence. No matter how much someone may try to clean up a crime scene, something is always left behind.

It's almost impossible for there to have been a violent crime without leaving some evidence. For Craig to be accused of body slamming, beating, and choking Melissa James, without leaving any physical evidence behind, or on Melissa's body, would be both problematic and improbable. Add in the autopsy report, where Melissa had no blunt force trauma, and the taser gun without any finger-print evidence, and the scenario changes from improbable to impossible.

So how could the prosecution pin a murder charge on Craig Titus, even though the evidence proved that Melissa James overdosed? Prosecution's answer: Have Megan tell the Grand Jury that Craig and Kelly injected Megan with the drugs that caused her overdose. This sounds far-fetched and utterly idiotic, but somehow it worked! They got Megan to say that Craig and Kelly injected Melissa with drugs!

Let's follow the not-recorded, hand written transcripts provided by the homicide detectives, to see what Megan actually said (repeated back) about Craig and Kelly injecting Melissa James with narcotics. "Craig held Melissa down, and told Kelly to get the morphine. Kelly shot a needle of morphine into Melissa's leg, and Kelly said that Melissa was resilient, because it did not do anything to her."

This was so eloquently worded by Megan Pierson (Detective Dean O'Kelley). The only problem was that the largest syringe in Craig and Kelly's house was a 3 cc (cubic centimeters) syringe, the standard unit for medication; and there would be no way that Melissa could have possibly overdosed from 3 cc of morphine.

According to Megan and Kelly's mutual friend, Megan truly did not want to turn on Kelly. However, when the investigators looked into the allegations of Melissa James committing identity theft and bank fraud, they discovered that the allegations were in fact true. In addition to this, they also discovered mortgage fraud. With this discovery, along with witness accounts of Megan's involvement in a cover-up, they were able to get Megan to say everything they needed to hear. This was important, because they had nothing else on Craig and Kelly that would justify charging them with murder.

Even though they knew that Megan had used drugs that night with Craig and Kelly, she was by far the most credible witness that would repeat back their theories as facts. Overlooking a witness that was not on drugs and had nothing to be held over her head, Mandy Polk was useless to the prosecution because her statements supported Craig and Kelly's claims of an accidental overdose. Never mind that this was hear-say (Kelly allegedly told Megan and Megan told the police); but given the source, and just by reading her first statement, second statement, and her grand jury testimony, Megan was not being truthful. And again, this was the prosecution's key witness. Without her testimony, they had nothing.

In America we convict people for the crimes they have committed. We do not invent crimes so that they will be convicted. After all was said and done, what happened to Melissa James was horrible. Craig was an asshole for disposing of her body because he was worried about his and Kelly's careers. Nonetheless, Craig should have only been charged with the crimes he committed: Arson, and Conspiracy to Conceal Evidence. Instead, those with power manipulated the system and charged him with something they deemed appropriate: Murder, even though Craig never committed that crime.

On Wednesday, December 28th Anthony Gross appeared in the Las Vegas court room of Judge Joe Bonaventure with his notoriously "connected" defense lawyer, Louis Palazzo. Gross was released on the surprisingly low bail amount of $13,000. As a condition of the bail, Judge Joseph Bonaventure said Gross would be under house arrest, and was not allowed to have any contact with Craig Titus or Kelly Ryan.

After Gross was released on bail, John Allen tried to report to the Clark County Detention Center authorities what Tony Gross told him; Allen didn't believe that either man should be charged with murder if the girl had died from a drug overdose. Allen told them exactly what Gross said, and the authorities didn't take notes nor did they ever get back with him. When he went back a few days later to check on the status of his report, he was told that the information had been given to the homicide investigators that were working the case, but Allen never heard back from anybody. Allen said, "I just thought, this was so fucking typical; you can't trust anybody in Vegas, least of all the fucking Metro police department! If they want someone to go away, they will either shoot you because nothing will ever happen to a LVMPD officer, or they frame you and put you away for the rest of your life!"

Craig and Kelly Waive Rendition

On January 9th, 2006 Craig Titus, and Kelly Ryan, and their lawyers waived Rendition in court. This meant that they were not fighting extradition, and would be moved to Las Vegas, Nevada within seven to ten days. Craig and Kelly left Massachusetts on January 16th in two different vans, taking two different routes back to Nevada. It took twelve days to transport Kelly Ryan from Massachusetts to Nevada; and on January 28th, she was arrested and booked into the Clark County Detention Center. The charges filed were- Accessory to Murder (help carry out or conceal a murder) and Third Degree Arson (set fire or aided another in setting fire to a vehicle); Kelly was now known as inmate # 01992276, case # 05F23407B. Kelly's parents, Tom Ryan and Nikki Ryan were there when she returned.

On January 30th, two days after Kelly returned, Craig arrived back in Las Vegas. His van took fourteen days to return home. Upon arrival, Craig was booked into the Clark County Detention Center with charges of Murder and Third Degree Arson. Craig would now be identified as inmate #01895641, case # 05F23407A. Craig's mother Sandi and sister Nicole were there when he arrived. Through Jeff Schwimmer, Craig and Kelly's parents hired the best defense lawyers in town, Richard Schonfeld and Thomas Pitaro. Pitaro recommended that Craig and Kelly hire Private Investigator Tom Dillard to join the defense. Pitaro had worked alongside Dillard on two previous high profile cases. He believed, "It's better having Dillard working for you than against you." They agreed, and Tom Dillard was hired and started working on their case immediately. Dillard's objective was: to find the physical evidence to counter the prosecution's accusations, and to discredit the witnesses that were not being truthful.

CHAPTER 4

The Binion Connection

Over the last several years, the Las Vegas Metropolitan Police Department has been involved in a number of cover-ups and scandals that have placed the spotlight on the perverse actions of those in authority. With no outside system of checks and balances, every outlet of power in Las Vegas has been crookedly interwoven with another. There doesn't appear to be a single, local institution that has not been tainted and damaged by the Las Vegas Metropolitan Police Department and the entire Clark County Judicial system.

Even the local newspapers have been exploited to print the District Attorney's bullshit propaganda. No one would dare stand up to a colleague or superior, lest they undermine their own future; yet a system is in place where the police, prosecutors, and judges were asked to hold each other accountable. If these stories of scandal stood alone, they would seem preposterous. However, lined up side by side, there seems to be a pattern of political and ethical depravity.

It would take another dozen books to document each and every nefarious activity whitewashed by this entire system in Las Vegas that is completely void of integrity. One trial stands out however: the Ted Binion Murder Trial. That case has an unusual number of similarities to the Titus' case. Because one case seems to be a duplicate of the other, in order to better understand Titus' case; it's important to look at the high profile murder case involving Sandy Murphy and Rick Tabish.

THE BINION CONNECTION

Coincidence or Connection? A few facts both cases have in common:

1. **Flawed police work, tunnel vision, and intimidation by the police** – The detectives conducting the investigation had tunnel vision, and decided that both Ted Binion and Melissa James were murdered, when in fact all of the physical evidence pointed towards an overdose. The investigators pointed their fingers at Sandy Murphy/ Rick Tabish and Craig Titus/ Kelly Ryan from the very beginning. In neither case did the police investigate the people that sold the drugs to the victims that overdosed; they were both pushed under the rug so that they could focus on the defendants. They built their case around a coerced witness testimony, and manipulated the system to convict the defendants.

2. **Autopsy reports reveal that both cases were an overdose.**

3. **Articles leaked by the prosecution and printed in newspapers.** A reporter from the Las Vegas Sun wrote weekly articles about the Binion trial and then published a book from leaked information from the prosecutor. A reporter from the Las Vegas Review Journal wrote weekly articles about the Melissa James trial then published a book before the trial ever started.

4. **Prosecutorial Misconduct.** Each prosecutor was politically motivated to secure a conviction. The prosecutor in the Binion trial, David Roger, ran for district attorney and won. The prosecutor for the Craig Titus case was running for Congress.

5. **Judicial Misconduct.** When there was a motion for the judges in both cases to step away from the trials because of conflicts of interests, neither judge stepped down. Either the judge themselves or a colleague ruled in the judge's favor.

Facts and History about Ted Binion and his Death:

Ted Binion was a wealthy gambling executive and one of the sons of famed Las Vegas casino magnate Benny Binion, owner of Binion's Horeshoe Casino. In 1964, Benny Binion regained control of the casino after he served time for tax evasion. Since he was a convicted criminal, Benny was no longer allowed to hold a gaming license so

SWIFT INJUSTICE

his twenty-one year old son, Teddy, took over the day-to-day operations of the casino. For the next 30 years, Ted Binion was the face of the Horseshoe's casino, and was drawing attention from the Nevada Gaming Commission because of his connection to the organized crime figure "Fat Herbie" Blitzstein.

In 1986 Ted Binion was arrested on drug trafficking charges. The NGC suspected that Ted Binion was using his live-in girlfriend, Sandy Murphy, as a bagwoman. The two met while she worked at Cheetah's Gentleman's Club; he would frequent this and other topless bars with his mob buddy, Fat Herbie.

In 1995 Binion's wife and daughter moved out, and Sandy Murphy moved into his home on Palomino Lane. In 1997 Ted Binion's gaming license was suspended after he failed a drug test, and in 1998 Binion's gaming license was permanently revoked for associating with known mafia- related criminals.

Teddy Binion was never to be associated with the family casino business again. His sister Becky (who had been feuding with him over the previous decade) had filed a lawsuit against him, and when Ted Binion was banned from the casino; his sister took over Ted Binion's job. Ted did not trust his sister Becky, or her husband, and so he hired a man named Rick Tabish to build a vault in the desert, and then removed all of the silver he had stored at the casino and put it into this vault.

After Binion lost his license, he became even more heavily involved in drugs- primarily black tar heroin, which he smoked every day. Ted Binion was found dead on a small mattress on the floor of his Las Vegas estate on September 17, 1998. Empty pill bottles were found near the body, and an autopsy and toxicology report revealed that he died of a lethal dosage combination of the prescription sedative Xanax and heroin.

The day before, Binion had himself purchased twelve pieces of black tar heroin from a street drug dealer, and had earlier gotten a prescription from his next-door neighbor (a doctor) for Xanax. Evidence introduced at trial showed that Binion personally took the prescription to be filled at a local pharmacy the night before his death. Binion's death was initially treated as a suicide by overdose; and the medical examiner documented these findings in the autopsy results.

His live-in girlfriend, Sandy Murphy, said that Binion had been suicidal ever since he lost his gaming license. His other sister Barbara, afflicted with the same kinds of drug problems as her brother, committed suicide in 1977, which also helped contribute to the perception that Ted could have been vulnerable to suicide as well.

However, Ted's living sister, Becky discounted any talk of suicide, saying that in her conversations with him he hadn't sounded despondent. She wanted to pin the murder on Sandy Murphy to ensure that Murphy did not inherit any of the Binion fortune.

Despite the urgings of Ted's sister, Metro refused to open a full-scale homicide investigation, so she paid Tom Dillard, a former homicide Metro detective, $250, 000 to investigate the death. Additionally, Tom Dillard would make another $250,000, if he could tie the case to Rick Tabish and Sandy Murphy, and persuade the District Attorney's office to change the cause of death from suicide to homicide and have charges brought up against the two.

For half a million dollars, Tom Dillard would make anything happen for the Binion Estate. Soon after, Tom Dillard turned up a trail of cellular phone conversations, and secret meetings between Rick and Sandy, as well as evidence that they had told people about their plot to kill Ted Binion.

Based on Tom Dillard's findings, a new theory emerged through David Roger at the District Attorney's Office – the levels of heroin and Xanax found in Binion's body were so lethal that there was no way he could have ingested this large amount of drugs on his own- and so he must have been a victim of a forced overdose. Soon after, the medical examiner changed his findings to "Homicide", and the Las Vegas Metropolitan P.D. began to investigate the death as a homicide.

Tom Dillard worked hand in hand with his best friend, the Deputy District Attorney for Clark County, David Roger. Roger impaneled a grand jury as a tool to continue the investigation that Dillard had started. Over the next three months Rogers called dozens of witness and gathered volumes of information. In an unprecedented fashion, Dillard worked closely with both the Homicide Detectives and Chief Deputy District Attorney David Roger. All the while Dillard had been building a civil case against Murphy and Tabish, who had been sued by the estate in District Court for allegedly causing Binion's death. On June 24, 1999, police arrested Sandy Murphy and Rick Tabish. They were charged with first-degree murder, grand larceny, and burglary.

The case attracted national media attention and everyone at the district attorney's office wanted a piece of the high profile case because a national win would help everyone involved to profit politically. During a 13-day Preliminary Hearing in September 1999, Chief Deputy District Attorney David Roger revealed a new theory to explain Binion's death: suffocation.

The prosecution brought to the case a New York pathologist of national repute, Michael Baden, and Baden testified that he believed the levels of heroin and Xanax in Binion's system were not enough to kill him, as the local medical examiner had initially concluded. Baden said congestion under Binion's eyelids and abrasions on his chest and back indicated he was suffocated in a nineteenth-century method called "burking." This occurs when someone sits on the victim's chest while covering his mouth and nose.

Prosecutors built their circumstantial case around this theory and then recruited witnesses to take the stand against the defendants. One such witness was the gardener, and the prosecution said that upon his arrival Sandy Murphy and Rick Tabish suffocated the victim. Another witness testified that Tabish told him about killing Binion.

Because of the testimony from witnesses that Tom Dillard personally recruited to testify in the case, without any physical evidence, Sandy Murphy and Rick Tabish were found guilty. Judge Joseph Bonaventure sentenced Tabish to 25 years to life in prison, while Murphy received 22 years to life. Later that year, David Roger (who prosecuted the Binion case) was elected Clark County District Attorney, and David Wall (who second-chaired the prosecution) was elected District Court Judge.

THE BINION CONNECTION

In May of 2002, Sandy Murphy filed a motion to dismiss, or a motion for a new trial based on prosecutorial misconduct and newly discovered evidence. A witness in the recent Binion evidentiary hearing, requested by Murphy and Tabish's attorneys, seemed to corroborate allegations that reward money offered by Binion's estate appeared to be in exchange for favorable testimony for the prosecution.

Key witness Kurt Gratzer said under oath that he was told by prosecutor David Roger that there would be $10,000 for him if he "cooperated fully." The prosecutors have publicly said the reward money was not offered until after the trial, but Gratzer said otherwise. Gratzer recently testified that the prosecution told him if he cooperated fully against Murphy and Tabish that he stood to gain the reward money for both ($20,000). **Gratzer was allegedly threatened by the prosecution that if he did not cooperate, the immunity agreement would be revoked and he would be prosecuted by the District Attorney's office.**

Court papers were also filed on the judge, Joseph Bonaventure, for Conflict of Interest and bias because he attended a book-signing at the Binion's casino that "demonized our clients." **The book was written by a Las Vegas Sun Crime reporter, and the defense attorneys said that the writer was fed information daily by the prosecution**, wrote articles that were entirely one-sided, and prejudiced the public against the defense. Also in attendance were the two prosecutors in the Binion Trial: David Roger and David Wall, now the newly elected District Attorney and District Court Judge.

The Nevada Supreme Court overturned these convictions, and the prosecution was able to further explore the circumstances around the prosecutorial misconduct. These allegations were substantiated, and it was found that witnesses for the prosecution received upward of $100,000 from the Binion estate through private investigator Tom Dillard. **It was also found that the prosecution's witness, Steven Kurt Gratzer, lied on the witness stand because he was bullied by Tom Dillard and David Roger. Gratzer said that he was told exactly what to say by the prosecution.**

The newly discovered evidence substantiated prosecutorial misconduct in the form of threats to one of the prosecution's key witnesses.

Gratzer said that he was also granted immunity by the prosecution for his testimony against the defendants. **The witness said that David Roger from the District Attorney's office told him that he could be charged and go to jail if he did not cooperate and implicate the defendants in the murder.**

After Gratzer testified in the first trial, he said that his drug charges in Montana were suddenly dismissed. Tom Dillard also testified that he paid Gratzer $20,000 from the Binion Estate for his testimony. Dillard also testified under oath that he paid Binion's housekeeper Mary Montoya $10,000 for her testimony against the defense.

Dillard said that during his tenure as a homicide detective with Metro, he had never before seen a reward of $100,000. Even Secret Service witnesses don't receive rewards to that extreme, he said. The defense also said that Jeff German from the Las Vegas Sun published articles every week that were pro-prosecution about the Binion case and then wrote a book that vilified the defendants. The defense attorney for Sandy Murphy said, "**I think this reporter was either in the pocket of the prosecution, which happens to almost every crime reporter, or heavily influenced by the Binion family.**"

The defendants were granted a new trial, which began on October 11, 2004 in Judge Bonaventure's courtroom with **Robert Daskas** and Christopher Lali prosecuting the case. **David Roger** had already capitalized on the first trial, and had become the **District Attorney**. It was then another deputy district attorney's time to shine, and move up the political ladder.

With a congressional seat being dangled in front of him, **Robert Daskas** (big surprise) trumped more charges up, so Murphy and Tabish then faced life in prison. This time Sandy Murphy was fighting back against the District Attorney's Office; Murphy was represented by a civil rights defense attorney from California and by defense attorneys **Michael Cristalli** and **Mark Saggese** from Las Vegas.

It would be political suicide to expose the Las Vegas District Attorney's office, so the local attorney's took a back seat as the California defense attorney exposed the corrupt side of the District Attorney's office. And according to the defense, **David Roger (through the Clark County Detention officers and Las Vegas Metro police) tampered with evidence, coerced the coroner's office, assisted the Binion estate and Tom Dillard, in paying witnesses for testimony, coerced witnesses by threat of indictment in other cases,** failed to release photos of Binion's sternum abrasions, and doctored tapes of phone conversations with Gratzer. **But most alarming, David Roger (from the Clark County District Attorney's Office) attempted to have an "In-house" snitch set Rick Tabish up on a phony "Murder for Hire" attempt. DOES ANY OF THIS SOUND FAMILIAR?**

Tabish and Murphy were each acquitted of murder in November 2004 but were convicted on lesser charges of burglary (12 to 60 months) and grand larceny (12 to 60 months) connected with the Binion case. For Murphy, it was time served, and she walked out of the women's prison a free woman. As the gates to the prison door opened, Ms. Murphy greeted reporters and exclaimed, "Michael Cristalli and Marc Saggese were the best criminal defense attorneys in Las Vegas."

The Murphy/Tabish trial appeared to be a blueprint for the Titus/Ryan case. Both had too many factors in common for it to be a coincidence; constitutional and due process rights were violated by the same people, under the same circumstances. Both cases had the same misconduct. Law enforcement manipulated the witnesses and the evidence.

Private investigators worked with the prosecution and provided information to the District Attorney's office. Prosecutors bullied the witnesses into perjury for their own political gain and leaked prejudicial information about the defense to the press. The defense attorneys frivolously spun their wheels with political aspirations cooperating with the prosecution. And, judges with a conflict of interest were patted on the back by colleagues, and allowed to stay on the case. Basically, those with power were able to do whatever the hell they wanted, and those without could not do shit about it!

A closer look at the two cases provides obvious connections:

1. Both cases had the same Defense Attorneys/Firms: Craig's original attorney was **Richard Shonfeld** of Chesnoff & Schonfeld Law firm;

while Sandy Murphy's original lawyers were **David Chesnoff** and **Oscar Goodman**. Goodman was a Las Vegas criminal defense attorney from 1968-2000 and well-known for notorious organized crime defendants like Chicago Mobster Herbert "Fat Herbie" Blitzsten (Ted Binion's best friend) and Chicago enforcer/ hit man Anthony Spilatro. Both mobsters managed to stay out of prison in Chicago and Las Vegas, with the help of his loyal criminal defense lawyer, Oscar Goodman.

Oscar Goodman was elected mayor in 1999, and had to step down from the Sandy Murphy case (and actually *did* stand down), but his partner, David Chesnoff, defended Murphy in the first trial. Ted Binion's best friend, top Chicago Lieutenant "Fat Herbie" Blitzsten was shot and killed in his own home a year before Binion died (Goodwin represented both men at different times). Herbie was shot by members of the Los Angeles crime family who were attempting to take over his racketeering and loan shark schemes. One of these mobsters, Stephen Cino, had hired **Louis Palazzo** and was acquitted on the murder charges.

Palazzo was also Anthony "Tony" Gross' attorney, who made all of his charges disappear, and who had deep connections with Goodman. Louis Palazzo and Oscar Goodman's son, Nick Goodman, were best friends and partners on various projects. They are both considered men that have walked in Goodman's footsteps, and reportedly defend the men connected with the mob. **Palazzo was also Rick Tabish's first attorney. In Tabish's appeal, he stated that Palazzo was purposefully ineffective, and implied that he "threw the trial." Murphy would hurl the same allegation at her attorney's Goodman and Chesnoff. Looking at the close connection between the attorneys, this could have been a real possibility.**

On May 20, 1999 attorneys Chesnoff and Palazzo withdrew from the case, and **Steve Wolfson (Judge Jackie Glass' husband) was hired as the defense attorney**. In the first trial, David Roger was the prosecuting attorney. After Murphy and Tabish were convicted of murder and sentenced to life in prison, Roger ran for District Attorney and won. **Robert Daskas** prosecuted the second trial and lost.

THE BINION CONNECTION

Working on Sandy Murphy's appeal was **Thomas Pitaro**, Kelly Ryan's first attorney. Both Kelly Ryan and Sandy Murphy fired Pitaro. Murphy fired him because he was **working with private investigator Tom Dillard** on another high profile case, defending Margaret Rudin. After Murphy fired Pitaro, she hired Michael Cristalli and Marc Saggese. After Craig fired Schonfeld, he hired Marc Saggese and Kelly Ryan hired Marc Saggese.

Tom Dillard was hired as a private investigator for Craig Titus and Kelly Ryan, however it seemed his information was used against the defense and given to his best friend, David Roger, in the District Attorney's office. When the Titus family tried to turn to Dillard for answers, he mysteriously disappeared for the remainder of the trial.

The judges, Joseph Bonaventure & Jackie Glass, sought out the high-profile cases (those that were to be featured on Court TV) in Las Vegas to hopefully get a reality court television show, Judge Joseph Bonaventure was the man in the 1990's who always seemed to land the high-profile criminal cases. There were 19 Clark County District Court judges, and supposedly a computer in the Court Clerk's office made random selections on what judge would get a case, however, this never happened with high- profile cases. The Court Clerk's computer assigned judges in numerical order. If the clerk was aware that a highly desirable case was about to be assigned, he/she could hold that case until the number of that judge who would like to preside over it was about to appear on the computer.

District Court Judge Joseph Bonaventure presided over both of the Binion trials, Margaret Ruden's trial, and Deen Cassim's trial and re-sentencing. Bonaventure was the judge that sentenced Cassim for aggravated burglary originally in March 2005, and then freed him a few months later after he cooperated with Robert Daskas to set Craig Titus and Ron Brady Jr. up for a "murder for hire" plot.

Judge Jackie Glass was another judge that would supposedly draw the high- profile cases. She was assigned to the Binion case, because her husband was the defense attorney. She was assigned to the Craig Titus case, however, and secretly met behind closed doors with the prosecutor and Tony Gross' attorney. Glass was informed of a murder for hire set-up, and Craig's attorneys were never notified of the illegal meeting. Judge Glass would sentence Anthony Tony Gross (Tony Palazzo's client) to probation. Robert Daskas recommended the slap on the wrist because Tony helped them try to set up Craig Titus. Of course, Judge Glass was also assigned the O.J. Simpson trial, where the District Attorney's office trumped up charges, and Judge Glass gave him a ridiculously long sentence for them.

2. Covering the Binion case for the Las Vegas Sun, Jeff German wrote articles about the trial with "insider information" handed to him by the prosecution. German wrote a victory article for the prosecution in May of 2000 called, "Private Detective Shrugged off Attacks by the Defense Team," where he featured Tom Dillard as the hero for the prosecution.

"To them, he was the private investigator who manipulated witnesses for the wealthy Binion estate, contaminated the death scene and manufactured evidence against the two people charged with killing Binion: his live-in girlfriend, Sandy Murphy and her lover, Rick Tabish. Though they hurled barb after barb at Dillard outside his presence in court, defense lawyers never bothered to call the 53-year-old ex-homicide cop to the witnesses stand for a direct assault.

The conviction of Murphy and Tabish gives Dillard an immense measure of satisfaction. Dillard said he was hired by the $55- million dollar estate on September 24, 1998, one week after Binion was found dead at his 2408 Palomino Lane home. His hiring occurred after estate lawyers Richard Wright and James J. Brown came away from a Sept. 21, 1998, meeting with Metro Police homicide supervisors, who were less than enthusiastic about launching a murder probe.

At that meeting, Brown for the first time revealed that Binion, fearing Murphy might try to kill him, had given orders the day before his slaying to remove Murphy from his will. Top homicide officials, aware of Binion's heroin habit and not being told of any immediate signs of foul play at the Palomino Lane home, thought it was more likely that he had died of an accidental drug overdose or had committed suicide.

THE BINION CONNECTION

Dillard said that one of his first tasks was to tour the death scene and take photographs. From there he paid a visit to lead homicide detective James Buczek, who let him see the crime photos. 'It got to the point where we really had two investigations going on,' Dillard said. 'They were doing their investigation for Metro, and I was doing my investigation for the estate.' Dillard said that he shared everything he picked up with homicide detectives, who were pursuing their own leads.

Dillard also said that he met with Clark County Coroner Ron Flud and Chief Medical Examiner Lary Simms, who performed the autopsy on Binion, to persuade them to take a closer look at homicide as the manner in which Binion had died. He even arranged for them to visit the death scene. The investigation really picked up, Dillard said, after his best friend, Chief Deputy District Attorney David Roger, was assigned to the case in late December 1998.

By March 1999 the Clark County Coroner was ready to declare Binion a victim of a homicide, and three months later Murphy and Tabish were arrested and charged with murder. 'David Roger feels very strongly about his ethical obligations, as an officer of the court and a prosecutor, and I didn't want to give the defense an opportunity to use our friendship against him in that area,' Dillard said."

In 2001, Jeff German, of the Las Vegas Sun, wrote a book with an "insider's account to the Ted Binion murder case." It's a book that German said contained "New, unpublicized details about the case." German, who covered the Binion saga for the Sun said, "I have come up with some sexy nuggets that will not be popular with Sandy Murphy and Rick Tabish. It's the inside story, the most comprehensive look at the most publicized murder case in Las Vegas history."

Inside the book, it said, *"Jeff German has been an award-winning writer for the Las Vegas Sun for more than two decades. As a columnist and the newspaper's senior investigative reporter, he has chronicled the activities of the mob and covered Las Vegas from its streets to casino boardrooms. His early reports on Ted Binion's death led police to conclude that the casino boss was the victim of a homicide. German later obtained hundreds of pages of confidential law enforcement* documents and broke a steady stream of stories that took his readers into the heart of the police investigation. He is regarded as one of the nation's foremost experts on this sensational case."

Just as German was a tool for the prosecution, publishing everything they leaked to him, Glenn Puit of the Las Vegas Review Journal was used in a similar way in the Craig Titus Case. Puit was also leaked information that the prosecution used to their advantage, and likewise Puit wrote weekly articles with a bias against the defense. Then much like German, he published a book about the case. Although German waited until after the trial, Puit wanted to be the first to cash in on Melissa James' misfortune, and published the book nearly two years before Craig Titus and Kelly Ryan were sentenced for a crime.

3. When Craig Titus hired Tom Dillard as a private investigator for both his and Kelly's defense, he had no idea that Dillard was actually working for the State. Craig Titus' family paid Tom Dillard a significant amount of money, and turned over all of their leads to this man. The state had no physical evidence, and completely relied on the witness testimony of Megan Pierson Foley.

Dillard worked as a double agent; he collected money and information from the Titus family, and passed over any information the defense had to the lead investigator Dean O'Kelley and the District Attorney's office. While the Titus and Ryan family thought that Dillard was investigating the testimony provided to the police by alleged drug dealers and addicts, he actually told the State of their plan to discredit the witnesses. Staying one step ahead of Titus, the investigators worked together with Dillard and the Clark County Detention Center and found a man willing to frame Craig Titus and another inmate for an alleged "murder for hire" plot.

It might sound ludicrous, but it had already happened once before. According to Rick Tabish's defense team, Tom Dillard and officers from the Clark County Detention Center attempted (but got caught trying) to do the exact same thing to Rick Tabish. In an article written for the Sun, the prosecution denied the allegations, but they sounded eerily similar to what happened in the Craig Titus case. Law enforcement

THE BINION CONNECTION

sources said detectives learned that the informant, David Gomez, was in the same protective custody cell block as Rick Tabish.

David Gomez said he had information that Tabish was plotting to kill Binion's gardener, Tom Loveday, who was a key witness. Jail officials declined to comment that morning. But late the following Tuesday Palazzo, joined by John Momot, (the lawyer for Tabish's co-defendant, Sandy Murphy), filed a motion charging that David Roger and jail officials planted Gomez next to Tabish to steal personal notes from Tabish before his March 13 trial. They then attempted to set his client up on a "Murder for Hire" charge to ensure that both Tabish and Murphy got charged with killing Binion in September 1998 and for stealing his valuables.

4. Both cases had in-house informants that attempted to set-up a Murder-for-Hire: David Gomez & Deen Cassim. Defense lawyers asked District Judge Joseph Bonaventure to dismiss the murder charges against their clients because of the alleged wrongdoing. *"The misconduct at issue is so flagrant that nothing short of dismissal will serve to deter such unlawful and egregious tactics in the future,"* Palazzo and Momot wrote in an affidavit. Palazzo charged that jail officials placed Gomez in the same protective custody block as Tabish, "for the purpose of invading the defense camp and seeking to undermine Mr. Tabish's defense in this case." Palazzo added, "Furthermore, it is believed that this informant has purloined personal notes and work product documentation relating to the defense of Mr. Tabish in the upcoming trial from Mr. Tabish's cell on behalf of the district attorney's office."

In their motion, the lawyers said Tabish reported the papers missing. "The documents at issue include matters impacting upon trial strategy, as well as matters concerning impeachment material of various state witnesses," Palazzo and Momot wrote. Law enforcement sources said Gomez provided detectives with documents but a handwriting analysis could not determine whether Tabish was the author. Roger also looked briefly at the papers and said he couldn't identify the handwriting as Tabish's, the sources said. "Detectives were convinced that the information provided (by Gomez) was not accurate information, and no further action was taken," one law enforcement source said.

The documents were believed to be in the custody of jail officials. Defense attorneys described Gomez as a "reputed snitch who has repeatedly worked on numerous cases for the state and federal government." Tabish was placed in protective custody, after jail officials reported they had received death threats against him.

Officials would not say how long Gomez had been in the same cell block with Tabish. Metro Detectives said, "You name the crime, short of murder, and David Gomez has probably committed it." Gomez, a reputed member of the Mexican Mafia, has convictions for battery, rape, assault with a deadly weapon, burglary and perjury.

While facing lengthy prison time, he became adept at earning favors from his jailers by snitching on fellow inmates, and he has become the biggest rat of all jailhouse rats, attaching himself to high-profile cases. A couple of years ago Gomez reportedly helped prosecutors, from his Los Angeles jail cell, convict Mikhail Markhasev of killing Bill Cosby's son, Ennis.

Later in Las Vegas he gave corrections officers the lowdown on his ex-Mexican Mafia pals, and proceeded to thrust himself into the Ted Binion murder case, the most well publicized criminal proceeding of all time in Las Vegas. But this time he's working for the defense. He has become important to Rick Tabish and Sandy Murphy as they try to persuade District Judge Joseph Bonaventure to toss out their murder convictions in Binion's Sept. 17, 1998, death.

The jail house snitch, David Gomez, was supposedly prepared to testify that Chief Deputy District Attorney David Roger conspired with Clark County Detention Center officials to plant him in the same protective custody cell block with Tabish to steal his confidential defense notes. It was later brought out that Gomez reported that Tabish told him he would pay him $200,000 to have Binion's gardener killed. When Murphy's lawyer brought this to the judge's attention, he said, "This case is fraught with immunity, paid testimony, perjury and heavy involvement of interested parties."

5. Both Roger and Daskas tried to threaten defense with having the "lawyer-client" right waived, and having original defense attorneys testifying against them. After the defense attorneys filled out a 30-page writ, outlining all of the specific misconduct by then deputy district attorney David Roger, Roger used his clout as the new district attorney, and personally wrote a response to the defense attorneys. But Roger did not respond to the points of the law presented as prosecutorial misconduct on his part. Instead, he put a spin on the defense's writ, and said that he wanted to call Tabish and Murphy's original defense lawyers up to the stand, and have their lawyer-client privilege waived.

Roger wrote, "The defendant has waived the attorney-client privilege by the mere filing of his affidavit." The next day, David Roger filed a motion asking that Tabish's attorney-client privilege be waived. If granted, it would have opened the unprecedented door to any and all conversations the defendant's had with their attorney, giving prosecutors an unusual inside look at previous legal strategies. (This unprecedented and unethical threat was also used by Greg Denue and Robert Daskas against Craig Titus when they were trying to dump Denue and hire a different attorney. This is nothing short of extortion, and a violation of the defendant's Sixth Amendment right to Due Process Rights.)

Where have we seen Tom Dillard's name before?

Tom Dillard was a detective who worked in Metro's homicide unit from 1983 until his forced retirement in 1993. Before making nearly half a million dollars for his work on the Binion case, he was being sued by Mr. Howard Haupt in court for withholding exculpatory evidence when he worked as a Las Vegas Metro Homicide detective.

In the Las Vegas Sun, in an article "Metro Settles Civil Rights Case for $800,000" in 1997, it states: "Metro Police must pay a San Diego man, Howard Haupt, about $800,000 not to pursue a $1 million judgment he won after being acquitted in a Las Vegas murder case. Howard Haupt sued after his civil rights were allegedly violated by Metro homicide detective Tom Dillard during his criminal trial. Haupt is expected to receive about $300,000, with the remaining $500,000 to pay his legal bills, the source said Monday." Tom Dillard was written up in 1989 by the Investigative Services Division of Metro for Tom Dillard calling District Court Judge Stephen Huffaker concerning the murder trial in which Howard Haupt was the defendant. Officer Dillard attempted to influence the judge's decision. A federal civil jury awarded Haupt $1 million in punitive damages for retired Metro Detective Tom Dillard's behavior during the criminal trial.

To this day, Tom Dillard is still duping unsuspecting clients (like Craig Titus' mother, Sandi) out of money on the pretense of working for them. Most recently it has been published that a mourning mother, Cynthia Turner, paid Dillard $5,000 to investigate her son's homicide. This homicide would have been bad publicity for the district attorney (Dillard's best friend David Roger). So Dillard pocketed the money, and did nothing to further the investigation. Apparently this last deed has turned some heads, and an investigation into this murder has pointed in the direction of a cover-up. The district attorney, Dillard's best friend, David Roger has since prematurely (3 years early) retired from his position.

CHAPTER 5

Checkmate

What do we know about the prosecutor, Robert Daskas? Not much! Robert Daskas is a riddle, wrapped in a mystery, inside an enigma, wearing elevator shoes to be able to see over the podium! There is not much information floating around in cyber-space, or anywhere else, about Robert Daskas, other than his height and salary: he is short (5ft. 4 inches) and makes a decent amount of money (annual salary +benefits- $204,209.52). Either nothing has been written about the man, good or bad; or he has one hell of a staff working overtime to keep his name off the internet grid.

One thing we do know about Robert Daskas is that he has prosecuted the most notorious, high- profile cases in Las Vegas over the past fifteen years, and has been seen on countless "current affair" news programs and "true crime" television shows. Daskas has logged in enough face time in front of the camera to have his name and "accomplished visual entertainment work" listed on the IMBD website (Internet Movie Database, a comprehensive list of celebrities, actors, and actresses with contributions in the entertainment media).

This is a man that loves the spotlight, and in an attempt to promote himself and become a "celebrity" prosecutor, he has taken advantage of every opportunity to make an appearance on national television. For whatever reason however, Daskas has gone to great lengths to keep his personal and private affairs out of the public eye. Almost every detail of his personal life has been sealed or deleted, making it difficult to procure an accurate depiction of this man. Not everything can be hidden however; and following the paper trail of misconduct has revealed a great deal about his character.

When Craig Titus was asked to use one word to describe Robert Daskas, he instantly said, "hypocrite." A hypocrite is a person that professes beliefs and opinions that he himself does not hold, in order to conceal the truth about himself. This word says it all, and the definition provides an accurate description of the man who set out with a personal vendetta to destroy Craig Titus and his entire family.

While Daskas shielded his own family from his past indiscretions, he was on a crusade to slander Craig Titus and his family in the media by leaking disparaging information that was irrelevant to the case. Titus' mother and sister were called, among many other things, "trailer park, white trash" in the media. (By the way, I have been to Sandi's house, and would hardly qualify this upscale, half a million dollar home, in an exclusive area of Houston, as a trailer.)

In several newspaper articles, Titus' mother and sister were even accused of being involved in a plot to have the prosecution's witnesses killed. These fabricated depictions of Craig's mother and sister hit below the belt. Craig adored these women, and has always been protective of them, his entire life. When he was unable to protect them from Robert Daskas, his resolve to continue fighting was ultimately destroyed.

In this smear campaign fueled by the prosecutor, innocent by-standers' reputations were ruined. The backlash was severe, and for his mother and sister, the fall out was unbearable. Both his mother and sister have talked about friends and family members turning their backs on them after these lies were printed in the newspaper. To this day, they live in isolation because they are still being accused of this crime that never took place. When Robert Daskas leaked information to the press, it not only prejudiced the public against Craig Titus, it prejudiced the public against his family members as well.

CHECKMATE

Robert Daskas would have made a great politician

With all of the attributes and qualifications to become a great politician, (lying, backstabbing, obfuscating, and double-dealing), Robert Daskas ran for Congress in the 2008 election (if you can call it that; he ran for a couple of months and then dropped out of the race). Strangely enough, very little was written about Daskas when he entered the political race. He claimed to be a democrat, but his views were too conservative to qualify as such. Daskas supported capital punishment, and when he prosecuted capital cases, he typically recommended the death penalty over life in prison. After Daskas appeared on Jon Ralston's *Face to Face*, Ralston described Daskas as being: *"Startlingly unprepared to answer some basic questions, especially about health care and immigration."*

Ralston said, "Robert Daskas did not know the answer to the most basic questions, and doesn't' seem to know enough yet to even know what he believes. I was most stunned by Daskas' refusal even to consider any broad policies for illegal immigrants here until the border is secured. He clung to a metaphor he seemed proud of, which was 'if Hoover Dam sprung a leak today and thousands or millions of gallons of water were flowing through the dam to the other side, it wouldn't make sense to take a bucket and start emptying out the water that's flowed through. The first step would be to block the dam.'

When I also pressed him on whether he supported any path to citizenship, Daskas took refuge in what has become the touchstone - and a misleading one - for candidates in this debate: driver's licenses for illegals. Putting on his prosecutor's hat, Daskas said, 'It causes me great concern that we could give someone incentive to come here by giving them some privilege like a driver's license ...

It defies common sense and logic.' Maybe he can defend that position and maybe he just wants to inoculate himself against GOP attacks on an issue that has been distorted to death. But it also defies common sense and logic that denying driver's licenses to illegals means they will stop coming."

This was the only interview that could be found during Daskas' short run for Congress; keeping his mouth shut probably gave him the best shot at winning the election. Robert Daskas' campaign literature provided a selected and limited insight into his professional and personal life. The "Daskas for Congress" campaign brochures said:

"Robert Daskas boasted winning 32 of 33 murder trials. He started his career in 1995 with Clark County District Attorney's Office, and he rose through the ranks in just six short months, and prosecuted his first murder case.

In 1999, Daskas was promoted to the Major Violator's Unit, an elite team, dedicated exclusively to prosecuting homicide cases. Time and again, Daskas had been selected to prosecute Nevada's most notorious criminals, and he has been featured on: 48 Hours Murder Mystery, America's Most Wanted, Dateline, and Court TV."

Daskas was a member of the undefeated 1984 Nevada State champion wrestling team." (Fun fact: Craig Titus won State in wrestling, and he also graduated from high school in 1984)

"Daskas has been married for ten years to his wife Julie Leimomilan-Sanpei, and they had two children, Nicole (8) and Dustin (3). With Julie by his side, Daskas entered the political race after he prosecuted his last high profile case, and resigned from the district attorney's office in November 2008." According to the Daskas for Congress campaign brochure, *"Robert Daskas' success as a prosecutor was attributed to his high conviction rate in high-profile cases."*

While Daskas measures success by the number of high profile cases he wins in the courtroom, the American Bar Association states:

(Standard 3-1.2c) **The primary duty of the prosecutor is to seek justice, not merely to convict.**

Before Robert Daskas ran for Congress, several articles in the newspapers called him the "anointed candidate that was guaranteed a win." Obviously Daskas was given this title long before anyone ever bothered to ask him about his views or heard him speak in public. In April of 2008, Robert Daskas unexpectedly dropped out of the Congressional race citing, "family considerations" as the reason for the abrupt departure, leaving the Democrats only a couple of weeks to find a replacement.

Robert Daskas and his wife Julie Sanpei-Daskas divorced within months of Daskas dropping out of the political race (sometime between April and August). This was discovered by looking at a Clark County Data website. The website provided the following information: Julie Sanpei-Daskas and Robert Daskas owned a mutual property on Brushwood Peak Ave. in Las Vegas until August 18, 2008 when Robert Daskas' name was taken off, and Julie Sanpei became the sole property owner. Robert Daskas and Julie Sanpei-Daskas shared that home together from 12/29/2003 – 08/18/2008 (four days before Craig Titus was sentenced in a plea deal.)

The District Attorney hands Robert Daskas the Craig Titus case

In December of 2005 Deputy District Attorney Robert Daskas was assigned the Melissa James case by Clark County District Attorney David Roger (the prosecutor-turned-D.A. that successfully convicted Sandy Murphy and Rick Tabish of First Degree Murder in the Ted Binion Murder Trial, and then had the decision overturned by the Nevada Supreme Court because of prosecutorial misconduct).

As the new district attorney, David Roger re-filed murder charges and assigned Robert Daskas to prosecute the case. Securing a conviction in the second trial was an unattainable feat primarily because Roger had already sabotaged the outcome by his egregious acts of misconduct during the first trial. Murphy and Tabish were predictably acquitted of murder, and Robert Daskas was handed his first defeat as a prosecutor.

David Roger placed Daskas in a "no-win" situation; and in their profession, prosecutors must always win if they want to advance their political careers. After Daskas "took one for the team," the District Attorney owed Daskas a big favor. David Roger needed to set Daskas up with a "sure win" the next time around, a high-profile case to vindicate the Binion loss.

In December of 2005, that "sure win" landed on the District Attorney's desk: one that would attract national attention with salacious details surrounding a celebrity bodybuilding couple involved in a love triangle resulting in the murder of their beautiful assistant.

The Craig Titus Case was not only guaranteed to be in the headlines of all the tabloids, it also appeared to be an easy win for the prosecution. With all of the physical and circumstantial evidence collected by the investigators, it seemed as if every element of this crime could be proven beyond a reasonable doubt. All the District Attorney's office had to do was "cut and paste" the evidence and Robert Daskas would be assured a victory.

The only obstacle appeared to be the autopsy results, and the cause of death being ruled "Undetermined." The toxicology report was not completed, yet it was clear Melissa James had enough drugs in her system to have overdosed (if there was an overdose, there was no murder). This was just a small snag for the prosecution; there was no way in hell Robert Daskas was going to lose this case. There was too much on the line after the Binion loss, and this trial would either make or break his future. A win would mean redemption, and could potentially launch his political career in Congress. A loss however would put an end to his political career before it ever got started.

From day one, every move Daskas made, starting with the arraignment hearing, had to be calculated and meticulously planned out; there was no room for error. Daskas' first order of business was to stack the charges against the defendants in order to ensure bail was denied, thus handicapping the defense from the start.

As Daskas stated to the judge, "Your honor, First Degree Murder is the only charge for which a person can be held without bail." The original charges against the defendants did not add up to first degree murder; however, throwing in additional charges bumped up the severity of the crime. With the amended charges, Craig Titus would not be able to secure bail, and he would be forced to plan his defense behind bars. This would make defending his case extremely difficult if not impossible.

Charge Stacking

Robert Daskas stacked the charges by slipping in "Kidnapping" to an amended criminal complaint. By adding "Kidnapping" to "Murder", the charges were automatically elevated to "First Degree Murder".

Charge stacking is a process by which a prosecutor creates a case with numerous charges or numerous instances of the same charge to: (a) manipulate the pretrial motions against the defense, (b) prejudice the public, judge, or jury against the defendant, (c) convince the defendant that the risk of not pleading guilty is too risky, forcing an innocent defendant into accepting a plea deal or an outrageous jail sentence.

This class of murder is one committed during the perpetration of kidnapping, and is deemed to be murder of the first degree, whether the murder was intentional or accidental. However, in order for the Felony Murder Rule to be applied, the intent to perpetrate kidnapping must be proven beyond a reasonable doubt.

Robert Daskas knew that Craig Titus and Kelly Ryan never kidnapped Melissa James because the autopsy report stated that Melissa James was dead prior to them moving her body. According to the Autopsy Report: (1) there was no soot in Melissa James' lungs, (2) she died from a Morphine/ heroin overdose around 3:00 p.m., (3) she still had food in her stomach, and in Nevada, for a kidnapping to take place, the victim must be alive in order to be "carried away."

The charge of Kidnapping should have never been added to the criminal complaint.
RPC 3.8(a) requires that the prosecutor refrain from prosecuting a charge not supported by probable cause, while national standards establish that a prosecution should only proceed on the basis of sufficient admissible evidence to support a conviction.

This was just the first of many pretrial moves that were strategically manipulated by Robert Daskas. Like a game of chess, Daskas was lining himself up to remove the King. Without any physical evidence, and an autopsy report that supported the defense's claim of an accidental overdose, Robert Daskas did not have a chance in hell of convicting Craig Titus of Murder, much less Manslaughter.

There has to be premeditation to convict somebody of Murder; it cannot be impulsive. Kelly Ryan and Melissa James' physical altercation was impulsive; it was not premeditated. The only thing that was premeditated was Craig purchasing Melisa James a hotel room and plane ticket to end all of the fighting between the two women.

The phone records confirmed that Craig Titus was not at the house when Melissa James passed away; and the toxicology report substantiates that Melissa James died of an overdose. Not only that, the AFIDS from the taser gun, and the autopsy report pinpoints Melissa's time of death being sometime between 2:15-2:45 p.m. on December 14th.

According to the prosecution's surveillance tapes and phone records, Melissa's body was transported from the Titus home to Sandy Valley road twelve hours after Melissa James had overdosed. This was not kidnapping; this was an unethical prosecutor trumping up the charges. With the added charge of Kidnapping, it did not matter if the act was impulsive or not however; it automatically became a First Degree Murder because of the Felony Murder Rule. And under Nevada law, bail is refused to anyone charged with First Degree Murder.

There was no turning back; Craig Titus was not guilty of murder, but the cameras were already lined up outside the court doors. Robert Daskas had already made a fool out of himself in the Ted Binion murder trial, and he had no intention of being made a fool of again in front of a national television audience. Daskas would do whatever it took to secure a conviction in the end, and he used a phony kidnapping charge, and the Felony Murder Rule, to ensure that Craig Titus would be stuck behind bars, unable to properly defend himself in court.

Craig Titus' case was a "Must Win" for the prosecution

To make it big as a prosecutor on the national stage, there is a formula to be followed:

Celebrity + Murder = High Profile Trial. If Melissa James overdosed, the spot light on Robert Daskas would have disappeared. What would

Daskas be able to charge Titus with? Desecration of a Grave is not even a crime in Nevada, and Arson would not have the cameras lined up outside the court doors.

Robert Daskas felt obligated to fudge the system in order to give everybody what they wanted: beautiful celebrities involved in a love triangle that ended in First Degree Murder, not an overdose. Throw in the words, "bodybuilders, drugs, swinging, and sex tapes," and everybody is lined up to get a piece of the pie! " Robert Daskas and David Roger both needed some good publicity through a high profile conviction in order to redeem themselves and progress forward in their political careers.

At the same time, the media needed sensational stories to keep their pockets lined with cash. A partnership between the prosecutor and the media became lucrative for both parties involved; everyone profits from the collaboration. Everyone wins except the American Judicial System, and anyone that ends up fighting for their life in a Las Vegas courtroom.

This is still going on in 2014: *The State of Nevada vs. Robert Cox*

Don't think this could happen to you? That's what California youth pastor, Rob Cox, thought this past summer when Robert Daskas unjustifiably prosecuted him. A member of Cox's congregation wrote this on a blog about their experience with Robert Daskas on July 4, 2014 titled: *"Prosecutor Robert Daskas vs. Robert Cox- What is Behind Prosecutor Robert Daskas' Ambitious Prosecution?"*

"It is my assertion that justice and political ambition are a mostly deadly combination when a man possesses the authority of the state; that is, to impose the rule of law upon another. With the combination of this power, there is likely another motive other than justice.

Herein is a prosecutor, Robert Daskas that has yet to explain himself in the prosecution of Robert Cox, a person of faith that was visiting Las Vegas with members of his church, when a large, intoxicated man attacked their group.

SWIFT INJUSTICE

Several people were injured by this man, and Robert Cox, though much smaller in stature defended those with him, including women and children; and he subdued the aggressor. In the scuffle, caught on video surveillance, the intoxicated man fell backwards and hit his head, falling into a coma.

After the event, Cox returned home, able to face not only his wife and children, but his congregation as well. The prosecutor sent Cox a letter saying that no charges would be filed; then six months later, the attacker died from his wounds. Another six months went by, and suddenly, Robert Cox found himself extradited and facing murder charges.

What happened? Robert Daskas filed 'Murder' charges against Cox, not 'Manslaughter' but 'Murder!' Cox had to post a $100,000 bond before the charges were finally heard by a judge, and she threw the charges out and ordered that the bond money be returned to him.

This would have appeared to be the end of this most strange and unusual prosecution; but Robert Daskas apparently didn't care how the judge ruled, and Daskas decided to take the case to the grand jury.

This means: a person with a law degree and enough experience to be appointed judge ruled against Daskas, but that's not what Daskas wanted to hear, so he goes against the judge's ruling, and decides to present the case in front of a group of people without a law degree.

Who is Robert Daskas, and why is he doing this? *I am wondering, along with commentators across the country: Does he have prejudice against Cox due to Cox' religious affiliation? Or, does he have his sights, as so many overly ambitious prosecutors do, on self-promotion and marketing?*

We learn that he appeared to have a political seat all but tied up in 2008 only to have to drop out, late in the almost won 'game' : **From the Las Vegas Sun**: *'In 2008, After months as the Democratic establishment's anointed candidate, Robert Daskas on Monday dropped out of the contest against Rep. Jon Porter, citing 'family considerations.'*

What "family considerations" caused him to bail out of his political ambitions? *Was it an embarrassing sexual scandal that derailed what appeared to be a slam dunk election? We do not know what "family considerations" caused him to drop out but we do know this: It had to do with family; that is, his wife and two children.*

Something within this circle of four human beings was something that would cause him, after raising more than $500,000 for his campaign, as well as the countless hours and leg work, and the backbreaking labors of all his team of supporters, to suddenly, just before victory, to quit.

The 'family considerations' can have lots of speculation but if it is due to sexual immorality, is it possible that Daskas was opposed by people of faith, who, at least in 2008, held that fidelity to family was a simple prerequisite to fidelity to the public.

After all, if a man cannot be trusted by those closest to him, can he really ask strangers to 'trust' him? Was the 'thou shalt not' so offensive and onerous to you that you've projected your anger towards an easy target? I do not know the answers; perhaps only Robert Daskas and his immediate family know the truth.

Perhaps it was not animosity; but a self-serving purpose, one of political gain *to make Daskas go after Robert Cox. How would we know if this was the case? We begin by asking, 'Has Robert Daskas ever used his office to get himself on television?' The answer is here in his own campaign blurb: 'At one point in his prosecutorial career, he 'won 32 of 33 murder trials, including convictions against single, double, triple and quadruple murderers' and was able to get himself on America's Most Wanted, Dateline NBC, 48 Hours, and Court TV.*

This may be the real reason Daskas is pursuing Cox: **Publicity; but is it to come at the expense of justice?** *Has he chosen an out-of-state easy target in an attempt to ingratiate himself to voters? Might this case help rejuvenate Robert Daskas political ambitions? He has had his eye on Congress in the past...is this what is driving him now?*

You, Prosecutor Robert Daskas, have had a solid record of murder convictions and have stated that the murderer forfeits his right to live when he took the life of another. Are you using your office for personal ambition? What is it about this case that you not only erroneously went after, but have refused the bench rebuke of your colleague? Already you've seen by the judge's de facto rebuke: 'You swung and missed!'"

This case received national attention, and Christians from the political left and right aligned in protest and outrage at Robert Daskas' malicious prosecution of an innocent man. At the end of June, the District Attorney, Steve Wolfson announced that the charges had been dropped, and they would not proceed further. Robert Cox was a man that never thought this could happen to him, and had it not been for the huge Christian media blitz against Robert Daskas. Daskas could have used his gift of rhetoric and manipulation to have this innocent man sentenced for a murder he did not commit.

The Amended Criminal Charges

When Robert Daskas added the false kidnapping charges to the criminal complaint, Craig Titus began fighting for his life. Daskas knew this was a false charge and that a kidnapping never took place; yet the prosecutor never dropped the charges, and in fact pursued it to the very end.

According to the autopsy results: (1) there was no soot in Melissa James' lungs, (2) she died from a Morphine/ heroin overdose around 3:00 p.m. on December 13th 2005, and (3) she still had food in her stomach at the time of her death. Melissa James was not killed as a result of being kidnapped. Her death was the result of a drug overdose, and Melissa James had been deceased for more than twelve hours before her body was removed from the house at 3:00 p.m. on December 14th 2005.

Never once was the kidnapping charge mentioned or justified during the arraignment, grand jury, bail, or habeas corpus hearings; there was not even an explanation for the charge at sentencing. In violating the Nevada Rules of Professional Conduct: *The prosecutor in a criminal case shall refrain from prosecuting a charge that the prosecutor knows is not supported by probable cause.* Robert Daskas engaged in prosecutorial misconduct (Prosecutorial misconduct occurs when a prosecutor breaks a law or a code of professional ethics in the course of prosecution).

Amended Criminal Complaint:
The State of Nevada - Plaintiff vs. Craig Michael Titus, Kelly Ann Ryan, Anthony Remo Gross - Defendants

The Defendants above named having committed the crimes of Murder With Use Of Deadly Weapon Accessory to Murder and Third Degree Arson *in the manner following, to-wit: That the Defendants, on or between the 13th day of December and the 14th day of December, 2005, at and within the County of Clark, State of Nevada.*

Count 1 - Murder With Use Of A Deadly Weapon
Defendants Craig Michael Titus, Kelly Ann Ryan, and Anthony R. Gross did then and there, willfully, feloniously, without authority of law, and with malice aforethought, kill Melissa James, a human being, by applying an "Air Taser" gun to the body of Melissa James and/or asphyxiating Melissa James and/or suffocating Melissa James and/or administering morphine and/or a related drug to Melissa James and/or manner; and means unknown, with a deadly weapon, to-wit: an "Air Taser'" gun and/or fabric ligature and/or wire ligature and/or other unknown object, the Defendants being responsible under one of more of the following principles of criminal liability; to wit:(1) by directly committing the acts constituting the offense; and or (2) by said Defendants aiding and abetting each other in its commission, by counseling, encouraging, hiring, commanding, inducing or otherwise procuring each other to commit the acts constituting the offense, as evidenced by the conduct of the Defendants before, during and after the offense, and/or (3) by the Defendants conspiring with each other to commit murder whereby each is vicariously liable for the acts of the other in the conspiracy, and/or (4) by committing the offense during the commission of a felony, to-wit: a kidnapping.

Count 2 - First Degree Kidnapping- Defendants Craig Michael Titus and Kelly Ann Ryan did then and there, willfully, unlawfully, feloniously, and without authority of law, seize, confine, inveigle, entice, decoy, abduct, conceal, kidnap, or carry away Melissa James, a human being, with the intent to hold or detain the said Melissa James against her will, and without her consent, for the purpose of inflicting substantial bodily harm or death; the Defendants being responsible under one or more of the following principles of criminal liability, to wit: (1) by directly committing the acts constituting the offense, and/or (2) by said Defendants aiding and abetting each other in its commission by counseling, encouraging, hiring, commanding, inducing, or otherwise procuring each other to commit the acts constituting the offense, as evidenced by the conduct of the Defendants before, during, and after the offense, and/or (3) by the Defendants conspiring with each other to commit the offense whereby each Defendant is vicariously liable for the acts of the other committed in furtherance of the conspiracy.

Count 3 - Accessory to Murder- Defendants Kelly Ann Ryan and Anthony R. Gross, did then and there willfully, unlawfully and feloniously harbor, conceal, or aid Craig Michael Titus with the intent that the said Craig Michael Titus might avoid or escape from arrest, trial, conviction, or punishment, having knowledge that the said Craig Michael Titus had committed a felony, to-wit: murder, and was liable to arrest therefore.

Count 4 - Third Degree Arson- Defendants did then and there willfully, unlawfully, maliciously, and feloniously set fire to, and thereby cause to be burned, the unoccupied personal property of another, to-wit: a 2003 Jaguar, bearing Nevada License No. 269PPL, the property of Kelly Ann Ryan and/or unknown financial institution, being then and there located at Clark County, Nevada, by use of open flames and/or combustible materials, and/or by manner and means *unknown; Defendants being responsible under one or more of the following principles of criminal liability, to wit: (1) by directly committing the acts constituting the offense, and/or (2) by said Defendants aiding and abetting each other in its commission by counseling, encouraging, hiring, commanding, inducing or otherwise procuring each other to commit the acts constituting the offense; and/or (3) by the Defendants conspiring with each other to commit arson whereby each Defendant is vicariously liable for the acts of the other committed in furtherance of the conspiracy.*

CHAPTER 6

The Arraignment & Bail Hearings

The Arraignment Hearing
On February 1st 2006, at their Arraignment Hearing, neither Titus nor Ryan were asked to enter a plea to the amended complaint. They appeared in court through closed-circuit television. Kelly appeared first, at 8:00 a.m. in the morning. She wore the standard blue jumpsuit, and politely answered Judge Joe Bonaventure when he asked her if she had received a copy of the amended complaint? "Yes Sir, Your Honor," Ryan said. Soon after, it was Craig Titus' turn. With his arms stretching out of his blue jail uniform, he appeared confidant and undeterred. When asked if he understood the charges, Titus said, "Absolutely!"

At this hearing, Daskas declined to describe a motive for the slaying. The complaint however, accused the two of using a taser stun gun, administering morphine or a related drug, and asphyxiating or suffocating James with a fabric or wire around the neck. Judge Bonaventure scheduled a formal bail hearing for Feb. 10th, and a preliminary hearing for March 29th.

Charges against Anthony Gross were the same, and he remained under house arrest after posting a $13,000 bond. His lawyer, Louis Palazzo, said that Gross remained in Las Vegas and did not try to flee. He cooperated with police when he was interviewed after James' body was found. "I'm certainly not going to let him be a scapegoat in connection with this case, and we'll meet these charges head-on," Palazzo said.

Kelly Ryan's lawyer, Tom Pitaro declined comment as he walked out of the court room. Craig Titus's attorneys met outside of the courtroom. Steven Boozang said, "On behalf of our client, he is 100 percent not guilty!" Richard Schonfeld spoke with Eyewitness News and said, "Our client is innocent and when all the facts and circumstances come to light, I think the public is going to have an entirely different perception of this case."

The Bail Hearing

At 1:00 p.m. on February 10th 2006, Craig Titus and Kelly Ryan appeared in a Clark County Judicial Court in front of Judge Joe Bonaventure with high hopes of posting bail; albeit an outrageously high bail because of the "flight risk" allegations. Nonetheless, Craig was confident and Kelly was hopeful, that at the conclusion of their hearing, they would be walking out of the courtroom doors, sleeping in their own bed, and focusing on their defense together.

With the exception of a Capital Murder/First Degree Felony Murder charge, almost every defendant is granted bail in a court of law. Going into this hearing, Craig assumed that it would be a fair battle between the prosecution and the defense. In reality, there would never be anything fair about this trial at all, as the prosecution used the media to take Craig Titus out below the knees before the fight ever started.

In an article written by Josh Longobardy for Las Vegas Weekly, he described that day in court as he "watched the bail hearing play out in real life". In his article entitled, "What Happened to Melissa James," Lombardy described Kelly Ryan and the moment she walked in escorted by the bailiffs... "Handcuffed and chained wearing a blue Clark County Detention Center jumpsuit. It was as if her reality has been flipped inside out- and not just because she was then charged with murder, kidnapping and third-degree arson, but because she had once been the epitome of a role model, popular for her stellar physique, her girl scout's charm and her sweet and innocuous nature. Also because today, February 10, 2006, after several cosmetic surgeries, countless libertine nights submerged in drugs, and two months in jail, she looked like an apparition of herself. This is how the media in the gallery exposed her, their collective stares and pitiless camera lights striking down on Kelly as she entered the Las Vegas Justice Court."

The article described Titus: "He had been ushered from his cell to the defendant's table minutes earlier, and was sitting there, all 215 muscular pounds of him, quiet and ineffable until he saw Kelly, the woman he had married in 2000 after a long and resilient courtship, the wife he would go on describing to friends as 'my best friend and my heart, the best thing that's ever happened to me.' Then he started to cry. Tears fell, and he sobbed. Kelly responded with an impulse of unadulterated affection: With her eyes opened wide, and her head tilted like that of a faithful hound, Kelly's full and salient lips began to quiver, and if she couldn't speak it was only because those omnipresent stares and oppressive lights from the media wouldn't permit her a word commensurate with the moment. The room was running over with them: journalists, local and national, and from every denomination, too. Newspapers, celebrity magazines, bodybuilding websites, prime-time newscasts—they were all there, come to see the unfolding story of two superstars in the world of muscle and fitness charged with the murder of Melissa James, a young woman who had lived, and worked and even played with the celebrity couple within the stucco walls of their home in southwest Las Vegas."

Longobardy then described the case, and the atmosphere of the court: "It has become a true-life crime story, one with a dramatic narrative written in case files and legal motions, orated by lawyers before overflowing courtrooms, and translated by journalists. It's become a hot topic not only of gym gossip and Internet message boards, but also for the world's untamable bloggers. It is a tragic yet enthralling story in which one life has ended and two others, no matter what happened next, are doomed."

And with the sensationalized opening lines of this article, the media was off to the races- trying to be the first with the scoop, topping each other with "sordid" details about the defendant's lives. Defendants were obviously "guilty before proven innocent." These not-so-objective reporters and writers were fed information by the investigators and prosecution, and the nation would take these articles in print as the facts of the case. Kelly was to be portrayed as the perfect, "Ozzy and Harriet, girl next door," torn down after years of abuse by her deviant, thug of a husband, the "Bad Boy of Bodybuilding" Craig Titus.

The media had been circling around Craig Titus and Kelly Ryan since the day the Las Vegas Metropolitan Police Department issued a warrant for their arrest, subsequently discovering the "Sexy Bodybuilding killers" had "fled" for Boston, Massachusetts attempting to "flee the United States to a non-extradition country like Greece." Craig Titus after all, according to Body Building message boards, is of "Greek decent," so this would only make sense.

With that kind of buzz, when the media was allowed into the courtroom at this bail hearing, the room was crammed full of reporters and journalists from all across the nation, ready to report on "Craig Titus and Kelly Ryan's first court appearance" (Actually it was the second, if we count the arraignment, but that's less dramatic) in Las Vegas since they had been extradited back from Massachusetts. "True Crime" stories were the pop culture genre of choice in the new millennium, and everyone was there to be the first to report on the celebrity bodybuilding couple.

Daskas' theatrical opening statement at the bail hearing

The Bail Hearing commenced for Craig Titus and Kelly Ryan in the courtroom of Justice of the Peace Joe M. Bonaventure. In his opening statement (Not sure if this is a statement or a soliloquy- a dramatic speech expressing inner thoughts to himself and to the audience- either way, it was dramatically theatrical for an arraignment hearing!), Chief Deputy District Attorney, Robert Daskas said, "The state asks this honorable court to hold defendants Craig Titus and Kelly Ryan without bail. Bail, at any price, is just not applicable to the defendants in this case, for not only are they charged with murder, but they are also high risks for flight, and one of them, Craig Titus, is of very dubious character. We have witnesses, statements, evidence that show on the date of December 13, 2005..." And then Craig Titus' defense attorney, Richard Schonfeld objected, "Your honor, the state is proffering, and I know this honorable court is well aware that a bail hearing is not meant to determine guilt." Then **Daskas replied, "Your honor, first-degree murder is the only charge for which a person can be held without bail, 'if the proof is evident or the presumption great.'** And that's what we intend to prove here today, that 'the proof is evident, the presumption great." Titus' attorney from Massachusetts, Steven Boozang said, "Plus, your honor, we filed a motion yesterday at 9:30 a.m. to suppress illegally obtained recorded statements from my client on December 24, 2005, in Massachusetts, and because those statements were recorded surreptitiously they should not be admitted to the court today." Judge Bonaventure said that he never received a copy of the Motion to suppress the 102 page interrogation by the Las Vegas homicide detectives, and so the motion was denied.

The judge instructed Robert Daskas to continue, but that disruption threw Daskas for a loop, and he looked like a painfully self-conscious 13- year old boy giving a speech in front of a bunch of girls in Sex Ed. He appeared to have forgotten everything he learned at his weekly Toastmaster workshops, and stood frozen for a few seconds, shuffling back through his papers, awkwardly starting his soliloquy from the beginning.

(Warning- Before reading the prosecution's opening, two page paragraph statement, it is recommended that the reader first take a bathroom break and a 5 hour energy shot- just sayin'!)

"There is overwhelming evidence that defendants Craig Titus and Kelly Ryan murdered Melissa James and they are of dubious character. Let's start with the evidence. On December 14, 2005, a dead body was discovered in the trunk of Mrs. Titus' red 2003 Jaguar. Six hours after the car had been lit on fire, Detectives Mogg, Hardy and Wilson traced the burnt Jaguar's license plates back to the home of the car's registered owner, a Mrs. Kelly A. Titus, and they knock on her door completely unfamiliar with her celebrity and the sport which has engendered it. When the detectives ask Kelly and her husband, Craig Titus, if they know the whereabouts of Kelly's 2003 Jaguar, the couple says, 'no, they had discovered it stolen from their garage at 5 o'clock that morning, and have reason to believe it was their roommate, Melissa James, who took it.'

THE ARRAIGNMENT & BAIL HEARINGS

After short preambles letting the couple know their respective interviews are being recorded, the detectives begin taking down Craig and Kelly's official statements. Detective Wilson asks Kelly why they didn't call the police, and Kelly replied, 'Craig thought it was a private matter, so he just called our friend Tony Gross, and asked him to help search for Melissa and the car. They went looking for about an hour, but didn't find anything, so Craig decided to wait here for Melissa to come back.'

Detective Wilson asks who Anthony Gross is, and Kelly says, 'he's just a friend. He's just a really good friend.' Detective Wilson then asked, 'So who is Melissa James?' Kelly said that she's a friend we hired to manage our personal affairs. She said that they invited her to live in their house free of rent because she was going through hard times. Furthermore, Kelly and Craig both say that Melissa has been stealing from them, taking money out of their bank accounts and charging items to their credit cards without permission.

Craig told Detective Mogg that Kelly confronted Melissa about the embezzling, and the tension between the two women rose to such combustible levels that he had to book Melissa a room for the past two nights at the La Quinta on Sahara and Fort Apache, whose records would confirm that Room 232 had indeed been reserved for Monday and Tuesday nights under the name of Craig Titus. Moreover, Craig Titus stayed with Melissa in her room for most of the first night. But on Tuesday afternoon when Melissa came back, Kelly Ryan told her, "you're no longer welcome in my house.' Craig had booked a flight for her to New Jersey, where her mother lives, to depart that night. So, Kelly says that she packed her things in a suitcase, and at about, um, 2:30 I think it was, she dropped her off at the convenience store around the corner, where she was supposed to get a ride to the airport. Detective Wilson asks, 'Do you remember what she was wearing?' Kelly Ryan said, 'yes, she had on a blue, long-sleeve top with a hoodie and denim jeans.' Now, of course, the defendants were being disingenuous because they offered contradictory statements in Massachusetts."

(Not trying to be "disingenuous", but Daskas' statement is not only full of lies, but it is "dubiously" long-ish!)

Daskas nervously rocked back and forth as he said, "Craig Titus and Kelly Ryan had a motive to kill Melissa James- they believed Melissa was stealing from them. And there is overwhelming evidence that defendants Titus and Ryan murdered James. On December 15, the day after the 2003 Jaguar was found burning in the desert, the Clark County Coroner performed an autopsy on Jane 'Sandy Valley' Doe, and through the use of dental records he would determine the victim to be Melissa James, a 28-year-old woman who once stood five-foot-three and 120 pounds, with blue eyes and white skin, before fire had charred her identity. Furthermore, upon unwrapping the blanket that covered her head, the coroner reveals that Melissa's face has been mummified with gray duct tape, sealing off four of her five senses, and that two ligatures, a piece of white fabric and an insulated wire, have been knotted around Melissa's neck, leading him to suspect she died from asphyxiation. But the findings also conclude that Melissa James had a toxic level of morphine in her system.

Also, the detectives dug up cell-phone records that indicate there were 14 calls between the phones of Kelly Ryan and Craig Titus on Tuesday, December 13, all occurring between 12:18 and 1:41 in the afternoon. Or, in other words, less than an hour before an Air Taser Gun had been shot six times in Melissa's room and in the living room, as detectives would learn a month later. And there were 13 calls between the phones of Anthony Gross and Craig Titus, with the first occurring at 3:28 pm on Tuesday afternoon, and the last at 4:28 Wednesday morning, just 13 minutes before Dick Draper received a dispatch to a burning vehicle on Sandy Valley Road. The morphine in her system supports the prosecution's belief that they drugged James, used a Taser gun on her, killed her, and then torched the body in the trunk of the car. There were levels of morphine in her system consistent with the way we've charged the case. In addition, we will be able to prove that the motive for murder, according to the defendant's first statements, was embezzlement.

The defendants believed that Melissa James was embezzling money, and they ended her life because of that. Craig Titus and Kelly Ryan should, furthermore, be denied bond because they are a flight risk and had intentions of fleeing to a country with a non-extradition

THE ARRAIGNMENT & BAIL HEARINGS

policy- either Greece or Mexico. They tried to sell their houses, and that they did not sleep in their own house again after the detectives questioned them on the morning of Dec. 14th. They stopped using their cell phones, and instead purchased pre-paid phones so that their number would not be traced. They traded in their truck, roared some 3,000 miles across the country with some $8,000 stashed away, refusing to sleep in motels due to the fear of recognition, and thus any notion that they were just vacationing together is altogether laughable! No, they were trying to escape the country because they knew they were going to be held in connection with the murder of Melissa James. And I ask that your honor takes a close at defendant Titus because his character is of question in this matter. Craig Titus- the man who failed to answer Maura James' frantic phone calls after her daughter did not arrive on the flight for which she had been scheduled, the man who finally called Melissa's mother back the Saturday after the incident and told her it wasn't Melissa's body that had been in the trunk, and the man who went on to tell Maura that her daughter faked her own death to assume a new identity- is dubious, and not worthy of bail."

Unlike most theatrical productions, Robert Daskas rambled on for over an hour, with no intermission- all for a bail hearing! Prosecutor 101- who does that? This just goes to show how desperate the prosecutor was to keep Craig Titus and Kelly Ryan behind bars. Daskas' lack of confidence in himself and the case he had built became crystal clear at the bail hearing.

Following Daskas, Kelly Ryan's attorney, Tom Pitaro began his opening statement. Pitaro did take Prosecution 101 in law school, so he gave Robert Daskas and the rest of the courtroom a thirty minute lesson on the fundamental principles of bail. Invoking the constitution, the country's forefathers, and a hundred precedent cases, Pitaro demanded that the judge grant Craig Titus and Kelly Ryan bail at a reasonable price- right then and there!

The fact that Robert Daskas was just capriciously throwing around theories, and not able to come up with a cause of death, should be reason enough for the judge to grant their bond, but should also throw the case out altogether. "Nobody knows anything for sure; so the prosecution is just trying to throw everything out there. They really don't even know how Melissa James died, not to mention, who is responsible. They've got more theories than you can shake a stick at. For all the sound and fury, the prosecution has nothing," Thomas Pitaro said.

Richard Schonfeld stepped in and tried to assure the judge that Craig and Kelly had no intentions of fleeing, stating that the hard evidence reflected it: "Craig Titus and Kelly Ryan stopped in Stoughton, Massachusetts to get an oil change, which would have been futile if they indeed planned on going to Mexico.

For why would they travel 3,000 miles east when they could have just headed a short way south to Tijuana? At any rate, at the oil lube station both Craig Titus and Kelly Ryan were described by witnesses as 'relaxed, talkative, and friendly,' and the manager even reported that Craig and he exchanged phone numbers, with Craig Titus saying, 'whenever you come to Vegas, call me up.' Also at that same oil lube station, a marked Massachusetts State trooper was getting work done on his vehicle, but neither Craig Titus nor Kelly Ryan appeared worried.

And furthermore, Kelly Ryan's passport was found in their Las Vegas home; this is not a sign of a person anxious to leave American soil. Even more interesting, both Kelly Ryan and Craig Titus both had a significant amount of money in each of their bank accounts. In fact, Craig Titus had written a check to his attorney in Las Vegas for $5,000 the day before they left for Boston, Massachusetts, and then turned around and paid another lawyer when he returned to Las Vegas. These were not signs of people running away from their home, ready to start all over in a new country."

After listening to both the prosecution and the defense present their reasons for and against bail, Judge Joe M. Bonaventure said that he needed time to think it over, and announced that the court would be in recess for twenty minutes. The defense attorneys, Tom Pitaro, Richard Schonfeld, and Steven Boozang conferred with Craig and then with Kelly, but mostly amongst themselves. Reporters and cameramen read over their notes, and gossiped amongst themselves.

THE ARRAIGNMENT & BAIL HEARINGS

Then the bailiff addressed the courtroom, and after his preamble, Judge Joe M. Bonaventure returned to his chair, and said to the court, "I've taken everything with which I was presented into deep consideration, and I believe I must uphold their current status. Defendants Craig Titus and Kelly Ryan will continue to remain in custody of the Clark County Detention Center without bail." After discussing some logistical matters, Richard Schonfeld told the judge, "For some reason, unknown to me or my client, Mr. Titus is being held in isolation at the CCDC, and that makes it difficult, if not impossible, for me to consult with my client about his defense." Schonfeld then asked the judge to talk with the prison to see if they could, "discontinue Craig's trips to the hole."

Craig Titus was isolated from everyone including his attorneys, and placed in Segregation as well. Planning a defense, with two defendants, on two different sides of a caged building, and three lawyers trying to zigzag their way through the jail's over-the-top rules and procedures was very difficult to say the least. The lawyers had to jump through hoops to even talk to their clients, and this created a world of chaos for those trying to represent Craig and Kelly in a court of law. In the end, on top of everything that was done to sabotage Craig Titus' defense, Robert Daskas "sank the ship" with his move to have the Criminal Charges Amended, making their "crime" a capital offense.

Daskas' big gamble paid off: Craig Titus and Kelly Ryan would have to remain behind bars. With everything on the line, the prosecutor had to hatch a plan, and then plot out every move with precision. He had to plan the details fast and furious, because he needed to secretly call a grand jury together if he wanted to have any chance of using Megan Pierson Foley's statement against Craig and Kelly. During the grand jury testimony, the defense would not be present, and thus would not be able to counter the presentation by the prosecution.

Grand Jury hearings are not adversary trials, meaning the defense does not present evidence, examine witnesses, or conduct cross-examinations. The defense does not yet know that the prosecution has called for a grand jury hearing. Additionally, jurors do not even get to see all of the evidence obtained by the prosecutor.

◄ SWIFT INJUSTICE

If the prosecutor has exculpatory evidence showing the accused did not commit the crime, the prosecutor generally does not tell the grand jury about such evidence. The grand jury does not get to see all of the evidence obtained by the prosecutor. Instead, the prosecutor selects what evidence he believes, as an officer of the courts, is enough to justify asking for (and almost always getting) an indictment, as jurors simply rubberstamp the prosecution's charges.

CHAPTER 7

The Grand Jury Testimony

Below are excerpts from the grand jury testimonies of relevant witnesses to Craig Titus' case.

> EIGHTH JUDICIAL DISTRICT COURT
> CLARK COUNTY, NEVADA
> BEFORE THE GRAND JURY IMPANELED BY THE AFORESAID
>
> THE STATE OF NEVADA,   Case No. 05BGJ079ABC   C220719
> Plaintiff, vs.
> CRAIG MICHAEL TITUS,
> KELLY ANN RYAN,
> ANTHONY R. GROSS, Defendants.
> Taken at Las Vegas, Nevada
> Thursday, March 2, 2006 8:40 a.m.
> REPORTER'S TRANSCRIPT OF PROCEEDINGS

Robert Daskas: Good morning everyone my name is Robert Daskas; my partner is Becky Goettsch. This morning we will begin the presentation of the State of Nevada –vs. - Craig Michael Titus, Kelly Ann Ryan, and Anthony Remo Gross. The defendants in this case are charged with Murder with use of a deadly weapon, 1st Degree Kidnapping, Accessory to Murder, and Third Degree Arson. I have a number of instructions that pertain to the elements of offenses with which the defendants are charged:

***Murder** is the unlawful killing of a human being with malice aforethought. Malice aforethought means the intentional doing of a wrongful act; it is not an accident.

***Murder of the First Degree** must have all three elements: Willfulness- an intent to kill, Deliberation- determining upon a course of action to kill as a result of thought, & Premeditation- an unconsidered rash impulse cannot be considered first degree murder.

*There is a class of murder, which is committed in the perpetration of such kidnapping is deemed to be 1st Degree murder, even if the killing was intentional or caused by accident, this is called the Felony Murder Rule. **In order to apply the Felony Murder Rule, the intent to perpetrate kidnapping must be proven beyond a reasonable doubt.** * **Voluntary Manslaughter** is the unlawful killing of a human being without the malice, and without deliberation. It occurs upon a sudden heat of passion, caused by provocation.

* Every person concerned in the commission of a felony, whether he or she directly commits the act, or **Aids or Abets** in its commission, and whether present or absent; every person who directly or indirectly counsels, encourages, hires, commands, or otherwise procures another to commit a felony, with the intent that the crime will be accomplished is a principal and shall be proceeded against and punished as such.

* **Conspiracy** is an agreement or mutual understanding between two or more persons to commit a crime.

* **When associated with the charge of murder, kidnapping does not occur** if the movement is incidental to the murder and does not increase the risk of harm over and above the necessarily present in the commission of such an offense.

* **The crime of kidnapping in the first degree**, as charged in this case is a specific intent crime. This means- more than the general intent to commit the crime. To establish specific intent the State must prove that the defendant knowingly did the act which the law forbids, purposely intending to break the law.

* Any person that willfully sets fire to any unoccupied personal property which has the value of $25 or more is guilty of **Arson in the 3rd Degree.**

THE GRAND JURY TESTIMONY

The questions are asked by the Deputy District Attorneys: Robert Daskas and Becky Goettsch.

Witnesses called to testify at the grand jury hearings:

1. MAURA JAMES- Mother of Melissa James

2. DICK DRAPER- Fire Chief that put out the Jaguar

3. JESSIE SAMS- Senior Crime Scene Analyst with LVMPD

Question: What did you find in the trunk of the vehicle?
Answer: There was a body in the trunk with a lot of charred debris. There were pieces of fabric that looked like blankets.

Question: Can you describe the position of the body that you found in the trunk?
Answer: Body was folded up. The head was to the right side of the vehicle or the passenger side and knees bent, and the feet were to the left side of the vehicle or driver's side. Her head was covered so you couldn't see the face.

Question: Was there any fabric in the trunk that stuck out as unusual?
Answer: There were three different ones that I remember. There were two fleece fabrics- one with purple, blue and some black in it, and another with orange and black tiger print. The third was a thick, white cotton fabric with a raised square pattern. The cotton blanket didn't burn all the way.

Question: You said the body was partially covered, can you describe that?
Answer: You couldn't see the face or head at all, it was covered with something.

Question: Was there anything else lying on the body that was unusual?
Answer: It looked like there was a wire that was like in the neck area.

Question: Could you determine what the face was covered with?
Answer: It appears to be a different type weave fabric.

Question: Could you tell whether it was secured to her head?

Answer: It appeared to be because it wasn't loose.

Question: Once you removed the body, what happened next?
Answer: The body was placed in a sealed body bag and removed by the mortuary to the coroner's office.

4. ROBERT WILSON- Homicide Detective LVMPD

Question: What was the first step in the homicide that occurred out at Sandy Valley Road on or about December 14th in Las Vegas, Clark County?
Answer: We received a call around seven in the morning; we were advised that there was a burnt vehicle and what was believed to be a human body in the trunk.

Question: How were you able to determine the owner of the car?
Answer: The first fireman on the scene documented the plate numbers before it was totally consumed by fire. Based on the plate information, the owner of the car was determined to be Kelly Ann Ryan.

Question: Did you make contact with Ms. Ryan?
Answer: Yes we went to her house and told her about the car, and she indicated that she knew that it was missing and invited us in to talk.

Question: Did you take a statement from Ms. Ryan?
Answer: Yes. We tape recorded a statement.

Question: What did Mr. Titus and the other detectives do during this time?
Answer: They gave us permission to search Melissa James room so Detective Hardy was involved in that while Detective Mogg interviewed Mr. Titus. Mogg and Titus were in the living room, and we were in the kitchen.

Question: Was Ms. Ryan a suspect at this time?
Answer: No, and after the interview she was free to leave.

Question: What did Kelly Ryan tell you about her car missing?
Answer: She said they had some friends over until two in the morning, and she stayed up a little bit longer and did a load of laundry. When she walked by the garage she noticed the posing lights were

on, so she went in the garage to turn them off and noticed the car was missing around four or five in the morning.

Question: Did she call the police? Did they have problems prior to this day?
Answer: No, they didn't call the police; but, yes they did have problems with Melissa prior to this. Prior to her car missing, she noticed things happening to their bank accounts and credit cards- charges on the ATM and things like that they had not authorized or even aware of.

Question: Did she talk to Melissa about it?
Answer: Yes, Kelly said she believed that Melissa was involved in some sort of fraud where Melissa was embezzling their money. Kelly said she confronted Melissa about it and they got into an argument so Craig got Melissa a hotel room at La Quinta. Kelly talked about a letter she gave Melissa that detailed all of the problems they had with her, and there was a second confrontation after Melissa returned from the hotel. Kelly told Melissa that she had to leave, and went to Melissa's room to help her pack. Kelly said that she was drove Melissa to the airport around 3:30 p.m. on December 13th and Melissa wanted to be dropped off at the Green Valley Grocery Store located at Ft. Apache and Hacienda. Kelly said this was the last time she saw Melissa.

Question: Did Kelly Ryan tell you how many friends came over that evening?
Answer: Yes, she said her friend Megan came over with her boyfriend, and they left around two the next morning.

Question: Did Ms. Kelly point anything else out about Melissa James?
Answer: They met in Florida, and she has lived with them off and on in California and in Florida. She moved in with them recently in October. She talked about Melissa's drug problem, and pointed out her drug paraphernalia and drugs they had thrown in the trash.

Question: Did Ms. Kelly mention Anthony Gross?
Answer: She said that when they discovered the car was missing, Craig and Tony went driving around to find her. She gave me his cell

phone number and her other friend's cell phone numbers that were over that night.

5. Clifford Mogg- Homicide Detective LVMPD

Question: Turn your attention to December 14th, and who did you interview?
Answer: I interviewed Craig Titus in the living room of his residence. The taped conversation began at 12:05 p.m. I explained to him that a body was found in the trunk of their Jaguar, and the car was set on fire. Craig Titus said that both his wife, Kelly Ryan and their friend, Melissa James had permission to drive the car.

Question: Did he explain who Melissa James was?
Answer: Yes, he said that she was their friend and she had been living in a downstairs bedroom located on the east side of the residence by the garage since October 2005.

Question: Did Titus mention any problems that either he or his wife had with her?
Answer: He told me that they had been concerned because of her drug use inside the house. He also said that they believed she had been using their identities to obtain money, take money from their checking accounts, things like that.

Question: Did he mention renting a hotel room for Melissa James?
Answer: He said that he rented her a room at La Quinta on Sahara; he paid for the room with his business credit card. Mr. Titus said he was with her when she checked in, and he was there with her off and on until one or two the next morning. He said that he went home and then returned to pick her up some time before ten am. Titus said he bought Melissa a plane ticket to go home for Christmas, and she was to leave later that evening.

Question: Did Mr. Titus explain to you what happened after he picked up Melissa James from the La Quinta and returned home on the morning of December 13th?
Answer: Mr. Titus said that his wife and Melissa had talked out their issues then Melissa packed her bag for her trip and then his wife dropped Melissa at Green Valley Grocery around 3:30 p.m. Green

THE GRAND JURY TESTIMONY

Valley is approximately a quarter mile from Craig and Kelly's house. After about a half hour, Titus said that Kelly returned home and they began to ransack Melissa's room and found information from Green Point Mortgage for their home, personal information about Craig, Kelly and her mother, and methamphetamines and needles.

Question: When you saw the bedroom, was it ransacked? Describe what you saw.
Answer: The bed was in disarray, things were piled up all over the floor, strewn all over the floor and the top of the bed. There was a small nightstand in the corner of the room and on top of that there was like a little metal strong box that had been forced open. There were some papers inside it. I saw numerous syringes and bloody tissue in the room. I also saw at least ten or fifteen bottles of some type of medication.

Question: Did Titus ever tell you about going out to look for Melissa James?
Answer: Yes he did, he drove to the Palace Station around midnight with Anthony Gross looking for a black Jeep Cherokee which was driven by an associate of Melissa's named Eddie. He said he never stopped anywhere, but drove around looking for Eddie. Titus said he wanted to make sure that she made her flight. Titus said he returned about thirty minutes later. At this time Craig said that the Jaguar was still in the garage.

Question: Did Craig Titus ever offer an explanation as to the missing Jaguar?
Answer: He said that at some point Melissa must have come home and taken the Jaguar without them knowing. After he discovered the car was missing, he said that he called her and sent her text messages. Titus showed me a text message he sent at 4:28 am asking "Where the fuck is my car?"

Question: Were all of the syringes and drugs sent off to the crime lab?
Answer: I think some were collected, but that wasn't my job, another detective was assigned to process that room with the crime scene analysts.

6. Robin Peterson- Asset Protection with Wal-Mart

Question: Please describe the surveillance system at Wal-Mart on 5200 South Fort Apache Road, and the images it caught at 3:30 a.m. December 14th.
Answer: There are sixteen cameras with 24 Hours Video Surveillance. They record the time, but are a few minutes off the register times; there's a five minute margin of error. The register times are more accurate than the camera times. There are two cameras on the outside of Wal-Mart that shoot nine still shots a piece of the parking lot. They keep an electronic journal, and Kelly Ryan's transaction at 3:30a.m. on December 14th was registered in her name, with her Wells Fargo Debit Card #4368 8400 2009 2014 with the store number 5070 reflected on the receipt.

7. Marnie Carter- Crime Scene Analyst for the LVMPD

Question: Were you dispatched to aid in the investigation of a possible homicide on Sandy Valley Road on December 14th 2005, and a follow-up investigation?
Answer: Yes, and I arrived at the scene to assist Jessie Sams collect evidence, and then I assisted the Coroner in the autopsy the next day on December 15th.

Question: What are your job duties as a crime scene analyst at an autopsy?
Answer: We take lots of photos, and collect any evidence pertaining to the body, whether it be clothing or anything that is actually in the body bag like money.

Question: Was there a forensic pathologist or medical examiner at the autopsy?
Answer: Yes, Dr. Kubiczek.

Question: When you first got to the autopsy what was the condition of the body?
Answer: The body arrived in a sealed body bag the day before, and when we started the autopsy, we broke the seal and wrote down the time then I took photographs of the body. We slowly removed each layer from the body, there were multiple layers of fabric; and I took

a photograph after each layer was removed. The body was severely burned.

Question: Explain each layer that was removed from the body?
Answer: The first layer had multiple layers of fabric that disintegrated as we touched them. We piled these pieces up on a sterile sheet as we went along.

Question: Okay, let's talk about the body's head area. What did you find there?
Answer: It was just completely covered in cloth of some sort, burned cloth that covered her head and torso. It didn't seem to be wrapped around her, but placed on top of her. There were coated wire substances lying across her on top of the material. They were at the scene as well on the body and all in the trunk; it appeared as if they came off of the burning car.

Question: And once you removed the top layer, were you able to determine whether or not the wire was just lying on top of the body or whether it was interspersed with the rest of her hair or other items on her?
Answer: Those initial wires that we looked at were just lying on top, they weren't intertwined with anything.

Question: When the outer cloth layer was removed, what did you find?
Answer: There was duct tape around another layer of meshed fabric. We found this all over the cloth, but it was also stuck to her hair and denim on her jeans.

Question: Was there anything significant underneath the duct tape?
Answer: There were what appeared to be bodily fluids all inside and also in her nose and mouth. I impounded this entire clump of duct tape and what was on it.

8. Megan Pierson- testimony documented in Introduction

9. Dean O'Kelley- Lead Homicide Detective on Titus case for LVMPD

Question: You were assigned the investigation of an apparent homicide involving a body found in the trunk of a car. As part of the investigation did you eventually contact a witness by the name of Megan Pierson?
Answer: Yes I did, it was on December 22nd 2005. I had been contacted by her attorney, Robert Langford, the previous day, and then I spoke with her with her at the attorney's office on 8th Street. We questioned her with the attorney present.

Question: Was this interview recorded?
Answer: No it was not.

Question: Did you meet with her again after this conversation?
Answer: Yes I did, a week later, and she provided me with a Nike, nylon bag that had several items inside it. She gave it to me at the conclusion of the interview.

Question: Was this interview recorded?
Answer: No it was not.

Question: What did you do with the gym bag?
Answer: It was taken back to the homicide office and the contents were examined with gloves, and on the inside we found a black, molded plastic case containing a civilian model, M-18 Taser conducted energy weapon, two cartridges that were shrink wrapped and appeared to have come with the weapon. There was an eight inch leather SAP, it's a weighted blunt force trauma type instrument.

Question: I want to ask you specifically about the taser gun, and the cartridges. How many cartridges were there? Are the cartridges associated with the taser?
Answer: Four total; two inside the box and two in a separate package. Yes, the cartridges were for the taser gun, they are inserted into the end of the weapon where you would see a barrel on a normal handgun. When the trigger is pulled with the cartridge in place there are probes inside with wires attached to them that deploy at the front of the cartridge. The little yellow blasters break away and those air fired cartridges make contact with the target and deliver an electric charge.

THE GRAND JURY TESTIMONY

Question: What was done with the taser that was provided to you by Ms. Pierson?
Answer: The taser gun was sent to Taser International in Phoenix, Arizona, by our sergeant, Rocky Alba.

10. Andrew Hinz- Law Enforcement Technical Coordinator for Taser Intl.

Question: What are your duties and responsibilities?
Answer: I analyze Taser units that are involved in investigations, analyze the data of download and how the taser unit functions.

Question: What type of information can you extract from a taser gun?
Answer: Taser units will record the time that the trigger is pulled.

Question: What can you tell us about this particular model, the M-18 civilian unit?
Answer: It shoots at a lower level, and the cartridge contains 15 feet of wire with two probes that are fired with compressed nitrogen. When the trigger is pulled the electricity will discharge a primer which pushes the nitrogen capsule down onto a tube that actually fires the probes up to fifteen feet. When the probes hit the intended target, the electricity will start to flow down the wires and it will deliver a neuromuscular interference at 50,000 volts. When a target is hit, it sends an electrical signal to the muscles, and where the two probe placements are, that muscle group creates white noise inside that muscle and it freezes the muscle so you are immobilized.

Question: When the M-18 unit is discharged, are remnants left behind?
Answer: Yes, every taser cartridge has AFID (Anti-Felon Identification) tags; there are approximately 30-40 yellow, pink and clear tags, and each one has a serial number of that particular cartridge. So when the taser is discharged it will disburse confetti like paper with a serial numbers to trace where the cartridge was purchased, and who it was sold to.

Question: Based on your analysis in this case what were your findings?
Answer: I found that on December 13th 2005 at 2:10 p.m., the unit was discharged six times (each shot lasts 5-6 seconds) with the last

shot being fired at 2:13 p.m. So within a 2 minute time frame the gun was discharged six times simultaneously.

Question: Can you hit somebody in the back of the neck?
Answer: The further away that a person is, the harder it would be. For every foot you're away there will be a seven-inch spread on the probes, so you would have to be very close to shoot someone in the neck.

Question: Can you adjust the voltage on a taser gun?
Answer: No you cannot. These tasers take 2 double a batteries, so I suppose the voltage could be less if the batteries are older, but you can't manually adjust it.

Question: Once you are shot with a taser, does your body go back to normal?
Answer: I have been tased myself four times in a row, and when the effect is over, it's over.

11. David Lemaster- Senior Crime Scene Analyst LVMPD

Question: What is a Crime Scene Analyst's job for the Las Vegas Metropolitan Police Department?
Answer: We respond to crime scenes and assist officers and investigators with those scenes in identifying, preserving, documenting, and processing evidence.

Question: What is a Senior Crime Scene Analyst?
Answer: It is the highest level of the three, basically saying you have more experience and passed more testing, so are assigned to the more difficult cases.

Question: Why were you called out to 9539 Adobe Arch Court in Las Vegas on December 5th, 2005 around 2:00 p.m. that afternoon?
Answer: Yes, to assist with a homicide investigation on a search warrant.

Question: And who all was there?
Answer: I went with another crime scene analyst, Jessie Sams, and Detectives O'Kelley, Wilson, Hardy and Mogg were already there.

THE GRAND JURY TESTIMONY

Question: Were you called back out on another warrant to the same residence on January 5th 2006, and what were you searching for?
Answer: Yes, and on this particular day we went back to look for some potential Taser evidence, and any other potential evidence we could find like blood.

Question: Did you find taser evidence? If so, what?
Answer: Yes, I impounded 26 small dots from Melissa's room and the living room. There were two different serial numbers on the dots, indicating it had been fired two different times on different dates. Also in the vacuum canister stored in the laundry room was a vacuum cleaner with some of the tags in the canister.

Question: What else did you find in the search?
Answer: We were looking for a woman's red matching sweat jacket and sweat pants with a white stripe, and we found that clothing. The same clothing that Kelly Ryan appeared to be wearing when she purchased lighter fluid from Wal-Mart.

12. Cherry Neff- The asst. manager at Short line Express #2 Shell gas station.

Question: Where is that located?
Answer: 9155 South Rainbow Boulevard off Rainbow and Blue Diamond Road.

Question: And as part of your duties as the assistant manager, are you familiar with the surveillance capabilities at the Shell gas station?
Answer: Right. At this time we have a surveillance system that has 26 cameras, four of them are outside and twenty-two are inside, and it is recorded on a DVD.

Question: Were you able to go back in your archives and find footage of the early morning hours of December 14th?
Answer: Yes I did, and I found the footage they were looking for; the surveillance is about two minutes fast for all of the cameras. The footage shows a date and time.

13. Jason Kiess- The I.T. manager with Green Valley Grocery. He oversees all of the computer systems for all 28 locations for the corporate office.

Question: I'd like to ask you specifically about the Green Valley Grocery located at 5325 South Fort Apache. Does this location have surveillance? And were you able to provide surveillance footage to the LVMD from Dec. 13th-14th?
Answer: Yes, and I provided a copy of surveillance of that time on CD format to the LVMPD of over 12 hours of footage.

14. David Levinson- Sales Associate at Integrity Chrysler Jeep Dodge.

Question: Did you see a customer Craig Titus on the morning of December 17th?
Answer: Yes I did, he was there to trade his existing vehicle (a 2005 Dodge SRT-10 quad cab) in to purchase another one. The SRT is a hot rod truck with a Viper V-1- motor. It's a high profile vehicle. I originally sold him this truck in May of 2005, and he was there that morning to look for a different truck, one that would get better gas mileage and make it across country.

Question: Can you describe Craig Titus' demeanor that morning and how long he was there?
Answer: He seemed fatigued, taking naps, but he also seemed jittery. He arrived somewhere around ten am, and was finished around 2pm that afternoon.

15. Dr. Piotr Kubiczek- the medical examiner at the Medical Examiner's office in Clark County that performed the autopsy on Melissa James.

Question: What are your duties and responsibilities?
Answer: I perform autopsies; investigate causes and manners of death.

Question: I'd like to direct your attention to December 15th 2005 and the autopsy you performed on Melissa Ann James. Please describe her external body, and what you found around the decedent's face and neck.

THE GRAND JURY TESTIMONY

Answer: Her body was charred in approximately seventy percent. There's fabric material and duct tape around this area. Some of the duct tape was adhered directly to the face. The duct tape was placed on in pieces like a mummy- so as to seal off fluids. On the neck there were two pieces of material that were tying the fabric around the head and those two pieces of material preserved this area from the fire that were charring the outlying areas. There were pieces of cord from the car and a necklace that were imbedded into the skin.

Question: Am I correct that once the fabric and the items securing the fabric were removed from Melissa's head and neck area there was a wire around her neck?
Answer: No that is incorrect, actually it was a piece of wire on her, on the right side of the neck, and that loose wire made an impression on the skin. This loose piece of wire was only five inches long.

Question: Were there any other significant external findings that you saw?
Answer: There were no blunt force trauma injuries upon external examination.

Question: What significant findings did you find during the internal exam?
Answer: Basically again, there was no blunt force injuries, and no other significant findings. There was no sign of strangulation- the hiatal and thyroid cartilage were still intact; not fractured as typically happens with a strangulation. The content in her stomach was a mixture of small white meat fibers with rice mixed in with a thick chunky fluid. In her lungs, there was congestion and edema (gathering of fluid), which is consistent with a drug overdose; and this is especially prominent in opiate intoxication such as morphine and heroin.

Question: What were the results of the toxicology tests?
Answer: Her peripheral blood was positive for morphine and 6-monocetyl-morphine (both constituents of heroin). There were highly toxic levels of Morphine: 472 nannograms per milliliter, and 6-monocetyl-morphine: 13 nannograms per milliliter. Both of these are constituents of heroin, so the combination of these two drugs indicates that Melissa was using heroin.

Question: Can you tell us with any degree of certainty whether both of these were originally heroin when they were introduced to her body.
Answer: Yes heroin was ingested, but if it was all heroin or just part of it.

Question: As a physician would you consider the dosage found in the decedent's body a lethal amount, or could it possibly be a therapeutic dose in any case?
Answer: This amount would be a lethal amount for anyone. But it is better to ask the toxicologist when they take the stand; they can better address this question. But it is definitely a toxic level.

Question: What were the results from the toxicology screen done on her hair samples?
Answer: The hair showed a presence of amphetamines, and this indicated chronic use of amphetamines (Crystal Meth).

Question: Were you able to determine a Cause of Death by the end of the exam?
Answer: Well, I called it Undetermined with the Contributory Finding of Opiate Intoxication.

16. Dean O'Kelley- testified previously so this is actually witness #15.

Question: Did you obtain surveillance that purportedly showed Kelly Ryan wearing a red jumpsuit on the early morning hours of Dec. 14th? The same sweat suit that was recovered during a search of the home in January?
Answer: Yes, in the Wal-Mart there are pictures of Kelly Ryan walking around in a red jump suit with a stripe down the arm and pant leg. She is shown purchasing lighter fluid with receipts that match her credit card in her name. The same credit card and jump suit was found in the Titus/Ryan home.

Question: Was there surveillance of Craig Titus and Kelly Ryan driving the 2003 Jaguar in question in the early morning hours of December 14th 2005?
Answer: Yes, there was footage at Wal-Mart, and an image of the jaguar pulling up and dropping off Kelly Ryan. Then there is surveillance

THE GRAND JURY TESTIMONY

of what appears to be Craig Titus pulling up at the exit after Kelly Ryan purchased the lighter fluid, and they load her purchases in the back seat of the Jaguar.

Question: As part of your investigation did you meet with and interview Anthony Gross? What did you discover from this first interview?
Answer: Yes I did on December 19th 2005. We spoke for probably forty-five minutes to an hour before we actually recorded the interview. The interview took place at his attorney, Louis Palazzo's office, and Detective Wilson and I interviewed him. We had obtained phone records prior to asking him questions. The phone was on his mother's account, and billed to her address on Beekman. Gross was not aware that we had this information before we questioned him. We asked him if he had talked to Craig Titus on December 14th, and he said that Titus called him when he was asleep early in the morning at his girlfriend's (Elizabeth Williams) house. He said he ignored the calls that he received between 2:30 a.m. and 3:00 a.m. Gross stated that he eventually picked the phone up, and Craig told him he needed his help. Gross said that he met Craig Titus and Kelly Ryan at the Shell Gas Station in a truck that was also registered to his mother. He originally told us, before we started the recording, Craig and Kelly were waiting on him; but we told him about the surveillance video, and he changed his story and said they came in together at the same time. Gross put gas in the red plastic gas can, and put it on his center console. Gross said that Craig called him and told him where to drive around 4:15 a.m.; and the video footage shows them driving off at this time. He said they drove 15-20 minutes out past the mountain range leading to Pahrump back down to a flat area and then they turned onto a dirt road, and he drove down a ways and then pulled over. Gross said that Kelly Ryan jumped out of the Jaguar and jumped into the passenger seat of his truck and told him to turn the vehicle around.

Gross said he pulled up about 2 car lengths past the Jaguar (20 feet), and then Gross said he passed the gas can to Craig Titus. Gross said that he was talking to Kelly Ryan, unaware of what Craig was doing, and then Craig came running up to the car, jumped in and yelled at him to go. Gross said he saw a glow behind him, and that was the first time that he realized what might have been happening. Gross said that he dropped Craig and Kelly off at their house without asking any questions.

Question: Gross told you that he met Craig and Kelly at the Short line Shell Gas Station, and did not meet with or talk to Titus before this point, correct? Did you confront him with further evidence that proved otherwise?
Answer: Yes, in the video obtained by Green Valley Grocery, when we tried to find Kelly Ryan and Melissa James, we instead found footage of Tony Gross around three a.m. of that morning which is around the block from Craig and Kelly's home, maybe a two minute drive.

Question: During your investigation did you obtain cell phone records for Mr. Titus? And did you analyze these cell phone records to determine when the two men contacted each other on December 13th and December 14th?
Answer: The earliest phone call we found on that day was placed from Craig Titus' cell phone to Tony Gross' cell phone at 3:28 p.m. There were 13 additional phone calls in that time frame: on Tuesday December 13th at 4:39 p.m., at 6:23 p.m., at 7:46 p.m., at 8:02 p.m.; then on Wednesday December 14th at 2:34 a.m., 3:22 a.m., 4:20 a.m., and the last call at 4:28 a.m.

17. Lauren Amanda "Mandy" Polk-

Question: Do you know Kelly Ryan? How do you know her?
Answer: Yes, I do through fitness competitions. We were introduced by a mutual friend, and we had contact over the phone and internet in early July of 2005. We started talking because I had an interest in renting a competition suit that I knew belonged to her and the woman who made the suit advised me to contact her about renting the suit.

Question: At this time what was your view of Kelly Ryan?
Answer: I really admired her and looked up to her. She influenced me from the very beginning in the way that, in my interest of the sport, and they way that I approached routine training, by seeing her routines and her willingness and ability to improve every competition, it inspired me to try to do the same.

THE GRAND JURY TESTIMONY

Question: Where were you living in July? When did you develop a professional relationship with Ryan, and what happened to influence you to move to Vegas?
Answer: I lived in Germantown, Tennessee in July, and when I contacted her about the suit, she began to give me professional advice on my fitness preparation. She gave me advice on visualization exercises, and sent me motivating text messages; she seemed to really care, and wanted me to do well in my competition in August. After that show I spoke to her, and I had placed 5th. To turn professional, a competitor must place in the two spots in the overall category, and Kelly believed that I could do this. Kelly mentioned working with me one-on-one with my routines. I was originally going to stay at her house for a week and train, but she said they had rental property, and asked if I was interested in moving to Vegas long-term. I agreed to do that, and my boyfriend and I moved to Las Vegas in October.

Question: Would you consider yourself friends with Kelly Ryan? How often did you speak to each other?
Answer: Yes we were close friends, and we talked at least twice a week.

Question: I'm going to fast forward to Thursday, Dec. 15th 2005. Did you get a call from Craig or Kelly that day, and what was it like?
Answer: Yes, I got a call from Craig at two in the afternoon. Craig had never called me before so it was unusual for him to call. In the call, he informed me that he and Kelly would be coming over later because they had run into some trouble; it was a long story, and shortly after they had to get out of town.

Question: What did you say in response to that?
Answer: Because he told me and did not ask me, I was hesitant, and told him to make sure that he called before he came over. He agreed, but never called, and showed up around 6:00 p.m. with Kelly and Joey, their dog.

Question: What happened after they arrived at your house?
Answer: I went to change clothes, and Kelly followed me to my room and wrapped her arms around me. She seemed panicky, and was crying, and seemed to be trying to hold back emotion. Kelly then

said, 'Oh my God, the police found my car burned with a body in it.' When I asked what she was talking about, she said, 'Homicide was at our house this morning, there's a dead body in my car and it was burned up in the desert.' After about ten minutes, Kelly indicated that her roommate was missing, and they thought that she stole their car, and was the dead body in the car.' I said that I didn't know that she even had a roommate.

Question: Did you ask her questions about what happened?
Answer: I did, and Craig came upstairs and said, 'The less you know the better; we really don't want to involve you guys. I will say that she was a drug addict and stealing from us.' (Unlike what the investigators and prosecutors told everyone else, including Megan Pierson, Polk said that Craig did not want to get them involved and wanted to tell them as little as possible.) When I looked at Kelly and asked, 'She was a drug addict?' Kelly responded, 'Yeah, she was a meth addict; a fucking tweaker.'

Question: Does there come a time when you and Kelly leave the house?
Answer: Yes, around seven we went to get Chinese food in my car.

Question: Did Kelly explain anything else about what happened to Melissa?
Answer: She said that Melissa had been a source of stress in her life, saying, 'Melissa was a drug user and her behavior was erratic; she was unreliable, and this made it stressful at home.' When pressed about details, Kelly broke down and confessed, 'Okay, Mandy I can't lie to you anymore; I found the girl dead in her room of a drug overdose.' (Why would the investigators not listen to this witness? Her story matched Craig and Kelly's story, and she was a credible witness.)

Question: So because you had been asking follow up questions, she confessed?
Answer: "Right, because I was confused and she seemed confused; she was my friend, and she knew I wanted to be there for her, so I asked her why she didn't call 911. If she found her dead from a drug overdose, that was not her fault and if she destroyed the evidence that would only incriminate her and Craig.

Question: What was her reply to that?
Answer: She said, 'I'm fucked; I bought seven bottles of lighter fluid with my credit card at Wal-Mart.' She said that she was freaked out when Melissa overdosed, and they decided it would be best to get rid of the body because of her career. Craig had a criminal record, and they were starting a new league, and they did not want to have any negative publicity over an overdose at their house.

Question: Did you ever ask her where they found Melissa's body?
Answer: Yes, she made it clear that they found Melissa in her room.

Question: What happened when you got back to your house?
Answer: I carried the food into my kitchen, brought it upstairs, brought plates and things upstairs and then went outside to get the cokes out of the car. Craig and Kelly started eating, so I pulled Ryan out into the garage with me and I told him quickly what she had told me, and I said, "Oh my gosh Ryan, Kelly told me that they burned the roommate in the car. Kelly said they found her dead of a drug overdose. But I'm not supposed to tell you or Craig because she doesn't want anyone to know, but I thought it was only fair that you know what's going on."

Question: Did you hear Craig make a statement about what happened to Melissa?
Answer: He said that she was shady and he thought she was trying to steal their identity. When Kelly and I were in the bathroom, I remember her saying that, you know, she had a lot of problems with her bank account because of Melissa. They tried to look on the computer for information on their credit card and bank account, but they passwords had been changed so many times, they could not get on to look.

Question: Did Craig every say anything in front of you about what happened to Melissa, whether she disappeared or overdosed or anything like that?
Answer: I remember him using the word overdose.

Question: At any time during the evening did you hear Craig say anything about Melissa falling down the stairs?

Answer: No.

Question: What happened the next morning?
Answer: After I woke up, Craig and Kelly were on their phones making plans about where they were going to go, and what they were going to do. I believe Craig called his attorney.

Question: Did they eventually leave your house that morning?
Answer: Yes, they asked if we could take them to La Quinta, so we drove them to La Quinta on West Sahara. They asked my boyfriend to go inside and pay for the room, but when he went inside, La Quinta did not accept cash, only credit cards; so he said we had to go somewhere else that would accept cash. We drove to them to the Holiday Inn across the street, and they accepted cash, so my boyfriend rented the room for Craig and Kelly.

Question: Did you talk to Kelly Ryan again after you dropped them off? If you did talk to her again please explain.
Answer: Yes, I called her around 5:30 in the afternoon, and this is going to sound horrible but honestly, curiosity; to see how she was doing and what was going on; I was honestly concerned about her because I cared about her.

Question: Did she explain anything else to you that night on the phone?
Answer: No.

Question: Have you talked to her again since that time?
Answer: No.

SPACKLING THE HOLES IN THE PROSECUTION'S CASE

CHAPTER

Spackling the Holes in the Prosecution's case

After reading over the Grand Jury Testimony there are two big questions:

1. Why was kidnapping never mentioned, not even once? Actus reus is a criminal act. Most crimes have two components: mens rea (intent) and actus reus (action). Both intent and action are required to find a person guilty of a crime under US Criminal law doctrines. However in this courtroom, the criminal intent in regard to Kidnapping was never discussed. How could Robert Daskas charge Craig Titus with Kidnapping, and never bring the topic up during the grand jury hearings?

2. Why was there no physical evidence anywhere to support the prosecution's claim of Murder? This was it, everything the prosecution had against Craig Titus and Kelly Ryan! There was physical evidence to prove they caught the car on fire, but absolutely nothing else (other than the "word" of Megan Pierson Foley) to prove there was a murder. Had Megan Pierson Foley picked one theory, and stuck with it, her story might have been a little more believable. To say that Craig Titus "beat up, strangled and injected Melissa James with morphine," was absurd.

In Megan's own words, she said that Kelly Ryan was the one that was shot with a taser. Megan was lying or being "disingenuous" when she said "Kelly did not have the voltage up high enough." The prosecution's own experts said the voltage was not adjustable, and a person could not die from a civilian stun gun; so throw that out! The taser gun is absolutely irrelevant; except to support the defense's claim that Melissa James shot Kelly Ryan before she overdosed on drugs.

The fact that Melissa's body was burned did not affect the internal examination, and according to the Medical Examiner, there was no blunt force trauma or broken bones anywhere in her body. There was no damage such as fractures or lacerations to the deep, solid tissues, such as the ribs and internal organs (notably, the spleen and liver) which would have been evident after a severe beating. There was absolutely no proof that she was repeatedly punched or body-slammed, and this would have certainly been seen in the x-rays and or in the examination of her skull.

If Craig Titus, a professional body builder weighing 240 pounds, had body-slammed Melissa James, a petite one hundred and twenty pound woman; without a doubt, there would have been some type of blunt force trauma! There was also no physical evidence to support that she had been choked.

The Medical Examiner said that there were pieces of electrical wires, five inches in length on top of her body, but not around her neck. These were pieces of wire from the car that melted off and fell on top of Melissa's body during the fire. Even so, five inches would not be long enough to wrap around a person's neck to strangle the individual. There were no broken bones or snapped muscles/ligaments to support that she had been either choked or beaten.

The only thing that the Medical Examiner could say beyond a reasonable doubt was Melissa James had enough morphine and heroin in her system to kill her. The report showed the drugs had metabolized, so they had been in her system for a while; and there was obvious proof of chronic drug abuse. This was all the physical evidence the prosecution had against Craig Titus and Kelly Ryan. All of it supported the obvious fact: Melissa James had overdosed, as Craig Titus and Kelly Ryan truthfully claimed all along.

Article published by Glenn Puit for the Las Vegas Review Journal- March 29th, 2006

"Kelly Ryan participated in the brutality that culminated in the death of her personal assistant by using a Taser gun on the victim; beating her and helping her inject the woman with a massive dose of morphine Ryan's self-described best friend told a grand jury. In her (Megan's) testimony to the grand jury that indicted Ryan and her husband, Craig Titus, on murder charges, Megan Pierson, 25, also said Titus demonstrated how he strangled 28-year old Melissa James."

The article goes on, "Pierson testified that Ryan told her that a confrontation had occurred between her and James at the home because she and Titus suspected James was stealing from them and was planning to steal their identities. 'They had gone into Melissa's room and found, opened up, a lock box that had credit cards, copies of credit cards, a home equity line of credit, and copies of ID's.' Craig was very, very pissed, adding Titus said that there are three things that you don't mess with 'friends, family, and his money.'

The article also quotes Pierson as saying that Kelly told her that "she tried to stun Melissa with a Taser in the back of the neck, but she didn't have the voltage up high enough so she yelled for Craig's help. Craig came upstairs, picked Melissa up, brought her downstairs and body slammed Melissa and started beating her up." Pierson said that Kelly told her that Melissa took a Xanax, and then Kelly went in her room and started punching her in the face. She said that she, 'punched her a couple of times,' and she 'showed me the marks on her knuckles from it,' and she said that Craig was holding her down and told Kelly to get the morphine and she shot a whole needle of morphine into her leg."

"Pierson said that later that evening, Craig demonstrated 'How you can strangle somebody,' then he placed Pierson in a chokehold. 'He did it on me, and you instantly stop breathing.' Pierson went on, 'Craig just walked in and started talking about it and, that's how he had killed Melissa, by strangling her.' Pierson then said that Titus mentioned James' body was in his wife's car and that Craig was going to drive the vehicle to Red Rock, 'scatter clothes around the car and set it on fire and make it look like a rape'".

Comparing this article to what Megan Foley actually said to the Grand Jury, (while being led by Deputy District Attorney, Robert Daskas).

What Megan actually said in her grand jury testimony:
1. About the Taser gun:

Megan Pierson: *Kelly was sitting upstairs and Melissa had the taser gun, and at some point it got into Kelly's hands, and she turned around and tried to use it.*

Daskas' Question: Who had the taser gun?
Megan Pierson's Answer: *Melissa had it at first and Kelly took it from Melissa.*
Then Kelly turned on the taser to use it, and it hit Melissa in the back of her neck. But it was not up high enough so it kind of just got Melissa's attention. Kelly tried to do it again, but she didn't have the voltage up high enough.

(This was significant, as Megan Pierson's "hear say" testimony was the only evidence that the prosecution had to prove that a murder actually took place. It took on a life of its own when the information was twisted for the newspaper, and this articles' version of what happened that day became the facts of the case. Megan clearly stated Melissa had the taser and used it on Kelly first. When she said Kelly took the taser from her and tried to use it on Melissa, but could not because the "voltage was not high enough," this was an obvious lie, refuted by the prosecution's witness from Taser International.)

According to the "Frequently asked questions" Page for Taser International: *TASER devices utilize electro-muscular distribution technology with a powerful 50,000 volt electrical signal to completely override the central nervous system and directly control all the muscles. The EMD effect causes an uncontrollable contraction of the muscle tissue, allowing the TASER device to physically debilitate*

SPACKLING THE HOLES IN THE PROSECUTION'S CASE

a target by directly telling the brain what to do, resulting in muscle spasms, until the target is in the fetal position on the ground. Upon firing, compressed nitrogen projects two 15 feet probes (hooks). An electrical signal transmits through the region where the probes make contact (it penetrates through clothes, but not a thick jacket because the needle is only 3/8- inches long. The voltage ensures that the target's nervous system does not recover instantly to remove the probes. It is highly unlikely the assailant will be able to get up and walk after they are hit with the gun.

(The Taser Intl. FAQ data tells me that absolutely nothing Megan Pierson said was truthful, because had Melissa shot Kelly with the gun, she would not have been able to pull the probes out and then turn around and fire it at Melissa. It would also be virtually impossible to hit somebody in the back of the neck with a full head of hair like both Kelly and Melissa had at the time.)

2. About Craig and Kelly beating Melissa up:

Daskas' Question: So Kelly's told you that she called Craig upstairs, and he took Melissa downstairs and body- slammed her in the living room? **Megan Pierson's Answer:** *Uh-huh.*

Daskas' Question: And you said he started to beat her up?
Megan Pierson's Answer: *Uh-huh.*

Daskas' Question: Are those the words that Kelly used?
Megan Pierson's Answer: *Uh-huh.*

Daskas' Question: Did she tell you anything else that happened to her?
Megan Pierson's Answer: *At some point she had taken a Xanax to fall asleep and while she was sleeping, Kelly went in the room and punched her in the face.*

Daskas' Question: You are talking about Melissa taking a Xanax and getting hit?
Megan Pierson's Answer: *Uh-huh.*

Daskas' Question: From your understanding of the conversation, was this after she was beat up and body slammed by Craig Titus?
Megan Pierson's Answer: *After.*

(The autopsy report showed that there were no broken bones and there was no blunt force trauma. If any of these things that Megan said, and the paper exaggerated actually happened, there would have been some type of internal trauma to this petite woman's body! Craig and Kelly both beat her in the face, and there's not a broken nose; Craig body-slams her, and there are no broken ribs? Where were the marks all over Kelly's hands that Megan was talking about?)

3. About injecting Melissa with Morphine:
Daskas' Question: What else does Kelly say happened to Melissa?
Megan Pierson's Answer: *Kelly punched Melissa a couple of times in the face, and she showed me the marks on her knuckles from it. After that, Craig was holding Melissa down and Kelly got a needle of morphine and shot it into her leg.*

4. What Megan actually said about Craig choking Melissa:
Daskas' Question: Was anything else said about Melissa that evening?
Megan Pierson's Answer: *Later on in the master bedroom Craig showed on Kelly how you can strangle somebody, and I kind of played dumb to see what he was talking about, and I was like, what are you talking about, let me see, and he did it on me; and you instantly stop breathing.*

Daskas' Question: You said later that he did this?
Megan Pierson's Answer: *Uh-huh*

Daskas' Question: This was after you were in the garage, correct?
Megan Pierson's Answer: *Uh-huh. Correct.*

Daskas' Question: What starts the conversation about choking someone?
Megan Pierson's Answer: *Craig just walked in and started talking about it, and he started talking more about how he said that he killed Melissa.*

Daskas' Question: "Who all was in the master bedroom at that time?"
Megan Pierson's Answer: *Myself, Kelly, Craig and I believe Jeremy was, if not he ran to the bathroom, I can't remember, I believe he was there.*

SPACKLING THE HOLES IN THE PROSECUTION'S CASE

Daskas' Question: Did Craig talk about doing this choking to Melissa?
Megan Pierson's Answer: *Uh-huh.*

Daskas' Question: And then you also said that he said he killed Melissa?
Megan Pierson's Answer: *Uh-huh.*

Daskas' Question: What did he say specifically that you can remember?
Megan Pierson's Answer: *He said that, uhm well, he said that he was joking around, but that is how he had killed Melissa, by strangling her.*

The million dollar question: why isn't there any DNA evidence left behind? If Melissa was beaten, body-slammed, choked, and injected with drugs in that house, there has to be some evidence! WHERE IS IT? Where's the physical evidence left behind: Was the taser tested for hand prints to see who last held it? Were the hundreds of needles left behind by Melissa James tested? Test both ends to prove that they injected her with drugs. If the prosecution believes this ludicrous statement, then there must have been some physical evidence left behind at the scene.

Based on the evidence tested by the defense, we do know that: There were close to 100 needles collected in Melissa's room that had different types of drugs in the syringe, and Melissa's DNA on the needle; she was a chronic user. Based on the hair follicle test, she had been abusing methamphetamines for years.

We also know that the statement made by homicide detective Dean O'Kelley on *48 hours* was a lie: the leather sap came back "inconclusive" when tested; it did NOT have Melissa's DNA on one end and Craig Titus' DNA on another.

This whole case was about to fall apart. The prosecutors and investigators were working in overdrive trying to spin Megan's statements, and get Ron Brady Jr. to connect with Deen Cassim. Nothing seemed to be working according to plan up to this point.

Investigators and Prosecution were in panic mode because:
- Ron Brady Jr. was avoiding Deen Cassim, and trying to back out,

◄ SWIFT INJUSTICE

- A witness (Tony Gross' cell mate) came forward and reported that Tony Gross and his attorney had worked out a deal to lie and set Craig up,
- Megan Pierson hurt the prosecution during her grand jury testimony,
- The witnesses for the prosecution were videotaped either buying or selling drugs.

Everything had back-fired so far. The investigators needed to light a fire under Cassim; and to do that, they threatened to send Cassim off to Ely Penitentiary two weeks earlier than planned if he did not deliver! They needed to make sure that Cassim was adding enough pressure to Ron Brady Jr. If the authorities wanted to trick Brady into showing up for a meeting with an undercover agent and handing over some money, Brady needed to feel trapped, like there was nowhere else for him to turn. Cassim needed to threaten Brady with his life in order to force his hand.

Additionally, the prosecutor needed to put the pressure on the witnesses to keep their noses clean, because if the defense discredited them, their deal would be tossed, and he would charge them with Conspiracy along with Craig and Kelly. Robert Daskas also needed to monitor every phone call between Craig Titus and Ron Brady Jr., and to do that, it was essential that he recorded and listened to every single phone call that Craig Titus made while he was held at the CCDC.

These men stepped it up, and did everything they could to get a murder conviction. Starting April 1st 2006, Robert Daskas recorded every conversation Craig Titus made on the telephone at the Clark County Detention Center. The prosecutor listened to every call that was placed by Craig Titus to his mother, father, brother, sister, daughter, private investigator, and Ron Brady Jr. Daskas was not just looking for evidence to use against Craig in court, but he was also looking for information to leak to the newspaper.

The Defense was tight lipped with all of their facts about the case. Daskas knew if he prosecuted Craig through the media and falsely portrayed him as a monster, Titus would eventually blow up and turn the defense upside down.

SPACKLING THE HOLES IN THE PROSECUTION'S CASE

Conversations between Brady and Titus were tape-recorded. In these taped phone calls, there is never mention of a "murder for hire", but rather information from Brady to Titus about the witnesses' narcotics trafficking and use. Brady said he had videotaped all of the illegal activity, and had turned all of the information over to Craig's private investigator.

Craig said, "Just talk to Dillard about that; I don't want to have any part of that!" Titus knew that none of the witnesses were real bright, and they would end up helping the defense because the truth would eventually come out. Brady on the other hand thought that it was bullshit that these guys were lying, and insisted on catching them at their own game. Brady knew how Craig felt about the whole thing, so he didn't dare mention the mess he was in with Cassim.

Using the media to put the pressure on Brady

Craig was more worried about having a steady flow of income coming in while he was stuck behind bars. Craig and Kelly had hired the best(and most expensive) lawyers in town, and Craig needed to make sure that he could keep them funded until it was all over. To do that, Craig knew he needed to sell his house and his rental property. Kelly's mother could help sell the property, but he would need to have the tenants evicted, and all of the properties cleaned out and ready to sell before she could do that. This was what the Brady family did for a living, so Craig hired Ron Brady Jr. and Sr. to clean out and fix up all of the properties.

Cassim tells Brady about Megan's testimony

On March 29th, 2006, (One of the few times that their conversation was recorded) Deen Cassim called Ron Brady Jr., and asked him if he had read the headlines in the Las Vegas Journal. When Brady said that he had not read the newspaper, Cassim told Brady about the transcripts of Megan Pierson's Grand Jury Testimony, and the article written by Glenn Puit. Cassim read the article to Brady word for word, and then said, "Number 23 is bad, but that Megan Pierson chick is really bad."

Cassim said he wasn't sure from the article what Jeremy Foley knew about what happened because he didn't testify. Brady responded, "He knows what she knows. They were both there and saw the body, and helped cover up the overdose." Cassim talked about a bag Craig had given Megan and Jeremy containing a stun gun. Brady said "They didn't use the stun gun on Melissa. Melissa got Kelly with it. He told me everything dude."

Cassim said that wasn't what Megan Pierson was saying, "She said that Kelly shot Melissa with it in the back of the neck." Brady said, "She's a fucking liar, and drug addict, she'll get hers!" Cassim said that he wasn't so sure, not unless they do something. "She's saying that Craig: beat, strangled and injected drugs into that girl, and the District Attorney's office always wins- Craig will go down for this shit!"

Brady said, "He didn't do anything, I know what happened, she died from an overdose." Cassim said that the only way Craig could stay out of prison would be to take care of everything with his friend's Edison and Fred. Cassim said, "Talk to your attorney, and ask him what he wants to do with Edison; Fred will be in town, and he will be pissed if you don't follow through." Brady said that he had talked to him, and he didn't want to do anything, and that was his call. Cassim told him, it would be bad if he backed out, saying "talk to his family and see if you can change their minds for him." Brady said, "Okay," and then they both hung up the phone.

Homicide Detective Dean O'Kelley's hand written account of conversation between Deen Cassim and Ron Brady Jr.:

The rest of the phone calls were not recorded. Homicide Detective Dean O'Kelley listened in via 3-way conferencing and took notes, writing down what each man said (Yeah, right!). Over the next couple of days, Detective O'Kelley documented (wrote hand notes): Brady told Cassim he spoke with Schonfeld, and Craig will get the attorney paid up front to handle things for Cassim.

Brady said Craig gave the go ahead to do the money up front, but since the amount went up because of the other two, he needed to get some more money together. Brady said, "Tell me exactly what

SPACKLING THE HOLES IN THE PROSECUTION'S CASE

I'm gonna need." Cassim said, "Pictures." Brady said, "I can get the pictures." Cassim told Brady he needed their first and last names, and Brady said that he already had their names.

Brady told Cassim, "I confirmed things this morning. I'm more confident about doing this than I've ever been. I've got the ok from both families. I spoke to them this morning. I ran into some friends of Megan and Jeremy's the previous week so I now have access to more information through them." Brady said he was going to try to get the pictures later that night. Brady also mentioned he might be able to find pictures of Megan online. Cassim suggested they could just stick with the plan on Number 23 only, but Brady interrupted by saying "That would defeat the purpose. I want them all gone."

Brady asked Cassim, "How long is the job gonna take?" Cassim responded back, "It will be quick. I don't see it taking more than a week. They won't show up and they won't be found." Cassim told Brady the money on the back end of the deal would only be due after the job was done. Cassim asked Brady if he had any problems with the actual envelope. Brady said, "No. That's easy." Brady volunteered that he was going to contact Craig's family members, to talk to them about the other two witnesses. Cassim said they may consider the other two, once it's found out the main witnesses doesn't want to testify and goes on vacation.

On Getbig.com, a bodybuilding website, the following messages were posted along with excerpts from Megan's actual testimony: *On Wednesday, March 29th, the entire Getbig.com community was anxiously awaiting the appearance of Craig, Kelly, and Anthony Gross in their preliminary hearing, and we were surprised that this hearing had been postponed because the prosecution called a secret Grand Jury hearing. Now I think some of us were under the notion that the Las Vegas Grand Jury witnesses and statements in the case were to be secret. Not so, and a few copies of the grand jury transcripts were leaked out earlier than expected. Perhaps one of the most interesting statements made was by Megan Pierson (Megan Foley). Now let's keep in mind that this is Megan's testimony, and the defense has not had a chance to refute or even challenge these statements. This is the reason* the prosecutor bypassed the preliminary hearing. But Megan's statements just bring more amazement and wonder to this saga of a case.

(Excerpts from Glenn Puit's article were referenced on the site.)

Message Board Responses to the article on titusandryan.com:

When we read the recent story in the Las Vegas Review Journal it had us convinced that Megan Pierson hung Craig and Kelly out to dry. It appeared that Ms. Pierson gave chilling details that incriminated Titus and Ryan. The story was the first to name Megan by name and quoted many of her statements to the Grand Jury. We've since read the entire transcript from the Grand Jury testimony and it paints a much different picture then what Glenn Puit did in his story "GRAND JURY TRANSCRIPTS: Friend: Pair told of violence". Mr. Puit picked key quotes from the testimony to sensationalize what Ms. Pierson said. In the full testimony, Ms. Pierson comes across nervous and appeared as if she is hiding something. We weren't there so we can only speculate, but based off the Grand Jury testimony, we feel the defense will be able to discredit many of the things Megan Pierson Foley has stated. Why? Simply because her story and the facts don't add up. We're confident there is much more to this story than Foley's testimony...

Responses to "GRAND JURY TRANSCRIPTS - Pierson speaks out:

> **No Name says:**
> I know Megan and Jeremy personally. Las Vegas is a very small place and to the most part tons of people know each other or know people that know other people, more so here than other cities because of how compact we are here. A lot of us here have known more about the case than the media has shared with the general public. I've known Craig and Kelly for years and know most of the people they associate with and more importantly all the drugs that they have and were using and Jeremy and Megan were right there beside them taking the same drugs of which I have witnessed so this isn't something that I was told!! Jeremy and Megan were out with all of them the night Melissa was killed, I also know the gentlemen that Melissa was talking to on the phone for an hour or so

SPACKLING THE HOLES IN THE PROSECUTION'S CASE

hours before her death. Jeremy and Megan should be on trial right alongside Craig and Kelly.

Megan and Jeremy kept key information about certain events hidden, and they know more than they are saying, but now with a little prison time being threatened now after all these months they are singing like a bird about anything and who knows if it is true and why they are now talking. If Craig was telling them that he was going to kill Melissa or had told them that he did then why not call the police unless they were involved and or part of the cover-up, either way their involvement isn't just "hey I heard something" or "hey Craig said this"

It was all over the news and Megan and Jeremy knew Melissa on a personal level, they would all hang out and party amongst other things if you know what I mean. I don't know the exact involvement and I don't want to know but they were involved and they should have to face the music as Craig and Kelly are. Look at the transcripts of what they said three months ago and now. The stories that they have said to everyone else are completely different than the ones told to the authorities, no matter how one slices it that is called being a liar!!!If one needs anymore proof than just read Megan's statements from then and now and talk to the people that they know and you will have your proof in less than a day!!

Again I think that Craig and Kelly are guilty but as far as Megan and Jeremy being credible witnesses, I don't think so, they were involved. I think everyone will be a bit surprised when these two are questioned and I wouldn't be surprised if the authorities don't get what they need from these two I think they will be prosecuted as well.

The Truth says:
Megan why are you hiding behind a keyboard, using different names, making every attempt you can to help the damage that you-Megan have caused by the lie's you have spread. Megan and Jeremy were close friends of Craig and Kelly and

now Megan and Jeremy's stories have changed more than once and Megan is upset that is viewed in a bad light!!

Come on now, Megan you were friends with Craig and Kelly, a little more than friends with Craig and now you are selling Craig up the river. Did Craig reject you the last time you were together is that why you are upset with him and now turning on him????I think you and Jeremy need to get your stories straight so you don't end up behind bars with Craig and Kelly.

Craig has never put his hands on a woman to my knowledge, and I have been friends with him almost my whole life! Megan remember that protecting your friends by lying can only put you in jail and ruin your reputation. It is fact that there stories have changed and that is in writing so please before defending them you might want to do a little research just to make sure that they aren't making you look foolish.

You are stating that they have told the truth then I guess the Grand Jury transcripts are a misprint then right? I know for a fact that Megan lied about doing drugs because I have personally witnessed then taking drugs, so please let me know now that I am blind and didn't see what I saw and then we can all sleep better at night.

I think that if a person is going to be a part of something then stand accountable and accept your mistakes and move on and don't be mad at others because they disagree with your choices when they are evidently wrong.

"She" lied to the authorities for Craig and Kelly so now take responsibility for those actions and don't get mad or blame others for your choices; "she" makes comments about others, if she only knew that makes her look more guilty than she already is.

We told Craig and Kelly from the beginning that Jeremy and Megan were bad apples and Craig and Kelly thought that they could use them for business and sex thus here we are today. So you know, I have known a handful of people that have *known Jeremy and Megan for years and they both are trouble makers and yes I do know them but not well and thank God for that. Megan please get help with your drug use since I know that you have one. You again have made yourself look foolish.*

Manslaughter, Murder, or None of the above

For a moment, let's assume that Craig or Kelly did beat up and/or body slammed Melissa James (they didn't, but for argument's sake, let's say they did). The fact that Kelly Ryan and Melissa James were physically fighting, and Craig Titus ran home to defend his wife has never been disputed by either the defense or the prosecution. (According to Robert Daskas, this is the only fact he knows to be true). If either Craig or Kelly had done any of those things, this would not be First Degree Pre-meditated murder; it would have been Manslaughter at best. The only way that it could ever be considered First Degree Murder would be if Craig and Kelly kidnapped Melissa, and she died as a result of them kidnapping her.

Kidnapping was never mentioned once, much less proven beyond a reasonable doubt. Because the prosecutor unethically added that charge in with the original charge, Craig Titus and Kelly Ryan's Due Process rights were blatantly violated. Craig and Kelly were not able to meet with their lawyers freely to build a defense, nor were they given a preliminary hearing to refute the charges. This prosecutor overcharged the defendants, and never provided one piece of evidence to back up the charges. There was no physical evidence presented to back up a murder charge; and there was no physical or circumstantial evidence to prove kidnapping.

According to the "Clarifying Nevada Kidnapping Law" section on the Nevada State of appeals website; "Overcharging and False charges of Kidnapping" by prosecutors was addressed on 06/09/08 as follows:

FIRST-DEGREE KIDNAPPING CASES IN CLARK COUNTY DISTRICT COURT DURING 2006: 57 Total cases, **41 Kidnapping charges dismissed:** with only 3 Guilty pleas on first-degree kidnapping charges, and 1 Guilty verdict on first-degree kidnapping charges.

◄ SWIFT INJUSTICE

The Supreme Court this year overturned a jury's guilty verdict on kidnapping against Juan Garcia, a Las Vegas man who robbed an auto shop in 2003. During the robbery, Garcia restrained two victims with duct tape, but the Supreme Court ruled that was not enough to sustain a kidnapping conviction. The Garcia ruling followed an earlier state high court decision that sought to better define kidnapping: To support a kidnapping conviction, the court ruled in Mendoza v. Nevada that movement or restraint of victims during a robbery "must substantially increase the risk of danger to the victim over and above that necessarily present" in a robbery. The ruling was accompanied by a new jury instruction for those crimes.

CHAPTER 9

Entrapment & Solicitation for Murder

Chief Deputy District Attorney, Robert Daskas was able to gain an indictment against Craig and Kelly, but that was not a surprise: almost every grand jury ends with an indictment in the Clark County judicial courts. The grand jury indictment was baseless, obtained through unethical manipulation, and Robert Daskas knew it. In interviews with the media, Daskas tried to come across as confident about securing a guilty verdict, but Daskas knew that he was actually fighting a losing battle.

Daskas needed to get aggressive and play dirty if he actually wanted to secure a "Win" for the prosecution. To do this, he would have to maneuver his way around a few American Bar Association rules, and leak specific details about the grand jury indictment. Even though the transcripts had been sealed, and everyone was ordered not to discuss anything that happened during the hearings, the District Attorney's office revealed a few select snippets from Megan Pierson Foley's testimony to the local newspaper. That was a huge gamble; after all, the District Attorney's office tried to sabotage Rick Tabish and Sandy Murphy by doing the same precise thing, and it ended up back firing on them.

Fortunately for Daskas, his boss, District Attorney David Roger, along with Roger's best friend, Tom Dillard (a former homicide detective and current private investigator for the defense) had a plan. Dillard was theoretically working for the defense, but this former metro homicide detective was more than willing to hand over all of his information to the prosecution, essentially pocketing a pay check from Titus and Ryan while feeding the prosecution every detail of their case.

The private investigator arranged a meeting with his best friend at the District Attorney's office, along with officials from the Clark County Detention Center, and the homicide detectives currently working the Craig Titus case. In this meeting, Dillard explained that he had received information that the prosecution's key witnesses were either involved in the purchasing or selling of illegal narcotics. After Dillard learned about this information, he made a call to the Narcotics division of the LVMPD, and they placed surveillance on Greg Ruiz, Tony Gross, Jeff Schwimmer, Jeremy Foley, and Megan Pierson Foley. After watching all of these individuals, Dillard learned that they were all in fact either using or selling illegal narcotics. In addition to this information, he was informed by intelligence at the CCDC that a cell mate of Anthony Gross had come forward, told authorities that Melissa James' death was an overdose, and Gross was going to work with the homicide investigators to pin a murder charge on Craig Titus.

Everyone knew this was huge. This case had absolutely no physical evidence, and the only thing they had that would hold up in a court of law were the testimonies from those people providing details about the case. Without those testimonies, the odds of Robert Daskas' case being thrown out was more likely than not. In order for these witness allegations to stick, and the prosecution having any chance of winning, the District Attorney's office needed to be proactive. They needed to make sure that a judge got assigned this case that would approve all of their decisions, and shoot down every motion that Craig Titus and Kelly Ryan's attorneys brought up in court; and they knew the perfect woman for the job. Dillard was not convinced that having a judge in their pocket was the only way to go; he had been sued before when he attempted to influence a judge's decision, and lost the lawsuit and his job.

He did however have a fool-proof plan. Something he had done time and again as a homicide detective and investigator, a plan that would be impossible to trace back to the police or prosecutors: a frame-up. If they wanted to keep Titus locked up indefinitely, they needed to take it one step further, and set him up for a completely different

ENTRAPMENT & SOLICITATION FOR MURDER

crime while Titus was already behind bars. A "murder for hire" charge would scare the shit out of Titus, and provide a cushion for the prosecution's witnesses.

A CCDC official with the intelligence unit said that he and his guys have had their eyes on Titus ever since they were forced to release him form segregation Unit 5 D to Unit 7B, in a general population module on February 19th. This is where they house the general population inmates, and it consists of 46 rooms with an adjoining day space area and outdoor recreation space.

While Titus was living in this module, intelligence reported that he had become tight with a man named Ronald Brady Jr. It was reported that this man followed Craig Titus around like he was a rock star, and a quick look at Brady's records revealed over a dozen nonviolent, drug related arrests over the previous twenty years. In psych records, it was reported that his mind was "off" because of heavy drug use in the past; "He had the mind of a young teenage child." While they had never been cell mates, everyone agreed that Brady would be the easiest target to help them set up Craig Titus.

The official said he would instruct select members of his staff to be on the lookout for someone to befriend Brady to turn state's witness against Craig Titus. Having experience with this from the Binion case, Dillard stressed the importance of not using one of "the friendlies" (an informant over-used by authorities; like David Gomez in the Binion trial) from the " informant tank"; this needed to be "new blood- an articulate loner." He then suggested that the Assistant Sheriff, the Metro affiliated official in charge of the Clark County Detention Center, put a tap on Titus' phone calls, and turn over all of the conversations to the prosecution. The "Good Ol' Boys" had formed a plan, and once they found an informant to place in a cell with Ron Brady Jr., they would set their plan in action to take Craig Titus down, for good..

Craig Titus meets Ron Brady Jr. for the first time

During the short time that Craig Titus had with Ron Brady Jr., the two men became close as they discussed their personal struggles with drugs. Craig shared with Ron his disdain for narcotics, methamphetamines in particular. At the time, Craig assumed that Melissa had died from an overdose of meth; he had not been told that it was actually heroin that caused her overdose. Many of Brady's problems were caused by meth, and he opened up about his addiction and his girlfriend's addiction to the drugs.

The men talked about Craig's case, and Craig said the detectives told him during his interrogation that some of his friends had already turned on him. Craig said they had to be lying to save their own asses, and the investigators were holding something over their heads. Craig told his new friend that they were all involved with drugs, and a couple of them were drug dealers.

Brady told Craig that he was getting out in a couple of weeks, and would help him out. Brady told Craig that he could call Narcotics and get them all busted; "their word wouldn't mean shit then!" Craig said, "Na, don't worry about it; I don't want a reputation as a snitch! My lawyers and family are handling it. Their lies will come out all on their own, you watch! They will turn on each other, I'm not even fucking worried about it bro! I got other worries like paying the bills, and getting all of my property sold!"

Brady was enamored with Craig, and was chomping at the bit to help him out. Ron Brady Jr. said, "Me and my dad got a business, and we can help you out. Anything you need done, brother, I will get it done… put notices on doors, kick people out of the houses. After we kick them out, we'll scrub the places down from top to bottom, fix everything up, and get that fucking property ready to sell!" Craig was excited; if this guy was for real, that would be a load off his mind. Craig gave Brady the phone numbers of both his family and Kelly's family that would be in Las Vegas. Once Brady got out of jail, he could take care of everything, so Kelly's mom could focus on selling all of the properties as soon as possible.

Finding just the right snitch

All of the Correctional Officers that had been selected to find a snitch were under a lot of pressure to deliver a potential informant to their boss, but nobody had any immediate luck. Everyone felt a heavy burden because time was quickly running out; Ronald Brady Jr.'s sentence was about to be up, and he would be released at the end of the

ENTRAPMENT & SOLICITATION FOR MURDER

following March. It was a "now or never" situation, and it was looking more like never, until a sociopathic criminal walked through the Clark County Detention Center's doors.

Deen Cassim was a violent felon that had just been sentenced by Judge Joseph Bonaventure to twelve years behind bars. Cassim would only be in the CCDC for a short time though, because after a quick couple of weeks, Cassim would be sent off to Ely State Penitentiary to do his time with other violent criminals like himself. When Cassim arrived at the Clark County Detention Center, he was booked and moved through the system faster than usual. After he was taken out of the holding cell, a CCDC officer escorted him down the hall.

Before they arrived at Deen Cassim's cell, Cassim asked the officer to speak with someone in Intelligence. It was not clear if Cassim's attorneys gave him a heads- up or if it was simply a coincidence; but Cassim met behind closed doors with Las Vegas Metropolitan's Clark County Detention Intelligence officials. Cassim told the Intelligence officials he would be willing to be an informant, and do everything asked of him if he could somehow have his sentence reduced or tossed out. Shortly after, the homicide detectives were called in with the officials for a meeting, and a verbal agreement was made between Cassim and the officers. The "good ol' boys," had their rat, and set their plan in motion.

Who is Deen Cassim? In December of 2004 Deen Cassim, along with an accomplice, attempted to rob the 2004 World Series of Poker Champion Greg "the Fossilman" Raymer. The victim had been staying at the Bellagio where he participated in the Five Diamonds World Poker Classic. After six hours of play, he decided to cash out and head back to his room on December 20th at 2: a.m. Raymer said that he was checking out of the Bellagio the next morning because he would be participating in a televised poker tournament called the "Battle of the Sexes" at the plaza. After he emptied his deposit box of, more than $150,000.00, and put it in a duffle bag; he took the elevator to the 20th floor and began to walk to his hotel room door.

Raymer said Cassim was walking about thirty feet ahead of him, and another man was walking 30 feet behind him. Cassim proceeded down the hallway and stopped at the door next to Raymer's hotel room. Raymer said, "He (Cassim) appeared to fish around in his pocket and then began knocking on the door and calling a woman's name saying "Let me in, I locked myself out, wake-up." Raymer said Cassim's action didn't seem unusual so he proceeded to unlock his door.

The poker celebrity, Greg Raymer, put the key in and had the door only open a few inches when Cassim and his accomplice grabbed him from behind. "They ambushed me, and pushed me into the room," Raymer said, "Once I was in the room, I began to push my way back to the hall, and I screamed, 'I'm being robbed, someone call security!'" Cassim pulled out a gun as he instructed Raymer to go back into the hotel room. "I knew it was a bad idea to allow two armed criminals push me into my room. I was being physically assaulted and was in fear for my life, so I pushed back with all of my weight." Raymer had them back in the hall, and protected the bag like a basketball player protecting the ball after a rebound, "I had it tucked in, with my elbows out, and I swung my elbows as hard as I could."

Deen Cassim raised his gun, but the other guy had already bolted down the hall. Raymer said that he saw the look in his eyes, and Deen Cassim was ready to kill him for that money. "If I cooperated and went into my room, they knew I could later identify them, and I would have been murdered, no doubt about it!" Cassim was charged with burglary while in possession of a firearm, attempted robbery with use of a deadly weapon, attempt to commit first-degree kidnapping with use of a deadly weapon, conspiracy to commit first-degree kidnapping, and conspiracy to commit robbery both with use of a deadly weapon. Cassim was convicted and sentenced by Judge Joseph Bonaventure (the same judge from the Binion trial) to 3-12 years in a maximum-security prison.

Cassim prepares to set up Ron Brady Jr. and Craig Titus
The homicide detectives provided Cassim with all of the details about the case, and instructed him step by step what they needed him to do if he wanted to be set free. They explained how Ron Brady Jr. was close on the inside with Craig Titus, who is "somewhat of" a star in bodybuilding. They said Brady was going to be released in a couple

of weeks, and should be easy to suck in because he's a drug addict. "Your job is to suck Brady in; he is in awe of Craig Titus, so use that against him. Once Brady leaves jail, he will become our bitch because he will be using drugs again the second he hits the streets!"

The detectives told Cassim he needed to convince Brady to hire a hit man on the outside to get rid of the witnesses. "If Brady acts hesitant, confuse him and make Brady think the witnesses will only be roughed up into telling the truth." They told Cassim to make sure Brady does not tell Craig what's going on yet. Instead, Cassim needed to convince Brady that if he quietly helped out Craig Titus with the witnesses, then Titus would always be indebted to him, and would remain friends with him on the outside.

After a couple of days of being briefed by the detectives, Deen Cassim felt that he had the script down, and was ready to take out both Ron Brady Jr. and Craig Titus. Cassim was never housed with the violent offenders. He had been assigned to that module with the violent offenders, but when he walked in and said that he wanted to be an informant, they placed him in a module with low level criminals that were about to be released from jail.

Deen Cassim and Craig Titus would never meet, but the officers at the CCDC were arranging for Ron Brady Jr. to become fast friends with Cassim by moving him into his cell on March 3rd 2005. When they moved Brady from the Violent Offender's Module 7B in the North Tower to Module 2M in the South Tower, Ron Brady Jr. was shocked.

This was an "Incentive Module"; a reward for the model prisoners that had been there longer than three months and had not gotten into any trouble. Brady had only been incarcerated for two months and seventeen days, that must have been his lucky day! He was bumped ahead of 4,000 other men, and got to stay his last month of jail in the lower level penthouse of the CCDC.

Ron Brady Jr. is moved to Deen Cassim's cell
He was taken aback, but Brady was not about to complain about the move. This was a country club compared to the north tower, and his new roommate, Deen Cassim seemed like a great guy. During their

short stay together, Cassim was able to get Brady to open up about Craig Titus by mentioning that he read about his case in the newspaper, and thought he was guilty of murder. Brady defended his friend, and told him Craig Titus' version of the story.

He told Cassim about the fight between Kelly and Melissa, and how Titus came home and found Melissa dead of a drug overdose. Brady talked about Craig being worried about their careers if the police were called. He said that Craig called his friend; Brady couldn't remember his name, and Cassim said, "Anthony Gross." Brady thought that sounded right but was not certain; but the friend helped Craig wrap the body and put it in the trunk of the car, and then they later burned the car.

When Cassim asked Brady about potential witnesses, Brady said that Craig's lawyer told him about his wife's best friend lying to police to cover a mortgage fraud scheme. He said Craig was told that the prosecution had lined up his "druggie friends" to testify against him to save their own asses. Cassim now had an opening, and jumped right on it, guiding the conversation towards a "murder for hire" set up. Deen Cassim was a very intelligent man, and after a few days with Ron Brady Jr., he knew how to exploit all of his weaknesses.

Brady was a man that was easily manipulated, and a soft target because he was so insecure. He has been described as "loyal until the end, a man that would do anything for anyone; he never wanted to let a single person down." Unfortunately, this devotion would be what Cassim would use against Ron Brady Jr. as he gradually gained dominance over him. Cassim was a predator, and bit-by-bit, he slowly gained control over him without Brady even realizing it.

Cassim told Brady that he knew someone on the outside that could scare the shit out of those witnesses and force them to tell the truth for a small amount of money. Brady wanted to do anything he could to help save Craig Titus, and he wanted Deen Cassim to know how much he liked him as well, so he listened and agreed with everything that Cassim had to say.

ENTRAPMENT & SOLICITATION FOR MURDER

Brady became easily confused, and started to feel threatened when Cassim's stories escalated from intimidation to physical violence. Cassim incessantly rambled without breaking eye contact with Brady. As Cassim stared him down, Brady didn't know if he was talking about intimidating and murdering Craig's friends or if he wanted to intimidate and murder Brady. Cassim had poured it on a little too thick, and Brady was starting to pull away from Cassim and distance himself from his new cell mate. Just when Brady was about to ask for a different cell mate, Ron Brady Jr. was mysteriously released, for no apparent reason, two weeks early on March 8th, 2005.

When Ron Brady Jr. was released from prison, he put Deen Cassim far out of his mind, but he still wanted to help his friend out. Brady was on a mission to discredit the "low life druggies that made shit up about his friend." Brady knew the drug world in Vegas; he had been a part of that community for nearly twenty years. After talking with several dealers and drug buddies of Megan, Jeremy, Greg, Jeff, and Tony around Vegas, and confirming they were a part of the drug scene, Brady wrote down every detail that would help lead to their arrest.

Anxious to discredit those potential witnesses, Brady reported everything he found to the Metro Narcotics department, and they in turn alerted the lead detective on the Titus case about the information; this stopped the drug investigation dead in its tracks. Brady had a feeling that would happen, so he took matters into his own hands.

Over the following couple of weeks, Brady tracked the "key witnesses" down and videotaped all of their potential drug activities on his video recorder. After talking with Craig's family, and informing them what he had done, they suggested that Brady give the tapes over to their private investigator, Tom Dillard. The private investigator handed the tapes over to the homicide detectives, and after that it became urgent to jump-start their sting operation!

They needed Cassim to start communicating with Brady as soon as possible. After another lengthy discussion, the homicide detectives decided the best way to maintain contact between Deen Cassim and Ron Brady Jr., without Brady suspecting the line was tapped, was to have a private investigator for the defense, place a call from the public defender's office. In the presence of the homicide detectives, the private investigator called Deen Cassim (who answered the phone at the CCDC) and Cassim then made a three-way call to Ron Brady Jr.'s cell phone. This was the first call placed on March 24th, 2006 in the collaborative effort to frame Ron Brady Jr. and Craig Titus on a Murder-for-Hire charge.

Deen Cassim calls Ron Brady Jr. - over and over again

Ron Brady, Jr. didn't want to have anything to do with Cassim, and did not answer the phone for two days. Brady thought that Cassim was a psycho, and that was confirmed after Cassim continuously called Brady's cell phone and left him over twenty phone messages. When Brady finally answered the phone, he did not know what Deen Cassim wanted; hell he could not even understand a word the man said!

With his thick accent, Cassim was difficult to comprehend. Brady could tell that Cassim was growing agitated with him when he repeatedly asked Brady to repeat back what he had just said. Brady just repeatedly said, "Okay, that's fine," or "alright that will work" after everything Cassim sputtered off in broken English.

In their conversation, Cassim talked about someone being in town staying at the Bellagio, and he wanted to place a bet on the number twenty-three; Brady did not have a clue what Cassim meant. Deen Cassim terrorized Ron Brady Jr. all day, every day for the next few days. Brady felt helpless, and he thought his life, and the life of his loved ones, were in danger because he befriended this crazy prisoner.

At first Brady did not know what Deen Cassim wanted from him, but after Cassim taunted him over and over, Brady realized Cassim was pressuring him to give Cassim's friend some money to put a hit on the witnesses in Titus' trial. Brady did not want to have anything to do with Deen Cassim or his crazy plan. Every time the phone rang, Brady felt so much anxiety that he finally put his phone away and turned back to drugs for some relief.

ENTRAPMENT & SOLICITATION FOR MURDER

Ron Brady Jr. tries to avoid Cassim and get out of this "deal"

Brady thought that if he didn't answer his cell phone, Cassim would leave him alone; but he was worried because his father's name and address was listed in the phone book, and he shared the same name as his father. After a couple of days, Brady thought he was in the clear, until his dad told him somebody named Dean Cassim was calling him on their home phone. Brady turned his cell phone back on, and within thirty minutes Cassim had started calling him back. When Brady answered, he made up a story, hoping that it would stop the phone calls from Cassim. Brady said he was being followed by narcotics agents after he purchased some weed from his dealer, and he didn't answer his phone because he was afraid they had his phone tapped.

Cassim didn't care about phones being tapped, and he started back in on Brady, demanding that he meet with his friend to pay him some money. When Brady tried to tell Cassim that he did not feel comfortable doing it, Cassim told him it was not his decision to make. Brady had no choice in the matter, and he had to show up to meet Edison, with five hundred dollars, or else; meaning there would be a hit placed on Ron Brady, Jr. if he did not cooperate.

Deen Cassim told Brady to pass the word on to Titus, "Number twenty-three was about ninety percent of the case against him; Titus better take care of the problem sooner rather than later." Cassim told Brady to inform Titus that the other two (Megan Pierson and Jeremy Foley) could also hurt him, and Edison would be willing to take care of them as well. Brady had never mentioned any of this to Craig Titus, and he didn't have five hundred pennies, much less five hundred dollars to his name. So the next day Brady turned his phone off, and was a no-show for the second time.

After Cassim heard the news of Brady's no-show, he started "blowing up" Brady's cell phone with repeated phone calls again. When Brady did not answer the phone for a couple of days, Cassim once again called Ron Brady Sr. and demanded that his son return his phone calls. Ron's father politely assured Cassim that he would pass the message on to his son. After Ron's father urged Ronnie to turn his cell phone back on and acknowledge this man's phone call (because he was now harassing the family on the home phone), Brady reluctantly turned his phone back on. He did not have to wait long before Cassim started calling.

When Brady answered the phone, he told Cassim he ran into a big problem: "Homicide detectives had contacted him about the case." Brady said he was too scared to meet with Cassim's friend, and even more scared to carry any of this out. Brady asked Cassim to please stop calling him because he did not want any part of this. Deen Cassim flipped his shit and started screaming and cursing at Brady. Brady asked Cassim to give him a couple of days to think about it, and Cassim grudgingly agreed. Ron Brady Jr. would later say that he was scared out of his mind because he knew Cassim had him trapped like an animal, and there was nowhere to run.

Ron Brady Jr. said, "I could never understand what the fuck that foreigner was saying half of the time! I think he did that on purpose to confuse me and mess with my head. He would sound normal at times and then start screaming psychotic threats. He was totally nuts; his threats were real off the wall, grotesquely violent threats. I honestly did not know what to do, so I would go hide and do dope like a coward."

The homicide detectives knew they had a problem: Ron Brady Jr. was backing out and ignoring Deen Cassim's phone calls. The investigators told Cassim to turn up the heat on Brady. They told him their conversations were not being tape recorded, so Cassim could say whatever he wanted, and nobody would get in trouble. The homicide detectives told Robert Daskas that Brady was backing out; and they agreed it was time to start leaking some of the grand jury testimony to the press. They were hoping that Megan's testimony would make both Brady and Titus angry enough to want to retaliate against her.

CHAPTER **10**

Who wants to be a Celebrity Judge?

Who would preside over the Craig Titus murder trial? The judge handpicked by the District Attorney's office for this must-win case was Judge Jackie Glass. Judge Joseph Bonaventure was not available. He was busy with another high-profile case, so the next best judge to rule in the prosecution's favor, and soak up all of the publicity, in hopes of becoming a famous celebrity judge, was none other than…Judge Jackie Glass.

Glass was first elected to the Clark County district court bench in 2002, and she was a controversial judge from the very beginning. Jackie Glass is known for giving severe sentences and many a tongue lashing to high-profile defendants. She graduated from the University of Georgia with a degree in Journalism. Glass moved to Las Vegas in 1978, beginning as a radio news reporter. She quickly moved to television and served as an anchor and crime beat reporter. As she followed trials she covered, and after she met her attorney husband in a courthouse hallway, she became interested in the field of law. Between 1984 and 1985, she graduated from San Diego School of Law, received her Juris Doctorate, passed the Nevada Bar Exam, and was admitted to the Nevada Bar Association. That same year she married fellow lawyer, Steven Wolfson. Wolfson, a past criminal defense lawyer and city councilman, is now the District Attorney in Las Vegas, Nevada.

◄ SWIFT INJUSTICE

Judge Glass was elected District Court Judge, December 5th, in the 2002 election, defeating incumbent Jeff Sobel. In an article written by Jeff German of the Las Vegas Sun (the same writer that penned the pro-prosecution articles and the controversial book about the Binion trial) about Judge Jackie Glass' win:

"A NASTY MIX: LAWYERS, POLITICIANS." *"The polls tell us that lawyers and politicians make up the least trusted professions in the country. So when we have a situation where lawyers turn into politicians, the potential for distrust is even higher. The race between District Judge Jeff Sobel and Jackie Glass is a prime example of why the public has a low opinion of these professions. And why reforms in how we select judges are needed. It was a nasty race from the start, with Glass accusing Sobel of being lazy, and Sobel attacking Glass saying she was inexperienced and carried a long list of DUI clients. More than two weeks after Glass handily defeated Sobel, sparks still are flying. The latest controversy is a letter Glass sent out to lawyers, many of whom likely will appear before her in court, soliciting contributions to retire her large campaign debt. Those being asked for money include lawyers who backed Sobel during the heated campaign. The pressure on these lawyers to help Glass pay for the mudslinging that ousted Sobel must be enormous; this is both distasteful, and a good reason why some states appoint their judges."I think it's an unfortunate situation when candidates in judicial campaigns have to raise money from lawyers who go before them, but that's the way it is," says Richard Morgan, dean of the Boyd School of Law at the University of Nevada, Las Vegas. Jeff Stempel, a Boyd Law School professor who specializes in ethics, says bitter races like the one between Sobel and Glass tend to undermine the entire judicial branch and give credence to the argument for appointing judges. "I don't think it's good for the judiciary when you have a rip-roaring campaign where candidates engage in negative advertising and have to shake down contributors," he says. Whether we need to appoint judges or merely reform campaign contribution laws, it's clear that something needs to be done to purify the selection process. The alternatives are there. If we do nothing, we can look forward to nastier versions of Sobel v. Glass in the future. Here's another example of why it's hard to trust lawyers who turn into politicians."*

WHO WANTS TO BE A CELEBRITY JUDGE?

Judge Jackie Glass is described as a "get-it-done" judge from 8-5 during the week, and a soccer mom of two when she gets home. But she has some harsh critics. The American Civil Liberties Union of Nevada has accused her of sacrificing defendants' constitutional rights for court efficiency. She has been criticized for making judgments against those that did not provide her campaign monetary support. This judge is a democrat in conservative clothes, with a past record of throwing the book at everyone that comes her way when the camera is running, unless the ruling is beneficial to her or her husband's law firm.

One such example: *The Case of Dominic Rizzolo,* **INSIDE LAS VEGAS written by Steve Miller** - *Convicted racketeer Rick Rizzolo in 1985 plea bargained with a friendly District Attorney to a gross misdemeanor after beating Rick Sandlin almost to death with a baseball bat. Sandlin died three years later of his injuries, and Rizzolo did not spend even one day in jail. Rizzolo's attorney was Oscar Goodman, who today is our town's Mayor. 24 years later, just before Christmas 2008, Rick Rizzolo was heard telling his friends that his son Dominic will also get off with a slap on the wrist and get one year probation for pleading guilty to Battery with Use of a Deadly Weapon.*

Dominic's prosecutor is current Clark County DA David Roger, a long- time friend of Rick Rizzolo and his family attorney Tony Sgro -- "an experienced defense attorney." Sgro donated Roger's campaign headquarters in 2007 when Roger ran for reelection. Roger was also the benefactor of a 2003 political fundraiser in the Rizzolo's Canyon Gate estate, and received over $50,000 in campaign contributions based on Rick Rizzolo's efforts. Dominic Rizzolo, 26, will be sentenced at 9 AM, Tuesday, January 13, in Clark County District Court, Department 5. This is Dominic's first felony offense. His judge is the honorable Jackie Glass who is best known for presiding over the 2008, O.J. Simpson robbery and kidnapping case. She's been described as "a no-nonsense judge known for tough sentences. Because "violent crimes are on the rise in most cities across the nation," Glass tried to set an example by sentencing Simpson to over 9-33 years in state prison; and he didn't cause his victims physical harm during his crime spree at the Palace Station Hotel. His associate did threaten several men with a gun, but never pulled a gun out. It was Simpson's first felony offense.

Judge Glass is married to prominent criminal defense attorney and Las Vegas City Councilman Steve Wolfson who serves at the side of Rick Rizzolo's former criminal defense attorney and corporate agent, Oscar Goodman. Wolfson would like to succeed Goodman as mayor, and needs Goodman's endorsement to be elected. Associates of Rick Rizzolo (below) were responsible for launching Goodman's career as a mob lawyer. (Steve Wolfson was appointed to take over David Roger's job as District Attorney on January 3, 2012 after Roger abruptly resigned,)At approximately 10 PM, January 21, 2008, Dominic Rizzolo reportedly drove to William Moyer's home in a dark colored SUV with the license place covered by a T-shirt. Moyer, 26, who was a class mate of Rizzolo at Gorman High School, reported he received a phone call on the night of the incident asking if he was staying home that evening. Fifteen minutes later, Rizzolo reportedly knocked at his door. Moyer's mother answered the door and summoned her son. The two men conversed on the front lawn for several minutes until Rizzolo reportedly asked Moyer, "Do you know who my family is?" then demanded $20,000. Moyer said he refused the demand and ordered Rizzolo off the property which he said inspired Rizzolo to strike him in the face with his fist. A fight ensued in which Rizzolo reportedly pulled a switch blade knife and stabbed Moyer in the upper abdomen. Moyer sustained life threatening injuries requiring emergency surgery and six days hospitalization. Moyer has not received compensation for his medical bills, pain, and suffering. He said he has hesitated suing Rizzolo in civil court to recover his expenses because Rizzolo does not work, have assets, or own property in order to satisfy a judgment.

NRS 200.481 Battery*:* **Definitions; penalties. a person convicted of a battery... shall be punished: (e) If the battery is committed with the use of a deadly weapon, and: (2) Substantial bodily harm to the victim results, for a category B felony by imprisonment in the state prison for a minimum term of not less than 2 years and a maximum term of not more than 15 years, and may be further punished by a fine of not more than $10,000. Judge Glass is guided by NRS**

WHO WANTS TO BE A CELEBRITY JUDGE?

200.481 to sentence Rizzolo to the state prison for a minimum term of not less than 2 years. Or she can suspend his sentence and place him on probation.

However, suspended sentences and probation is not Judge Glass's style. While the world watched, she threw the book at Simpson, and he never shot or stabbed anyone that fateful day at the Palace Station. By coincidence, this is the second concurrent case involving a member of the Rizzolo family that has been randomly assigned to Judge Glass. In 2003, Judge Glass was assigned to preside over Kirk Henry's Attempted Murder civil lawsuit against Rizzolo's corporation, The Power Company. Because Dominic Rizzolo was a "person who (used) a... deadly weapon... in the commission of a crime," and William Moyer almost died of his injuries, it's expected that Judge Glass will heed the words of her husband who stated: "People convicted of violent crimes have their prison sentences impacted by the harm done to their victims," and she will impact Dominic Rizzolo's sentence, fine, and victim restitution by the harm he did to Mr. Moyer. Hopefully, her sentencing will not be impacted by Dominic's father's close connections to the DA and Mayor. Re-elected in 2008 without opposition, Glass drew national attention over the Simpson case and was noted for her personality that she herself described as "probably more animated as what you expect of a judge." In the Las Vegas Review Journal's 2010 "Judging the Judges" survey, Glass received a 60 percent retention rating; this score was below 19 of her 24 district court colleagues. She scored low because she did not do a good job explaining her decisions, or applying the law to her decisions.

Arraignment Hearing after Grand Jury Indictment: Judge Glass' debut

On March 30th, 2005 The "Honorable" Judge Jackie Glass made her first appearance in the Craig Titus/Kelly Ryan/Anthony Gross murder trial at their Arraignment Hearing, three months after their arrest in Boston, Massachusetts. At the hearing, the charges (not the evidence) were to be presented to the judge. The indictment was to be "unsealed," for the first time, but it had obviously been "unsealed and leaked" to the Las Vegas Review Journal the day before.

SWIFT INJUSTICE

An article had already been written, demonizing both Craig Titus and Kelly Ryan. When Craig Titus was asked by the judge if he pled, "Guilty or Not Guilty to First Degree Murder, First Degree Kidnapping, and Arson," the raspy, deep voiced Craig Titus exclaimed, "100 percent not guilty." In a more subdued, high-pitched voice, Kelly Ryan responded with a "Not Guilty" to the outrageous charges. The judge then asked Craig Titus and Kelly Ryan about their education level, and Ryan told the judge that she had a Bachelor's in Journalism, and Titus said that he was a high school graduate. When the judge asked Anthony Gross how he pled to Accessory to Murder and Arson, Gross also said that he was "Not Guilty." A trial date was set, and Titus' defense attorney said that he would file motions, "asking the judge to set bail for Titus so that he could have a chance to await trial outside the confines of the CCDC."

If the name Judge Jackie Glass still does not ring a bell, maybe this will: (Cue the corny court television music) Sashaying across the television screen is a woman with an open smock, who appears to be late to a hair appointment. She glides from one end of the screen to the other and back (over and over). After a few minutes of aimless walking, the judge stops and looks at the camera. The narrator says: "She was a judge and a defense attorney in Las Vegas for nearly 20 years. She is the judge who put O.J. Simpson away for 33 years. The cases are real, her rulings are final, and justice will be swift- Swift Justice with Jackie Glass."

Nevada Commission on Judicial Discipline
P.O. Box 48
Carson City, Nevada 89702

VERIFIED STATEMENT OF COMPLAINT

On or about Oct. 19, 2007, Judge Jackie Glass ruled to deny a warrant for the arrest of Jason and Keith Overton on charges of Felony Battery with Substantial Bodily Harm. (Exhibit 2) To do this, Judge Glass left her District Court Bench and sat in for Judge Bonaventure, presumably for just this one case. Judge Glass denied the Request for Warrant in spite of the evidence and both defendants' violent criminal history. (Exhibit 3)

Judge Glass was conflicted as her husband's name, defense attorney Steven Wolfson, was prominently displayed on the Declaration of Warrant (Exhibits 4 and 5) as representing Jason and Keith Overton, the Defendants, and having supplied LVMPD with statements from both of the Defendants. Judge Glass ignored this conflict and ruled to deny the warrants in spite of witness statements, hospital reports (exhibit 6 - partial hospital report) showing substantial bodily injury including a fractured spine, broken rib, broken nose and various other injuries, in what one witness described as an "attempt to kill" (Exhibit 7). It is suspected that the only reason Judge Glass ruled on this case was because her husband was representing the Overton Defendants, and any other Judge would have issued the Warrant for Arrest.

Although Detective Merrick claimed in his Declaration of Warrant that he had no information that would lead to the identity of assailants 3 and 4, that has also been found to be untrue as subsequent discovery requests from the LVMPD Records Department revealed that Mr. Wolfson supplied statements from all four assailants and Det. Merrick left them out of his packet prepared for the DA. The other two statements identifying suspects 3 and 4 (Jonathon Rosati and Joseph J. Martin) were obtained through additional discovery of LVMPD records and also were shown to have come from Mr. Wolfson's office. Witness reports state that Joseph Martin, the largest of the four trained fighters, was the first to attack the victim, although all four assailants took part in the brutal beating.

The supporting documents were received from the DA through a FOIA request dated February 15, 2011. Included is the DA's cover letter (Exhibit 1) and the original incident report (Exhibit 8). This was the second FOIA request presented to the DA. The first response did not include most of this information, and therefore the delay in filing this complaint.

I pray that the Nevada Commission on Judicial Discipline strongly consider these allegations and investigate to the fullest extent possible.

Signature of Complainant

Dated
March 14, 2011

CHAPTER **11**

Book Deal or Murder Plot?

The pressure was on Deen Cassim, and law enforcement was gearing up to kick Cassim out of his informant/rat bachelor pad and place him into general population with the other violent offenders. On April 1st, Deen Cassim called Ron Brady Jr. over and over, and Brady would not pick up the phone. Cassim informed him that he wasn't playing around, "This ain't no April fool's joke!" Cassim's "friends" were tired of fucking with him, and he was about to get hurt if he didn't pick up the phone.

Brady should have known that Cassim would not let up, but Brady still tried to hold him off as long as possible, hoping the harassment would stop, but it never did. Then on April 3rd, Brady finally answered the phone. Cassim began to berate him while he cussed him out and threatened his life over the phone. Deen Cassim demanded that Brady show up the next day at a Starbuck's and give Edison some money, or somebody was going to get hurt. Brady believed him and was scared out of his mind. Because he didn't want anybody to get hurt, he turned to drugs, and stayed high, hoping to avoid the situation all together, but the situation never went away. Instead, Brady missed another meeting, and Cassim threatened to come slit his throat and his Dad's throat himself.

On April 4, 2006 Detective O'Kelley did not record, but "monitored, and took notes" another call between Brady and Cassim. Dean O'Kelley documented, "Cassim told Brady he has spoken with Edison

& the deal is off. Cassim recommended Brady save himself money by going to the west side and getting some gang member to do the job for 5 K. He told Brady it would be messy, the bodies would be found, but he could save money." Dean O'Kelley wrote down Brady's response, "Just give me one more chance, I swear to God I will get the money to Edison tomorrow. I will talk to Richard Schonfeld about representing you right now, and tell Craig that this is going down. His family really wants this to happen, however you want to do it I will do anything, I swear."

Neither Craig Titus nor his family had a clue that any of this was going down. And, according to Brady, this conversation never happened the way O'Kelley documented it. In their conversation, Brady said that he would talk to Craig and his attorney, but he never had any intention of talking to either one. Brady also said that he never talked to Craig's family about hiring a hit man, the detectives just wanted to take down Craig Titus, and nailing his family would be a bonus.

Once again, for the next several days Brady turned his phone off to avoid Cassim. Brady thought by ignoring Cassim, maybe he would drop the bullshit and move on to something or someone else to exploit. Brady kept himself busy by cleaning out Craig's houses with his dad, and doing repairs to all of Craig's properties. Craig and Kelly's house at 9539 Adobe Arch Court was finished and listed on Re/MAX:
- Beautiful Two Story Home
- built in 2002, approximately 3,034 square feet
- for $550,000.00
- 5 Bedrooms, 3 Full Baths with 3 Car Garage
- Custom Paint & Upgraded Flooring Throughout
- Beautiful Kitchen w/ Built-In Refrigerator, Granite Countertops & Tile Back Splash & Walls
- Upstairs Loft w/ Sunken Family Room w/ Built-In Entertainment Center
- Open Living Room w/ Fireplace
- Pebble Tech Pool and Spa
- Furnishings Available Separately.

The house sold for the asking price the same week it went on the market!

Craig talks to Brady about his "Titus Tells All" book deal

After Brady was finished working on all of the properties, he was eager to tell Craig about everything he had done. Since Ron Brady Jr. could not call Craig at the Clark County Detention Center, he decided to turn his phone back on, and wait for Craig to call him.

This however was like playing Russian roulette, because when Brady's phone rang and the ID shows "CCDC," he would have no idea if it was Craig Titus or Deen Cassim on the other side of the phone. Brady did not have to wait for long; within minutes of turning his phone back on, it started to ring. The call was from the Clark County Detention Center, and Brady held his breath, hoping it was Craig on the other line. Breathing a sigh of relief, it was his buddy, Craig Titus, with an upbeat greeting the second he answered the phone.

Both men had good news to report, and Brady went first. Brady told Craig that all of the rental houses were empty, cleaned and fixed-up, and ready to be put on the market. Brady said it was a collaborative effort to get Craig and Kelly's houses on the market, with Brady's dad and Craig's mother working with him around the clock. Kelly's mom, Niki Ryan, had listed the house, and potential buyers were lined up to purchase the house.

Craig was both ecstatic and relieved, and he continuously thanked Ron over the phone. Craig then told Ron about his good news: he had been contacted by a writer/publisher that wanted to write a book about him. Craig said that he had been corresponding with a writer, Dennis Bates, founder of Muscle Missions; and Bates said he would draw up a contract and start writing the book immediately. Bates was a former bodybuilder, and he exposes the "cult of bodybuilding" and helps those that are "trapped within it to escape its clutches."

Craig said, "Bates wanted to know if I would be interested in exposing all of the corruption involved in the world of professional body building? It didn't take me long to say, 'Hell yes!' They have fucked me and Kelly over in the past, so I have wanted to do this for years." Craig said Bates told him he would fly to Vegas in a few weeks, and attend the upcoming court hearings. Craig told Brady, "After the hearings, he will come to the jail and interview me, but we have already started the book with phone interviews." Brady asked, "So is it just about bodybuilding, or will you talk about this murder case too?" Craig said, "No, for now it's just about exposing bodybuilding; after the trial he agreed to write a book about this case." Brady was excited, "That's going to be fucking huge man! I bet it turns into a movie or something. What's the title going to be for the book?" Craig said, "Titus tells all."

Cassim threatens Brady with violence but Brady still does not show up

The next morning on April 10th, Deen Cassim started calling Ron Brady Jr. again. Brady apologized for not picking up the phone for a week, but he had been busy doing some work for Craig on his rental properties. Brady told Cassim about all of the surveillance he did on the witnesses, and that he no longer needed Cassim's assistance with anything else.

This infuriated Cassim, he had worked too hard to have Brady fuck him over and drop all of his plans. Deen Cassim told Brady if he fucked this up for him (and Cassim had to do his 12 years stint at Ely State Penitentiary), he would put a hit on Brady himself! Cassim started yelling and threatened to have Brady and everyone he loved murdered in their sleep if Brady backed out at the last minute!

Brady tried to back track and explain to Cassim, "Titus has no fucking clue what's going on man. I fucked up, and want out. Titus will never be okay with any of this, much less put down a dime to have it done. Titus wants all those dumb fucks to take the stand because every time they open their mouths, he has a better case. Every single one of them is stupid as hell, especially the dumb whore!" Cassim said, "No you are the one that is stupid as hell!"

Brady still tried to reason with Cassim, "All we wanted to do was expose those pieces of shit for what they are: drug addicts, thieves, and dope pushers. Nobody wants them hurt or anything. I have video and pictures of them buying and dealing dope. Craig's lawyers have documents implicating them in embezzlement and insurance fraud. These three will end up doing more time than Titus; so we don't want anything to happen to them! Titus' revenge will be throwing those mother fuckers right back under the bus they threw him under! Titus only talked about discrediting the witnesses; and I don't want to fuck anything up for him."

Cassim said, "Well where the fuck does that leave me?" Brady said, "Look man, we got what we needed. Everything is taken care of. I am sorry to have wasted your time, but I'm fucking done with you! Kill me, what the fuck ever, just stop calling, and leave me the fuck alone!" Brady hung the phone up on Cassim, and Cassim called him right back with a less aggressive attitude.

The power struggle shifted, and Cassim had to be very careful with his words in order to continue manipulating Ron Brady Jr. Cassim knew he had to trap Brady into something, and the investigators could doctor or accidentally delete the recordings. Brady answered the phone by telling Cassim to "stop fucking calling me!"

With a calmer tone, Cassim picked right back up where he left off. Cassim said, "Look I understand where you're coming from, but I can't just leave these guys hanging. These guys are connected, and they are some bad mother fuckers! They won't just do something to you; they will clip me for fucking vouching for you. Look man, you got this fucking thing rolling, not me, and it's out of my fucking control. If we back out, there will be bloodshed. How is that fair to me, I was just trying to help you out? You're a good guy; you know this is wrong! If you don't give them something, they will kill me, and I am scared!"

Brady sat in silence, and his conscience was eating him up; he did lead Cassim on, and he was responsible for all of this. Cassim said, "Listen what we could do is just have the witnesses scared shitless and nobody will get hurt. This would be about half, $10,000. What do you say?" Brady did not have that kind of money. His conscience was killing him, but there was nothing left for him to do; the only way he knew how to cope was through drugs. In an effort to step away from reality, Brady went on a drug binge. He was wired out of his mind on meth, and tweaked out for over 48 hours without any sleep. After a few days, Brady crashed, and went to bed and slept for a day and a half; when his cell phone eventually woke him back up.

On April 14th, at approximately 12:40 p.m. Cassim called Brady, and their conversation was recorded on the jail monitoring system. Brady could barely remember his last conversation with Cassim, but he remembers feeling guilty because Cassim told him his guys were going to kill him. Still, Brady was flipping back and forth, and this was irritating Cassim. In a somber voice Cassim told Brady, "I have given up on this whole thing because you are not serious at all. You are playing games with my life man, and it's all over for me; I am fucking done. I thought you were my friend, but you stabbed me in the back! How could you fucking do this to me man?"

Brady told Cassim, "I am not going to do that to you. You are my friend, and I don't want anything to happen to you." Cassim said he did not want anything to happen to Brady or his family either. Brady said, "I want to go through with this, but I only want to scare those guys into telling the truth on the stand. My problem is, I don't have thousands of dollars in my back pocket, and I don't want to fuck this case up for Titus. You know what I'm sayin'? Everything is going according to plan, and Titus needs those mother fuckers around; his defense lawyers will get the truth out of them. With the autopsy report and the witness' bull shit stories, Craig will be a free man. I can't fucking screw this up for him! You know what I mean?"

Cassim could tell that he was getting nowhere being nice to Brady, so he flipped his switch, and started back up with the physical threats. Cassim said, "You are the one who started this whole fucking thing, and it will end with you, one way or another." Cassim had a piece of paper with all of Brady's personal information about his family. He started to read aloud all of the details and then told Brady that the killers had the same information. Cassim said, "You need to come up with $10,000 by tomorrow. I don't give a shit how you get it, you can fucking rob a bank for all I care, but you better fucking have it by tomorrow. Talk to Titus' family, and tell them you need it for something with Craig."

Scared out of his mind, Brady told Cassim, "I will talk to his mother, and see if she can help me out." Cassim said, "Uou better! No more second, third, or fourth chances again! When you get the money, you will give it to my ex-girlfriend. Edison and all of those other guys are out. Meet her at Starbucks tomorrow at noon, and I'm not playin' with you, you better fucking have it." On April 11th an undercover officer, disguised as Cassim's ex-girlfriend, sat at the Starbuck's for over an hour, and Ron Brady Jr. never showed up.

(At this point, the investigators should have backed off, but they of course did not since the entire frame-up was unethical and illegal to begin with.)

Deen Cassim incessantly called Ron Brady Jr. at all hours of the day, and Brady continued to ignore the phone calls. Brady wanted to talk to Titus, but did not want to risk answering the phone and having Cassim on the other line. After a couple of days, Brady thought, "fuck it," and answered the next call he received from the jail. To his relief, it was Craig Titus, wanting to talk to him about the book deal. Craig told Brady the book was going to be huge, and someone had contacted his family about possibly writing a "made for television" movie or a "screenplay" about his case. Ron was pumped, hell he could have a part in this movie; both men talked about all of the possibilities. Craig said, "Look, it's not a done deal; I don't even know if it is a legitimate deal. That's what fucking sucks about being behind bars. I want to personally look into it, and make sure it's not just a scam, or someone trying to take advantage of my mom."

Brady asked if it was the guy from Muscle Missions, and Craig said, "No, it's someone else, totally different; this would be about this case." Brady said he would get the information from Craig's mother, and see what he could find out. Craig thanked Ron, and told him he was a loyal friend. He asked Ron if he was keeping his nose clean on the streets, and Ron lied and said that he was; Craig was so proud of him, and Ron did not want him to know how he had majorly fucked up!

Ron Brady Jr. had been a "fuck-up" for most of his life, and for the first time, he felt as if he was important. Brady was ready to tackle the world, and turn his life around. The first step was to stay away from drugs. Brady vowed to himself, starting that day, he would never touch that shit again. For nearly two weeks, Brady avoided Deen Cassim, and Cassim was beyond livid. Cassim started intimidating Brady's father this time. When Brady's dad approached his son about the phone calls, Ronnie opened up and told his dad some bits and pieces about everything.

Brady told his dad that Cassim had tricked him into thinking he had a friend that could follow and intimidate the witnesses in Craig Titus' case. Brady said the witnesses were lying, and doing drugs, so he only wanted to scare or discredit them. Cassim wanted more, and had been threatening his life if he didn't give him money to do something to these witnesses. Brady said that he didn't want anything done to anyone, but he was afraid for his life. Brady's dad said, "Ronnie, I want you to listen to me, more likely than not, this is just a scam, a desperate criminal trying to shake you down. But you can't just turn off the phone and ignore this guy forever. You have to tell him that you are not interested, nobody has that kind of money, and you will call the police if the threats don't stop." Ron Brady, Sr. had never been to prison, and he did not understand, those guys don't just go away when you politely ask them to stop. Brady thanked his dad and gave him a hug; and his dad said, "Ronnie I love you, do the right thing son."

More than anything Brady wanted to do the right thing; he did not want anybody hurt, and he was willing to do whatever it took to make it right. Brady decided that when Cassim called again, he would answer and say whatever he needed to say, to stop anything bad from happening. Brady would give him all the money he had, and tell Cassim it was all he could do, "Take the money and leave me alone!"

Dennis Bates coming to Las Vegas to write "Titus Tells All"

Craig thought that the president of "Muscle Missions" was a little off of his rocker, with his radical views on Satanism and Bodybuilding; but at that point, the entire bodybuilding world had turned their back on him, and Dennis was the only guy that reached out to help. Craig actually enjoyed talking with Dennis and his wife on the phone, and looked forward to their upcoming visit. Bates and his wife would be attending a fitness workshop in Las Vegas, and they planned an extended visit to help Craig and his family out.

At this time, they could also work on the book Bates planned on writing and publishing about bodybuilding. Dennis Bates, through

Muscle Missions, wrote and published a book called: "Anabolic Outlaw"; a story about a man that was a "pot smoking, cocaine snorting, pill popping, acid dropping, whiskey drinking, steroid shooting bodybuilder." In the fickle world of bodybuilding, Craig Titus knew he had to remain relevant if he was going to be able to pick back up where he left off with his federation when he returned. He was excited about the book because it would help him do that.

Every time he talked to Ron Brady Jr., Craig bounced ideas off of him to get his opinion about the upcoming book. The conversation would inevitably lead to talk about the potential movie script, and they had fun talking about plot lines and characters. What actor would play their character on the big screen was discussed on a daily basis. Ron Brady Jr. jokingly said, "Brad Pitt or Tom Cruise will play me; and all those mother fuckers that lied about everything, they ain't gonna be in shit. Their ass has already been written out of the script." Brady laughed and said, "What gay actor will play Shawn Ray? There can be a love story about him taking it up the ass by his transgender boyfriend/girlfriend Sasha!" Craig busted out laughing; he had not laughed that hard in a long time. It felt good to laugh, and with this book, he saw a silver lining at the end.

Homicide Detectives are 0 for 2 in the Evidence Department

Clark County Officials were taping every single one of Craig Titus' phone calls, and Dean O'Kelley, Rob Wilson, and Robert Daskas were all listening to each and every word that came out of Titus' mouth. In the taped conversations between Brady and Titus, Brady never brought up anything about Deen Cassim, and there was never a word mentioned about a "Murder for Hire."

Craig Titus had no idea that O'Kelley and Wilson were doing everything in their power to frame Ron Brady Jr. in order to charge Craig Titus with the crime. Unfortunately for these homicide detectives, nothing they were doing, with either the murder or the murder-for-hire investigation, was working. Not only did they fail to provide any physical evidence linking Craig Titus to a murder; they had no evidence to frame him with the murder for hire allegations. The investigators and prosecutor wanted their bonuses and promotions; but most importantly, they wanted to "save face!" They did not want to look like huge assholes on national television in such a high-profile case.

Most frustrating for the authorities were the hours poured into taping and listening to all of Craig Titus' phone conversations without coming up with a single lead. They could not tie either Ron Brady Jr. or Craig Titus to a crime. In fact, Brady was doing the opposite of what the veteran detectives expected him to do; Brady appeared to turn his life around, and stay away from drugs. Ron Brady Jr. was thinking clearly, staying out of trouble, and avoiding Deen Cassim like the plague.

With nothing else to go on with the murder-for-hire plot, they decided to point a finger at Titus' book deal, and authorities insisted the book deal was code for the plot to kill the witnesses in the Titus' murder trial. The authorities said Titus and Brady were speaking in code, and justified no longer recording Brady's phone calls. Instead, homicide detective Dean O'Kelley would "transcribe" every phone encounter between Ron Brady Jr., Deen Cassim, and Craig Titus. When the incessant phone calls from Deen Cassim started back up, Brady turned back to drugs in order to cope with the mess. The investigators knew that they needed some money to switch hands if they wanted to frame Craig with the crime, so they put the pressure on Deen Cassim to close the deal out.

On April 20, 2006 Brady felt brave and answered Deen Cassim's phone call; Cassim laid into Brady, cussing him out, telling Brady that he was a worthless piece of shit that was going to get them both killed. He said, "I trusted you, and you fucked me over, and now they are going to fuck you over!" Brady talked Cassim down, and said that he had some money, but not much. He would give him what he had if he would please stop calling and harassing he and his family. Brady told Cassim that he did not want to get rid of anybody because that would hurt the case, and get Craig in more trouble.

Brady said, "If your guys have to do something, just have them tell the witnesses they have pictures of them buying and selling drugs, and make them tell the truth on the stand!" Cassim yelled, "What the fuck are you talking about you moron?" Brady said, "I will give you every fucking thing I have, if you will just stop calling and threatening me; I want you to leave me the fuck alone!" Deen Cassim was furious, "The guys I work with murder people; they don't just scare people, or take pictures of them selling dope." Brady said, "I don't want them to do shit; just take my fucking money and leave me alone!" Cassim said that he didn't know if they would go for that, but it would buy Brady a little time for now.

Brady said, "All I have is $500 dollars, but I could put that down and pay another $500 in May." Cassim told Brady he would talk to his guys and get back with him, but only if Brady agreed to talk to Craig one last time. Brady had never said a word to Craig about any of it, and was not going to bring it up then; but he told Cassim he would talk to Craig just to get Cassim off his back.

The investigators knew that Ron Brady Jr. was vulnerable, and they could eventually get him to put some money down. As an addict, Brady's mind was jumping back and forth; trying to do the right thing and wanting to do the wrong thing. He didn't want to use drugs anymore, but felt like that was his only escape. Brady was weak because the drugs clouded his mind, and he was not making rational decisions. In spite of it all, Ron Brady Jr. knew the difference between right and wrong; and no matter how clouded his mind became, he refused to take another person's life.

Deen Cassim called Ron Brady Jr. on April 21st, 2006, and told Brady that the hit- man was not happy, but he would take the down payment as they had discussed the day before. Cassim told Brady he had a couple of days to come up with $1,500, and he would call him later to make arrangements to make the trade. Brady argued with Cassim and said they had discussed $1,000 not $1,500. Cassim snapped back, "Are you fucking kidding me? He is giving you a gift! The extra five is for his travel expenses!" Brady agreed to pay the money, even though he did not have a dime to his name. He was relieved to have a few days to come up with the cash, but did not know where to turn; so he turned back to the pipe to escape from the world. Getting lost in drugs helped him forget everything else; and with his phone turned off, he put Deen Cassim out of his mind for good.

BOOK DEAL OR MURDER PLOT?

On April 27th 2006, Dennis Bates met with Craig Titus for the first time at the Clark County Detention Center. Over the previous few years, Bates and his wife had handed out free copies of his book, "Anabolic Outlaw" and other "Muscle Missions" pamphlets about the "Evil of bodybuilding" at IFBB and NPC sanctioned events like the Arnold and Olympia. Bates' wife remembers trying to give Craig Titus some information a year before in Ohio, and Titus respectfully declined the hand-outs. Bates had been a thorn in the side of the bodybuilding community for years. As a former addict and bodybuilder, he felt led by his Christian faith to expose and help others that struggled as he once did.

Bates and Titus had shared many letters back and forth, and talked on the phone several times while he was incarcerated, and Dennis felt like Craig would recognize him when they finally saw each other for the first time at Clark County Detention Center. When they met, it was not "in person," because communication was through a video camera and monitor, but Craig was excited about the meeting nonetheless.

As the video camera came on, and Craig saw Dennis Bates for the first time, Craig did not recognize him; Titus apologized, and said that he "runs into so many people, it's hard for him to remember everybody's faces." The two men only had ten minutes to talk, but they had time to exchange ideas, and Craig asked Bates if he and his wife could visit with his wife, Kelly Ryan? Bates said that they would take the time to schedule a visit, and then the screen cut off at the CCDC.

Dennis Bates called the Religious Coordinator at the CCDC, making arrangements for religious visitations with both Craig and Kelly. This allowed them to visit daily, rather than just twice a week. The general population could only have two visits a week per visitor; this would add up to twenty minutes a week; so they were both fortunate that the man writing his book was a minister.

After the second visit, Craig had a name for the book that he wanted written and published by Muscle Missions, "How to Be an IFBB Pro Bodybuilder - The Truth and Nothing but the Truth!" Craig said that he wanted to expose all of the drugs that it took to be an IFBB pro like himself; Craig had journals that he had kept from way back that listed all of the drugs, dosages, etc. and that they could publish those as a way of exposing the horrendous amounts of drugs that he used to become an IFBB pro.

Bates shot this idea down however; he wanted to take more of an autobiographical approach, and he didn't want to glorify drugs in any way. Craig reluctantly agreed with Dennis Bates, and both men were onboard to have Bates write and publish the Craig Titus story. Dennis Bates was from Columbus, Ohio, but said he could record all of their exchanges over the phone, and write the book from their taped conversations.

Before Dennis Bates and his wife flew back to Ohio, they placed money in both Craig and Kelly's accounts for commissary, and handed Craig a copy of the drafted agreement that he wrote up prior to his last visit to allow Muscle Missions permission to write his "Tell All" book. After Craig signed the agreement, the two men discussed some more details, and then Bates said that he would begin working on the book once he got back to Ohio. Dan Solomon read a letter written by Titus on his bodybuilding talk radio show on air, and he said that Craig Titus wanted all of his fans to know that he was 100 % not guilty, and he's working on a book, set to be published in the future called: "Titus Tells All."

Craig Titus: "The only evidence Daskas had on me was the words he put in Megan Foley's mouth. Once I outed his affair, it became a vendetta. I screwed up his run for Congress, and he made me pay the price."

Section Four: Corruption in the System

CHAPTER 1

Prosecutorial and Judicial Misconduct

Second Bail Hearing
Craig and Kelly's second Bail Hearing was on April 18, 2006 in the courtroom of the "Honorable" Judge Jackie Glass. Lawyers for Kelly Ryan and Craig Titus argued that the prosecutors had not shown *how* they thought Melissa James died before her body was found in the trunk of Ryan's car. The Defense lawyers told the judge that the prosecution "had not proven that Melissa James was either kidnapped or murdered. All the prosecution did was pitch a lot of circumstantial theories out there without any physical proof to back the theories up; just testimony from a witness that had credibility issues."

When the judge mentioned she believed Craig Titus and Kelly Ryan might be a flight risk, their defense attorneys said they were willing to put down a significant amount of money for bail. They said, "$25,000 for Ryan and $250,000 bail for Titus would ensure the couple would not skip town before the trial," but the judge was not convinced. Judge Jackie Glass denied the couple bail, and ruled that they were to remain at the Clark County Detention Center.

Defense Motion to have charges thrown out
The defense lawyers' next move was to challenge the grand jury indictment, so they filed a motion to have it thrown out of court. Attorney Richard A. Schonfeld filed a petition seeking oral arguments in support of a petition for Writ of Habeas Corpus in State v. Titus, Ryan and Gross. Schonfeld detailed why the complaint charging

Craig Titus with murder, kidnapping and arson should be dismissed: "Craig Titus was indicted by a Clark County Grand Jury on March 23, 2006 and charged with Murder with Use of a Deadly Weapon, First Degree Kidnapping, and Third Degree Arson following the death of Melissa James."

Titus' defense lawyers claimed there was no evidence presented to the Grand Jury related to the charge of First Degree kidnapping. There was also no evidence presented that a taser gun was used on Melissa James, or that duct tape or a wire ligature were used as deadly weapons. A detailed list of "claims of no evidence during testimony" was presented. Also cited in the petition was that: "The State presented absolutely no evidence related to the kidnapping charge. In fact, the State did not even present one theory as to a kidnapping charge. The word kidnapping was never even used."

Also stated was: "According to police interrogations, and evidence submitted to the court, Jeff Schwimmer testified that he observed Megan Pierson, Jeremy Foley, and Greg Ruiz all using Cocaine, Xanax, OxyContin. This statement contradicts Megan Pierson's statement on the stand, and is apparent that Megan Pierson lied under oath when she said she did not drink or do drugs when she was with Titus and Ryan. The Supreme Court held that 'habitual users of drugs become notorious liars who cannot distinguish images and facts from illusions and realities.'"

Defense Attorney Richard Schonfeld asserted that during the grand jury hearings, Craig Titus' Due Process Rights were violated because the Deputy District Attorney engaged in malicious and unethical prosecution when Robert Daskas added the charges of kidnapping to the complaint in an effort to trump up the charges against the defendant.

It stated the prosecutor provided no evidence to the grand jury that explained the kidnapping charges. His document claimed the charges were never addressed, and there was absolutely no probable cause to warrant the additional charges. The charge was added to Kelly Ryan's complaint to punish her for not testifying against her husband. It was added to both of their charges, to stack the charges, which resulted in a charge of First Degree Murder that was not supported by probable cause.

According to the NVPAC, the Nevada Advisory Council for Prosecuting:

The Role of the Prosecutor – Seeking Justice

The prosecutor is held to a higher standard than other attorneys in our legal system due to the great responsibility that comes with the position. As the United States Supreme Court proclaimed in ***Berger v. United States***:

> The *[prosecutor]* is the representative of sovereignty whose obligation to govern impartially is as compelling as its obligation to govern at all; and whose interest, therefore, **in a criminal prosecution is not that it shall win a case, but that justice shall be done**. As such, he is in a peculiar and very definite sense the servant of the law, the twofold aim of which is that guilt shall not escape or innocence suffer. He may prosecute with earnestness and vigor - indeed, he should do so. But, while he may strike hard blows, he is not at liberty to strike foul ones. **It is as much his duty to refrain from improper methods calculated to produce a wrongful conviction as it is to use every legitimate means to bring about a just one.**

Exercising Prosecutorial Discretion:

The prosecutor's authority to exercise discretion in charging decisions is a key component of our criminal justice system. RPC 3.8(a) requires that the prosecutor refrain from prosecuting a charge not supported by probable cause, while national standards establish that a prosecution should only proceed on the basis of sufficient admissible evidence to support a conviction. **The prosecutor should only file charges that adequately encompass the offense or offenses believed to have been committed and that rationally address the nature and scope of the alleged criminal activity.**

Fairness at Trial & Trial Publicity:

Prosecutors are subject to intense scrutiny of statements at any stage of trial that may constitute prejudicial misconduct. The standard is "whether a prosecutor's statements so infected the proceedings with unfairness as to make the resulting conviction a denial of due process."

The prohibition on extrajudicial statements set forth in RPC 3.6(a) extends to statements by the prosecutor in a criminal proceeding likely to increase public condemnation of the accused.

Kelly Ryan's mother passes away

Unfortunately for Craig and Kelly, they did not have an ethical prosecutor or judge, and were denied bail once again. Sadly, on April 22nd, Kelly Ryan's mother, Nikki Ryan, passed away from a heart attack at the age of 61. Most heartbreaking was that Kelly Ryan would never see her mother again due to the fact that she had been denied bail by Judge Jackie Glass. Had Robert Daskas not stacked the charges to punish Kelly Ryan for not testifying against her husband, she would have been granted bail, and had the opportunity to spend time with her mother before she passed away.

To Robert Daskas, it was all just a game; strategizing and making moves to ensure a conviction. To Craig Titus and Kelly Ryan, it was their life. Kelly's life was robbed of those last three days to spend with her mother here on earth. If anyone ever found out everything Robert Daskas had done, and word ever got out how his misconduct resulted in Kelly Ryan not receiving bail or being able to attend her mother's funeral, his political career would be over before it ever got started!

Put up or Shut up Time for Deen Cassim and Ron Brady Jr.

Deen Cassim had been trying to reach Ron Brady Jr. for over two weeks, but Brady had ignored him, and had made himself scarce. The homicide detectives had completely lost their patience with Deen Cassim, and told him they were done fucking around. It was either "put up" or "shut up" time, and if Cassim could not deliver what he promised, their deal was off, and Cassim would be sent directly to prison.

PROSECUTORIAL AND JUDICIAL MISCONDUCT

The game of cat and mouse had been going on between Cassim and Brady for over six weeks. The detectives put Cassim in a room, and told him he could not leave until Ron Brady answered the fucking phone! The detectives had given him Brady's home phone number before, and nobody would answer that phone anymore, so they gave him Brady's dad's cell phone number. They hoped that having that number would change everything, and Cassim planned on scaring the shit out of Brady and his family to finish everything off.

Brady did not want to give Deen Cassim money, and he sure as hell did not want anyone hurt. Brady had his cell phone and home phone turned off, but that would not be enough; he would eventually be forced to give in to the authorities. Cassim called Ron Brady Sr., and asked to speak with his son. His father thought that Ronnie had dealt with that thug a while back, and was reluctant to take the phone to him.

Brady knew he could no longer blow Cassim off or both he and his family would be dead. Brady told Cassim he did not have $1,500, but he could try to find a grand. Cassim told Brady he would give him a pass one more time; he only needed to show up with a thousand dollars for wasting everybody's time. Brady knew he could no longer blow Cassim off or both he and his family would be dead. Brady told Cassim he did not have $1,500, but he could try to find a grand. Cassim told Brady he would give him a pass one more time; he only needed to show up with a thousand dollars for wasting everybody's time.

Brady agreed to the deal, and Cassim told him to meet his ex-girlfriend the next day at Starbucks to give her the cash. Brady didn't know where he would come up with the money, but he would try to find it somehow before he met Cassim's ex-girlfriend; he had 24 hours. Brady took all of his valuables to a pawn shop, and came up with $500 dollars. He tried to wheel and deal all night; but the night soon turned to morning, and yesterday was now today. On May 17th 2006, Brady took everything he had, and hoped for the best. Around 1:30 p.m. Brady drove to meet Cassim's ex-girlfriend (actually an undercover agent); he felt nervous but was mostly relieved to finally put an end to the harassment by Deen Cassim.

SWIFT INJUSTICE

At 1:55 p.m., Cassim called Brady to make sure he was following through, and Brady told him that he had just pulled up at the Starbuck's. As he walked to the front door, he told Cassim that he was wearing a button down shirt, blue jeans, and white tennis shoes. After he sat down at a table, he told Cassim that he had a black suitcase on the table.

Still on the phone, at 2:02 p.m. the undercover officer posing as Cassim's ex-girlfriend is heard greeting Brady in the background. Brady handed the agent an envelope with $500, he told her he would give her the rest of the money the next day. Cassim was on the phone the entire time the transaction went down, and he was upset with Brady because it was short.

Cassim didn't know if this would be enough money to have him released from jail, so he again threatened Brady's life to show up the next day, at the same time, with the rest of the money; Brady swore to Cassim that he would, saying he told him he wouldn't let him down. After the "drop-off" was over, the detectives photo-copied, processed, and impounded the cash that Brady had given the undercover agent.

Brady was forced to sell drugs on the street to come up with the remaining money. The entire time he was working the streets, Cassim called him every five minutes harassing Brady about the money. Cassim became belligerent, threatening to slit Brady's throat and Brady finally told Cassim to fuck off and stop calling him, and he would have the rest of the money in his girl's hands the next day. Brady kept his word, and met the ex-girlfriend/undercover agent and gave her the remaining amount. After the second "drop off", the additional five hundred dollars were photo-copied, processed and impounded just like the day before.

On phone patrol at the CCDC, Robert Daskas listened to every single conversation that Craig Titus made on the phone. In the conversations between Craig Titus and Ron Brady Jr., they never once discussed anything about a "Murder for Hire," or anything remotely close to it. So what was Robert Daskas thinking, had he lost his mind? (To give him the benefit of the doubt, if I was as obsessed over Craig Titus as Robert Daskas appeared to be, and I spent thousands of hours listening to every single one of his phone calls, and came up with nothing, I would probably go a little nuts too!)

Robert Daskas had nothing on the phone recordings to implicate Craig of any crime, so he asserted that Craig and Brady must have been speaking in "code" about the murder when they were talking about the "book deal." Whether Daskas had actually lost his marbles or he really believed that this legitimate book deal was a huge ruse laced with secret messages and code words will probably never be revealed.

Dennis Bates and Craig Titus had started the book writing process, and talked to each other every day at length. Bates recorded their phone calls all summer long, and he started turning Titus' words into a book. Muscle Missions was billed $1,056.74 for all of the collect phone calls made to Bates' office from the Clark County Detention Center. Craig offered to help pay for the bill by donating some of his workout equipment to Muscle Missions, but Bates thought it would be too expensive to get all of the equipment back, so he offered to sell Titus' gym equipment online instead. The gym equipment was sold on eBay, and the two continued to work on his tell-all book.

Robert Daskas knew there was a legitimate book deal, and they were not speaking in "code". With nothing to lose, and in a pathetic attempt to get ahead, Daskas leaked more of Craig Titus' phone conversations to the press. Craig's friend read him the article, and Craig felt betrayed by all of his so-called friends. He was even more shocked at how low the prosecution would sink to drag Craig's name through the mud before the case even went to trial.

Murder case records detail of sordid lives

GLENN PUIT REVIEW-JOURNAL: For more than a decade, Craig Titus and Kelly Ryan knew what it was like to be at the pinnacle of fitness and weightlifting competitions. But as their careers on the national fitness stage wound down, the two at times were living a wild, drug- and sex-fueled lifestyle in Las Vegas, according to police statements and grand jury testimony in the couple's murder case.

For example, **according to a police inventory report observed by the Review-Journal, police searched the couple's home in southwest Las Vegas in December and found a videotape depicting "footage of a sexual encounter with Titus, Ryan and an unidentified female." The report does not indicate that Melissa James, the couple's personal assistant and the woman who Titus and Ryan are now accused of killing, is on the tape.**

According to police reports obtained by the newspaper, Gregory Ruiz of Las Vegas told homicide detectives, **'Titus and Ryan were into an alternative lifestyle; they are into swinging;** they like having girl-friends over. Titus used to go tell me all the time to have sex with Kelly.' Ruiz said that he was not into that because he was in a 'straight up family; me and my wife aren't into that.'

Ruiz told police he went into a clothing line business venture with Titus because Titus was a huge celebrity in the weightlifting world, but he soon realized Titus had a drug problem. Ruiz said he witnessed Titus injecting OxyContin, a strong and often-abused narcotic pain reliever.

'Titus didn't seem to care who saw him doing it,' he said. Ruiz said that he would get embarrassed because he would do it in front of everybody. Ruiz said, 'He always carries little needles ... and it was the most awful thing ever.' Titus had already told police he had steroids in his house at the time of his arrest in James' death.

In addition, Ryan's self-described best friend, Megan Michelle Pierson, told police James once told her Ryan was shooting cocaine with a needle; Megan believed 'she was becoming very addicted to cocaine.' Pierson said she and a friend were planning an intervention for Ryan. Gregory Ruiz, although he admitted he had never seen Kelly shoot up drugs, he knew that she did a lot of drugs, and he said that both Craig and Kelly had a serious drug problem.

Titus' defense attorney, Richard Schonfeld said that the drug allegations against Titus will be contested. In addition, Schonfeld said the credibility of several witnesses who gave statements to authorities will come into serious question once the trial unfolds. 'Drug use affects *peoples' credibility,' Schonfeld said. 'There is case law on it.' A motive in the case remains convoluted. Titus and Ryan originally told police they suspected James, who has an arrest history for identity theft, was stealing from them and possibly planning to steal their identities."*

The sole purpose of leaking the police reports to the Las Vegas Review Journal was to make Craig and Kelly look like they were morally defunct, and to further prejudice the end results of the Melissa James Murder case. Why else would the Las Vegas Homicide Detectives release information about "swinging, and sex tapes" to the Las Vegas Review Journal? This had nothing to do with the case, but they knew if they released it, the Las Vegas Journal would print it. The paper sensationalized the trial to turn a buck, and sparked interest by dumbing down the audience, and "tabloiding" up the story.

Robert Daskas also knew that most of the "druggie" friends' statements made during the police interrogations would never make it to trial, and those witnesses would never take the stand because of their involvement in narcotics. The investigators purposefully leaked their interviews, so that it would show up in print, and hopefully seep into the subconscious of everyone in Las Vegas.

If they were called to serve on a jury in the case, in the back of their minds, they would believe that Craig Titus led a "sordid life," and would already be prejudiced against him. This was a mind game Robert Daskas played with Craig Titus, knocking him down through the media. If Titus went into a trial already defeated, then Daskas would have a huge advantage going into plea negotiations. Robert Daskas also knew that a potential run for congress was in his future, and the bigger the headlines, the bigger the audience!

Deen Cassim is re-sentenced by Judge Bonaventure
One of the greatest miscarriages of justice, and proof that prosecutorial and judicial misconduct are alive and well in the Las Vegas judicial system, was on June 10th 2006 when Deen Cassim was released from the Clark County Detention Center after he worked as an informant for the investigators and prosecution.

SWIFT INJUSTICE

Robert Daskas and Judge Joseph Bonaventure had Cassim's original sentence revoked. He was resentenced to probation and was able to walk out of the Clark County Detention Center a free man. The district attorney (and former prosecutor in the Binion trial) attempted to do the same thing with David Gomez. Gomez was caught stealing legal papers from Rick Tabish, and the set up fell apart. He later confessed that the prosecutor, David Roger, pressured him into setting Tabish up on a Murder for Hire plot against the gardener, and they set him up to testify against Tabish. The second time around, with Cassim, they were successful when Robert Daskas and the District Attorney's office did the exact same thing.

Isn't it strange how anytime there is corruption involved in a high-profile case, the same people are always involved? Take a look at Judge Jackie Glass; she sentenced O.J. Simpson to 33 years for "kidnapping and robbery" because he was with a group of men trying to collect what had been stolen from him. They told the men not to move, and because one man said he had a gun, Simpson was charged with kidnapping. Deen Cassim pushed a man into a room at gun point (which actually *is* kidnapping) and assaulted the victim as he attempted to rob him of $150,000. Comparing these two crimes, O.J. Simpson and Deen Cassim: Judge Bonaventure and Robert Daskas threw out Cassim's sentence letting him walk free, while O.J. is serving a 33- year sentence handed down to him by Judge Glass.

Marc Saggese said that the benefits afforded to Cassim by authorities were inappropriate and that he now thinks Titus was the victim of a setup. "Deen Cassim is a violent criminal, and they've let a violent criminal out on the streets," Saggese said. "I've never seen anything like this." **Saggese said he has never seen a defendant who already has been sentenced to prison resentenced in the same case after cooperating with authorities. "Do you know how hard it is to amend a sentencing like this**? Saggese said. "I'm floored. I have never, ever, heard of a resentencing of a convicted felon like that." The prosecutor in the case that recommended Cassim be released, Robert Daskas, declined comment, which was odd. Robert Daskas never declined comment about Craig Titus after he leaked information to the press.

Meeting between the detectives, prosecutor and Tony Gross to strike a deal

The lengths that homicide detectives Dean O'Kelley and Rob Wilson, and prosecutor Robert Daskas, went to, in an effort to destroy Craig Titus were extraordinary. Since there was not enough evidence to convict Craig Titus of murdering Melissa James, their focus turned to framing Craig Titus with Solicitation for Murder. To do this, five days after Deen Cassim was released from prison, on June 15th, Homicide Detectives Dean O'Kelley, Rob Wilson, and Prosecutor Robert Daskas met with Anthony Gross, his parents and Gross' attorney to discuss an unusual deal concocted by the prosecution pertaining to an arrangement to set Craig Titus up on a fake "Murder for Hire" plot.

At the meeting, an agreement was made between the prosecution and the defense that if Gross cooperated with the investigation, posed dead in the trunk of a car, as though he had been murdered, and allowed them to take pictures, the prosecution would request that the judge cut Tony Gross from Craig Titus and Kelly Ryan in the trial. When Gross had a separate trial in front of Judge Jackie Glass, Daskas would also request that Gross receive probation, and not have to serve any time in prison. In addition, the prosecution would fly Tony Gross to Chicago to stay with family members until he had to return back in court.

The deal was unbelievable; Gross' posse jumped right on it, and without hesitation, agreed to help the detectives and prosecutor set-up Craig Titus in an effort to frame him for Solicitation of Murder. With this phony picture of a murdered Anthony Gross, the detectives believed that this would trick Titus into thinking that a hit had actually taken place. With a little luck, it would force Titus into a false confession, and it would seal the murder deal for O'Kelley and Daskas.

Detectives have Tony Gross "play dead" while they take pictures

On June 22nd the elaborate hoax was carried out in the parking lot of Home Improvement. The detectives placed Tony Gross in the trunk of a car and laid him on his side. Gross' wrists were duct-taped behind his back, and he had duct tape over his mouth and ankles. With the help from the Metropolitan Police Department's Crime Scene

Analysts, they applied make-up and prosthetics on Anthony Gross' face to make it appear as if he had been shot, and poured fake blood from the "bullet wound" and made it appear as if the blood was pouring out of his head and all over his clothes and the inside of the trunk.

Several photographs were taken of Gross while he pretended to be dead in the trunk of his mother's white Lexus. The detectives cut Anthony Gross' electronic ankle monitor off that allowed authorities to track his whereabouts under the terms of his release. Dean O'Kelley claimed he did this to make it more believable. (But in the pictures, the monitor would have never been seen. He was wearing pants, and they had duct tape all over him; they could have simply placed the duct tape over the device.) This was just an excuse, because they knew that once the monitor was cut, the judge would be alerted, forcing him to have a meeting with everyone about the situation. By cutting off the monitor and forcing the meeting, the judge would be prejudiced against Craig Titus. This made it more likely she would rule against him the next month in court, during his hearing to have his charges dismissed due to prosecutorial misconduct during the court hearings.

Tony Gross flies to Chicago

Gross had already packed his bags for Chicago, anticipating that he would be there for a couple of months until he had to return to court. After he took a shower, and got his bags ready to go, Detective Dean O'Kelley picked Tony Gross up and took him back to his office at the Metropolitan Police Department. Gross remained in Dean O'Kelley's office until 5:00 a.m. the next morning, at which time he escorted Gross to the McCarran International Airport in Las Vegas, Nevada, where Gross had an early morning, cross-country flight to Chicago, Illinois courtesy of the Clark County District Attorney's office.

The "vacation" was not for his protection. If that were the case, they would have had him in hiding, along with Megan and Jeremy, back in March when the alleged "hits" were being set up. Ron Brady Jr. was able to take photos and videos of all three of these people buying, selling, and using drugs from March through the first week of June 2005. If their lives were in danger, they would have been warned and hidden by the government, and an outside entity like the FBI would have been brought in to investigate the alleged hits on these witnesses.

The alleged "Murder for Hire" would have never been investigated and set up by the same detectives and prosecutor working on the original Craig Titus case, the "murder"/overdose of Melissa James. (It appears Tony's big talk about his family being "connected in Chicago" was actually true! It would become even more intriguing as his "mob defending" attorney would later pull out even more tricks from his hat, eventually making all of Tony Gross' charges disappear.)

After Tony Gross flew off across country, his House Arrest Officer from the Metro police department realized that Tony's ankle monitor had been cut. The Metro Homicide detectives claimed they had to cut the monitor to make it look believable in the pictures. It just slipped their mind to notify Gross' House Arrest officer, that they cut the monitor off and flew him to Chicago. This justification by was laughable!

For one, the second that the ankle bracelet was cut on this "violent" criminal (he was charged alongside Craig Titus and Kelly Ryan for Melissa James' death), the House Arrest officer would have been notified through Metro. The Homicide Detectives and Crime Scene Analysts were colleagues with the House Arrest Officer, since they all worked for the Las Vegas Metropolitan Police Department. (Remember, everybody has one boss: the Sheriff; and all agencies are merged into one under Metro.)

Oops, we forgot to inform the officer we cut off Gross' monitor

According to the court and police documents, later the next day, the House Arrest Officer stopped by Tony Gross' parents' home (where Tony Gross lived) and asked why he removed the monitor. George Remo Gross, Tony's father, told him that he could not answer that question. When the officer asked where Tony was located, Mr. Gross once again refused to cooperate.

According to Gross' father, "The officer monitoring the house arrest status seemed to be very upset about Anthony having gone missing. When I contacted homicide detective O'Kelley, he told me to tell the officer that a high-level supervisor with the House Arrest Section of Metro had just been advised about the situation, and to call him directly if he had any other questions."

When the Metro officer attempted to call the detective, he received no reply, so he was forced to report Anthony Remo Gross missing to the Clark County courts. According to the report filled out by the detectives, this officer "Called the homicide detectives to inform them that he had secured an arrest warrant from District Judge Jackie Glass."

Bullshit! If this really happened, any parent would become defensive and upset that their son was going to be wrongfully arrested and brought back for another charge, after homicide detectives and the district attorney just set everything up for his release! A parent would think, "They just set up an innocent man on a fake murder- for- hire-plot, and let a violent criminal free just to send Craig Titus to prison! What's to stop them from setting up my kid as well to further the witch hunt against Craig and Kelly?"

Any normal parent in that situation would not arrogantly brush this Metro officer under the rug when his son's freedom was in jeopardy. No, what a parent would have done (especially those as over-protective of their son as the Gross' were) would have said, "Look, I can't go into details, but call Metro Homicide Detectives Dean O'Kelley and Rob Wilson, and they will fill you in on what's happening.")

Had Anthony Gross Sr. done that, it would have been end of story, no big deal. But of course he didn't do that, and "He refused to tell the officer anything about his son." Now, big surprise: Robert Daskas had to let the "honorable" Judge Glass in on this other Murder-for- Hire case, so that Tony Gross would not be arrested. (In my opinion, all of these men are either stupid, or liars; they did this on purpose so they could have a secret meeting with the judge.) Up to this point, with respect to the Melissa James' murder case, both the District Attorney's office and law enforcement's actions were deplorable.

Robert Daskas amended criminal charges, and included 1st Degree Kidnapping, even though, according to the autopsy report, Melissa James died around three in the afternoon on December 13th. The overdosed body was moved between three and four in the morning on December 14th; and a person must be alive to be kidnapped. Daskas then presented no evidence to prove that Melissa James was either kidnapped or murdered to the Grand Jury. He also allowed a coerced witness to testify. When she was clearly being dishonest with her contradictory statements provided under oath, the hearing completely fell apart. Knowing this case would likely be dismissed, the prosecutor leaked the grand jury testimony in an attempt to discredit Craig Titus and strong-arm him into agreeing to a murder-for-hire plot against the witnesses.

The Metro homicide detectives' actions were egregious the moment they walked through Craig and Kelly's front door on December 14th, began interviewing them, and refused to leave when Craig asked for an attorney. And then once Craig Titus was arrested, these investigators made it clear in their illegally tape recorded interrogation of Kelly Ryan that they believed Craig Titus murdered Melissa James; Detective O'Kelley then attempted to coerce Kelly into changing her statement to implicate Craig Titus in the murder (as he appeared to do with Megan Pierson and later with Ron Brady Jr. as well.) The same detectives then encouraged a convicted violent felon to entrap Ron Brady Jr. into providing a down payment on a fictitious murder for hire plot.

Brady was threatened and harassed all hours of the day, did not show up for three meetings, and tried to get out of the transaction. The detectives targeted Ron Brady Jr. because they knew he was a drug addict, and repeat offender. Someone they believed would be easy to manipulate, and would seem culpable of the crime because of his past drug arrests.

The detectives recorded over 200 conversations between Craig and Ron, and Ron and Deen Cassim (most of the conversations were between Craig and Ron, where nothing was ever mentioned about a murder for hire.) There were hundreds of other calls that, for some reason, "wink, wink," were not recorded between Ron Brady Jr. and Deen Cassim. In those unrecorded phone calls, Dean O'Kelley wrote notes as the two men talked, and he turned over his transcription as evidence.

Ron Brady Jr. was a pawn in their twisted scheme, and they thought he would flip on Craig when they charged him with a crime. According to their jail house snitch, Cassim, the day that he was resentenced, and his charges were dropped, the District Attorney's office attempted to distance him from the defense by paying for the informant's flight to England, where he was to stay until Ron Brady Jr.'s trial (but he was told it would more than likely not go to trial). They also paid for his rent and living expenses out of a fund that was set aside for such purposes.

(The District Attorney's office has money set aside to pay for an informant's testimony, and other miscellaneous bills like rent, cell phone, etc.) The amount provided to the informant/snitch is based on the severity of the crime, and the number of victims. It was never disclosed how much money was spent on Deen Cassim, and that information has now disappeared. Given the circumstances, and Cassim's remarks in the media, it was apparent that Cassim was paid a considerable amount of money to set Ron Brady Jr. up, with the ultimate goal of securing a conviction against Craig Titus.

According to Ron Brady Sr., Robert Daskas has also never disclosed why Ron Brady Jr. was moved from his cell into Deen Cassim's cell a week before they released Brady from Clark County Detention Center. Requests for this information were made by the defense, and to this day, Robert Daskas has only replied that he would "get back to them with that information," and he never has. Withholding this information is clearly prosecutorial misconduct, and both Brady and Titus should have their convictions overturned. However, their appeals will always be denied because the judges for the Nevada State of Appeals are colleagues with the district court judges, and they rarely rule against their comrades.

Misconduct on every level: Ex Parte Communication

On June 26th 2006 (this is un-freaking-believable, so pay close attention!) the Deputy District Attorney Robert Daskas (the lead prosecutor for the Melissa James Murder case), James Oronoz (Tony Gross' newly- hired defense attorney to work with Louis Palazzo on the Melissa James case), and the "honorable" Judge Jackie Glass (assigned to the

PROSECUTORIAL AND JUDICIAL MISCONDUCT

Melissa James murder trial, and who has already denied Craig Titus and Kelly Ryan bail. She was set to decide a motion in a couple of weeks to have the murder case thrown out due to prosecutorial misconduct by Robert Daskas) all meet behind closed doors in the judge's chambers to discuss, "Why Tony Gross was in Chicago."

In the meeting, Robert Daskas explained all of the details in the Murder for Hire case built against Craig Titus. He told the judge that the homicide detectives received information that Titus was directly involved in a murder for hire hit to take out the prosecution's key witnesses in the upcoming murder trial of Melissa James. Daskas told the judge about their (homicide detectives) sting operation, and he said that they had recorded phone calls directly implicating Craig Titus.

Daskas explained every detail of their Murder for Hire case against Craig Titus, including taking pictures of Tony Gross pretending to be dead in the car. He told her that they planned on mailing the pictures to Titus in a week, and they fully expected him to make the final payment to have the other two witnesses assassinated before the court hearing in July.

(Craig Titus had a court hearing scheduled in front of Judge Jackie Glass to have the murder case thrown out in July. According to the defense attorneys and Craig himself, they fully expected to win their argument, and the Kidnapping and Murder charges in the Melissa James case would be dropped. So why would Craig Titus pay someone to kill witnesses in a case that was about to be dropped? That does not make sense.

What does make sense is setting Craig up, and filling the judge in on what has happened so that she did not dismiss the case before it all went down. Tony Gross was never seen as a threat. For one, he was dumb as rocks, so the truth would inevitably come out. But most important, he was also on trial for murder and arson alongside Craig Titus and Kelly Ryan. It would be more logical to send off Megan Pierson, and if her life was actually in danger, why didn't they make an attempt to hide her? Because, everyone knew there was no real threat to any of their lives, because those idiot witnesses' testimony helped the defense!)

Neither Judge Jackie Glass nor the Deputy District Attorney ever disclosed any information about this meeting to Craig Titus' defense attorneys. When Judge Glass was questioned about it months later, she insisted that she could still be impartial as a judge, and refused to recuse herself from the case. One has to ask, was she really impartial and unbiased?

It certainly did not seem so in the subsequent decisions she made against Craig Titus and Kelly Ryan. She shot down their legitimate argument to have the case thrown out because of prosecutorial misconduct, and later agreed to have Tony Gross tried separately because of the newly alleged charges against Craig Titus. No effort was ever made to include the defense in the secret meeting, nor was there ever an attempt made by either Daskas or Glass to notify the defense team that the meeting had taken place.

Titus' defense team filed motions and appeals, requesting that Glass step away from the case; they were certain both she and Daskas would deliberately sabotage the outcome of the case. Those requests were scoffed by Glass, and rejected by her colleagues that ruled in her favor. This was a slap in the face to the "blind eye of justice" as both Daskas and Glass should have been reprimanded for misconduct. According to Nevada law, Judge Glass engaged in misconduct when she held a prohibited conversation with a prosecutor and another attorney.

It was not only the same homicide detectives working the Melissa James case, but the court was in on the ruse when Judge Jackie Glass and Robert Daskas teamed up and became active participants in the plot to set up Craig Titus on Solicitation for Murder. To make matters worse, Anthony Gross' attorney, James Oronoz, was invited into the meeting without Craig's defense counsel, behind closed doors. This was a huge conflict of interest and justice, since Craig Titus was fighting a murder charge in that same courtroom. Behind those walls, "Las Vegas Justice" at its finest allowed a violent criminal, Deen Cassim, to walk free, and the message was sent out loud and clear: rules don't apply to Las Vegas, Nevada!

For Daskas, who was being wooed by members of the Democratic Party to run for political office, securing a conviction in this high-profile case was the only thing that mattered! Ron Brady Jr. and his family were collateral damage to Robert Daskas; his public image could not be tarnished and he had to win at all costs! Ironically, just as Craig and Kelly could not turn back after they had already put Melissa James' body in the trunk of the car; Robert Daskas could not turn around after they placed Tony Gross in the trunk of a car, and tried to frame Craig for a fake crime. Thirsty for more power, Daskas had an image to protect, and he would step on anyone in his way, on the road to success.

Was this private meeting against the law? Yes!

According to the Nevada Code of Judicial Conduct:
RULE 2.9 Ex Parte Communications:

(A) A judge shall not initiate, permit, or consider ex parte communications, or consider other communications made to the judge outside the presence of the parties or their lawyers, concerning a pending or impending (a matter that is expected to occur in the near future) matter. (1) When circumstances require it, ex parte communication for scheduling, administrative, or emergency purposes, which does not address substantive matters, is permitted, provided: (a) the judge reasonably believes that no party will gain a procedural, substantive, or tactical advantage as a result of the ex parte communication; and (b) the judge makes provision promptly to notify all other parties of the substance of the ex parte communication and gives the parties an opportunity to respond. If a judge inadvertently receives an unauthorized ex parte communication bearing upon the substance of a matter, the judge shall make provision promptly to notify the parties of the substance of the communication and provide the parties with an opportunity to respond. **RULE 2.11 Disqualification:** *(A) A judge shall disqualify himself or herself in any proceeding in which the judge's impartiality might reasonably be questioned if the judge has a personal bias or prejudice concerning a party or a party's lawyer, or personal knowledge of facts that are in dispute in the proceeding. A judge should disclose on the record information that the judge believes the parties or their lawyers might reasonably consider relevant to a possible motion for disqualification, even if the judge believes there is no*

basis for disqualification. A judge making such a disclosure should, where practicable, follow the procedure set forth in Rule 2.11(C).

In 1991 the U.S. Supreme Court said: The outcome of a criminal trial is to be decided by impartial jurors, who know as little as possible about the case, based solely on material admitted into evidence before them in a court proceeding. Extrajudicial comments on, or discussion of, evidence which might never be admitted at trial and ex parte statements by counsel giving their version of the facts obviously threaten to undermine this basic tenet. Gentile v. State Bar of Nevada, 501 U.S. 1030, 1070 1991.

Mailing Craig Titus the phony pictures

Something needed to happen soon, because the hearing to have the murder case thrown out in court was fast approaching. On July 11th, Robert Daskas notified the detectives that they needed to mail the phony picture of Anthony Gross to Craig Titus at the Clark County Detention Center, along with a note to request payment for the hit. Daskas explained how urgent it was to get Titus to fall for the setup because of the Habeas Corpus hearing that was coming up. Daskas was certain that he had Judge Glass wrapped up, but he didn't want anything to go wrong. The detectives assured him they would do everything in their power to trap Craig Titus on this charge, and they would keep in constant communication with Daskas about the results.

Police set up an "undercover" checking account at the Bank of America, and detectives obtained a cellular phone that could be called directly from the Clark County Detention Center. Police contacted the Federal Bureau of Investigation, which was given a letter authored by Detective Rob Wilson. The letter was to be printed on attorney stationery and mailed by the FBI to Titus at the jail. The homicide detectives mailed Craig Titus the phony pictures taken of Tony Gross posing dead in the trunk of his mother's car, and enclosed with the picture was a postcard from the purported hit man.

The note read: "In town for a few days. Thinking of you and wondering why I haven't heard from you with that address. I'm running short on funds. No money in my bank account, waiting for payday, and will be heading back to L.A. on the 16th, so I won't be here for your 'big day.' Expect to hear from you before then. Fred. 702-469-1942." The card was addressed to Craig Titus with a return address of "Fred Hitterman." When Craig Titus received the postcard, he immediately turned it over to his attorney Richard Schonfeld instead of calling the hit man on a police-monitored phone or wiring the hit man money, as the homicide detectives had hoped he would do. Marc Saggese said that he believed the homicide detectives and district attorney crossed the line in the investigation.

Acting as if nothing ever happened while ruling on dismissal

Less than a week later on July 18th, Craig Titus and Kelly Ryan, along with their defense attorneys, appeared in the district courtroom of the "Honorable" Judge Jackie Glass. They were prepared to present legal arguments for the Defendant's Request for a Writ of Habeas Corpus in State v. Titus, Ryan, and Gross (a request to have the charges dismissed and be released from custody).

At question in the courtroom was whether an unsubstantiated murder and kidnapping charge should be dismissed against all three defendants. In true Robert Daskas fashion, the little man made a grandiose statement that he would not be able to back up with physical evidence.

The Las Vegas Prosecutor told Judge Jackie Glass that Kelly Ryan was an active participant in the slaying of their personal assistant Melissa James. Daskas said, "It was Kelly Ryan herself who was involved in the fight with Melissa James." Daskas with a raised voice proclaimed, "It was Kelly Ryan who used a taser gun on the victim, and it was Kelly Ryan who injected Melissa James with morphine."

The courtroom became tense when Craig Titus suddenly yelled out, "No she did not!" With a sarcastic smirk, looking Craig square in the eyes, Daskas said, "Well, let's ask Mr. Titus who did it!" When his counsel tried to calm him down, Craig said, "I am getting tired of him lying and saying that." Craig was fed up, and the judge belittled him and let him know that he was nothing here, simply a body without a voice, as she told him to "be quiet or I will kick you out of the building!"

SWIFT INJUSTICE

The defense argued that the charges against the couple were flawed, and there was never any proof that the couple kidnapped Melissa James. This charge was simply added on to bump the charges to 1st Degree Murder. They discussed the autopsy results, and the only thing that could be proven was that Melissa James died of a drug overdose. According to the defense, the only witness the prosecution had was involved in drugs at the time, and should be charged with conspiracy alongside everyone else. It was obvious that this particular court hearing was just for show. There was no way in hell that the judge ever had any intentions of dismissing the unfounded and unsupported charges. That afternoon the "Honorable" Judge Jackie Glass dismissed the case, and set a trial date for January 22nd 2007.

Robert Daskas did not have enough evidence to prove that it was "more probable than not" that Melissa James was ever murdered, much less kidnapped. This was a legitimate motion to have the entire murder case thrown out, and in most courts it would have been tossed because the kidnapping charge was never addressed, NOT ONE TIME, during the Grand Jury Testimony.

RPC 3.8(a) requires that the prosecutor refrain from prosecuting a charge not supported by probable cause. The prosecutor should only file charges that adequately encompass the offense or offenses believed to have been committed and that rationally address the nature and scope of the alleged criminal activity.

Looking back at this court room and the hearing that took place, laying out all of the documents from February 2005- July 2005, piecing together a time line of events leading up to this hearing, and seeing, in black and white, the injustice that took place was appalling! Walking into that courtroom on July 18th, Craig Titus, Kelly Ryan, and their defense attorneys had no idea what all had happened over the previous few months, or even the few weeks prior. Tony Gross sat next to his co-defendants in the courtroom, as if he had never posed dead in a car a few weeks earlier. Gross' attorneys pretended as if it was business as usual, and they hadn't met with Daskas earlier in the month and struck a verbal deal for their client, Tony Gross. The biggest question was, after Judge Jackie Glass met with Daskas, Oronoz, and the detectives in private, and according to the detectives, was made aware of Craig Titus' involvement in a Solicitation for Murder, how did the judge play it off, as if she was going to give Craig Titus a fair hearing? They (Glass, Daskas, Oronoz, Palazzo, O'Kelley and Wilson) all went through the motions, but as it turned out, this "Habeas Corpus" hearing was as fake as the "Murder for Hire" charges!

Working on the "Titus Tells All" Book

After Judge Jackie Glass denied the motion to dismiss the charges against Craig Titus, Kelly Ryan, and Anthony Gross in the Habeas Corpus hearing, Titus was resolved that he would be prejudicially incarcerated in the Clark County Detention Center for quite a while. He decided to make the most out of his time and called Dennis Bates and wrote him notes about the book every opportunity he had. The two men talked on the phone twice a day, every day, if not more, and Bates recorded every phone conversation. By the end of August, Bates began to put Craig Titus' words into print in what would have been a controversial "tell-all" behind-the-scenes look at the world of professional bodybuilding.

Nothing would be written about the upcoming murder trial in this "tell all" book; and Craig had no idea the authorities were in the process of trying to frame him for another crime. This book was strictly about Titus' experience as a professional bodybuilder. However, Daskas listened in on these "book deal" conversations and "suspected" this book was a cover for the "Murder for Hire" plot. After the phony Tony Gross death photos and the postcard from "Fred Hitterman" to Craig Titus failed, the uncomfortable farce of a hearing was cutting it too close for Robert Daskas. He became paranoid about being exposed.

Following that court hearing, Daskas obsessed over the hundreds of hours of phone calls Craig made while he was at Clark County Detention Center. Daskas decided he would claim Craig Titus was speaking in "code" with book publishing terms, and was actually talking about the "Murder for Hire." With the Olympia just two months away, Dennis Bates wanted to put something out as soon as possible. He was still interviewing Craig Titus and writing the book, but he had some of the most scandalous information on the audio recordings between him and Craig Titus.

◂ SWIFT INJUSTICE

In order to have something available before the crowds of bodybuilders and fans arrived in Las Vegas for the Mr. Olympia on September 29th, Bates and Titus agreed to take the audio recordings, with the actual jailhouse conversations between the two men, and make the first part of the story an audio book. Bates began advertising and getting the word out about the Craig Titus expose on the IFBB. Over the next month, he meticulously edited the interviews and packaged the project into a series of compact discs. On September 22nd, 2006, "Titus Tells All" officially went on sale and the audiobook became available through eBay and Amazon.

CHAPTER 2

Out with the old, and in with the De-new

(That was actually the line used by Greg Denue when he ran for district court judge- and lost!)

September 2006 Titus fires legal team

That same week, Craig Titus and Kelly Ryan decided to become more proactive in their defense and fired their defense lawyers. Richard Schonfeld and Tom Pitaro were out. The defense team that represented Sandy Murphy and Rick Tabish during the Binion trial, exposed corruption in the District Attorney's office, and handed Robert Daskas his first loss as a prosecutor (the dynamic defense duo of Marc Saggese and Michael Cristalli) were in. Or as Megan Pierson would put it, "in-ish". There was a temporary glitch in bringing both lawyers in to handle the couple; according to Judge Jackie Glass, having both Saggese and Cristalli represent the couple would be a conflict of interest. So Cristalli was sidelined while Judge Glass checked into the matter further. For the time being, Judge Glass assigned Kelly Ryan a temporary public defender: Greg Denue.

After dismissing their defense lawyers, Craig decided to go public, which was a complete about-face from his prior legal team's strategy. Schonfeld and Pitaro would rarely comment on the sensationalized exaggerations published in the media, and they never allowed Craig Titus to speak out and defend himself when the media ripped his character a part. For a man like Titus, who has always been vocal and was known for speaking his mind, confronting anyone that spread shit about him, being silent was a tough pill to swallow.

This legal approach was somewhat beneficial in the beginning, because after they allowed the prosecution to incessantly blab about everything they had against Craig Titus, the defense was able to discern that the prosecution had a weak circumstantial case with no physical evidence. However, after the grand jury transcripts were released by the prosecution at the end of March, it was apparent how the prosecution was going to play the game.

A competent defense attorney would have filed a motion to have the judge place a gag order on the case. An unbiased Judge would have placed a gag order on this case from the beginning to ensure the trial was as fair as possible by impeding the public from discussing intricacies associated with an active case. This was not just any judge though, this was the judge that used her celebrity status after she sentenced O.J. Simpson to prison, and received her own court television show- *Swift Justice with Jackie Glass*. This judge needed all the media attention she could get, and wanted salacious gossip publicized because the more scandalous this high-profile trial became, the more notoriety she received.

Why was there not a gag-order placed on the trial by the judge?

A gag-order is a gift to those defending themselves in a court of law, handed down from the Supreme Court, to protect the accused in high profile cases. It ensures their constitutional rights to a fair trial. A gag order would have prevented the investigators and prosecution from leaking taped interviews, sex tapes, and recorded personal phone calls that would have never been permitted during the trial and that were ultimately twisted into tabloid trash.

Most importantly, a gag order would have prohibited Robert Daskas from trying the case through the media in the form of newspaper articles and books written and published months before Craig Titus had his day in court. Had Marc Saggese and Michael Cristalli been hired from the beginning, there's no doubt that they would have demanded Judge Glass enforce a gag order.

OUT WITH THE OLD, AND IN WITH THE DE-NEW

When their law firm represented Sandy Murphy in the second Binion trial, that was the first thing they did, and a reluctant Joseph Bonaventure had no choice but to enforce it. By the time Saggese and Cristalli went to work, the damage had already been done, and Daskas had already spewed his prejudicial venom all over the media. If Saggese and Cristalli insisted on having a gag order in place at that point, it would have most likely only hurt the defense because they needed to utilize the media to do damage control at that point.

Their first step in untangling the web of lies released by the prosecution and published in the press was to allow Craig Titus an opportunity, without revealing too much, to share his side of the story. Craig released a statement through his new lawyers explaining why he fired his previous lawyers: "There were too many sketchy things going on behind the scenes, and instead of fighting, they let it slide, and told me to be quiet. I didn't want to be quiet because then it makes me look guilty, and I am not guilty! I have never been scared to talk to the press; I want the world to know that we are 100 percent Not Guilty! And to be completely honest, these guys weren't fighting for me, and at times it seemed like they were actually working against me. Kelly and I needed a defense team that listened to us, and had our best interest at heart. Things that have happened in court are not right, and these attorneys will make it right. They are not afraid of the prosecution or the judge; they are in it to win it!"

Saggese boldly stated, "My client is totally innocent, and I'm going to personally walk him out of the court house in January!" Craig was overjoyed because he felt like someone finally had his back. Saggese was personally invested in having Titus acquitted, because he was not just his client, they had become good friends. The two men became so close, and Saggese was so convinced of Craig's innocence, that he put off his wedding until after Craig was to be set free, and asked him to be a part of the wedding party.

Marc Saggese went on to explain, "So far, the public has only had a completely one-sided story as to what the facts are in this case." He assured the public that the facts would eventually come out, and he would allow his client to speak out against all of the exaggerations and untruths presented by the prosecution at the appropriate time. Saggese said, "My client has wanted to talk publicly about the charges against him since the moment the authorities voiced their suspicions that he and his wife were murder suspects, and when the time is right we will expose their lies."

Craig's first article since fired attorneys
With his lawyer by his side, Craig Titus was interviewed by the journalist that had been writing all of the slanderous articles about him, and who was also about to release a book about the case. Titus was instructed to hold back verbally on the specifics of the case, but he could not help himself. He was unable to hold back emotionally when he talked about Melissa James, and how devastated he was by her overdose.

In the article, Craig stated, "Kelly and I both loved Melissa, and the image depicted in the media about me and my wife has been totally fabricated. My wife and I are caring people. We are loving people. We are not the horrific monsters we've been portrayed as being. Melissa was our friend, she was our family; and she was one of my best friends." Titus steadfastly maintained that they did not murder Melissa; she died from a drug overdose. He said, "We are not guilty of murdering anybody!"

Although Titus' lawyers would not let him discuss exactly what happened that evening, Craig told police that James overdosed on drugs at the couple's southwest Las Vegas home. He panicked and tried to get rid of the body to avoid any negative publicity that would have ruined the couple's careers. "I'm guilty of some very, very bad judgment. I'm guilty of some very poor decisions. I wish I would have just listened to my wife and called the police," Titus said as he choked back the tears and emotion.

The article mentioned Melissa James, and said that she spent a lot of her time running a dance studio and teaching young children how to dance in Florida. Right before she moved in with Craig and Kelly in California, James became addicted to methamphetamine. "The drug use became prevalent; and we had to ask Melissa to move out." Titus said that James later rejoined the couple when they moved to Las Vegas in 2003, and that she continued to struggle with methamphetamine use. "I watched a human being disintegrate in front of my eyes." When asked about how he was handling being incarcerated during this time, Craig said that he has had a tough time, but has been able to endure the nearly nine months behind bars because he and Kelly have been allowed to have video conference meetings twice a week because of their marital status.

While Craig was interviewed by Puit, he refrained from disclosing too much information at the request of his new legal team, but Craig was about to burst trying to keep his mouth shut. He desperately wanted to tell the world what he really thought about the 5 foot 4 inch, one hundred and thirty pound weasel in a cheap suit prosecuting his case.

Robert Daskas was destined to become a politician, he was a master at spinning stories and spreading lies with his smear campaign he launched in the media against Titus. Titus' lawyer could not stand Daskas, nor the newly elected district attorney, and the corruption behind the scenes. Saggese witnessed David Roger's prosecutorial misconduct in the first Binion trial; conduct that was so unethical, the Nevada State Supreme Court overturned the guilty verdict.

As a result, Saggese and Cristalli's client, Sandy Murphy was given a new trial. Roger became the district attorney on the coattails of that win, and now both Daskas' and Roger's underhanded deeds were being swept under the rug as their political careers took off. Those around them simply looked away at the corruption in the system, because when it came to convictions in high-profile trials, a win for the State meant bonuses, promotions, and notoriety for everyone involved!

As much as both Saggese and Cristalli would have loved for Craig to expose Robert Daskas, they were savvy enough to not allow Titus to say too much. Daskas had already lifted up his dress, and showed everybody his tiny package; which was why he was running around leaking false information to the media and trying to set up innocent people for crimes that did not exist. The new defense team wanted to knock Daskas on his ass, and to do that, they needed to be smarter than him. They needed to be patient, hold their information tight, and throw everything at Daskas at the trial.

CHAPTER 3

The Dynamic Defense Duo

Who are Marc Saggese and Michael Cristalli?

Marc Anthony Saggese was born in 1973, and was raised in Utica, New York. He attended State University of New York at Cortland and earned his Bachelor of Arts Degree (cum laude) in Political Science. Saggese received his Juris Doctorate degree from Catholic University of America, Columbus School of Law, in Washington, D.C. After obtaining his law degree, Saggese served as a Captain in the United States Army, Judge Advocate General Corps. Saggese had been practicing law for 10 years as a civil and criminal trial attorney. He is also a pro tempore Judge for the Las Vegas Municipal Court System, as well as a Small Claims Court Judge. He is licensed in Nevada, Georgia, the United States Court of Appeals for the 3rd Circuit, the United States Court of Appeals for the 5th Circuit, and the United States Court of Appeals for the Armed Forces. Saggese is a professional boxer and has a record of 3-0 (all first round KO's). Saggese is also the inspiration for the character, Pete Kaczmarek on CBS's Wednesday night TV drama, *The Defenders*. He works closely with the writers on all scripts and provides the legal and storyline authenticity for the show. Marc Saggese has appeared nationally on *Fox and Friends*, *On the Record with Greta VanSusteren*, *The Line-up* with Kimberly Guilfoyle, CBS's *48 Hours* with Peter Van Sant, CNN's *The Burden of Proof*, *Catherine Crier Live*, The New York Post, USA Today, Vegas Magazine, The New York Times, Muscle Missions Radio, and Entertainment Weekly. He has also been featured in the Las Vegas

Review Journal, the Las Vegas Sun, CBS's local affiliate KLAS-TV's 8 News Now This Morning, KTNC-ABC Action News, KLAS-TV 8 News Now, KSNV-TV NBC News 3, Fox 5 News, *Face to Face* with Jon Ralston, KXNT Talk Radio with host Alan Stock. Saggese also makes regular appearances on X-107.5's Dave and Mahoney in the Morning on their "Ask a DAM Lawyer" segment.

Michael V. Cristalli was also born and raised in Utica, New York. Cristalli holds a Bachelor of Science in Political Science from the University of Rochester and received his Juris Doctorate degree from Syracuse University. He is licensed to practice in all federal and state courts in the State of Nevada, and specializes in both criminal and civil litigation. He has successfully litigated some of the highest profile cases in the state of Nevada. Cristalli has represented clients both nationwide and internationally and is regarded as one of the premier trial lawyers in Nevada. He possesses unequaled expertise in the areas of civil and criminal litigation. He has litigated on behalf of plaintiffs who have been harmed by the negligent and intentional acts of others. His experience with criminal cases is unparalleled, including capital murder, and securities fraud cases. Mr. Cristalli has also handled many civil rights cases protecting the interests of people whose constitutional rights have been violated. He is active in both community and professional organizations in Nevada as well as nationally. He is a member of the Nevada Attorneys for Criminal Justice, the Augustus Society, and serves as a Board of Director for La Voce. He is also a member of the National Association of Criminal Defense Lawyers and is active in the First Amendment Lawyers Association and the American Bar Association. Cristalli has made appearances on many national and local TV shows. He's been interviewed by Larry King on *Larry King Live*, *Greta Van Susteren,* and *Good Morning America*. There have been programs and movies produced about his cases. Those shows include *Dateline* NBC, CBS *48 Hours*, and *Snapped*.

You hired whom?
After reading over all of the notes pertaining to Craig Titus' case, one person stuck out like a sore thumb: private investigator Tom Dillard. The attorneys knew that he was a former Metro homicide detective,

and he had been sued in court numerous times for coercing witnesses, wrongfully setting up defendants, and trying to manipulate a judge. Law suits had been awarded to numerous defendants, and convictions had been over turned, costing the Las Vegas community millions of dollars, all because of Tom Dillard's corruption. Cristalli and Saggese were fresh off the Binion trial, working for Sandy Murphy. They saw Tom Dillard's under-handed actions first hand. They knew that Dillard was best friends with the District Attorney, David Roger; there were several articles written about their friendship in the local newspapers.

Here's an article in the Las Vegas Sun where Tom Dillard acknowledges that he and District Attorney David Roger are best friends:

Las Vegas Sun: Murphy defense on attack over private detective's role
Sunday, Jan. 30, 2000 | 10:23 a.m.

"Defense lawyers are turning up the heat on the private detective who broke open the investigation into Ted Binion's slaying. Last week, attorneys for Sandy Murphy and Rick Tabish, the two people charged with killing Binion, filed a motion attacking Tom Dillard, who has made life difficult for them in the biggest murder case in Las Vegas history.

The motion seeks to declare Dillard an "agent of the state" and suppress any evidence he may have gathered for police. Dillard, a former homicide detective working for Binion's $50 million estate, spent countless hours interviewing more than 100 witnesses and providing leads to police investigating the 55-year-old gambling figure's Sept. 17, 1998.

Dillard has been open about his role in the Binion investigation. **From the beginning he has acknowledged being best friends with Chief Deputy District Attorney David Roger, the lead prosecutor in the case,** *and he has told both sides that his marching orders were to provide police with every piece of information he picked up while helping the estate pursue its wrongful death lawsuit against Murphy and Tabish.*

Essentially wearing twin hats of state investigator and private detective, Dillard was the primary individual through which the Las Vegas police department and district attorney developed their case," Murphy's lawyer, John Momot, wrote in his motion."

What does Dillard know?

Marc Saggese knew that any information Craig Titus handed over to Tom Dillard would have been placed right into the hands of the district attorney. So without alarming Titus, they needed to fire Tom Dillard, and hire another investigator, and find out everything Craig Titus told the private investigator because they would need to do a lot of damage control. Before Saggese met with Craig Titus, he sat down with his family to ask them some questions about the private investigator they had hired.

When he sat down with Craig's mother, Sandi Titus, Saggese asked to look through all of their private investigator's files, and she informed him that they did not have any files. Shocked, Saggese said, "What do you mean there are no files?" Sandi told him that she had not heard from Tom Dillard since the end of May; "He just up and disappeared; I could not believe it! His secretary didn't even know where he was at! We kept giving him money, and he would say that he needed more. This went on for some time, and then he just up and disappeared! We gave him over $10,000; it was just horrible! His secretary was so nice, and she was worried about him too. I hope nothing happened to him!" Saggese was not surprised, Dillard had done this to people before, and he has both law enforcement and the district attorney's offices in his back pockets. Dillard gets sued all of the time, but criminal charges are never brought against him. Sandi asked Saggese, "Do you think you can find him? I mean I'm sort of worried about him, and we really need to get all of Craig's files back. When we asked his secretary for Craig's information, she said that Mr. Dillard must have taken them with him." Saggese asked her what information Tom Dillard had on Craig, and she said, "Well that's the thing, I am not completely sure. It was so strange, we kept giving him money, but it didn't seem like was really doing anything."

After Sandi thought about it for a minute, she blurted out, "Oh shit, I almost forgot, Tom Dillard has a video tape of that Tony Gross fellow, and a bunch of other people set to testify against Craig, buying and selling dope." With a "What the fuck?" look on his face, Saggese asked Sandi Titus, "A video of who buying what?" Sandy said, "Oh I can't remember all of their names, I know there's a Megan. They were supposedly friends with Craig and Kelly, and in some sort of trouble with the law, so they made shit up about Craig to save their own asses!" Saggese said, "Yeah, that usually happens when the prosecution doesn't have anything else! So you say that Tom Dillard recorded these people buying and selling drugs?" Sandi said, "Hell no, Dillard's lazy ass did not record them, he just has all of the tapes. Let me back up a little bit. Did you read that article about the grand jury indictments a couple of months ago, where that Morgan, Megan, or whatever the hell her name is; where she made up all of those crazy ass stories?"

Saggese said, "Oh yeah, yeah, yeah, I know exactly what article you are talking about. I've heard all about this girl, so there's surveillance on Megan Foley, this is the first I've heard about this." Sandi told him, "There's surveillance on all of those losers; every last fucking one of them! With everything going on, you would think they would be more careful than that; but they just buy it in the open for anyone to see, and this video just dropped in our laps!"

Saggese asked her how that happened, and Sandi told him about Ron Brady Jr. Sandi explained, "Craig made friends with this really nice guy while he was in jail; Ronnie was down on his luck, and was about to be released from jail, and he needed to find a way to get back on his feet. We needed work done on all of Craig's properties; a shitload of work, work that most people would not want to do, or if they did do it, they would charge a fortune. So anyways, Craig gave Ronnie my phone number, and I arranged to have Ronnie and his dad clean out those houses. Afterwards I cooked for everybody, and we had a really nice visit. Ronnie told us that he was a recovering addict, and he knew a lot of those people that were making shit up about Craig and Kelly, because he had been so heavily involved in the drug community for years. He said that he was friends with their 'connection,' whatever the hell that means. Ronnie knew where they 'partied,' and said he could get a video of them buying and selling drugs. So anyways, I thought he was just talking big, and didn't think anything of it; but I will be goddamned if he didn't show up with a video of all of those losers using drugs! I didn't want anything to happen to it, so I told Craig's lawyer, Richard Schonfeld about it, and he said to give the tape to the private investigator. Tom seemed so excited about it, and had Ronnie give him anything else he had that would help the defense. Ronnie did a few more things, and then Tom asked us for more money and disappeared!"

Saggese knew that Craig's mother was already sick with worry about her son, so he didn't want to worry her any more than he had to. Saggese told her that he would do his best to get everything back from Dillard, and suggested they hire new private investigators. Craig's mother thanked Saggese over and over for helping her son. With his confident charm, Saggese gave Sandi a hug, and assured her that they would beat this thing! Just the words Sandi Titus needed to hear. This was something Marc Saggese the man and lawyer was very good at doing. He made his clients and their families feel at peace because he truly cared, and this was something that Sandi Titus desperately needed at that time. Sandi was thousands of miles away from her home, and she was mentally and physically exhausted. She knew that she needed to be strong for Craig, but felt like she was about to break.

Craig's mother had built a strong relationship with Kelly's mom Niki Ryan; she was the only woman that honestly knew what Sandi was going through, because she was going through the exact same thing herself. When Nikki Ryan died unexpectedly from a heart attack in April, Sandi was devastated, and felt all alone. Fortunately for Sandi, she had a special relationship with her daughter, and considered Nicole to be her best friend. Nicole was not able to be there in Las Vegas with her mother all of the time, but the times that she was there, gave Sandi the strength to make it through another day.

As Saggese made his way to the Clark County Detention Center, he thought about the conversation he had with Craig's mother. He had promised her that Craig would be a free man by his birthday on January 14th; and now driving in his car to visit with Craig, he hoped that he had not given her a false sense of hope. Saggese knew that Craig was innocent, and any jury in America would look at this case and unanimously vote "Not Guilty."

But they weren't in just any city in the United States, they were in the "Corruption Capital of the World": Las Vegas, Nevada. With all of the depravity infested deep inside each branch of the government in this county, it was going to be hell trying to win this battle! But if ever there was a battle to be fought, it would be right now for this guy and his family. Craig Titus and Marc Saggese had a special bond, and he would do everything in his power to make his promise to Sandi Titus become a reality!

Marc Saggese arrived at the detention center and met with Titus. He debated telling Craig about Dillard, but decided not to say anything just yet. Dillard was a man with connections, and he would gladly fuck over anybody that crossed him or exposed him in anyway. If Craig found out about his past, he would find a way to go off on Dillard's ass, and that would just end up being an added headache to deal with down the road.

Saggese was not even 100 % sure that Dillard had even done anything wrong. All he knew for a fact was he wanted to get Dillard as far away from his client as possible. Saggese told Craig that defense attorneys usually hire their own private investigators, using the same guys every time, because it has to be someone they feel comfortable with and know well enough to trust. He asked Craig if he would be okay with letting Dillard go, and bringing on someone else to assist them in the investigation, and Craig said of course he did not have any problem with that. Craig said, "My mom can't even find him anyway; he skipped town or something."

Marc Saggese asked Craig if Tom Dillard had any information that Saggese needed to know about that would possibly help him with the defense, and Craig dropped a bombshell: there was a witness out there that could possibly exonerate Craig! According to Titus, the witness, John Allen was housed with Gross before Christmas, and Gross told Allen that Craig and Kelly did not kill Melissa James; James overdosed on drugs. Tony Gross told Allen, in a jail house confession, that he walked in on Craig Titus giving Melissa CPR, and then wrapped her up in blankets, bound the blankets together with duct tape, and placed her in the trunk of the car. Gross admitted finding a place to take her body earlier in the day, and he said that Craig wanted him to drop the body before they lit the car on fire in the desert, but he tricked Craig into lighting the body and the car on fire at the same time. Gross said that his attorneys were going to help get him a deal if he lied about Melissa James, and said that Craig Titus murdered her.

When Craig was finally moved out of solitary after his first bail hearing in February, and into the general population, Allen approached Craig and told him the story. John Allen told him that he tried to report it twice to the CCDC, and nothing was ever done about it. Craig said that he told his lawyers about it, and they arranged for Tom Dillard to interview Allen as a potential witness for the defense. Dillard interviewed him and said John Allen was believable, and after checking his records, he said Allen would be a credible witness. With Allen's approval, he tape-recorded Allen's statements, and wrote down all of the details, and then supposedly turned all of that information over to the authorities. Craig told Saggese, "This guy, John Allen, didn't want any kind of deal, or a reduced sentence. He didn't want shit in return. Allen just thought it wasn't right, and wanted to make me aware of what the detectives were doing to me. Allen said he was willing to testify in court, and do whatever he had to do to help me out, but we have never heard anything else about it after Dillard took off."

Judge Glass won't allow Cristalli to represent Kelly Ryan
Both Craig and Kelly wanted to stand united to prove Melissa James died of a drug overdose, and that they did not murder her. This was almost impossible with the couple stuck behind bars (because of the prosecutor overcharging the case to bump it up to first degree murder). There was chaos and confusion when they had different attorneys fighting for the same goal. Craig Titus and Kelly Ryan needed to stay focused as a team to fight and win this battle, and in order to do this, they wanted another power team leading the charge: Michael Cristalli and Marc Saggese.

◄ SWIFT INJUSTICE

Unfortunately, Judge Jackie Glass was not going to allow this to happen. She said, "Their dual representation would cause a potential conflict of interest at trial." Glass was not concerned about any conflicts of interest up to that point, so why would she be concerned then? Could there be an ulterior motive in denying Kelly's request to retain Michael Cristalli as her counsel? Perhaps it's because Michael Cristalli and Marc Saggese exposed both prosecutorial and judicial misconduct during the Binion trial, and Glass was afraid that they would do it again in this case? It's curious that this judge would take such a stand on this "conflict of interest" when she refused to recuse herself from this exact same case when there clearly was a "conflict of interest" because of her ex-parte communication with the prosecution.

This was a conflict of interest that affected Judge Jackie Glass' ability to be objective and rule fairly. The judge would be placed in a courtroom where she would have to rule on a judgment; with a prosecutor she just had a prohibited conversation with, about the defendants in the case. With Glass blocking Cristalli from representing Kelly Ryan, she now had to appoint a Contract Public Defender (defense attorney that works for the Clark County Court System). Public Defenders are associates with the District Attorney's office and the District Court Judges. In fact, the attorney Glass appointed, Greg Denue, had worked closely with or "against" Robert Daskas many times in the past on different court cases and trials. During these trials, the Public Defender appeared to make decisions that were unexpectedly favorable to the prosecution. Given Daskas and Denue's history together, it was not a surprise to see Greg Denue make several moves that appeared to be advantageous for the prosecution. Most notable, as soon as Denue was assigned to Kelly Ryan, he immediately began to distance her from Craig Titus. Many people, including Marc Saggese, have speculated that Greg Denue had been hired by the State, and had teamed up with Robert Daskas in an effort to turn Kelly against her husband, and have her turn State's witness.

What is known about Greg Denue, the man hand-picked to represent Kelly Ryan by Judge Jackie Glass? The Las Vegas Review-Journal did a series called "Conflicted Justice;" where they exposed flaws in the

THE DYNAMIC DEFENSE DUO

judicial system of assigning private lawyers to the public defendant's office. District Court Administrator Chuck Short said his office has taken action in response to the articles, and Greg Denue was highlighted as one of the three attorneys that would be investigated for overbilling the State, and there would be possible civil or criminal action against Denue.

It was found that Denue repeatedly billed for more than 24 hours in a given day. County records showed Denue, who declined repeated interview requests, devoted more than 950 hours in the first six months of last year to a small group of cases that qualified him for a $100-per-hour fee. These three lawyers billed the county for a combined $1 million last year; he billed the county $400,000 for the previous work year.

In a letter to the Review-Journal in the fall of 2005, Denue reflected on an earlier job he had as a public defender in New Orleans. He referred to people in the hard-hit Ninth Ward of New Orleans as "an entire class of people hooked to the government welfare check I V." Greg Denue wrote, "Victims of Hurricane Katrina were no different when it comes to their mental outlook than the plantation slaves who waited for the 'massa' to feed them and clothe them. The hurricane victims suffered no losses because they really had nothing but their welfare checks to begin with."

Greg Denue ran for Clark County District Court Judge with the phrase, "Out with the old, and in with the De-nue." Fortunately for Las Vegas, the small- minded public defender didn't "De-win." But unfortunately for the Titus-Ryan team, this classless human being was appointed to represent Kelly Ryan while they were forced to file an appeal to the Nevada Supreme Court to ask permission to have Michael Cristalli represent Kelly in court.

CHAPTER 4

Cruel and Unusual Punishment

The calm before the storm: Craig continued his phone conversations with Dennis Bates from Muscle Missions, and they tirelessly worked on: "Titus Tells All," a book about the inside world of professional bodybuilding. On the evening of October 18th, Titus and Bates talked to each other about the book, and Craig Titus said he would call Bates back in an hour or two. Two hours had passed and the phone rang; Bates assumed that it was Craig Titus calling him back. Titus was not on the other line however; instead, it was the clergy from the Clark County Detention Center. Craig had asked him to call Bates and his attorney because the Correction's Officers came in and took him out of his cell, placing Craig Titus in Solitary Confinement without any justification. The clergy said this was an unusual occurrence, and he was concerned about Craig Titus' welfare.

Ron Brady Jr. arrested

The next day, October 19th, 2006 Ron Brady Jr. was arrested on three counts of Solicitation to Commit Murder. The police and prosecution alleged through the media that Titus had ties with Brady for years, and the two men attempted to hatch a plot to put out a hit on three key witnesses in Craig Titus' case.

The same homicide detectives that were trying to put Craig Titus behind bars for the rest of his life for the alleged murder of Melissa James, were now sitting in front of Ron Brady Jr., singing the same song they sang to Megan Pierson, Kelly Ryan, and Tony Gross: "Implicate Craig

Titus with the crime, and you will walk. If you don't, we will put you away for the rest of your life." Metro Homicide Detective Dean O'Kelley told Brady that he did not want to see him spend the rest of his life in prison because he chose to protect Craig Titus, the man responsible for all of this pain and heartache. He said, "You tell me that Craig Titus arranged the hits on these witnesses, and his family paid the down payment to make it all happen, and you will be a free man. Every charge against you will be dropped."

The homicide detectives were shocked when Brady refused to lie, and told them to "Go fuck your selves!" They never dreamed in a million years that this man with dozens of drug arrests would not save his own ass and bow down to their demands. That was not the way it was supposed to happen! In their eyes Ron Brady Jr. was a junkie, and a junkie would not have enough integrity to do the right thing.

They fully expected him to turn on Craig Titus the second he sat down for questioning. These homicide detectives, with over three decades of experience combined, completely misjudged Brady's character. Ron Brady Jr. was nothing like Deen Cassim or Tony Gross, he had a back bone. Ron Brady Jr. was not going to allow those asshole detectives use him to frame Craig Titus for a bullshit crime; a crime thrown together because they couldn't find enough evidence to convict Titus for the murder of Melissa James.

Solitary Confinement

The homicide detectives weren't panicked yet; they knew that Brady would eventually come down from the drugs he was on, and when he began to feel the excruciating pain from detox, they were convinced that he would talk. To make it even tougher on Brady, they placed him in "Disciplinary" Solitary Confinement, where Brady became violently ill from withdrawal. In a tiny isolated cell, Brady was denied sunlight, showers and food for a few days. The investigators told Brady he could either do this the hard way, or the easy way, but either way, he would eventually give them what they wanted! Detective O'Kelley told Brady they would check on him later to see if he had changed his mind, and until he changed his mind, Solitary would be his home for the next couple of years while he waited to be sentenced to life without parole along with Craig Titus.

The atrocities that happened to Ron Brady Jr. while he spent his time in Solitary Confinement were nothing short of barbaric. The authorities were punishing Brady because he would not tell their lies and testify against Craig in court. There were convicted murderers, rapists, and child molesters who were treated better than Ron Brady Jr. while they awaited their sentences; yet everyone looked away, and pretended it was not happening.

Deen Cassim guaranteed the detectives that Brady would turn on Craig Titus; it was a "fucking foolproof plan!" Everything could fall apart if Brady did not turn on Craig Titus; O'Kelley was about to lose his shit, because he no longer controlled the situation. The seasoned homicide detective could not let Brady see that though; he had to play if off as if it were no sweat off his brow. O'Kelley told Brady, "You know where you can find me if you change your mind!" From that point on, Brady and O'Kelley played the waiting game, and only time would tell who would win in the end.

Both Craig Titus and Ron Brady Jr. were placed in "Disciplinary Solitary Confinement" or "Segregation" as the Clark County Detention Center refers to it. Brady was told by the investigators that he was there because he would not rat out Titus, and he would remain there until he changed his mind. Craig Titus, on the other hand, had no clue why he had been placed there. Only two reasons exist why an inmate is placed in Solitary Confinement: "Disciplinary Segregation" is used when an inmate has violated facility rules while they are incarcerated, and they are to be isolated for two weeks at a time. "Administrative Segregation" is used when the CCDC authorities believe that an inmate poses a danger to other inmates, and must therefore be isolated from the general population.

Solitary Confinement is to be a "last-resort measure" reserved for the "worst of the worst." However for many in the Clark County Detention Center, including Craig Titus and Ron Brady Jr., Solitary Confinement is a first-resort control strategy implemented by members of the Las Vegas Metropolitan Police Department, as Metro controls the

Detention Center. Inmates housed in Segregation are held in a 24-hour locked down section of the jail. They are virtually free of human contact, and are only allowed out of their cell one hour a day.

During this hour, the prisoner is allowed "recreation" time which consists of standing in a concrete enclosed yard alone, with no other inmates around; allowed the "privilege of breathing in the outdoor air." At this time, they are permitted ten minutes to use the shower or place a phone call. The other 23 hours are spent in their 6 x 9 foot cell. They are provided three small meals a day, dropped on the ground through a slot in the metal door; and the authorities made sure that the meals were prepared "special" and "strategically" dropped for both Craig Titus and Ron Brady Jr.

The cells in Segregation are smaller than most closets, and isolated from all of the other inmates, including other inmates in Solitary. In fact, the only verbal or physical contact an inmate has with another human being takes place once a day when the inmate is placed in handcuffs and chains by the guard before they are escorted out of their cell for their "recreation" hour.

What these detectives did to both Craig Titus and Ron Brady Jr. were a violation of their civil rights. Under no circumstance are inmates, especially those whom have not even been proven guilty in a court of law yet, to be held in Solitary Confinement or Segregation without just provocation or explanation.

Supreme Court Rulings on inmates in Solitary Confinement:
The Supreme Court explicitly stated that "a detainee may not be punished prior to an adjudication of guilt in accordance with due process of law." (Sandin, 515 U.S. at 484 quoting Bell, 441 U.S. at 535). This distinction between convicted prisoners serving a sentence and pretrial confinees has been recognized by the courts of appeals that have addressed this issue. The First and Ninth Circuits have recognized specifically that pretrial detainees may constitutionally be punished for infractions committed while awaiting trial, but also have recognized the need for procedural protections prior to the imposition of any punishment.

The court explained that, in contrast to convicted prisoners, pretrial detainees have no sentence that could be deemed to encompass such disciplinary confinement. (See id. at 524-25.) Moreover, the court noted, "a due process hearing helps to ensure that disciplinary punishment is what it purports to be, rather than punishment in advance of conviction for the crime that led to detention."

The court explained that, in contrast to convicted prisoners, pretrial detainees have no sentence that could be deemed to encompass such disciplinary confinement. See id. at 524-25. Moreover, the court noted, "a due process hearing helps to ensure that disciplinary punishment is what it purports to be, rather than punishment in advance of conviction for the crime that led to detention.

High Security Extraction of Craig Titus: Mission- Humiliation

Punishing Ron Brady Jr. and Craig Titus by confining them in Disciplinary Solitary Confinement or Segregation was not only unethical, it was unconstitutional. As outrageous as this behavior by the authorities was, what happened to Craig Titus next, paralleled abuse only seen in third-world countries. In an attempt to frighten and humiliate Craig Titus into submission, rendering him physically and mentally powerless while being held captive in the Clark County Detention Center, on October 23rd, 2006, Assistant Sheriff Ray Flynn through Metro Deputy Chief Michael Holt ordered a very rare, Code Orange, High Security Extraction.

Four days after Ron Brady Jr. was arrested, and refused to turn State's witness in exchange for his freedom, and thus placed in Solitary Confinement, sirens and buzzers blared through the Segregation unit, and "Code Orange" was repeatedly uttered over the loud speakers. Correctional Officers rushed down the hall to the front of Titus' metal door, and yelled, "Inmate Titus, get down on the floor, head towards that wall. Down on the floor, on your belly, now!"

Craig had absolutely no idea what was going on. Scared out of his mind, he respectfully obeyed every command barked at him when all of a sudden, a dozen specially trained SWAT team officers wearing full riot gear, burst down the hall and stormed into Craig's tiny cell. Laser dots were shining on his body, as high- powered shot guns were pointing directly at him. Lying flat on his stomach, face down, a SWAT team officer yelled at Craig Titus, "Cross your legs, bring them up to your butt, put your hands straight out, straight out to the side like an airplane with your palms up, not down, up, up, up, now! Stay there in that position and do not move! Do you understand? If you do not comply, force and or (unintelligible) will be used against you. It will create pain and it possibly will create death. Do you understand?" Craig replied, "Yes, sir; what is happening sir? What the heck is going on?"

The SWAT Team did not explain to Craig what was happening, but warned him if he asked questions, and was uncooperative, he would experience a whole lot of that pain as explained. Even though he did as the officer asked, Craig still felt a lot of pain when they physically hog-tied him with his arms and legs restrained together behind his back, and forcefully extracted him out of his cell. Feeling like his bones and muscles were ripping out of his shoulders, Craig was in a tremendous amount of pain when the officers brutalized him, but he was afraid to let on that he was physically injured because they might make it even worse for him. With lasers and shotguns still pointed at him, Craig Titus was placed in a large black wheel chair as the officers readjusted the restraints, and strapped him into the chair designed for extremely violent inmates.

While the officers fastened every last body part into this chair, Craig scanned the room with his eyes, and saw a man with a video camera that appeared to be mocking him as he videotaped the attack. The officer, and several other officers beside him, seemed to be enjoying themselves as they humiliated the former bodybuilder. Every officer around undoubtedly wanted Craig Titus to not only feel completely degraded, but wanted to scare the shit out of him as well. And it wasn't over, as the SWAT Team then placed a blacked-out pair of goggles over his eyes so that Craig Titus was then strapped down in total darkness.

Craig Titus was so scared that his body began to physically shake; tears ran down his face, and he was petrified because he could not control his body from trembling in fear. He tried to keep his body from quivering because he knew these men would use that as an excuse to assassinate him. Craig didn't know if they were actually a Metro Swat team, or if they were terrorists holding him captive. Either way, Craig Titus believed that his time on earth was about to come to an end, and those men were about to execute him.

Titus was wheeled around the building, and he could tell by the noise and smell in the air that they were no longer on the same floor. He was taken by elevator down to the basement, and in an effort to keep Craig Titus confused and disheveled; the officers pushed him into a dark room and then immediately pushed him back out. Still strapped to the chair and blind folded, the officers forcefully backed the chair out and into another cell or room. This went on for a few minutes, then they stopped in a room, and an officer started to talk to Craig. In total darkness, the officer said, "Inmate Titus, we're gonna unstrap you from the chair, lay you down on the bunk, strip your clothes off of you, and restrain you with your arms and legs behind your back."

There was a sinister presence in the room, as Craig was taken over to a bunk bed, told not to resist, and placed flat on his stomach with the blind fold still on his face. They physically restrained Craig with the bulk of their weight pushing his body into the mattress while they took his handcuffs off. With his faced shoved down into the mattress, and a crowd circled around him to gawk, his underwear and pants were pulled off and dropped on the ground.

Totally naked, Craig thought that he was about to either be raped or executed when someone ripped off his goggles and pulled his head back, yelling at him to stare straight forward at the laser dot from his shotgun on the wall. The officer pointed the laser to his head then back to the wall, and asked Titus if he knew what that red dot was for. Paralyzed in fear, Craig acknowledged that he knew what it was; it was for the bullet that would go in his head if he moved an inch. The officer said, "Be still, don't move, and don't take your eyes off of that dot as we exit from the cell." Still being videotaped, Craig Titus was asked if he had any injuries, while two female nurses took his vital signs, and Craig said, "Only my pride."

This video was not released for over a month, so the Clark County Detention Center had a long time to come up with a story to explain

CRUEL AND UNUSUAL PUNISHMENT

why this barbaric atrocity was done to Craig Titus. Assistant Sheriff Ray Flynn came up with some bullshit excuse saying that someone reported a man working near the ducts on the roof, and some Correctional Officers thought he might be helping Craig Titus escape from jail. Titus of course was not a part of any plan to escape from jail, and after further investigation, it was proven that this story was a lie, and the CCDC refused to explain why this extraction ever took place at all.

After the video became public, these smug officials justified the brutality of their actions by saying, "Titus was currently a suspect in a murder for hire plot, and faced First Degree Murder Charges against another woman." Sherriff Ray Flynn said, "Although it is not a common occurrence, this tactic is used occasionally when someone is thought to be an escape risk, or pose a threat to the well-being of the officers."

Craig Titus' defense attorney, Marc Saggese had a different take on the incident after viewing the video footage: "I am shocked and horrified! This is a man, who, by law, is presumed innocent, and he is being treated like an animal. There was no truth behind an escape attempt; this was psychological warfare. They had moved him multiple floors, he was in the basement, he was surrounded by security guards, he was in cuffs, strapped, everything you could name, but they had to take his pants and underwear off so he was naked? I mean, what does that reek of? That reeks of misconduct. It serves no purpose to do that, other than to humiliate Craig Titus and they were successful."

This traumatic incident left Craig Titus both physically and mentally scarred for life. Shell-shocked, and to this day, Craig lives every day in fear that this will happen to him again. Craig was not the only one that suffered from the brutality by the Clark County Detention Center. Craig's mother, to this day, becomes emotional when she talks about what "those monsters did to my son." Sandi Titus said that Dennis Bates, the man that was writing Craig's book, called her and told her to turn on the news. She said that her heart sank when she watched the officers terrorize her child. She subsequently sank into a depression because she knew there was nothing she could do about it. To this day, both Craig and Sandi Titus are afflicted with nightmares and bouts of depression, from the abuse needlessly inflicted on Craig Titus while he was housed at the Clark County Detention Center.

The reaction around the nation

Court TV's Catherine Crier said that it was, "a scene straight out of Silence of the Lambs!" Marc Saggese asked Catherine Crier "Was it necessary for them to have him naked and 'hog-tied'?" Tony Papa, author of "15 Years to Life" answered Saggese, "This is a classic case of authoritative overkill, and it is a human violation, used to intimidate the inmate." The activist encouraged Craig Titus' lawyer to file a lawsuit on his behalf, and Saggese replied, "First things first; I need to get this innocent man into courts to get him free."

Shortly after the videos were shown across the country, an article appeared in the Las Vegas Tribune, alleging wrongdoing on the part of officials at the Clark County Detention Center. The paper cited Titus' treatment in the expose:

Jail incident involving Craig Titus fearing escape attempt removed from cell

"At the Clark County Detention Center Rights Violations Are Taking Place" Picture of Craig Titus strapped to a wheel chair, naked, bound and blindfolded by Rolando Larraz Tribune Media Group Once again authorities have created a phantom scenario in order to excuse their inexplicable behavior, violation of rights, and abuses of power.

This time they have accused nationally known bodybuilder Craig Titus, who has been at the Clark County Detention Center in Solitary Confinement, of planning an escape and then tied him with belts, completely naked to a wheel chair. Their story is so well planned and manufactured that even the American Civil Liberties Union did not consider their actions human rights violations.

Titus and his wife, Kelly Ryan, have been in the Clark County Detention Center for a year, accused of murdering their personal assistant, Melissa James. During the one-year stay in the county jail, authorities have accused Titus of several infractions, including an escape attempt, and a plot to kill three witnesses in their case.

CRUEL AND UNUSUAL PUNISHMENT

The Associated Press has reported that a jailhouse informant, Dean Cassim, was the driving force behind the murder for hire investigation of Titus, according to a review of more than one hundred phone calls recorded by police. On the tapes, Cassim is repeatedly heard prodding Nelson Brady Jr., a jail house acquaintance of Titus, to meet with an undercover detective to pay for the services of a hit man named "Fred" who "was willing to kill as many as three witnesses in the Titus murder case for the right price." As part of the deal with the authorities, Cassim is now in London, from where he called the Las Vegas Tribune trying to sell his story.

When the Las Vegas Tribune told him that the newspaper does not pay for stories and does not deal with snitches, he tried to borrow $500.00 from the newspaper. He left a phone number "in case we should change our minds." Three separate meetings were set by Cassim for Brady to meet with the undercover officer. Brady failed to show up at all three meetings to hire "Fred" (the undercover officer) to kill the witnesses. Cassim then became irritated, making it a case of entrapment, almost forcing Brady to commit a crime. Cassim told Brady that we were disrespecting him (Cassim) and reminded him of what happens to people who disrespect someone in prison. Intimidated by Cassim's pressure, Brady eventually participated in two meetings with an undercover officer.

Back in October, Titus became the subject of an attempted escape investigation that placed him in solitary confinement until last week when jailed when officials uncovered "another escape attempt." Because jail officials and Public Information Office of the Las Vegas Metropolitan Police Department are not allowed to communicate with the Las Vegas Tribune (which is an obvious display of discrimination) reporters could not verify the accounts of the alleged escape attempt.

However, Deputy Chief Michael Holt, who oversees the Clark County Detention Center, told the rest of the Las Vegas media that "someone had crawled up onto the roof, directly where Mr. Titus was housed." Director Holt also told the Las Vegas media that "being that Mr. Titus was already in disciplinary housing, and that it was close to this area, we did not know whether or not there had been a breach of security to the outside of the building. We felt for security measures, it was best to use basically a high security or a high risk extraction and move him until we were able to search the room and get the full story of what was going on. The operation was recorded by jail officials and reviewed by high ranking police officials who believe that the actions the corrections officers used were appropriate and showed the officers acting courteously toward Titus, but no references were made when the cameras were off, both before and after the incident.

A copy of the tape was obtained by a request for the records by the review journal & viewed by the Director of the American Civil Liberties Union of Nevada Gary Peck told the Las Vegas Tribune, "We have serious concerns and questions based on the facts that we now know. I am hard pressed to understand why Mr. Titus was treated that way and what the department's policies are with respect to those matters. It would be nice if the department could offer some sort of explanation."

Peck from the Civil Liberties Union went on, "The other two things that are troubling me, when Mr. Titus was extracted from his cell, officers had a high powered rifle aimed at him and then later on had to have a taser drawn and aimed, and asked him if he knew what that taser was for- which is obvious to intimidate him and scare him- it is to shoot him in the head. I would like to know what the policies are in regard to those matters."

Craig Titus' attorney told the Las Vegas Tribune, "They treated Titus like an animal, as if he was trying to an escape; I believe they wanted him to try and escape so they could have shot him down like a hunted animal. After viewing the video, I am shocked and horrified. This is a man, who by law is presumed innocent until proven guilty," Saggese said. "They have now admitted that my client was not involved in any escape attempt. It was psychological warfare," Saggese said.

Saggese also said that jail officials moved Titus through multiple floors. While he was in the basement, he was surrounded by security guards. He was in cuffs, strapped, everything you could name, but did they have to make him walk around naked? That reeks of misconduct. It *served no purpose to do that, other than humiliate Craig Titus and they were successful."*

What was the purpose of the high- security extraction? Let's cut the shit and be real, it was not because they thought Craig Titus was about to escape! Examining everything that had happened thus far, their (Daskas, O'Kelley, Wilson and Glass) house of cards was about to collapse. Ron Brady Jr. was not going to flip on Craig Titus, and their plot from the top down would more than likely be exposed. Looking at the actions and behavior of the SWAT team, they gave Craig Titus a warning that if he did not do exactly what they said, they would kill him.

Given Craig's past, and his recent outbursts at Robert Daskas and Judge Jackie Glass in the courtroom, he could have very likely exploded and acted out against the SWAT team. It would only be human nature for a person to defend themselves when that person is threatened and attacked like Craig Titus was during this extraction. (It is my opinion, though there is no proof to back it up, looking at all of the circumstantial leading up to this event, this extraction was most likely a setup designed with the intention of pushing Craig to lose his temper. Once he lost his temper, he would have more than likely acted out, and the officers could have justifiably ended Craig Titus' life.)

CHAPTER 5

Making Sense out of Nonsense- The Case Against Ron Brady Jr.

Ron Brady Jr.'s Arraignment Hearing

Being housed in a completely different unit in isolation, Ron Brady Jr. had no idea what was going on with Craig. In fact nobody heard about it for nearly a month. On October 26th, 2006, Brady appeared in court for the first time at his arraignment hearing. The charges were explained to him, and he plead, "Not Guilty" to the Solicitation to Commit Murder, and the judge set his preliminary hearing for November 27, 2006.

Nothing about the murder for hire plot added up, and for the first time, the public began asking questions: "Is this just an incredible situation, or was this actually a book publishing deal that the police have turned into a murder for hire?" Why, if they interviewed Deen Cassim in March, and the facts of this case and evidence obtained were completed on May 19th, did it take six months to arrest Ron Brady Jr.? It made no sense, especially if he was a crazed man setting up three different murders? How could Robert Daskas comment to the newspaper that the three witnesses "were never in any real danger," unless it was because there was no Solicitation to Commit Murder? Six months is a long time to leave a "dangerous criminal" loose to walk the streets among his make-believe possible targets.

MAKING SENSE OUT OF NONSENSE- THE CASE AGAINST RON BRADY JR. ➤

Over a week after Ron Brady Jr. was booked, processed, interrogated, and placed in solitary confinement, the following warrant was issued for his arrest:

October 28, 2006: Declaration of Warrants/Summons (Event #060522-1455) for Nelson Ronald Brady Jr. ID # 1067408 executed on Sept. 15, 2006 - Homicide Detectives Robert Wilson and Dean O'Kelley were assigned to investigate the crimes of Solicitation of Murder, 3 Counts, **committed on or about May 22, 2006**, which investigation has developed Nelson Ronald Brady Jr., as the perpetrator thereof. The facts in wit:

* **On March 21, 2006**, Detective O'Kelley spoke to Sergeant Forbus with the CCDC Intelligence Section, he said an inmate had information to relay to detectives about Craig Titus.

***On March 22, 2006** at 1525 hrs. Detectives Wilson and O'Kelly conducted a preliminary interview, **which was not recorded** (this is curious because when they explained why they illegally tape recorded Craig Titus and Kelly Ryan in Boston, they stated that they always record every witness' testimony) *with Deen Cassim, ID# 1944564, During the interview, Cassim told detectives he had been solicited for the contract killing of Anthony Gross and the possible killing of two other witnesses in the case against Craig Titus and Kelly Ryan.*

Cassim said that Brady talked with him about the need to get rid of Anthony Gross. They spoke about a possible $25,000 up front payment and a $25,000 supplemental payment when the job was done. Cassim explained to Brady how the deal could be coordinated from inside the detention facility.

Cassim would contract a hit man on the outside to kill Anthony Gross. Brady would meet with the hit man and provide them with an envelope containing the up- front money.
(How would Deen Cassim know how to set all of this up? He wouldn't- this was an elaborate plan that could have only been though out and organized by an expert. Homicide Detectives O'Kelley and Wilson laid out the plan, and arranged to have Ron Brady Jr. transferred to Deen Cassim's cell.)

On March 23, 2006 Detectives Wilson & O'Kelley again meet with Cassim and his attorney Marty Hart. This interview was taped: Cassim consented to have the detectives monitor three way phone calls between him and Brady. Detectives developed a plan- Cassim would arrange for Brady to meet with Cassim's trusted friend, Edison. An undercover officer would pose as Edison. Brady would give Edison two envelopes. One envelope would contain money and another envelope would contain Gross' photograph and contact information. Edison would then pass it on to the supposed hit man named Fred, who would allegedly eliminate the intended target, Anthony Gross.

On March 24, 2006, the first call detectives monitored (not recorded) between Cassim and Brady occurred at 1635 hours. Cassim called Brady on his cell phone. Cassim told Brady he was going to get "Fred" to do the job for $25 K, $15 K of which would be covered by Cassim's credibility. Cassim told Brady that Edison was in town and he needs to give him $500 for expenses; he said it would come out of the back end of the deal unless Richard Schonfeld took his case. (This is interesting- why were the investigators trying to set-up Craig's attorney Richard Schonfeld?) *Cassim said to Brady 'I don't know what Craig told you about what happened but it looks like this number 23 is about 90 percent of the case against him.*

*** On March 25, 2006***, the meeting between Brady and the undercover officer posing as Edison did not occur. Brady did not show up at the appointed place and time. Several attempts were made to contact Brady over the next few days. Messages were left and Cassim spoke to Brady's father, Ron Brady Sr. & he said he would attempt to help Cassim stay in contact with his son.

On March28, 2006, at 1343 Cassim contacted Brady via telephone, Brady told Cassim he ran into a big problem- Brady claimed he was contacted by homicide detectives about the case. This alleged meeting never took place. Brady told Cassim the contact with the police scared him so much he did not want to meet with Edison for fear the police were watching him.

(Brady did not meet with the "go between" the first time, and then made up a story about the homicide detectives being on to him, and not wanting to have any part of this.)

MAKING SENSE OUT OF NONSENSE- THE CASE AGAINST RON BRADY JR.

* **On March 29, 2006-** *at 1440 hrs. Cassim called Brady and asked him if he read the mornings paper. When Brady said he had not, Cassim told Brady about the transcripts of Megan Pierson's Grand Jury Testimony. Cassim talked about a bag Craig had given Megan and Jeremy containing a stun gun. Brady said, 'They didn't use the stun gun on Melissa. Melissa got Kelly with the stun gun.'*

(Cassim called Brady to stir the shit, in an attempt to make him angry with Megan Pierson, and want to have her taken out. This proves that Craig and Ron had no idea that Megan was lying in court. It also explains why Daskas leaked the information; he was using Puit to set these guys up. If Daskas truly cared about the safety of Megan Pierson, he would have never leaked that info. Daskas knew this was all a set-up, but what if it backfired, and someone did get killed? Robert Daskas plays with people's lives like it's all just a big game.)

Several other calls were made and monitored in the same fashion as the others by Detective O'Kelley. He listened in on 3-way and took notes on the conversation.

*On April 2, 2006 Brady failed to show up for a second meeting scheduled with the undercover officer. Brady claimed he was on his way to the meeting but got pulled over by an officer. (Brady has not shown up twice, and actually told Cassim he didn't want to do this.)

*On April 4, 2006 Detective O'Kelley monitored another call between Brady and Cassim. Cassim told Brady he has spoken with Edison and the deal is off. Cassim recommended Brady save himself some money by going to the west side and getting some gang member to do the job.
(Brady is relieved to be off the hook. He ignores phone calls from Cassim, because he does not want to have any part in Deen Cassim's Murder-for- Hire!

*On April 10, 2006, Brady and Cassim had a phone conversation recorded on the jail monitoring system. Cassim says he gives up on this because Ron is not serious. Ron says "I am not going to do that to you." Cassim sets up another meeting, this time with his "ex-girlfriend."

* **On April 11, 2006** Brady failed to meet at the Starbucks with the undercover officer posing as Cassim's ex-girlfriend. Several attempts were made to contact Brady which were not successful.
(This is the third time that Brady has not shown up, but they don't back down!)

* **On April 11, 2006** at approximately 2250, Brady received a call from Titus on a recorded jail line. Brady begins by telling Titus that he wanted to talk to him about the book publishing deal. Brady said that he had been on the internet to see which characters are going to be in the book. Titus said, 'Yeah. No shit. Yeah, from the screenplay. Yeah." Brady says that he thinks the book will go great anyway and that he will make good money on it.
(How could anybody think this was code for a murder hit?)

* **On April 21, 2006** Cassim calls Brady and explains that Fred would be willing to accept an envelope with a thousand dollars. Cassim said if they decided not to do the deal, they still owed Fred a thousand dollars for his troubles.

(So now they try to set Brady up by telling him he can pay money for the hit man's troubles, and everything will be dropped. Brady didn't have this kind of money, and wanted Cassim to just get tired of calling him and give up on the whole thing, but Cassim stalked, and threatened Brady every day, until Brady finally gave up, got the money together and answered Cassim's calls. He felt duped out of a thousand dollars, but he would give them this cash to leave him alone and stop harassing him twenty times a day.)

* **On May 17, 2006** at 1248, Cassim called Brady and he agreed to meet Cassim's ex-girlfriend at 2:00 pm at Starbuck's. At 1402, the undercover officer posing as Cassim's ex-girlfriend is heard greeting Brady. Brady was heard describing the two envelopes he was handing to the detective. One was for the attorney's fees and the other was for the book publication. The detective said there was $500 in the attorney's fee envelope. Brady said he would be able to give her the other $500 the next day. After the meeting was over, the envelopes were opened and the money was photocopied and impounded.

CHAPTER **6**

Exposing the Unbelievable Truth

It is ironic how back in June, the Metro detectives were not smart enough to notify men in their own office about cutting off Tony Gross' ankle monitor. Because of this "accidental oversight", Robert Daskas, Tony Gross' attorney, and the investigators had to meet in private with Judge Glass (in person- a phone call would not do) to explain everything that had happened. Yet, in November, Daskas was cunning enough to tactically arrange to have Anthony Gross severed from *the State vs. Titus, Ryan & Gross* during a time when the other lawyers were preoccupied with the chaos going on around their clients.

Tony Gross and his lawyers helped Robert Daskas set Craig Titus and Ron Brady Jr. up (Seriously, that's one huge ass favor- play dead in a car with fake blood, fly him off to Chicago where he's promised he could stay until it was over. However after detectives hit a snag when Craig Titus didn't fall into their trap and pay money for a hit, Tony had to come back and do a pretend trial where he and everyone else already knew the outcome: Motion Denied.)

Daskas would inevitably reward him with having his charges dropped, but they had to be very careful with how they handled the pay off. On November 7th, 2006 Anthony Gross appeared with his attorney's Palazzo & Oronoz in front of Judge Jackie Glass in a court hearing where the attorneys would ask to have all ties cut with Titus and Ryan in a Motion for Relief from Prejudicial Joinder. Robert Daskas was of course there to argue in favor of Gross during the motion.

According to the Court Minutes: "Mr. Daskas advised that the State does not oppose the defendant's motion because as far as the State knows at this point, the defendant was not part of the conspiracy to kill the victim; the defendant is not charged with the murder itself, and there is evidence of a recent plot by co-defendant Titus to kill defendant Gross. The court FINDS there will be prejudice to defendant Gross if the matter is not severed. Why was Robert Daskas never called out on this? First, Robert Daskas states, "as far as the State knows at this point, the defendant was not part of the conspiracy to kill the victim." (Are you kidding me?)

Let's take a moment to look back at your own words, Robert Daskas and Dean O'Kelly's testimony as you questioned him under oath:

Robert Daskas: "Good morning everyone my name is Robert Daskas. This morning we will begin the presentation of the State of Nevada –vs.- Craig Michael Titus, Kelly Ann Ryan, and Anthony Remo Gross. The defendants in this case are charged with Murder with use of a deadly weapon, 1st Degree Kidnapping, Accessory to Murder, and Third Degree Arson. Every person concerned in the commission of a felony, whether he or she directly commits the act, or **Aids or Abets** in its commission, and whether present or absent; every person who directly or indirectly counsels, encourages, hires, commands, or otherwise procures another to commit a felony, with the intent that the crime will be accomplished is a principal and shall be proceeded against and punished as such. **Conspiracy** is an agreement or mutual understanding between two or more persons to commit a crime."

Robert Daskas' Question: *As part of your investigation did you meet with and interview Anthony Gross? What did you discover from this first interview?*

Dean O'Kelley's Answer: *Yes I did on December 19th 2005. We spoke for probably forty-five minutes to an hour before we actually recorded the interview. The interview took place at his attorney, Louis Palazzo's office, and Detective Wilson and I interviewed him. We had obtained phone records and surveillance images prior to asking him questions. Gross was not aware that we had this information before we questioned him. We asked him if he had talked to Craig Titus on December 14th, and he said that Titus called him when he was asleep early in* the morning at his girlfriend's (Elizabeth Williams) house. He said he ignored the calls that he received between 2:30 and 3:00 am. Gross stated that he eventually picked the phone up, and Craig told him he needed his help. Gross said that he met Craig Titus and Kelly Ryan at the Shell Gas Station in a truck that was also registered to his mother. He originally told us, before we started the recording that Craig and Kelly were waiting on him but when we told him about the surveillance video, he changed his story and said they came in together at the same time. Gross put gas in the red plastic gas can, and put it on his center console. Gross said that Craig called him and told him where to drive around 4:15 am; and the video footage shows them driving off at this time. He said they drove 15-20 minutes out past the mountain range leading to Pahrump back down to a flat area and then they turned onto a dirt road, and he drove down a ways and then pulled over. Gross said that Kelly Ryan jumped out of the Jaguar and jumped into the passenger seat of his truck and told him to turn the vehicle around. Gross said he pulled up about 2 car lengths past the Jaguar (20 feet), and then Gross said he passed the gas can to Craig Titus. Gross said that he was talking to Kelly Ryan, unaware of what Craig was doing, and then Craig came running up to the car, jumped in and yelled at him to go. Gross said he saw a glow behind him, and that was the first time that he realized what might have been happening. Gross said that he dropped Craig and Kelly off at their house without asking any questions.

Daskas' Question: *Gross told you that he met Craig and Kelly at the Short line Shell Gas Station, and did not meet with or talk to Titus before this point, correct? Did you confront him with further evidence that proved otherwise?*

O'Kelley's Answer: *Yes, in the video obtained by Green Valley Grocery, when we tried to find Kelly Ryan and Melissa James, we instead found footage of Tony Gross around three a.m. of that morning which is around the block from Craig and Kelly's home, maybe a two minute drive.*

Daskas' Question: *During your investigation did you obtain cell phone records for Mr. Titus? And did you analyze these cell phone records to determine when the two men contacted each other on December 13th and December 14th?*

O'Kelley's Answer: *The earliest phone call we found on that day was placed from Craig Titus' cell phone to Tony Gross' cell phone at 3:28 pm. There were 13 additional phone calls in that time frame: on Tuesday December 13th at 4:39 pm, at 6:23 pm, at 7:46 pm, at 8:02 pm; then on Wednesday December 14th at 2:34 am, 3:22 am, 4:20 am, and the last call at 4:28 am.*

Daskas has Anthony Gross separated from Craig Titus and Kelly Ryan

It's interesting to watch Robert Daskas on National Television: every time he appears on a true-crime show (*48 Hours, Snapped, Wicked Attraction* to name a few) about the Craig Titus case, he talks about Craig Titus constantly changing his story. When in reality, Robert Daskas is the one who was always changing his story! Not just on shows, but in court as well. Daskas called Craig "disingenuous, and a man of dubious character," on numerous occasions, but these are actually the perfect words to describe Robert Daskas.

Talk about deceitful- Robert Daskas argued in front of Judge Jackie Glass that Anthony Gross was not a part of the conspiracy, when Daskas under oath during the grand jury hearings presented evidence that Tony Gross was in fact involved in the conspiracy to commit murder. Daskas' own evidence presented to the grand jury showed phone records between Craig and Anthony (14 total in 24 hours).

The first call at 3:28 p.m. was right after Melissa overdosed, and Craig called Tony to help him out. There is surveillance coverage of Gross at Green Valley Grocery, surveillance of Gross leading Craig and Kelly into a Shell station where he put gas in a gas can, and surveillance of Tony leading Craig and Kelly out of the parking lot, and onto the highway where they burned the car. The Prosecution's key witness even said that Tony helped them conceal the body right after she died, and then had a set time to meet them to dispose of the body.

According to Daskas' explanation for the Joinder of Defendants when he charged the three with the crime, "Two or more defendants may be joined in the same indictment or complaint if the charges against them arise out of the same criminal conduct or episode or out of a course of criminal conduct or series of criminal episodes so connected as to constitute parts of a single scheme, plan, conspiracy or joint enterprise."

When they went before the grand jury, Daskas wanted to lock Gross up and throw away the key. A few months later, Robert Daskas was making deals with Tony Gross to set Craig Titus up. A few months after that, Daskas asked the judge to separate Gross from Craig and Kelly, saying he had nothing to do with Melissa James' death. No surprise, Judge Jackie Glass ruled: COURT ORDERED, Defendant's motion is GRANTED, defendant GROSS IS SEVERED FROM THE CO-DEFENDANT'S TRIAL matter reset for trial.

As Information is released to the media- the public begins to ask questions

During the first days of December, the truth began to come out, and people began to question the homicide detectives and prosecutor in the case. The name of the jail house snitch (Deen Cassim) that set Craig Titus and Ron Brady Jr. up was published in the newspaper, and people were outraged to learn about his violent history and that his sentence of three to twelve years had been erased! Robert Daskas, the same man that had a negative comment to add about every article written about Craig Titus, when asked if he had a comment about the release of Deen Cassim, had no comment.

Craig Titus' defense attorney Marc Saggese had plenty to say however: "The benefits afforded to Cassim were inappropriate; and it leads me to conclude that there was a set-up. Deen Cassim is a violent criminal, and they've let a violent criminal out on the streets. I've never seen anything like this before! A defendant who already has been sentenced to prison, resentenced in the same case after cooperating with authorities. Do you know how hard it is to amend a sentencing like this? I'm floored. I have never, ever, heard of a resentencing of a convicted felon like that."

If Saggese was not bewildered and outraged enough over Deen Cassim being set free, the plot to arrange the "Murder for Hire" scheme was revealed in the Las Vegas Review Journal, and it sent him over the edge!

(I start to wonder if Puit began to realize that he had been duped by Robert Daskas over the previous year.)

BODYBUILDER CASE: Police Tried Ruse of Phony Corpse
December 5, 2006 *By GLENN PUIT REVIEW-JOURNAL*

Anthony Gross is very much alive! But in June, when Las Vegas police suspected that Craig Titus had ordered the slayings of Gross and two other witnesses in the bodybuilder's murder case, Gross agreed to play dead. According to police reports, Gross posed as a corpse at the behest of detectives, and he was photographed by police in the trunk of a car- bound with duct tape, bloodied and seemingly lifeless.

Las Vegas detectives planned to use the bogus death photos to make Titus believe a hit man had killed Gross. But Titus, who was locked up at the CCDC, didn't bite on the law enforcement trickery. When Titus received a postcard at the jail from the supposed hit man, Titus turned it over to his attorney instead of calling the hit man on a police-monitored phone or wiring the hit man money, as detectives had hoped he would do. Clark County prosecutor Robert Daskas declined to comment Monday.

Titus' defense attorney, Marc Saggese, said he thinks authorities crossed the line in the investigation. Saggese said, "Titus' actions in the face of the police ruse confirm what Titus has said all along, he had nothing to do with the murder-for-hire plot. It is just more evidence as to the great lengths the state and police will go to smear the character and reputation of my client."

The particulars of the murder-for-hire investigation are detailed in a 28-page police report. In October, police arrested an acquaintance of Titus, Nelson Brady Jr., on charges of trying to hire a hit man to kill three witnesses in Titus' case. One of the individuals authorities said was targeted in the plot was Gross. Two other witnesses targeted, authorities said, were Megan Pierson Foley and her husband, Jeremy Foley. Titus has not been charged in the murder-for-hire plot, but authorities have voiced suspicions that he was behind the scheme. He was recorded twice on jail phones talking to Brady about a "book *deal" and screenplay, which authorities suspect was code for the murder-for-hire plot.*

According to police reports, the origins of the murder-for-hire inquiry date to March, when a jailhouse informant named Deen Cassim approached authorities and claimed "he had been solicited for the planned killing of Anthony Gross and the possible contract killing of two other witnesses in the case against Craig Titus." Over the following weeks and months, police carried out an elaborate investigation with the help of Cassim working in the role of informant. Cassim was still in custody at the time, but Brady was out of jail.

According to the reports, police decided the best way to maintain contact between the two men was to have a detective pose as an investigator with the public defender's office. The detective would call Cassim, who then made three-way calls to Brady without Brady suspecting the phone line was being recorded because calls between the public defender's office and inmates at the jail are not recorded. The police reports said that Cassim was in repeated contact with Brady.

Three separate meetings were set up with Brady in which he was scheduled to meet with an undercover detective posing as a go-between for a hit man named "Fred," but Brady failed to show at each meeting. A fourth meeting was arranged by Cassim, and this time, Brady showed. Police alleged that during the meeting and a subsequent meeting, Brady paid an undercover detective $1,500...

On June 15, the reports said that detectives met with Gross, his parents and his attorney, James Oronoz. Gross was on house arrest at the time and wearing an electronic ankle bracelet that allowed authorities to track his whereabouts under the terms of his release. "Several photographs were taken of Gross while lying on his side in the plastic lined trunk of a white Lexus wearing his (employee) uniform," the report said. "Gross had his wrists duct taped together, a strip of duct tape across his mouth, and fake blood dripping down the side of his head and face. The fake blood was pooled around Gross' head and upper body."

On June 21, police met with Gross again at a Home Depot parking lot and "cut the ankle monitor off. Gross was kept at the police homicide office until 5:00 a.m. the following morning, then taken to McCarran International Airport and flown to Chicago.

But police had not told Gross' house arrest officer of the murder-for-hire investigation. That same day, the officer monitoring Gross' house arrest called homicide detectives to let them know he had secured a warrant from District Judge Jackie Glass' court to arrest Gross.

On June 26, the prosecutor on the case, Daskas, met with Glass and Gross' attorney, Oronoz, regarding Gross' disappearance. "Judge Glass was informed of the actual circumstances regarding Gross' disappearance and his current location/status," the reports said.

On July 11, detectives told Daskas they were going to send a postcard to Titus from the supposed hit man, then see whether he called the cell phone or whether any money was placed in the bank account for the purported hit on Gross. The postcard sent to Titus from the supposed hit man read: "In town for a few days. Thinking of you and wondering why I haven't heard from you with that address. I'm running short on funds. No money in my bank account. Waiting for payday. Will be heading back to LA on the 16th, so I won't be here for your 'big day.' Expect to hear from you before then. Fred. 702-469-1942." The card was addressed to Craig Titus with a return address of "Fred Hitterman."

Saggese said that when Titus received the postcard, he immediately turned it over to his prior attorney, Richard Schonfeld. Saggese also said that based on the contents of the police report read to him by the Review-Journal on Monday evening, he plans to explore the timing of the meeting with Daskas, Oronoz and Glass, and whether procedure was followed.

According to the police report, the prosecutor and Gross' attorney met with Glass in June about Gross' disappearance, but there is no mention in the documents of the previous attorneys for Titus and Ryan (Tom Pitaro and Richard Schonfeld) being present at the same meeting. Judicial rules prevent a judge from meeting with one party of a case without all other parties to the same case being present. Such a meeting is referred to as an ex parte communication which is prohibited. In July, nearly a month later, Glass denied motions from Titus, Ryan and Gross to dismiss the criminal case against them. Saggese said. "I have to protect the procedural due process rights of my client."

With the article about the phony "Murder-for-hire" death scene, orchestrated by the homicide detectives and Tony Gross, many were left asking themselves, "What the hell is going on?" Nobody wanted to believe that law enforcement, prosecutors, and judges would be in on a plan to destroy an innocent man; but with the release of the article, it was not hard to put things together, and conclude that nothing was adding up!

Time Line:

April 18th Judge Jackie Glass Denies Bail

April 22nd Kelly Ryan's mother passes away

June 15th Homicide Detectives Dean O'Kelley and Rob Wilson meet with Tony Gross and his parents to discuss the phony murder plot.

June 21st Homicide Detectives Dean O'Kelley and Rob Wilson meet with Tony Gross, and stage a murder scene placing Gross in the trunk of a car with duct tape and fake blood. They cut his ankle monitor, and fly him to Chicago.

June 26th Gross is reported missing and the Detectives, Prosecutor, Tony Gross' attorney, and Judge Jackie Glass all meet to discuss why Tony Gross is missing.

July 11th Homicide Detectives Dean O'Kelley and Rob Wilson notify Prosecutor Robert Daskas that they have sent Craig the letter to solicit money.

(Everyone involved in the Melissa James case knew this set-up was taking place, a few days before a court appearance to have charges dismissed because of prosecutorial misconduct by Robert Daskas in the Grand Jury Hearings.)

◂ SWIFT INJUSTICE

July 18th Craig Titus, Kelly Ryan, Anthony Gross appear in court in regard to arguments for the defendant's request for a Writ of Habeas Corpus (dismissal of charges and release from custody) because of failure of the prosecution, Robert Daskas, to prove that either a kidnapping or murder occurred.

How was Anthony Gross able to sit next to Craig Titus and Kelly Ryan, pretend like nothing was going on, after he had just had fake blood poured all over him and flown to Chicago and back? How was the judge able to sit there in court, knowing everything that happened, and act like she could rule on the motion fairly? She dismissed all the charges against everyone, including Tony Gross. Can you honestly tell me it was not prearranged for the judge to separate Gross from Titus and Ryan's trial in November, and dismiss all of Gross' charges in the near future? Robert Daskas tried to set Craig Titus up with a picture of Anthony Gross posing as a corpse. The same co-defendant Robert Daskas was appointed to prosecute in court! Isn't it logical both Robert Daskas and the "honorable" Judge Jackie Glass should have stepped away from this case, due to a conflict of interest? That would require an ethical compass, so instead of doing the right thing, they fought to stay on the case.

Many times defense attorneys can be full of shit, and say whatever they have to in order to win a case. That was not what Marc Saggese was doing when he filed a motion to have Judge Jackie Glass removed. Having her stay in that position and preside over that trial was unethical on so many levels. When Saggese stood up and said that both Daskas and Glass were liars and the judge needed to step down, he was not grandstanding. It was a bold move from this young lawyer! Saggese did, however, recognize that doing so could be political suicide for his career as a lawyer in Las Vegas. He was well aware of how the game was played: everyone "on the in" scratches each other's backs, they don't stab each other in the back.

Everything that happened in the courts to Craig Titus, happened in the Binion trial, and the Nevada Supreme Court threw out the decision. In the second trial, a jury acquitted the defendants. This made Saggese and Cristalli nationally famous, but they now had a big target on their backs. They had been black balled from their fraternity

EXPOSING THE UNBELIEVABLE TRUTH

brothers in the Vegas Legal community. The District Attorney's office appeared to be incompetent after the Binion trial, including Robert Daskas, and they were not going to let that happen again.

In the Nevada Judicial System there's an inbred posse of lawyers that are all connected to each other. These lawyers maneuver themselves through the system and into the next position of power. They start off as a deputy district attorney, five- ten years later they become a district court judge. Five to ten years after that they become a Nevada Supreme Court judge. So there are very few rulings against the prosecutors by the judges, and there are very few rulings against the judges by the Nevada Supreme Court judges; because they are all colleagues who cover each other. When the Supreme Court ruled against the District Attorney's office in the Binion trial, everyone was shocked!

After the ex parte communication discovery, Marc Saggese asked Judge Jackie Glass to recuse herself from the case, and she refused. So when Saggese decided to file a motion to have her dismissed, it was the right thing to do, but he knew that lightening striking twice was probably not going to happen. Making it even more difficult, it would not even be sent to the Nevada Supreme Court. It got tossed down the hall, a few offices over, to the "Chief of Judges." (This is another district court judge that has volunteered to organize the other judge's case loads, throws out motions by defense attorneys, and organizes the Christmas party every year.)

CHAPTER 7

Judge Jackie Glass refuses to step down

Marc Saggese files a motion to get Judge Glass removed
On December 24th 2006, Craig Titus' attorney Marc Saggese filed a motion to remove Judge Jackie Glass from the trial for engaging in a prohibited conversation with a prosecutor and another attorney about the case. Saggese said, "Judge Glass engaged in misconduct by holding a prohibited conversation with a prosecutor and another attorney." Judge Jackie Glass never recused herself from Craig's Murder case, and remained the judge while trying to set him up on a fictitious Murder for Hire plot.

The motion stated: "On June 26, Robert Daskas and an attorney for Anthony Gross, James Oronoz, met with Judge Jackie Glass about the matter. According to a Las Vegas police report, "Glass was informed of the actual circumstances regarding Gross' disappearance and his current location and status." Saggese said the meeting was improper and prejudiced his client. Under Nevada Judicial rules, a judge cannot meet with one party of a case unless the other parties of that case are present. Saggese and Titus' and Ryan's attorneys at the time were not invited to the meeting.

Furthermore, he said, he suspected Glass was told that Titus might be involved in a plot to kill Gross. A little more than a month later, Glass denied important legal motions for Titus and Ryan that sought to dismiss the charges against the couple. At the time, Glass did not mention her meeting with Daskas and Oronoz. "Knowledge of that investigation could not do anything but impact her neutrality," Saggese said. "It's only human." In his motion, Saggese sought Glass' removal from the case. It also asked for a chance to re-argue Titus' and Ryan's legal motions in front of another judge.

According to the Nevada Code of Judicial Conduct, Judge Jackie Glass should have been thrown off that case.

RULE 2.9 Ex Parte Communications: *(A) A judge shall not permit communications made to the judge outside the presence of the all the parties or their lawyers, concerning a pending or impending (a matter that is expected to occur in the near future) matter.*
RULE 2.11 Disqualification: *(A) A judge shall disqualify himself or herself in any proceeding in which the judge's impartiality might reasonably be questioned if the judge has a personal bias or prejudice concerning a party or a party's lawyer, or personal knowledge of facts that are in dispute in the proceeding.*

In an affidavit filed Thursday, Glass said Saggese' allegations are not accurate. "I was not advised of the actual circumstances regarding Mr. Gross' disappearance…I was told by Mr. Daskas and Oronoz that Mr. Gross had not absconded (escaped) and that I did not need to issue a warrant," Glass said. "I do not believe I acted improperly, and I believe I can be fair and impartial," Glass said. (If that were the case, then wouldn't a phone call from Metro to the judge would suffice? Why did the judge have to meet behind closed doors with everyone except the attorneys for Craig Titus and Kelly Ryan? Why did the report say that the details of the case were discussed?)

In Saggese' opinion, judicial rules make it clear that the meeting of the judge, the prosecutor, and Gross' attorney means that Glass cannot preside over the case. Saggese said he was prepared to litigate the matter to the Nevada Supreme Court if necessary, "This is not a discretionary recusal," he said. "It's mandatory."

Nobody was surprised on January 2, 2007, when District Court Judge Kathy Hardcastle ruled in favor of Jackie Glass stating, "I reviewed the allegations against Glass and determined that the judge did nothing wrong, and she would be allowed to stay on the case. What is presented here is nothing more than a bare motion supported by suspicions and assumptions about why events turned out the way they did. This court cannot disqualify a judge on such a motion."

Saggese said he was disappointed with the ruling, and felt that a hearing on the matter should have been held. He said given the facts presented to him, he had a legal obligation to pursue Glass' removal. "I just want to make sure everyone is playing by the rules," Saggese said. "Don't fault the defense for taking the words of an officer as true."

It is actually rare for a judge to recuse him or herself from a case, and even more rare to have an appointed "Chief" Judge make the decision to have their colleague step down because of judicial misconduct. Craig Titus, along with any other defendant in the same situation would be powerless to obtain due process when conflicted judges refuse to recuse themselves in the State of Nevada.

The Law of Recusal is clear cut: "It's not enough for judges to act in an unbiased manner when suspected of a potential conflict of interest. A judge must avoid even the appearance of bias. The test for impropriety is whether the conduct of the judge would create in any independent and reasonable observer a perception that the judge's ability to carry out judicial responsibilities with integrity, impartiality, would think that an appearance of bias is likely. If so a judge must withdraw from supervising a case." In reality, defendants have almost no power to enforce the rule, especially when the judge is determined to retain control.

According to the United States Supreme Court Law: "A judge must bow out of a hearing in which his or her impartiality might reasonably be questioned."

Corruption is a huge problem in the judicial system in Nevada because prosecutors, judges and defense lawyers are being "held accountable" by other prosecutors, judges, and defense lawyers all having the same motive. This would be the equivalent of a student being assigned "hall monitor," and reporting his friends and fellow classmates in to the principal.

Just like friends don't want to tattle on friends, lawyers don't want to report on other lawyers for ethical violations. When Defense Attorneys report prosecutorial misconduct or judicial misconduct, those attorneys and their clients will be targeted in the future, much like what happened with Saggese and Cristalli after the Ted Binion case. When Saggese reported Robert Daskas and Judge Jackie Glass for violating Craig Titus' due process rights, the prosecutor and judge teamed up together and made Craig Titus' life even more unbearable than they already had before.

Saggese reported the ethical violation to the courts, and a fellow judge shot it down. Even though judges are bound by a code of judicial conduct, and are actually instructed to "report and assist in misconduct investigations," judges rarely ever do that. In reality, it is absurd to have judges discipline other judges.

"Judging the Judges" gave both Glass and Hardcastle "F's"

As a side note, in the Review-Journal, in an article titled, "Judging the Judges: Lawyers gave an "F" rating to three Clark County Judges on a report card;"...Guess who made the list? Judge Kathy Hardcastle and Judge Jackie Glass! In the report, Las Vegas lawyers were asked to anonymously critique, evaluate, and rate the performances of the Clark County District Court Judges. A majority of the lawyers believed that both Judge Kathy Hardcastle and Judge Jackie Glass should not be re-elected, and they received failing marks from the attorneys. Hardcastle's worst scores (48 % less than adequate) were on appropriate rulings, applying law and rules, and courtesy. One lawyer wrote that while Hardcastle previously excelled in the administrative role of chief judge, she seems less effective since returning to the trial bench. Glass had similar scores, with 56 % opposed to her retention. Nearly half called her less than adequate on appropriate rulings, proper application of law and courtesy.

If this was true, why was Glass assigned the biggest trial in Nevada history (the O.J. Simpson trial) a couple of months after she sentenced Craig Titus? My theory is that the District Attorney's office knew that Glass had an agenda, retribution for O.J. being acquitted of murder in 1995, and that she would follow right along as the prosecution over charged Simpson for crimes he did not commit. It's curious how the District Attorney's office operates: Deen Cassim, who actually had a gun in his hand, and did attempt to kidnap and kill a victim in an armed robbery, was set free. While O.J. Simpson's was convicted of armed robbery and kidnapping for going into a hotel room and demanding to have his things back that had been stolen from him. Simpson did not have a gun, and they all stayed in one room. Of course, everyone knows the story, and O.J. was handed an outrageous sentence by Judge Jackie Glass, which catapulted her Hollywood career.

Daskas and Denue team up

With all the craziness going on, Kelly Ryan's temporary public defender, assigned to represent her while the courts ruled on Cristalli, made every attempt to have Kelly separated from Craig in the upcoming trial. Without Kelly's knowledge, Denue filed a Motion for Relief from Prejudicial Joinder on his client's behalf (after consulting with the prosecution) then he never bothered to tell Ryan about it, or even show back up to work for that matter.

Denue pulled a Dillard, and was nowhere to be found for a couple of weeks. During this time, Kelly Ryan began to panic. She was told about the motion, but Denue never came around to explain it himself. Robert Daskas offered the same deal to Denue, that he had originally offered Ryan in the beginning: if she blames everything on Craig and testifies against him, charges will eventually be dropped down the line.

The move to Denue seemed like a no-brainer: convince the court that Titus abused Kelly, have her testify against Craig in court, and she would walk out the doors a free woman. Denue saw what happened to people that refused to cooperate and testify against Titus; they were stuck in solitary confinement, facing years in prison. Those who cooperated, walked out the prison doors, and were provided with an all-expense paid vacation with a round-trip flight to the destination of their choice by the District Attorney's Office.

The only problem for Denue was that Kelly had "found God" in prison. It would be even harder to convince Ryan to jump on the band wagon and tell a few lies under oath. She would, after all, be breaking one of the Ten Commandments: "Thou Shall Not Lie or Bear False Witness." He knew the church lady would never go for that, so he moved forward with the motion without her approval. With Daskas pulling the strings, Denue said he would tell a jury that Kelly Ryan was a battered woman and under the control of her husband, knowing that she would not be willing to say it herself.

During this time, Craig was informed by Saggese what was going on; Craig attempted to make contact with Denue, and Denue blew him off. Kelly corresponded with Craig through letters, communicating to him that she was confused and scared, and Denue was nowhere to be found. Craig asked Saggese to go check on Kelly for him as a friend. It was at this time that Kelly Ryan had a complete breakdown, and told Saggese that she wanted to fire Greg Denue.

Fire in the Desert is released

In the Binion trial, a local crime reporter was fed information by the prosecution, and he wrote a book about the case. Now we see history repeating itself as another crime reporter from another local newspaper is fed information about the Titus case from the prosecution, and he has also written a book. There is a slight difference this time. The last reporter waited until the trial was over before he published the book, this reporter wrote a book and had it published a year and a half *before* the case went to trial!

One would hope lessons were learned from the first go around, and Judge Glass and Robert Daskas wouldn't show up at a book signing for autographs like Judge Joseph Bonaventure and District Attorney David Roger did right after the first Binion trial.

On January 8th 2007, Las Vegas Review Journal's Glenn Puit released the book, "Fire in the Desert: The True Story of Craig Titus- Kelly Ryan Murder Mystery." According to the book, the author had the inside scoop gathered by the Las Vegas Police against Craig Titus and Kelly Ryan. The book was said to offer an independent examination of the fitness couple's actions before and after their personal assistant was found dead.

SWIFT INJUSTICE

It seems peculiar to have a book written about a murder trial a year and a half before the case even went to trial: with no preliminary hearing, only testimony from a grand jury hearing; testimony where the defense was not present, and not able to cross-examine any of the prosecution's witnesses. How can the book's title claim to be the "True Story" about Craig and Kelly, when there had not even been a trial to prove their guilt or innocence yet? The only information this reporter had was information provided to him by the corrupt Las Vegas police department and court system. Craig and Kelly's family and friends were never interviewed in order to provide a more balanced description of the couple.

When asked why Glenn Puit would publish this book so early, he provided the following response: "I've been asked why I did this book, and why I also decided to come out with it pretrial. At the time I took this on, I was coming off a very successful run with my first book. It did very well, it's a great book, and as a result, I'm always on the lookout for other cases that would make for a good book. I like writing true crime books, and, it's pretty obvious to everyone that the Titus-Ryan affair is a very, very interesting case. Primarily, however, the reason I did this book was because I had the chance to. I was fortunate to have a **source that was willing to give me the entire police investigative case file early on in the case**. We put some of the major stuff in the Review-Journal from the file as news content, and in the meantime, I also felt the contents of the police file would make for a good book. Bottom line was the opportunity presented itself, so I chose to follow up on it as opposed to letting it get away from me. Regarding the idea that I somehow have a potential conflict as a reporter and author, I'm not agreeing with that at all, although I respect everyone's opinion and I believe such skepticism is healthy. In fact, there is too little of it in the news business. There are two reasons why I released the book pretrial. One, there is a competitive advantage in being the first book out. It's certainly not a perfect situation, but the cold hard truth in the media business is that being second is worthless, and my goal is to have my work read. Second, and most importantly, I was in the unique position where I had enough information in front of me, i.e. exclusive content about the case, to warrant publishing the book pretrial. I think the book is very good, and I'm proud of it."

CHAPTER 8

That would be a Conflict of Interest!

Greg Denue —vs. - Marc Saggese and Michael Cristalli

The sparks began to fly in February at a pretrial hearing when Kelly Ryan announced that she fired her attorney Greg Denue, and that she would be replacing him with Michael Cristalli. Cristalli said Titus and Ryan had signed a "joint defense agreement," meaning they would pursue the same line of defense. Judge Jackie Glass had already denied Kelly Ryan's request, saying that it was a conflict of interest.

With the help of Marc Saggese, Kelly Ryan appealed that decision in the Nevada Supreme Court. With the exception of the Titus/ Ryan team, everyone in the courtroom was unhappy, including the prosecutor Robert Daskas. Of the over 30 trials Robert Daskas had won as a prosecutor, Cristalli was the only one to hand him a defeat in the highly publicized Ted Binion murder trial. Cristalli announced that Craig and Kelly would attack the charges in a united defense, much like Tabish and Murphy did in the Binion trial.

The judge was displeased because according to her, she would have to delay the trial once again. (Actually, she was the one causing the delays by not allowing Kelly to choose who she wanted to represent her during the trial.) Greg Denue said he had preliminary discussions with Clark County prosecutor Robert Daskas about the possibility of Ryan pleading guilty to lesser charges, but any plea would require Ryan to testify against her husband, and Ryan would not even consider that.

Denue said, "They (prosecutors) wanted to know what she could give them, and the deal was contingent upon how much information she was willing to provide to the prosecution. Kelly Ryan has declined to provide them with anything, because she was adamant that Craig Titus did not kill this girl. Even if Kelly Ryan was able to walk, she won't do it. She refuses to say that Craig murdered this girl because she says he did not do it, and insists Melissa James died of a drug overdose."

Greg Denue explained that everything was more complicated than just dropping him as her attorney. He said, "With the murder for hire case pending against Craig Titus, it changes the dynamics of everything." Denue tried to file motions to have her case heard a part from Titus' because she appeared to him to be a "battered wife;" Kelly didn't approve of this move, and decided to fire Denue in return, and insisted on having Cristalli represent her.

Denue believed Kelly was confused, and did not know where to turn, so she wanted the Nevada Supreme Court to decide how it will would be handled. Denue believed he needed to stay and fight "for the best interest of Kelly Ryan." Denue said the prosecution revealed to him that they were likely going to charge Titus with trying to kill three witnesses and this will imperil Ryan's right to a fair trial if the couple is tried together." "Although Ryan's name is not mentioned in the police reports regarding the murder-for-hire plot, if Titus is charged in the scheme, a jury will not be able to look past the allegations when mulling Ryan's fate," Denue said. "I've got the motion for severance in my brief case, and with the support of the prosecution, I am about to file it."

(Once again Daskas was attempting to influence and prejudice the courts in the decisions made about Craig Titus, by falsely claiming that Craig Titus was tied to the "murder for hire" plot.)

Denue stated to the court that he believed his firing was the result of Titus' controlling his wife's legal defense. Denue said, "That will be detrimental to Ryan in the long run. Who is looking out for Kelly? I think Titus has been pulling the strings." Denue said that Titus had repeatedly tried to communicate with him since he started representing

Ryan. Denue said he never responded to Titus' inquiries. "I won't return phone calls. He sent me letters, and I put them in an envelope and sent it back to him without opening it. He's not happy because he knows I have adverse interests, so I have to go," Denue said.

In the courtroom of District Judge Jackie Glass on Friday, attorneys were scheduled to argue a multitude of pretrial motions for the couple's murder trial in April. But once the proceedings started, it became clear that the issue of the day was Denue's firing. Titus smiled broadly at the sight of Cristalli in court. "I've been trying to do this for a year now...This is what I've been trying to do since day one," Titus said loudly. Cristalli said his proposed representation of Ryan was not dictated by Titus; ultimately it was Kelly Ryan's choice as to who her attorney would be.

Cristalli said, "She has a Sixth Amendment right to the counsel of her choice." He said that even though he is Saggese' law partner, he would pursue whatever defense was best for Kelly Ryan. He also said that any talk of a plea deal for Ryan was not feasible for one reason: she did not want to make a deal. "It ain't never going to happen," Cristalli said. Judge Glass said she would appoint an independent attorney to speak with Kelly Ryan regarding the matter.

Greg Denue loses his shit in front of the cameras

On February 25th, Greg Denue announced to the media that Kelly Ryan was a "battered woman," and he "plans to tell a jury that she was under the control of Craig Titus when Melissa James was found dead in the desert." Denue said that he was seeking a court order to have Ryan examined by an expert on battered women syndrome, and he also planned to argue at Ryan and Titus' murder trial that Ryan did whatever Titus wanted her to do because she was an abused spouse.

Denue also announced Tuesday that if he was forced off the case, he would have Craig Titus' defense lawyer, lawyer Marc Saggese, kicked off the high-profile murder case for visiting Ryan at the Clark County Detention Center even though he was not Ryan's attorney. "His visits have made him a witness in this case," Denue said; but Cristalli said that Denue was lying, and that Ryan had no interest in blaming her husband for the fate of Melissa James. "That is completely inconsistent with what I've heard from her," Michael Cristalli said.

Denue came across as a certified crazy person when he started telling the press a flat out lie that Kelly Ryan had second thoughts, and wanted to keep him as her attorney. He then stated, "She wants it to play out in front of the Supreme Court, and she believes whatever happens is God's will," Denue said. Denue, on Tuesday, filed the motions seeking to have Ryan tried separately from Titus, and to have Saggese tossed off the case. Then he went on an unprofessional rant saying, "Craig Titus found the sock puppet lawyer he has been searching for in Marc Saggese. When three of this town's top lawyers refused to dance to the Titus Two-Step, he choreographed their removal. Now, because I likewise refuse to do the two-step, I am targeted for legal amputation by Craig Titus and his errand boy, Marc Saggese." In his motion to have Kelly removed from Craig's case, Denue wrote that Saggese was seeking to have Ryan "Sacrificed at the altar of Craig Titus." Judge Glass appointed a veteran attorney, William Terry, to meet with Kelly Ryan. After their consultation, William Terry concluded that the joint defense agreement was "Essentially an unenforceable contract."

Saggese, on Tuesday night, countered that Denue was attacking him because he does not want to be taken off the high-profile case, and that Kelly Ryan's problems with Greg Denue resulted from the attorney never visiting with Ryan at the Clark County Detention Center. Saggese said, "I feel sorry for him. It's an act of desperation. It's not my fault he didn't have the competence to represent her. Kelly Ryan literally cried to me in desperation to have a lawyer really represent her. He is lashing out at me because of his shortcomings as an attorney. If he was a good lawyer, he would be a good lawyer."

Robert Daskas gave Saggese notice he will be called as a witness

Saggese also confirmed Tuesday that Clark County Prosecutor Robert Daskas has given him notice that he planned to call Saggese as a witness in the trial, but Saggese said he would never testify in the Titus-Ryan trial. Marc Saggese said, "I think Denue conspired with Daskas, just like Daskas has conspired with everyone else to eliminate Craig Titus. Now Daskas is conspiring with Denue to eliminate me from the case. I would never practice law for a second, ever again, for the rest of my life, if I was in some way forced to testify against Kelly Ryan or Craig Titus. I would give up all I have or ever will have to stand by the attorney-client privilege. No person, no entity, and no agency could ever get me to testify against my client."

It didn't seem possible that Robert Daskas could sink any lower, but he did! After his plot to have Greg Denue represent Kelly Ryan flopped, Daskas told Saggese that he had teamed up with Denue, and they were going to force him to do the most unethical thing a lawyer could be forced to do- testify against their own client. Daskas was a bully and he punishes everyone around him that will not cooperate in his witch hunt!

The bullying tactics against Craig Titus worked, and when Titus saw Robert Daskas destroy Ron Brady Jr., just to get revenge on him- it played with his mind. Titus started to believe that no matter how innocent he was, Daskas was powerful enough to turn anything around on him. Daskas' bullying had to have an effect on Saggese as well because Daskas' had twisted things, for so long, and all Saggese could do was sit by and watch it happen because everyone of his motions were tossed out.

Now, if this went to trial, Daskas would force Saggese to take the stand against Titus, which must have frightened him to the core. When it came closer to the trial, Saggese lost his confidence, and was hesitant to encourage Craig to fight for his freedom. More than likely because of this move, Daskas scared Saggese into a plea deal by threatening Saggese he would have to take the stand against his client.

Nevada Supreme Court Ruling
Over a year after Kelly Ryan first requested to have Michael Cristalli represent her in a joint defense with her husband and Marc Saggese, the Nevada Supreme Court handed down their decision; and they ruled in favor of Kelly Ryan.

◄ SWIFT INJUSTICE

RYAN v. EIGHTH JUDICIAL DISTRICT COURT COUNTY OF CLARK
Kelly RYAN, Petitioner, v. THE EIGHTH JUDICIAL COURT of the State of Nevada, In and For the COUNTY OF CLARK, and The Honorable Jackie Glass, District Judge
No.49114 Oct. 11, 2007 Cristalli & Saggese, Ltd., and Michael V. Cristalli, Las Vegas, David J. Roger, District Attorney, and Robert Daskas, Deputy District Attorney.
Conclusion: Ryan and Titus appear eager to present a unified front against the prosecution and have expressed as much through their joint defense agreement and waiver of conflict-free representation. Ryan and Titus have been advised of the potential pitfalls of conflicted dual representation, and they knowingly, intelligently, and voluntarily embrace a potentially conflicted dual representation, the conflict of interest is forever waived. We grant Ryan's petition for a writ of mandamus in part and direct the clerk of this court to issue a writ of mandamus directing the district court to hold a new canvass of both defendants.

In a nutshell, the Nevada Supreme Court ruled against Judge Jackie Glass and said Kelly Ryan could select a lawyer of her choosing, even though her prospective attorney's law firm would also defend her husband, Craig Titus. In the decision, the justices said there was a strong presumption in law that "non-indigent" criminal defendants can choose their own lawyers if they voluntarily waive their right to a "conflict-free" counsel. "When a defendant knowingly, intelligently, and voluntarily waives the right to conflict-free representation, the district court must accept that waiver," the court stated. The justices also said if Ryan agreed to representation with the firm that also represented her husband, she could not later claim she was ineffectively represented.

The Nevada Supreme Court told Greg Denue to hit the road

In response to the appeal, Greg Denue stated that he planned on testifying in court that Kelly Ryan was a battered woman, and at that time, he would disclose everything Kelly Ryan told him in confidence when she was his client. He added that he planned to be called as a witness by the prosecution (Robert Daskas- how unethical is that?) at the upcoming trial and tell the jury that Craig Titus poured lighter fluid all over the victim and burned her to death. That Kelly Ryan had no part in it, but she was under the control of her husband, and was a battered woman. Denue said he would also testify that Craig Titus would likely be charged with a murder-for-hire conspiracy.

Denue's unprofessionalism violated numerous ABA Rules of Professional Conduct. Most alarming, Robert Daskas appeared to encourage Denue to act out in retaliation after he was fired by Kelly Ryan and subsequently ruled against by the Nevada Supreme Court. Under no circumstances should a prosecutor urge a public defender that has been fired by their client to engage in a prohibited activity.

*Client-Lawyer Relationship-*Rule 1.6 Confidentiality of Information: A lawyer shall not reveal information relating to the representation of a client unless the client gives informed consent, the disclosure is impliedly authorized in order to carry out the representation or the disclosure.

Craig and Kelly's Defense Team would have to try and move forward, past all of the immaturity and misconduct that had taken place over the previous year and a half in and outside the courtroom. Saggese and Cristalli needed to pour all of their energy into defending their clients, and they only had a few short months to prepare for the trial of their lives.

Making it twice as difficult for the defense, bail had been repeatedly denied to Craig and Kelly, so they would have to plan their defense with Saggese and Cristalli in the couple of hours they were allotted every day while they were incarcerated at the CCDC. There was a sense of urgency for the defense during the pretrial preparation which included: client interviewing and counseling, fact investigation, witness interviewing, finding and selecting experts, brainstorming and developing a case theory, discovery, etc. There was a lot to get done, and only a few months to do it- so the defense kicked it into high gear.

CHAPTER 9

Daskas, Brady, Titus: Lives intertwined

Daskas for Congress

On August 12th 2007, Robert Daskas announced that he was considering a run for Congress, seeking the Democratic nomination of 2008 to challenge Representative John Porter, a Republican from Nevada. Daskas told the Las Vegas Review Journal: "I have not announced anything yet, but I have been talking to state and national officials about the possibility. My biggest concern is timing. I need to ensure that I have sufficient time to commit to a campaign without abandoning my obligation to my cases."

Daskas announced he was only "considering" the Democratic Nomination, and look who had first lined up with their checkbooks to make a donation to Robert Daskas:

08/22/2007- Tony Gross' Attorney- Louis Palazzo donates $2,300 to Daskas for Congress.
08/22/2007- Tony Gross' Attorney- James Oronoz donates $2,300 to Daskas for Congress.
08/22/2007- James Oronoz donates another $2,300 to Daskas for Congress.
09/04/2007- Gregory Denue donates $1,000 to Daskas for Congress
09/14/2007- Judge Jackie Glass' husband, attorney Steven Wolfson (future Clark County District Attorney) donates $1,000 to Daskas for Congress

Daskas had not even declared that he was a candidate, yet the "key players" in the Craig Titus cases had already started giving him "the maximum amount" in donations. Robert Daskas made it official on September 19th, 2007 and formally announced that he was running for the suburban Las Vegas congressional district. In an article in the Las Vegas Sun titled "OK, he was fourth on the list, but he's taking on Porter," the paper announced that Robert Daskas had filed the papers to run against an unpopular pro-war republican candidate.

The article by David McGrath Schwartz said, *"Invitations went out to the big dance off, and it had to be tempting. Challenge a Republican congressman who has been unwavering in his support of an unpopular war.*

Get millions of dollars in assistance from national Democrats. And do all of this when voters are leaning towards Democrats. The cool kids, though, decided not to show. So a political neophyte will be the candidate. Robert Daskas, a chief deputy district attorney, filed papers last week announcing his intention to run against Rep. Jon Porter, a three-term incumbent.

Daskas has the support of Senate Majority Leader Harry Reid and Rep. Shelley Barkley of Nevada. But that doesn't' mean he was the first choice. At least four others passed up a chance to run. So what does Daskas say about this? He is not commenting; instead, in a written statement, Daskas said he filed his papers to run 'based on the overwhelming encouragement and financial support I received.' Better late than never."

Daskas' statement was very true: many interesting people, mostly defense attorneys, had contributed significant amounts to his campaign. None contributed as much however, as Anthony Gross' attorneys James Oronoz and Louis Palazzo. Daskas must have really appreciated their deep pockets to help him jump start his campaign! If Robert Daskas already owed Oronoz and Palazzo a big favor for having Tony Gross play dead in an attempt to set up Craig Titus; he would really owe them then!

Another book was written and published on September 13th, 2007 about the Craig Titus/Kelly Ryan murder trial. This one was published only eight months before the scheduled trial date: "Killer Bodies... They Were Perfectly Fit for Murder: A Glamorous Bodybuilding Couple, A Love Triangle, and a Brutal Murder," by Michael Fleeman, an associate bureau chief for People magazine. With the title of the book saying "they were perfectly fit for murder," along with pictures of Craig and Kelly on the cover; once again a book was written presuming that Craig and Kelly were guilty before they ever went to trial. (I understand Freedom of the Press, and writing articles about the case, but publishing two pro-prosecution books well before the trial is hard for me to understand. And we have to remember the first book was written with leaked information from the prosecution to prejudice the public against Craig Titus.)

On October 8th, Robert Daskas verbally announced that he would run for congress, and would resign as Clark County Deputy District Attorney after the completion of the Darren Mack case that was set to begin in the following two weeks. Daskas did not believe that the trial would take long, because they planned on offering Mack a plea deal. Daskas was also close with Mack's attorneys, and was certain they could talk Mack into the deal, especially if Mack was faced with Capital Murder. Mack was resolved to fight the battle in court, and turned down the initial offers.

That did not sit well with Robert Daskas, because he was ready to hit the campaign trail. Daskas was already months behind the other candidates, and the longer the Mack trial played out, the tougher his campaign would be trying to prepare for the election. Daren Mack didn't care about Daskas' campaign schedule, and demanded to have his right to a trial before a jury of his peers. To the dismay of the prosecution and the defense, the trial was going to take place, and only time would tell how long Daskas would have to wait before he could resign from the District Attorney's office. Mack was represented by David Chesnoff (Richard Schonfeld's law partner, Craig Titus' first attorney) and Scott Freeman. Prosecutors Robert Daskas and Christopher Lalli were teamed back up again, coming off an embarrassing loss in the Binion trial.

Darren Mack's trial

Darren Mack's trial began on October 24th, 2007. The first week of the trial, the prosecution presented its case to the jury in the courtroom of the Honorable Judge Douglas Herndon in Las Vegas, Nevada. This would be Robert Daskas' farewell conviction before he hit the campaign trail. During his presentation, Robert Daskas said, "Darren Mack is essentially, he's a spoiled brat. I mean the kid was raised with a lot of money. He got everything he ever wanted, and now he found himself in family court. Things weren't going his way. He wasn't getting what he wanted, and he took matters into his own hands." (Don't judge the grammar, the "anointed fourth choice candidate" was probably nervous about coming up with some catchy lines about immigration to repeat over and over when he was stuttering through his opening lines in court).

After seven full days of testimony the prosecution rested, and the defense was to begin presenting their side on the following Monday morning. In an unusual move, the prosecution offered Darren Mack a plea deal after their closing arguments on Friday, but Mack turned it down.

Despite wanting the trial to move forward, Mack said that his defense attorneys went after him hard, trying to convince him to take a plea deal, but Darren Mack refused. Then in a surprising move on the Monday morning when the defense was to begin presenting their case to a jury, Mack's attorneys (Scott Freeman and David Chesnoff) told the court he had agreed to a plea deal. According to Darren Mack, his attorney's bullied him into the deal, and "broke his spirit" by insisting that he take it. Whatever the case may be, an agreement was struck that morning before the defense had an opportunity to present their case.

On November 5, 2007 Darren Mack pleaded "Guilty to First-Degree Murder" in exchange for a recommendation by the prosecutor, Robert Daskas, for life in prison with the possibility of parole after 20 years. Robert Daskas was then free, thanks to the plea agreement he arranged with Darren Mack and his defense attorneys, Freeman and Chesnoff; Daskas could now resign from the District Attorney's office, and pour all of his energy into his campaign.

Just three weeks later, Darren Mack announced he had fired his attorney, Freeman and Schonfeld, and said that he wanted to withdraw his guilty plea. Mack alleged that he was pressured into signing the plea deal, and when he would not sign it, his signature was forged. He said that his attorneys were just in it for the money. "It was great until they got all my money and then it was take the deal 'cause we have no hope," he said in an interview. Scott Freeman and David Chesnoff were out, and local Reno attorney William Routsis was in, and his first order of business was to try and get Darren a whole new trial.

Judge Douglas Herndon denied Mack's motion to withdraw his plea, and request for a new trial; and because he wasn't bound to the sentencing recommendations of the prosecution, Judge Herndon imposed the maximum terms of the plea deal by sentencing Mack to "Life in prison" with the possibility of parole after 36 years.

Mack was outraged, because he believed the prosecutors tricked him into believing he would be able to get out on parole in 20 years, and he didn't understand how a judge could just change their agreement. According to the judge, in handing down the sentence, he cited the heinous nature of the crime, and Mack's lack of remorse for his decision for the harsher sentence. "The truth is Mr. Mack is guilty of these crimes, but he doesn't want to hear anything about that," the judge said. According to Darren Mack, "The prosecutors conspired with his defense attorneys to coerce him into a plea deal that they knew the judge would not honor."

Plea Bargains

A plea bargain is simply an agreement between the defendant and the prosecution where both parties agree to do something for some type of benefit. The question here is, if the defendant and prosecution had a deal, and the defendant agreed to plead guilty, and then honored that agreement by pleading guilty, how is it okay for the judge not to honor the State's end of the agreement?

One would think the judge and prosecutor would be on the same page, because they are both officers of the State. Nevertheless, apparently this is perfectly legal because the judge has "discretion" to change a ruling and give a harsher sentence when he or she deems it appropriate, but just because they "can," does that make it right? According to statistics, this rarely happens and only once in a while is the judge's hand is forced to ignore the prosecutor's recommendations and give a harsher sentence.

In this case, just by glancing at the circumstances, it could be assumed that Robert Daskas, realizing how long winded the defendant was (Mack spoke for over two hours at his sentencing), and recognizing that the defense was calling over 100 witnesses, wanted to corner Darren Mack into a plea deal because this trial could have possibly taken a month or two longer than he had originally anticipated. Mack seemed adamant, and had refused every deal up to that point, and the only way to get him to agree to a plea deal would be to give him an offer he could not refuse. The question: What's to stop a prosecutor from doing what Mack claimed Robert Daskas did, and offer an amazing deal, knowing the judge would not follow that recommendation? Answer: there is nothing to prevent that from happening!

There is a pattern: it sucks to be a defendant in a high-profile case in Las Vegas, but it's great to be Robert Daskas, a prosecutor racking up all of those wins! With Mack taking a plea, Daskas was able to claim yet another victory for the District Attorney's office, and make his Congressional run for Congress official and stronger.

On November 30th 2007, Robert Daskas resigned from his post as Clark County Deputy District Attorney, and formally announced his bid to challenge incumbent Republican Jon Porter for the Congressional seat. At his alma mater, (Basic High in Las Vegas, Nevada) Robert Daskas, along with his wife of ten years Julie, and their two children, stood in front of about 50 supporters and said, "I'm not a career politician, I'm a career prosecutor. I've devoted the last 12 years of my life to a courtroom prosecuting criminals and protecting families in the community. When I go into court, I'm the voice of the victims who otherwise can't be heard. Now I want to be the voice for you in Congress."

Daskas leaks private phone conversations to the paper
Robert Daskas got one last jab in at Craig Titus before he flew off on the campaign trail. Daskas handed the Review Journal private taped

conversations between Craig Titus and his sister, with sensitive information pertaining to Titus' under age daughter. Yet again, Robert Daskas crossed the line. The article states:

"Titus is heard telling his sister about catching his daughter sneaking home around 3:00 a.m. wearing no underwear under her skirt. 'That's when I grabbed her and threw her across the room. Man I was hot. Anyways, it wasn't good.' Craig Titus, involved in a domestic dispute with his daughter does not indicate whether the incident was ever reported to police or investigated by authorities. The recordings, obtained by the Review-Journal this week, are among more than 120 calls recorded by police as part of an investigation into allegations that Titus tried to orchestrate the murders of three witnesses in his upcoming murder trial. Titus' defense attorney, Marc Saggese, said Thursday that the contents of the latest police recordings are irrelevant to Titus' murder case, and that Titus always has acknowledged having a stormy relationship with his teenage daughter. 'Titus has struggled for years to steer the girl onto the right path in life but never has harmed the young woman,' Saggese said."

These recordings had absolutely nothing to do with Craig Titus' case, much like the "sordid lives" article published in the Review Journal before where details of Craig and Kelly's sex lives, were revealed. The previous articles were bad enough, but releasing this tape to the Review Journal and having the paper write an article about Craig's daughter that publicly humiliated her, took things too far! Craig bit his tongue, and didn't say anything right then, but he was determined to somehow humiliate Robert Daskas! "Just like that asshole humiliated me and every single member of my family over the past two years!" Craig said, "I couldn't believe what fell into my lap a few months later! I knew if I released the information, there would be hell to pay, but by this point, I thought what else can this guy do to me that he hasn't already done?"

Judge Jackie Glass is the big winner- landing the O.J. Simpson Trial

Also announced in November, there was another celebrity making it big while working on the Craig Titus case, the "Honorable" Judge Jackie Glass was selected to be the Judge to preside over the O.J.

Simpson trial. AP: *Titus and Ryan Judge to preside in the O.J. Simpson Case:*

"As if things in the Titus and Ryan trial weren't bizarre enough... Judge Jackie Glass will now preside over the O.J. Simpson trial. In an earlier time, Jackie Glass would have been covering O.J. Simpson's trial instead of presiding over it. Before becoming a lawyer and being elected Clark County District Court Judge, Glass was a television journalist covering courts in Las Vegas. Glass has covered several high-profile cases. Most recently, Glass was assigned the case of husband-and-wife professional bodybuilders Craig Titus and Kelly Ryan, accused of slaying their assistant, their trial is set to begin in June. Glass has dropped in ratings by county bar association members, from 80 percent favoring retention in 2004 to 71 percent in 2006. One critic surveyed in 2004 said Glass worked hard and meant well but needed training in "rules of evidence, law and procedure."

On December 9th 2007, Jon Ralston of *Face to Face* was less than impressed with the prosecutor-turned-politician! On the December 9th airing of *Face to Face*, the Las Vegas Sun reported: *"It's early but here is what we know about Robert Daskas, the latest repository of all Democratic hopes in Congressional 3: He has the acute smarts of a career prosecutor. He has the ebullient earnestness of a political newcomer. But despite his announcement 10 days ago (Nov. 27), Daskas is not yet ready to take on Rep. Jon Porter."*

Donations from attorney's directly involved with Titus case donate:
12/10/2007- David Chesnoff donates to $2,300 Daskas for Congress
12/10/2007- David Chesnoff donates to $2,300 Daskas for Congress
12/13/2007- Louis Palazzo donates $2,300 to Daskas for Congress
12/14/2007- Louis Palazzo donates another $2,300 to Daskas for Congress
12/28/2007- Richard Schonfeld donates $500 to Daskas for Congress

On the campaign trail, or down the street in Vegas, Robert Daskas was handing out "Daskas for Congress" pamphlets at a rally featuring Bill and Hillary Clinton at Greenspun Junior High. At least 5,000 people crammed into the gymnasium to see the Clintons. Daskas' first campaign literature, showed the candidate in a courtroom with a giant fingerprint on a screen behind him and the words, "A Prosecutor Makes the Case for Change in Washington." The flier touts his record of 32 convictions in 33 murder trials. "The people of Clark County counted on Robert to protect their safety and he delivered," it says. On the back, Daskas stands next to the letters "JUSTICE" etched in marble and readers are urged to "Examine the Evidence on Robert Daskas".

Interview with Ron Brady Sr. on the news

In an interview with NBC News 3 Las Vegas, Ron Brady Sr., Ron Brady Jr.'s father, talked about his son's upcoming trial. Ron Brady Sr. said, "This Murder for hire is a set-up with one purpose, to convict Craig Titus. Ronnie spent sixteen days in the same module as Craig Titus in February of 2006. When Ronnie was released, he tried to help Titus by gathering information about the case. But prosecutors say what Ronnie was doing was trying to find a hit man to eliminate witnesses that could testify against Titus. There is absolutely no proof of this and this never happened. Metro claims there are recordings of Ronnie discussing the murder-for-hire scheme but Robert Daskas from the DA's office has refused to turn over those tape recordings or any information supporting that allegation. They have kept my son in Solitary Confinement for the last nine months in an attempt to convince him to fabricate a story to help strengthen their case against Craig Titus."

News 3 asked the county jail what their procedures were for keeping inmates in solitary confinement. An official at the jail said they could not get them copies of those policies, but did say that certain high profile cases and certain charges could warrant a spot in their single cell maximum custody unit. But they also said they try to move those inmates back into the normal prison population as soon as they can.

The ACLU Speaks Out: "To shroud that in secrecy is simply unacceptable," Gary Peck with ACLU (American Civil Liberties Union) said. Peck said the detention center should be required to disclose the reasons behind keeping Ron Brady Jr. in solitary confinement. "To say we don't have to tell you… we don't have to show you our manuals, we don't have to talk about it, we run the jail, and we do what we want. That is not unacceptable. Not in America, not in a democracy!" To add insult to injury, The DA's office did not return their phone calls and to this day have not acknowledged why Ron Brady Jr. was kept in Solitary Confinement every day, even after his trial had begun. It was confirmed however that Ron Brady Jr. was not in solitary confinement for either disruptive or violent behavior.

Ron Brady Jr. phone interview

Ron Brady Jr. was interviewed from the Clark County Detention Center over the phone, and asked how long he had been locked up in solitary confinement, and why he thought he was placed there. Ron Brady Jr. said, "I've been locked down in the hole for so long, I can't even tell you how long I've been here. Let's see, over a year. I've been here since the day they arrested me, and interrogated me; I wouldn't say what they wanted to hear. I told them it wasn't a murder for hire, and Craig had nothing to do with it, and they told me I could sit in the hole and think about it until I decide to tell them otherwise. I'm in the hole because I won't tell the lie they want me to tell. How is that right? They act like my friends, like they are trying to do me a favor, and tell me I could walk today, just like Cassim. The district attorney will have all of the charges dropped, and I can walk out the door. Every day, they interrogate me and say the same thing over and over, telling me they know Craig masterminded the murder- for- hire, and every time they say that, I tell them that there was no murder for hire, and he had nothing to do with it."

When asked about the conditions in segregation, Ron Brady Jr. said, "It gets worse every day. At first I got an hour a day to get out, now it's down to 30 minutes, and some days I can't come out at all. They have even come in desperate just recently saying they'd have some of my past convictions taken off if I talked, but you know what? They can all kiss my ass. They could promise me a million dollars, and I still wouldn't make something up. That's bullshit! It seems like these people that are police officers and lawyers would know that, but oh well; I have made it this far, I can make it a little longer. It's hard to have faith in the justice system when I live every day before my trial in such injustice!"

In spite of everything that has happened to him, Ron Brady Jr. still held out hope in the American Justice System. Brady said, "I think people will see what's going on, and I will get a fair trial, I pray I will anyway. This is America right? No matter what your thoughts and feelings are about a crime, a person charged with any crime in the United States of America is innocent until proven guilty; that goes for me, and it goes for Craig. What's been done here is wrong, it really is; I wish someone would just take a look at everything that has happened, and look at it close because it's clear these people are corrupt; and once they have looked at everything, stand up and say that this ain't right!"

Ron Brady Jr. finally gets his day in court

Finally, on February 6th 2008, judgment day had arrived for Ronald Brady Jr. After unjustly sitting in solitary confinement for sixteen months, Brady would finally have his day in court in front of a jury of his peers. Maybe an unbiased jury would take a closer look at everything that has happened thus far, and justice would truly be served.

The trial lasted for more than a week. The three jail house taped interviews were played in court, and the homicide detectives' notes were presented to the jury. The video of Ron Brady Jr. handing "Cassim's ex-girlfriend" $1,000 to call the whole thing off was played, as the prosecutor read the detectives' notes about the details during the exchange with the undercover police officer.

In Robert Daskas' place was Josh Tomsheck from the District Attorney's office. Tomscheck described Brady as "an awestruck fan that worshipped Craig Titus" who met the bodybuilder while serving time in the county jail. The prosecutor said that Brady approached another inmate, Deen Cassim about killing witness' in Craig Titus' case, and Cassim in turn notified the police.

To back up the prosecutor's story, Tomsheck called homicide detectives Dean O'Kelley and Rob Wilson to the stand. Both of the detectives testified under oath that Deen Cassim came to them because Brady wanted to put a hit on key witnesses set to appear in Craig Titus' trial. There was never any mention that they were the same homicide detectives working the Craig Titus "murder" trial, and no explanation why an outside agency wasn't called in to investigate the case as would have been proper procedure do to conflict of interest.

Deen Cassim was flown back from England to testify in court against Ron Brady Jr. Of course, it was never mentioned that Cassim had his sentence of 3-12 years revoked for his violent crime against a poker player because he set Ron Brady Jr. up for this crime.

It would have been interesting to hear the detectives' explanation for taking down a man for "solicitation of murder"; where the accused gave an undercover agent $1,000 to scare the witnesses into telling the truth. Subsequently, the man on trial only wanted to stop the threats made by the "State's witness", a man that had just been convicted of assaulting a man at gunpoint in an attempt to steal $150,000 from him. This is 150 times the amount that Brady handed the undercover agent, and there was never any weapons or violence involved.

Many questions needed to be addressed about these "witnesses"

1. Why did the Clark County Deputy District Attorney, Robert Daskas cut that deal with a violent felon, and recommend that Judge Joseph Bonaventure revoke Cassim's sentence? This could not be viewed at as a reasonable exchange: $150,000 vs. $1,000, a violent offender with gun vs. drug related charges without a weapon.

2. How much money did this cost the Las Vegas' tax payers to fly Tony Gross to Chicago and back twice, and Deen Cassim to England and back, all the while paying for their living expenses?

3. How did the District Attorney, David Roger (the prosecutor that won the district attorney's race after the Binion trial and won a second term after the O.J. Simpson trial; then one year after being elected for a second term, abruptly resigns amid a huge HOA scandal conducted by the FBI, and then accepted a job with the LVMPD Protective Association.) justify spending that much money from the District Attorney's Victim/Witness Assistance Fund? And why wasn't the total amount of money spent on these witnesses disclosed to the defense?

4. All of these witnesses that were either directly or indirectly involved in the Craig Titus case, what was their motivation to cooperate with the prosecution, and say exactly what Robert Daskas wanted them to say?

5. If Ron Brady Jr. would have given the homicide detectives what they wanted (Craig Titus' head) would there even be a State of Nevada vs. Nelson Ronald Brady Jr.?)

Brady's defense attorney, Michael Schwarz, said that his client was taken out of a cell and placed in a cell with Deen Cassim without explanation. According to Schwarz, homicide detectives Dean O'Kelley and Rob Wilson set that "coincidence" up, in order to frame Brady for a "solicitation" charge. This "solicitation" charge in turn would have been "null and void", if Brady had cooperated, and testified against Craig Titus.

The defense attorney said that Deen Cassim initiated the conversation the minute Brady was placed in his cell. Cassim then led Brady to believe, at first, that it was to simply intimidate the witnesses into telling the truth at Craig Titus' trial. Once Ron Brady Jr. realized what Deen Cassim was doing, and Cassim began to threaten his life and the lives of Brady's loved ones, Brady felt threatened into paying Cassim. Brady did not show up three times to meet with undercover agents because he did not want to go along with what Cassim was planning.

Ron Brady Jr. even turned his cell phone off, in an attempt to rid himself of Deen Cassim. Then the homicide detectives gave this convicted, violent felon Brady's dad's cell phone number! Deen Cassim then started harassing Ron Brady's father, demanding to talk to his son. This father and son duo are best friends, and now his father had innocently been pulled into all of this; Cassim had already told Brady what he was in prison for, and said that all of these people involved were connected to the mafia.

Brady was terrified, Deen Cassim was violent, and threatened to use his violent connections to assassinate Brady and his family. And now Deen Cassim is calling his father's private cell phone. How would Cassim have access to this cell number behind bars unless he was in fact connected to somebody in a powerful position? After Cassim called his father's cell phone demanding to talk to him, Brady was panicked. When Cassim finally told him he could have an out, but had to pay the hit man $1,000 for taking up his time, Brady did just that, and was falsely arrested for three counts of Solicitation to Commit Murder a few months later.

If I were Brady's defense attorney, questions I would ask the detectives

Questions for the homicide detectives:

If this alleged hit was in the works, beginning in March and ending with a payment from Brady to Cassim in May, why was Ron Brady Jr. not arrested until mid- October?

If Brady really wanted these people dead, and had been videotaping the three of them in the drug community for months, why would homicide detectives not have him locked up in May to protect them? That leaves six months unaccounted for. If Brady wanted them dead, he could have killed them or had them killed without going through Deen Cassim!

Why was Ron Brady Jr. not tape-recorded when he was arrested and interrogated in October? If it's legal, wouldn't it protect honest detectives, and make sense to record everything? "Important" phone calls between Craig Titus and his sister were recorded, and when Titus made a joke about "having sex with a cousin", this vital piece of recorded information was handed to the Las Vegas Review Journal to write an entire article about Craig Titus' "sordid life!" The homicide detectives didn't forget to turn on the tape recorder in Boston (where it's against the law to tape-record a defendant) to record Craig Titus' and Kelly Ryan's interrogation. Those tapes were shortly leaked to the newspaper, and an article was subsequently written. Why are the accused only recorded when it's beneficial to the prosecution?

Detectives, why isn't there a recording of the two of you interrogating Ron Brady Jr.? Why isn't there a recording with the two of you homicide detectives on the Titus' case telling Ron Brady Jr. that you will turn on the recorder when he tells you Craig Titus set this whole thing up? Why isn't there a recording of the tow of you telling Brady that he could walk, all he had to do was testify against Craig Titus? Why isn't there a recording telling Brady he could sit in the hole until he changed his mind, where he sat until the day he went to trial? That's too convenient to be true for the prosecution!

What I would say in my closing statement to the jury

Okay now really think about this! Is it plausible to believe that Ron Brady Jr. paid a professional hit man $333 per person ($1,000 total) to assassinate the criminal witnesses for the State in a capital murder trial? After this professional hit man had already flown in from Los Angeles and stayed at the Bellagio hotel for a week waiting on a payment and information from Ron Brady Jr. One thousand dollars would not have even paid for Fred Hitterman's round-trip flight and week stay at the Bellagio.(I have a hard time typing in "Fred Hitterman" and keeping a straight face; I really don't know how Detective Wilson was able to type out an entire letter from "Mr. Hitterman" with a fake execution picture of Tony Gross, and keep a straight face.)

Ron Brady Jr. takes the stand and the jury returns with a verdict

Ron Brady Jr. took the stand in his prison scrubs and testified that he never wanted to hire a hit man. Brady said that while he was in the Clark County Detention Center, he was pulled out of his cell and placed in a cell with Deen Cassim. Brady described himself as a people person, and he and Cassim talked about a lot of things. It was during this time Cassim first mentioned Craig Titus, because they were talking about famous people in jail. Brady told Cassim about Craig's case, and how he was charged with the murder of a girl who had overdosed in his home. Brady also explained how Craig's friend helped him get rid of the body after she overdosed. He told Cassim about his other friend's helping Titus and his wife cover-up the overdose.

Brady told Cassim that all of these friends were drug- addicts, and were possibly lying to the police about what really happened to cover their own asses. Cassim and Brady talked about ways to get these drug-addicted friends to tell the truth. Not long after this conversation, Brady was released from the CCDC. Brady said that he had forgotten about their conversation, and a few days after he was released, Deen

Cassim started calling him up. Brady talked about trying to ignore Deen Cassim, but Cassim was relentless and called him non-stop. He talked about turning off his phone, and not showing up to meet with Cassim's friends when Cassim started to physically threaten both Brady and his family.

Brady said he panicked, and began to fear for his life, and his family's life as well. Brady said, "I never wanted anybody to be killed, and I was never told by Craig to kill anybody, and that's the truth, as God is my witness that is the truth!" Brady's lawyer said it was not until Mr. Brady and his family were threatened with acts of physical violence, insinuating death, by the state's jailhouse informant Deen Cassim that Brady eventually exchanged a small sum of money with an undercover officer just to make the stalking and harassment stop.

When the jury returned, Ron Brady Jr. would not get to experience justice as he had been hoping; instead, on February 21st, 2008 the jury declared, "Nelson Ronald Brady Jr., guilty on all Three Counts of Solicitation to Commit Murder. Brady faced two to fifteen years behind bars for each count (6-45 years). Before Ron Brady Jr. was sentenced, he looked at Judge Herndon and said, "Your honor, I'm sorry for getting caught up in this mess; I truly was scared, but that's no excuse. But I can look you in the eyes and tell you I am innocent of this crime. This was never a murder-for-hire plot, and I'd rather be in the position I'm in right now, and even do life in prison, than be involved in bringing harm, much less killing another human being."

Brady's defense attorney, Michael Schwarz, pleaded with the judge for a shorter prison term, hoping the judge had looked over this case and would take the ethical high ground and make things right. But Judge Herndon told his lawyer that there was overwhelming evidence showing that Brady wanted three witnesses in Craig Titus' case dead. Herndon said that Brady's prior criminal record, along with the fact he wanted to kill witnesses in a murder case, meant that Brady deserved a stiff penalty. "Giving him leniency would be a slap in the face to the people who have been willing to come and testify in this case," Judge Douglas Herndon said. In the end, Brady was sentenced to 8-25 years by the judge.

Brady's attorney responded to the ruling by saying, "This was a sad day for the court! Ron Brady Jr. was merely used as a pawn to build a stronger case against Titus; this is truly a sad day for justice." In one of the most touching moments, the man that had been fighting for his son since day one, his Dad, Ron Brady Sr., stood up and told his son that he had made mistakes and let him down in the past, but he has never been more proud of him. Ron Brady Sr. said: "I can look you in the eyes and tell you this was never a murder-for-hire plot. I'd rather be in the position I am in now, and even do life in prison, than be involved in bringing harm, much less killing anyone." Ron Brady Sr. said, "I am so proud of my son for doing the right thing. He never turned on Craig, and that would have been the easy way out. The homicide detectives and prosecutors thought my son would be an easy target because of his mistakes in the past, but my son showed them how a man with true character behaves, and he held firm to the truth. My son was framed and threatened by a jail house snitch- a violent man that had just been sentenced to 3-12 years in prison and then had his conviction overturned because of his cooperation with the authorities. My son was singled out and set up because they thought he was an easy target, and boy were they ever wrong! They kept my son in solitary confinement, and told him he would stay there until he turned on Craig, but my son never budged and held the truth close to his heart. My son saw Deen Cassim walk out of prison, a free man because of his deception and lies; Ronnie could have walked out too if he would have turned on Craig. My son by his example taught these men in power a lesson in what is right and what is wrong. For all of the wrong things my son has done in his life, he made up for it today, and I could not be more proud of him than I am right now!"

(These words from this dad's mouth gave me goose bumps. What a beautiful story about a father's unconditional love for his prodigal son who had lost his way, became involved in drugs, had lied and stolen from his dad, and been arrested time and again. This was a man that the detectives and prosecutor saw as "easy bait", a drug addict, from a working class family, with very little money. If anyone would flip on Craig, everyone thought it would be this guy, Ron Brady Jr., but not his father. This was his son, and he raised "Ronnie" to do the right thing, and his father knew that he would eventually find his way back home, and become the man he raised him to be. Ron Brady Jr. lost everything because he did the right thing. How many people would have been able to do that? I don't know if I could have. I for one think Ronnie is amazing, and pray that the Nevada Innocence Project will pick up this case, and look at the facts, and then fight to get him out of prison!)

Craig Titus' reaction to the Brady conviction

When Craig heard the words "Guilty," he made up his mind to just throw in the towel. If these men could set up this ridiculous plot that made absolutely no sense and convince a jury to find Ron Brady Jr. guilty, there was no way in hell that Craig would walk away a free man! They had been playing a game of chicken for the last couple of years, and come "crash" or "jump" time, Craig had to jump! When Craig sat in Solitary Confinement, he made peace with the people that had caved in and given O'Kelley and Daskas what they wanted; had they not lied, they would be in the same predicament that Ron Brady Jr. was in, facing time in prison over a bullshit crime! He put himself in Maura James' shoes, and wished he could reach out and express how sorry he was that Melissa overdosed because he could have possibly prevented that from happening. He wanted to tell her how sorry he was for being so selfish, and not just calling the police after she overdosed. Their careers might have been over, but her mother would have been spared from so much pain. Craig decided to make things right with his heart, and forgive those who have hurt him, and he could only pray that those he has hurt would forgive him as well.

There was one person that Craig could never forgive no matter how hard he tried. Craig hated Robert Daskas with all of his entire being. Craig fucked up when he didn't call the police that day, and he was willing to suffer the consequences for his crimes; but he did not murder or kidnap Melissa James, and Robert Daskas knew it! Craig's mind was racing, "How could anyone look at the autopsy report, and believe that anything other than a drug overdose happened in his house? They fucking couldn't! Daskas had to know, how could he not?" Craig got even more pissed thinking about, "That little prick, stepping and shitting on me, to get to that Congressional Seat!"

The next day, Marc Saggese was able to meet with Craig, and he knew that this would be a low point for him. Saggese needed to keep Craig positive, maybe give him some encouraging lines from "Rocky". Hell, even Rocky got knocked out and lost the fight in the first movie! Saggese tried to give him a pep talk, friend to friend; and he told Craig that he, "believes him, and he believes in him; and they were going to fight this thing together!" The hardest thing for Marc Saggese was that he knew Craig Titus was telling the truth; it would be a hell of a lot easier if he didn't. Saggese could see it in Craig's eyes, this was a blow that he might not recover from. He told Craig that he would fight until the end to have those charges dropped, and Craig wasn't convinced. Saggese looked at Craig and said, "Hey man, it's gonna happen; and when it does, I want you to be a groomsman in my wedding!" That put a smile on Craig's face. Just to have at least one person that believed in him, and would fight for him, gave Craig hope.

His attorney said, "If for nothing else, we got to finish this out just to see Daskas' face when the jury returns a 'Not Guilty' verdict!" Craig said after he walks out of the Clark County Detention Center doors, he's going to file a lawsuit against the whole fucking justice department, and expose every one of their lies! Craig smacked the table and said, "God, Daskas is such a pussy! He's behind everything that has happened; he makes me want to fucking puke!" Saggese made some jokes about Daskas to try and lighten the mood, when one of the private investigators arrived with some information; talk about perfect timing. Craig had just started into another rant about the prosecutor, when the investigator said, "You are going to love this, listen what I just heard about Daskas!" Craig hoped it was something good; and boy, was it ever! And what came out of that private investigator's mouth, and went into Titus' ears would change both Craig Titus and Robert Daskas' lives forever.

Craig throws a "kink" in Daskas' run for Congress

The next day at the CCDC, Craig called his sister, and with an extra pep in his voice said, "Guess what I heard?" His sister could tell by his tone, it must be something good; and she replied, "Dunno what?" After a couple of smart ass remarks, Craig proceeded to spill every last detail told to him by the private investigator, hoping word would get back to Daskas. Or better yet, Daskas would hear it for himself when he eavesdrops on his conversations. Craig said, "I always assumed Daskas was a queer because he had such a hard-on for me, but turns out, he's not!" His sister laughed and said, "What the hell are you talking about?" Craig said, "Word on the street, or gossip around the D.A.'s office, is that he got caught fucking a red-headed deputy district attorney named Cara in the office! He's apparently running around trying to keep people quiet; but shit if I'm going to keep it quiet!" His sister asked Craig if he thought Daskas would leak this tape to the newspapers like he did with all of the other tapes about him; Craig said, "no but I will!" Craig said, "I didn't know that Napoleon had it in him. Apparently even he thinks that Campbell soup is uhm, uhm good!" His sister said, "What are you talking about? Oh never mind, I am sure I don't want to know. Hey I wonder if he will still be the anointed candidate when word leaks out about his sordid life. He may be even more dubious than you big brother, if that is possible!" They both laughed, which felt good because it had been a while since they had something to laugh about. Craig didn't really have any intention of sharing the information with the public; but if word did leak out, the little prick would get what he deserved!

Word traveled fast, and Daskas had not even let the shit dry in his pants before he was telling Craig how he was going to destroy him! Titus had all of his "privileges" stripped from him in the hole, and wasn't allowed to talk to anyone on the phone. Craig was not completely sure if word leaked out from those who worked with Daskas, or if somebody listened in on Craig's conversation with his sister, and word spread from there; but word definitely got out, and rumors were floating around. All the while, Craig and Kelly were in and out of court pending motions in their case. Ironically enough, Josh Tomsheck was now on the case, apparently undaunted by rumors of Daskas possibly dropping out of the Congressional race. On April 17th, 2008 the momentum seemed to be behind the defense. Motions were heard, and ruled in their favor, in an effort to have the state pay for more independent testing of evidence that would undoubtedly put a nail in the coffin of the prosecution's case.

SWIFT INJUSTICE

Nearly two weeks later the headline of the Las Vegas Sun Read: *Daskas pulls out of race against Porter... By <u>Michael Mishak</u> Monday, April 28, 2008 | 4:10 p.m. Robert Daskas withdrew today from the race to unseat Republican Rep. Jon Porter in Nevada's 3rd Congressional District.* And Nevada's top party leader expressed disappointment, "We are sorry to hear that Robert Daskas has decided not to run for Congressional District 3," Nevada Democratic Party Chairman Sam Lieberman said in a statement released this afternoon. "Robert would have made an excellent candidate and member of Congress. Senate Minority Leader Dina Titus has the track record, the experience and the know-how to serve Nevadans well in Congress, and has proven she can win this District."

Daskas' campaign issued the following press release this morning: "Citing family considerations, Robert Daskas has announced his decision to withdraw his candidacy for Nevada's Third Congressional District. The Daskas campaign has every confidence that another strong, viable candidate will enter the race and unseat incumbent Jon Porter. Daskas thanks everyone for their support and asks supporters to stay focused on the common goal of changing our representative in the Third Congressional District. Democrats now hold a 22,500 voter registration advantage over Republicans in the district." Democratic congressional candidate Robert Daskas abruptly withdrew from the race for Nevada's 3rd District on Monday, citing "family considerations", Daskas' brief statement didn't elaborate on the reasons behind his surprise exit from a contest in which the political newcomer was thought to have a good shot at victory. "The Daskas campaign has every confidence that another strong, viable candidate will enter the race and unseat incumbent Jon Porter," the statement said. "Daskas thanks everyone for their support and asks supporters to stay focused on the common goal of changing our representative. "Daskas, a former prosecutor, had been the Democrats' handpicked candidate to challenge Republican Rep. Jon Porter in what is seen as one of this year's hottest House races in the country. Immediately after Daskas' surprise announcement, Democrats began touting state Senate Minority Leader Dina Titus, D-Las Vegas, as a replacement candidate. "I'm seriously considering it," Titus said, adding that she planned to make a decision by the end of the week. Daskas' brief statement didn't elaborate on the reasons behind his surprise exit from a contest in which the political newcomer was thought to have a good shot at victory. "The Daskas campaign has every confidence that another strong, viable candidate will enter the race and unseat incumbent Jon Porter," the statement said. "Daskas thanks everyone for their support and asks supporters to stay focused on the common goal of changing our representative" Daskas had raised $453,213 through March 31, according to the Federal Election Commission. He cannot simply turn it over to another candidate, although he can ask his donors to redirect their contributions. Under FEC rules, Daskas also could donate the funds to charity or to national, state and local party committees. Any contributions out of the campaign fund to other candidates would be subject to state or federal limits.

The Bitch is back in town

Little can be found about Robert Daskas' divorce from his wife, but on the Clark County Data website, their mutual property on Brushwood Peak Ave. in Las Vegas was purchased and owned by Robert Daskas from 12/29/2003- 08/18/2008 when his ex-wife became the owner of the property. From this, it's apparent that he got a divorce prior to August 18th, 2008 (4 days before Craig Titus and Kelly Ryan were sentenced.)

So what would cause Daskas to drop out of the race for Congress on April 29, 2008, and get divorced before August 18, 2008? Nobody knows for certain. All that's known for sure is: Daskas was placed back on the Craig Titus case, and he vowed to send Craig away for the rest of his life. How ironic, and quite likely uncomfortable, Robert Daskas was once again the Lead prosecutor and Josh Tomscheck stepped aside to assist Daskas with the Craig Titus/Kelly Ryan "Murder" trial. When the local media asked if they could televise alongside court TV, Judge Jackie Glass of course approved. The more cameras in the court room, the more angles to choose from when she sends her audition tapes to Hollywood.

Robert Daskas visited with Craig Titus before the trial took place, letting him know that he had a score to settle. He told Craig, "You picked the wrong guy to fuck with; I'm about to destroy you and everyone around you!" The environment was surreal; as Daskas just stepped right back into his role at the District Attorney's office, as if nothing had ever happened.

It was obvious Robert Daskas had a vendetta against Craig, but nobody knew exactly why, and nobody seemed to care. If anything, the atmosphere was electric, with the surge now behind the prosecution. When Daskas first picked this case up in December of 2005, he believed it would be his ticket up and out of his current position as a Deputy District Attorney, where he had been stuck for the past ten years. Daskas dreamed of a position more powerful and prestigious in the world of politics. This was a man that couldn't sit still, and was constantly moving; he was never complacent to just stay in one spot. According to his own literature, he was promoted to the second most powerful position at the District Attorney's office, Deputy D.A. right out of law school, just six months after he first took this job. Daskas had the drive to take his career to the next level, he was just waiting on the perfect case to drop in his lap.

The District Attorney, David Roger, still owed Daskas a favor after the Binion debacle, and it appeared as if Roger would deliver by placing the Titus case in his lap. Before long, it became apparent that the case was nothing more than an overdose and arson, but Daskas was determined to try this case as a Capital Murder. Robert Daskas' motivation for convicting Craig Titus by May of 2008 had taken a dramatic turn. Daskas no longer needed to use the conviction to promote himself in politics; in his mind, Craig Titus had obliterated that dream already. No, Robert Daskas was now fueled by rage, and he had a score to settle with Craig Titus; he was determined to manipulate the system to the very end in retaliation for what Craig had done.

Apparently not everyone got the memo that Robert Daskas had dropped out of the Congressional race. Defense lawyers connected to or directly involved with Craig Titus' case were still giving sizeable donations to the "Daskas for Congress" fund. It is curious, now that a timeline has been established, to see these donations made and what appear to be favors done in return. Whether there's a connection or not, who knows? But it would be something interesting for the Las Vegas Tribune to look into!

Donations to Daskas for Congress by key players in Craig Titus case. Keep in mind that Daskas announced his run for Congress on Nov. 28th 2007 and withdrew from the race on April 29th 2008:

1. Louis Palazzo (Anthony Gross' attorney):

08/22/2007: $2,300

12/13/2007: $2,300

12/14/2007: $2,300

05/05/2008: $2,300

Total contributions to Daskas for Congress: $9,200

2. James Oronoz (Anthony Gross' attorney that met behind closed doors with Judge Jackie Glass and Robert Daskas)

08/22/2007- $2,300

08/22/2007-$2,300

05/05/2008- $2,300

Total contributions to Daskas for Congress: $6,930

3. Greg Denue (Kelly's public defender, assigned to her by Judge Jackie Glass while Kelly Ryan attempted to hire Michael Cristalli.)

09/04/2007- $1,000

4. Steven Wolfson (Current D.A., Judge Jackie Glass' husband- Judge that sentenced Craig Titus harsher sentence after Titus' attorneys agreed to a plea deal.   09/14/ 2007- $1,000   06/18/2008- $1,000

Total Contributions- $2,000.

CHAPTER **10**

The Plea Deal & Sentencing

The prosecutor has more control over life, liberty, and reputation than any other person in America. While the prosecutor at his best is one of the most beneficent forces in our society, but when he acts from malice, he is one of the worst- Former U.S. Attorney General Robert Jackson.

The Plea Negotiations

Daskas could not let the Titus case go to a jury; a plea bargain in this case would whitewash all of the misconduct, which occurred during the case, because Titus would admit to being guilty. That admission of guilt would trump any claim he had against the prosecution. In the Titus case, a plea bargain was offered because of all the potential prosecutorial misconduct. After all of the misconduct was brought to light by Marc Saggese, Daskas came back with a favorable offer to the defense, because he did not want to see it litigated.

From the beginning, Daskas stacked the charges to control the climate of the court, and keep Craig and Kelly from being able to bail out of jail. It was used against Kelly Ryan tin attempt to scare her into turning on Craig Titus, and to intimidate witnesses into testifying against the couple. As a final blow, Daskas used the charge stacking to bully Craig Titus into pleading guilty, rather than go to trial and risk the possibility of a longer sentence. Daskas is essentially letting Craig know he will be punished for exercising his constitutional rights and having his case heard in front of a jury.

THE PLEA DEAL & SENTENCING

On May 30th, 2008 the State and Craig Titus entered into a plea deal negotiation marathon, overseen by the "Honorable" Judge Jackie Glass in District Court Department 5, with Titus' attorney Marc Saggese, Ryan's attorney Michael Cristalli, and Clark County deputy district attorneys Robert Daskas and Josh Tomsheck. With negotiations lasting over 7 ½ hours, just outside the judge's office, both sides made repeated visits to her office to fine-tune and adjust some of the issues in an attempt to come to a resolution.

According to the court documentation, at about 4:30 p.m., Judge Jackie Glass told Marc Saggese and the prosecutors needed to "either fish or cut bait;" time was running out, and the district court's jury services needed to be notified by 4:45 p.m. that day whether the trial was going forward. Judge Glass then invited both the prosecutor, Robert Daskas, and defense attorney, Marc Saggese into her chambers to confer over the hold up in the negotiations. Counsel for both parties then entered in the chambers and told her the defendant's encumbrance.

The final issue was the minimum of 15 or 17 years. Based upon court documents and a sworn affidavit by Marc Saggese, he told the Judge the tipping point for Titus was whether or not the arson charge would be sentenced consecutive or concurrently, being the difference between fifteen and seventeen years. The "honorable" Judge Jackie Glass told the defense counsel, "He's getting 17." Marc Saggese repeated back to the Judge, "Seventeen, correct?" To which the judge nodded her head yes, and Saggese asked the same question one last time, stating that he wanted to be clear before he advised his client, at which time, the judge raised her voice in aggravation, and said, "I told you, he is getting seventeen years!"

The deal was set in stone, and Saggese believed that he would not be able to make either the judge or the prosecution budge. Saggese then went back and told Craig that he only had a couple of minutes to decide, but both the prosecution and the judge said that seventeen years was set in stone, and Saggese recommended that Titus take the deal. Craig had said all along that he wouldn't take anything more than fifteen, but he was backed in a corner and had to make a snap decision right then.

Craig shook his head, and told Marc that this just wasn't right; "I didn't do this bro; and I can't do seventeen years for something I didn't do." Saggese told him it was only two more years than what he had been fighting for all day, and if they went to trial, he risked spending the rest of his life behind bars. Saggese hated this as much as Titus; he knew Craig was innocent, but the defense attorney felt like he did everything he could in an attempt to stand up against a system plagued with misconduct in every direction. Saggese was stuck between a rock and a hard place. Ethically, he needed to fight until the end, but Titus could end up with life without parole, and Saggese' career would take a nosedive for standing up against the power hitters in the game.

Charging Craig Titus with First Degree Murder, Kidnapping and Arson gave Daskas an unfair advantage out of the gate, and at the finish line in the end. A kidnapping never occurred, so the Felony Murder rule was never applicable. This negated both First and Second Degree Murder, and in any other courtroom in America these charges would have never held up past the Grand Jury hearings.

Overcharging or "make-believe" charging by Robert Daskas kept both Craig and Kelly behind bars for over two years, and gave him a huge advantage going into the plea negotiations. He then had the ability to play God, and decide how long he wanted to keep Craig in prison. When Daskas said Craig would get seventeen years, Craig was forced to decide whether going to trial was worth the risk of the devastating penalties the inflated charges carry.

Would it be likely he could be found "Not Guilty?" The answer should have been "no," but it should have been "no" with Brady's trial, and he was found "Guilty" and given the maximum sentence. Craig had no other choice, he had to plead guilty because the consequences of requesting a trial by jury were too high. Before he agreed to anything however; Craig had to be certain that what everyone agreed to earlier in the day was still on the table.

If Craig agreed to the prosecution's agreement with him, Kelly would get to walk and be sentenced to time served. Saggese said it was a done deal. Craig said, " I don't have a fucking choice then, I don't want my wife to suffer anymore. Okay, let's do this." After two and a half years, Craig Titus and Kelly Ryan agreed to a plea deal in the 11th hour in connection with the death of Melissa James. Kelly Ryan plead guilty to Arson, and entered a No Contest "Alford" plea to Battery with a Deadly Weapon.

Craig Titus pled to three charges: (1) 2nd Degree Murder (10-25 years); (2) Kidnapping (5-15 years); and, Arson (2-15 years). It was agreed that Counts I and II would be consecutive and that the parties would argue at sentencing as to whether or not the court should run Count III concurrent or consecutive.

* If concurrent- Titus' bottom end would be 15 years.
* If consecutive, Titus' bottom end would be 17 years.

Judge Jackie Glass accepted the pleas Friday evening, bringing to a close the high- profile case that was set to go to trial on the following Monday after years of delays.

After the plea deal: Media

After the plea agreement was announced, both the prosecution and the defense spoke with the media: Robert Daskas commented, "It is a fair deal. It's one both the victim's family and detectives in the case agree with, because it makes Craig Titus admit to murder and his wife helping destroy evidence. I think both defendants recognize that a train was coming down the tracks and either they resolved it today or we were going to a jury trial and leave it up to a jury.

With Craig Titus and Kelly Ryan both facing possible life sentences for murder, Titus moved to save both himself and his wife. We had strong evidence that they purchased lighter fluid that was used ultimately to light the car on fire with Melissa James in the trunk. Daskas went on, "While there are still and always will be unanswered questions, we have always believed, and I think the guilty pleas reflect, that there was a confrontation between Kelly and Melissa and that Craig intervened, and ultimately it was Craig Titus that killed Melissa James."

(Yes Mr. Daskas, we realize you had evidence that lighter fluid was purchased. It was all the evidence you ever had, and proved arson not murder. If you believed that Craig intervened in a fight between Kelly and Melissa which resulted in her death, that would be Manslaughter. Now what about the KIDNAPPING CHARGES? Robert Daskas never once talks about the bogus kidnapping charges before or after the sentencing.)

Saggese told the press, "As we approached trial, Craig Titus became more and more worried about the exposure his wife was going to have to first degree murder. Titus agreed to plead guilty to second degree murder in the death of Melissa James, along with kidnapping and arson. He did accept responsibility and this is evidenced by his entering a guilty plea."

Saggese has to be questioned, however, because what defense attorney would have his client plead guilty to the kidnapping of a woman that was dead from an overdose? There was not kidnapping, so why in the hell would he have Craig Titus plead guilty to it? The one who actually got into the fight with Melissa James was given the best deal, and Craig Titus would once again fall on his own sword to keep the damsel in distress out of trouble. For Kelly Ryan, when she admitted to murder, she was cleared of murder and charged with battery with a deadly weapon and first degree arson. "She was faced with more serious charges, significantly more serious charges. We feel that this is a fair resolution for her," said Ryan's attorney Michael Cristalli. She now faces no criminal liability in James' death. But with overwhelming evidence, both had to admit arson.

Craig Titus recants his guilty plea on a local news interview

After Craig and Kelly accepted the plea, the matter was referred to the Division of Parole and set for sentencing. The original trial date of July 18th was vacated, and at the request of the court, the sentencing was pushed back to August 22nd, 2008. On June 2, 2008 on a local news station, Craig gave his first interview since his guilty plea in court. In the interview, Craig Titus said that he was willing to sacrifice his freedom for his wife, Kelly Ryan. Titus denied claims that he murdered Melissa James, but said the plea deal was the only way to spare his wife a lengthy prison sentence. "I never said I killed Melissa James," Titus told News 3's Dana Wagner, "I said I would plead guilty if you give my wife an opportunity to have a life." Titus would not explain the details of Melissa James' death out of respect for the judge and court system, but he said that he never wanted any harm to come to her, and he wishes to explain what really happened in the future. He also said that he wants to tell Melissa's mother that he loved her daughter and he is nothing like the prosecution painted him out to be.

Sentencing
Discussing the news interview where Titus said he was not guilty

On August 22, 2008 Craig Titus and Kelly Ryan appeared before Judge Jackie Glass where she accepted their pleas, and was ready to announce the sentence. However, Judge Jackie Glass said that she had concerns whether the plea was, "freely and voluntarily given" because on the following Monday after the plea, Titus gave an interview to two news stations in which he said the Second Degree Murder did not happen and the crimes alleged did not occur, and he "took a plea deal to a crime he did not commit."

During that proceeding, the judge confronted Titus with the fact that he had done a television interview on June 2nd, three days after the plea agreement, and the day that his trial was supposed to have begun. In an effort to "maintain the integrity of the process," the court inquired if Craig Titus entered the plea voluntarily. Titus responded by saying, "What I pled guilty to is not actually what happened." As Craig tried to explain, Judge Glass cut him off, and asked Titus' counsel, Marc Saggese about the comments made on the news. Saggese stated, "Defendant Titus' concern is with the language contained in the original charges, but Titus accepts the language in the Second Degree Murder."

When Judge Jackie Glass asked Craig Titus if he was in fact pleading guilty to Second Degree Murder, Titus hesitated. He looked over at his defense attorney to see if he had to do this, and say that he was guilty of a crime he didn't commit. Saggese gave him an affirmative nod, and Craig reluctantly told the judge that he was pleading guilty to Second Degree Murder, First Degree Kidnapping and First Degree Arson.

Craig Titus was only guilty of the arson, but he felt trapped after Ron Brady Jr.'s verdict, and believed he and Kelly both would face the rest of their lives behind bars if they did not agree to this plea deal. Craig said, "At my sentencing, Judge Glass would not allow me to speak and answer her questions. I wanted to say that I was taking this deal so my wife can go home on probation as promised to us. Every time I tried to talk, I was admonished by the judge. I didn't know what to do, what does anybody do in that position? Both the prosecutor and judge said that if I didn't take this deal, they would charge me with capital murder. They already convicted Brady on those fake charges, and I was the next one on their hit list. I was scared to death because I knew that Robert Daskas would follow through with threats to me, and he would destroy both me and my family! The plea deal seemed like the only out, and I was left with no other choice."

According to Titus' appeals, Michael Schwarz wrote, "This case was intricately tied to the Ron Brady Jr. case. For one, the State alleged, throughout Craig Titus' case, on numerous occasions, in the press and courtroom that Craig Titus had also engaged in criminal conduct to eliminate several of the State's witnesses. Second, both cases had the same prosecutors and same homicide detectives. So the State, through the same prosecutors and same homicide detectives, acted in concert with the Clark County Detention Center- Intelligence Unit to take down Titus. The State used the Brady case to undermine Titus' resolve, and force him into a plea agreement. Craig Titus believed, from the beginning that it would be impossible for the State to obtain a conviction in the Brady case, because all of his conversations regarding the witnesses in his case were related to 'discrediting: the witnesses by initiating their arrest for narcotics trafficking.' Brady did contact these entities and provided them with drug trafficking information regarding the State's witnesses. However, all of the evidence showing that these contacts were made was successfully suppressed by the State in the Brady case by merely refusing to provide it. Brady's conviction shocked Titus to the core because "he knew" that Brady did not commit the crime alleged. It was solely because of the State's success in the Brady case that Titus started leaning toward taking a plea. Titus realized that if a conviction could be so easily obtained on the allegations in Brady's case, which he knew to be false, that the

State's ability to manipulate information was so powerful and he did not stand a chance at a trial."

Prosecution addresses the court

Robert Daskas addressed the judge and said that James' head was encased in duct tape, and he showed the court graphic photos of a "death mask formed by her face when it peeled away with the heavy tape during her autopsy." Daskas told the court and judge before sentencing, "Melissa James was beaten, drugged, stunned with a taser, injected with morphine and strangled before she was burned beyond recognition in the trunk of Ryan's car. The investigators could never say for sure whether James was still alive in the back of the car caught on videotape outside a Wal-Mart where Ryan bought charcoal starter fluid at 3:30 a.m. or at a gas station where Titus, Ryan and their friend bought another $2.66 worth of gasoline to pour on the car. Along with those homicide detectives, I too question whether in fact Melissa James was even dead while she was in the back of the trunk of the car at Wal-Mart while Ms. Ryan was so casually buying seven bottles of lighter fluid because, 'that's all they had.' Oh my God, what if she wasn't dead?"

This statement was the promised "blow" to Craig Titus when he swore to "destroy" him. Robert Daskas' statement to the court at sentencing was not just disingenuous, but insincere, dishonest, deceitful, hypocritical, misleading, and duplicitous as well. Under no circumstances was Melissa James alive when they arrived at Wal-Mart or the Shell gas station.

According to the first and second autopsy report, she died around 3:30 pm on December 13th from a likely drug overdose. Robert Daskas even mentioned the time of death at the grand jury hearing. That of course, was before he and the investigators arranged for Tony Gross to be a part of a fictitious "murder for hire," and argue that he had nothing to do with disposing of James' body. When Daskas argued that Tony Gross was involved with the crime at the hearings, his proof were all of the telephone calls placed between Craig and Tony, the first being at 3:28 p.m.- TUESDAY AFTERNOON- "at the time of Melissa James' death!"

Robert Daskas manipulated the courts at every hearing leading up to the trial, and then did it one last time when he lied and said that Melissa James might have still been alive before they set the car on fire. It was the cherry on top of the sundae, because this inflammatory statement would prove to be prejudicial to the Judge when she ruled against the plea agreement (which is allowed, but rarely happens). In doing this, Robert Daskas once again made a deliberate and conscience false statement about Craig Titus, with complete indifference and disregard for Titus' Constitutional Rights to fairness to the proceedings in a court of law. The State is to be a justice seeker not a retribution seeker; and once again, at the most crucial time for a defendant (the sentencing phase of a trial) Robert Daskas blatantly commits misconduct.

Standard 3- 2.8 Relations with the Courts and Bar (a) A prosecutor should not intentionally misrepresent matters of fact or law to the court.

The Defense' statement: Marc Saggese said Melissa James' death occurred after Craig Titus defended Kelly Ryan from James during a fight between the two women. Saggese said that James had taken enough drugs to cause an overdose, and then turned on Craig Titus and attacked him before going into her bedroom and consuming more drugs and alcohol. James then tore her room a part, and they heard crashing noises, and then silence. They later found her dead in the room. "Under no circumstances did Craig Titus premeditate anything. He came home, defended his wife, and then later Melissa was found dead; the contributing factor, according to the autopsy was, opiate intoxication. It was after Melissa James passed that the brutal chain of events starts; once they decide they're going to dispose of the body."

Kelly and Craig address the court: After the judge affirmed that Craig and Kelly were in fact pleading guilty, she allowed them to address the court. Both Craig and Kelly begged for forgiveness, with Kelly Ryan saying, "I am truly, truly sorry. I know that I did not kill her, but I did aid in the events after she overdosed. I know I was not in a state of mind emotionally or physically to make the right decisions, or to, Oh God, to take appropriate control of what was happening. I am so sorry, and ask forgiveness of both this court and Melissa's family."

THE PLEA DEAL & SENTENCING

Craig asked to address Melissa's mother Maura James, and with tears streaming down his face, apologized for letting things get out of control. "I am ashamed and sickened of my actions after Melissa passed away; I let drug use get way out of control in my home. I failed my wife, I failed my family; and most regretfully, I failed Melissa, who was my friend."

Glass did not believe the couple was sorry for the 'killing'. She described the lengths to which Titus and Kelly went to, to destroy James' body, and then repeated back the comments from the State, "which included wrapping her head with duct tape, binding her, and without knowing if she was dead or alive, burning her so badly authorities had to use DNA to identify her." After which the Honorable Judge Jackie Glass singled Craig Titus out, and admonished him saying that she didn't believe a word that came out of his mouth. Judge Glass told Craig Titus to "Save your tears, those tears are crocodile tears and mean nothing." Glass wasn't done with Craig yet. She made one last, unprofessional dig: "Mr. Titus came into this process a big man with muscles. famous, and in control. Now look at him, he is nothing, nothing but a murderer!"

The State made representations at sentencing that Melissa James was alive at the time of the arson, and Judge Jackie Glass said that she took this into consideration before sentencing. The "Honorable" Judge Jackie Glass then proceeded to sentence Defendant's Kelly Ryan and Craig Titus. For Defendant Titus, after the judge attacked Titus' character, sentenced Craig Titus to Counts I and II as agreed and then **deviated on the sentence of Count III (the deal maker or breaker at the negotiations on May 30, 2008) and instead of sentencing Titus to the statutory minimum or bottom time, she expanded the bottom time to 40 % of the entire sentence and gave Titus 6 years on the bottom. Negating the previously discussed parole eligibility of 17 years, and expanding it to 21 years.**

Craig Titus said, "When Judge Glass sentenced Kelly to prison, I wanted to withdraw my guilty plea right there in court. This was not what Robert Daskas promised, he said that Kelly would walk free with probation, and I would be eligible for parole in 15 to 17 years. I tried to withdraw my guilty plea, and the judge told me to shut my mouth, it was not an option." Titus' appeal lawyer responded to the verdict, "The State made false and misleading statements to the sentencing judge regarding the condition of the victim, alleging that the victim was alive while she was burned in the vehicle. The response of the sentencing court to the State's improper statements was to accept them as fact and she immediately reacted by excoriating Mr. Titus and his wife."

Marc Saggese calls the judge and prosecutor out for misconduct

Marc Saggese started in on the either forgetful or unethical judge, and he brought up the conversation that he had with both Robert Daskas and Judge Glass on the record. Saggese said, "Your honor, I feel completely blindsided by a 21 year sentence that was inconsistent with what we discussed in your chambers. Your honor gave me the marching orders to leave your office and tell Mr. Titus he would be eligible for parole in 17 years. Judge Glass became enraged and told Saggese to "Keep his smart remarks to himself." Titus' trial counsel continued to zealously argue, showing complete disgust with the court because he said, "Your honor, you told me to leave your office, tell Mr. Titus that if what's holding you up is the difference between fifteen and seventeen years, tell him he is getting seventeen." Counsel continued, "You, your honor, adamantly said he was getting seventeen. I went to speak, you interrupted me and you said, 'He is getting seventeen!' I left your chambers, misinformed my client, and Mr. Titus put pen to paper and signed that guilty plea agreement under auspices that he'd be receiving 17-55 years with no variation. Now I've been blindsided with a six-year sentence that was completely inconsistent with what we discussed in chambers. Never in a million years would I believe that you would do this or that this could even happen."

When Titus' counsel brought this information to the court's attention at sentencing, Judge Jackie Glass became so enraged, that when Marc Saggese assisted the judge with his name, the judge exploded and stated, "I know who you are. I'd appreciate it if you kept the smart remarks to yourself at this point." But that didn't stop Saggese, because he could not believe that a district court judge would actually be so blatantly unethical.

THE PLEA DEAL & SENTENCING

Saggese said, "Everyone involved in these negotiation knows for a fact the difference that we were going to argue for, was whether or not the two years, the additional two years- whether it was going to be fifteen or seventeen years. I was going to argue for fifteen years, which I did. They were going to argue for consecutive, which they did, which would constitute seventeen years. Your honor, you had given me the marching orders to leave your office, tell Mr. Titus, 'If what is holding you up is the difference between fifteen and seventeen or more, tell him he's getting seventeen.'"

Glass looked at Saggese, and said, "Um-hm." Saggese said, "I didn't know that it worked that way, and that it wasn't even possible, given those particular marching orders. Your honor, you said that he's getting seventeen; the State said that, but you repeated it back to me not just once, but three times! My client relied on your statement, and Mr. Titus would have never entered into a guilty plea if he was not promised seventeen years! So my client certainly…" Judge Glass interrupted, "All right, Mr. Saggese, go ahead and have a seat." The Judge said she wanted to bring counsel back to her chambers.

The court recessed from 11:56:30 a.m. until 12:31:20 p.m., at which time Judge Jackie Glass took both the prosecution and defense back to her chambers and attempted to do damage control, given that it was now in the record that the Judge had clearly participated in the marathon settlement session. For the next 35 minutes, the Judge spoke off the record with the attorneys. In chambers, Saggese was outraged with both the judge and the prosecution. He said that before Craig Titus pled guilty, he was assured by both the prosecution and judge that he would have a chance at parole after 15 to 17 years in prison.

Judge Jackie Glass' reply to Saggese was that he could seek to invalidate the plea agreement after sentencing, but **he needed to be aware that would open Titus up to 1st Degree Murder,** and it could be later tried as a capital offense. Daskas agreed with Judge Glass; and by doing this, Daskas did not fulfill his end of the plea deal, and once again committed prosecutorial misconduct.

Standard 3-4.2 Fulfillment of Plea Discussions- (a) A prosecutor should not make any promise or commitment assuring a defendant

609

or defense counsel that a court will impose a specific sentence or a suspension of sentence; a prosecutor may properly advise the defense **what position will be taken concerning disposition. (c) A prosecutor should not fail to comply with a plea agreement, unless a defendant fails to comply with a plea agreement or other extenuating circumstances are present.**

Court resumed at 12:31:20 pm, and the "Honorable" Judge Jackie Glass said, "Okay, we are back on the record in the Titus and Ryan sentencing. Where we left off before I called counsel out to meet with the Court in chambers was I was sentencing Mr. Titus on Count 3, the First Degree Arson. There apparently is some discrepancy in people's recollections. However, the Court is going to stand by its sentence on Count 3 of seventy-two to one eighty consecutive." In the end, the judge did not honor the understood negotiation that Mr. Saggese represented to, and his client embraced as his understanding and inducement to enter into the negotiations.

FACTS RELATING TO PROSECUTORIAL MISCONDUCT:
Sentencing

The State erroneously and improperly argued at sentencing that it was Titus who dragged this through the system for three years and, as such, was evidence of his disingenuousness. Obviously, the sentencing court bought into this absurd position of the State. The sentencing court showed its own obvious bias, because when the court sentenced Titus, it turned the exercise of his legal rights into improper and offensive dilatory tactics. Nothing could be farther from the truth, it was the State that strategically delayed the Titus case, not Craig. The State wanted to pin a murder charge on Titus and they knew they had problems with their case, such as:

- The only two witnesses of the facts and events leading up to the death of Melissa James were Craig Titus and his wife, Kelly Ryan;
- The cause of death of James was undetermined;
- The coroner stated in his report that James had a toxic or lethal dose of morphine (heroin) in her system;

THE PLEA DEAL & SENTENCING

- The coroner found "no blunt force trauma" on any part of James' body;
- Melissa was a known drug addict and known intravenous drug user;
- Melissa James had previously been stopped and arrested for possession of hypodermic devices;
- Melissa was alive when she injected

The State's statements at Titus' sentencing were **intentional and clearly constituted misconduct.** Although the State's unsubstantiated allegations would surely offend any sense of fairness and justice, apparently it is just business as usual for the State.

CHAPTER **11**

After the Verdict

Directly after the sentencing took place, Marc Saggese on Craig Titus' behalf, submitted a motion to withdraw his guilty plea, and was notified that he would be back in court on October 14th, 2008. In the motion, Craig Titus gave his explanation for pleading guilty to a crime he didn't commit. Craig said he did this primarily because he saw an innocent man, his friend, Ron Brady Jr. sentenced for a crime he did not commit, and "I was broken from that point on." Looking in from the outside, it seemed crazy for Craig to plead Guilty because the prosecution had absolutely no physical evidence.

When the witnesses were cross-examined, the truth would have inevitably come out, and with the autopsy report "undetermined" the case would have been impossible to prove to a jury beyond a reasonable doubt. All of Melissa's criminal records, and drug arrests would have been brought into court, and her toxicology results that showed she had ingested a slew of drugs in a short amount of time, and the amount of ethanol, heroin, morphine, and amphetamines in her system killed her. With all of these drugs in her system at one time, it suggested she was "speed balling" to produce bursts of energy, and then allow her to come down and relax after a certain amount of time. The toxicology results proved

Melissa had been abusing drugs for a number of years, and it would be preposterous to believe that someone else injected drugs into her when she had been an intravenous drug user for so long.

The Nevada Code of Judicial Conduct: RULE 2.6 Ensuring the Right to Be Heard efforts *to further settlement do not undermine any party's right to be heard according to law. The judge should keep in mind the effect that the judge's participation in settlement discussions may have, not only on the judge's own views of the case, but also on the perceptions of the lawyers and the parties if the case remains with the judge after settlement efforts are unsuccessful. Among the factors that a judge should consider when deciding upon an appropriate settlement practice for a case are whether:*

(1) the parties have requested or voluntarily consented to a certain level of participation by the judge in settlement discussions, (2) the parties and their counsel are relatively sophisticated in legal matters, (3) the case will be tried by the judge or a jury, (4) the parties participate with their counsel in settlement discussions, (5) any parties are unrepresented by counsel, and (6) the matter is civil or criminal. [3]

Judges must:

(A) A judge shall accord to every person who has a legal interest in a proceeding, or that person's lawyer, the right to be heard according to law.

(B) A judge may encourage parties to a proceeding and their lawyers to settle matters in dispute but shall not act in a manner that coerces any party into settlement.[1] The right to be heard is an essential component of a fair and impartial system of justice. Substantive rights of litigants can be protected only if procedures protecting the right to be heard are observed. [2] The judge plays an important role in overseeing the settlement of disputes, but should be careful that be mindful of the effect settlement discussions can have, not only on their objectivity and impartiality, but also on the appearance of their objectivity and impartiality. Despite a judge's best efforts, there may be instances when information obtained during settlement discussions could influence a judge's decision making during trial, and, in such instances, the judge should consider whether disqualification may be appropriate. See Rule 2.11(A).

In court papers, Saggese said he was negotiating with county prosecutors Robert Daskas and Josh Tomsheck outside Glass' courtroom on May 30th the last business day before the June 2nd trial was set to start. The parties could not agree on what the sentence Titus would receive if he pleaded guilty to second-degree murder, first degree kidnapping, and first-degree arson. Saggese was asking for a minimum of 15 years while prosecutors wanted 17 years, according to court documents. About 4:30 p.m., Judge Glass told Saggese and the prosecutors that time was running out, court records state.

The District Court's Jury Services needed to be notified by 4:45 p.m. that day whether the trial was going forward. When Glass learned the sticking point in the negotiation was whether Titus would get 15 years or 17 years, she told them "He's getting seventeen," the court record states. Saggese stated that Glass repeated this twice. He said he relied on her statement when he brought the agreement to Titus. Titus would not have entered into a guilty plea if he had not been promised 17 years. Judges can give whatever sentence they deem appropriate and are not bound by plea agreements. Prosecutors declined to comment and judges do not discuss cases publicly that are before them. Saggese raised the issue when Glass sentenced Titus and his co-defendant, Kelly Ryan on Aug. 22nd. After Glass sentenced Titus to 21-55 years, Saggese said in court that he believed she would sentence Titus to 17-55 years. Oct. 14th, Titus' hearing was postponed until Nov. 18th and then moved to Dec. 4th.

10/14/2008- Craig Titus was set to appear in court; however, authorities did not transport Titus from jail to court, so it was postponed until Nov 18th.

11/06/2008- 48 HOURS airs

11/18/2006- Craig Titus was set to appear in court, but Judge Jackie Glass postponed the hearing until the next month.

12/04/2008 Craig Titus was finally able to make his case in front of the Honorable Judge Jackie Glass (via video conference). Craig Titus wanted Judge Glass to cut four years off his prison sentence or let him go to trial. Judges are not bound to plea agreements; however,

AFTER THE VERDICT

Saggese said in court documents that Glass made a 17 year assurance as "a matter of fact," to break a stalemate in pretrial negotiations between him and county prosecutors. When Glass learned the sticking point in the negotiations was whether Titus would get 15 or 17 years, Glass told them, "He's getting seventeen." Saggese said that Glass repeated this twice. He said he relied on her statement when he brought the agreement to Titus. Craig Titus would have never entered a guilty plea if he was not promised at the very least 17 years. When Saggese brought it up at sentencing, Glass flippantly remarked that she did not agree with his recollection of the agreement. Judge Jackie Glass refused sentence reduction/ new trial (why didn't another judge rule on this- of course she is going to refuse a sentence reduction or withdraw of plea). She said it was because Craig Titus and his counsel were aware that she had the discretion to sentence Mr. Titus to 17 years or more for pleading guilty to Second Degree Murder.

The last chapter in the Craig Titus and Kelly Ryan bodybuilder murder case came to an emotional finish Tuesday in District Court. In May of 2009, Anthony Gross pleaded No Contest to Accessory to Arson, and Conspiracy to Commit Arson. Judge Glass sentenced Gross to probation, saying that he helped law enforcement. "The Prosecution had agreed to grant him probation as part of his plea deal." Robert Daskas said, "The District Attorney's Office agreed to give Gross this deal because he helped authorities in a separate Murder for Hire Plot, involving Ronald Brady Jr."

This decision was made even though he had a previous arson record with a "stolen vehicle", and according to phone records and surveillance he was an accessory/accomplice to the crime. If Gross successfully completes his probation, Gross will be permitted to withdraw his guilty plea to the two felony offenses, plead guilty to the misdemeanor charge of Conspiracy to commit 3rd Degree Arson and receive credit for time served.

Maura James spoke during the sentencing for Anthony Gross, the final co-defendant in the case. Gross, 26, earlier pleaded no contest to charges of accessory to arson and conspiracy to commit arson. "My daughter, Melissa James, went up in flames on the side of a desolate desert road," Maura James said. "Because of Anthony Gross, I will never know what her last hours and minutes were like, or what it was to hold her just one last time." During the hearing, the victim's sister wept in the back of the courtroom. District Judge Jackie Glass sentenced Gross to probation, saying that he had helped law enforcement and that prosecutors had agreed to grant him probation as part of a plea deal. "I hope the James family can move forward and have some sense of closure," Glass said.

Judge Jackie Glass then spoke to the defendant. "I hope we never see you again Mr. Gross," she said. Gross was initially charged as an accessory to murder for the slaying of Melissa James. Prosecutor Robert Daskas said the district attorney's office agreed to give Gross a deal in part because he helped authorities in a separate murder-for-hire plot, involving Ronald Nelson Brady Jr. Daskas also said Gross had stayed out of trouble during the case. He described Gross as a star-struck fan of Titus, who was a Mr. Olympia competitor and world-class bodybuilder. "I live with regret for answering the phone that night," Gross said. "I thought I was helping someone, but I really wasn't helping." Maura James said she didn't buy the argument that Gross deserved a second chance because he was still young. Her daughter, she said, is dead. "I will continue to lose sleep each and every night of my life wondering," she said. "Tell me, does Anthony Gross wonder?"

Appeals- Nevada Supreme Court United States Supreme Court
IN THE EIGHTH JUDICIAL DISTRICT COURT OF THE STATE OF NEVADA IN AND FOR THE COUNTY OF CLARK

Craig Michael Titus, Appellant, v. The State of Nevada, Respondent
PETITION FOR WRIT OF HABEAS CORPUS (POST CONVICTION)

Length of Sentence: Count 1- Second Degree Murder (Category a Felony); Maximum of 25 years with a MINIMUM parole eligibility of TEN (10) years.

Count 2- First Degree Kidnapping (Category A Felony); Maximum of 15 years with MINIMUM parole eligibility of FIVE (5) years, to run CONSECUTIVE to Count 1

Count 3- First Degree Arson (Category B Felony); Maximum of ONE HUNDRED EIGHTY (180) MONTHS, to run CONSECUTIVE to COUNT 2.

Grounds raised: That the plea was not freely and voluntarily given; That Craig Titus did not understand the nature of the offense and the consequences at the time of entry of plea; Detrimental reliance on the courts representations by Craig Titus; The District Court's interjection and representations in plea agreement.

GROUNDS ON WHICH THE APELLANT IS BEING HELD UNLAWFULLY:
(a) Ground One: Defendant Titus' Due Process Rights were violated because he did not believe he would receive a fair trial after false allegations of a murder plot for hire that he was never even charged with were addressed at several hearings. **(b) Ground Two:** The defendant's' Due Process Rights were violated because the Court and the Prosecution made false allegations that were knowingly false. **(c) Ground Three:** The defendant's Due Process Rights were violated because of incompetent counsel. Defense counsel had been ineffective communicating the plea offer & Titus' defense counsel's deficient performance caused him prejudice, pleading guilty of a crime he did not commit. **(d) Ground Four:** The defendant's Due Process Rights were violated due to Prosecutorial Misconduct.

THE CORONER'S REPORT- the State made false and misleading statements to the sentencing judge regarding the condition of the victim, alleging that the victim was alive while she was burned in the vehicle. The response of the sentencing court to the State's improper statements was to accept them as fact and she immediately reacted by excoriating Mr. Titus and his wife. These allegations were simply untrue, and their undocumented allegations, contradicted the existing documents in the Coroner's report. If the State is entitled to bring up these facts, without submitting documents, then the Appellant is entitled to refute the lies with the actual facts.

Counsel Misinformed Titus- Titus' counsel never informed him that the Court could change the bottom end. Proof of this is the utter shock expressed by Marc Saggese, Titus' trial counsel when the trial court made the adjustment at sentencing.

CONCLUSION: What does the State have to worry about? Isn't their search for truth and for justice? Apparently, it is just more than a little uncomfortable for the State when an Appellant, such as Titus, is able to demonstrate that the State does not operate with a sense of fairness, **but is continually tipping the scales of justice toward their own ends.** Even though the evidentiary rules for argument at sentencing are more relaxed than at a trial, it surely does not include providing false evidence that contradicts the facts of the case. Even the State's own evidence does not substantiate their allegations. The State's statements at Titus' sentencing were **intentional and clearly constituted misconduct.** Although the State's unsubstantiated allegations would surely offend any sense of fairness and justice, apparently it is just business as usual for the State.

The Appellant is entitled to have a complete picture before this Honorable Court- although justice is supposed to be blind; it surely is not supposed to be ignorant. Presenting a full picture of the events and circumstances below, of necessity, means that the record must be expanded to include information that literally has no way of making it into record because of the very nature of the information itself. Surely this Court knows and must consider that these types of communications are never part of the record and, therefore, could never be included in a normal record. Regarding the Coroner's Report, the only one to blame is the Prosecutor, Robert Daskas when he argued at sentencing that the victim was still alive while in the trunk of the car. This being the sole cause of the judge modifying what had been a 2-15 year sentence and 6-15 year sentence, the Appellant is entitled to refute the allegations and disclose them for what the are- lies.

The information is relevant and necessary to fairly present the factual situation of the Appellant at his sentencing. Perhaps what troubles the State is that this Court may view their overt manipulation of the Plea below as offensive to justice and fairness.

The Nevada Supreme Court repeatedly denied Titus' appeals; Craig Titus' case will be presented to the United States Supreme Court on October 20, 2014. A recent Supreme Court decision, "The Plea Bargaining Law" should be beneficial as Craig Titus appeals his case to the court.

SUPREME COURT OF THE UNITED STATES NO. 10-444
MISSOURI, PETITIONER V. GALIN E. FRYE MARCH 21, 2012

Justice Kennedy delivered the opinion of the Court. The Sixth Amendment, applicable to the States by the terms of the Fourteenth Amendment, provides that the accused shall have the assistance of counsel in all criminal prosecutions. The court determined Frye met both requirements for showing a Sixth Amendment violation under Strickland. The Court next concluded Frye had shown his counsel's deficient performance caused him prejudice. To implement a remedy for the violation, the court deemed Frye's guilty plea withdrawn and remanded to allow Frye either to insist on a trial or to plead guilty to any offense the prosecutor deemed it appropriate to charge. This Court granted certiorari.

JUSTICE'S RULING EXPANDS RIGHTS OF ACCUSED IN PLEA BARGAINS:

Criminal defendants have a constitutional right to effective lawyers during plea negotiations, the **SUPREME COURT** ruled on Wednesday, March 21, 2012 in a pair of 5-to-4 decisions that vastly expanded judge's supervision of the criminal justice system. The decisions mean that what used to be informal and unregulated deal making is now subject to new constraints when **bad legal advice leads defendants to make a decision regarding plea deals.** "Criminal justice today is for the most part a system of pleas, not as system of trial," Justice Anthony M. Kennedy wrote for the majority. "The right to adequate assistance from counsel cannot be defined or enforced without taking account of the central role plea bargaining takes in securing convictions and determining sentences."

The Plea Bargaining Law "The Supreme Court's decision in these two cases constitute the single greatest revolution in the criminal justice process since Gideon v. Wainwright provided indigents the right to counsel." Said Wesley M. Oliver, a law professor at Widener University, referring to the landmark 1963 decision. In the context of trials, the Supreme Court has long established that defendants were entitled to new trials if they could show that **incompetent work by their lawyers probably affected the outcome.** The Supreme Court has also required lawyers to offer competent advice in urging defendants to give up their right to a trial by accepting a guilty plea. Those cases hinged on the right to a fair trial guaranteed by the Sixth Amendment. "In today's criminal justice system," Justice Kennedy wrote that plea bargaining "is not some adjunct to the criminal justice system; it is the criminal justice system." Adding that, "Longer sentences exist on the books largely for bargaining purposes."

The Sixth Amendment right to effective counsel extends to the consideration of plea offers that lapse or are rejected. That right applies to "all critical" stages of the criminal proceedings. (Montejo v. Louisiana, 566 U.S. 778, 786. **Hill v. Lockhart, 474 U.S. 52**, established that Strickland's two-part test governs ineffective assistance in the plea bargain context. In Padilla v. Kentucky, 559, "the negotiation of a plea bargain is a critical stage for ineffective-assistance purposes, id., and rejected the argument made by the State in this case that a knowing and voluntary plea supersedes defense counsel's errors. Plea bargains have become so central to today's justice system that defense counsel must meet responsibilities in the plea bargain process to render the adequate counsel of the Sixth Amendment requires at critical stages of the criminal process. **As a general rule, defense counsel has the duty to communicate formal prosecution offers to accept a plea on terms and conditions that may be favorable to the accused. The "Hill Standard"** requires a defendant complaining that ineffective assistance led him to accept a plea offer instead of going to trial to show "a reasonable probability that, but for counsel's errors, he would not have pleaded guilty and would have insisted on going to trial."

When Craig takes his case to the United States Supreme Court, he will have Marc Saggese' affidavit stating that he was misled by both the judge and prosecution while in negotiations in the judge's chambers. Saggese was led to believe that this deal was set in stone, and as a defense attorney, he gave Craig Titus wrong advice, that proved to be detrimental in the end.

AFTER THE VERDICT

Although Titus won't face life in prison, we feel like we got what we wanted out of him. We may never know exactly what happened in that house between the three, but Craig Titus will go to prison for Melissa James' death and that's all we wanted. Robert Daskas

www.ingramcontent.com/pod-product-compliance
Lightning Source LLC
Chambersburg PA
CBHW052335230426
43664CB00041B/1470